The Biolinguistic Enterpr

Oxford Studies in Biolinguistics

General editor: Cedric Boeckx, Catalan Institute for Advanced Studies (ICREA) and Center for Theoretical Linguistics at the Universitat Autònoma de Barcelona

Advisory editors:
Anna Maria Di Sciullo, Université du Québec à Montréal; Simon Fisher, The Wellcome Trust Centre for Human Genetics; W. Tecumseh Fitch, Universität Wien; Angela D. Friederici, Max Planck Institute for Human Cognitive and Brain Sciences; Andrea Moro, Vita-Salute San Raffaele University; Kazuo Okanoya, Brain Science Institute, Riken; Massimo Piattelli-Palmarini, University of Arizona; David Poeppel, New York University; Maggie Tallerman, Newcastle University

Published
The Biolinguistic Enterprise
Edited by Anna Maria Di Sciullo and Cedric Boeckx

In preparation
The Phonological Architecture: A Biolinguistic Perspective
By Bridget Samuels

The series welcomes contributions from researchers in many fields, including linguistic computation, language development, language evolution, cognitive neuroscience, and genetics. It also considers proposals which address the philosophical and conceptual foundations of the field, and is open to work informed by all theoretical persuasions.

The Biolinguistic Enterprise

New Perspectives on the Evolution and Nature of the Human Language Faculty

Edited by
ANNA MARIA DI SCIULLO AND CEDRIC BOECKX

OXFORD
UNIVERSITY PRESS

OXFORD

UNIVERSITY PRESS

Great Clarendon Street, Oxford OX2 6DP

Oxford University Press is a department of the University of Oxford.
It furthers the University's objective of excellence in research, scholarship,
and education by publishing worldwide in

Oxford New York

Auckland Cape Town Dar es Salaam Hong Kong Karachi
Kuala Lumpur Madrid Melbourne Mexico City Nairobi
New Delhi Shanghai Taipei Toronto

With offices in

Argentina Austria Brazil Chile Czech Republic France Greece
Guatemala Hungary Italy Japan Poland Portugal Singapore
South Korea Switzerland Thailand Turkey Ukraine Vietnam

Oxford is a registered trade mark of Oxford University Press
in the UK and in certain other countries

Published in the United States
by Oxford University Press Inc., New York

British Library Cataloguing in Publication Data

Data available

Library of Congress Cataloging in Publication Data

Library of Congress Control Number: 2010930309

Typeset by SPI Publisher Services, Pondicherry, India
Printed in Great Britain
on acid-free paper by
MPG Books Group, Bodmin and King's Lynn

ISBN 978–0–19–955327–3 (Hbk)
      978–0–19–955328–0 (Pbk)

3 5 7 9 10 8 6 4 2

Contents

General Preface

This series aims to shed light on the biological foundations of human language. Biolinguistics is an important new interdisciplinary field that sets out to explore the basic properties of human language and to investigate how it matures in the individual, how it is put to use in thought and communication, what brain circuits implement it, what combination of genes supports it, and how it emerged in our species. In addressing these questions the series aims to advance our understanding of the interactions of mind and brain in the production and reception of language, to discover the components of the brain that are unique to language (especially those that also seem unique to humans), and to distinguish them from those that are shared with other cognitive domains.

Advances in theoretical linguistics, genetics, developmental and comparative psychology, the evo–devo program in biology, and cognitive neuroscience have made it possible to formulate novel, testable hypotheses concerning these basic questions. *Oxford Studies in Biolinguistics* will contribute to the emerging synthesis among these fields by encouraging and publishing books that show the value of transdisciplinary dialogue, and which highlight the unique research opportunities such a dialogue offers.

Contributions to the series are likely to come from researchers in many fields, including linguistic computation, language development, language evolution, cognitive neuroscience, and genetics. The series welcomes work that addresses the philosophical and conceptual foundations of the field, and is open to work informed by all theoretical persuasions. We expect authors to present their arguments and findings in a manner that can be understood by scholars in every discipline on which their work has a bearing.

The Biolinguistic Enterprise launches the series. It showcases some of the most important work in progress, especially those aspects of biolinguistics that bear on the evolution of the language faculty and observed variations of the linguistic phenotype.

Cedric Boeckx
Barcelona, May 2010

The Contributors

ROBERT C. BERWICK is Professor of Computer Science and Computational Linguistics in the Department of Electrical Engineering and Computer Science at the Massachusetts Institute of Technology. Professor Berwick is the recipient of a Guggenheim Fellowship and co-Director of the MIT Center for Biological and Computational Learning. He is the author of ten books covering language acquisition, computational complexity and language, and parsing.

CEDRIC BOECKX is Research Professor at the Catalan Institute for Advanced Studies (ICREA), and a member of the Center for Theoretical Linguistics at the Universitat Autònoma de Barcelona. Most recently he was Associate Professor of Linguistics at Harvard University. He is the author of *Islands and Chains* (John Benjamins, 2003), *Linguistic Minimalism* (Oxford University Press, 2006), *Understanding Minimalist Syntax* (Blackwell, 2007), *Bare Syntax* (Oxford University Press, 2008) and *Language in Cognition* (Wiley-Blackwell, 2009); he is founding co-editor, with Kleanthes K. Grohmann, of the Open Access journal *Biolinguistics*.

CARLO CECCHETTO received his Ph.D. from the University of Milan and is currently Professor of Linguistics at the University of Milan-Bicocca. He has published several papers in major journals on the following topics: the theory of Quantifier Raising and the syntax–semantics interface, labeling and phrase structure theory, the syntax of left and right dislocation, sign-language syntax, and the role of memory resources in (spoken and sign) language comprehension. He has previously taught at the University of Siena and at UCLA.

NOAM CHOMSKY was born on December 7, 1928 in Philadelphia, Pennsylvania. He received his Ph.D. in linguistics in 1955 from the University of Pennsylvania. During the years 1951 to 1955, Chomsky was a Junior Fellow of the Harvard University Society of Fellows. The major theoretical viewpoints of his doctoral dissertation appeared in the monograph *Syntactic Structures*, 1957. This formed part of a more extensive work, *The Logical Structure of Linguistic Theory*, circulated in mimeograph in 1955 and published in 1975. Chomsky joined the staff of the Massachusetts Institute of Technology in 1955 and in 1961 was appointed full professor. In 1976 he was appointed Institute Professor in the Department of Linguistics and Philosophy. Chomsky has lectured at many universities across the globe, and is the recipient of numerous honorary degrees and awards. He has written and lectured widely on linguistics, philosophy, intellectual history, contemporary issues, international affairs, and U.S. foreign policy. Among his recent books are *New Horizons in the Study of Language and Mind* and *On Nature and Language*.

ANNA MARIA DI SCIULLO is Full Professor of Linguistics at the University of Quebec in Montreal, and the director of Major Collaborative Research Initiatives on Asymmetry and Interfaces. She held visiting positions at MIT and at the University of Venice. She published several books, including *Hedges, Heads, and Projections* (John Benjamins, 2010), *Asymmetry in Morphology* (MIT Press, 2005), *UG and External Systems* (John Benjamins, 2005), *Asymmetry in Grammar* (John Benjamins, 2003), *Projections and Interface Conditions: Essays on Modularity* (Oxford University Press, 1997), and, with Edwin Williams, *On the Definition of Word* (MIT Press, 1987). She is the founder of the International Network on Biolinguistics.

W. TECUMSEH FITCH is Professor of Cognitive Biology in the Department of Cognitive Biology, University of Vienna. His main interests are in bioacoustics, especially vertebrate vocal production, and the evolution of cognition, particularly the evolution of human speech, language, music, and art, all studied from a strongly comparative perspective. His research focuses on experimental investigations of vocal production and cognition in humans and a wide range of vertebrates, including chimpanzees, monkeys, seals, deer, dogs, alligators, ravens, and parrots.

ALESSANDRA GIORGI studied in Rome, University La Sapienza, in Pisa, Scuola Normale Superiore, and in the Department of Linguistics and Philosophy at MIT. She is presently Professor of Linguistics at the University Ca' Foscari of Venice, Italy. She is the author of the following monographs: *The Syntax of Noun Phrases* (Cambridge University Press, 1991, with G. Longobardi); *Tense and Aspect: From Semantics to Morphosyntax* (Oxford University Press, 1997, with F. Pianesi); and, most recently, *About the Speaker: Towards a Syntax of Indexicality* (Oxford University Press, 2010).

CRISTINA GUARDIANO is currently assistant professor at the University of Modena and Reggio Emilia. She earned her Ph.D. in historical (Greek) linguistics from the University of Pisa in 2003. Her research interests are historical syntax, parametric theories, and the syntax of the nominal domain.

WOLFRAM HINZEN is a professor in the department of philosophy at Durham University, United Kingdom, where he moved coming from the University of Amsterdam in 2006. He is the author of the books *Mind Design and Minimal Syntax* and *An Essay on Names and Truth*, both published by Oxford University Press.

LYLE JENKINS studied problems in theoretical syntax (modality and the existential construction) at MIT under Noam Chomsky within the Extended Standard Theory, one of the first theories of generative grammar to address the study of language from a biolinguistic perspective. After completing his Ph.D., Jenkins taught at a number of universities, including the University of Vienna, the University of Salzburg, and the University of Paris VIII (Vincennes). At Salzburg he helped to organize the Linguistic Society of America's (LSA) Summer Institute on the Biology of Language, which included the participation of Konrad Lorenz and other biologists. While a Visiting Fellow at the Department of Biological Chemistry, Harvard University, Jenkins worked on the SV-40 monkey virus. Together with Allan Maxam, who (with Walter Gilbert) had developed the chemical method of DNA sequencing and done pioneering work in the area of immunology, Jenkins helped organize the Harvard Medical School Biolinguistics Group and later the Biolinguistics Institute in Cambridge, Massachusetts, to promote interdisciplinary work in the field of biolinguistics.

RICHARD S. KAYNE received his Ph.D. from MIT in 1969 and his Docteur ès Lettres degree from the University of Paris VIII in 1976. In 1995, he was awarded a Doctorate *honoris causa* by the University of Leiden, the Netherlands. His work over the years has concentrated on syntactic theory, with recent emphasis on comparative syntax. He is the editor of *Oxford Studies in Comparative Syntax*, and has published six books: *French Syntax* (MIT Press, 1975); *Connectedness and Binary Branching* (Foris, 1984); *The Antisymmetry of Syntax* (MIT Press, 1994); *Parameters and Universals* (Oxford University Press, 2000); *Movement and Silence* (Oxford University Press, 2005); *Comparisons and Contrasts* (Oxford University Press, 2010). He is currently Silver Professor in the Department of Linguistics at New York University.

HOWARD LASNIK is Distinguished University Professor of Linguistics at the University of Maryland. He has played a prominent role in syntactic theorizing in the Chomskyan framework, starting with the Extended Standard Theory, through Government–Binding theory, to Minimalism. His main research areas are syntactic theory and the syntax–semantics interface. Alongside more foundational issues of language learnability and the general properties of linguistic theories, among the specific topics he has worked on are scope, anaphora, ellipsis, verbal morphology, Case, and locality constraints on movement.

RICHARD K. LARSON held appointments at the University of Pennsylvania (1984–5) and the Massachusetts Institute of Technology (1985–9), before joining the faculty at the University at Stony Brook, where he is currently Professor of Linguistics. His research has examined a wide variety of topics in syntax and semantics, including relative and adverbial clauses, NP adverbs, disjunctions, prepositional phrases, double objects, and clausal complements. It has also involved a wide variety of languages, including Warlpiri, Japanese, Korean, Mandarin Chinese, Persian, Zazaki, Gilaki, and Pashto.

GIUSEPPE LONGOBARDI is Professor of General Linguistics at the University of Trieste. He has held positions at the Scuola Normale Superiore in Pisa, the University of Venice, University of Vienna, UCLA, USC, Harvard, CNRS, and published extensively on syntactic theory and historical syntax.

MARIA RITA MANZINI is Professor of General Linguistics at the University of Florence, studied at MIT (Ph.D., 1983) and held the positions of lecturer and then reader at University College London. She is the author of several books, including *Locality* (MIT Press, 1992), and, in collaboration with Leonardo Savoia, *A Unification of Morphology and Syntax* (Routledge, 2007) as well as the three-volume work *I dialetti italiani*

(Dell'Orso, 2005). She is the author of several dozen articles in international journals and books.

Costanza Papagno received her M.D. and her Ph.D. at the University of Milan and is currently full professor of Neuropsychology at the University of Milan-Bicocca. She has published several papers in major journals on the following topics: verbal short-term memory and language acquisition and comprehension, aphasia, figurative language processing, and impairment of semantic memory. She has previously worked at the MRC Applied Psychology Unit in Cambridge and at the University of Palermo.

Massimo Piattelli-Palmarini is Professor of Cognitive Science at the University of Arizona. From January 1994 to July 1999 he was the director of the Department of Cognitive Science (Dipsco), of the Scientific Institute San Raffaele, in Milan (Italy), and professor of Cognitive Psychology at the San Raffaele University. From September 1985 to December 1993 he was Principal Research Scientist at the Center for Cognitive Science at MIT. He has been a visiting professor at the University of Maryland, at MIT, at the Collège de France, at Rutgers University, and at Harvard University. He is the author of *Inevitable Illusions* (Wiley, 1994), the editor of *Language and Learning: The Debate between Jean Piaget and Noam Chomsky* (Harvard University Press, 1980, translated into eleven languages) and the co-editor of *Of Minds and Language: A Dialogue with Noam Chomsky in the Basque Country* (Oxford University Press, 2009).

Leonardo M. Savoia is Full Professor of General Linguistics at the University of Florence, Director of the Department of Linguistics, and has been Head of the Faculty of Education (*Magistero*) at the same university. He is the author of several books, including *A Unification of Morphology and Syntax* (Routledge, 2007) and the three-volume work *I dialetti italiani* (Dell'Orso, 2005), in collaboration with Rita Manzini, as well as of several dozen articles in journals and books.

Juan Uriagereka's research ranges from comparative grammar to the neuro-biological bases of language. He has (co-)directed twenty Ph.D. theses, (co-)authored/edited eight books, eighty-five articles and chapters, and given two hundred talks, including a dozen keynote speeches. He has received several awards for his research, advising and teaching, and has worked at various universities in four continents. Participating in many professional groups internationally, he has obtained a dozen research grants.

Charles Yang is Associate Professor of Linguistics at the University of Pennsylvania. His book, *Knowledge and Learning in Natural Language*, was published by OUP in 2001. His interests include language acquisition and change, computational linguistics, morphology, and psycholinguistics.

Abbreviations

1	first person
2	second person
3	third person
A	Adenine (as used in Berwick chapter)
ABS	absolutive
ACC	accusative
AD	Alzheimer's dementia
Adj	adjective
AFP	anterior forebrain pathway
AKEFI	affected KE family individuals
AR	Ariellese
ASL	American Sign Language
ASP	aspect
AUX	auxiliary
BEI	passive marker in Mandarin
C	Cytosine
C	Complementizer
C_{HL}	computational system of human language
C-I	conceptual–intentional
CD	Complementizer Deletion
CG	Classical Greek
COMP	Complementizer
COP	Copula
CS	computational language system
CypG	Cypriot Greek
D	determiner
D-structure	Deep structure
DAR	double-access reading

DAT	dative
DECL	declarative
Det	determiner
DP	determiner phrase
DVD	Developmental Verbal Dyspraxia
ECP	Empty Category Principle
EM	external merge
EPP	Extended Projection Principle
EST	Extended Standard Theory
evo–devo	evolutionary–developmental biology
F	Feminine
FA	Fallese
FI	full interpretation
FL	faculty of language
FLB	faculty of language in the broad sense
FLN	faculty of language in the narrow sense
fMRI	functional magnetic resonance imaging
FUT	future
G	Guanine
GB	Government–Binding
GEN	genitive
GR	Grico
H	head
HCN	human congnition in the narrow sense
HLN	human language in the narrow sense
HOX	Homeobox
HVC	high vocal center
I	inflection
ILF	interpreted logical form
IM	internal merge
Imp, IMPF	imperfect
IND	indicative

INTR	intransitive
IT	Italian
ITV	intentional transitive verb
LCA	last common ancestor
LCA	linear-correspondence axiom
LDA	long-distance anaphor
LF	Logical Form
LIS	Italian Sign Langauge
LMAN	lateral magnocellular nucleus of the nidopallium
LOC	locative
LOTN	language of thought in the narrow sense
M	middle/intransitive marker
M	masculine
MA	Marcillian
MASC	masculine
MG	Modern Greek
MGP	Modularized Global Parametrization
MP	Minimalist Program
MtB	*Mitteilungsbedürfnis*
N	noun
NOM	nominative
NTC	no-tampering condition
O	object
P&P	Principles and Parameters
PART	partitive
PCM	Parametric Comparison Method
PDH	pervasive deep homology
Perf, PRF	perfect
PF	Phonological Form, Phonetic Form
Pl, PL	plural
PP	prepositional phrase
PRED	predicate

PRES	present
PRO	pronoun
PRT	participle
PS	phrase structure
REFL	reflexive
S	subject
S	singular
S-M	sensory-motor
S-R	stimulus–response
S-structure	Surface structure
Sg, SG	singular
SLI	specific language impairment
SMT	Strong Minimalist Thesis
SNP	single nucleotide polymorphism
STM	short-term memory
STP	superior temporal plane
SUBJ	subjunctive
SUT	Strong Uniformity Thesis
T	Thymine (as used in Berwick chapter)
T	Tense
Tns	tense
TOP	topic
TV	transitive verb
UG	Universal Grammar
USV	ultrasonic vocalization
V	verb
V2	Verb second
VP	verb phrase
WBS	Williams–Beuren syndrome
WGA	whole-genome (or genome-wide) association studies
WM	working memory

1

Introduction: Contours of the Biolinguistic Research Agenda

ANNA MARIA DI SCIULLO AND CEDRIC BOECKX

The term *biolinguistics* is currently enjoying a new lease of life, and the interdisciplinary research program behind it, renewed appreciation. The first mention of the term (Meader and Muysken 1950) went largely unnoticed, as far as we have been able to determine from the vanishingly few references to it in the literature. It was not until the early 1970s that the term caught on. It was used in the title of a conference "A Debate on Bio-Linguistics," organized by Massimo Piattelli-Palmarini in 1974, and it figures prominently in an address at the annual meeting of the American Association for the Advancement of Science made by Salvador Luria in 1976, which we will come back to in this introduction. After that, the term went underground and did not reappear until the turn of the millennium, as the title of a book by Lyle Jenkins (2000). Since then it has figured prominently in titles of talks, courses, articles, books, workshops, and conferences; it even became the title of a new journal and is the rallying call behind the formation of various research initiatives in Montreal, Barcelona, and elsewhere, and an international biolinguistic network was created in 2007. The present volume itself is the fruit of two conferences on biolinguistics that took place in Santo Domingo and Venice in 2007. Because of this recent re-emergence of the term, many who come across it feel the need for clarification, which we hope to provide in this introduction, meant to provide a context for the chapters that follow.

"Biolinguistics" expresses more transparently than any other term we know of what defines modern linguistics since the 'cognitive revolution' of the 1950s. Back then, under the impetus of Noam Chomsky, Eric Lenneberg, and Morris Halle, the field of linguistics abandoned its focus on external behavior and followed a path that was more decidedly cognitive—indeed biological—as it turned its attention to the organism that makes language possible. Chomsky's devastating review of Skinner's *Verbal Behavior* in 1959 (Chomsky 1959a) quickly became a landmark, and, combined with the analysis of English verbal morphology in *Syntactic Structures* (1957), laid the foundations of generative grammar masterfully articulated in the introductory chapter of *Aspects of the Theory of Syntax* (1965). At the same time Eric Lenneberg was working on his *Biological Foundations of Language* (1967), where he stressed the need to study "language as a natural phenomenon—an aspect of [man's] biological nature, to be studied in the same manner as, for instance, his anatomy."

Biological Foundations of Language was a seminal, ground-breaking work that anticipated many of the issues in the agenda of contemporary research programs concerned with the biology of language. Even a cursory look over the table of contents of the monograph shows that the book discusses and/or foreshadows such topics as the genetics of language, the biological (physiological) correlates of language, the growth of language in the individual (i.e. the progress of language acquisition), the interplay of brain processes (e.g. lateralization) with the growth of language, the neurological aspects of speech and language, the neural mechanism supporting language, and the evolution of language in the species. It also contains an appendix, written by Noam Chomsky, on formal aspects of grammar, and another by Otto Marx on the history of this research program. Each of these topics has spawned many areas of research that are currently being intensely explored anew in a necessarily interdisciplinary framework.

We believe that the renewed appreciation for biolinguistic research questions is due to a variety of factors. First, the decidedly interdisciplinary perspective adopted in introductory texts such as Uriagereka (1998) and Jenkins (2000) no doubt led many linguists to reopen the dialog with their colleagues in adjacent disciplines. Both Jenkins and Uriagereka stress the importance of addressing head-on the "logical problem of language evolution" (how could such an object as the human language faculty have emerged in the species?) from a multi-disciplinary perspective, to avoid the facile adaptationist, just-so story traps that are all too familiar (cf. Pinker and Bloom 1990). Interestingly, the same message in favor of a pluralist, less genocentric/adaptationist approach to central issues in biology can be seen with the rise of the evolutionary developmental (evo–devo) paradigm (see, among many others, Carroll 2005a) that (bio)linguists are now appealing to on a regular basis.[1]

---

[1] Incidentally, Jenkins's and Uriagereka's messages are not without antecedent. Both refer to Piattelli-Palmarini's (1989) compelling rejection of adaptationist scenarios in the context of language evolution (the article that sparked Pinker and Bloom's 1990 response), and both point out that Chomsky has voiced the same concerns on numerous occasions since his earliest writings. For an excellent collection of relevant passages from the Chomsky corpus, see Otero (1990).

   At roughly the same time, geneticists in Europe made the breakthrough discovery of a link between the language deficit manifested by the now famous KE family members and a specific gene (FOXP2). Though long suspected, the genetic basis of language received a tremendous boost from this (still ongoing) research. Although it is crystal clear that FOXP2 is not *the* language gene, investigations into the role of this gene brought linguists, cognitive scientists, neurologists, and biologists to ask one another questions, and to learn from one another's fields how to interpret the data, and this discovery would be our second force behind the renewal of interest in biolinguistics. This process requires temporarily abandoning, and at least moving beyond the jargon of one's field to articulate linking hypotheses. The need to adopt concepts that would be commensurable across disciplines has been stressed for several years by neurolinguists such as David Poeppel in an attempt to circumvent the sterile interactions among subfields of linguistics and adjacent disciplines that so far have led many to express skepticism about the very feasibility of biolinguistics. Fortunately these calls to develop a lingua franca for biolinguistic investigations have been taking place at a time when theoretical linguists themselves, under Chomsky's impetus, decided (for largely independent reasons) to revisit the very foundations of their field, and explore the plausibility of a 'minimalist' program for linguistic theory—the third force, in our opinion, behind the re-emergence of biolinguistics.

   Let us (all too briefly) sketch what the minimalist program amounts to. After roughly fifteen years of intensive work on properties of the language faculty under the banner of 'generative grammar' (more accurately, the extended standard theory), Chomsky got the impression in the late 1980s that the overall approach was well established, and that it was time to take the next step on the research agenda of the generative enterprise. This next step amounts to an attempt to go beyond explanatory adequacy. Chomsky (1965) distinguishes between three kinds of adequacy: observational, descriptive, and explanatory; not surprisingly, he puts a premium on explanatory adequacy. The aim of (generative) linguistics was first and foremost to account for the amazing feat of human language acquisition in all its subtleties. Once it was felt that the model was sufficiently well established, it became natural to ask how one could make sense of the properties of the language faculty that the model posits— how much sense can we make of this architecture of language? Put differently, why does the language faculty have this sort of architecture?

   Quite reasonably, Chomsky formulated this quest beyond explanatory adequacy in the most ambitious form (what is known as the strong minimalist thesis), in the form of a challenge to the linguistic community: Can it be shown that the computational system at the core of the language faculty is optimally or perfectly designed to meet the demands on the systems of the mind/brain it interacts with? By optimal or perfect design Chomsky meant to explore the idea that all properties of the computational system of language can be made to follow from minimal design specifications, also known as "bare output conditions"—the sort of properties that the system would have to have to be usable at all (e.g. all expressions generated by the computational system should be legible, that is, formatted in a way that the external systems can handle). In other words, the computational system of language, minimalistically construed, would consist solely of the most efficient algorithm to interface with the other components of the mind, the simplest procedure to compute (generate) its outputs (expressions) and communicate them to the organs of the mind that will interpret them and allow them to enter into thought and action. If the strong minimalist thesis were true, the language faculty (FL) would be an "ideal" linguistic system. But it should be stressed that the point of the minimalist program is not to prove the validity of this extreme thesis, but to see how far the thesis can take us, how productive this mode of investigation can be. The strong minimalist thesis amounts to asking whether we can make perfect sense of the FL. Asking this question is the best way to find out how much sense we can make out of the FL. The points where the minimalist program fails will mark the limits of our understanding. If one cannot make perfect sense of some property P of the FL (i.e. if P cannot be given a minimalist rationale in terms of computational efficiency towards interface demands), then P is just something one must live with, some accident of history, a quirk of brain evolution, some aspect of the FL that one must recognize in some brute force fashion.

Strategically speaking, the minimalist program forces linguists to reformulate previous findings in terms of elementary units, operations, and interface conditions. Many of these, minimalists anticipate, will have such a generic flavor to them ("combine," "map onto a linear sequence," etc.) that they are plausibly not specific to the language faculty. This should be very good news to researchers in other areas, as the concepts articulated by minimalists may find an equivalent in their own field or be more readily testable using familiar techniques. At the same time, these generic operations make it more plausible to entertain "descent with modification" scenarios concerning the evolution of language.

In sum, linguistic minimalism contributes to the end of what we would like to call linguistic isolationism—an inevitable period of over-modularization in generative grammar during which the language faculty as a whole was studied *sui generis*, as an autonomous system bearing little or no resemblance to other cognitive modules in humans, or in other species.

We realize that by placing the minimalist program at the center of the revived field of biolinguistics (both in this introduction and in the contributions to this volume) we are formulating a controversial hypothesis—at the very least one that runs the risk of alienating those who view the theoretical aspects of 'Chomskyan' linguistics with skepticism (not to say contempt), but still see language as a biological object, to be studied 'biolinguistically.' Let us be clear. Biolinguistics is a fairly broad research program, and allows for the exploration of many avenues of research: formalist; functionalist; nativist and insisting on the uniqueness of the language faculty; nativist about general (human) cognition, but not about language per se; etc. From Chomsky to Givón, from Lenneberg to Tomasello—all of this is biolinguistics. In practice, though, it is fair to say that the term "biolinguistics" is more narrowly construed as a more transparent label for generative-oriented studies (but see Givón 2002 for an important exception). This narrower characterization is perhaps in part due to the fact that the term biolinguistics was first used with the generative enterprise in mind (Piattelli-Palmarini 1974; Luria 1976; Jenkins 2000). But we think that it also reflects the fact that despite much criticism, the basic tenets of the generative approach to the language faculty remain the very best bet we have to carry the biolinguistic program forward. One should bear in mind that the latest instantiation of the generative enterprise, the minimalist program, is just as broad and 'theory-neutral' as biolinguistics itself. As Chomsky himself has remarked (2007c: 4):

Recent inquiry into these questions in the case of language has come to be called "the minimalist program", but there has been so much misunderstanding, even within professional circles, that it is perhaps worth reiterating that it is a *program*, not a *theory*, and a program that is both traditional in its general flavor and pretty much theory-neutral, insofar as the biolinguistic framework is adopted. [...] And whatever one's beliefs about design of language may be, the questions of the research program arise. It may also be worth mentioning that the program can only be pursued, whatever theoretical framework one adopts, insofar as some descriptive account of the phenomena to be explained is reasonably unproblematic, often not the case of course, as expected with any system of at least apparent intricacy.

In other words, there are many alternative minimalist visions one can entertain. As soon as one begins to ask "why is the language faculty that way," like it or not, we are in minimalist territory as well as in biolinguistic territory.

We regard Eric Lenneberg's book, *Biological Foundations of Language*, published forty years ago, as the best example of interdisciplinary research in biolinguistics. We feel that with the advent of the minimalist program and its emphasis on interfaces and primitive operations, it has become harder to formulate "purely" theoretical proposals, without any regard to interdisciplinary issues. It has certainly become more common to see theoretical linguists speculate on some of the biolinguistic implications of their proposals, or even motivate their premises on biolinguistic grounds. Thus it is more and more common to find introductory statements such as this (taken from Yang, this volume):

How much should we ask of Universal Grammar? Not too little, for there must be a place for our unique ability to acquire a language along with its intricacies and curiosities. But asking for too much won't do either. A theory of Universal Grammar is a statement of human biology, and one needs to be mindful of the limited structural modification that would have been plausible under the extremely brief history of *Homo sapiens* evolution.

This is what Chomsky has in recent years called "Approaching UG from Below." The present volume contains contributions to biolinguistics; but even in those contributions that are less explicit about interdisciplinary issues we hope that the biolinguistic implications will be fairly clear. Most of these contributions have been placed in the computation section of the book, but as editors we insist that this was not in any way intended to marginalize them against the (necessarily) interdisciplinary contributions in the section on evolution. We regard issues of computation as central to the biolinguistic enterprise, and just as we have encouraged the authors of these contributions to formulate their hypotheses in a way that would be transparent to experts in other fields (a request facilitated by the authors' adoption of the minimalist perspective), we urge non-theoretical linguists to take these claims about linguistic computation very seriously indeed, for failure to do so has almost invariably led to unconstrained, unrealistic, and ultimately doomed hypotheses regarding the evolution, neural implementation, acquisition, and use of language (witness the obvious limitations of adaptationist and connectionist hypotheses concerning language, both in terms of empirical coverage and explanation).

In addition to the sections on computation and evolution that we just mentioned, the present volume offers contributions pertaining to variation. In many ways variation is the natural 'interface' or meeting ground between language and biology. Both linguistics and biology have long focused on diversity, its nature and origin. Both biolinguistics (of a generative persuasion) and what biologists (following in Goethe's footsteps) call (Theoretical) Morphology are interested in defining the limits of variation (the 'morphospaces') for the language organ and organisms more generally. Furthermore, Chomsky has long made clear that the concept of parameter grew out of interactions with biologists like Jacob and Monod, whose works gave rise to the modern evo–devo paradigm (see Chomsky 1980). These forces conspire to making variation a central aspect of the biolinguistic agenda. The contributions included in this volume are not intended to provide an exhaustive list of issues that arise in biolinguistics but we feel that as a whole they offer a representative panorama of current research in this growing field.

In an address delivered at the 1976 AAAS meeting, Nobel laureate Salvador Luria said this about biolinguistics:

In closing, let me single out one frontier that today may seem as unreachable as Mount Everest seemed to be 50 years ago. And yet, it is exciting enough to warrant serious attention. I refer to what I may call Biolinguistics, or the biology of human language. The reason for singling out this field is two-fold. First, human language is the special faculty through which all conscious human activity is filtered; a faculty whose development may well have played the driving role in the almost catastrophic evolution from ape-kind to human-kind. And second, language alone, among the uniquely human faculties of the human brain offers to the scientist a systematic theory, the structural linguistics developed by Chomsky and his colleagues, which may be amenable to confrontation with biological data. What I mean is that formal language structure, plus some facts already known about language and brain structure, plus the advancing knowledge of brain organization provided by physiologists, hold some promise that between linguistics and neurobiology a kind of convergence may soon be possible that may provide a wedge into the biological exploration of the human mind.

The confrontation, and possible unification, envisaged by Luria strikes us as more feasible now than ever before. Work in theoretical linguistics to which most of the contributors of this volume have actively contributed over the years has re-opened the necessarily interdisciplinary dialog that defined the biolinguistic agenda; they have provided us with a new golden opportunity to shed new light on the language faculty, its nature, origin, acquisition, and use, an opportunity that the present volume hopes to highlight.

Summary of the contributions

The Biolinguistic Enterprise: New Perspectives on the Evolution and Nature of the Human Language Faculty brings together three sets of chapters. The first addresses the evolutionary origin of language: How could such an object as the human language faculty have emerged in the species? They also speak to the unification problem. The second part addresses the question of why languages vary. The chapters in this section provide evidence that understanding language variation from a biolinguistic perspective may lead to a deeper understanding of linguistic diversity. Part 3 is concerned with questions of computation. The chapters explore the properties of the computational system in the faculty of language, narrowly construed (FLN), as well as its relation to the broader language faculty (FLB), which includes the sensory–motor and conceptual–intentional systems. Within the foundational assumptions of the minimalist program, these chapters show that it has been a productive assumption that the FLN is an optimal solution to certain legibility conditions imposed by the sensory–motor and conceptual–intentional systems. Taken has a whole, the chapters contribute to the biolinguistic program, a program that specifically asks why-questions (why these principles not others) and raises issues related to biology, evolution, and neural representations. The following paragraphs summarize them.

Part I: Evolution

Robert Berwick and Noam Chomsky's chapter focuses on the dual questions of language's origin and variation, in particular how these questions may be informed by both recent biological work on evolution and development and the framework provided by the Minimalist Program. Human language appears to be best regarded as an internal computational system driven by a single recursive operator yielding hierarchical structure, with its particular functional design shaped by the link to systems of thought and action, rather than by the secondary process of externalization, that is, sensory-motor parsing or speech/sign. What relevant biological and evolutionary results there are, including recent results on FOXP2 and its analogous effects in other species such as songbirds, as well as computational considerations of parsing efficiency, all point to this conclusion. This chapter also reviews how an account of the apparently recent and saltational evolutionary emergence of this recursive system of "discrete infinity," apparently unique to the human species, profits from an examination of the ongoing revision of evolutionary explanation in light of new research on the link between evolution and development, which highlights the possibility of relatively rapid shifts in an organism's biology, given even minor genomic variation.

Cedric Boeckx goes in the same direction in drawing a parallelism between the problem in biology of explaining how language, with no apparent homolog in the biological world, originated in humans, and the problem of explaining how language growth is possible through interaction with an environment lacking in negative evidence (Plato's problem). Boeckx examines the nature of lexicalization and suggests "that turning concepts into lexical items that can merge at infinitum goes a long way toward characterizing the source of what makes humans cognitively special." The chapter also highlights a certain degree of convergence between recent developments in biolinguistics and evo–devo biology.

The chapter by Robert Berwick is related to the preceding two. It too points out that the fact that human language seems to be unique in the biological world presents a problem for an evolutionary theory of language based on the assumption that the evolution of language has proceeded on the basis of a continuous, adaptive process. This is because language is unique and therefore apparently a discontinuous trait. Berwick considers how to resolve the discontinuity problem, arguing that the micromutational adaptationist view adopted in the modern synthesis theory of evolution need not hold, and is replaceable by a deeper deductive system of regulatory interaction, or, alternatively, by single adaptive changes with far-reaching effect. Capitalizing on Hauser, Chomsky, and Fitch's (2002) proposal that, of the components of the FLB, only the FLN is unique to the human species, he argues that if the FLN consists of a single structure-building operation with many cascading effects, human language is less discontinuous than previously thought. The punchline is that only merge is to be explained and so far seems to remain discontinuous; there is no need to look for adaptive explanations for each of the cascading effects following automatically from the operation.

The following chapters in this section, too, are concerned with questions of methodology in biolinguistics, dealing, even if indirectly, with questions pertaining to the unification problem. They relate to the preceding chapters as they also discuss questions on the evolution of language, taking into consideration what we know of the genetic basis of language, in particular the evolution of FOXP2, and comparative studies on humans and non-human primates.

Massimo Piattelli-Palmarini and Juan Uriagereka point out that much publicity has been given to the identification of a specific mutation in the FOXP2 gene that causes various language impairments in the affected members of a British and Canadian family designated by the letters KE. Myrna Gopnik and collaborators had initially diagnosed a very specific "feature blindness" (problems with tense, number, agreement, and gender) in otherwise perfectly normal subjects, a perfect case of dissociation between general intelligence and language. Subsequent refined neurological (PET and fMRI) analyses and a rich battery of tests have corrected this claim. Orofacial dyspraxia and a limited capacity to learn complex sequences of oral movements have been proposed (contra Gopnik and colleagues) as the cause of reduced morphosyntactic "skills" [*sic*]. A reconstruction of the evolution of the FOXP2 gene in the mammalian world has prompted claims of an adaptive "sweep" from chimpanzees to humans, stressing the role of communication in the shaping of language. The most detailed genetic analysis today possible and a very detailed analysis of the neuronal correlates of the mutation seem to lead to a conception of language that many find quite problematic (language as part of motor planning and language acquisition as a step in the learning of complex motor sequences). The authors present the case and suggest that this picture of language (offered by distinguished neurologists and geneticists, but non-linguists) is objectionable. A different lesson from this case is proposed, centrally involving the evolution of language.

Jenkins argues for a comparative method under the assumption that homologs to natural language could be found in other organisms and domains. Jenkins starts by stating that the study of the biology of language, *biolinguistics*, encompasses the study of knowledge of language, its development in the child, and its evolution in the species. Each of these areas can be studied while abstracting away from underlying physical, neural, and genetic mechanisms. For example, one can study the language faculty by studying properties of language such as word order and distribution of pronouns and anaphors. The development of language can be investigated by looking for both universal principles and language-specific variation across many languages. Language evolution, its use and development, can be studied by mathematical models, simulating language change in time. Jenkins emphasizes that the biolinguistic program hopes to relate the properties of the language faculty discovered in linguistics (and in particular in the research areas outlined above) to physical mechanisms at the level of language micro-circuits of the brain and of language genetics. Finally, he emphasizes that abstract principles of language such as (a)symmetry and minimization principles may be related to and be illuminated by similar kinds of mechanisms found in other biological systems.

Tecumseh Fitch argues that many of the brain components that interact with the faculty of language are widely shared with other species although some seem to be uniquely human (unusual) in the biological world. Fitch points out that some of the novel capacities may depend on different underlying mechanisms that have a separate evolutionary history. Addressing how the mechanisms in question evolved, Fitch argues, requires a comparative approach that goes beyond the study of non-human primates to include virtually any living organism. "Only data from widely disparate species will allow us to determine selective forces that might drive convergent evolution... and determine the time depth of homologous mechanisms that are broadly shared." Recent molecular and developmental data offer an exciting and unexpected additional argument for a very broad comparative approach: shared traits that were not present in a common ancestor (and thus are not homologies in the traditional sense) may nonetheless derive from shared genetic and developmental mechanisms. Here, Fitch advances the hypothesis that such "deep homology" is characteristic of language evolution as it is for other traits (eye and limb evolution). To the extent that this hypothesis of "pervasive deep homology" is correct, molecular and developmental data from a very wide range of species, from flies and worms to mice and birds, will offer us a powerful and exciting new set of insights into the mechanisms underlying the workings of the human mind.

Part II: Variation

Lyle Jenkins observes that biolinguistics studies language as a biological system and, as such, investigates language in the traditional areas of biology: form–function, development, and evolution. The biolinguistic perspective concerns itself with the interplay between what Chomsky has termed the "three factors" in language design: genetic endowment, experience, and principles not specific to the faculty of language. Taking into consideration properties of relations that have been shown to be central in different fields, including physics and linguistics, Jenkins discusses the role of concepts such as symmetry in the language design. Such concepts, Jenkins argues, are non-domain specific and non-species specific, but can contribute to the variation in biological systems seen in development and evolution. Lyle Jenkins's chapter is related to Anna Maria Di Sciullo's, which argues that concepts such as anti-symmetry and asymmetry contribute to an explanatory account of variation and change in language, as they do in biology.

Charles Yang presents a further step toward the incorporation of methods of evolutionary genetics into the study of language acquisition and change. The author explores how, as a result of learning, syntactic variations may originate from and spread within a specific set of lexical items, and these variations then cause further changes in the global properties of the grammar. He shows that the mathematical models of genetic drift can be used to capture the stochastic aspects of linguistic transmission, with implications in the study of linguistic typology as well. Yang's chapter is related to Chomsky and Berwick's with respect to the relation between language variation and language acquisition, as well as to Guardiano and Longobardi's chapter on the relation between parametric syntax and phylogenetic variation. It is also related to Cedric Boeckx's chapter, which relates parameter settings, learning, and optimization.

In Chapter 10, Cedric Boeckx outlines a new theoretical framework to understand the nature and limits of language variation. Although it is often said that minimalism grew out of the perceived success of the principles-and-parameters approach at solving "Plato's problem," the classical notion of parameter, with its attendant "hierarchy," does not fit well with the attempt to approach Universal Grammar from below. Boeckx claims that parameters can affect only the morpho-phonological expressions, and that the FLN is therefore non-parametrized/truly universal, as one might expect if much of it is the result of "third factor" effects. Furthermore, the way language develops must be taken into consideration, and Boeckx proposes a Superset Bias, which amounts to saying that the child entertains a certain setting for parameters that minimizes the learning required, and only resets the value of the parameters involved if there is too much contrary evidence from the linguistic input. If correct, the Superset Bias suggests that recurrent patterns of variation show signs of optimization.

Rita Manzini and Leonardo Savoia analyze variation in auxiliary choice in the present perfect of Romance and Albanian, arguing that it reduces to the lexical, selectional, properties of *have* and *be*—and ultimately to the interaction of primitive notions of person split, transitivity, and voice. They characterize the person split in terms of event- vs. discourse-anchoring, while we take it that transitivity involves the *n*-adicity of the predicate—the basic split being between monadic and polyadic. The authors conclude that the unification of reflexives, anticausatives, passives, and impersonals in the middle-passive voice (such as Italian *si*) cannot be achieved on the basis of movement from object to subject position, as in the classical generative account of passives, proposing instead that voice distinctions require reference to notions of open/generic variables in the argument structure. This amounts to upholding the minimalist hypothesis of lexical parametrization. Manzini and Savoia also suggest that variation in the so-called functional lexicon is not distinguishable from variation in the substantive lexicon. This supports the hypothesis presented in Richard Kayne's chapter that the distinction between functional and lexical categories is not part of the primitives of the language faculty.

In Chapter 12, Giuseppe Longobardi and Cristina Guardiano state that in addition to its theoretical impact, the development of molecular biology has brought about the possibility of extraordinary historical progress in the study of phylogenetic classification of different species and human populations. The authors argue that parametric analyses of grammatical diversity in theoretical linguistics can prompt analogous progress in the historical classification of language families, by showing that abstract syntactic properties are reliable indicators of phylogenetic relations. The pursuit of this approach radically questions the traditional belief in the orthogonality of grammatical typology and language genealogy and ultimately contributes to establishing formal grammar as a population science and historical linguistics as an important part of cognitive inquiry.

Anna Maria Di Sciullo's chapter relates to Richard Kayne's regarding the idea that parametric variation is a property of unvalued features. It is also related to Cedric Boeckx's chapter with respect to the role of third factors in variation and to the view that the FLN is immune to variation. Furthermore, it also echoes Longobardi and Guardiano's and Berwick and Chomsky's chapters on the role of parameters in language and in biology. Di Sciullo formulates new links between variation in language and variation in biology, focusing on asymmetry. She starts by relating the dynamics of Homeobox (HOX) genes to the dynamics of parameters, and suggests that they too have an asymmetric if–then logic. She then relates the directionality of language change to anti-symmetry breaking. She suggests that anti-symmetry breaking might be part of language evolution as well as it is part of the evolution of body plans. Finally she asks the question why asymmetry should be a core concept of the language faculty.

Part III: Computation

Richard Kayne starts by assuming that recursion is unique to the FLN, asks the question why the FLN is not available to other species, and lists several properties of the FLN that could be absent in other species. He focuses on the role of the antisymmetry property (Kayne 1994) as a differentiating property. He points out that if antisymmetry is correct, and if there is no mirror-image language of English, the question arises whether this is a possibility in a given species of bird, for example. He then discusses issues related to the notion of optionality of projection in the case of head–head merger, and proposes a solution in terms of singleton-set formation and antisymmetry/antioptionality, which he suggests could be a property of the FLN. Kayne proposes to derive what we think of as the open–closed-class items distinction, the noun–verb distinction, as well as other properties of nouns from the antisymmetry-driven approach to the lexicon.

Howard Lasnik's chapter asks what kind of computing device the FLN is. He reconsiders the question of the generative power of the syntactic system associated with the FLN. To generate such common linguistic expressions as those involving agreement among certain constituents at least the power of context-free procedures is needed over the less powerful finite-state Markov model (an argument used by Chomsky 1957). This is because context-free grammars introduce structures that are not visible on the surface or linearized linguistic expressions. Lasnik points out that there are areas of syntax that appear to involve a flattened structure. Such structures were used as motivation for the move into transformational grammar. Lasnik expresses uncertainty as to whether transformations can solve the problem of coordination and wonders if the lower power of Markov procedures for such cases should be retained. Arguing that Markovian vs. non-Markovian properties have been discussed with respect to transformational derivations too, Lasnik notices that there have been early and recent arguments for globality in derivations and discusses the implications of some such cases.

Richard Larson discusses the computation of propositions and their interpretation by the psychological faculty. Larson observes that the minimalist view raises the clear expectation that one will find significant properties of linguistic representations, and perhaps of the architecture itself, that can be traced back to the articulatory–perceptual or the conceptual–intentional systems. Larson suggests that semantic intensionality and its representation in syntax are a promising place to seek such properties. More precisely, he argues for the following three points. First, that natural language seems to project the semantic property of intensionality uniquely into the syntactic domain of clausal complement, although this can be concealed by grammatical phenomena to some extent. Second, that children's mastery of intensionality appears to be crucially tied to mastery of clausal complementation, which also correlates with the development of the child's theory of mind. Third, that the correlation between intensionality and clausal complementation ("sententialism") plausibly reflects an interface constraint: roughly, that the conceptual–intentional system inputs propositions derived by the language faculty only when these are presented in appropriate format. These results suggest an attractive view of the syntactic notion of "phase" rather different from the current one, which adverts to grammar-extrinsic notions like memory and processing load. Phases can be seen as the point where the language faculty computes propositions for the psychological faculty.

Alessandra Giorgi's chapter focuses on the computation of temporal dependencies, and thus is related to the other chapters in this section. It also considers temporal dependencies across languages from the point of view of Universal Grammar, and thus her chapter is related to the chapters on variation, including Rita Manzini and Leonardo Savoia's chapter on variation in auxiliary choice. Giorgi argues that temporal relations are usually implemented in the various languages (mostly) by means of verbal morpho-syntax. Temporal, aspectual and modal morphemes codify the possible relations between events in main and embedded clauses. However, whereas on the one hand the inventory of the possible interpretive relations is universal—as well as relatively limited—on the other, verbal morpho-syntax varies across languages. On the other hand, the ability of expressing a preceding relation—that is, past or future—between events does not significantly differ among languages, and in a way, this relation is not expected to vary. The presence of considerable morpho-syntactic differences is therefore rather puzzling. The important issue is to reduce language variability—by means of an appropriate level of abstraction—in order to predict and explain the rise of the various language types, by identifying the relevant dimensions and their universal properties.

Like Richard Larson, Wolfram Hinzen addresses questions related to the computation of semantics in Chapter 18. He notes that minimalist inquiries often assume that semantics comes for free: semantics or "thought" is what so-called conceptual–intentional systems incorporate, and the primary task is that of explaining the emergence of a syntactic system that interfaces with these pre-given systems, so as to express the relevant "thoughts." Taking that as a basis, various syntactic constraints are rationalized as answering various "conditions imposed" by the conceptual–intentional systems, in optimal ways. On this model, internal computational complexity matches some specific task domain (composing predicates, taking arguments, thematic relations, "discourse," etc.). In this chapter, Hinzen pursues an alternative which he argues to be both conceptually superior and more in line with plausible principles of economy and conservativity in the building of adaptive complexity in biological evolution. In particular, he argues that syntactic structure should be regarded as radically underspecified with regard to the semantic task performed; domain-general principles of organizing information economically lend themselves to semantic uses, they engender semantic consequences.

In Chapter 19, Carlo Cecchetto and Costanza Papagno consider the questions related to processing of syntax by the brain, which are also discussed in Richard Larson's chapter, albeit from a different perspective. Cecchetto and Papagno start with the premise that working memory (WM) is involved in language comprehension, since this requires the temporary storage of the linguistic information. The most established model of WM is Baddeley and Hitch's. A crucial question is whether natural-language processing relies on one component of this model, namely the Phonological Loop (or Phonological Short-Term Memory, STM). Although the prevailing answer in the literature is negative, after reviewing the available evidence and reporting ongoing research, Cecchetto and Papagno claim that the Phonological Loop plays an important role in language processing. Finally, they discuss possible consequences for theoretical models of linguistic competence and for brain activation studies.

In the last chapter, Robert Berwick discusses theoretical issues on the computation of linguistic expressions within the Minimalist Program. He states that the basic question underlying the Strong Minimalist Thesis is how little can be attributed to Universal Grammar while still accounting for the variety of I-languages attained, relying on third-factor principles. The author notes that it has recently been argued that interface conditions at the conceptual–intentional side may largely fix the design properties of Univeral Grammar. Thus, his chapter relates to Cedric Boeckx's and Wolfram Hinzen's on the underspecification of the FLN. Berwick shows that these design properties also dovetail nearly perfectly with constraints on the sensory–motor side, with, for example, the no-tampering condition, Edge labels, binary Merge, and the like all meshing with a computational model that imposes the minimal possible cost for sensory–motor system. In this restricted sense, then, the entire system, from sensory–motor through to conceptual–intentional, is optimal.

The issues related to the mergence of language evolution and variation are central in the biolinguistic enterprise, which seeks to understand why certain principles and not others are part of the language faculty, why variation and change as well as language acquisition have certain formal properties and not others. Such questions can be raised only when questions on the form of computation have been addressed and at least partially resolved. We hope that this book will strengthen the import of biolinguistics and the Minimalist Program for the understanding of the properties of the human specific faculty of language and will foster research in this exciting interdisciplinary field.

Acknowledgments

We would like to thank Calixto Aguero-Bautista, who was part of the organization of the Biolinguistic Conference in Santo Domingo, which was sponsored by the Government of the Dominican Republic. We also wish to thank Guglielmo Cinque, who participated in the organization of the Biolinguistic Conference at the University of Venice. This conference was sponsored by the Social Sciences and Humanities Research Council of Canada, whose aid to research we gratefully acknowledge: a Major Collaborative Research Initiative project directed by Anna Maria Di Sciullo on Interface asymmetries and cognitive processing (SSHRCC #412-2003-1003). Finally we are grateful to the students that helped us at different stages of the editing of this book, Paul John, Calin Batori and Stanca Somesfalean at the Université du Québec à Montréal, Adriana Fasanella and Carlos Rubio at the Universitat Autònoma de Barcelona.

Part I
Evolution

2

The Biolinguistic Program: The Current State of its Development

ROBERT C. BERWICK AND NOAM CHOMSKY

Before discussing language, particularly in a biological context, we should be clear about what we mean by the term, which has engendered much confusion. Sometimes the term "language" is used to refer to human language; sometimes it is used to refer to any symbolic system or mode of communication or representation, as when one speaks of the language of the bees, or programming languages, or the language of the stars, and so on. Here we will keep to the first sense: human language, a particular object of the biological world. The study of language, so understood, has come to be called the *biolinguistic* perspective.

Among the many puzzling questions about language, two are salient: First, why are there any languages at all, evidently unique to the human lineage, what evolutionary biologists call an "autapomorphy"? Second, why are there so many languages? These are in fact the basic questions of origin and variation that so occupied Darwin and other evolutionary thinkers and comprise modern biology's explanatory core: why do we observe *this* particular array of living forms in the world and not others? From this standpoint, linguistic science stands squarely within the modern biological tradition, despite its seemingly abstract details, as has often been observed.

According to a fairly general consensus among paleoanthropologists and archaeologists, these questions are very recent ones in evolutionary time. Roughly 100,000 years ago, the first question did not arise, because there were no languages. About 50,000 years ago, the answers to both questions were settled: our ancestors began their trek from Africa, spreading over the entire world, and as far as is known, the language faculty has remained essentially unchanged—which is not surprising in such a brief period. An infant from a Stone Age tribe in the Amazon, if brought to Boston, will be indistinguishable in linguistic and other cognitive functions from children born in Boston who trace their ancestry to the first English colonists; and conversely. The actual dates are uncertain, and do not matter much for our purposes. The general picture appears to be roughly accurate.

We are therefore concerned with a curious biological object, *language*, which has appeared on earth quite recently.It is a species property of humans, a common endowment with no significant variation apart from serious pathology, unlike anything else known in the organic world in its essentials, and surely central to human life since its emergence. It is a central component of what the co-founder of modern evolutionary theory, Alfred Russell Wallace, called "man's intellectual and moral nature": the human capacities for creative imagination, language and symbolism generally, recording and interpretation of natural phenomena, intricate social practices and the like, a complex that is sometimes simply called "the human capacity." This complex seems to have crystallized fairly recently among a small group in East Africa of whom we are all descendants, distinguishing contemporary humans sharply from other animals, with enormous consequences for the whole of the biological world. It is commonly and plausibly assumed that the emergence of language was a core element in this sudden and dramatic transformation. Furthermore, language is one component of the human capacity that is accessible to study in some depth. That is another reason why even research that is purely linguistic in character actually falls under the heading of biolinguistics despite its superficial remove from biology, as exemplified in the chapters by Lasnik and Larson in this volume.

From the biolinguistic perspective, we can think of language as, in essence, an "organ of the body," more or less on a par with the visual or digestive or immune systems. Like others, it is a subcomponent of a complex organism that has sufficient internal integrity so that it makes sense to study it in abstraction from its complex interactions with other systems in the life of the organism. In this case it is a cognitive organ, like the systems of planning, interpretation, reflection, and whatever else falls among those aspects of the world loosely "termed mental," which reduce somehow to "the organical structure of the brain," in the words of the eighteenth-century scientist and philosopher Joseph Priestley. He was articulating the natural conclusion after Newton had demonstrated, to Newton's own great dismay and disbelief, that the world is not a machine, contrary to the core assumptions of the seventeenth-century scientific revolution—a conclusion that in effect eliminated the traditional mind–body problem, because there is no longer a coherent concept of *body* (*matter, physical*), a matter well understood in the eighteenth and nineteenth centuries. We can think of language as a *mental organ*, where the term "mental" simply refers to certain aspects of the world, to be studied in the same way as chemical, optical, electrical, and other aspects, with the hope for eventual unification—noting that such unification in these other domains in the past was often achieved in completely unexpected ways, not necessarily by reduction.

As mentioned at the outset with regard to the curious mental organ *language*, two obvious questions arise. One is: Why does it exist at all, evidently unique to our species? Second: Why is there more than one language? In fact, why is there such a multitude and variety that languages appear to "differ from each other without limit and in unpredictable ways" and therefore the study of each language must be approached "without any preexistent scheme of what a language must be," here quoting the formulation of the prominent theoretical linguist Martin Joos 50 years ago, summarizing the reigning "Boasian tradition," as he plausibly called it, tracing it to the work of one of the founders of modern anthropology and anthropological linguistics, Franz Boas. The publication that was the foundation of American structural linguistics in the 1950s, Zellig Harris's *Methods in Structural Linguistics* (1951), was called "methods" because there seemed to be little to say about language beyond the methods for reducing the data from limitlessly varying languages to organized form. European structuralism was much the same. Nikolai Trubetzkoy's classic introduction to phonological analysis was similar in conception. More generally, structuralist inquiries focused almost entirely on phonology and morphology, the areas in which languages do appear to differ widely and in complex ways, a matter of broader interest, to which we will return.[1]

The dominant picture in general biology at about the same time was rather similar, captured in molecular biologist Gunther Stent's observation that the variability of organisms is so free as to constitute "a near infinitude of particulars which have to be sorted out case by case" (as quoted in Carroll, 2005a: 24).

In fact the problem of reconciling unity and diversity has constantly arisen in general biology as well as in linguistics. The study of language that developed within the seventeenth-century scientific revolution distinguished universal from particular grammar, though not quite in the sense of the contemporary biolinguistic approach. Universal grammar was taken to be the intellectual core of the discipline; particular grammars were regarded as accidental instantiations of the universal system. With the flourishing of anthropological linguistics, the pendulum swung in the other direction, towards diversity, well articulated in the Boasian formulation we quoted. In general

---

[1] See Joos (1957); Trubetzkoy (1939, trans. 1969).

biology, the issue had been raised sharply in a famous debate between the naturalists Georges Cuvier and Geoffroy St. Hilaire in 1830. Cuvier's position, emphasizing diversity, prevailed, particularly after the Darwinian revolution, leading to the conclusions about the near infinitude of variety that have to be sorted out case by case. Perhaps the most quoted sentence in biology is Darwin's final observation in *Origin of Species* about how "from so simple a beginning, endless forms most beautiful and most wonderful have been, and are being, evolved." It is unclear if the irony was intended, but these words were taken by evolutionary biologist Sean Carroll as the title of his introduction to "the new science of evo-devo," which seeks to show that the forms that have evolved are far from endless, in fact are remarkably uniform.

Reconciliation of the apparent diversity of organic forms with their evident underlying uniformity—why do we see *this* array of living things in the world and not others, just as why do we see *this* array of languages/grammars and not others?—comes about through the interplay of three factors, famously articulated by the biologist Monod in his book *Le Hasard et la Nécessité*: (1970; *Chance and Necessity*, 1972). First, there is the historically contingent fact that we are all common descendants from a single tree of life, and so share common ancestry with all other living things, which apparently have explored only a minute fraction of a space that includes a much larger set of possible biological outcomes. It should by now be no surprise that we therefore possess common genes, biochemical pathways, and much else.

Second, there are the physio-chemical constraints of the world, necessities that delimit biological possibilities, like the near-impossibility of wheels for locomotion due to the physical difficulty of providing a nerve control and a blood supply to a rotating object. Third, there is the sieving effect of natural selection, which winnows out from a pre-existing menu of possibilities—offered by historical contingency and physio-chemical constraints—the actual array of organisms that we observe in the world around us. Note that the effect of the constrained menu of options is of utmost importance; if the options are extremely constrained, then selection would have very little to choose from: it should be no surprise that when one goes to a fast-food restaurant one is usually seen leaving with a hamburger and french fries. Thus, just as Darwin would have it, natural selection is by no means the "exclusive" means that has shaped the natural world: "Furthermore, I am convinced that Natural Selection has been the main but not exclusive means of modification" (Darwin 1859: 7).

Recent discoveries have reinvigorated the general approach of D'Arcy Thompson (1992) and Alan Turing on principles that constrain the variety of organisms. In Turing and Wardlaw's words, the true science of biology should regard each "living organism as a special kind of system to which the general laws of physics and chemistry apply," sharply constraining their possible variety and fixing their fundamental properties (Turing and Wardlaw 1953). That perspective may sound less extreme today after the discovery of master genes, deep homologies and conservation, and much else, perhaps even restrictions of evolutionary–developmental processes so narrow that "replaying the protein tape of life might be surprisingly repetitive," quoting a report by Weinreich et al. (2006) on feasible mutational paths, reinterpreting a famous image of Steven Gould's, who had suggested that the tape of life, if replayed, might follow a variety of paths. As Michael Lynch further notes (2007: 367), "we have known for decades that all eukaryotes share most of the same genes for transcription, translation, replication, nutrient uptake, core metabolism, cytoskeletal structure, and so forth. Why would we expect anything different for development?"

In a recent review of the evo–devo approach, Gerd Müller (2007) notes how much more concrete our understanding of the Turing-type patterning models have become, observing that several

Generic forms ... result from the interaction of basic cell properties with different pattern-forming mechanisms. Differential adhesion and cell polarity when modulated by different kinds of physical and chemical patterning mechanisms ... lead to standard organizational motifs .... differential adhesion properties and their polar distribution on cell surfaces lead to hollow spheres when combined with a diffusion gradient, and to invaginated spheres when combined with a sedimentation gradient.... The combination of differential adhesion with a reaction-diffusion mechanism generates radially periodic structures, whereas a combination with chemical oscillation results in serially periodic structures. Early metazoan body plans represent an exploitation of such generic patterning repertoires.   (Müller 2007: 947)

For example, the contingent fact that we have five fingers and five toes may be better explained by an appeal to how toes and fingers develop than that five is optimal for their function.[2]

Biochemist Michael Sherman (2007) argues, perhaps more controversially, that a "Universal Genome that encodes all major developmental programs essential for various phyla of Metazoa emerged in a unicellular or a primitive multicellular organism shortly before the Cambrian period" about 500 million years ago, when there was a sudden explosion of complex animal forms;

---

[2] As Ahouse and Berwick (1998) note, "Five fingers and toes were not the original number of digits in tetrapods (see the discussion by M. I. Coates and J. A. Clark in *Nature* 347, 1990, 66–9) and amphibians probably never had more than four digits (and generally have three) on their front and back feet. There is a clever explanation from molecular developmental genetics that rationalizes why there are at most five different types of digits even if some are duplicated."

and, further, that the many "Metazoan phyla, all having similar genomes, are nonetheless so distinct because they utilize specific combinations of developmental programs." On this view, there is but one multicellular animal from a sufficiently abstract point of view—the point of view that might be taken by a Martian scientist from a much more advanced civilization viewing events on earth. Superficial variety would result in part from various arrangements of an evolutionarily conserved "developmental–genetic toolkit," as it is sometimes called. If ideas of this kind prove to be on the right track, the problem of unity and diversity will be reformulated in ways that would have surprised some recent generations of scientists. The degree to which the conserved toolkit is the sole explanation for the observed uniformity deserves some care. As mentioned, observed uniformity arises in part because there has simply not been enough time, and contingent ancestry-by-descent bars the possibility of exploring "too much" of the genetic–protein–morphological space—particularly given the virtual impossibility of "going backwards" and starting the search over again for greater success. Given these inherent constraints, it becomes much less of a surprise that organisms are all built according to a certain set of *Baupläne*, as Steven Gould has emphasized, among others. It is in this sense that if sophisticated Martian scientists came to earth, they would probably see in effect just one organism, though with many apparent superficial variations.

The uniformity had not passed unnoticed in Darwin's day. The naturalistic studies of Darwin's close associate and expositor Thomas Huxley led him to observe, with some puzzlement, that there appear to be "predetermined lines of modification" that lead natural selection to "produce varieties of a limited number and kind" for each species (Maynard-Smith et al. 1985: 266). Indeed, the study of the sources and nature of possible variation constituted a large portion of Darwin's own research program after *Origin*, as summarized in his *Variation of Plants and Animals under Domestication* (1868). Huxley's conclusion is reminiscent of earlier ideas of "rational morphology," a famous example being Goethe's theories of archetypal forms of plants, which have been partially revived in the evo–devo revolution. Indeed, as indicated earlier, Darwin himself was sensitive to this issue, and, grand synthesizer that he was, dealt more carefully with such "laws of growth and form": the constraints and opportunities to change are due to the details of development, chance associations with other features that may be strongly selected for or against, and finally selection on the trait itself. Darwin noted that such laws of "correlation and balance" would be of considerable importance to his theory, remarking, for example, that "white cats if they have blue eyes are almost invariably deaf" (Darwin, 1856 letter to W. D. Fox).

When the evolutionary Modern Synthesis, pioneered by Fisher, Haldane, and Wright, held sway through most of the last half of the previous century, emphasis in evolution was focused on micro-mutational events and gradualism, singling out the power of natural selection operating via very small incremental steps. More recently, however, in general biology the pendulum has been swinging towards a combination of Monod's three factors, yielding new ways of understanding traditional ideas.

Let us return to the first of the two basic questions: Why should there be any languages at all, apparently an autapomorphy? As mentioned, very recently in evolutionary time the question would not have arisen: there were no languages. There were, of course, plenty of animal communication systems. But they are all radically different from human language in structure and function. Human language does not even fit within the standard typologies of animal communication systems—Marc Hauser's, for example, in his comprehensive review of the evolution of communication (1996). It has been conventional to regard language as a system whose function is communication. This is indeed the widespread view invoked in most selectionist accounts of language, which almost invariably start from this interpretation. However, to the extent that the characterization has any meaning, this appears to be incorrect, for a variety of reasons to which we turn below.

The inference of a biological trait's "purpose" or "function" from its surface form is always rife with difficulties. Lewontin's remarks in *The Triple Helix* (2000: 79) illustrate how difficult it can be to assign a unique function to an organ or trait even in the case of what at first seems like a far simpler situation: bones do not have a single, unambiguous function. While it is true that bones support the body, allowing us to stand up and walk, they are also a storehouse for calcium and bone marrow for producing new red blood cells, so they are in a sense part of the circulatory system.

What is true for bones is also true in spades for human language. Moreover, there has always been an alternative tradition, expressed by Burling (1993), among others, that humans may well possess a secondary communication system like those of other primates, namely a nonverbal system of gestures or even calls, but that this is not language, since, as Burling notes, "our surviving primate communication system remains sharply distinct from language."[3]

Language can of course be used for communication, as can any aspect of what we do: style of dress, gesture, and so on. And it can be and commonly is used for much else. Statistically speaking, for whatever that is worth, the

---

[3] Laura Petitto's work on the acquisition of sign language (1987) demonstrates Burling's point rather dramatically—the same gesture is used for pointing and pronominal reference, but in the latter case the gesture is counter-iconic at the age when infants typically reverse "I" and "you."

overwhelming use of language is internal—for thought. It takes an enormous act of will to keep from talking to oneself in every waking moment—and asleep as well, often a considerable annoyance. The distinguished neurologist Harry Jerison (1973: 55) among others expressed a stronger view, holding that "language did not evolve as a communication system... the initial evolution of language is more likely to have been... for the construction of a real world," as a "tool for thought." Not only in the functional dimension, but also in all other respects—semantic, syntactic, morphological, and phonological— the core properties of human language appear to differ sharply from animal communication systems, and to be largely unique in the organic world.

How, then, did this strange object appear in the biological record, apparently within a very narrow evolutionary window, perhaps about 50–100,000 years ago? There are of course no definite answers, but it is possible to sketch what seem to be some reasonable speculations, which relate closely to work of recent years in the biolinguistic framework.

Anatomically modern humans are found in the fossil record several hundred thousand years ago, but evidence of the human capacity is much more recent, not long before the trek from Africa. Paleoanthropologist Ian Tattersall reports that "a vocal tract capable of producing the sounds of articulate speech" existed over half a million years before there is any evidence that our ancestors were using language. "We have to conclude," he writes, "that the appearance of language and its anatomical correlates was not driven by natural selection, however beneficial these innovations may appear in hindsight"—a conclusion which raises no problems for standard evolutionary biology, contrary to illusions in popular literature (Tattersall 1998). It appears that human brain size reached its current level recently, perhaps about 100,000 years ago, which suggests to some specialists that "human language probably evolved, at least in part, as an automatic but adaptive consequence of increased absolute brain size" (neuroscientist Georg Striedter 2004). With regard to language, Tattersall concludes that "after a long—and poorly understood—period of erratic brain expansion and reorganization in the human lineage, something occurred that set the stage for language acquisition. This innovation would have depended on the phenomenon of emergence, whereby a chance combination of preexisting elements results in something totally unexpected," presumably "a neural change... in some population of the human lineage... rather minor in genetic terms, [which] probably had nothing whatever to do with adaptation" though it conferred advantages, and then proliferated. Perhaps it was an automatic consequence of absolute brain size, as Striedter suggests, or perhaps some minor chance mutation. Sometime later—not very long in evolutionary time—came further innovations, perhaps culturally driven, that led to behaviorally modern humans, the crystallization of the human capacity, and the trek from Africa (Tattersall 1998, 2002, 2005).

What was that neural change in some small group that was rather minor in genetic terms? To answer that, we have to consider the special properties of language. The most elementary property of our shared language capacity is that it enables us to construct and interpret a discrete infinity of hierarchically structured expressions: discrete because there are five-word sentences and six-word sentences, but no five-and-a-half-word sentences; infinite because there is no longest sentence. Language is therefore based on a recursive generative procedure that takes elementary word-like elements from some store, call it the lexicon, and applies repeatedly to yield structured expressions, without bound. To account for the emergence of the language faculty—hence for the existence of at least one language—we have to face two basic tasks. One task is to account for the "atoms of computation," the lexical items—commonly in the range of 30–50,000. The second is to discover the computational properties of the language faculty. This task in turn has several facets: we must seek to discover the generative procedure that constructs infinitely many expressions in the mind, and the methods by which these internal mental objects are related to two *interfaces* with language-external (but organism-internal) systems: the system of thought, on the one hand, and also to the sensory-motor system, thus *externalizing* internal computations and thought. This is one way of reformulating the traditional conception, at least back to Aristotle, that language is sound with a meaning. All of these tasks pose very serious problems, far more so than was believed in the recent past, or often today.

Let us turn then to the basic elements of language, beginning with the generative procedure, which, it seems, emerged some time in the 50,000–100,000 year range, barely a flick of an eye in evolutionary time, presumably involving some slight rewiring of the brain. At this point the evo–devo revolution in biology becomes relevant. It has provided compelling evidence for two relevant conclusions. One is that genetic endowment even for regulatory systems is deeply conserved. A second is that very slight changes can yield great differences in observed outcome—though phenotypic variation is nonetheless limited, in virtue of the deep conservation of genetic systems, and laws of nature of the kind that interested Thompson and Turing. To cite a simple illustration, there are two kinds of stickleback fish, with or without spiky spines on the pelvis. About 10,000 years ago, a mutation in a genetic "switch" near a gene involved in spine production differentiated the two varieties, one with spines and one without, one adapted to oceans and the other to lakes (Colosimo et al. 2004, 2005; Orr 2005a).

Much more far-reaching results have to do with the evolution of eyes, an intensively studied topic. It turns out that there are very few types of eye, in part because of constraints imposed by the physics of light, in part because only one category of proteins, opsin molecules, can perform the necessary functions. The genes encoding opsin had very early origins, and are repeatedly recruited, but only in limited ways, again because of physical constraints. The same is true of eye lens proteins. The evolution of eyes illustrates the complex interactions of physical law, stochastic processes, and the role of selection in choosing within a narrow physical channel of possibilities (Gehring 2005).

Jacob and Monod's work from 1961 on the discovery of the "operon" in *E. coli* for which they won the Nobel Prize, led to Monod's famous quote (cited in Jacob 1988): "what is true for the colon bacillus [*E. coli*] is true for the elephant" (Jacob 1988: 290). While this has sometimes been interpreted as anticipating the modern evo–devo account, it seems that what Monod actually meant was that his and François Jacob's generalized negative regulation theory should be sufficient to account for all cases of gene regulation. But this conjecture turned out to be incorrect. Eukaryotes (non-bacteria) do not (cannot) use the operon regulatory machinery that bacteria (Prokaryotes) use, because they do not have their genes lined up neatly in a linear fashion, strung out like beads along a string, without breaks and without intervening non-protein coding regions (introns). Roughly, it is this arrangement in Prokaryotes that permits the negative feedback operon system to work. Indeed, much of the modern evo–devo revolution is about the discovery of the rather more sophisticated methods for gene regulation and development employed by Eukaryotes. Nonetheless, Monod's basic notion that slight differences in timing and arrangement of regulatory mechanisms that activate genes could result in enormous differences did turn out to be correct, though the machinery was unanticipated. It was left to Jacob (1977) to provide a suggestive model for the development of other organisms based on the notion that "thanks to complex regulatory circuits" what "accounts for the difference between a butterfly and a lion, a chicken and a fly ... are the result of mutations which altered the organism's regulatory circuits more than its chemical structure" (1977: 26). Jacob's model in turn provided part of the inspiration for the Principles and Parameters (P&P) approach to language, a matter discussed in lectures shortly after (Chomsky 1980: 67).

The P&P approach is based on the assumption that languages consist of fixed and invariant principles connected to a kind of switchbox of parameters, questions that the child has to answer on the basis of presented data in order to fix a language from the limited variety available in principle—or perhaps, as Charles Yang has argued (2002), to determine a probability distribution over languages resulting from a learning procedure for parameter setting. For example, the child has to determine whether the language to which it is exposed is head-initial, like English, a language in which substantive elements precede their objects, as in *read the book* or *in the room*; or whether it is head-final, like Japanese, where the counterparts would be *book read* and *room in*. As in the somewhat analogous case of rearrangement of regulatory mechanisms, the approach suggests a framework for understanding how essential unity might yield the appearance of the limitless diversity that was assumed not long ago for language (as for biological organisms generally).

The P&P research program has been very fruitful, yielding rich new understanding of a very broad typological range of languages, opening new questions that had never been considered, sometimes providing answers. It is no exaggeration to say that more has been learned about languages in the past twenty-five years than in the earlier millennia of serious inquiry into language. With regard to the two salient questions with which we began, the approach suggests that what emerged, fairly suddenly in evolutionary terms, was the generative procedure that provides the principles, and that diversity of language results from the fact that the principles do not determine the answers to all questions about language, but leave some questions as open parameters. Notice that the single illustration above has to do with ordering. Though the matter is contested, it seems that there is by now substantial linguistic evidence that ordering is restricted to externalization of internal computation to the sensory-motor system, and plays no role in core syntax and semantics, a conclusion for which there is also accumulating biological evidence of a sort familiar to mainstream biologists, to which we return below.

The simplest assumption, hence the one we adopt unless counter-evidence appears, is that the generative procedure emerged suddenly as the result of a minor mutation. In that case we would expect the generative procedure to be very simple. Various kinds of generative procedures have been explored in the past 50 years. One approach familiar to linguists and computer scientists is phrase-structure grammar, developed in the 1950s and since extensively employed. The approach made sense at the time. It fit very naturally into one of the several equivalent formulations of the mathematical theory of recursive procedures—Emil Post's rewriting systems—and it captured at least some basic properties of language, such as hierarchic structure and embedding. Nevertheless, it was quickly recognized that phrase-structure grammar is not only inadequate for language but is also quite a complex procedure with many arbitrary stipulations, not the kind of system we would hope to find, and unlikely to have emerged suddenly.

Over the years, research has found ways to reduce the complexities of these systems, and finally to eliminate them entirely in favor of the simplest possible mode of recursive generation: an operation that takes two objects already constructed, call them X and Y, and forms from them a new object that consists of the two unchanged, hence simply the set with X and Y as members. Call this operation Merge. Provided with conceptual atoms of the lexicon, the operation Merge, iterated without bound, yields an infinity of hierarchically constructed expressions. If these can be interpreted by conceptual systems, the operation provides an internal language of thought.

A very strong thesis, called the "strong minimalist thesis," is that the generative process is optimal: the principles of language are determined by efficient computation and language keeps to the simplest recursive operation, Merge, designed to satisfy interface conditions in accord with independent principles of efficient computation. Language is something like a snowflake, assuming its particular form by virtue of laws of nature—in this case principles of computational efficiency—once the basic mode of construction is available, and satisfying whatever conditions are imposed at the interfaces. The basic thesis is expressed in the title of a recent collection of technical essays: "Interfaces + Recursion = Language?" (Sauerland and Gärtner 2007). Optimally, recursion can be reduced to Merge. The question mark in the title is of course highly appropriate: the questions arise at the border of current research. We will suggest below that there is a significant asymmetry between the two interfaces, with the semantic–pragmatic interface—the link to systems of thought and action—having primacy. Just how rich these external conditions may be is also a serious research question, and a hard one, given the lack of much evidence about these thought–action systems that is independent of language. A very strong thesis, suggested by Wolfram Hinzen (2006) is that central components of thought, such as propositions, are basically derived from the optimally constructed generative procedure. If such ideas can be sharpened and validated, then the effect of the semantic–pragmatic interface on language design would be correspondingly reduced.

The strong minimalist thesis is very far from established, but it looks much more plausible than it did only a few years ago. Insofar as it is correct, the evolution of language will reduce to the emergence of the operation Merge, the evolution of conceptual atoms of the lexicon, the linkage to conceptual systems, and the mode of externalization. Any residue of principles of language not reducible to Merge and optimal computation will have to be accounted for by some other evolutionary process—one that we are unlikely to learn much about, at least by presently understood methods, as Lewontin (1998) notes.

Notice that there is no room in this picture for any precursors to language—say a language-like system with only short sentences. There is no rationale for postulation of such a system: to go from seven-word sentences to the discrete infinity of human language requires emergence of the same recursive procedure as to go from zero to infinity, and there is of course no direct evidence for such protolanguages. Similar observations hold for language acquisition, despite appearances, a matter that we put to the side here.

Crucially, the operation Merge yields the familiar *displacement* property of language: the fact that we pronounce phrases in one position, but interpret them somewhere else as well. Thus in the sentence *Guess what John is eating*, we understand *what* to be the object of *eat*, as in *John is eating an apple*, even though it is pronounced somewhere else. This property has always seemed paradoxical, a kind of *imperfection* of language. It is by no means necessary in order to capture semantic facts, but it is ubiquitous. It surpasses the capacity of phrase structure grammars, requiring that they be still further complicated with additional devices. But it falls within Merge, automatically. To see how, suppose that the operation Merge has constructed the mental expression corresponding to *John is eating what*. A larger expression can be constructed by Merge in two ways: Internal Merge can add something from within the expression, so as to form *what John is eating what*; and External Merge can add something new, yielding *Guess what John is eating what*.

That carries us part of the way towards displacement. In *what John is eating what*, the phrase *what* appears in two positions, and in fact those two positions are required for semantic interpretation: the original position provides the information that *what* is understood to be the direct object of *eat*, and the new position, at the edge, is interpreted as a quantifier ranging over a variable, so that the expression means something like "for which thing x, John is eating the thing x."

These observations generalize to a wide range of constructions. The results are just what is needed for semantic interpretation, but they do not yield the objects that are pronounced in English. We do not pronounce *guess what John is eating what*, but rather *guess what John is eating*, with the original position suppressed. That is a universal property of displacement, with minor (and interesting) qualifications that we can ignore here. The property follows from elementary principles of computational efficiency. In fact, it has often been noted that serial motor activity is computationally costly, a matter attested by the sheer quantity of motor cortex devoted to both motor control of the hands and for oro-facial articulatory gestures.

To externalize the internally generated expression *what John is eating what*, it would be necessary to pronounce *what* twice, and that turns out to place a very considerable burden on computation, when we consider expressions of normal complexity and the actual nature of displacement by Internal Merge. With all but one of the occurrences of *what* suppressed, the computational burden is greatly eased. The one occurrence that must be pronounced is the most prominent one, the last one created by Internal Merge: otherwise there will be no indication that the operation has applied to yield the correct interpretation. It appears, then, that the language faculty recruits a general principle of computational efficiency for the process of externalization.

The suppression of all but one of the occurrences of the displaced element is computationally efficient, but imposes a significant burden on interpretation, hence on communication. The person hearing the sentence has to discover the position of the gap where the displaced element is to be interpreted. That is a highly non-trivial problem in general, familiar from parsing programs. There is, then, a conflict between computational efficiency and interpretive–communicative efficiency. Universally, languages resolve the conflict in favor of computational efficiency. These facts at once suggest that language evolved as an instrument of internal thought, with externalization a secondary process. There is a great deal of evidence from language design that yields similar conclusions; so called "island properties," for example.

There are independent reasons for the conclusion that externalization is a secondary process. One is that externalization appears to be modality-independent, as has been learned from studies of sign language in recent years. The structural properties of sign and spoken language are remarkably similar. Additionally, acquisition follows the same course in both, and neural localization seems to be similar as well. That tends to reinforce the conclusion that language is optimized for the system of thought, with mode of externalization secondary.

Note further that the constraints on externalization holding for the auditory modality also appear to hold in the case of the visual modality in signed languages. Even though there is no physical constraint barring one from "saying" with one hand that *John likes ice-cream* and *Mary likes beer* with the other hand, nevertheless it appears that one hand is dominant throughout and delivers sentences (via gestures) in a left-to-right order in time, linearized as in vocal-tract externalization, while the non-dominant hand adds markings for emphasis, morphology, and the like.

Indeed, it seems possible to make a far stronger statement: all recent relevant biological and evolutionary research leads to the conclusion that the process of externalization is secondary. This includes the recent and highly publicized discoveries of genetic elements putatively involved in language, specifically, the FOXP2 regulatory (transcription factor) gene. FOXP2 is implicated in a highly heritable language defect, so-called verbal dyspraxia. Since this discovery it has been intensely analyzed from an evolutionary and comparative standpoint, with small amino-acid differences between the human variant and other primates and non-human mammals posited as the target of recent positive natural selection, perhaps concomitant with language emergence (Fisher et al. 1998; Enard et al. 2002); and with similarities between those same two amino acids in humans and Neandertals also suggested as possibly significant with respect to language (Krause, Lalueza-Fox, et al. 2007; *Science Daily*, 21 Oct. 2007).

However, we might ask whether this gene is centrally involved in language or, as now seems more plausible, is part of the secondary externalization process. Recent discoveries in birds and mice over the past few years point to an "emerging consensus" that this transcription factor gene is not so much part of a blueprint for internal syntax, the narrow faculty of language, and most certainly not some hypothetical "language gene" (just as there are no single genes for eye color or autism) but rather part of regulatory machinery related to externalization (Vargha-Khadem et al. 2005; Groszer et al. 2008). FOXP2 aids in the development of serial fine motor control, orofacial or otherwise: the ability to literally put one sound or gesture down in place, one point after another in time.

In this respect it is worth noting that members of the KE family in which this genetic defect was originally isolated exhibit a quite general motor dyspraxia, not localized to simply their oro-facial movements. Recent studies where a mutated FOXP2 gene built to replicate the defects found in the KE family was inserted in mice confirm this view: "We find that Foxp2-R552H heterozygous mice display subtle but highly significant deficits in learning of rapid motor skills . . . These data are consistent with proposals that human speech faculties recruit evolutionarily ancient neural circuits involved in motor learning" (Groszer et al. 2008: 359).

If this view is on the right track, then FOXP2 is more akin to the blueprint that aids in the construction of a properly functioning input–output system for a computer, like its printer, rather than the construction of the computer's central processor itself. From this point of view, what has gone wrong in the affected KE family members is thus something awry with the externalization system, the "printer," not the central language faculty itself. If this is so, then the evolutionary analyses suggesting that this transcription factor was under positive selection approximately 100,000 years ago (in itself arguable) could in fact be quite inconclusive about the evolution of the core components of the faculty of language, syntax, and the mapping to the "semantic" (conceptual–intensional) interface. It is difficult to determine the causal sequence: the link between FOXP2 and high-grade serial motor coordination could be regarded as either an opportunistic prerequisite substrate for externalization, no matter what the modality, as is common in evolutionary scenarios, or the result of selection pressure for efficient externalization solutions after Merge arose. In either case, FOXP2 becomes part of a system extrinsic to core syntax/semantics.

There is further recent evidence from Michael Coen (p.c.) regarding serial coordination in vocalization suggesting that discretized serial motor control might simply be a substrate common to all mammals, and possibly all vertebrates. If so, then the entire FOXP2 story, and motor externalization generally, is even further removed from the picture of core syntax/semantics evolution. The evidence comes from the finding that all mammals tested (people, dogs, cats, seals, whales, baboons, tamarin monkeys, mice) and unrelated vertebrates (crows, finches, frogs, etc.) possess what was formerly attributed just to the human externalization system: each of the vocal repertoires of these various species is drawn from a *finite* set of distinctive phonemes (or, more accurately, songemes in the case of birds, barkemes in the case of dogs, etc.). Coen's hypothesis is that each species has some finite number of articulatory productions, for example, phonemes, that are genetically constrained by its physiology, according to principles such as minimization of energy during vocalization, physical constraints, and the like. This is similar to Kenneth Stevens's picture of the quantal nature of speech production (Stevens 1972, 1989).

On this view, any given species uses a subset of species-specific primitive sounds to generate the vocalizations common to that species. (It would not be expected that each animal uses all of them, in the same way that no human employs all phonemes.) If so, then our hypothetical Martian would conclude that even at the level of peripheral externalization, there is one human language, one dog language, one frog language, and the like.

Summarizing, FOXP2 does not speak to the question of the core faculty of human language because it really has nothing to do with the core language *phenotype*, Merge and syntax. From an explanatory point of view, this makes it quite unlike the case of, say, sickle-cell anemia where a genetic defect directly leads to the aberrant trait, the formation of an abnormal haemoglobin protein and resulting red blood cell distortion. To be sure, FOXP2 remains a possibly necessary component of the language system in the same way that a printer is part of a computer system. But it is not human language *tout court*. If all this is so, then the explanation "for" the core language phenotype may be even more indirect and difficult than Richard Lewontin (1998) has sketched.[4]

In fact, in many respects this focus on FOXP2 and dyspraxia is quite similar to the near-universal focus on language as communication.[5] Both efforts examine properties apparently particular only to the externalization process, which, we conjecture, is not part of the core faculty of human language. In this sense both efforts are misdirected, unrevealing of the internal computations of the mind/brain, the cognitive revolution notwithstanding. By expressly stating the distinction between internal syntax and externalization, many new research directions may be opened up, and new concrete, testable predictions posed particularly from a biological perspective, as the example of animal vocal productions illustrates.

Returning to the core principles of language, unbounded Merge (hence displacement) must have arisen from some rewiring of the brain, hence in an individual, not a group. The individual so endowed would have had many advantages: capacities for complex thought, planning, interpretation, and so on. The capacity would be partially transmitted to offspring, and because of the selective advantages it confers, it might come to dominate a small breeding group, though as with all such novel mutations, there is an issue about how an initially small number of copies of such an allele might survive, despite a large selective advantage. As first noted by Haldane (1927), the probability of even a highly advantageous heterozygous mutation with a selective advantage of 1 percent—about an order of magnitude greater than any selective advantage found in field measurement—would nevertheless have approximately a $1/e$ or about a 30 percent chance of going extinct within one generation. Gillespie (1991) notes that a 99 percent certainty of fixing such an advantageous mutation is attained only after reaching approximately 4000 copies of such an allele. Assuming an effective population size of about

---

[4] Note that the argument still goes through if we suppose that there's another possibility: that FOXP2 builds part of the input–output system for vocal learning where one must externalize and then re-internalize song/language—sing or talk to oneself. This would remain a way to "pipe" items in and out of the internal system, and serialize them, possibly a critical component to be sure, in the same sense that one might require a way to print output from a computer.

[5] This is much like attending solely to the different means by an LCD television and the old cathode-ray tube TVs display moving images without paying any attention to what image is being displayed. The old TVs "painted" a picture by sweeping an electron beam over a set of chemical dots that would glow or not. Liquid crystal displays operate by an entirely different means: roughly, they pass light or not through a liquid crystal array of dots depending on an electric charge applied to each dot, but there is no single sweeping beam. One generates the same flat image by an entirely different means. Similarly, whether the externalized, linear timing slots are being set out by motor commands to the vocal tract or by moving fingers is irrelevant to the more crucial "inner" representations.

this number—not unreasonable for what we understand about early demography in Africa at this time, albeit poorly—this would suggest that such a beneficial allele would have to spread to the entire breeding group in order that natural selection could operate unimpeded to sweep the mutation to fixation. This is not paradoxical, but simply reflects the stochastic character of evolution by natural selection itself; the same principle applies to all beneficial mutations. What it implies is that the emergence of language in this sense could indeed have been a unique event, accounting for its species-specific character. Such founder effects in population bottleneck situations are not uncommon.

When the beneficial mutation has spread through the group, there would be an advantage to externalization, so the capacity would be linked as a secondary process to the sensorimotor system for externalization and interaction, including communication as a special case. It is not easy to imagine an account of human evolution that does not assume at least this much, in one or another form. Any additional assumption requires both evidence and rationale, not easy to come by.

Most alternatives do in fact posit additional assumptions, grounded on the language-as-communication viewpoint, presumably related to externalization as we have seen. In a recent survey Számado and Szathmáry (2006) list what they consider to be the major alternative theories explaining the emergence of human language. These include: (1) language as gossip; (2) language as social grooming; (3) language as outgrowth of hunting cooperation; (4) language as outcome of motherese; (5) sexual selection; (6) language as requirement of exchanging status information; (7) language as song; (8) language as requirement for tool making or the outcome of tool making; (9) language as an outgrowth of gestural systems; (10) language as Machiavellian device for deception; and finally, (11) language as internal mental tool.

Note that it is only this last theory, language as internal mental tool, that does not assume, explicitly or implicitly, that the primary function of language is for external communication. But this leads to a kind of adaptive paradox, since animal signaling ought to then suffice. Számado and Szathmáry note:

Most of the theories do not consider the kind of selective forces that could encourage the use of conventional communication in a given context instead of the use of 'traditional' animal signals . . . thus, there is no theory that convincingly demonstrates a situation that would require a complex means of symbolic communication rather than the existing simpler communication systems.   (2006: 679)

They further note that the language-as-mental-tool theory does not suffer from this defect. However, they, like most researchers in this area, do not seem to draw the obvious inference but instead maintain a focus on externalization and communication.

Proposals as to the primacy of internal language—similar to Harry Jerison's observation, already noted, about language as an "inner tool"—have also been made by eminent evolutionary biologists. At an international conference on biolinguistics in 1974, Salvador Luria was the most forceful advocate of the view that communicative needs would not have provided "any great selective pressure to produce a system such as language," with its crucial relation to "development of abstract or productive thinking." The same idea was taken up by François Jacob, who suggested that "the role of language as a communication system between individuals would have come about only secondarily.... The quality of language that makes it unique does not seem to be so much its role in communicating directives for action" or other common features of animal communication, but rather "its role in symbolizing, in evoking cognitive images," in molding our notion of reality and yielding our capacity for thought and planning, through its unique property of allowing "infinite combinations of symbols" and therefore "mental creation of possible worlds." These ideas trace back to the cognitive revolution of the seventeenth century, which in many ways foreshadows developments from the 1950s (Jacob 1982; Luria 1974).

We can, however, go beyond speculation. Investigation of language design can yield evidence on the relation of language to the sensory-motor system and thought systems. As noted, we think there is mounting evidence to support the natural conclusion that the relation is asymmetrical in the manner illustrated in the critical case of displacement.

Externalization is not a simple task. It has to relate two quite distinct systems: one is a sensory-motor system that appears to have been basically intact for hundreds of thousands of years; the second is a newly emerged computational system for thought, which is perfect insofar as the strong minimalist thesis is correct. We would expect, then, that morphology and phonology— the linguistic processes that convert internal syntactic objects to the entities accessible to the sensory-motor system—might turn out to be quite intricate, varied, and subject to accidental historical events. Parameterization and diversity, then, would be mostly—possibly entirely—restricted to externalization. That is pretty much what we seem to find: a computational system efficiently generating expressions interpretable at the semantic–pragmatic interface, with diversity resulting from complex and highly varied modes of externalization which, furthermore, are readily susceptible to historical change.[6]

If this picture is more or less accurate, we may have an answer to the second of the two basic questions: Why are there so many languages? The reason might be that the problem of externalization can be solved in many different and independent ways, either before or after the dispersal of the original population.

We have no reason to suppose that solving the externalization problem involved an evolutionary change—that is, genomic change. It might simply be a problem addressed by existing cognitive processes, in different ways, and at different times. There is sometimes an unfortunate tendency to confuse literal evolutionary (genomic) change with historical change, two entirely distinct phenomena. As already noted, there is very strong evidence that there has been no relevant evolution of the language faculty since the trek from Africa some 50,000 years ago, though undoubtedly there has been a great deal of change, even invention of modes of externalization (as in sign language). Confusion about these matters could be overcome by replacing the metaphoric notions "evolution of language" and "language change" by their more exact counterparts: evolution of the organisms that use language, and change in the ways they do so. In these more accurate terms, emergence of the language faculty involved evolution, while historical change (which continues constantly) does not.

Again, these seem to be the simplest assumptions, and there is no known reason to reject them. If they are generally on the right track, it follows that externalization may not have evolved at all; rather, it might have been a process of problem solving using existing cognitive capacities. Evolution in the biological sense of the term would then be restricted to the mutation that yielded the operation Merge, along with whatever residue resists explanation in terms of the strong minimalist thesis and any language-specific constraints that might exist on the solution to the cognitive problem of externalization. Accordingly, any approach to evolution of language that focuses on communication, or the sensory-motor system, or statistical properties of spoken language, and the like, may well be seriously misguided. That judgment covers quite a broad range, as those familiar with the literature will be aware.

Returning to the two initial salient questions, we have at least some suggestions—reasonable ones we think—about how it came about that there is even one language, and why languages appear to vary so widely—the latter

---

[6] Positing an independent, recursive, "language of thought" as a means to account for recursion in syntax leads to an explanatory regress as well as being unnecessary and quite obscure.

partly an illusion, much like the apparent limitless variety of organisms, all of them based on deeply conserved elements with phenomenal outcomes restricted by laws of nature (for language, computational efficiency).

There are other factors that may strongly influence language design— notably properties of the brain, now unknown—and there is plainly a lot more to say even about the topics to which we have briefly alluded here. But instead of pursuing these questions, let us turn briefly to lexical items, the conceptual atoms of thought and its ultimate externalization in varied ways.

Conceptual structures are found in other primates: probably actor–action– goal schemata, categorization, possibly the singular–plural distinction, and others. These were presumably recruited for language, though the conceptual resources of humans that enter into language use appear to be far richer. Specifically, even the "atoms" of computation, lexical items/concepts, appear to be uniquely human.

Crucially, even the simplest words and concepts of human language and thought lack the relation to mind-independent entities that appears to be characteristic of animal communication. The latter is held to be based on a one–one relation between mind/brain processes and "an aspect of the environment to which these processes adapt the animal's behavior," to quote cognitive neuroscientist Randy Gallistel, introducing a major collection of papers on animal communication (Gallistel 1990a). According to Jane Goodall, the closest observer of chimpanzees in the wild, for them "the production of a sound in the *absence* of the appropriate emotional state seems to be an almost impossible task" (Goodall, cited in Tattersall 2002).

The symbols of human language and thought are sharply different. Their use is not automatically keyed to emotional states, and they do not pick out mind-independent objects or events in the external world. For human language and thought, it seems, there is no *reference* relation in the sense of Frege, Peirce, Tarski, Quine, and contemporary philosophy of language and mind. What we understand to be a river, a person, a tree, water, and so on, consistently turns out to be a creation of what seventeenth-century investigators called the human "cognoscitive powers," which provide us with rich means to refer to the outside world from intricate perspectives. As the influential neo-Platonist Ralph Cudworth put the matter, it is only by means of the "inward ideas" produced by its "innate cognoscitive power" that the mind is able to "know and understand all external individual things," articulating ideas that influenced Kant. The objects of thought constructed by the cognoscitive powers cannot be reduced to a "peculiar nature belonging" to the thing we are talking about, as David Hume summarized a century of inquiry. In this regard, internal conceptual symbols are like the phonetic units of mental representations, such as the syllable [ba]; every particular act externalizing this mental object yields a mind-independent entity, but it is idle to seek a mind-independent construct that corresponds to the syllable. Communication is not a matter of producing some mind-external entity that the hearer picks out of the world the way a physicist could. Rather, communication is a more-or-less affair in which the speaker produces external events and hearers seek to match them as best they can to their own internal resources. Words and concepts appear to be similar in this regard, even the simplest of them. Communication relies on shared cognoscitive powers, succeeding insofar as shared mental constructs, background, concerns, presuppositions, and so on, allow for common perspectives to be (more or less) attained. These properties of lexical items seem to be unique to human language and thought and have to be accounted for somehow in the study of their evolution. How, no one has any idea. The fact that there even is a problem has barely been recognized, as a result of the powerful grip of the doctrines of referentialism.

Human cognoscitive powers provide us with a world of experience, different from the world of experience of other animals. Being reflective creatures, thanks to the emergence of the human capacity, humans try to make some sense of experience. These efforts are called myth, or religion, or magic, or philosophy, or, in modern English usage, science. For science, the concept of reference in the technical sense is a normative ideal: we hope that the invented concepts *photon* or *verb phrase* pick out some real thing in the world. And of course the concept of reference is just fine for the context for which it was invented in modern logic: formal systems, in which the relation of reference is stipulated, holding for example between numerals and numbers. But human language and thought do not seem to work that way, and endless confusion has resulted from failure to recognize that fact.

We enter here into large and extremely interesting topics that we will have to put aside. Let us just summarize briefly what seems to be the current best guess about unity and diversity of language and thought. In some completely unknown way, our ancestors developed human concepts. At some time in the very recent past, maybe about 75,000 years ago, an individual in a small group of hominids in East Africa underwent a minor mutation that provided the operation Merge—an operation that takes human concepts as computational atoms, and yields structured expressions that provide a rich language of thought. These processes might be computationally perfect, or close to it, hence the result of physical laws independent of humans. The innovation had obvious advantages, and took over the small group. At some later stage, the internal language of thought was connected to the sensory-motor system, a complex task that can be solved in many different ways and at different times, and quite possibly a task that involves no evolution at all. In the course of these events, the human capacity took shape, yielding a good part of our "moral and intellectual nature," using Wallace's phrase (1871). The outcomes appear to be highly diverse, but they have an essential unity, reflecting the fact that humans are in fundamental respects identical, just as the hypothetical extraterrestrial scientist we conjured up earlier might conclude that there is only one language with minor dialectal variations, primarily—perhaps entirely—in mode of externalization.

To conclude, recall that even if this general story turns out to be more or less valid, and the huge gaps can be filled in, it will still leave unresolved problems that have been raised for hundreds of years. Among these is the question of how properties "termed mental" relate to "the organical structure of the brain," in the eighteenth-century formulation; and the more mysterious problems of the creative and coherent ordinary use of language, a central concern of Cartesian science, still scarcely even at the horizons of inquiry.

3

Some Reflections on Darwin's Problem in the Context of Cartesian Biolinguistics

CEDRIC BOECKX

3.1 Darwin's Problem and Rationalist Commitments

Already in the early days of modern science (seventeenth and eighteenth centuries) it was clear to natural philosophers like Descartes, Hobbes, Humboldt, and Hume that a detailed understanding of the human language faculty (FL) would be critical to the development of a genuine "Science of Man." As Chomsky has remarked on numerous occasions (see Chomsky 1965, 1966, 1972b), the "Cartesians"[1] saw in the essence of language the direct reflex of Man's most distinctive cognitive attributes at work—most prominent among which the unbounded creativity that is so unique to us. Under Chomsky's impetus modern linguistics has recaptured the central themes of the first cognitive revolution and is now a core area of modern cognitive science, a branch of biology. It is in order to emphasize the true nature of this research program that linguists of a generative orientation have begun to use the term

Early versions of the present work were presented in talks at the Universitat de Barcelona (Grup de Biolingüística), Potsdam University (Workshop on Biolinguistics), the University of Maryland, and at the San Sebastian encounter with Noam Chomsky, organized by Massimo Piattelli-Palmarini, Pello Salaburu, and Juan Uriagereka in the summer of 2006. I am grateful to the organizers of these venues for inviting me, and to the participants in these events for comments. For invaluable discussions of the issues touched on here over the years, I thank Noam Chomsky, Norbert Hornstein, Massimo Piattelli-Palmarini, Juan Uriagereka, Marc Hauser, Paul Pietroski, and Dennis Ott. Thanks also to the participants in my Spring 08 seminar on Biolinguistics at Harvard University for penetrating questions, and to Anna-Maria di Sciullo for her interest in this piece, and her support.

[1] To the dismay of historians of philosophy, Chomsky (1966) lumps together traditional rationalists and empiricists under the umbrella adjective *Cartesian*. I will follow him in this regard, as I believe that empiricists like Hume and Hobbes were much more rationalists than their modern reincarnations (behaviorists, connectionists, etc.). For further evidence, see Jerry Fodor's treatment of Hume in Fodor (2003).

"Biolinguistics," a term first used with this intention by Massimo Piattelli-Palmarini at a meeting in 1974.

The immediate aim of biolinguistics is still to reveal as accurately as possible the nature of the FL, but biolinguistic inquiry does not stop there. It also seeks to understand the course of development of language in the organism and the way it is put to use once it has reached its mature state; in particular, how linguistic form may give rise to meaning. Ultimately, biolinguists hope to contribute to our understanding of how core properties of language are implemented in neural tissues and how it evolved in the species. These last two tasks have an obvious interdisciplinary character, requiring linguists to join forces with psychologists, biologists, philosophers, and so on. I firmly believe that the linguists' own works on the nature of the FL will be of critical importance in the formulation of detailed hypotheses to be tested at different levels of scientific analysis. Furthermore, with their emphasis on formal/structural aspects of the FL and on the existence of both universality and diversity in language, biolinguists also hope to contribute significantly to the emergence (currently underway) of an expanded modern synthesis in biology, about which I will have more to say in this chapter.

After 50 years of research in this domain, we can say with some confidence that progress has been made on two fronts: what Chomsky calls Humboldt's Problem (the characterization of what the FL is) and Plato's Problem (how the FL grows into a mature state in the individual).[2] How FL is put to use ("Descartes' Problem") remains as much a mystery to us as it was to the Cartesians. Likewise, the issue of brain implementation remains elusive.[3] The evolutionary question—what one might call, for obvious reasons, Darwin's

[2] In laying out the research agenda of modern (bio-)linguistics, Chomsky appeals to important historical figures like Plato, Humboldt, and Descartes, who not only worried about the very questions generative grammarians focus on, but also made insightful suggestions that ought to be incorporated into current discussions.

[3] To the best of my knowledge, Chomsky has not given a venerable name to this problem. This is not because no important historical figure thought about the mind/brain (Descartes, Spinoza, and many others did), but because virtually no one managed to formulate insights that could be useful at this stage in our understanding. Perhaps one could call it Broca's Problem, or Gall's Problem (I am here referring to Gall's desire to "put an end to the highhanded generalizations of the philosophers," and his wish to study language as the "creation of our internal faculties, the latter being represented in the brain by organs"). But one should bear in mind that at this stage this is more of a mystery than a genuine problem (on the distinction between problem vs. mystery, see Chomsky 1975). Although the concern of mind/brain unification is certainly legitimate, it is often thought that solving this problem is a prerequisite for the legitimacy of the biolinguistic enterprise. This is incorrect, in my opinion. Just like it would be incorrect to characterize Mendel's results as not part of genetics. At numerous levels, it can be shown that linguistic inquiry, taking place in a generative/biolinguistic context, is continuous with research in various areas of the life sciences. I refer the interested readers to Boeckx and Piattelli-Palmarini (2005) and Boeckx (2006).

problem[4]—was consciously set aside for much of the past five decades[5] but it has gained momentum in recent years, for reasons that I think are worth detailing.

3.1.1 *The conceptual relationship between Plato's Problem and Darwin's Problem*

The central problem in generative grammar, as made explicit in Chomsky (1965: ch. 1), is to account for the human capacity for language acquisition; how any child, short of pathology or highly unusual environmental circumstances, acquires at least one language by the time they reach puberty (at the very latest) in a way that is remarkably uniform and relatively effortless. The acquisition of language is all the more remarkable when we take into account the enormous gap between what human adults (tacitly) know about their language and the evidence that is available to them during the acquisition process. It should be obvious to anyone that the linguistic input a child receives is radically impoverished and extremely fragmentary. It is in order to cope with this "poverty of stimulus" that Chomsky claimed that humans are biologically endowed with a capacity to develop a language. The biological equipment that makes language acquisition possible is called Universal Grammar (UG). In positing UG, Chomsky was doing what ethologists like Lorenz and Tinbergen had been led to do to account for the range of highly specific behaviors that many animals display. At a more general level, Chomsky was doing for language what Plato had done in *Meno* for geometry and what the Rationalists (Descartes, Leibniz, etc.) had done for ideas more generally. All of them were making it possible in principle for information to be gathered from experience (i.e. for learning to take place). In the absence of some innate bias toward interpreting incoming data in specific ways, knowledge (of language, mathematics—of anything!) would never be attained.[6] As the structure of UG became clearer in the Principles-and-Parameters era, attention shifted away

---

[4] Like Humboldt, Plato, and Descartes, Darwin recognized the distinctive character of our ability to pair sound and meaning and was fascinated with the nature of our language faculty, our "'instinctive tendency to speak," as he called it; an ability he related to birdsong, as in the following passage):

The sounds uttered by birds offer in several respects the nearest analogy to language, for all the members of the same species utter the same instinctive cries expressive of their emotions; and all the kinds that sing, exert their power instinctively; but the actual song, and even the call notes, are learnt from their parents or foster-parents.   (Darwin 1871: 108)

In addition, like Humboldt, Plato, and Descartes, Darwin made observations that are variants of, or sources of hypotheses entertained today. Koji Fujita has brought to my attention that he independently coined the term "Darwin's problem" in Fujita (2002).

[5] Although the problem was set aside, a very insightful discussion of many relevant issues can be found in Lenneberg's work (Lenneberg 1967).

[6] On this point, see Gallistel (2007).

from the logical problem of language acquisition and toward its cousin, the logical problem of language evolution.

It was already evident to the Rationalists that a discussion of the origin of the FL would be relevant to our understanding of the nature of the FL (see e.g. Viertel's discussion of Herder's theory of language origin (Viertel 1966)—after all, any investigation into the emergence of some faculty *x* depends on specific hypotheses regarding what *x* is[7]—but our notion of what the FL was likely to be first had to rest on somewhat secure grounds to prevent evolutionary scenarios from being more than fanciful just-so stories.

Once linguists felt the foundations were solid, they indeed began to approach UG "from below," and formulate informed speculations (hypotheses) concerning the emergence of language in the species, beginning with Hauser, Chomsky, and Fitch (2002). In the preceding paragraph I referred to Darwin's Problem as the cousin of Plato's Problem. This is because the logical structure of Darwin's Problem turns out to be very similar to that of Plato's Problem.[8] Both revolve around a Poverty of Stimulus situation. In the context of Plato's Problem, the argument goes like this: Given the richness and complexity of our human knowledge of language, the short time it takes for children to master their native languages, the uniformity displayed within and across languages during the acquisition process, and the poverty of the linguistic input to children, there does not seem to be any way out of positing some head start (in the guise of some innate component, UG) in the language acquisition process. This head start not only allows linguists to make sense of the speed at which (first) languages are acquired, but also why the acquisition process takes the paths it takes (as opposed to the paths it could logically take). By minimizing the role of the environment, UG allows us to begin to grasp how Plato's Problem could be solved.

Similarly, when it comes to Darwin's Problem, everyone seems to grant that the FL emerged in the species very recently (within the last 200,000 years, according to most informed estimates). Everyone also seems to grant that this was a one-time event: the faculty is remarkably uniform across the

---

[7] This is the very reason why Hume put so much emphasis on developing a theory of history as part of his Science of Man project.

[8] In the context of language, the similarity between the two issues, acquisition and evolution, had not escaped Skinner, as Chomsky points out in his famous 1959 review. I first discussed the similarity between the two problems in a minimalist context in Boeckx (2009). Hornstein (2009) pursues this similarity as well.

At a more general level, the relationship between ontogeny and phylogeny is one of the great themes in biology; see Gould (1977). The similarity is nicely captured in German, where issues in both ontogeny and phylogeny are referred to as issues of *Entwicklungsgeschichte* (lit. 'history of development').

species, a fact that is most likely the result of the faculty having emerged in a small group that spread (*Homo sapiens*). In light of the extremely recent emergence of the FL, one ought to welcome a hypothesis that minimizes the role of the environment (read: the need for several adaptive steps), and, more generally, one that minimizes what had to evolve. Just as in the context of Plato's Problem, the individual in which the FL emerged must be given a head start: the key evolutionary event must be assumed to have been small, and many cognitive structures available to our ancestors must have been recruited (with minimal modifications, to avoid the need for many adaptive steps). In Kirschner and Gerhart's (2005) terms, the emergence of this biological novelty had to be facilitated. As far as I can see, this is exactly the logic laid out in Hauser, Chomsky, and Fitch (2002), who take the FL to consist of a variety of shared cognitive structures (what they call the Faculty of Language in the Broad sense, FLB), and a minimal amount of genuine novelty/specificity (their Faculty of Language in the Narrow sense, FLN). My point in this section is that this sort of evolutionary scenario makes a lot of sense once we recognize the similarity between the logic of Darwin's Problem and that of Plato's Problem. (I guess one could say that in the context of language, the argument about phylogeny (Darwin's problem) recapitulates the argument about ontogeny (Plato's problem).)

3.1.2 *(Neo-)Cartesian linguistics meets (neo-)rationalist morphology*

It is customary to allude to Theodor Dobzhansky's well-known dictum that "nothing makes sense in biology except in the light of evolution" whenever questions of origin are raised (Dobzhansky 1973). The exquisite complexity of organisms can only be accounted for, so it seems, by means of natural selection. As Dawkins (1996: 202) puts it, "whenever in nature there is a sufficiently powerful illusion of good design for some purpose, natural selection is the only known mechanism that can account for it." Questions of origin pertaining to the mind, the "Citadel itself," as Darwin called it, are no exception. Indeed, the assumption that natural selection is the "universal acid" (Dennett 1995) is perhaps nowhere as strong as in the study of mental faculties, being the motto (credo?) of evolutionary psychology (witness Pinker 1997, Marcus 2008). But the simplicity of Dobzhansky's assertion conceals layers of necessary refinements that cannot be ignored. Its meaning very much depends on what it means to make sense of life (including mental life), and what we understand by (Darwinian) evolution.

As Fox-Keller has made clear in her book *Making Sense of Life* (Keller 2002), the notion of explanation, of "making sense of life," cannot be uniformly defined across the life sciences.[9] As for Darwinian evolution, Gould, more than anyone else, has stressed the richness and complexity of evolutionary theory (see Gould 2002), and stressed the limitations of ultra-Darwinism and its narrowly adaptationist vision. One can, and must, preface any study of origin by "ever since Darwin," not, I think, by "ever since Dawkins." And one must bear in mind that Darwin himself was explicit about the fact that "natural selection is ... not [the] exclusive means of modification" (Darwin 1859: 6) There are signs that the tide is changing. The promises of genome sequencing, and of the selfish gene, have not been met, and a growing number of biologists side with Lynch's (2007) opinion that "many (and probably most) aspects of genomic biology that superficially appear to have adapative roots ... are almost certainly also products of non-adaptive processes." Speaking for all evo–devo adherents, Carroll (2005a) points out that the modern synthesis has not given us a theory of form. A theory of form is at the leart of what Kirschner and Gerhart call "Darwin's Dilemma." When Darwin proposed his theory of evolution, he relied on two ingredients: variation and selection. Although he could explain selection, he could not explain variation. The forms on which selection operated were taken for granted. Since *The Origin of Species*, at repeated intervals, and with accelerated pace in recent years, it has been suggested that several factors giving direction to evolution (facilitating variation, biasing selection, etc.) must be taken into account.

As Gould (2002: 347) clearly states,

simple descent does not solve all problems of "clumping" in phenotypic space; we still want to know why certain forms "attract" such big clumps of diversity, and why such large empty spaces exist in conceivable, and not obviously malfunctional, regions of potential morphospace. The functionalist and adaptationist perspective ties this clumping to available environments, and to shaping by natural selection. Structuralists and formalists wonder if some clumping might not record broader principles, at least partly separate from a simple history of descent with adaptation principles of genetics, of development, or of physical laws transcending biological organization.

In this respect Gould (2002: 21) calls for a renewed appreciation for "the enormous importance of structural, historical, and developmental constraints in channeling the pathways of evolution, often in highly positive ways, adding that "the pure functionalism of a strictly Darwinian (and externalist) approach

---

[9] Mayr (2004) says nothing different when he calls our attention to two fields of biology, with radically different methodological assumptions: functional biology (biochemistry) and evolutionary biology.

to adaptation no longer suffices to explain the channeling of phyletic directions, and the clumping and inhomogenous population of organic morphospace."

Echoing Gould, Pigliucci (2007) writes that biology is in need of a new research program, one that stresses the fact that natural selection may not be the only organizing principle available to explain the complexity of biological systems. It is not just all tinkering; there is design too.[10] Pigliucci (2007) reviews numerous works that provide empirical evidence for non-trivial expansions of the modern synthesis, with such concepts as modularity, evolvability, robustness, epigenetic inheritance, and phenotypic plasticity as key components.

Amundson (2005) points out correctly that many of the themes at the heart of the expanded modern synthesis (a more enlightened version of Darwinian evolution) hark back to all the major theorists of life before Darwin, especially those that are often called the Rationalist Morphologists. All major theories of life before Darwin followed a tradition reaching back to Plato in presenting a fundamentally "internalist" account, based upon intrinsic and predictable patterns set by the nature of living systems for development through time, as the term "evolution" (*evolutio*, "unfolding") reveals. As one of the foremost exponents of such internalist accounts, and the person who coined the term "morphology," Goethe writes (second essay on plant metamorphosis, written in 1790):

In my opinion, the chief concept underlying all observation of life—one from which we must not deviate—is that a creature is self-sufficient, that its parts are inevitably interrelated, and that nothing mechanical, as it were, is built up or produced from without, although it is true that the parts affect their environment and are in turn affected by it.

By analogy with Chomsky's distinction between I(nternalist)-linguistics and E(xternalist)-linguistics introduced in Chomsky (1986), we could call the modern synthesis E-biology and the return to pre-Darwinian concerns, I-biology. As a common thread, internalist accounts deny exclusivity to natural selection as the agent of creativity, viewing "adaptation as secondary tinkering rather than primary structuring" (Gould 2002: 290). Internalists claim a high relative frequency of control by internal factors, emphasizing notions like Unity of Type and Correlation of growth. At the heart of internalist

---

[10] Not only design but perhaps simplicity too; see my remarks on Alon (2007) in Boeckx (2010). Note, incidentally, that the more good design and simplicity one finds in nature, the less one should be tempted to regard the brain (or any other organ) as a kluge (contra Marcus 2008).

frustrations is the linkage between natural selection and contingency. In the words of Kauffman (1993: 26):

We have come to think of selection as essentially the only source of order in the biological world. It follows that, in our current view, organisms are largely ad hoc solutions to design problems cobbled together by selection. It follows that most properties which are widespread in organisms are widespread by virtue of common descent from a tinkered-together ancestor, with selective maintenance of useful tinkerings. It follows that we see organisms as overwhelmingly contingent historical accidents, abetted by design. My own aim is not so much to challenge as to broaden the neo-Darwinian tradition. For, despite its resilience, that tradition has surely grown without attempting to integrate the ways in which simple and complex systems may spontaneously exhibit order.

Despite the fact that various biologists have complained that phrases like "adaptation to the edge of chaos," and "order for free," repeatedly used by Kauffman, Goodwin, and other proponents of Neo-rationalism in biology, lack clear scientific definition and operational utility, Gould (2002: 1213) argues that Kauffman et al. are groping toward something important, a necessary enrichment or broadening of biology, with important implications.

Of great significance is the fact that the concerns that animate the return to the insights of the Rationalist Morphologists are the very same concerns that animate research in (Cartesian) biolinguistics. By using Cartesian Biolinguistics I intend to point to an important distinction within those who conceive of linguistics as a branch of biology (at a suitable level of abstraction). I suspect that most biolinguists make the very same "bet" that Dawkins does,[11] and privilege adapation as the sole source or order and complexity. Let us call them neo-Darwinian biolinguists (see Givón 2002, Marcus 2008). By contrast, those that I would call Cartesian biolinguists follow Chomsky in (i) favoring internalist explanations, (ii) seeing design and topology where others would see tinkering, and (iii) focusing on Form over Function.[12] Indeed, once the complexity of biology as a whole, and evolutionary biology in particular, is clear, any perceived conflict between "Chomsky and Darwin" (Dennett 1995), or any need to reconcile them (Calvin and Bickerton 2000), quickly evaporates.

As a matter of fact, once the richness of evolutionary biology is taken into consideration, it seems to me that one can begin to approach Darwin's problem with some optimism toward its resolution. I am here relying on the fact that a neo-Darwinian view of the type advocated by Pinker and

---

[11] On Dawkins's bet, and how it contrasts with the one made by Gould, see Sterelny (2007).
[12] For converging remarks pertaining to cognitive science as a whole, see Fodor (2008).

Bloom (1990) still strikes me as hopeless, as Piattelli-Palmarini (1989), and more recently, Uriagereka (1998) and Lorenzo and Longa (2003), have made clear. But it is fair to say that the alternative, neo-rationalist scenario was hard to entertain until the advent of the minimalist program in linguistic theory. As I discussed in Boeckx (2006: ch. 4), the standard Principles-and-Parameters model of the FL focused on the specificities of the language organ, and made it very unlikely that central linguistic concepts such as c-command, government, empty categories, and cyclicity, just to name a few, may have emerged from any sufficiently general theory of form. The standard Principles-and-Parameters architecture, with its richly modular structure, offered a picture of the language faculty that was too complex for structural constraints (of the sort explored by D'Arcy Thompson) to realistically account for its emergence.

Put differently, the idea that the language faculty was not shaped by adaptive demands, but by physical constraints ("Turing's thesis," as Chomsky sometimes calls it)—a recurring theme in Chomsky's writings (see Jenkins 2000, Otero 1990, for relevant citations)—did not fit snugly in past frameworks. It found its niche only recently, as part of the Minimalist Program for linguistic theory, in the same way that the pre-Darwinians' speculations about a general theory of biological form seem to be finding their niche in the extended modern synthesis advocated by a growing number of biologists.

At the risk of oversimplifying, I will say that the core idea behind linguistic minimalism is that all the apparent complexity revealed in the course of pursuing a Cartesian Linguistics program is the result of few very simple computational mechanisms. Although the Minimalist Program as a whole may still be premature, there is little doubt that it offers an extremely useful perspective from a biological point of view, especially in the context of evolution.[13] With its emphasis on virtual conceptual necessity, minimalism reduces considerably the burden any evolutionary story has to bear. This is a welcome consequence because, to repeat, according to everyone's best guess, the human language faculty emerged very, very recently in the species, which makes it hard to seriously entertain an adapatationist, gradualistic story. There is just not enough time for such a complex object to be built step by step.

3.2 The Key Novelty

The hypothesis formulated in Hauser et al. (2002) and refined in Fitch, Hauser, and Chomsky (2005) offers a concrete example of the sort of research program

---

[13] As I argued in Boeckx (2006) (see also Hornstein 2009), linguistic minimalism may also form the basis for a more fruitful research program for addressing "Gall's/Broca's problem," or the question of how the FL is implemented in the brain.

that minimalism makes feasible in the study of Darwin's problem.[14] According to Hauser et al., what distinguishes humans from other species is the FLN: the computational system that constitutes Narrow Syntax, specifically its recursive quality (the ability for unbounded embedding) and the way syntactic expressions maps the syntactic objects it constructs to the conceptual–intentional and sensory–motor systems. They claim that there is evidence that other species possess sensory–motor and at least some conceptual-intentional systems similar to our own (on the sensory-motor side, see also Samuels 2009; for some of the conceptual richness in animals, see Hauser 2000, Carruthers 2006, Cheney and Seyfarth 1990, 2007, among many others). These constitute the FLB. (Hauser et al. 2002 leave open the possibility that once the FLN was in place, its presence led to modifications of FLB-components. For some evidence that this was the case on the sound side, see Samuels (2009). See also next section.) Hauser et al. (2002: 1574) point out that their hypothesis may have important consequences for how we think about the evolution of cognition:

[The hypothesis that only the FLN is unique to humans] raises the possibility that structural details of [the FLN] may result from preexisting constraints, rather than from direct shaping by natural selection targeted specifically at communication. Insofar as this proves to be true, such structural details are not, strictly speaking, adaptations at all.

It may be useful to point out that the evolutionary novelty that Hauser, Chomsky, and Fitch dub the FLN need not conflict with Darwin's important claim that novelty is often the result of descent with some significant modification. Indeed, genuine novelty, in the sense of emergence of completely new processes, is extremely rare in the biological world. Nature, as Jacob famously pronounced, is a tinkerer. But although many have seized on Jacob's pronouncement to stress the klugy, higgledy-piggledy aspect of evolution, I do not think that this is Jacob's most important lesson. I think Jacob wanted to emphasize that novelty in the organism's physiology, anatomy, or behavior arises mostly by the use of conserved processes in new combinations at different times and in different places and amounts, rather than by the invention of completely new processes. This is exactly what Darwin meant by his

[14] As Fitch et al. (2005) observe, although their hypothesis is logically independent from the minimalist program, the latter renders the former far more plausible. This plausibility is nowhere clearer than in the way minimalist proposals, with their focus on elementary operations, provide the basis for comparative, cross-species studies. This new chapter in comparative syntax and the way syntax interfaces with external systems is one of the ways in which our evolutionary narratives will be testable. It is not the case that comparative studies were impossible earlier, but the notions the various disciplines made use of were incommensurable.

term "descent with modification" (a term which he preferred to "evolution"). Germans would say that novelty is characterized by *Um-bildung* ('reformation', 'recombination'), not by *Neu-bildung* ('new formation')—topological variations, not introductions of novel elements. As Gould (1977: 409) clearly stated, "there may be nothing new under the sun, but permutations of the old within complex systems can do wonders." Novelty in biology arises the same way water arises from combining the right amount of H and of O. Notice that if this characterization of biological novelty is borne in mind, the fact that specificity is not consistently reflected in brain images, genetic disorders, etc. need not lead to a crisis for cognitive sciences, as is sometimes thought (see the literature against modularity). It is just what you expect if novelty arose through recruitment and subsequent diversification. It may well be that we are not yet at a stage where we detect diversification among recruited parts, a message which I think goes along the lines stressed by Josef Grodzinsky in recent work (see also Marcus 2006).

3.2.1 *The lexical envelope as the locus of linguistic specificity*

The literature following Hauser et al. (2002) has focused on their claim that a key property of the FLN is recursion (ignoring the fact that Hauser et al. explicitly mentioned the possibility that the FLN may be empty, as well as their emphasis on the issue of interfaces—the mapping of syntactic expressions onto the right mental components). Here I will show how a specific characterization of recursion may have important consequences for another seemingly unique and language-specific property of human cognition, the ability to build a lexicon.

Chomsky (2004a) has identified *Merge* as the most basic procedure that could yield recursive structures of the sort that the FL makes use of. In its simplest form, Merge takes two elements α and β and combines them into a set, $\{\alpha, \beta\}$. Iterative applications of Merge yield recursive structures $\{\delta, \ldots \{\gamma, \{\alpha, \beta\}\} \ldots \}$.[15] Here I would like to concentrate on the property that makes elements mergeable. After all, set formation is a very basic computational operation, one that is unlikely to be unique to humans or specific to language. What is remarkable and unique about the FL (and perhaps derivative systems like our improved number sense) is the fact that Merge is recursive in other words, what makes Merge possible in the first place remains available throughout a linguistic computation. Following a suggestion of Chomsky's

---

[15] Descriptively speaking, one can, following Chomsky (2004a)—in a move whose significance has not been fully appreciated in my view—distinguish between "external" Merge, which combines two previously unconnected elements (i.e. two elements selected from the lexicon), and "internal" Merge, which combines two elements, one of which was already contained inside the set to which the other element is merged. Internal Merge yields configurations manifesting displacement ("movement").

(see Chomsky 2005), I would like to attribute this fact to the idea that lexical items are sticky. They have what Chomsky calls an *edge feature*. The following passage, from Chomsky (2008: 6) makes this clear:

For a L[exical] I[tem] to be able to enter into a computation, merging with some [syntactic object], it must have some property permitting this operation. A property of an LI is called a feature, so an LI has a feature that permits it to be merged. Call this the edge-feature (EF) of the LI.

As I suggest elsewhere (Boeckx, in progress), we can think of the process of lexicalization as endowing a concept with a certain inertia, a property that makes the lexical item active (i.e. allows it to engage in Merge relations).[16]

We can represent a lexicalized concept C endowed with an edge feature as: $\{C\}$ (a concept with a lexical envelope), or $+\{C\}$, with the + sign representing the edge property that allows further combination, much like a free electron allows bonding in chemistry.[17] We can also think of the lexical envelope as a mapping instruction to the Conceptual–Intentional system to "fetch a concept C" (see Pietroski, to appear). Thus conceived, the process of lexicalization not only makes Merge possible, it also achieves what amounts to a demodularization of concepts. We can in fact think of lexicalization as the mental analog of the hypothetical creation of a truly universal currency, allowing transactions to cross formerly impenetrable boundaries.

I take it that Jerry Fodor is right to think of the mind as consisting at least in part of a variety of modules (the exact number and identity of which are not important for my purposes). I also assume that the modular mind is not a uniquely human attribute, but is in fact quite widely shared with other species. The ethology literature is replete with evidence that throughout the animal kingdom creatures are equipped with specialized behaviors, many of which require a certain amount of highly specific triggering experience, which crucially transcend the limits of any behaviorist stimulus–response schema. I follow Gallistel, Hauser, Marler, Cheney, and Seyfarth, and many cognitive ethologists in claiming that animals come equipped with learning organs (a.k.a. modules or core knowledge systems). Remarkably, as I will emphasize in the next section, humans appear to be uniquely endowed with the ability to consistently go beyond the limits of these modules and engage in systematic cross-modular combinations (i.e. cross-modular thought). I would like to claim that it is the process of lexicalization that underlies this ability to

[16] In Boeckx (in progress) I build on Marantz (2008) and take lexicalization to be a phase transition, induced by the combination of a 'root' (concept) with a lexical categorizer (Marantz's "little x"); that is to say, $\{C\} = \{x, \sqrt{C}\}$.

[17] Hiroki Narita (p.c.) points out that the set-formation capacity that is Merge leads us to expect the existence of "unvalued" features, giving rise to agreement relations (Chomsky 2000a), if we understand "unvalued feature" as a feature whose value has merged with the empty set.

extract concepts from their modular bounds. It is as if the lexical envelope (the edge feature) on the one hand makes the content of a concept opaque to the computational system (a hard atom in Fodor's 1998 sense), and, on the other, frees this concept from its limited (modular) combinatorial potential (for a similar view, see Pietroski, to appear). Once lexicalized, concepts can be combined freely (via Merge) as expressions like Chomsky's *Colorless green ideas sleep furiously* or Lewis Carroll's "Jabberwocky" attest. Syntactic relations cease to depend on (semantic/conceptual) content; presumably, by the same token, the semantics of "words" cease to be tied to (externalist) notions like reference (which may well be at work inside modules).

I am surrounding the term "word" with quotation marks because I want to emphasize the fact that linguistic words are not merely sound–meanign pairs; they are mergeable items. Word formation (in this sense) is as specific and unique to the FL as recursion. Accordingly, the oft-made claim that members of other species may acquire words, but may lack the ability to combine them (see Anderson 2004 on Kanzi) must be qualified. Acquiring words in the context of the present discussion cannot be dissociated from being able to freely combine them. If one insists on designating the sound–meaning associations attested in others species as "words," then we should say that FL lacks words, but instead possesses lexical items.

My claim in this section is that the edge feature, the catalyst for recursive Merge, is the one key property that had to evolve. I am silent on precisely how it evolved. It may be the result of random mutation, or an exaptation. Perhaps we will never know for sure, but it is something that is now part of our biological endowment (albeit maybe indirectly coded, perhaps as part of brain growth)—what Chomsky (2005) would call a first factor component. Other properties standardly attributed to Merge, such as binary branching or the phasal property of certain nodes (the ability of certain nodes to trigger transfer of their complements to the interfaces), may instead be the result of non-genomic, third factor principles.[18] In the remainder of this section I will focus on binary branching, and assume that cyclicity (spell-out by phases) is a specific implementation of the general chunking strategy that pervades the cognitive world, especially when working memory is involved (see Miller 1956, Feigenson and Halberda 2004, Terrace 2005, among many others).[19]

---

[18] Other properties of the FLN, for example, the mapping instructions to external mental components may have been recruited. Indeed, the sort of mapping instructions discussed by Pylyshyn (2007) in the context of vision may be sufficient to carry out the required operations, especially if the mapping is as simple and transparent as Pietroski (to appear), Kayne (1994), and others claim.

[19] For material that directly bears on the relevance of subitizing and chunking in language, see ? (?).

3.2.2 *On the distribution of lexical material in natural languages*

Since Kayne (1984) it has been standard to take syntactic representations to be constrained by a binary branching requirement; in modern parlance, Merge can only combine two elements at a time. For Kayne, the binary branching requirement on syntactic structures was imposed to ensure that paths (the set of nodes between two elements establishing a syntactic dependency) be unambiguous (basically, binary branching reduces the number of routes an element might take to connect to another element). Chomsky has also at times suggested that binary branching may be imposed by an overarching requirement of efficient computation (see Chomsky (2004a: 115), and especially Chomsky (2005: 16), where "minimization of search in working memory" is hinted at). I would like to claim in this subsection that the intuition that binary branching may be the result of third-factor considerations is on the right track, and can in fact be strengthened by taking into account results achieved on completely independent grounds in Bejan (2000).

For a number of years Bejan has been studying systems that exhibit binary-branching (bifurcation, pairing, dichotomy) properties, and has hypothesized that all these systems are organized in this way as a result of an optimization process. Specifically, he has established on the basis of a wide range of examples (from systems of nature to artificial systems in engineering) that flow systems that connect one root point to a finite-size area or volume (an infinity of points) display tree-shaped networks. He claims that the shape of the network can be deduced from considerations guaranteeing easiest access (optimal flow). Bejan is careful to stress that exactly what flows is largely irrelevant (it can be electricity, water currents, and, I would add, information such as lexical/conceptual information); what matters is how what flows flows. Bejan is able to show mathematically that the binary branching the networks he studies exhibit is one of constant resistance—that is, one that defines the path of least resistance for all that points in an area/volume that have to be squeezed through a single exit (one that minimizes entropy generation). The basic intuition is one that Galileo already had, when he investigated ways of defining a beam of constant strength. Galileo concluded that a beam of constant strength is one in which the maximum stress (pressure) is spread as much as possible through the body of the beam. This is equivalent to a binary-branching tree. It is indeed easy to see that a uniformly binary-branching tree is better equipped to provide the least resistance for whatever is flowing from a terminal node to a root note. The maximum resistance is defined by the maximum number of branches meeting at a single point. In a binary branching tree, the maximum number (n^{max}) is 2. This is less than if the tree exhibits uniform ternary branching (($n^{max} = 3$), or if the tree varies in its branching configuration (making some points of access more resistant than others). This is equivalent to minimizing the maximum pressure difference across points.

Bejan notes that dendritic patterns occur spontaneously in nature when flow systems are large and fast enough, because it is Y-shaped flow systems that minimize volume/area-to-point resistance (thermodynamic optimization). By the same reasoning, he is able to predict the shape of snow flakes, the emergence of fractal structures, and even deduce Fermat's Principle of Least Time/Maupertuis's Principle of Least Action (Path of Least Time = Path of Easiest/Fastest Access = Path of Least Resistance). A binary-branching tree is thus one that achieves constant minimax stress/resistance across the length of a derivation—a sort of smooth design, where no single point bears more than two relations at any given time.

Nature thus appears to favor slender trees, achieving resistance minimization through growth. It optimizes access by optimizing the internal geometry of the system, achieving a stationary optimal configuration, an optimal space allocation, which patterns according to a scaling law already recognized by Murray (1926), where $W = 2d$ (W = width, d = depth).

I submit that syntax performs its objective (providing instructions to external mental systems; squeezing a phrase structure representation through a spell-out point; a volume/area-to-point situation) in the best possible manner; with binary branching emerging as a balancing act that guarantees equipartition (optimal spacing, or uniform spreading) of terminals.

By focusing on the structure of flow systems, Bejan reveals nature's urge to optimize. Bejan notes that the tree-shaped networks he studies are astonishing in simplicity and robustness, holding across the inanimate, the animate, and the engineered realms. By bringing optimization considerations to bear on issues such as why tubes and streams bifurcate, Bejan can rationalize the geometry of all these structures. But it is important to stress that the optimization at issue is one without search; it is emphatically not the sort of optimization that ultra-Darwinists like Dawkins advocate (see e.g. Dawkins 1982). For them, optimal structures are the inevitable result of trials-and-errors over a very long period. Ultra-Darwinists study the slow making of the fittest, whereas Bejan studies the spontaneous emergence of the best. (It is interesting to note that the very same optimization considerations led Bejan in recent work to vindicate Galileo's intuition that animal locomotion is optimal; see Bejan and Marden 2006.)

Bejan explicitly sees his work as consolidating Leibniz's intuition that of all the possible processes, the only ones that actually occur (spontaneously) are those that involve minimum expenditure of "work (action)." Reinforcing rationalist tenets, Bejan stresses that only explanations of this kind—ones that appeal to nature laws—enable the scientist to make better sense (I would say, perfect sense) of the object of study. Only the appeal to general laws lends a certain sense of inevitability to the explanation, and hence a certain sense of genuine satisfaction, to the explanation—a sense that one has gone beyond explanatory adequacy, an indication that nature can be understood more simply, a sign that it is not chance, but necessity alone that has fashioned organisms.

In sum, Bejan's work suggests that there is at least one way in which the shape of Merge can be understood as the optimal distribution of terminals ("an optimal distribution of imperfections," as Bejan puts it), the result of optimization of lexical access. Like traffic patterns, Y-shaped phrase structure representations seek to spread out flowing material to avoid bottleneck effects. This need not be coded in the genome. As soon as Merge is available (as soon as edge features/lexical envelopes have emerged), it would follow as a matter of course that Merge will exhibit a binary branching character if the FL is optimally designed.

3.3 The Seat of Humaniqueness and the Ascent of *Homo combinans*

In this section I would like to return to the process of lexicalization, the key event in the evolution of the FLN, and suggest that it may be the source of Man's unique abilities (humaniqueness, as Hauser felicitously dubbed it), that Great Leap Forward that gave us our niche. It is commonly assumed that the key evolutionary step that gave us our distinctness is cognitive in nature.[20] Accordingly, the quest for humaniqueness amounts to identifying the factors that make human cognition special. In the words of Hauser (2008),

[a]nimals share many of the building blocks that comprise human thought, but paradoxically, there is a great cognitive gap between humans and animals. By looking at key differences in cognitive abilities, [we hope to] find the elements of human cognition that are uniquely human. The challenge is to identify which systems animals and human share, which are unique, and how these systems interact and interface with one another.

The program can be seen as an extension of Hauser et al. (2002), from the FLN to HCN (Human Cognition in the Narrow sense; that which is specific and

---

[20] Needless to say, it is perfectly possible that our special cognitive features are the result of more basic anatomical changes. Tattersall (1998) even suggests that the emergence of language was the result of epigenetic processes.

unique to human cognition), or (building on Fodor 1975), LOTN (Language of Thought Narrow).

Hauser presents four evolved mechanisms of human thought that give us access to a wide range of information and the ability to find creative solutions to new problems based on access to this information:

1. the ability to combine and recombine different types of information and knowledge in order to gain new understanding;
2. to apply the same rule or solution to one problem to a different and new situation;
3. to create and easily understand symbolic representations of computation and sensory input; and
4. to detach modes of thought from raw sensory and perceptual input.

Details of formulation aside, Hauser's hypothesis is a very familiar one. The essence of Hauser's claim really goes back to the Descartes's fascination with human cognitive flexibility, its fluidity, its detachment from perception, and its unbounded character—in short, its creative character. This is what led the Cartesians to claim that Man has no instinct, by which they meant that Man's cognitive faculties rise above the *hic and nunc*. This was clear to Konrad Lorenz as well, who said that "man is a specialist in not being specialized" (Lorenz 1959). As Marc Hauser likes to put it, while other animals display laser-beam-like intelligence (highly precise specificity), humans intelligence is floodlight-like (generalized specificity) in character. Tattersall (1998: 197) calls it "the human noncondition" and writes:

… [O]ver millenia now, philosophers and theologians have made something of an industry of debating the human condition. Even if inevitable, it is rather ironic that the very species that apparently so much enjoys agonizing over its own condition is, in fact, the only species that doesn't have one—or at any rate, whose condition, if any, is most difficult to define. Whatever condition is, it is surely a lot easier to specify it in the case of an amoeba, or a lizard, or a shrew, or even a chimpanzee, than it is in our own.

Elsewhere (p. 207), Tattersall notes that in our case, "natural selection has gone for 'flexibility' instead of specificity in behavior" (something which one may attempt to relate to Gould's 1977 discussion of "neoteny").

To be sure, scientists have found that some animals think in ways that were once considered unique to humans. For example, some animals have episodic memory, or non-linguistic mathematical ability, or the capacity to navigate using landmarks. In sum, animals have a rich mental life, full of modules or what Liz Spelke calls "core knowledge systems." What Man seems to have in addition is the ability to systematically transcend the boundaries of modular thought and engage in cross-modular concept formation.

I would like to claim that this ability of building bridges across modules is directly related to language, specifically the ability to lexicalize concepts (uprooting them from their modules) and combine them freely via Merge.

I am by no means the first to speculate along these lines. Spelke (2003), Carruthers (2006), Pietroski (2007), Tattersall (1998), Chomsky (2005), and, to some extent, Mithen (1996), all agree with Descartes that language plays a significant role in human cognition. Darwin himself appears to be in agreement when he writes in *The Descent of Man*,

> If it could be proved that certain high mental powers, such as the formation of general concepts, self-consciousness, etc., were absolutely peculiar to man, which seems extremely doubtful, it is not improbable that these qualities are merely the incidental results of other highly-advanced intellectual faculties; and these again mainly the result of the continued use of a perfect language. (p. 126)

The emergence of lexical items was the sort of perfect storm that gave Man his niche. Once concepts are dissociated from their conceptual sources by means of a lexical envelope, the mind truly becomes algebraic and stimulus-free.

The creation of the human lexicon, which, if I am correct, goes hand in hand with Merge, is what lies behind the creative aspect of our thought process, which fascinated both Descartes and Chomsky. Edge features are the set of humaniqueness. With language, creativity emerged, understood (as did Arthur Koestler) as "the sudden, interlocking of two previously unrelated skills or matrices of thought," an almost limitless capacity for imagination, metaphorical extension, etc.[21] Note that one need not follow Hauser (2008) in positing four distinct mechanisms to account for humaniqueness. One key event (the emergence of edge features) suffices. Going back to Hauser's four ingredients for human specificity listed above, we can now claim that by means of lexical envelopes, humans are able to "detach modes of thought from raw sensory and perceptual input," and lexicalize at will ("create and easily understand symbolic representations of computation and sensory input"). Via Merge, humans have "the ability to combine and recombine different types of information and knowledge in order to gain new understanding, and apply the same rule or solution to one problem to a different and new situation."

---

[21] It may be interesting to note that Mithen's (1996) characterization of the evolution of mind in three stages—primitive general intelligence, specialized intelligence (modules), and cross-modular intelligence—mirrors Fitch's (2008) three stages of consciousness. Perhaps one may attempt to make precise the link between language and consciousness that Jackendoff (1987, 2007) has tried to establish.

With edge features and Merge, the human mind became capable of true Swiss-army-knife style cognition. Before that the tools at the animal's disposal were exquisitely tuned to their tasks, but too isolated. Their effects could only be combined sequentially; they could not be seamlessly and smoothly integrated with one another. With language, the human mind developed into a key ring, where all keys (concepts) can be combined and available at once, thanks to the hole (edge feature) that they all share.

One could say that the ability to endow a concept with an edge feature was, to paraphrase Armstrong, a relatively small step for a man, but a giant leap for mind-kind (and mankind). As Dennett (1996: 17) puts it (in agreement with the intuition behind Cartesian dualism), "perhaps the kind of mind you get when you add language to it is so different from the kind of mind you can have without language that calling them both minds is a mistake."

Merge/edge features gave Man a truly general language of thought, a *lingua franca*, where previously there were only modular, mutually incomprehensible, dialects/(proto-)languages of thoughts. It significantly altered Man's conceptual structures—how humans think the world. By merging lexicalized concepts, Man was able to hold in mind concepts of concepts, representations of representations, and associations of associations. *Homo* became *Homo combinans*.

The result of the emergence of the FLN was a creative, cultural explosion well attested in the archeological record (art, symbol, music, notation, feelings of mystery, mastery of diverse materials, true innovation in toolmaking, sheer cleverness), a "quantum leap," as Tattersall (1998) calls it.

I agree with Tattersall (1998: 171) that "it is very hard to avoid the conclusion that articulate language is quite intimately tied up with all the other mysterious and often unfathomable aspects of modern human behavior."[22] Tattersall (1998: 186, 228) notes further,

Almost all of the unique cognitive attributes that so strongly characterize modern humans—and that undoubtedly also distinguished our fellow *Homo sapiens* who eliminated the Neanderthals—are tied up in some way with language. Language both permits and requires an ability to produce symbol in the mind, which can be reshuffled and organized by the generative capacity that seems to be unique to our species. Thought as we know it depends on the mental manipulation of such symbols, which are arbitrary representations of features belonging to both the internal and outside world.

[22] Tattersall is quite careful, as is Chomsky (see Chomsky 2008) to distinguish between language [the FLN] and speech, which he regards as an "adjunct" (p. 186) to language. It is quite possible that this adjunction was a recruitment of old circuits specialized in externalization of the sort we find in songbirds. For relevant discussion, see Piattelli-Palmarini and Uriagereka (this volume) on the possible role of FOXP2 in this respect.

... virtually any component of our ratiocinative capacities you can name—from our sense of humor to our ability to entertain apocalyptic visions—is based on those same mental abilities that permit us to generate language

Through Merge/edge features, we became the symbolic species—a transformative experience that is directly reflected in the archeological records. As Camps and Uriagereka (2006) have noted, aspects of *Homo sapiens*'s tool-making seem to require the kind of mental computation that are distinctive of the FLN (the discussion in Mithen 1996: 76 can also be interpreted in this way).

Monboddo—one of the forefathers of evolutionary thought—was clearly correct in his belief that language is "necessarily connected with an[y] inquiry into the original nature of Man." As Tattersall (1998: 58) writes, "universal among modern humans, language is the most evident of all our uniqueness." Tattersall goes on to note (p. 68) that our closest relatives "do not display 'generativity,' the capacity that allows us to assemble words into statements or ideas into products." It seems to me that edge features are a good candidate for the source of this very generativity, and humaniqueness.

3.4 On the Importance of Distinguishing between Language and the Language Faculty

The scenario I have sketched does not account for all aspects of the FL, but it surely alleviates the explanatory burden that evolutionary hypotheses face in light of the rapid emergence and spread of "Merge-man" (*Homo combinans*). And perhaps it is just as well that the hypothesis I have sketched does not cover all aspects of what we would call language, because it is not at all clear that unification of all aspects of language is desirable. Language is almost surely not a natural object. It is an object of our folk psychology/biology. The FL is the real object of study. The FL, like the hand, the nose, and other properties of our organism, is put to use in countless ways, and it would be foolish to expect any theory to capture all these aspects. The term "language" is a remnant of philological thinking; ignoring the basic distinction between competence and performance is bound to lead to the claim that language is messy or klugy. Instead, if one focuses on the language organ, I think that signs of good design emerge very quickly.

This said, the discussion above has left out important aspects traditionally associated with the FL. For example, I have said very little about the way linguistic expressions are externalized. I have tacitly assumed the correctness of a long-standing intuition (already present in the writings of the Cartesians) that the FL's core function is basically that of providing a syntax of thought (Language of Thought in the narrrow sense, LOTN). As Chomsky (2008: 136) remarks,

It may be that there is a basic asymmetry in the contribution to language design of the two interface systems: the primary contribution to the structure of [the] F[aculty of] L[anguage] may be optimization of the C-I [sense] interface.

From this perspective, externalization appears to be an addendum—(quite literally) an afterthought. This may explain why the nature of morpho-phonology appears to be radically different (see Bromberger and Halle 1989, Blevins 2004). This is not to say that morpho-phonology is not part of language. It clearly is. But it is just that the syntax–phonology connection is much looser, and less constitutive of the FL than the mapping from syntax to thought.

I also said nothing regarding the size of the lexicon, or the way words are acquired. Although I have argued that the nature of lexicalization is crucial to the FLN, I do not think that the size of the lexicon or some of the strategies used in its acquisition must be regarded as unique to language (or specific to humans). Clearly, syntax plays a role in carving the path of acquisition to some extent (as Lila Gleitman and colleagues have revealed over the years; Gleitman et al. (2005); see also Borer 2005), but other aspects, not specifically linguistic, surely come into play (see Bloom 2000). As for the size of our vocabulary, it is likely to be tied to our ability to imitate—unique to us, but not specific to language (Hauser 1996, 2000; Tomasello 1999).

Finally, there is another aspect of the FL that I have not touched on and that many would have regarded as central to language (indeed part of the FLN) until recently, and that is parameters—the points of variation pre-defined by Universal Grammar, the open variables in universal linguistic principles. I argue in Boeckx (this volume) that perhaps UG is not as overspecified as traditionally thought in generative grammar. There is indeed a case to be made that parameters are not constituents of the FLN. Rather, they may be the necessary result of a very impoverished, underspecified system (that is to say, some parametric effects may be epigenetic). Let me illustrate what I mean with one clear example. Take the fact that phrases are headed (a property known as endocentricity). Under most accounts (but see Kayne 1994), phrases in natural language are assumed to be underspecified with regard to the directionality of headedness. One can formulate this as a principle with open values, as in "syntactic projections must be [right/left] headed." From the acquisition standpoint, children know that projections have to be headed, but have to figure out whether their language is head-initial or head-final. They must pick one or the other option. However, note that instead of building the parametric variation into linguistic principles (FLN), we could get the same result from letting it follow (logically) from the fact that each phrase must be linearized, and, since externalization proceeds through a narrow, one-dimensional channel, the physics of speech will force the very choice that the head parameter is supposed to code for.

Generally speaking, I believe that a more minimalist understanding of parameters ought to move underspecification from the domain of individual principles to the system as a whole. It is because the system is not richly specified in the genome, because the FLN is so minimalist, that not every aspect of the FL is fixed once and for all, and therefore variation is expected. This view on variation meshes well with Kirschner and Gerhart's (2005) theory that variation results from underspecified parts of system that allow organism to explore the fullness of space pre-defined by their flexibly connected constituents, freeing the genome from registering rigidly the space of variation. The same logic underlies the temporal retardation of development, especially prominent in humans—with absence of early rigidification leading to bigger potential (neoteny; see Gould 1977). Less is indeed more.[23] Once available, non-genomic parametric dimensions would be made use of, in the same way that colored patterns on wings are used in butterflies to reinforce group boundaries, preventing possible interbreeding (a state of artifical speciation) (see Lukhtanov et al. 2005).

3.5 By Way of a Conclusion

The formulation of concrete minimalist hypotheses, combined with recent developments in genetics that re-establish the balance between genes, environment, and organism (Lewontin's 2000 triple helix) and allow us to extrapolate back to our ancestors when the fossil record fails (see Kirschner and Gerhart 2005, Wade 2006), should enable us to not only regard the much-publicized 1866 ban imposed by the Linguistic Society of Paris on any debate concerning the origin of language as *passé*, but more importantly relieve Lewontin's (1998) unremitting attack on the plausibility of evolutionary studies of cognitive faculties. I will not review Lewontin's points in detail here. Suffice it to say that he saw the problem of reconstruction in the absence of

---

[23] This view also fits in well with recent attempts to minimize the structure and format of parameters by reducing their size and macroproperties (see Kayne 2005b). It also fits well with recent criticism leveled at (macro-)parametric approaches (see Culicover 1999, Newmeyer 2005, who, unfortunately, made the mistake of throwing away the baby with the bathwater; for further discussion, see Boeckx, in progress).

record as insuperable, and therefore all evolutionary account of cognition as Just-So stories. In his own words (p. 130):

the best lesson... is to give up the childish notion that everything that is interesting about nature can be understood.... It might be interesting to know how cognition... arose and spread and changed, but we cannot know. Tough luck.

It is hard to dismiss the views of giants like Lewontin, but those interested in Darwin's problem will no doubt find comfort in the following assertion made by Darwin himself in *The Descent of Man*:

It has often and confidently been asserted, that man's origin can never be known: but ignorance more frequently begets confidence than does knowledge: it is those who know little, and not those who know much, who so positively assert that this or that problem will never be solved by science.   (p. 3)

One could indeed point to many episodes where the end of a field has been announced right before important advances took this field to new heights. Perhaps we will never know for sure whether certain aspects of the FL emerged via adaptation or some other means, but already now it seems we can make some educated guesses about and some progress toward understanding how the FL could have evolved. But there is no doubt that if we are to vindicate Darwin's view, the task that lies ahead will be supremely interdisciplinary and therefore extremely hard. To address Darwin's problem, it will be imperative to ask—simultaneously—distinct, but inextricably related questions, which I borrow from Piattelli-Palmarini and Uriagereka (2005): What is language such that it may have evolved? and, What is evolution such that it may have applied to language?

Jackendoff (2002) is right: One's view on the evolution of language depends on one's view of language. But it also depends on one's view on evolution, which too many students of language have taken to be fixed along Dawkinsian lines. The point here is not to revive creationism or promote intelligent design. It is simply an attempt to strike a non-dogmatic balance between Form and Function, between Necessity and Chance. What I find most fascinating, from the perspective of a linguist, is that seemingly arcane discussions about Merge and the nature of lexicalization may contribute to our understanding of evolutionary theory. The language organ may become a model organism in the context of an extended modern synthesis in biology—extremely useful because surprisingly simple and optimal in its design.

4

Syntax Facit Saltum Redux: Biolinguistics and the Leap to Syntax

ROBERT C. BERWICK

I have been astonished how rarely an organ can be named, towards which no transitional grade is known to lead. The truth of this remark is indeed shown by that old canon in natural history of *Natura non facit saltum*. We meet with this admission in the writings of almost every experienced naturalist; or, as Milne Edwards has well expressed it, nature is prodigal in variety, but niggard in innovation. Why, on the theory of Creation, should this be so? ... Why should not Nature have taken a leap from structure to structure? On the theory of natural selection, we can clearly understand why she should not; for natural selection can act only by taking advantage of slight successive variations; she can never take a leap, but must advance by the shortest and slowest steps.   (Darwin 1859: 194)

4.1 Introduction: Language, Biology, and the Evolution–Language Gaps

For hundreds of years, long before Darwin's publication of *Origin of Species* (1859) and his *Descent of Man* (1871) that explicitly brought language into the fold of modern evolutionary thinking, the evolution of language has captured the imagination of biologists and linguists alike. Among many evolutionary puzzles, one that stands out is the obvious discontinuity between the human species and all other organisms: language is evidently unique to the human lineage—being careful here to define language properly as distinct

This research was supported by NSF grant 9217041-ASC and ARPA under the HPCC program. Noam Chomsky, Samuel Epstein, Anna Maria Di Sciullo, Charles Yang, and Morris Halle provided many valuable comments; all remaining errors are our own.

from general communication, a matter addressed in Berwick and Chomsky (this volume) and considered further below.

Such gaps, or evolutionary novelties, have always posed a challenge to classical Darwinian analysis, since that theory is grounded fundamentally on the notion of gradualism—incrementally fine steps leading from a trait's precursor, with adaptive, functioning intermediates at every step along the evolutionary path, ultimately culminating in an "organ of extreme complexity and perfection," as with the vertebrate eye. Add one extra layer of light-sensitive membrane, so the argument goes, and an eye's photon-trapping improves by a fractional percent—a smooth incline with no jumps or surprises. Indeed Darwin himself devoted considerable effort in *Origin* to analyzing precisely this problem with this assumption (Chapter VI, "Organs of extreme perfection"), using the evolution of the eye as his make-or-break case study for his gradualist model, the very heart and soul of the theory itself, since, as he himself insists, "If it could be demonstrated that any complex organ existed, which could not possibly have been formed by numerous, successive, slight modifications, my theory would absolutely break down" (1859: 189):

To suppose that the eye, with all its inimitable contrivances for adjusting the focus to different distances, for admitting different amounts of light, and for the correction of spherical and chromatic aberration, could have been formed by natural selection, seems, I freely confess, absurd in the highest possible degree. Yet reason tells me, that if numerous gradations from a perfect and complex eye to one very imperfect and simple, each grade being useful to its possessor, can be shown to exist; if further, the eye does vary ever so slightly, and the variations be inherited, which is certainly the case; and if any variation or modification in the organ be ever useful to an animal under changing conditions of life, then the difficulty of believing that a perfect and complex eye could be formed by natural selection, though insuperable by our imagination, can hardly be considered real.   (1859: 186)

From this perspective, human language seems to be exactly the kind of unwanted biological surprise Darwin sought to avoid. Indeed, it apparently stands squarely as a counter-example to his entire theory of evolution via descent with modification, at least if we are to take Darwin at his word. Perhaps that is why ever since Darwin nearly all researchers seem to abhor even the slightest hint of a non-gradual, non-adaptationist account of human language evolution.

It is perhaps worth recollecting that this picture of evolution-as-minute-accumulation of small changes was not always so strongly embraced. As the evolutionary theorist Allan Orr notes in a recent review (2005a), in the late nineteenth and early twentieth centuries, Mendelians like William Bateson argued that the "micromutational" view was simply a path of least effort:

"By suggesting that the steps through which an adaptive mechanism arises are indefinite and insensible, all further trouble is spared. While it could be said that species arise by an insensible and imperceptible process of variation, there was clearly no use in tiring ourselves by trying to perceive that process. This labor-saving counsel found great favor" (Bateson 1909). The gradualist position became the dominant paradigm in the field in the 1930s via the analytical unification marrying Mendelism to Darwinism forged by R. A. Fisher, S. Wright, and J. B. S. Haldane, dubbed the "Modern Synthesis": on this view, micro-mutational particulate events—tiny changes, perhaps at the level of single nucleotides (the DNA "letters" Adenine, Thymine, Guanine, and Cytosine), and correspondingly small steps in allele (gene variant) frequencies—comprise the bulk of evolutionary change. The Modern Synthesis too suggests that a Big-Bang emergence of language might be quite unlikely.

How then can one reconcile evolutionary theory's Modern Synthesis with the apparent discontinuity, species-specificity, and distinctive syntactic competence of human language? A familiar line of thinking simply denies that a gap exists at all: other hominids also possess human syntactic abilities. A second position embraces the Modern Synthesis and rejects discontinuity, asserting that all the particular properties of human language have been specifically selected for as directly adaptive, with small gradual changes leading from non-language using ancestors to the present, a position perhaps most strongly advocated by Pinker and Bloom (1990). Other researchers deny that there are properties proprietary to human syntax, instead grounding them on principles of general purpose cognition, like those found in connectionism (Rummelhart and McClelland 1987). Still other approaches call for development from a proto-language to full language (Bickerton 1990). Perhaps the only proposals made previously that avoid an outright appeal to gradualism are those that involve exaptation in the sense of Gould and Vrba (1982), or genetic draft (Gillespie 1991)—that human language hitch-hiked on the back of a related, already adaptively advantageous cognitive subsystem, such as motor-gesture articulation, hierarchical tool-making, or social grooming. While these last approaches remain possibilities within a classical gradualist framework, they all focus on some external aspect of language-as-communication, rather than internal syntax *tout court*, a matter discussed elsewhere (Berwick and Chomsky, this volume). Berwick and Chomsky note that all recent relevant biological and evolutionary research leads to the conclusion that the process of externalization is secondary, subsequent to conceptualization and the core principles of human syntax. If this conclusion is on the right track, we are left with the same puzzling gap as before.

Besides this unsettling discontinuity, human language poses a second challenging gap, a classic and also familiar biological one: how to bridge between a genotype and a phenotype, in this case perhaps the most complex behavioral phenotype we know. Linguistics has cast natural language's intricate and ultimately behavioral "form that shows" (its phenotype) at an abstract level, far removed from language's computational and biological "inner form" or genotype. Linguistic science's successful program over the past fifty years has resulted in perhaps the richest description of a human genotype-to-phenotype mapping that we know of—the initial substrate for human language and how language develops in an individual.

However, until recently progress at bridging from the language genotype to phenotype has been difficult. In part this is because we simply do not know much about the human language genotype, and we often run aground by misidentifying the language phenotype with communication, as mentioned above. Further, the gulf separating computation, biology, and language has been equally long-standing—in large measure resulting from the abstraction gap between linguistic and biological description: we do not expect to literally find a "passive grammar rule" inside a person's head. The history of the field here from Fodor, Bever, and Garrett's summary of work from the 1960s (1974) to Berwick and Weinberg (1986), Di Sciullo (2000), Phillips (2003), Reinhart (2006), and many others might be read as one long attempt to find more-to-less isomorphic mappings between linguistic rules and representations and computational rules and representations.

In this chapter we show how to resolve both the evolutionary and the genotype–phenotype gaps in a new way, emphasizing that the species-specificity and novelty of human language need not conflict with Darwinian thinking—indeed, that modern evolutionary theorizing and discoveries have moved past the "micro-mutational" gradualist view so as to become quite compatible with modern linguistic theory, with both linguistic theory and evolutionary theory contributing theoretical insights to each other. This synergy is not a new development. It is one that itself has evolved over the past two decades: the Principles-and-Parameters (P&P) approach to language (Chomsky 1981) was directly inspired by the biologist Jacob's (1977) remarks about how the apparent diversity of biological forms might be produced by an underlying parameterization of abstract genetic regulatory switches, a view that Chomsky then imported into linguistic theory. On the biological side, the so-called evo–devo [evolution–development] revolution (see Carroll, Grenier, and Weatherbee 2001; Carroll 2005a; Chomsky 2007c; Müller 2007), along with new results on genomic and regulatory networks, new simulation results on the apparently much larger size of adaptive mutational change

(Orr 2002, 2005a), and a more widespread acknowledgment of homeoplasy or horizontal gene transfer (Warren et al. 2008), have moved evolutionary theory well past the Fisher–Wright gradualist, particulate, micro-mutational view. We shall see below that historically developments in both linguistic theory and evolutionary theory are in many respects parallel and mutually reinforcing.

To resolve these two gaps, in this chapter we move beyond the 1980s viewpoint on both the biological and linguistic fronts, showing how the most recent developments in linguistic research, dubbed the Minimalist Program (MP) (Chomsky 1995, 2005, 2007a) can bridge the biology–language divide. The MP demonstrates that despite its apparent surface complexity, language's core might in fact be much simpler than has previously been supposed. For biologists pursuing clues left by the linguistic phenotype's fault lines down to the level of the real genotype, this is a promising development. The refinement of our understanding of the linguistic phenotype comes at a particularly apt time, since in the last decade there has been an ever-growing, though still small, range of work on genetics and language, as exemplified in the work of Gopnik and colleagues (Gopnik 1990), and many others since, including the extensive recent findings on locating specific genetic variation in language, namely, the mutations in the FOXP2 gene (Marcus and Fisher 2003; Enard et al. 2002). (But see Berwick and Chomsky, this volume, for a critique of naive genetical interpretations of single mutations.) This is because the Minimalist Program is eliminative in exactly the right way, and so can serve as a case study for how a complex behavioral phenotype emerges from the interactions of a much simpler genotype. In particular, the Minimalist Program posits that the human syntactic engine consists of just two components: (1) words and word features; and (2) a single, simple recursive operation, Merge, that glues together words and word complexes into larger units.

This chapter demonstrates how *just* these two components, without further stipulation, interact to yield many, perhaps all, of the special design features of human language syntax. If this is so, then we have no need for specific, adaptive accounts of these particular features. By design features we mean familiar properties of human language syntax such as the following:

- digital infinity and recursive generative capacity, the familiar "infinite use of finite means": sentences may be arbitrarily long and novel; there are 1-, 2-, ... word sentences, but there are no $5\frac{1}{2}$ -word sentences;
- displacement: human languages move phrases from their natural argument positions, as in *This student, I want to solve the problem* where the subject

of the verb, *solve*, namely *This student*, appears at the front of the sentence instead of in its normal position after the verb;

- locality constraints: displacement does not act over unbounded domains— in *Who do you wonder Bill thinks solved the problem*, *who* cannot be interpreted as the subject of *solve*;
- restricted grammatical relations: out of a potentially infinite set of logically possible relations that might be defined over configurations of syntactic structures, only a handful ever seem to play a role in human syntax. For example, human languages often match verbs to objects (in terms of predicate–argument structure); demand agreement between tense/inflection and subjects as in the case of subject–verb person–number agreement; or verbs may select either subjects or objects, as in the familiar contrast between *John admires honesty/Honesty admires John*. Yet most logically possible syntactic rules and relations are unattested—for instance, there is apparently no analog to "object-of," say subject-object-of, where the subject and object of a sentence must agree.

For the evolutionary biologist seeking to answer *why* we see this particular distribution of organisms or traits in the natural world and not others—one of the central questions of biology being to reconcile this pattern of variation both present and absent with the apparent commonalities of organisms, just as with language—such a finding is central. If observed patterns follow from a single, central principle, then there is no need to invoke some special adaptive explanation for any of them. There is no locality "trait" and no grammatical relation trait that must be acquired in an evolutionary piecemeal fashion. One does not need to advance incremental, adaptationist arguments with intermediate steps between some protolanguage and full natural language to explain much, perhaps all, of natural language's specific design.

Note that from a logical or communicative standpoint, these particular design properties are otherwise mysterious. For instance, there is no immediately obvious computational or communicative reason why languages ought *not* to relate subjects and objects. Communicatively, a sentence's subject, usually an agent, and its object, usually the affected object, form just as natural a class as subject and predicate. Further, as is easy to see from the transitivity of conditional probabilities that can be simply multiplied together, nothing blocks a purely statistical conditional relationship between subject and object. However, it seems that no such connections are to be found in human languages. Indeed this is another clear limitation of the currently popular statistical approach to language description, which otherwise offers no barrier to such unattested relations. Similarly, as pointed out in Berwick and Chomsky (this volume), displacement makes language processing and communication *more* difficult, not *less* difficult—yet another argument that language is not designed for communication. The ultimate explanation for language's design must be, obviously, biological, but on the view here, not at the level of expressiveness or communicative efficiency. This chapter offers an alternative, deeper, possibility: the reason why human syntax looks the way it does rather than some other way—why natural languages have an object-of grammatical relation but not a subject-object-of grammatical relation—*follows* from the fundamental principles of the basic combinatorial syntactic engine itself.[1]

As to the evolutionary origin of the fundamental combinatory ability itself, Merge, we leave this topic largely unexplored here. Along with the evolutionary theorist G. C. Williams (1996: 77), one might speculate that the hierarchical combinatorial ability possibly appeared just as other evolutionary novelties do: "new structures arise in evolution in one of two ultimate ways, as redundancies or *spandrels*"—a structure arising as an incidental consequence of some other evolutionary change. Where we part ways with Williams's classical account is in the nature of evolutionary change itself, as we describe in Section 4.2, below. Berwick and Chomsky (this volume) provide additional details on how a singular event of this kind might arise and spread in a small group, some 50,000 to 100,000 years ago.

This minimalist reformulation also has important consequences for models of language processing, and so ultimately for descriptions of the linguistic phenotype as it is externalized. The most minimal conception of a processor or parser for natural language takes the relation between basic parsing operations and the abstract linguistic system as simply the identity function. As it turns out, this leads to the most efficient processor achievable, left-to-right,

---

[1] We note that it is more difficult than sometimes supposed to give a purely functional communicative justification for some of the more patent universal properties of natural-language syntax. For instance, it is sometimes suggested that recursive generative capacity is somehow *necessary* for communication, thus bridging the gap between protolanguage and recursive human syntax. But is this so? There seem to be existing human languages that evidently possess the ability to form recursive sentences but that apparently do not need to make use of such power: a well-known example is the Australian language Warlpiri, where it has been proposed that a sentence that would be recursively structured in many other languages, such as 'I think that John is a fool' is formed via linear concatenation, 'I ponder it. John is a fool'; or to take a cited example, *Yi-rna wita yirripura jaru jukurrpa-warnu wiinyiinypa*, literally, 'little tell-PRESENT TENSE story dreaming hawk,' translated as 'I want to tell a little dreaming story about a hawk' (Nash 1986, Swartz 1988). Evidently then, recursion is not essential to express "the beliefs about the intentional states of others," quite contrary to what some researchers such as Pinker and Bloom (1990) and more recently Pinker and Jackendoff (2005) have asserted. This seems again to be an example of the confusion between externalization-as-communication and internal syntax. Apparently the same was true of Old English, if the data and linguistic arguments presented in O'Neil (1976) are correct. There is nothing surprising in any of this; it is quite similar in spirit to the observed production/perception limitations on, for example, center-embedded and other difficult-to-process sentences in English.

real-time, and deterministic to the extent this is possible at all, and at the same time replicates some of human language's known psychophysical, preferential "blind spots." For example, in sentence pairs such as *John said that the cat died yesterday/John said that the cat will die yesterday*, *yesterday* is (reflexively) taken to modify the second verb, the time of the cat's demise, even though this is semantically defeasible in the second sentence. In this sense, this approach even helps solve the secondary process of externalization (and so communicative efficiency, again to the extent that efficient communication is possible at all).

If all this is correct, then current linguistic theory may have now attained a better level of description in order to proceed with evolutionary analysis. In this sense, using familiar Darwinian terms, the syntactic system for human language is indeed, like the eye, an "organ of extreme complexity and perfection." However, unlike Linnaeus's and Darwin's slogan shunning the possibility of discontinuous leaps in species and evolution generally—*natura non facit saltum*—we advocate a revised motto that turns the original on its head: *syntax facit saltum*—syntax makes leaps—in this case, because human language's syntactic phenotype follows from interactions amongst its deeper components, giving it a special character all its own, apparently unique in the biological world.

The remainder of this chapter is organized as follows. Section 4.2 serves as a brief historical review of the recent shift from the "gradualist," micro-mutational Modern Synthesis in evolutionary biology to a more ecumenical encompassing the evo–devo revolution and macro-adaptive events. Section 4.3 follows with an outline of parallel shifts in linguistic theory: from highly specialized language-particular rules to more abstract principles that derive large-scale changes in the apparent surface form of syntactic rules. This historical shift has two parts. First, the change from the atomic, language-particular rules of the *Aspects* era, the Extended Standard Theory (EST) to a system resembling a genetic regulatory–developmental network, dubbed the Principles-and-Parameters (P&P) theory; and second, the more recent shift to the Minimalist Program. Putting to one side many important details irrelevant for our argument, we outline how sentence derivations work in the MP. By examining the notion of derivation in this system, we demonstrate that all syntactic "design features" in our list above follow ineluctably, including all and only the attested grammatical relations, such as subject-of and object-of. Section 4.4 turns to sentence processing and psychophysical blind spots. It outlines a specific parsing model for the minimalist system, based on earlier computational models for processing sentences deterministically, strictly left to right. It then shows how reflexive processing preferences like the one described above can be accounted for. Section 4.5 concludes with observations on the tension between variation and uniformity in language, summarizing the evolutionary leap to syntax.

4.2 Ever since Darwin: The Rise and Fall of Atomism in Modern Evolutionary Biology

As we noted in the introduction, by the mid-1930s the micro-mutational, atomistic picture of evolution by natural selection held sway, admirably unified on the one hand by particulate Mendelism and on the other hand by Darwinism, all unified by the "infinitesimal" mathematical theory established by Fisher, Wright, and Haldane. However, by the late decades of the twentieth century and on into the twenty-first, this Modern Synthesis paradigm has undergone substantial revision, due to advances on three fronts: (1) the evo–devo revolution in our understanding of deep homologies in development and underlying uniformity of all organisms; (2) an acknowledgment of a more widespread occurrence of symbiotic evolutionary events and homeoplasy; and (3) the erosion of the Fisher-inspired adaptationism-as-incrementalism model.

First, the evo–devo revolution has demonstrated that quite radical changes can arise from very slight changes in genomic/developmental systems. The evolution of eyes provides a now-classic example, turning Darwin's view on its head. While perhaps the most famous advocate of the Modern Synthesis, Ernst Mayr, held that it was quite remarkable that 40 to 60 different eyes had evolved separately, thus apparently confirming that micro-mutational evolution by natural selection had a stunning ability to attain "organs of perfection" despite radically different starting points and different contexts, in reality there are very few types of eye, perhaps even monophyletic (evolving only once) in part because of constraints imposed by the physics of light, in part because only one category of proteins, opsin molecules, can perform the necessary functions (Salvini-Plawen and Mayr 1961; Gehring 2005). Indeed, this example almost exactly parallels the discoveries in linguistic theory during the 1980s, that the apparent surface variation among languages as distinct as Japanese, English, Italian, and so forth are all to be accounted for by a richly interacting set of principles, parameterized in just a few ways, that deductively interact to yield the apparent diversity of surface linguistic forms, as described in the next section.

This move from a highly linear model—compatible with a "gradualist, incrementalist" view—to a more highly interconnected set of principles where a slight change in a deep regulatory switch can lead to a quite radical surface change, from vertebrate eyes to insect eyes—follows the same logic in both linguistics and biology. The parallel is much more than superficial. Gehring (2005) notes that there is a contrast to be made in the evolution of biosynthetic pathways, for instance for histidine, as proposed by Horowitz (1945), as opposed to the evolution of morphogenetic pathways, as for the vertebrate eye. In the case of biosynthesis, the linear model can proceed backwards: at first, histidine must be directly absorbed from the environment. When the supply of histidine is exhausted, then those organisms possessing an enzyme that can carry out the very last step in the pathway to synthesize histidine from its immediate precursor are the Darwinian survivors. This process extends backwards, step by step, linearly and incrementally. We might profitably compare this approach to the one-rule-at-a-time acquisition that was adopted in the Wexler and Culicover (1980) model of acquisition in the similarly atomistic linguistic theory of the time.

However, quite a different model seems to be required for eye morphogenesis, one that goes well beyond the incremental, single nucleotide changes invoked by the Modern Synthesis. Here the interplay of genetic and regulatory factors seems to be intercalated, highly interwoven as Gehring remarks. That much already goes well beyond a strictly micromutational, incremental view. The intercalation resembles nothing so much as the logical dependencies in the linguistic P&P theory, as illustrated in Figure 4.1; see p. 82. But there is more. Gehring argues that the original novelty itself—a photoreceptor next to a pigment cell—was a "purely stochastic event," and further, that there is reasonable evidence from genome analysis that it might in part be due to symbiosis—the wholesale incorporation of many genes into an animal (Eukaryotic) cell by ingestion of a chloroplast from *Volvox*, a cyanobacter. Needless to say, this completely bypasses the ordinary step-by-step nucleotide changes invoked by the Fisher model, and constitutes the second major discovery that has required re-thinking of the gradualist, atomistic view of evolution:

The eye prototype, which is due to a purely stochastic event that assembles a photoreceptor and a pigment cell into a visual organ, requires the function of at least two classes of genes, a master control gene, *Pax6*, and the structural genes encoding on rhodopsin, for instance, the top and the bottom of the genetic cascade. Starting from such a prototype increasingly more sophisticated eye types arose by recruiting additional genes *into* the morphogenetic pathway. At least two mechanisms of recruitment are known that lead to the intercalation of additional genes into the genetic cascade. These mechanisms are gene duplication and enhancer fusion.... For the origin of metazoan photoreceptor cells I have put forward two hypotheses: one based on cell differentiation and a more speculative model based on symbiosis.

(Gehring 2005: 180; emphasis added)

The outcome is a richly interconnected set of regulatory elements, just as in the P&P theory. Further, we should note that if the origin of the original novelty assembling photoreceptor and pigment cell is purely stochastic then the "cosmic ray" theory of the origin of Merge, sometimes derided, might deserve more serious consideration, though of course such a view must remain entirely speculative.

Second, the leaps enabled by symbiosis seem much more widespread than has been previously appreciated. As Lynn Margulis—the biologist who did much to establish the finding that cellular mitochondria with their own genes were once independent organisms ingested symbiotically—has often remarked, "the fastest way to get new genes is to eat them." To cite yet another recent example here out of many that are quickly accumulating as whole-sale genomic analysis accumulates, the sequencing of the duckbill platypus *Ornithorhynchus anatinus* genome has revealed a substantial number of such horizontal transfers of genes from birds and other species whose most recent common ancestor with the platypus is extremely ancient (Warren et al. 2008). (Perhaps much to the biologists' relief, the crossover from birds does not seem to include the genes involved in the platypus's duck bill.)

Of course, at the lowest level, by and large genomic changes must of necessity be particulate in a strong sense: either one DNA letter, one nucleotide, changes or it does not; but the by-and-large caveat has loomed ever larger in importance as more and more evidence accumulates for the transmission of genes from species to species horizontally, presumably by phagocytosis, mosquito-borne viral transmission, or similar processes, without direct selection and the vertical transmission that Darwin insisted upon.

The third biological advance of the past several decades that has eroded the micro-mutational worldview is more theoretical in character: Fisher's original mathematical arguments for fine-grained adaptive change have required substantial revision. Why is this so? If evolutionary hills have gentle slopes, then inching uphill always works. That follows Fisher chapter and verse: picture each gene that contributes to better eyesight as if it were one of millions upon millions of fine sand grains. Piling up all that sand automatically produces a neatly conical sand pile with just one peak, a smooth mound to climb. In this way, complex adaptations such as the eye can always come about via a sequence of extremely small, additive changes to their individual parts, each change selectively advantageous and so seized on by natural selection.

The key question is whether the biological world really works this way, or rather, how often it works this way. And that question divides into two parts. Theoretically speaking: what works better as the raw material or "step size" for adaptation—countless genes each contributing a tiny effect, or a handful of genes of intermediate or large effect? Empirically speaking: how does adaptation really play out in the biological world? Are large mutations really always harmful, as Fisher argued? Do organisms usually tiptoe in the adaptive landscape or take larger strides? Are adaptive landscapes usually smooth sand piles, jagged alpine ranges, or something in between?

Fisher addressed the theoretical question via a mathematical version of the familiar "monkey wrench" argument: a large mutation would be much more likely than a small one to gum up the works of a complex, finely constructed instrument like a microscope, much as a monkey randomly fiddling with the buttons on a computer might likely break it. It is not hard to see why. Once one is at a mountain top, a large step is much more likely to lead to free-fall disaster. But the microscope analogy can easily mislead. Fisher's example considers a mutation's potential benefits in a particularly simple setting—precisely where there is just one mountain top, and in an infinite population. But if one is astride K90 with Mt. Everest just off to the left, then a large step might do better to carry me towards the higher peak than a small one. The more an adaptive landscape resembles the Himalayas, with peaks crowded together—a likely consequence of developmental interactions, which crumple the adaptive landscape—the worse for Fisher's analogy. Small wonder then that Dawkins's topographic maps and the gradual evolutionary computer simulations he invokes constantly alter how mountain heights get measured, resorting to a single factor—first for eyes, it's visual resolution; next, for spider webs, it is insect-trapping effectiveness; then, for insect wings, it is aerodynamic lift or temperature-regulating ability. An appropriate move, since hill-climbing is guaranteed to work only if there is exactly one peak and one proxy for fitness that can be optimized, one dimension at a time.

Even assuming a single adaptive peak, Fisher's microscope analogy focused on only half the evolutionary equation—variation in individuals, essentially the jet fuel that evolution burns—and not the other half—the selective engine that sifts variations and determines which remain written in the book of life. Some fifty years after Fisher, the population biologist Motoo Kimura (1983) noted that most *single* mutations of small effect do not last: because small changes are only slightly selectively advantageous, they tend to peter out within a few generations (ten or so). Indeed, most mutations, great or small, advantageous or not, go extinct—a fact often brushed aside by pan-adaptationist enthusiasts (see also Berwick and Chomsky, this volume). Kimura calculated that the rate at which a mutation gains a foothold and then sweeps through a population is directly proportional to the joint effect of the probability that the mutation is advantageous and the mutation's size. Moreover, even if medium-scale changes were less likely to fix in a population than micro-mutations, by definition a larger change will contribute correspondingly more to an organism's overall response to natural selection than a small one.

However, Kimura neglected an important point: he calculated this relative gain or loss for just a single mutation, but the acquisition of some (perhaps complex) trait might take several steps. This alters Kimura's analytical results, as has been more recently studied and thoroughly analyzed by Orr via a combination of mathematical analysis and computational simulations (2002, 2005a), and extended to discrete molecular change in DNA sequence space via other methods by Gillespie (1984). The upshot seems to be that beneficial mutations have exponentially distributed fitness effects—that is,

adaptation is therefore characterized by a pattern of diminishing returns—larger-effect mutations are typically substituted earlier on and smaller-effect ones later, . . . indeed, adaptation seems to be characterized by a 'Pareto principle', in which the majority of an effect (increased fitness) is due to a minority of causes (one [nucleotide] substitution).

(Orr 2005a: 122, 125)

Thus, while Kimura did not get the entire story correct, Fisher's theory must be revised to accommodate the theoretical result that the first adaptive step will likely be the largest in effect, with many, many tiny steps coming afterwards. Evidently, adaptive evolution takes much larger strides than had been thought. How then does that connect to linguistic theory? In the next section, we shall see that linguistics followed a somewhat parallel course, abandoning incrementalism and atomistic fine-grained rules, sometimes for the same underlying conceptual reasons.

4.3 Ever since *Aspects*: The Rise and Fall of Incrementalism in Linguistic Theory

Over the past fifty years, linguistic science has moved steadily from less abstract, naturalistic surface descriptions to more abstract, deeper descriptions—rule systems, or generative grammars. The Minimalist Program can be regarded as the logical endpoint of this evolutionary trajectory. While the need to move away from mere sentence memorization seems clear, the rules that linguists have proposed have sometimes seemed, at least to some, even farther removed from biology or behavior than the sentences they were meant to replace. Given our reductionist aim, it is relevant to understand how the Minimalist Program arose out of historical developments of the field, partly as a drive towards a descriptive level even farther removed from surface behavior. We therefore begin with a brief review of this historical evolution, dividing this history into two parts: from the Extended Standard Theory of Chomsky's *Aspects of the Theory of Syntax* (1965) to the P&P model; and from P&P to the Minimalist Program.

Before setting out, it perhaps should first be noted that the 'abstraction problem' described in the introduction is not unfamiliar territory to biologists. We might compare the formal computations of generative grammar to Mendel's Laws as understood around 1900—abstract computations whose physical basis were but dimly understood, yet clearly tied to biology. In this context one might do well to recall Beadle's comments about Mendel, as cited by Jenkins (2000):

> There was no evidence for Mendel's hypothesis other than his computations and his wildly unconventional application of algebra to botany, which made it difficult for his listeners to understand that these computations *were* the evidence.
>
> (Beadle and Beadle 1966)

In fact, as we suggest here, the a-biological and a-computational character sometimes (rightly) attributed to generative grammar resulted not because its rules were abstract, but rather because rules were not abstract enough. Indeed, this very fact was duly noted by the leading psycholinguistic text of that day: Fodor, Bever, and Garrett's *Psychology of Language* (1974: 368), which summarized the state of psycholinguistic play up to about 1970: "there exist no suggestions for how a generative grammar might be concretely employed as a sentence recognizer in a psychologically plausible system."

In retrospect, the reason for this dilemma seems clear. In the initial decade or two of investigation in the era of modern generative grammar, linguistic knowledge was formulated as a large set of language-particular, specific rules, such as the rules of English question formation, passive formation, or topicalization (the rule that fronts a focused phrase, as in, *these students I want to solve the problem*). Such rules are still quite close to the external, observable behavior—sentences—they were meant to abstract away from.

4.3.1 *All transformations great and small: From* Aspects *to* Principles and Parameters

By 1965, the time of Chomsky's *Aspects of the Theory of Syntax*, each transformational rule consisted of two components: a structural description, generally corresponding to a surface-oriented pattern description of the conditions under which a particular rule could apply (an 'IF' condition), and a structural change marking out how the rule affected the syntactic structure under construction (a 'THEN' action). For example, an English passive rule might be formulated as follows, mapping *Sue will eat the ice cream* into *The ice cream will be+en eat by Sue*, where we have distinguished pattern-matched elements with numbers beneath:

Structural description (IF condition):

Noun phrase	Auxiliary Verb	Main Verb	Noun Phrase
1	2	3	4
Sue	will	eat	the ice cream

Structural change (THEN):

Noun phrase	Auxiliary Verb	be+en Main Verb	by + Noun Phrase
4	2	3	1
The ice cream	will	be+en eat	by Sue

In the *Aspects* model a further housekeeping rule would next apply, hopping the *en* affix onto *eat* to form *eaten*.

This somewhat belabored passive-rule example underscores the non-reductionist and atomistic, particulate, flavor of earlier transformational generative grammar: the type and grain size of structural descriptions and changes do not mesh well with the known biological descriptions of, for example, observable language breakdowns. Disruption does not seem to occur at the level of individual transformational rules, nor even as structural descriptions and changes gone awry generally.

The same seems to holds true for many of the biological/psycholinguistic interpretations of such an approach: as Fodor, Bever, and Garrett remarked, individual transformational rules did not seem to be engaged in sentence processing, and the same problems emerge when considering language learnability, development, or evolution. Indeed, the biological/evolutionary picture emerging from the *Aspects*-type (Extended Standard Theory or EST) grammars naturally reflects this representational granularity. For any given language, in the EST framework, a grammar would typically consist of many dozens, even hundreds, of ordered, language-specific transformations, along with a set of constraints on transformations, as developed by Ross (1967), among others. This "particulate" character of such rules was quite in keeping with a micro-mutational view: if the atoms of grammar are the bits and pieces of individual transformations, structural descriptions and changes, then it is quite natural to embrace a concomitant granularity for thinking about language learning, language change, and language evolution. It is quite another matter as to the empirical reality of this granularity.

Consider by way of example the Wexler and Culicover (1980) model of the late 1970s, establishing that EST grammars are learnable from simple positive example sentences. In the Wexler and Culicover model, what was acquired at each step in the learning iteration was a single rule with a highly specific, structural description/structural change, as driven by an error-detection principle. This atomistic behavior was quite natural, since it mirrored the granularity of the EST theory, namely, some sequence of transformations mapping from a base D-structure to a surface S-structure.

But equally, this extreme particulate view was embraced in other contexts, notably by Pinker and Bloom (1990), who argued that language evolution must follow a similar course: *all* of the specific design features of language *must* have arisen by incremental, adaptive evolutionary change. What Pinker and Bloom did in part is to run together two distinct levels of representation: what of necessity must be true, barring horizontal transfer—that genomic evolution lies, ultimately, at the level of single DNA letters or nucleotides—with what need not, and we shall argue, is not true—that language evolution, a distal behavior, proceeds apace at the level of the granularity set by the EST linguistic theory, with all evolutionary change incremental and adaptive. Such a position can lead to difficulties. It argues in effect that each and every property of syntactic design that we see must have some measurable outcome on fitness—perhaps quite literally, the number of viable offspring. As Lightfoot (1991a) notes, this entails what might be dubbed the "Subjacency and Sex Problem"—there are important syntactic constraints, like the one called "subjacency," a restriction on the distance that a phrase can be displaced—that have no obvious effect on the number of offspring one might have, absent special pleading: "subjacency has many virtues, but...it could not have increased the chances of having fruitful sex." Further, this stance seemingly entails connecting all such "inner" constraints once again somehow to external communication—a delicate, probably incorrect link, as we have seen. Indeed, Pinker and Bloom do not advance any specific evolutionary modeling details at all about which syntactic structures are to be linked to particular aspects of fitness so as to construct a proper evolutionary model. Fortunately, we do not have to resort to this level of detail. As we have outlined in the previous section, such incrementalism and pan-adaptationism is now known to be far from secure quite generally in evolutionary biology, even assuming the conventional Fisher model. If one in addition takes into account our more recent, nuanced understanding of the rapid evolution that can occur due to developmental changes as well as the widespread possibility of homeoplasy, then this micro-mutational view of language evolution fares even worse.

Given such rule diversity and complexity, by the mid-1960s the quasi-biological problems with surface-oriented rules—problems of learnability and parsability among others—were well known: how could such particular structural conditions and changes be learned by children, since the evidence that linguists used to induce them was so hard to come by? The lack of rule restrictiveness led to attempts to generalize over rules, for example, to bring under a single umbrella such diverse phenomena as topicalization and question formation, each as instances of a single, more general, Move *wh*-phrase operation. By combining this abstraction with the rule Move Noun phrase, by the end of the 1970s linguists had arrived at a replacement for nearly all structural changes or displacements, a single movement operation dubbed Move alpha. On the rule application side, corresponding attempts were made to establish generalizations about constraints on rule application, thereby replacing structural descriptions—for example, that noun phrases could be displaced only to positions where they might have appeared anyway as argument to predicates, as in our passive example.

Inspired in part by a lecture given by Jacob at MIT's Endicott House in 1974 on the topic of biological variation as determined by a system of genetic switches (see Berwick and Chomsky, this volume), Chomsky had already begun to attempt to unify this system of constraints along the same lines—a concrete example of linguistics inspired by biology. By the 1980s, the end result was a system of approximately 25 to 30 interacting principles, the so-called Principles-and-Parameters (P&P) or Government-and-Binding approach (Chomsky 1981). Figure 4.1 sketches P&P's general picture of sentence formation, shaped like an inverted Y. This model engages two additional representational levels to generate sentences: first, D-structure, a canonical way to represent predicate–argument thematic relations and basic sentence forms—essentially, "who did what to whom," as in *the guy ate the ice cream* where *the guy* is the consumer and *ice cream* is the item consumed; and second, S-structure, essentially a way to represent argument relations after displacement—like the movement of the object to subject position in the former passive rule—has taken place. After the application of transformations (movement), S-structure splits, feeding sound (phonological form, PF) and logical form (LF) representations to yield (sound, meaning) pairs.

Overall then, on the Principles-and-Parameters view, sentences are derived beginning with a canonical thematic representation that conforms to the basic tree structure for a particular language, and then mapped to S-structure via

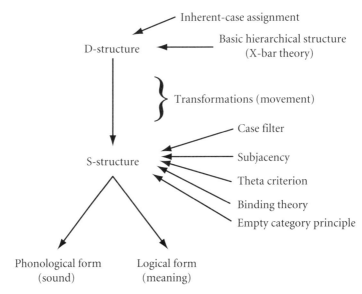

FIGURE 4.1 A conceptual picture of the traditional transformational generative-grammar framework (applying equally to the Extended Standard Theory, Government–Binding, and Principles-and-Parameters, approaches). Thin arrows denote constraints that possible sentence forms must satisfy, like the case filter. We do not describe all the depicted constraints in this chapter

a (possibly empty) sequence of displacement operations. For instance, one could start with *the guy ate the ice cream* in hierarchical form with a thematic or D-structure; via displacement of *the ice cream* this initial representation can be mapped to the topicalized form, *ice cream, the guy ate*. To use another conceptual picture that has been developed for computer implementation, in the P&P approach, sentence generation can be viewed as starting at D-structure and then running a gauntlet through a set of constraint boxes placed at D-structure and S-structure, as shown in Figure 4.1. A sentence is completely well formed if it passes all the constraints and emerges at the two interfaces of phonological form and logical form as one or more sound–meaning pairs.

Akin to atomic theory, this small set of constraints may be recombined in different ways to yield the distinctive syntactic properties of diverse natural languages, just as a handful of elements recombine to yield many different molecular types, or, anticipating the evo–devo revolution, the way that the same regulatory genes might readjust their timing and combinations to yield "endless forms most beautiful," in Darwin's famous closing lines, the title of Carroll's (2005a) book on evo–devo. For example, one of the principles, X-bar theory, constrains the basic D-structure tree shapes for phrases—whether phrases can appear in function–argument form, as in English verb–object or preposition–object combinations, for example, *eat ice cream* or *with a spoon*, or alternatively, in argument–function form, as in Japanese object–verb or postposition–object combinations, such as *ice cream-o tabeta* or *spoon-ni*.

The X-bar module constrains just a small part of the ultimate surface form of sentences and must conspire with other principles to yield the surface complexity that one actually sees. In order to replicate the passive rule, at least three other general principles constraining displacement and S-structure come into play. One such constraint is the so-called theta criterion: if one pictures a verb as a predicate taking some number of arguments—its thematic roles, such as *drink* requiring something to be drunk—then at the end of a derivation, all of the verb's arguments must have been discharged or realized in the sentence, and every possible argument in the sentence must have received some thematic role. A second constraint is the Case filter: any pronounceable noun phrase, such as *the guy*, must possess a special feature dubbed Case, assigned by a verb, preposition, or tense/inflection.

Now the former passive rule follows as a theorem from these more basic principles. Starting from the D-structure *was eaten ice cream*, since *eaten* does not assign Case (analogously to an adjectival form, like *tired* or *happy*), the object *ice cream* must move to a position where it does get case—namely, the position of the subject, where *ice cream* can receive case from the inflected verb *was*. We thus derive the surface form *the ice cream was eaten*. The thematic association between *eat* and *ice cream* as the material eaten is retained by a bit of representational machinery: we insert a phonologically empty (unpronounced) element, a trace, into the position left behind by *ice cream* and link it to *ice cream* as well. In a similar fashion one can show that approximately thirty such constraints suffice to replace much of syntax's formerly rule-based core. The end result is a system very close to Jacob's system of genetic regulatory "switches," with variation among languages restricted to the choice of parameters such as function–argument or argument–function form, possibly restricted further to choices of lexical variation. The language phenotype now looks rather different; it has far less to do with the surface appearance of structure descriptions and structural change, but is constituted entirely of the parameters and their range of variation, a rather different picture. This P&P approach to language variation was quite fruitful, and led to models of language acquisition, change, and parsing that differed substantially from the *Aspects* view, more closely mirroring the possibilities of radical surface differences given just a few underlying changes. For example, in the domain of language acquisition and change, Niyogi and Berwick (1996) demonstrated the possibility of rapid phase changes from one language type to another, for example, from the verb-final form of earlier English to modern-day English. In the domain of parsing, Fong (1990) implemented a uniform computational engine with twenty-odd modular components, corresponding to the Case filter, thematic role checking, X-bar theory, and so forth, parameterized along narrow lines like genetic switches to yield a unified parser for English, Japanese, German, Hungarian, Turkish, and many other languages. None of these possibilities were realizable under the *Aspects* model.

4.3.2 *From P&P to the Minimalist Program: Reducing the language phenotype*

The Minimalist Program goes the Principles-and-Parameters approach one better: it aims to eliminate all *representations* and *relations* that can be derived from more primitive notions. Syntax still mediates form and meaning in the classical Saussurean sense, as in Figure 4.1 with its paired sound and meaning interfaces—but the representations of D-structure and S-structure are eliminated. To build syntactic objects and relations, minimalism invokes only the notion of a word construed as a list of features plus a generalized hierarchical derivation operator, called Merge. For example, it is Merge that glues together *eat* and *ice cream* to form the verb phrase *eat ice cream* and tacks the *en* morpheme onto the end of *eat* to form *eaten*; a sequence of Merges generates a sentence. In fact, relationships among syntactic objects established by Merge constitute the totality of syntactic structure, and, as we shall see, also fix the range of syntactic relations. In other words, those elements that enter into the Merge operation are precisely those that can be syntactically related to each other. Merge thus delimits the atoms and molecules visible for chemical combination. At the sound–meaning interfaces, the only available entities are syntactic objects and the syntactic structures these objects form. These entities contain inherent word features that impose constraints on articulatory generation or parsing and conceptual–intentional interpretation. What drives the generative process is feature matching and feature elimination, as we now describe.

4.3.2.1 *Deriving sentences in the minimalist approach*   To see how this generative machinery works, let us consider a concrete example that we will follow through the remainder of this chapter. The following two figures illustrate, with Figure 4.2 providing a conceptual overview and Figure 4.3 more detail. We retain the basic syntactic categories from previous syntactic models, considered as features, both open-class categories such as n(oun) and v(erb), as well as grammatical categories like d(eterminer), t(ense) (or i(nflection)), c(omplementizer), and so forth. Conceptually, in Figure 4.2 we begin with

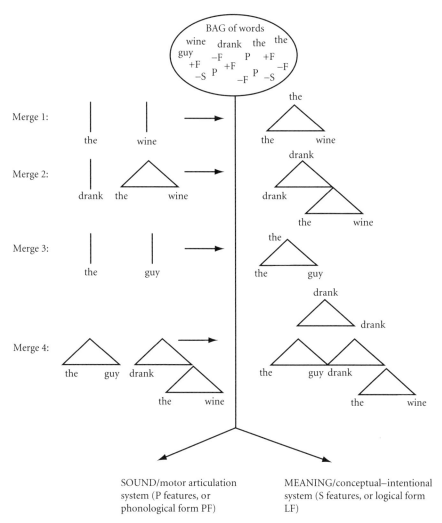

FIGURE 4.2 Merge maps from an initial array of words to a (sound, meaning) pair—representations containing only phonological or semantic features, respectively. A sequence of Merge operations constitutes a derivation in the Minimalist Program, generating a sentence from an initial unordered word set. *P*, *S*, and *F* denote phonological, semantic, and formal (syntactic) features, respectively

an unordered bag of words (formally, a multiset, since some words may be repeated), where words are just feature bundles as we describe in more detail later. In our example, we begin with {the, guy, drank, the, wine} and via four derivational steps, four Merges, wind up with the syntactic structure corresponding to *the guy drank the wine*, which is then spun off to both

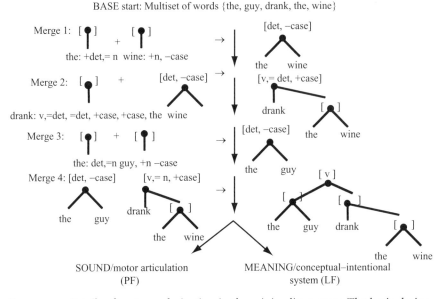

FIGURE 4.3 Details of sentence derivation in the minimalist system. The basic derivational operator, Merge, applies four times, starting with an unordered word multiset. Each Merge combines either two words, indicated by straight lines, into a hierarchical superword, indicated by a triangle, or else combines two word/hierarchical superwords into a new hierarchical combination. Merger continues until all possible formal features have been eliminated

phonological and semantic interpretation. We should emphasize at the outset that these figures depict just one possible, successful, derivational sequence. In fact, with five words there are 5! or 120 possible basic derivational possibilities, but most of these, as we shall see, do not lead to well-formed structures.

Adhering to the chemical analogy of sentence derivation, minimalism deploys Merge to combine words into larger, hierarchical superwords via a notion somewhat like chemical valency. All structure-building is feature-driven, via words with formal (F), phonological/sound (P), and semantic (S) features. Figure 4.2 depicts these as F, P, and S features in an initially unordered word soup (a lexicon). Roughly, phonological features are those that can be interpreted, or 'read' by the articulatory/perceptual interface—such as classical distinctive features that refer to articulation, like ±Coronal; semantic features are those that can be read by the conceptual/intentional interface—such as ±Past; while formal (or syntactic) features include those such as ±Tns or ±Case that play no role in sound or meaning. Syntactic features also encompass the traditional notion of *selection*, as in the sense of agreement or a verb–argument relation: a feature attached to a word can select for a particular syntactic category feature to its right or left. Following Stabler (1997) we use the notation $= x$ to denote such a requirement; for example, the feature $= n$ means that a verb like *drink* could select a word marked with the feature n (for noun) to its right or left. (Again, a more careful approach like that advanced in Di Sciullo 2005 ought to be able to derive this asymmetrical selection from asymmetrical Merge itself.)

Merge combines two words, a word plus an affix, or two word complexes into a single new superword, with one of the two elements being selected as the head of the new hierarchical structure, as shown schematically as the combination of two vertical lines into a triangle or two triangles into a larger one. Merge is triggered in two ways: (1) either $+f$ and $-f$ formal features on two words or word complexes can cancel, erasing the formal feature f; or (2) a $= x$ feature can select a $+ x$ category. For example, we take *the* to be a determiner, $+det$, selecting the feature n(oun), so it has the formal features $-det$, $=n$; while *wine* is marked $+n$, $-Case$. The $=n$ feature can select the $+n$ feature, so Merge can apply in this case. (Right/left order is irrelevant for selection; we put to one side the important question of how actual word order is fixed, for instance, why the combination *wine the* is barred.) Merging these two words, *the* is taken as the head of a new hierarchical complex, which one can write as {the {*the, wine*}}, and which would traditionally have been written as a phrase-structure tree. The process of matching and canceling features, or matching and selecting features, is called *feature checking*. Note that it is possible for Merge to fail if features do not cancel or match: for instance, we cannot Merge *wine* and *guy*. Finally, it is important to add that Merge is driven by a locality notion of economy: a feature $-f$ must be checked done "as soon as possible"—that is, by the closest possible corresponding $+f$ feature. (For a much broader and more sophisticated view of selection and feature checking that can derive some of these properties, driven by the asymmetrical nature of syntactic relations generally, including morphology, see Di Sciullo 2005.)

After Merge applies, any features that remain unchecked are copied or projected to the top of the new hierarchical structure, so our example complex has the features $+det$, $-Case$; conventionally, a noun phrase. (We could just as easily envision this as copying the entire word *the* to the head of the new structure, as shown in Figure 4.2.) Note that on this view, it is only words and affixes—the leaves of a syntactic structure—that have features; the head of a hierarchical structure receives its features only from these.

Merge operations repeat until no more features can be canceled, as shown in Figure 4.2, and in detail in Figure 4.3—note that after step 4, all formal syntactic features have been eliminated and only sound and meaning features remain to be read by the phonological and conceptual–intentional machinery, a process dubbed spell-out. Note that in fact spell-out is possible at any time, so long as the structure shipped off to PF or LF is well formed.

Step by step, generation proceeds as follows (see Figure 3). Selecting a possible Merge at random, *the* { $+det$, $=n$} can combine with *wine* {$+n$, $-case$}, selecting the $+n$ feature, and yielding a complex with $+det$, $-case$ at its root. Note that we could have combined *the* with *guy* as well. For the next Merge operation, one might combine either *the* with *guy* or *drank* with *the wine*, selecting the $+det$ feature and canceling the $-case$ requirement corresponding to the noun phrase argument *wine*—this corresponds to a conventional verb phrase. The root of this complex still has two unmet feature requirements: it selects a noun ($=n$), and assigns a case feature ($+case$). Note that an attempted Merge of *drank* with *the* before a Merger with *wine* would be premature: the *v*, $=det$, features would be percolated up, to a new *wine-the* complex. Now *wine* could no longer be combined with *the*. (On the other hand, there is nothing to syntactically block the sentence form, *the wine drank the guy*; presumably, this anomaly would be detected by the conceptual–intentional interface.)

Proceeding then with this path, depending on whether *the* and *guy* had been previously merged, we would either carry out this Merge, or, for the fourth and last step, Merge *the guy* with the verb phrase, in the process canceling the $-case$ feature associated with *the guy*. At this point, all formal features have been eliminated, save for the *v* feature heading the root of the sentence, corresponding to *drank* (in actual practice this would be further Merged with a tense/infl(ection) category). We can summarize the generation process as follows:

1. Merge 1: combine *the* and *wine*, yielding *the wine*.
2. Merge 2: combine *drank* and *the wine*, yielding *drank the wine*.
3. Merge 3: combine *the* and *guy* yielding *the guy*.
4. Merge 4: combine *drank the wine* and *the guy* yielding *the guy drank wine*.

Summarizing, Merge works on the model of chemical valency and feature cancellation. The core idea is that Merge takes place only in order to check features between its two inputs—a functor that requires some feature to be discharged, and an argument that can receive this discharged feature. The feature is then eliminated from further syntactic manipulation. After any Merge step, if a feature has not been canceled by a functor–argument combination, that feature is copied to the root of the combination and further Merges attempted until we are left with only phonological and logical form features. After exhausting all possible Merge sequences, if any nonphonological or LF features remain then the derivation is ill-formed.

4.3.2.2 *Minimalism and movement* So far we have described only how a simple sentence is derived. Following Kitahara, as described in Epstein (1999), one can see that displacement or movement can be handled the same way, as a subcase of Merge. Figure 4.4 shows how. Suppose one forms the question, *What did the guy drink* by moving *what* from its canonical object position after the verb *drank*. Recall that we may define Merge as Merge(X, Y), where X and Y are either words or phrases. If X is a hierarchical subset of Y (roughly, a subtree), then this is a case of movement, as illustrated in the figure: $X = what$ is a subtree of $Y = the guy drink what$. As usual, Merge forms a new hierarchical object, selecting and projecting one of the items, in this case *what*, as the root of the new tree. As usual, we must assume that Merge is driven by feature checking: we assume that there is some feature, call it Q for "question," that attracts *what*, while *what* possesses a $-Q$ feature as before, *what* moves to the *closest* position where its feature may be checked. Note that movement now amounts to copying the displaced element to its new position, forming literally *what the guy drink what*. Presumably a general phonological principle at PF avoids pronouncing *what* a second time, yielding the sentence that actually surfaces beyond the PF interface.

As we shall see in the next section, this approach also accounts for several of the formerly stipulated properties of movement. Perhaps more surprisingly, the notion of merge-as-derivation suffices to fix precisely the syntactic

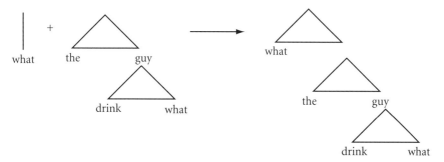

FIGURE 4.4 Movement or phrase displacement as a subcase of Merge. In this figure, *wh*-question formation is depicted as the Merger of two elements, *what* and a (traditionally named) sentence phrase, *the guy drink what*. Details about the inflection of *drink* and insertion of *do* to bear inflection information are omitted

relations appearing in natural languages, in this sense deriving a complex phenotype from a much simpler genotype.

4.3.3 *Deriving syntactic relations and constraints from Merge*

As described in the introduction, natural languages are characterized by certain specific properties, syntactic relations obtaining only among certain syntactic elements, under certain circumstances. These are seemingly forced by the minimalist framework and Merge itself. Let us review these properties here, showing how each follows from Merge without further stipulation. This of course is the key to establishing that we do not need separate, adaptive accounts for each of these properties, only for Merge.

- *Recursive generative capacity*   This is a basic inherent property of Merge. Since Merge can apply recursively to its own output, indefinitely large hierarchical structures can be generated.

- *Structure dependence*   Algebraically, Merge works via the concatenation of two (structured) objects. It is therefore a noncounting function: its inputs can be any two adjacent elements, but by definition it cannot locate the first auxiliary verb *inside* a string of elements (unless that element happens to appear at the left or right edge of a phrase), nor, *a fortiori*, can it locate the third or seventeenth item in a string. Note that given a "conceptually minimal" concatenative apparatus, this is what we should expect: clearly, Merge could not operate on a single argument, so the minimal meaningful input to Merge is two syntactic objects, not one or three.

- *Binary branching phrases*   Since Merge always pastes together exactly two elements, it automatically constructs binary branching phrase structure.

- *Displacement*   Given Merge, the previous section showed that a mechanism to implement displacement exists. Again, whether and how a particular human language chooses to use displacement is an option dependent on the features of particular words (up to the constraints enforced by Merge). For example, English uses displacement to form *wh*- questions, given a *Q* attractor in C(omplementizer) or root position, but Japanese does not. If displacement is a subcase of Merge, then the following constraints on displacement follow—constraints that are all in fact attested.

  - Displaced items *c-command* their original locations. C-command is the basic syntactic notion of scope in natural language; for our purposes, c-command may be defined as follows (Reinhart 1978):
  A c-commands B if and only if

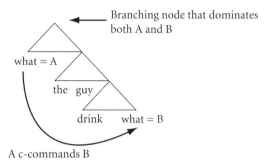

FIGURE 4.5 C-command is an asymmetrical grammatical relation between two hierarchical nodes in a sentence structure. This example shows that displaced elements
always c-command their original locations

1. The first branching node dominating A dominates B
2. A does not dominate B
3. A does not equal B

Figure 4.5 illustrates. As one can see, in our displaced question sentence
the first *what* (= A) c-commands the second *what* (= B), the object of the
verb, because the first branching node above *what* dominates (lies above)
the second *what*. Note that the c-command relation is asymmetric: the
second *what* does not c-command the first.

   The c-command relation between displaced elements and their original
locations follows from a general property of Merge: given any two inputs
to Merge, *X* and *Y*, where *X* selects *Y*, then *X* c-commands *Y* and all the
subcomponents of *Y*, because by the definition of Merge we always form
a new hierarchical structure with a label dominating *both X* and *Y*. In
particular, for displacement, when *X* is a subset (conventionally, a subtree)
of *Y*, the displaced *X* must dominate the original location that is a subpart
of *Y*. Below, we show how to derive the form that c-command takes from
more primitive properties of Merge.

- *Locality conditions*   Displacement is not totally free, because feature checking is local. What blocks question-formation such as *What do you know
  how the guy drank?*, while allowing *How do you know what the guy drank?*
  This too has a direct answer, given Merge. Note that any phrase such as
  How the guy drank what is "locally convergent" in the sense that all its
  case and other feature-checking requirements have already been satisfied—
  this is what is called in linguistics an adjunct phrase. In other words, *How*
  satisfies any feature-checking requirement for the full sentence's aspect.

Another way to think of the same situation is that at this particular point in the derivation only phonological and semantic features remain in this subphrase. Therefore, this phrase may already be shipped off to LF—spelled-out—and is thereby rendered opaque to further syntactic manipulation. If this is so, then there is nothing that allows *what* to participate in further Merges—that is, it can no longer be displaced or moved. In contrast, the hierarchical object corresponding to *did the guy drink what* is still open to syntactic manipulation, because (in English) the aspectual/question feature associated with the full sentence has yet to be satisfied—and in fact, can be satisfied by Merging *what* with the sentence, moving *what* to the front: *what did the guy drink what*. Finally, such a sentence may be combined as an argument with *How do you know* to yield *How do you know what the guy drank*. In other words, given the local feature-checking driven properties of Merge, plus its operation on simply adjacent syntactic domains, we would expect locality roadblocks like the one illustrated.

To conclude our summary of how basic syntactic properties and relations can be derivable from the fundamental generative operator, following Epstein (1995) we can demonstrate that natural languages can express only a limited set of relations like subject-of, object-of, and c-command.

For example, the c-command relation holds between the subject noun phrase *the guy* and the object *the wine*, but not vice versa. Why? In so-called representational theories of syntax, such as government-and-binding theory, the notion of c-command is given by definition (Reinhart 1978). Its exact formulation is stipulated. However, c-command is derivable from properties of Merge and the derivational formulation presented earlier, as are the other basic syntactic relations.

To see why, consider again the Merge operation. Merge takes a pair of syntactic objects items and concatenates them. Syntactic structure is thus a temporal sequence of Merges, a *derivational history*. Given a derivational history and the sequence of syntactic structure the history traces out, we obtain the set of syntactically possible relations among syntactic objects. Let us see how. The derivation of our *wine* example is repeated below:

1. Merge 1: combine *the* and *wine*, yielding *the wine*.
2. Merge 2: combine *drank* and *the wine*, yielding *drank the wine*.
3. Merge 3: combine *the* and *guy* yielding *the guy*.
4. Merge 4: combine *drank the wine* and *the guy* yielding *the guy drank the wine*.

Now the notion of a possible syntactic object and relation can be expressed via the following definitions.

Definition 1
Let A be a *syntactic object* if and only if it is a selected word or a syntactic object formed by Merge.

Definition 2
A syntactic object is said to *enter in the derivation* if and only if it is paired with another object via Merge.

Definition 3
We say A and B are *connected* if they are parts of another (larger, common) syntactic object C.

We can now *deduce* c-command from Merge:

Theorem 1
Let A and B be syntactic objects. A *c-commands* B if A is connected to B at the step when A enters into the derivation.

Proof sketch.   Without loss of generality, let us see how this works with our example sentence. When *the* and *wine* are merged, they both enter into the derivation, and thus either may c-command the other, as is required. Merge creates a new hierarchical object, essentially the projection of *the*. Analogously, the verb *drank* and the object (the traditional object noun phrase) *the wine* c-command each other, because *drank* is connected to *the wine* at the time of their merger. These are the straightforward cases. The property that is more difficult to see is how one can derive the asymmetry of c-command. For instance, *drank* also c-commands all the subparts of *the wine*, namely, *the* and *wine*, but *the* and *wine* do not c-command *drank*. This is because at the Merger step when *drank* entered the derivation it was *connected* to *the* and *wine*. But the converse is not true. At the time when *the* and *wine* entered into the derivation (when they were Merged to form *the wine*), *drank* was not yet part of the derivation, hence was not visible. Hence, *the* and *wine* do *not* c-command *drank*, as is required. Similarly, the subject phrase *the guy* c-commands *drank the wine* and vice versa—because these two objects are Merged. Letting A = *the guy* and B = *drank the wine*, we see that the subject noun phrase is by definition connected to all the subparts of *drank the wine* because it is connected to them at the time it enters the derivation. Therefore, the subject c-commands these subparts, as required. The converse is not true—neither drank, nor the, nor wine c-commands the subject—because for A = *wine* for instance, A was not connected to the subject *at the time* it entered into the derivation.

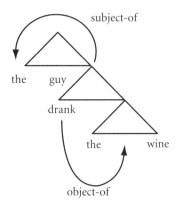

FIGURE 4.6 The core syntactic relations are fixed by visibility at Merger time. This figure depicts the *subject-of* and *object-of* relations, with the 'selected' or functor-like pair of the Merger drawn as the source of the arrow

Indeed, it appears that if we take our definitions as specifying syntactic visibility, then all other syntactic relations reduce to subcases of the same criterion. Figure 4.6 illustrates the possibilities.

- *Object-of* is the relation: Merge and select a word base (functor) with either another word or a hierarchical structure.
- *Subject-of* is the relation: Merge a previously-merged hierarchical structure with a second hierarchical structure, selecting the first element as the new hierarchical root, and the second as the 'subject' (left-to-right order irrelevant—that is, the subject can appear either to the right or to the left).
- *Head-of* is the relation already described as the projection of features after Merge.
- No other (natural) syntactic relations are expected to be attested in natural languages, e.g. *subject-object-of*, relating, say, *guy* to *wine*, since these items are not *connected* at the time of their mutual participation in Merge.

4.4 From Merge to Language Use

A Merge-based model also meets a psychological-fidelity requirement for efficient language processing and accurate breakdown processing, beyond the broader kinds of language breakdown just described. There is a natural, transparent relation between a Merger sequence and the operation of the most general kind of deterministic, left-to-right language analyzer known in computer science, namely, the class of LR parsers or their relatives, as we demonstrate below. In other words, given that the general hierarchical Merge operator forms the basis for natural language syntax, then an efficient processor for language follows as a by-product, again without the need to add any new components. Of course, as is well known, this processor, like any processor for human language, has blind spots—it will fail in certain circumstances, such as garden path sentences like *the boy got fat melted*. However, we can show that these failings are also a by-product of the processor's design, hence indirectly a consequence of the Merge machinery itself. In any case, these failings do not seem to pose an insuperable barrier for communicative facility, but rather delimit an envelope of intrinsically difficult-to-process expressions that one then tends to avoid in spoken or written speech (Miller and Chomsky 1963).

First let us sketch the basic relationship between Merge and efficient LR parsing; see Berwick and Epstein (1995) and Stabler (1997) for details and variations on this theme. The basic insight is simple, and illustrated in Figure 4.7: a merge sequence like that in the figure mirrors in reverse the top-down expansion of each Rightmost hierarchical phrase into its subparts. Thus, since parsing is the inverse of top-down generation, it should be expected to follow nearly the same Merger sequence 1–4 as in Figure 4.7 itself, and it does. Consequently, all that is required in order to parse strictly left to right, working basically bottom-up and building the Leftmost complete sub-tree at a time, is to reconstruct almost exactly the Merger sequence that

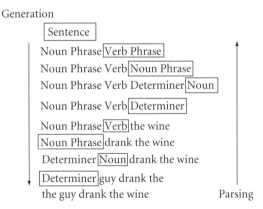

FIGURE 4.7 LR parsing is the mirror image of a top-down, rightmost sentence deriva-tion, and mirrors the Merge sequence for a sentence. This figure shows a line-by-line derivation for *the guy drank the wine*, where the boxed portion of each line shows that we expand the rightmost possible portion at each step in a top-down generation. Naturally, in a bottom-up parse, we reverse this process, and recover the leftmost complete hierarchical structure (the boxed portion) at each step

generated the sentence in the first place. We assume in addition that if there is a *choice* of actions to take, then the processing system will again mirror the grammar, and so favor the economy condition that the closest adjacent feature should be checked, rather than delaying to a later point in the derivation.

Such a parser can work with a simple push-down stack, and has just two possible operations: either *shift* a word (a feature bundle) onto the stack, analyzing its features; or *reduce* (that is, Merge) the top two items on the stack, yielding a new hierarchical structure that replaces these items on the stack, forming what is traditionally known as a "complete subtree." Figure 4.8 shows

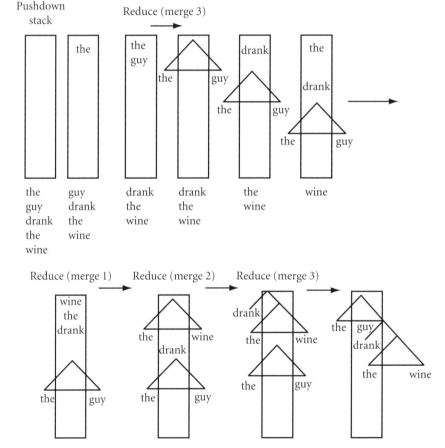

FIGURE 4.8 This figure shows how a step-by-step LR parse for the sentence *the guy drank the wine* mirrors Merger steps 1–4 for the same sentence. Each reduction corresponds to a Merge step

the blow-by-blow action of such a machine operating on our example *drank* sentence.

As each complete subtree is produced, we envision that it is shipped off to the conceptual–intentional component for interpretation, up to the as-yet-unmet features still left at the top of each hierarchical structure. Recall that this is possible for locally convergent categories. For example, after *the* and *guy* are analyzed and then Merged, all the internal features of *the* and *guy* have now been accounted for, aside from those that play a role *external* to the entire phrase, such as the phrase's thematic role—but these are precisely any features that have not yet been "canceled" and are percolated to the head of the phrase for further processing. Thus these individual words may be interpreted. This proposal of incremental interpretation is essentially that found in Berwick and Weinberg (1986), and improved by Reinhart (2006). The basic principle amounts to what Chomsky (2001) called "derivation by phase": the bottom-up construction of complete thematically satisfied syntactic units.

We can trace through the parse of our example sentence in detail as follows, relating Merge to parsing actions.

Step 1. Shift *the* onto the stack, recovering its features from the lexicon. (From now on, we shall omit the phrase *recovering its features from the lexicon* for each shift.)

Step 2. Shift *guy* onto the stack, on top of *the*.

Step 3. Merge 1: combine *the* and *guy*. Parser action: reduce *the* and *guy* to a complete phrase (leftmost complete subtree) replacing *the* and *guy* on top of the stack with any uncanceled, projected features.

Step 4. Shift *drank* onto the stack.

Step 5. Shift *the* onto the stack.

Step 6. Shift *wine* onto the stack.

Step 7. Merge 2: combine *the* and *wine* into a new hierarchical object, replacing both on the stack (this is the object of the sentence). Parser action: reduce.

Step 8. Merge 3: combine *drank* and the object into a new hierarchical structure, traditionally known as a verb phrase, *drank the wine*. Parser action: reduce.

Step 9. Merge 4: combine *the guy* and *drank the wine* into a complete sentence. Parser action: reduce. The parse is complete.

In many cases the choices for either shift or reduce (Merge) are deterministic, and allow such a device to work in the fastest possible time, namely, linearly in the length of the input sentence; but as is well known, in order to handle the ambiguity present in natural language, we must generalize an LR machine to work in parallel simply by carrying along multiple possibilities;

there are known efficient algorithms for this (see Tomita 1986). In other cases, choices can be resolved by appeal to the local feature checking or economy condition imposed by the grammar; this leads directly to an account of some known language processing blind spots. Consider as one example the reflexive attachment of *yesterday* in sentences such as *John said that the cat will die yesterday*, described in the introduction. Why does the human sentence processor work this way? If in fact Merge proceeds by the most local feature cancellation at each step, then the answer is clear: *yesterday* can be merged with the lower verb *die*, so this choice is made rather than waiting for so-called late attachment—and this occurs before the *die* verb complex is shipped off for semantic interpretation. Hence, this is an operation that should be impervious to semantic effect, as indeed it seems to be. Similarly, such an approach also accounts for familiar cases of garden-path sentences, such as *the boy got fat melted*. Here too the basic situation, putting to one side many complexities, is that the noun–verb combination *boy got* is Merged "too soon" and taken as to be the main sentence—a processing error that we attribute to the local character of feature matching. It remains to see whether all psycholinguistic blind spots of this kind can be accommodated in the same way.

4.5 Conclusions

Taking stock, we see that Merge covers much ground that formerly had to be assumed in traditional transformational generative grammar. Many fundamental syntactic particulars are derivative: basic skeletal tree structure; movement rules; grammatical relations like object-of; locality constraints; even the cyclic character of grammatical rules—all these fall into place once the fundamental generative operation of Merge is up and running. These features are no less than the broad-brush outlines for most of human syntax—so nothing here has to be specifically selected for in a gradualist, pan-selectionist sense.

Of course, Merge will have little or nothing to say about the details of word features particular to each language—why English has a question word that sounds like *what*, or why such a word in English has features that force it to agree with an abstract question marker, while this is apparently not so in Japanese. Similarly, Chinese has no overt markings for verbal tense. The different words and associated features each language chooses ultimately lead to different possibilities for "chemical combinations," hence different "chemical compounds" or sentence construction types. But there is no need to invoke an array of distinct rules for each language, just as there is no need to invoke different laws of chemistry, once the basic principles are known.

As Chomsky (1995) has remarked, echoing the structuralists, while universal grammar has a long history, nobody has ever assumed there would be a universal morphology. Different languages will have different words with different features, and it is precisely here, where variation has been known all along, that languages would be expected to vary. In this sense, there is no possibility of an intermediate language between a non-combinatorial syntax and full natural language syntax—one either has Merge in all its generative glory, or one has effectively no combinatorial syntax at all, but rather whatever one sees in the case of agrammatic aphasics: alternative cognitive strategies for assigning thematic roles to word strings. Naturally, in such a system that gives pride of place to word features, one would expect deficits in feature recognition or processing, and that these could lead to great cognitive difficulties; many important details remain to be explored here. But if the account here is on the right track, while there can be individual words, in a sense there is only a single grammatical operation: Merge. Once Merge arose, the stage for natural language was set. There was no turning back.

5

A Geneticist's Dream, a Linguist's Nightmare: The Case of FOXP2

MASSIMO PIATTELLI-PALMARINI AND
JUAN URIAGEREKA

5.1 Introduction

The integration of language pathologies, genetics, brain imaging, molecular embryology, and sequential gene expression by means of DNA/RNA/proteomics is a remarkable open possibility. When it comes, however, to how this can help our understanding of cognition, and, more specifically, linguistic competence, everything gets complicated. This can be illustrated with the interesting saga of the FOXP2 gene. As it turns out, the most detailed genetic, developmental, and brain-activation analyses to date lead to conclusions that in many instances clash with those derived from over fifty years of linguistic inquiry in generative grammar. Though we have no reason to question the accuracy of the genetic, brain-imaging, and developmental studies as such, when it comes to mapping a very specific point mutation of the FOXP2 gene onto the differential activation of brain areas (with respect to normal subjects), we do question the interpretations and conclusions that we find in the technical literature. We will show here that, for each one of the brain regions cited in the literature as pertinent to what the gene is really up to in linguistic behavior, other neurological publications suggest different functions. We stress that remarkable genetic and biochemical analyses are being mapped onto imperfect knowledge of the brain, rather arbitrary evolutionary reconstructions and, alas, a very naive linguistics. Linguists should of course welcome a prospective integration of different domains of inquiry. But in the present case, if these distinguished geneticists, neurologists, and embryologists are right, then a lot of linguistic theory and data are deeply wrong and vice versa. Our aim is to show that this need not be the case, and that both fields may in the end be correct, albeit under a significantly different interpretation of the facts.

5.2 The Discovery of the KE Family

In the last decade of the twentieth century, an entire English family was brought to the attention of neurologists and logopedists at the Institute of Child Health in London working with Jane A. Hurst and her team. Over three generations, about one half of the family members showed a remarkable language deficit, which presented the textbook characteristics of an inheritable condition. Psycholinguist Myrna Gopnik studied this deficit and was able to track the family (ever since known as KE) also in Montreal (Gopnik 1990). Although we will not describe the condition in great detail here (we refer the reader to the review in Vargha-Khadem et al. 2005), we would like to present the basic phenotypic traits of the affected KE family individuals (AKEFI). We should start by saying that their sociability is normal, they are painfully aware of their deficit, and their efforts to make themselves understood are relentless. A precise estimate of their level of general intelligence has been a thorny issue, to which we will return shortly. Suffice it here to summarize what we think goes generally unquestioned: that there is a dissociation, in the population of AKEFIs, between general intelligence and their linguistic impairment (there are cases of normal to high nonverbal IQ with heavy linguistic impairment, and of low nonverbal IQ with only minor linguistic impairment).

In order to evaluate their verbal and general cognitive ability, various tests were administered to AKEFIs, comparing them to subjects with left-hemisphere stroke aphasia, matched for age, sex, and general education, as well as non-affected members of the KE family. These tests include the Standard Wechsler non-verbal IQ test; lexical decision tasks (real vs. nonsense words); receptive grammar (understanding subordinate clauses); word and non-word repetition and decision (for tokens like *thimble, hampent*); naming objects presented with line-drawings; verbal fluency (generating as many words as possible in 2 min.) and written verbal fluency (writing down as many words as possible in 5 min.); derivational and inflectional morphology production (*small–smallest, ski–skiing*) upon presentation of sentences to be completed; regular and irregular past-tense production (*walk–walked, teach–taught*); reading and spelling pronounceable monosyllabic non-words; reading aloud and repeating poly-syllabic non-words; limb praxis (trace a circle in the air, etc.); oro-facial praxis (blow up your cheeks, bite your lower lip, etc.) and consecutive oro-facial movements (first blow up your cheeks, then bite your lower lip, etc.).

If these seem a bit haphazard, we admit that we find the matter under-standable for a new syndrome evaluated by clinical experts and psychologists. A variety of constraints, not the least of which are ethical, have made it so far impossible to have narrow experts (e.g. syntacticians) evaluate more nuanced aspects of the condition.

Caveats aside, however, the results were quite striking. They can be summa-rized as follows:

(a) Performance is equally impaired in both AKEFIs and traumatic aphasics, as com-pared to the controls, in the following areas:
  (i) The "coding" test (arbitrary pairings of symbols and digits).
  (ii) The standard naming test.
  (iii) Non-word repetition of complex articulation words.
  (iv) Morphosyntax and word-order receptivity.
  (v) The execution of inflectional and, especially, derivational morphology, and more for non-words than for real words.

(b) Performance is superior in aphasics than in the AKEFIs in:
  (i) Lexical decision (words vs. non-words).
  (ii) Simple word repetition (hardly affected in aphasics).

(c) Performance is superior in AKEFIs than aphasics in:
  (i) Complex word repetition.
  (ii) Fluency (rapid production of words).
  (iii) AKEFIs and traumatic aphasics are equally impaired in the naming tasks, but the longest reaction times are witnessed in the aphasics.

In sum, despite the very different nature of the respective deficits (innate in AKEFIs, acquired in traumatic aphasics), their overall characteristics are relatively similar, particularly in tasks that require repeating non-words and understanding complex syntactic and related morphological nuances.[1] That said, although AKEFIs show a significant deficit relative to unaffected mem-bers in generating words from different categories, their impairment is less severe than that of aphasics. Furthermore, unlike aphasics, AKEFIs do not differ from unaffected members in their latencies to produce single-word responses, for example in naming tasks, and they do not have noticeable word-finding problems during conversational speech. The standard view seems to be that, if one symptom only had to be selected as discriminatory for the AKEFIs,

---

[1] This characterization is overly simplistic for the aphasics, as we think it may well be for the AKEFIs. Broca's aphasics have quite selective comprehension deficits for complex passives, object relatives, object gaps, and object clefts, but not for other kinds of syntactic constructions (such as complex actives, subject relatives, subject gaps, and subject clefts). See Grodzinsky (2000), Grodzinsky and Amunts (2006), and the March 2008 special issue of the *Journal of Neurolinguistics* for perspective and references.

that would be difficulties in the repetition of articulatorily complex poly-syllabic non-words. Finally, it should be noted, regarding non-verbal tasks, that although limb praxis is not affected for either group, oro-facial praxis is, and equally in AKEFIs and aphasics, particularly in the domain of sound articulation.

5.3 The Controversy Begins

In a letter to Nature, Gopnik (1990) described the syndrome in the KE family as an instance of what she called "feature blindness" (see also Gopnik and Crago 1991). She emphasized, in particular, how AKEFIs show normal intelli-gence (in some cases over the norm—see n. 8), and yet are incapable of dealing with some basic featural specifications of language (notably verbal inflec-tion, subject–verb agreement, and gender agreement in the French-speaking members of the family). However, the head of cognitive neuroscience at the Institute of Child Health, the neurologist Faraneh Vargha-Khadem, sharply disagreed with Gopnik's analysis. This remains a controversial issue, indirectly bearing, also, on the nature of the so-called Specific Language Impairment (SLI), which AKEFIs were initially considered a paradigm case of.[2] SLI is generally characterized as a developmental language disorder, affecting both expressive and perceptual aspects of the language faculty. That much seems clear, but the description of the phenomenon as *specific* remains contentious, meaning that the syndrome is not related to or caused by other developmental disorders, such as hearing acuity or loss, acquired brain injury or innate brain defects, or even problems affecting "general intelligence." Recognized hallmarks of SLI are an excessive use of infinitives (with omission of the sub-ject), difficulty with inflections in words, and, more specifically, the repetition of non-words containing complex articulation patterns. However, there are many diagnosed instances of SLI that improve with training—unlike what is seen in the KE family—suggesting that it is very complicated to identify the genetic underpinnings of SLI. Certainly, a variety of patients diagnosed with SLI do not exhibit at least the specific mutation we discuss below (see Barry, Yasin, and Bishop 2007), which suggests that SLI, as presently understood, is an umbrella term for various, indeed possibly unrelated, conditions, in all likelihood with little bearing on what afflicts AKEFIs (see n. 2). Be that as

---

[2] At present, few researchers would classify AKEFIs as suffering from SLI (Kenneth Wexler, pers. comm.). For progress in SLI see Rice, Wexler, and Clieve (1995), Van der Lely and Stollw-erck (1996), Wexler (2002), Levy and Schaeffer (2003), Bishop and Snowling (2004), Falcaro et al. (2008).

it may, the issue with AKEFIs is still whether their condition, whatever it is, can be directly related to language, and thus whether it can ultimately be considered the first *specific* linguistic pathology of an inheritable sort caused by a precisely identified point mutation.

Vargha-Khadem to this day insists that the central deficit is a severe oro-facial dyspraxia, combined with developmental cognitive deficits which somehow affect the learning of fine sequences of subtle motor controls. To make her case, she undertook a series of precise analyses of the deficit, accompanied by PET and fMRI scans, and found over-activation of a part of the basal ganglia, called the caudate nucleus, in two affected individuals of the KE family when executing (poorly) a word-repetition task. This was interpreted as the sign of intense effort that involves that brain region (Vargha-Khadem et al. 2005). Again, comparison with aphasics is interesting also in this domain, suggesting that rather different—and non-focal—brain abnormalities can lead to similar linguistic deficits. In aphasics, the general case is one of strictly unilateral left-hemisphere lesions (opercular region), sometimes extending to the sub-cortical regions. The insular and dorsolateral prefrontal cortex is also usually affected. In contrast, in AKEFIs bilateral, though asymmetric, abnormalities can be found in the caudate nucleus (concretely in the density of grey matter), and in cortical motor- and speech-related regions. These include the left-anterior insular cortex (thought to be crucial for speech articulation), two cortex ridges—the posterior middle temporal gyrus (somehow involved in the representation of actions) and the left supra-marginal gyrus (involved in phonological processing)—and another part of the basal ganglia, called the putamen (which together with the caudate nucleus forms the dorsal striatum), and specifically the neostriatum. It should be noted that acquired damage to the neostriatum in adulthood can result in language deficits similar to the one observed in the KE family. More generally, these cerebral areas, together with the cerebellum (which later on turned out to be relevant too, as we discuss below), are implicated in motor co-ordination. Significant under-activation of Broca's area and the putamen were observed during both overt and covert language tasks. Given these observations and correlations, Watkins, Dronkers, and Vargha-Khadem (2002) and Watkins et al. (2002) suggested that verbal and non-verbal deficits in AKEFIs "arise from a common impairment in the ability to sequence movement or in procedural learning." Both linguistic and non-linguistic difficulties take place if one adopts this point of view, because these are mere superficial manifestations of the very same core deficit. We return to a critique of this approach.

5.4 The Genetic Basis

Quite aside from those controversies as to what exactly the syndrome boils down to, in 1996 this fascinating case was brought to the attention of Anthony Monaco and Simon Fisher at the Wellcome Unit of Human Genetics in Oxford. With Vargha-Khadem, this group then tried to track the genetic and brain correlates of the deficit. As luck would have it, the deficit segregates according to the classic Mendelian single autosomal dominant gene pattern, and so a genome-wide search for a gene became then possible. In 1997, region 31 of chromosome 7 was singled out, via positional cloning and linkage analysis, as the relevant one where the gene may be found, which was initially labeled SPCH1 (for a later review see Fisher et al. 2003). The singled-out region had between fifty and a hundred candidate genes, and about eight million bases, so although the screening and sequencing had become possible, it was also rather time-consuming. But then a new patient, totally unrelated to the KE family, was discovered by Jane Hurst at the Oxford Radcliffe Hospital. As luck would again have it, this boy, known as CS, exhibited both a deficit very similar to the one described for AKEFIs and also a visible defect in chromosome 7. The karyotype in CS shows a breakage and translocation from chromosome 5 to a precise locus of chromosome 7, specifically in the q31 region. At that point the definitive identification of the gene became almost immediate. Surprisingly, "SPCH1" turned out to be a member of the FOX (forkhead/winged-helix replicator genes) family, of which several other genes are known all across the animal world. It was then labeled FOXP2, that being its current, and more conventional, name.

In 2001, the group determined the exact locus and nature of the mutation affecting the KE family (Lai et al. 2003). In one copy of the gene only (the maternal one), in exon 14, an arginine aminoacid goes to histidine, a mutation that is not found in non-affected individuals in the KE family, nor in hundreds of controls for the normal population. For perspective, this mutation alone turns out to be necessary and sufficient for whatever AKEFIs ultimately exhibit, a situation that can be fairly characterized as a geneticist's dream. Moreover, the identification of a specific point mutation affecting a single nucleotide in a known position in the gene, producing a single aminoacid substitution in the expressed protein, is as detailed a result as one can hope for: the ultimate contribution of genetics to the analysis of a phenotype. Importantly, also, this mutation in one copy of the gene only, from what is presently observable, does not affect the development of the various other organs in the development of which FOXP2 is implicated.[3]

The forkhead domain codes for a transcription factor, a regulatory protein that modulates the transcription of other genes from DNA into RNA. Note: greater activity of the protein(s) produced by this gene means less activity in the genes that they regulate. As far as one can tell, therefore, and contrary to naïve intuition, a defect in this gene causes *more* other proteins to be synthesized and/or a *greater quantity* of those proteins. In the regulatory proteins that are the products of FOX genes, the forkhead binding domain allows them to bind to the promoter region of hundreds of genes.[4] As it turns out, the arginine residue in the precise position just mentioned, mutated for the affected KE family members, happens to be extremely conserved across species all the way down to yeast. That suggests that its stereochemical role in the final folding of the protein turns out to be central. So much so that a single change of that aminoacid into histidine has the same observable effect on the gene as a radical translocation that disrupts its open reading frame, as observed in patient CS. This may well be because, being a transcription factor, FOXP2 directly or indirectly affects a very large set of target genes, including some that appear to regulate the development of the brain tissues.

A metaphor to underscore this point is to think of a transcription factor like FOXP2 as the ancient Chinese irrigator Li Bing, who according to Kurlansky (2003) was the inventor of massive irrigation by controlling the water levels of the Minjiang River to divert it into channels, depending on both rain conditions and agricultural needs. A vast network of possibilities and potential disasters depended more on Li Bing's repressing or liberating the Minjiang's waters than on the weather itself. Imagine that the emperor had imprisoned Li Bing, cut his tongue, making him go mad, or, even worse, killed him. This would have spelled disaster for the irrigation network, affecting millions of families in Eastern Sichuan. Well, our job in attempting to understand the role of FOXP2 is the equivalent of guessing Li Bing's actions merely from (a) knowing his whereabouts and (b) observing the ensuing variable wealth of the ancient Chinese economy at large. This metaphor might actually be too favorable, for unlike Li Bing, who was a single governor giving orders to many people, there is no single "regulator" that gives orders to his subordinates on how to "select" the relevant channels. FOXP2 is one among

---

[3] It has not been determined yet how the expression of FOXP2 in these quite different organs correlates with alternative variants of the gene produced by alternative splicing (see Lopez 1998, Blencowe 2006, Parmley et al. 2007, and also n. 13 for important clarifications and extensions).

[4] Two hundred and eighty-five have been recently identified in the fetal brain alone (Spiteri et al. 2007).

scores of other transcription factors, in fact acting at different times in developmental sequencing in one of the many complex genetic regulatory networks that govern the development and the functioning of biological organisms (Davidson 2006; Davidson and Erwin 2006).

5.5 A Rather Hasty Interpretation

Naturally, such a great finding, with a level of refinement on which one could hardly improve, had an immediate impact on the press even if the subtleties just mentioned could not have been reported. This is understandable for popular venues, but it is less so for journals like Nature, which came up with the front-page title "Language gene found." A number of commentators and the authors themselves—Anthony Monaco being reported as very explicit on this caveat (see for instance Trivedi 2001)—have correctly pointed out that this is, at best, misleading. Words of prudence have also been expressed by Dorothy Bishop (2002). On the one hand, surely many other genes are implicated in language,[5] so there is no sense in which FOXP2 could be *the* language gene. On the other, a regulating gene of this sort is involved in a variety of physiological and anatomical processes, as we have just seen, and it is plainly parochial to concentrate on the language aspect, even if it may be the most interesting to some of us.

That said, we find that it is also misleading, possibly even mistaken, to go in the exact opposite direction, taking the view that the only reason FOXP2 is relevant to language has to do with its effect on those linguistic observables that mere common sense would grant us. Language is, well, a bunch of noises that we make with vocal gestures; so if somehow the ability to articulate such gestures is impaired, then the corresponding ability to analyze the corresponding sounds would fall apart. This is the line of reasoning which stems from the initial localization of the gene (Fisher et al. 1998), later followed, as we said, by an analysis of functional and structural abnormalities in brains affected with the syndrome that occupies us, the most significant being a bilateral reduction in the size of the caudate nucleus, together with abnormal high activity in the left caudate nucleus during speech tasks. Since, again, that cerebral area, plus the cerebellum (where FOXP2 is now known to be expressed as well), are implicated in motor co-ordination, a line of rapid inference ends up in statements that leave many of us quite perplexed. These are some revealing quotes:

---

[5] A recent study by Benítez-Burraco (2007) mentions at least one hundred and fifty.

It is possible that the accompanying linguistic and grammatical impairments observed in the KE family are secondary consequences of basic deficits in motor planning and sequencing.   (Lai et al. 2003: 2458—Though they admit that "it is equally plausible that the motor and cognitive problems arise simultaneously" [ibid.])

Impaired phonological analysis resulting from poor subvocal rehearsal of incoming speech could interfere with the ability to draw analogies between words with articulation patterns in common and, particularly in a developmental context, to learn implicitly the rules of syntax.   (Watkins, Dronkers, and Vargha-Khadem 2002: 463)

These findings indicate that one core deficit in affected family members is a higher order orofacial motor impairment or dyspraxia that is best exemplified in speech, because speech requires the precise selection, coordination and timing of sequences of rapid orofacial movements.   (Vargha-Khadem et al. 2005: 132)

The extensive behavioral data on the KE family, combined with the success of linkage analysis, support the proposal that there is at least one core deficit—orofacial dyspraxia—underlying the speech and language disorder of the affected members. However, it is unclear whether their associated grammatical, semantic and other cognitive impairments are all secondary consequences of this fundamental deficit, or whether they point instead to the existence of additional core deficits.

(Vargha-Khadem et al. 2005: 132)

The FOXP2 gene may therefore have an important role in the development of a putative frontostriatal network involved in the learning and/or planning and execution of speech motor sequences, similar to that involved in other types of motor skills.

(Liegeois et al. 2003: 1234)

To us these commentaries are akin to saying that, since, as the governor that he was, our friend Li Bing was implicated in ceremonies and rituals of all sorts that occupied most of his time, the marvelous rice economy in China was a "secondary effect" of praying.

5.6 The Geneticist's Dream Turning into the Linguist's Nightmare

For those of us raised within the Cognitive Revolution—a response to the inability of associationism and behaviorism to say anything truly significant about the mind—it is disheartening to have to listen to rehashed claims about silent monologues ("subvocal rehearsal"), "drawing analogies between words," to "learning the rules of syntax," and see language equated with "other motor skills." Ideas of this sort are at best irrelevant, and it is impossible to see how they would have anything to contribute to explicating even the most basic facts of the language faculty, as understood by professional linguists.

Take for instance the problems with morphology that both aphasics and AKEFIs exhibit. Half a century of syntactic study shows that there is nothing trivial or low-level about such marks of tense, plurality, and the like. It is precisely because of agreement phenomena of this sort that Chomsky first proposed in 1955, and ever since has defended with strong evidence, the idea that the computations of language must be context-sensitive, in technical parlance. This can be illustrated with a simple example.

The agreement between the subject of a sentence like the present one (which the reader can easily see starts with the words *the agreement*) and the predicate it combines with (which the reader will easily see is about to be pronounced) *is* an affair that can span arbitrarily many words. In the case just parsed (whose crucial component is "agreement...is"), precisely forty words. What AKEFIs seem to be having difficulties with is, so it seems, finding the right form in words like *is* and comparable examples.[6] This is why Gopnik had the intuition that these patients specifically exhibited "feature blindness", a testable hypothesis which, as such, of course is either right or wrong. But what opponents of this approach do not seem to even realize is that standard linguistic practice takes the dependency between words like *is* and whatever triggers its morphological shape to be *the* central phenomenon in linguistic structuring, which predictably goes by the name of the Agree operation. In other words, AKEFIs appear to be lost with the central phenomenon of linguistic structuring, and this should not be dismissed via one-liners about grammatical skills learned by analogy. What Chomsky showed long ago, and it resists all the attacks of half a century of rather brutal scrutiny, is precisely that agree conditions cannot be learned by analogy, indeed cannot be learned at all in any serious sense of the word "learn," and in the end are simply not at all skills.[7]

Ultimately, nobody knows what is really happening, deep down, with AKEFIs. We linguists and cognitive scientists are the first who would want to find out, and many of us are willing to offer our expertise in seriously analyzing the available data and even building revamped tests to acquire new information. The risk is that our linguist and cognitive colleagues, when they see the matter

---

[6] Shorter sentences make the same point, across languages. Consider, for instance: *The books that the boy reads are expensive.* Why does the verb not agree with the noun that is closest to it in the (surface form of) the sentence? Why do we not have, something like the ungrammatical **The books that the boy read is expensive.* Physical proximity is not the relevant factor, but rather syntactic hierarchy is. (For a recent restatement of these considerations, see Chomsky's contributions to Piattelli-Palmarini, Uriagereka, and Salaburu 2009.)

[7] The argument is based on showing how so-called context-sensitive conditions in language (e.g. of the sort arising for a series of precisely *n* elements arbitrarily distant from another series of precisely *n* elements followed by yet another such exact series) cannot be generally modeled in finite-state terms. The latter, however, are the standard way in which local associations (of the stimulus–response sort) can be, and have been, simply modeled (standard connectionist networks are more or less elaborate extensions of such systems). As an exercise, proponents of purely associative theories should attempt to model the agreement dependency in **these** *(that we're talking about and anyone can parse...)* **are** *(extremely simple agreement...)* **facts**, where the important point is that the agreement dependency in *these are facts* can be dissociated by an arbitrary number of intervening elements.

trivialized to these extremes, will turn their attention elsewhere. But this would be a mistake, because we have here the best instance of a possible, though extremely complex, bridge between language and genes, something many of us have been wishing to see happen for decades. Our point is that, in truth, none of the assumptions customarily made to allow for the hasty inferences discussed above holds water under closer scrutiny.

The matter starts with considerations of general intelligence, which of course critics contend that—contrary to what Gopnik had initially reported— is lower in affected members, on average. However, it is not clear what considerations "on average" mean in this instance, particularly when to this day intelligence remains such an elusive notion. As we mentioned earlier, in the KE family there are cases of normal to high nonverbal IQ with heavy linguistic impairment,[8] and of low nonverbal IQ with only minor linguistic impairment, for what such correlations are worth. So, plainly, there is some dissociation between these two variables. Moreover, IQ is itself an average, lumping together roughly pre-theoretical notions (at least from the point of view of cognitive scientists) deciding on what is verbal and what is not. The fact remains, though, that the only nonverbal task responsible for lower nonverbal IQ in AKEFIs is the arbitrary pairing of symbols with digits. But is this a non-verbal task? Is it a task that parasitizes on verbal (syntactic) conditions? Is it one that exemplifies some deeper condition that underlies structural dependencies of various, still poorly understood, sorts? Nobody knows, but these wizards of neurobiology and genetics seem to presuppose an easy answer. Which, to be candid about the matter, is a bit as if those of us who are not geneticists were to gallantly presuppose that genetic soups are nothing but trivial amino-acid associations.[9] The nightmare worsens in the following domain of inquiry.

---

[8] One affected male member of the family is a highly accomplished computer programmer (Myrna Gopnik, pers. comm.).

[9] Not even high-school genetics is taught these days without noting that, together with linear DNA base-triplet to aminoacid associations, a variety of more complex groupings and dependencies exist as well, such that linearly distant elements end up associated after some topological rearrangement of a DNA or RNA sequence, for instance in pseudo-knots. Similar considerations apply for protein folding, and matters are probably on the verge of a new frontier as the role of introns and epigenetic considerations at large is beginning to be unearthed. Curiously, this morass of new facts and ideas has led researchers like Searls (2002) to suggest that molecular biologists would do well to introduce tools from linguistics—and very specifically context-sensitive dependencies—into the modeling of such nuanced and complex structures (developing a suggestion that goes back at least to Niels Jerne's 1984 Nobel Award address). It is incomprehensible to us that both the richness of genomic and proteomic analyses and the tools that linguistics has proposed, which aptly describe its own equally rich structures, can be ignored.

5.7 Brain Correlates

Let us focus on the most paradigmatic correlations between brain areas and phenotypic manifestations of the behavioral sorts: the cerebellum, the caudate nucleus, and the motor system. This sort of correlation is even coarser than the one suggested above for the molecular level. To consider such correlations causal would be, again, like having the entire Chinese economy caused by prayer, except this conclusion would now be reached even without knowing that Li Bing is responsible for irrigation: simply noting that there is an organized system of religion in ancient China, and concomitantly observing that this place has a rice economy. Of course, in this instance we happen to know the details, but to make the troubling analogy complete, all that we have to do is pretend for a moment that, in fact, there *had not* been an irrigation system in China, and plentiful crops were the mere consequence of a favorable climate. The correlation would still hold, and we would jump, making it causal, to simply the wrong conclusion.

As it turns out—although even Wikipedia tells us that the cerebellum "is a region of the brain that plays an important role in the integration of sensory perception and *motor* control" [*sic*]—studies of unrelated patients with acquired lesions have revealed a role of the cerebellum in at least procedural learning (detection and generation of event sequences) and in rather nuanced linguistic functions. Typically, as Fiez et al. (1992) show, lesions to the cerebellum cause gait ataxia (problems with walking), dysmetria (problems with the distance, power, and speed of movements), dysarthia (articulation difficulties), abnormal eye movements, and vertigo (balance problems). Spontaneously occurring and laboratory-induced mutants in mice and rats carrying a disruption of the cerebellum show strange uncontrollable global movements, such as reeling, "waltzing," circling, staggering, lurching (for an early review see King 1936, and Millen et al. 1999 for a comparative analysis of the development of the cerebellar system in the mouse and the human embryo). It is also involved in timing, rhythm, and the sequencing of events. Then again, procedural learning of several tasks is under the control of the cerebellum, in particular the learning and execution of motor sequences (Riva and Giorgi 2000), as well as various timing functions, such as maintaining a rhythm and discriminating interval durations (Fiez et al. 1992).[10] Indeed, the cerebellum is also thought to be involved with emotional processes of the

---

[10] "Roles of the cerebellum in cognitive functions are suggested by deficits induced by cerebellar lesions in cognitive planning, in practice-related learning and error detection, in judging time intervals, in rapidly shifting attention between sensory modalities, and in cognitive operations in three-dimensional space..." (Ito 2000a: 159; see also Ito 2000b).

motivation and reinforcement sort (Fiez et al. 1992) and, more relevantly, even language.

Now Gebhart et al. (2002) argue that the cerebellum is implicated in "mental movement" tasks.[11] This study shows that the posterior-lateral part of the cerebellum is activated in the procedural learning of lexical tasks of this sort. Damage to the right posterior-lateral region of the cerebellum impairs verb and antonym generation, blocks insight into relevant errors and any tendency to self-correct even when presented with nouns seen in a list earlier. This seems to have little to do with movement or even a mental rehearsal thereof. Descriptively, constrained semantic association (choosing from a range of appropriate lexical candidates) may be under the control of the right posterolateral regions of the cerebellum, a cognitive aspect of language that would appear extraneous to a motor component. Comparative fMRI data by Dogil et al. (2002) on the comprehension of sentences involving syntactic displacement in Danish (of the sort illustrated by the topicalization in *This, I cannot understand*) reveals the following: phrasal displacement to the left-periphery of clauses activates Broca's area and the temporal–occipital–parietal junction, including the cerebellum, whereas a non-syntactic rearrangement of words does not, but activates instead the left anterior temporal cortex (though see Christensen 2008 for perspective). The point is: many things are going on in the cerebellum, which does not license the inference that, because it is implicated, it should be in terms of its canonical motor "function."

Similar considerations apply to the basal ganglia. Here is a relevant quote:

Although the mammalian basal ganglia have long been implicated in motor behavior . . . [Parkinson's disease being the best known example] extensive evidence now indicates a role for the basal ganglia, in particular the dorsal striatum, in learning and memory. One prominent hypothesis is that this brain region mediates a form of learning in which stimulus-response (S-R) associations or habits are incrementally acquired.   (Packard and Knowlton 2002: 563)

In a nutshell, lesion studies in humans and brain imaging in controls show involvement in "habit learning" of this area, and simultaneous activation with the medial temporal lobe memory system (accompanied by hippocampal activation) with competitive interference. Similarly, Levitt et al. (2002) emphasize involvement of the caudate nucleus in short-term memory (and the onset of episodes of schizophrenia). Interestingly, neuroleptic medication reduces the volume of the caudate nucleus, and reduced volume in the caudate leads to abnormalities in short-term memory (Ullman 2004). Motor control? Well, again, who knows? But whatever is going on seems pretty sophisticated, and

---

[11] Intuitively, the lexical pair *bike–ride* involves mental movement, while the pair *moon–glow* does not.

certainly not enough to make fast inferences whose implied consequence is to deny what serious linguistics has been doing for the best part of the twentieth century.

In sum, if someone wants to argue that impairments in sequencing of movement and procedural learning (knowing *how*) are central to the speech and language disorder caused by a mutated FOXP2, they owe us a better line than to later claim that oro-facial dyspraxia is later accompanied by impairments in the development of a wide range of linguistic and grammatical skills. We fail to see how this tells us anything relevant to the conditions under which what linguists call Agree, and which is so obviously implicated in these instances, should break down. To insist: the errors found in AKE-FIs are not slips of the tongue, stutterings, lisps, or anything in that league. They appear to be structural, syntactic difficulties, whether or not they have non-linguistic correlates (or whether the latter are parasitic on underlying syntactic conditions). Explaining this simple situation would be a plus, and claiming that it simply follows from some vague motor conditions seems to us wrong-headed. In our view, the now popular link between motor controls and language "learning" still has to be seriously substantiated, as does the "common underlying cause" identified as the learning of sequential actions. A finer-grained analysis of the involved brain regions may well reveal more interesting differences, particularly as all these brain correlates are, well, that: purely correlational. In truth, no genuine "computational" difference is available yet for the different brain regions that researchers have identified; they are a series of black boxes, at best. At worst, they may even be the wrong units to be looking for answers, as a genuine integration of linguistics, genetics and the neurosciences is yet to be constructed (as pointed out by Poeppel and Embick 2006). And yet, what we are reporting here is really the mainstream view, which, as we are about to see, only got reinforced when evolutionary studies of FOXP2 were released—again introducing information which, in itself, is certainly very important.

5.8 FOXP2 Evolving

First the good news: in 2002, the Oxford group, and a group at the Max Planck Institute for Evolutionary Anthropology led by Svante Pääbo and Wolfgang Enard at Leipzig, reconstructed the phylogenesis of Foxp2 (see n. 12 for this spelling), across the mammalian world.[12] Foxp2 is ubiquitous, which allows researchers to see its variants for the expressed region. Genes have

---

[12] The human variant of the gene is indicated in capital letters (FOXP2), while the non-human mammalian and avian versions are indicated as Foxp2 or FoxP2. Recently the expression of a honeybee FoxP2-homologue, *AmFoxP*, was investigated in the honeybee brain (Kiya et al. 2008).

both intragenic and expressed regions (introns and exons, respectively), and only the latter express a protein.[13] The major splice form of the protein that FOXP2 encodes has a whopping 715 aminoacids, and yet it is largely identical in various primates, including the apes. With one glaring exception: humans, for whom *two* point mutations are shown in exon 7: T (threonine) to N (asparagine) in position 303 and N to S (serine) in position 325 (though see also n. 30 for the bat case). To put this in perspective, although only three (out of 715 possible) point mutations exist between humans and, say, mice (distant about 150 million years, having had a common ancestor some 75 million years before present), two of those exist between humans and chimps (distant some 11 million years). In other words, two recent mutations in the expressed region of the gene took place in our lineage, while things remained pretty much stable in our joint primate lineage with mice for the best part of our common evolution. It should be noted that the change in position 325 creates a potential target site for phosphorylation,[14] together with a change in the predicted secondary structure in the protein. Phosphorylation of forkhead transcription factors can be a mechanism mediating transcriptional regulation, and so it may have functional consequences.

That said, it would be inaccurate to say that N-to-S in position 325 of exon 7 of FOXP2 is a specifically human mutation, which is where the not-so-good news start in this ongoing story. The mutation in question is also found, at least, in hogs, badgers, cats, and at least six species of bats (see n. 30). As Robert Berwick suggests (pers. comm.), the mutation in question, for all we know so far, could have had an effect on diet, for instance, which would probably be irrelevant to all our concerns. Enard et al. (2002), too, revealed that no variation exists in the expressed region of FOXP2 within the human species,

---

[13] In a typical gene within eukaryotes (multicellular organisms), an entire DNA sequence is initially transcribed, by the specialized enzymatic machinery of the cell, into one long sequence of RNA. Then the RNA sequences that correspond to the introns are cut out and the terminal ends of the exons are joined (or "spliced") together, before the final mRNA (messenger RNA) is formed. This is what then migrates from the nucleus into the cytoplasm, into the apparatus that synthesizes the proteins (the ribosomes), and finally expressed into a protein (whence the term "exons"). The role of introns, which are ubiquitous in the genome of eukaryotes, remains somewhat unclear, although it is more and more evident that they have a crucial role in regulating the expression of genes. Quite commonly, as it has become evident in the last few years, the cutting and splicing process allows for an alternative splicing of a gene, producing several different proteins expressed from the very same gene. We mention this mechanism for FOXP2 as well, which may have unforeseen consequences, including the possibility that different proteins originating from a same FOXP2 initial DNA sequence and sharing long sequences, but having ultimately different functions, could be regulating different genes in the various tissues in which FOXP2 is expressed.

[14] Phosphorylation is the addition of a phosphate group to a protein. Reversible phosphorylation of the proteins that form the histones (the drum-shaped complexes around which DNA is coiled in the chromosomes) is an important regulatory mechanism in gene expression, with methylation and acetilation.

at least for dozens of individuals tested, each from a different ethnic group and geographical area.[15] These facts are no doubt surprising, emphasizing in both instances a high conservation, both within humans and across species. But conservation of what? This is a much more subtle issue that deserves to be seriously worked out, particularly when we see FOXP2 expressed, in humans alone, in the spleen, muscle, the liver, skin, the uterus, the eye, the mammary glands, the testes, the kidneys, the lungs, and the intestine—at the very least, and quite aside (or so it seems) from its clear expression both in the brain and within the "speech organs" at large (ear, tongue and trachea); for germane considerations, see Marcus and Fisher (2003) and the bibliography therein.

It should give us pause (a) to find the gene doing something apparently rather basic in all those instances having little or nothing to do with language, and (b) doing so across species, expressing pretty much the same protein in one of its major splicings at least all the way up to fish. Precisely why are we supposed to be moved by the two point mutations in humans that many authors are talking about? Should we be more moved than, say, when witnessing that there have also been mutations in other mammals?[16] Or to put this differently: surely FOXP2 is playing an important role in *some* aspect of the language faculty—we are the first to admit that. But the mutation in the KE family, which leads to the syndrome in AKEFIs, was *in exon 14*, a totally different one from the one now being considered (and see n. 16). How do we even know that what was found is relevant *to language*, as opposed to, say, diet (as Berwick this volume suggests)? Or for that matter any other aspect of our complex anatomy and physiology? Only the narrowest view of genetics would link,[17] in a more or less bijective way, point-mutations at the genotypic level to punctate changes in the phenotype. Situations of that sort are rarely ever present in biology, perhaps never when it comes to complex mechanisms like the language faculty. In any case, only the most careful negative control experiments would help the scientific community determine the validity of claims about this or the other mutation being relevant to God-only-knows what phenotypic

[15] One subject per ethnic group was examined, for the expressed part of the gene only. Differences in the intronic sequences could not, thus, be revealed, or for that matter variants at low frequency (in sequenced human genes, many are typically revealed as being only a few percent in frequency).

[16] For instance, as Li et al. (2007) show, S to P in 302, T to A in 304, and I to M in 316 in cetaceans, or scores of point mutations in various bat species, all of them within positions 278 and 326 of the very same exon under discussion (and see n. 30 in this regard).

[17] A consensus is beginning to emerge among geneticists studying complex diseases that success in mapping one mutation in a gene to one specific altered phenotype (as in the textbook cases of phenilketonuria or hemoglobin S) is more the exception than the rule (Carlson et al. 2004). It can hardly be questioned that "language" is a paradigmatically complex phenotype.

inference. Richard Lewontin has emphasized this simple point in a recent talk (at the 2008 gathering of the AAAS in Boston), which goes back to his central and little known (1998) article "The evolution of cognition: Questions we will never answer."

Let us be very clear: we are not suggesting that one should not be bold in attempting to understand what role this or other relevant genes may be playing in language and cognition. What worry us are not the daring moves, but (a) the lack of basic control experiments, and (b) what the moves being made may in the end buy us, in terms of what we have come to understand, over the years, about the relevant structures at a cognitive level. How can this wealth of data be seriously ignored? Yet these very fine scientists unearthing the building blocks of cognition are fast to jump into very poor evolutionary moves, coupled with even poorer cognitive science, thereby finding "selective sweeps"—a favorite catchword[18]—predictably "accounting," for instance, for the two mutations separating humans from chimps. The bandwagon is so eager to march into a selective explanation that fast calculations done by the Enard team in 2002 triumphantly concluded that, with 95 percent accuracy, the fateful FOXP2 mutation had taken place 120,000 years before the present— and with 100 percent accuracy within the last 200,000 years. We ourselves were delighted with such a finding, even if already at the time Robert Berwick had warned us about the calculation (see n. 19). Needless to say, the transition to the Upper Paleolithic is a topic that everyone is interested in, and linguists who actually suspect that this is the time in which Universal Grammar—in some form or another—became useable by humans (see Hauser, Chomsky, and Fitch 2002, Fitch, Hauser, and Chomsky 2005) are of course perfectly willing to entertain the possibility that something in the genetic machinery of either UG itself or some sub-component thereof suddenly, for some reason irrelevant to the argument, came into place roughly at that time. Indeed, as these authors themselves were quick to point out, this state of affairs pre- dicted that not even our Neanderthal cousins (separated from us within the last 300,000 years or so) would have had the relevant allele of FOXP2 that interests us.

---

[18] A selective sweep is taken to occur when a beneficial mutation rapidly settles on a population, eliminating alternative alleles of the gene where the mutation has occurred, and reducing polymor- phisms in linked genes. Having found evidence of such a sweep both in FOXP2 introns and recom- bining loci, Enard et al. interpret it in "selective" terms, suggesting that its origin was one or both of the mutations discussed above. They go on to explicitly speculate that this change was critical in the evolution of speech, indeed by enabling fine oro-facial movements. That the sweep is present is not indisputable, and we are not convinced that, even if so, it has a selective origin, or that, if it did, it can be attributed to a speech improvement leading to language as we know it.

5.9 The Neanderthals Too?

But, alas, things have turned out to point in a different direction, again with good and bad science playing a decisive role in this never-ending saga. A subset of the Leipzig team (Krause, Orlando et al. 2007) recently teamed up with Spanish scientists to go directly to the archeological field in Asturias, Spain, to test with the best of present techniques whether Neanderthals had the right FOXP2 allele (Krause, Lalueza-Fox et al. 2007). The genomic analysis of two well-preserved Neanderthal specimens showed that the two mutations discussed above were perhaps inherited both by Neanderthals and modern Sapiens from their last common ancestor (around 400,000 years before present). These authors, moreover, conclude that the relevant genetic "function" was nothing short of the modern faculty of language, thus operative in Neanderthals! What happened, then, with that 100 percent certainty that the pertinent mutation had taken place within the last 200,000 years? Answer: different statistical methods were used to calculate things in either instance, as Robert Berwick explained to us. Which is fine; but then this should all be put into perspective, lest innocent consumers (ourselves included) would have to do for themselves the control recalibration, adjusting for sensitive parameters the way some of our colleagues can. This does not help anyone, and plain honesty in the exposition and a less grandiose presentation would be good first steps. Second, if someone is arguing for such a tricky "selective sweep," one should probably see what it really buys for the whole thing whose architecture and evolution we are attempting to model.[19]

But remember, in this instance the argument is really pretty trivial. Are we supposed to take seriously the idea that enhanced vocal abilities in *Homo sapiens* led to *all* that we can really tell the language faculty is? If someone is making such a claim, they really should show us how even the most basic properties of the faculty (and any linguistics textbook lists them) would follow from that. Otherwise, the claim is vacuous. Then again, for this kind of adaptive explanation to work, perhaps it is as well that underlying claims be vacuous so that nothing prevents tweaking them back and forth. New evidence emerges that Neanderthals too had FOXP2? No problem: we will give them "language" too. In the trivial sense we are now identifying this putative faculty, it does not really matter that all the traits which archeologists commonly associate to the language faculty *strictu sensu* (rich, constantly evolving cultures; highly flexible and yet specific cognitive abilities; representational

---

[19] Moreover, Robert Berwick (pers. comm.) has applied the same statistical algorithm as in the original Enard article, but relaxing two rather implausible idealizations that were made there: random mating and fixed population size. Without these crucial idealizations, the sweep disappears.

manifestations; a massive diaspora; etc.) are patently not present in Nean-derthals (see Balari et al. 2009 for perspective and references). "Language" in this sense is a metaphorical term, on a par with "culture," "symbol" (and the alleged science concentrating on symbols qua symbols—semiotics) or other such terms. If so, however, modeling the evolution of *that* may not be worth it, just as it probably is not worth modeling the biological *evolution* of, say, religion.

We hasten to add that we have no idea whether Neanderthals had a form of language or proto-language, or for that matter what the significance of the FOXP2 allele is that has been found in the two specimens mentioned above. As Benítez-Burraco et al. (2008) discuss, (too) many scenarios are compatible with the available data: (1) the mutations could be transferred into Neanderthals from modern humans through hybridization; (2) they could be present but unselected in Neanderthal's genetic endowment; (3) they could be selected, but for some non-linguistic function. Thus the analysis in Krause et al. does not confirm either the antiquity of the human faculty of language or the linguistic capabilities of Neanderthals, and more reliable data are needed to settle this question.

5.10 Waking up from the Linguist's Nightmare

In closing, we wish to switch to a more positive mood and suggest future avenues of inquiry that can more profitably integrate genetics, neurobiol-ogy, developmental studies, and linguistics (a consummation devoutly to be wished for). These final reflections still involve FOXP2, but the link between genes and phenotypes is made in them at a different level of "granularity." It is quite doubtful, in fact, that genes and brain loci may map neatly onto components of language that have been demarcated one from the other mostly (and justifiably) in view of organizing academic disciplines. In other words, it is doubtful that brains may really (not just metaphorically or approxi-mately) possess distinct areas for phonology, morphology, syntax, semantics, pragmatics, and the like. Even less so, as we have just seen, may genetic variants map onto even broader functions encompassing language and motor sequencing or language and a general capacity to discover analogies. More plausibly, different brain areas implicated in linguistic computations are likely to be specifically responsible for bona fide components such as hierarchical organization, linearization, concatenation, recursion, and so on (Poeppel and Embick 2006). Assuming, plausibly, that these are the truly elementary ingre-dients of the language faculty, it stands to reason that sometimes the most interesting counterparts of each one of them may be found in different species, even distant ones in different genera.[20] It may repay to be reminded that the essentials of genetic recombination have been best evidenced at first in the study of bacteria and the fruitfly, the mechanisms of embryonic development in the study of the sea urchin and the dynamics of the nervous impulse in the study of the squid's giant axon. In recent years it has become standard to explore mental retardation in children by studying specific mutants in drosophila (Restifo 2005; Didelot et al. 2006). Obviously, we humans did not directly evolve from any of these species, but there are enough commonalities in particular organs and functions to make these model-systems interesting analogs, and thus looking into what a gene like FoxP2 may be doing in other species is very telling.

Since advanced knock-out technology exists for them, mice are the first good candidates to explore the matter thoroughly. As it turns out, the relevant allele of Foxp2 in mice appears involved on how pups ultrasonically communicate with their mothers (Holy and Guo 2005; Shu et al. 2005). This, of course, seems totally removed from speech in the usual sense, and it is already an indication that things are more subtle than anticipated (Suthers 2004). A team of Japanese neuroscientists has recently generated a knock-in (KI) mouse for Foxp2, corresponding precisely to the human FOXP2 mutation, by homologous recombination (Fujita et al. 2008). Mice that are homozygous for this Foxp2 mutation show reduced weight,[21] immature development of the cerebellum, and achieved crisis stage for survival three weeks after birth.[22] More important for us here, at postnatal day 10, these mice also showed severe ultrasonic vocalization (USV) and motor impairment.[23] These authors state specifically (p. 3117) that

The heterozygous Foxp2 mice [see our n. 21, MPP JU], which showed modest impairment of USVs with different USV qualities and which did not exhibit nuclear

---

[20] Marc Hauser has cogently defended the interest of looking for model systems in a large variety of species in the study of cognition (Hauser 2005). See also his contribution to Piattelli-Palmarini et al. (2009).

[21] Homozygous individuals carry the mutation on both copies of the gene, one on each chromosome. The heterozygous mice, carrying the mutation on one copy only, show more modest impairments and are the more direct analogs to the affected members of the KE family, where only one copy of the gene is mutated.

[22] Severe weight reduction in the mutated homozygotes is mentioned in this paper, but not whether epithelial gut linings and lung tissue were also compromised, as might perhaps be expected given the known multiple regulation of FoxP2 target organs.

[23] Similar to the wild-type protein, the mutated Foxp2 localized in the nuclei of the cerebellar Purkinje cells and the thalamus, striatum, cortex, and hippocampus neurons of the homozygous Foxp2 mice, and some of the neurons showed nuclear aggregates of Foxp2. In addition to the immature development of the cerebellum, nuclear aggregates of the defective protein of the mutated Foxp2 may further compromise the function of the Purkinje cells and neurons of the homozygous mice, resulting in their premature death.

aggregates, should provide insights into the common molecular mechanisms between the mouse USV and human speech learning and the relationship between the USV and motor neural systems.

So a lesson emerges already from these studies: could it be that Foxp2 is playing a more relevant role for "language" in mice than in chimps? Of course, it may turn out that we will also find a quasi-linguistic role for the gene in chimps (for which ethical considerations prevent knock-out experiments), but the other possibility is that the relevant brain circuits that FoxP2 regulates in both mice and humans turn out not to be active in the chimp, even if in other regards such a brain is closer to ours than a mouse's. These are the kinds of surprises that emerge from molecular biology, which moves us to the most interesting example to date of what FoxP2 can do in species other than humans.

5.11 The Songbird Case

A variety of songbirds, like zebra finches, are relatively easy to study in the lab, and they have been thought to be interesting because many of them exhibit a form of learning of the song the male woos the female with, at a critical period a few weeks after hatching. Brain studies had long shown how the bird brain presents two relevant circuits, one for song acquisition, and a differentiated one for its performance (Haesler et al. 2004; Scharff and Haesler 2005; Haesler et al. 2007). Interestingly, FoxP2 is expressed in both, especially in a region called Area X that connects the acquisition and production circuits. It is expressed in the acquisition circuit while the male bird is acquiring the song, and later on in the production circuit as he sings it.[24] Quite recently, also, specific "mirror" neurons have been identified in the swamp sparrow that respond in a temporally precise fashion to the auditory presentation of certain note sequences in this songbird's repertoire, and to similar note sequences in other birds' songs (Prather et al. 2008). These neurons display nearly identical patterns of activity when the bird sings the same sequence. Furthermore, these neurons innervate striatal structures important for song learning, raising the

---

[24] If FoxP2 levels of expression in Area X are reduced during song development (a knock-down of the gene produced by RNA-interference) the result is an incomplete and inaccurate imitation of the tutor song. Inaccurate vocal imitation is already evident early during song ontogeny and persists into adulthood. Basically, the acoustic structure and duration of adult song syllables become abnormally variable. These authors say: "Our findings provide the first example of a functional gene analysis in songbirds and suggest that normal auditory-guided vocal motor learning requires FoxP2" (Haesler et al. 2007).

possibility that singing-related activity in these cells is compared to auditory feedback to guide vocal learning.[25]

A note of caution is of course necessary. Much as we would like to see such parallels firmly established, the different techniques applied to the different cases (knock-down in birds, knock-out and knock-in in mice, fine sequence analysis in humans) make a direct comparison only tentative.[26] The role of alternative splicing (see n. 13) could be crucial, if different proteins encoded by the same DNA sequence migrate to different target organs, possibly including target brain regions. Moreover, in humans and birds we have both learning and production, while in mice (as far as one can tell so far) only production of ultrasound vocalizations, not a comparable learning of an elaborate song-like sequence. But the field is rife with new ingenious experiments as we speak, so the next few years will reveal much more precise contours of similarities and differences.

But no matter how many caveats one may want to add, interesting considerations have emerged already from the study of birdsongs. The bird produces characteristic chirpings through two separate channels in its syrinx, and they appear to have no (compositional) semantics to them. So plainly this is a behavior different from language—functionally and structurally—yet it shares abstract properties with it. Quite aside from the acquisition issues just raised, by all accounts birdsongs are pretty complex structures, and yet they are "squeezed out" into a uni-dimensional sound. In a sense this happens in language too, of course in much more complex terms: this

---

[25] Another interesting passage from this paper: "To enable learned vocal communication, the brain must establish a correspondence between auditory and motor representations of the vocalization and use auditory information to modify vocal performance. Individual neurons that display a precise auditory-vocal correspondence could enable auditory activity to be evaluated in the context of the animal's vocal repertoire, facilitating perception. These neurons could also play an important role in vocal learning, because their motor-related activity could be compared with auditory feedback to modify vocalizations adaptively. Despite their potential importance to learned forms of vocal communication, including human speech, single neurons displaying a precise auditory-vocal correspondence have not been identified" (Prather et al. 2008: 305). See also Woolley and Doupe (2008).

[26] The knock-down of a gene (as in the birds) is the result of introducing a variable dose of a specific "mirror" (complementary) messenger RNA that competes with the normally transcribed RNA of the gene by hybridizing with it and thereby sequestering it. The procedure is modulable by dosage, and selectively targeted to specific organs at different times in development. In contrast a knock-out (as in the mice example) consists in selectively deactivating a gene in the whole organism, by means of various techniques. The knock-in is basically the reverse of this technique: inserting a specific gene into an organism. The resulting animals with the genetic change in their germline cells can then often pass the gene (knock-out or knock-in) to future generations. In our case, supposing that different alternatively spliced proteins encoded in FoxP2 migrate to different target organs (a live possibility as far as we can tell), a knock-in mouse will have the mutated proteins distributed uniformly to all the target tissues, and a knock-out to none. This is a different case from a selective and suitably timed knock-down (in birds).

very sentence has an internal structure, yet the reader is now parsing it one word at a time after it was squeezed out by us into writing. Obviously, writing (a cultural creation) is not the issue, but the speech that underlies it, for which this linearization problem is equally patent: humans parse sentences one word—nay, one phonological unit—at a time. Could the fact that FoxP2 is apparently involved in the birdsong, and also speech or language, be merely accidental?

Importantly from our perspective, a study by Teramitsu and White (2006) shows how the mRNA of FoxP2 *sub*-regulates in Area X as males sing to themselves, in effect practicing small variants of the song, while when the action is directed to a female it slightly *up*-regulates. As the authors point out, in both instances the same abstract motor control is at stake. So the role that FoxP2 plays in all of this cannot just mean "motor control" in any flat sense.[27] We do not know, yet, whether non-singing females also show up- or down-regulation of FoxP2 in their partially atrophied Area X as they listen to the male's song. But if they do, and this can be detected, it would clearly indicate that FoxP2 has a bearing not just on actions, but also on reflections thereof.[28]

The correlations between humans and songbirds are even more remarkable. As Sebastian Haesler, Erich Jarvis, Constance Scharff, and colleagues (2005) have argued, the brain circuit operative in birdsong is functionally equivalent to one of the circuits involved in human language, which clearly expresses FOXP2. Birds lack a neo-cortex, which of course is key to human language (Broca and Wernicke's areas, at least); but the inner brain, from the cerebellum down to the basal ganglia, is also centrally involved in language performance and acquisition, as we have noted earlier. In particular the caudate nucleus, which is functionally equivalent to the bird's Area X, seems critically involved

---

[27] "This *FoxP2* downregulation cannot be a simple consequence of the motor act because birds sang in both directed and undirected contexts. Our data suggest that *FoxP2* is important not only for the formation but also for the function of vocal control circuitry. Social context-dependent, acute changes in *FoxP2* within the basal ganglia of adult songbirds also suggest, by analogy, that the core deficits of affected humans extend beyond development and beyond basic central motor control" (Teramitsu and White 2006: 7390).

[28] Woolley and Doupe (2008) found that both mated and socially naive females discriminate between directed and undirected song—and preferred the former. These preferences, which appear to reflect attention especially to aspects of song variability controlled by the Anterior Forebrain Pathway (AFP), are enhanced by experience, as they are strongest for mated females responding to their mate's directed songs. Neural activity was measured using expression of the immediate early gene product (ZENK), associated with memory formation and plasticity. They found that social context and song familiarity differentially modulate the number of ZENK-expressing cells in telencephalic auditory areas. Specifically neurons in the caudomedial mesopallium are most affected by whether a song is directed or undirected, whereas the caudomedial nidopallium is most affected by whether a song is familiar or unfamiliar.

in what may be thought of as operational memory, as Michael Ullman has emphasized (see Ullman and Pierpont 2005). This memory is of the sort one needs to rapidly remember the sequential interplay of one's fingers, let's say, as they touch a keyboard (whether typing or playing the piano), tying one's shoelaces, dancing or clapping in rhythmic fashions, or as one speaks. In work in progress we suggest that this sub-cortical area may be key to what linguists call "parsing"; that is, the process that allows us to reconstruct complex sentences as we hear or see them, or to produce them to start with, or obviously to acquire the fundamental parameters of one's particular language as first experienced, during language acquisition. In our view birds too may well need a parser, in a non-metaphorical sense of the term: they may not be processing propositions, but their songs are complex enough, and reconstructing them is a remarkable computational task, especially after they are linearly squeezed out of the bird's brains, one note at a time.

5.12 Towards a New Synthesis?

Here is, then, a suggestion of what may be going on at least abstractly, from a perspective that is not violent to linguistic theorizing. Nature has many genes in its tool kit, some of them regulatory like those in the Fox family. These activate proteins with a variety of consequences, from cell aggregation to, it seems, regulating aspects of structural behavior, in as of yet practically unknown ways. One such gene, FoxP2 in birds and FOXP2 in humans, appears at least implicated in operational memory regulation, perhaps indirectly so, thus constituting a central aspect of a parser, which songbirds (and perhaps other species) have used for communicating through the air waves extremely intricate structures, which are reconstructed back in the receptor bird's brain. The gene may have remained active throughout the eons in various chordates, often not serving memory purposes, but other functions the gene also regulates, whatever those are.[29] Then enter the apes, which follow whatever evolutionary path brings them in our direction. The present idea has had nothing to say about that, the "semantic path"—interesting though it obviously is. Nothing, however, in that path entails being able to *express* the wonderful thoughts that a chimp certainly has into something remotely like our language. Indeed, all indications are that Neanderthals too surely had great thoughts (enough to bury their dead or control fire), but we would be very surprised if they had a way to externalize them. They may have lacked, merely, the parser

---

[29] Though there is also a remarkable record of genes being present, but inactive, in ancestral species for very long evolutionary times (see Sherman 2007).

that FOXP2 regulates—pace the Krause, Lalueza-Fox et al. (2007) findings. We got lucky: for some reason that we at least do not understand, our species could recruit an ancient gene with a relatively ancient function (very possibly among many) to help us squeeze our thoughts out into the airwaves, much as a male finch does with his. Granted, the complexity of the thoughts themselves is quite different, including the associated semantics in only one instance. But the sub-cortical circuits regulating the parsing of the structure probably do not care about that: just to reconstruct the original abstract structure (whether music or a full proposition) into a receptor brain.

This theoretical approach is fully testable. As interest in songbirds develops, knock-down technology already exists (Haesler et al. 2007) and knock-out technology, we understand, is being developed. When it is perfected, we will be able to know more precisely what happens to a bird's brain as the gene is affected in various ways. In the meantime, new studies come out weekly, for instance recent results show echolocating bats exhibiting behaviors also regulated by a hyper-mutated variant of FoxP2 (Li et al. 2007),[30] which need to be integrated into this picture (some species of bats have also been claimed to be vocal-learners, but it remains to be seen whether they are the ones for which the gene is indeed active in relevant brain circuits, a matter presently being investigated by Jerry Wilkinson and his associates at the University of Maryland). Meanwhile, in-vitro experiments should continue with FOXP2, to see what happens, to start with, to a chimp's cell when this bit of human DNA is inserted. Eventually, we have little doubt that non-invasive technologies will emerge that will allow us to see the exact role of FOXP2 in language performance. Of course, as is to be expected also, new genes implicated in the process will be isolated and discovered; then all the issues raised here will arise again, for each one of those genes. Last but not least, language theoreticians have to become aware of the matters just discussed. In our view they must be prepared both to see how their standard findings regarding language structure can be integrated into this (or a similar) picture, and possibly also how the molecular mechanisms being analyzed—which touch on such fundamental dimensions as memory regulation, a prerequisite for complex syntactic structuring—may also affect their theoretical conclusions. In the end, the issue is to be ready for what amounts to a new step in the sciences of language and human cognition

---

[30] These authors found that, contrary to previous reports emphasizing the conservativeness of the FoxP2 protein across all nonhuman mammals, it is actually extremely diverse in echolocating bats. They claim to have detected divergent selection (a change in selective pressure) at FoxP2 between bats with contrasting sonar systems, suggesting the possibility of a role for FoxP2 in the evolution and development of echolocation. They also speculate that observed accelerated evolution of FoxP2 in bats supports a previously proposed function in sensorimotor coordination.

more generally, with concrete hypotheses that can be evaluated and improved on, as new data emerge.

This incommensurabilty in basic assumptions and a slack in the granularity of the respective scientific domains was to be expected, as different sciences deepen along different trajectories. But some of it is unnecessary, particularly the sweeping general conclusions we reported above on the nature of language. Instead we wanted to offer an alternative way of integrating these important studies into what we take to be the best linguistic theory available. Our aim here was, on the one hand, to show to linguists why it is imperative that they pay attention to what molecular genetics and related disciplines are telling us about the cognitive phenomenon of human language. On the other hand, symmetrically, we invite geneticists, neurophysiologists, speech pathologists, and evolutionary biologists to take into consideration the results of several decades of linguistic inquiry, involving thousands of linguists who have attained unprecedented insights into the nature of the language faculty after having examined data from hundreds of the world's languages. Having offered accounts both of the underlying commonality and the manifest differences among languages, these linguists are really not enemies competing for turf but partners from whom a deeper understanding can be gained.

6

Biolinguistic Investigations: Genetics and Dynamics

LYLE JENKINS

6.1 Introduction

Biolinguistics is concerned with the traditional fields of interest in biology such as (1) the form/function of language, including knowledge and use of language, (2) the development of language, and (3) the evolution of language. There is currently much interest within the Minimalist Program in the question of "principles not specific to the faculty of language" or what is sometimes called the "third factor," the first two being the more thoroughly investigated topics of genetics (UG) and experience/language environment (Chomsky 2005, 2007b). One area of linguistic study that falls under this rubric is the study of principles of efficient computation.

Another kind of body of principles not specific to the faculty of language might be those principles related to symmetry of systems. It has often been found to be the case that many systems in physics, chemistry, and biology that are asymmetric are symmetric at a deeper level. However, the symmetric state is not necessarily the most stable state of the system. Hence the system will adopt a more stable asymmetric state. Below we will see a few cases of systems that have this property (see e.g. the lateralization of birdsong, below). Since many linguistic systems exhibit asymmetric properties one should always ask whether these may have arisen from the general principles of symmetry that we find operative in physics and the other sciences (Jenkins 2000: 161). Although it is undoubtedly premature to expect to find immediate answers to these questions, it may turn out to be a useful perspective as research advances. Much of current work in syntax on the operation Merge (within the framework of Minimalism) involves building structures that reflect language asymmetries (e.g. the theory of binding of anaphors) (Boeckx 2006; Chomsky 2007b). For work on the antisymmetry properties found in the study word order and hierarchy, see Kayne (1994); for work on asymmetry in morphology, see Di Sciullo (2005).

There has been increased interest in questions of self-organization and dynamics in other areas of biology, such as cell biology, as we will see. In fact, much of this work has led to the founding of new research institutes around the world as well as the creation of new journals, under the rubric of systems biology (Karsenti 2008). A recent review of this work notes that "in a sense we are moving back to the views of D'Arcy Thompson, who thought that biologists overemphasize the role of evolution over that of physical laws in the origin of growth and form" (Thompson 1992). Part of the reason for this renewed interest is that more concrete empirical data has become available as a result of the Human Genome Project and work in such fields as evolutionary–developmental biology (evo–devo), which has led to and accelerated our current understanding of many biological models. For example, researchers in Germany have provided what some regard as one of the most convincing experimental candidates for the Turing reaction-diffusion mechanism in biological pattern formation (Sick et al. 2006). They found that the spacing and density of hair follicles in the skin are regulated by skin proteins in accordance with the Turing model (Turing 1952). In addition, there is renewed interest in the Turing reaction-diffusion system to help explain patterning of digits in the vertebrate limb (Tickle 2006).

As another example, studies have been made to determine the principles, such as "minimization of wiring," that might underlie the formation of neural connections. Much of this work has been done with the organism *C. elegans*, which has a small number of neurons, and hence fewer neural connections to keep track of (Chen, Hall and Chklovskii 2006). The origin of this work is attributed to the "wiring economy principle" of the famous neuroanatomist Ramón y Cajal in his seminal work from over a hundred years ago (1899). According to Chen et al. (quoting Ramón y Cajal), the wiring economy principle "postulates that, for a given wiring diagram, neurons are arranged in an animal to minimize the wiring cost."

6.2 Investigations in Genetics

There has been an explosion of information in genetics due to the completion of the Human Genome Project and such projects as HapMap, which is a catalog of common genetic variants in humans. The most common variation is a difference in one of the DNA bases which are called *single nucleotide polymorphisms* or SNPs. The existence of millions of such SNPs allow one to perform what are called *whole genome* (or *genome-wide*) *association studies*

(WGA studies) to efficiently track down genetic disorders. Two groups of people are taken, one group with the disorder or disease of interest, and one group without the disorder (the control group). DNA is taken from each person representing that person's entire genome. This DNA is placed on small chips (microarrays). Automated machines scan each person's genome and identify the SNPs present. If more SNPs (variations) are present in people that have the disorder than in the controls, then we say that these variations are associated with the disease. Since the locations of the SNPs are known, we can then zero in on the region of the genome where the gene(s) involved in the disorder are located.

These WGA studies are particularly powerful in tracking down multifactorial diseases, that is diseases that come about from combinations of many gene alleles. The method has been successful with identifying a number of diseases, including genetic variations that contribute to risk of type-2 diabetes, Parkinson's disease, heart disorders, obesity, Crohn's disease, and prostate cancer (National Human Genome Research Institute). In one interesting case a type of blindness called age-related macular degeneration was associated with a variation in the gene for complement factor H, which regulates inflammation. This connection was totally unexpected.

One can readily envision applications of WGA studies to human language and other cognitive domains. For example, many disorders such as developmental dyslexia (Galaburda et al. 2006) and Specific Language Impairment (Wexler 2004) may be multifactorial in nature. Moreover, some kinds of autism are related to language problems. It has become clear that autism is not a single entity, but is a spectrum of many disorders, some associated with language problems, some not. A WGA study of autism was recently completed (Weiss et al. 2008). Cases of autism were discovered that were associated with spontaneously occurring (*de novo*) mutations (deletions and duplications).

Another application of the microarray technology has been to identify some candidate targets for the much studied *FOXP2* gene, which has been associated with deficits in articulation, language, and cognition (Spiteri et al. 2007; Vernes et al. 2007). Since the product of this gene is a transcription factor, meaning it is involved in gene regulation, and since it acts in combination with other transcription factors to function in a variety of tissues (including brain, gut, and lung), *FOXP2* is not a "language gene" per se. Hence it is of importance to identify its downstream targets, so as to locate genes involved more directly with the specification of neural circuits subserving language. Vernes et al. employed chromatin immunoprecipitation and promoter microarrays to identify candidate targets for the transcription factor (the first time this method has been used to assess transcription factor targets in the human fetal brain). The candidates possibly include "modulating synaptic plasticity, neurodevelopment, neurotransmission, and axon guidance and represent novel entry points into *in vivo* pathways that may be disturbed in speech and language disorders" (p. 1232).

The notion of a critical period for language acquisition was proposed by Lenneberg (1967) and has received support from studies of language acquisition, including second-language learning and the acquisition of sign language by deaf children and children deprived of language. Many questions remain open about the critical period such as the timing: how long does the critical period last, and what is its onset and end? How does it differentially affect one language module as compared with another? For example, the acquisition of vocabulary seems to extend far beyond the critical period for other modules, such as the acquisition of the phonetic system of the language.

Some of these questions are more amenable to study in other organisms, but hopefully part of what is learned at the molecular level will carry over to the more complex case in humans. In one such case, the critical period for ocular dominance has been examined in the visual cortex of mice (McGee et al. 2005). Normally the critical period for ocular dominance lasts about one month. However, researchers found that they could extend the critical period beyond one month by disabling the Nogo-66 receptor (NgR) protein.

In normal mice, roughly the same amount of the visual cortex is devoted to the left eye as to the right eye. If one eye is sutured shut during the first month, then more of the visual cortex is taken over by the other eye. This does not happen at the end of the critical period (after one month). However, in mice that were genetically engineered so that they did not have the Nogo receptor, it was found that an eye could be sutured shut four months after birth and still cause the visual cortex to reorganize.

Moreover, it was found that one of the proteins that binds to the Nogo receptor, Nogo A, was also involved in regulating the end of the normal critical period. If the mouse did not have Nogo A, then the critical period did not shut down at the end of a month. This in turn provided a clue that myelinization was somehow involved in shutting down the circuits for the critical period. Nogo A is one of the components of the myelin sheath on neurons. Furthermore, it was known that myelinization of visual cortex neurons occurred around the end of the critical period. The researchers hypothesize that this in turn may block axon growth, hence preventing new neuron connections from forming. This would be consistent with what was already known about the

Nogo system's role in inhibiting nerve regeneration after injury. Interestingly, mutations to the Nogo/NgR pathway did not alter the end of the critical period for whisker barrel fields. This suggests that a separate (nonmyelin) (perhaps subcortical) pathway may be involved in the latter case.

The critical period for pure-tone exposure on the auditory cortex (A1) in the rat has also been studied (de Villers-Sidani et al. 2007: 185); this was the "first study determining the onset, duration, and offset of the critical period (CP) in A1, in any mammalian species." It was found that the critical period lasts for three days (from postnatal day 11 to postnatal day 13). Only during this time did exposure to tone result in alterations of the auditory cortex that were both profound and persistent.

Biolinguistics stresses the importance of comparative work with humans and other species to evaluate what is or is not uniquely human (Hauser, Chomsky and Fitch 2002). There is known to be a region which prefers "human voices and vocalizations over other animal vocalizations, acoustical controls and natural sounds" (Petkov et al. 2008). It is located in the temporal lobe anteriorly and on the upper bank of the superior–temporal sulcus. It appears to have several functions. For one, it can distinguish the "voice of our species." In addition, it can differentiate and identify different kinds of human voice.

Prosopagnosia, problems with face recognition, is a well-known neurological disorder, which has been studied for over sixty years. Neurological substrates have been identified, as well as homologs in the monkey. However, there is another disorder, called phonagnosia, a voice-recognition and discrimination disorder, which has been less well studied.

It has been known that people could lose the ability to recognize voices after strokes. However, recently a 60-year-old British woman (KH) surfaced who appears to have never had this ability (annual meeting of the Cognitive Neuroscience Society, April 13, 2008, work reported from the lab of Bradley Duchaine) (Miller 2008). She read an article about face-recognition problems (prosopagnosia) and realized that she had always had a similar problem with voices and had not been able to differentiate between the voices of her close relatives.

When examined, KH successfully passed tests on memory and reasoning, her hearing was normal, and no problems were revealed by an MRI brain scan. However, she failed to perform better than chance when she tried to recognize sentences spoken by famous actors, politicians, or other celebrities, doing much worse than control subjects. She also had trouble learning and distinguishing new voices from the voices of strangers. She could however identify the gender of the voice as well as the speaker's emotional state, indicating the deficit was specific to voice recognition.

Since it is important for vocal animals to be able to recognize the vocalizations of conspecifics in day-to-day interactions and in order to survive, the question arises as to whether a similar region might exist in nonhuman primates. Petkov et al. (2008) used functional magnetic resonance imaging (fMRI) to show that a voice region existed in the rhesus macaque monkey. This voice region was preferentially activated by species-specific vocalizations and was able to differentiate the identity of individuals. The studies located the monkey voice region in the middle of the anterior portion of the superior temporal plane (STP). They also identified several other areas that show a less reliable preference for species-specific vocalizations. They noted that these areas needed further study and additional primates should also be included.

6.3 Investigations in Dynamics

The well-known mathematician Turing proposed a reaction-diffusion mechanism for pattern formation, sometimes called the Turing model, which he suggested might be applicable to patterns in biological development. These systems postulate morphogens, including a short-range activator and a long-range inhibitor with specific constraints on their behavior. Under certain conditions these systems are subject to symmetry-breaking and can produce patterns like stripes and spots (Maini, Baker and Collins 2006). However, work on *Drosophila* led researchers to different developmental mechanisms based on positional information and no conclusive evidence was forthcoming for the Turing model in the biological domain (Akam 1989). However, work continued on Turing models, for example, on skin appendages like hairs and feathers. Nagorcka is credited with first proposing the Turing model for hair formation (Nagorcka 1983–4). Finally, a model was proposed with a particular molecular mechanism for the Turing model for feather formation (Jung et al. 1998).

Now researchers at the Max-Planck Institute in Freiburg have proposed that hair-follicle spacing can be explained by a reaction-diffusion mechanism (Turing model). They postulate that the signaling molecule WNT plays the role of activator in the system and induces the formation of hair follicles. DKK is the inhibitor. They employed both experiments and computational modeling to provide evidence for their hypothesis. Maini et al. (2006: 1397) note that the model predicts and confirms that "moderate overexpression of activator (WNT) increases follicular density, whereas moderate overexpression of inhibitor (DKK) during the initial inductive wave increases the interfollicular spacing." Therefore the molecules appear to be "acting as morphogens in the true Turing sense" (p. 1397). Nevertheless, as they go on to point out, to nail down the analysis, one needs to perform additional experiments to measure such parameters as rates of production, decay, diffusion coefficients, and so on.

Other kinds of optimization that could potentially play a role as a third-factor principle are minimization principles, for example, least effort in syntactic computation. Chklovskii and colleagues have investigated the possibility that there are general principles of wiring optimization for neuronal placement in the brain that help account for the positions of neurons (and ultimately some of their properties) (Chen et al. 2006). This work may be thought of as an application of the wiring economy principle of Ramón y Cajal. The idea is that "neurons are arranged in an animal to minimize the wiring cost" (p. 4723). Although the cost is due to a number of factors, including wire volume, signal delay and attenuation, and metabolic expenditures, one can make the assumption that the connection between two neurons is more costly the farther apart they are. Hence the wiring cost is expressed as a function of distance between neurons and is minimized.

Chen et al. studied the neuronal layout of the complete nervous system of the nematode *C. elegans*, considering 279 non-pharyngeal neurons. They were able to predict the position of most neurons along the anterior-posterior axis of the worm. The analysis revealed some discrepancies; namely, groups of outlier neurons "with stereotypical roles in the network, such as developmental pioneers and command interneurons" (p. 4728). Moreover, Wen and Chklovskii (2005) also propose that a possible explanation for the segregation of the brain into gray and white matter results from another minimization design principle that minimizes conduction delays.

Another design principle, symmetry breaking, has also proven useful in modeling neural behavior in systems such as singing in songbirds, for example canaries (Trevisan, Cooper et al. 2007). The physical and neural substrates for song-production do not exhibit any obvious asymmetries. The avian vocal organ (a bipartite organ called the syrinx) is controlled by muscles that control the tension of the oscillating labia, which modulates the vocal frequency. In addition, other muscles control the air passage through the syrinx by opening and closing both sides. This respiratory activity is bilaterally symmetric. However, one or the other side of the sound sources (or both) can be active during vocalization. Since the morphology of the system is symmetric the question is how the song vocalization can exhibit asymmetrical (lateralized) patterns.

Trevisan et al. proposed that the neural circuits that control the muscles can be modeled as a set of non-linear equations. And, although these equations are underlyingly symmetric, consistent with the hypothesis that both the neural circuitry and the vocal organ are perfectly symmetric, the solutions to the equations reflect spontaneous symmetry breaking bifurcations.

The authors note that there is a range of lateralization in songbirds from unilateral dominance (white-crowned sparrows, chaffinches) to those exhibiting equal contributions from each side of the syrinx (brown thrashers, gray catbirds, and zebra finches). They speculate that there may be a "different degree of departure from a perfectly symmetric neural substrate" (p. 5). They conclude that spontaneous symmetry breaking is "another example of how nature can achieve complex solutions with minimal physical requirements" (p. 5).

As a last example, involving human language, there are a number of studies which analyze evolutionary and historical change in populations of speakers using dynamical systems methods (Mitchener 2003; Niyogi 2004, 2006; Nowak 2006). In this approach a population of speakers is assumed to possess a language-learning mechanism constrained by a Universal Grammar. Furthermore, the population is modeled by a dynamical system called the language dynamical equation. Mitchener (2003) studies the special case where the parameters are chosen so that the dynamical system is highly symmetric. Two kinds of population state are considered, a coherent population where the majority of members speak one language and an incoherent population where many languages are spoken by a significant fraction of the population. He presents a bifurcation analysis of the language dynamical equation to determine under what conditions populations approach the coherent or incoherent steady state. He discusses how one might apply this kind of analysis to problems of language change such as the transition from Old to Middle English under the influence of Scandinavian invaders.

6.4 Conclusion

We have seen how research on a number of fronts in biology, including biolinguistics, involves sometimes complex interactions between the genetics of systems and the dynamics of those systems. Ian Stewart referred to this as the partnership of physics and genetics (Stewart 1995). He had in mind the model proposed by Douady and Couder for the spiral phyllotaxis in the sunflower (Douady and Couder 1992). We have seen this interaction for a number of systems earlier: reaction-diffusion mechanisms, wiring diagrams, birdsong, and language change and language evolution. However, this partnership will certainly continue to be central to much of the work at the frontier of work in biology and biolinguistics.

7

"Deep Homology" in the Biology and Evolution of Language

W. TECUMSEH FITCH

7.1 Introduction: FLB and the Comparative Approach

Most recent discussions of language evolution agree on the necessity of a comparative approach to language evolution: one that uses data from animals to help analyze the mechanistic and evolutionary basis of this crucially human characteristic (Lieberman 2000; Hauser, Chomsky, and Fitch 2002; Pinker and Jackendoff 2005; Hurford 2007). Nonetheless, there is some disagreement concerning the scope of the comparative data which are thought to be useful. Traditional anthropological approaches seeking homologues of linguistic traits have focused on primates to the exclusion of other taxa (e.g. Leakey 1994), implicitly assuming that most of the traits that make humans special have their antecedents in primate dexterity, intelligence, sociality, vision, or other traits. However, while this may be true in many cases, it is by no means a logical necessity. Thus, there is no reason why the search for homologs to human cognitive traits should stop with primates, given that most aspects of human brain structure are shared with mammals in general, and indeed that the most salient organizational principles of the nervous system characterize all vertebrates (Striedter 2004). We are mammals, and vertebrates, just as surely as we are primates. Furthermore, as recognized at least since Darwin, the closest animal analog to certain human characteristics is found not in primates or other mammals, but in birds (e.g. habitual bipedalism, or vocal learning; Darwin 1871). Understanding both the biological basis for, and constraints on, such traits and their evolutionary origins in terms of adaptive function, we need to cast the net wider than primates or mammals, and perhaps in some cases beyond our own vertebrate phylum.

In this chapter I discuss three reasons why the traditional comparative focus on primates, to the exclusion of other clades, is misguided. First, each of the many components of language may have separate evolutionary histories. Many of the human mechanisms which *have* homologs derive from ancestors that lived long before the last common ancestor of the Order Primates (e.g. neurons are shared with all animals, the larynx is shared with all tetrapods, and the neocortex is shared with all mammals), and it would be wholly arbitrary to restrict investigation to primates in such cases. Second, a crucial source of information about past adaptive *function* is to be found in examining cases of convergent evolution, and here the wider we search, the better. If we want to understand which aspects of a trait like bipedalism or vocal learning are incidental, versus either phylogenetically or developmentally necessary, our best source of empirical data will be from multiple species that have evolved that trait independently of one another. For example, anyone who suggests that the human larynx descended automatically with bipedalism (see e.g. Wind 1976; DuBrul 1977) must explain why this did not occur in bipedal birds. Although these first two points may be unfamiliar to some linguists or psychologists, both constitute standard operating procedure in biological and evolutionary biology since Darwin, so I will not make them my focus here (for more detailed review and discussion see Fitch 2005, 2007b).

The thrust of the present chapter is to examine a third argument. This argument hinges upon the existence of a phenomenon that would have been quite surprising to Darwin, or even to most biologists, 15 years ago: the phenomenon of *deep homology*. Deep homology exists when the developmental mechanisms responsible for generating a trait are shared by common descent, even though the phenotypic trait itself was not present in the common ancestor (Shubin, Tabin, and Carroll 1997; Hall 2003). For example, the wings of flies and those of birds are not homologous in any traditional sense (the common ancestor of birds and flies did not have wings). Nonetheless, the genes and developmental processes that generate wings turn out to be shared between these species. Thus, in cases of deep homology, the developmental mechanisms generating a trait are homologous, but the trait itself is not.

While the probability of deep homology seemed very slim indeed to the architects of the neo-Darwinian synthesis (e.g. Mayr 1970), the recent revolution in molecular genetics and developmental biology has revealed deep homology to be common, or even typical, due to the previously unsuspected degree to which genetic and developmental mechanisms are shared among all living organisms. Based upon these new molecular data, we now know that many key aspects of human biology are shared, at a detailed mechanistic level, with amoebae, yeast and fruit flies (not just vertebrates or primates).

Indeed the new science of evolutionary developmental biology (evo–devo), which constitutes a long-awaited phase transition in biological thinking about the mechanisms underlying evolutionary change, has reversed previous expectations regarding homology. Based on the systems we currently understand relatively well (e.g. eye or limb development), deep homology appears to be a norm, not an exception, even in similar traits that arose by "convergent" evolution (Carroll 2008).

In at least one trait relevant to language—the evolution of complex vocal learning in birds and humans—deep homology applies to the case of the FOXP2 gene, which is involved in complex oral motor control in humans and in song learning in birds (Haesler et al. 2007). Thus, the traditional distinction between homology and analogy (or homoplasy) needs to be reconsidered in the light of new mechanistic conceptions of evolution revealed by molecular and developmental data. Although it is certainly too early to say whether deep homology typifies the multiple mechanisms that played a part in language evolution, I suggest here that this is a quite viable hypothesis: that deep homology, even for traits as novel as language, is pervasive. The purpose of the present chapter is to give this idea careful consideration, and to consider its potential implications for future research in biolinguistics.

Before discussing the explanatory role of deep homology in language, it is worthwhile to consider carefully what we hope to explain. A crucial first step is the recognition that "language" is not a monolithic whole, but must be treated as a set of interacting but semi-independent mechanisms. Thus, I will start the chapter with a brief review of the multi-component approach, and three components (roughly speaking speech, semantics, and syntax) that need to be explained. This is both to give focus to my later discussion and to illustrate by example the value of a broad comparative approach in terms of tangible results, already achieved. In each case I will give some examples of my own work, to provide concrete evidence supporting the following, highly personal, point: my work on primates has garnered considerable attention, has been published in high-profile journals and widely cited, and has been readily funded by granting agencies. In contrast, broad comparative work that I believe is as important, on a variety of species including cranes, dogs, deer, and seals, has been harder to publish, is more rarely cited, and has proven difficult to fund. The reason for this neglect, when stated at all, has consistently been that "deer (or seals, or dogs) aren't primates, and thus aren't relevant to language." The arguments I make here about the necessity of a broad comparative approach beyond primates are not made in a vacuum, but in the real-world everyday context of what I see as a quite pervasive misconception that is detrimental to scientific progress. My personal experience is relatively unusual in that there are not that many people who do research on both primates and non-primates, but my conclusion is broadly consistent with that of others in my shoes. And my reaction to this experience is not just sour grapes (after all, I am getting cited and funded for my primate work!). But I hope these personal examples will provide some foundation for the core argument about deep homology that will follow.

7.2 Background: Three Components of FLB

The language faculty, in its broad sense (FLB hereafter, following Hauser et al. 2002; Fitch, Hauser, and Chomsky 2005), comprises many interacting components that, working together, give humans our unique power to express an unlimited range of thoughts. Many (probably most) of these components (memory, vocal production, perceptual systems, etc.) are widely shared with other species. In contrast, a few are unusual or possibly even unique to our species, and clearly differentiate us from our last common ancestor with chimpanzees. These include our capacity for complex vocal imitation, and our apparent drive to freely share information with others (our *Mitteilungs-bedürfnis*). Although the comparative data concerning syntax remain sparse, it is plausible that one or more specific abilities to extract complex hierarchical structure from acoustic sequences differentiate humans from other primates. Each of these capacities, underlying speech, semantics, and syntax, respectively, may depend on different underlying neural mechanisms that have a separate evolutionary history. Unfortunately, at present we have only sketchy knowledge of the genetic and developmental mechanisms underlying any of these unusual capacities, and must rely at present almost exclusively on comparative data to understand their provenance. I will briefly discuss these comparative data relevant to the three components of the FLB here; a more extensive discussion can be found in Fitch (2005, 2010).

7.2.1 *Vocal control*

Because speech is the default modality for communicating linguistically, the human capacity for speech has always figured prominently in discussions of language evolution. Despite considerable intelligence and imitative ability in many other domains, chimpanzees raised in a human home will not learn to speak at even a rudimentary level (Hayes 1951; Kellogg 1968). Neither general intelligence nor generalized motor control appear to be the limiting factor preventing ape speech—something more specific is involved.

A debate has gone on for centuries about whether the factor preventing chimpanzees (or indeed most animals) from speaking was their peripheral vocal anatomy or the central neural control over this vocal production system. Aristotle argued that it was the inflexible tongue of dolphins that prevented these large-brained mammals from speaking (Aristotle 350 BC), and with the discovery by Europeans of the apes, some anatomists concluded that the presence of laryngeal air sacs prevented orang-utans from speaking (Camper 1779). Darwin, considering these anatomical arguments, concluded instead that *neural* factors were key in preventing most animals from speaking (Darwin 1871). The question was reawakened, however, with the better mechanistic understanding of speech production attained in the mid-twentieth century, when Philip Lieberman and colleagues suggested that the unusual anatomical feature of a descended larynx and tongue root was a crucial prerequisite for modern human speech (Lieberman, Klatt, and Wilson 1969; Lieberman and Crelin 1971). Until recently, this reconfigured vocal anatomy was thought to be unique to *Homo sapiens*. Although these scholars never claimed that this feature was required for linguistic communication of any sort, this aspect of human vocal anatomy has been considered by many subsequent scholars to be a specific and necessary adaptation for spoken language (e.g. Pinker 1994b; Carstairs-McCarthy 1999). Unfortunately, all of this work was based on anatomical investigations of dead animals, and such data do not provide an adequate basis for understanding vocal production in living animals. X-ray investigations of vocal production in several mammal species reveals the vocal tract to be a highly dynamic and flexible system (Fitch 2000). All mammals examined thus far can dynamically lower their larynx to (or beyond) the human level. Furthermore, broader comparative study has now revealed permanently descended larynges in a variety of other mammals, including several species of deer and big cats (Fitch and Reby 2001; Weissengruber et al. 2002; Frey and Riede 2003). These new data indicate that a permanently descended larynx is neither necessary nor sufficient for attaining a human-like vocal tract configuration, consistent with Darwin's suggestion that neural control, rather than vocal anatomy, is the key factor underlying speech production in humans.

What are these neural bases of complex vocal control and imitation? The most compelling hypothesis currently available is that humans have, and other primates lack, direct connections between motor cortex and the brainstem motor neurons that control the larynx and respiration (Kuypers 1958; Jürgens 1995). Innate vocalizations in all mammals appear to be driven by the brainstem alone (for example, cats whose telencephalon has been disconnected from their brainstem can still produce normal growling, hissing and purring, in response to appropriate stimuli (Bazett and Penfield 1922)). In most mammals, this brainstem-based system has exclusive connections to the motor neurons involved in vocal production. In contrast, humans have direct (mono-synaptic) connections between cortical neurons and the laryngeal and other vocal motor neurons. The Kuypers–Jürgens hypothesis suggests that such connections are a necessity for detailed, volitional control over vocalization, and for the complex vocal imitative abilities typical of our species (Striedter 2004).

This hypothesis clearly predicts that other animals with complex vocal imitation should also possess such direct connections. This prediction is met, *mutatis mutandis*, in song-learning birds, who have direct telencephalic connections to the syringeal and respiratory motor neurons (Wild 1993). This is a beautiful example of how a convergently evolved trait can be used to test a mechanistic hypothesis, in this case yielding supportive data. However, because the avian brain and vocal production system differ considerably from that in mammals, a stronger test of the hypothesis would come from mammals capable of complex vocal learning (including some seal, whale, and dolphin species, and possibly bats and elephants as well (Janik and Slater 1997; Poole et al. 2005, Knörnschild et al. 2010)). The prediction is particularly strong for seals, which use an ordinary mammalian tongue and larynx for vocal production, and which can produce extremely convincing imitations of human speech (Ralls, Fiorelli, and Gish 1985) but there has to date been virtually no exploration of the mechanisms of vocal control and production in this or other pinniped species. My colleagues and I are currently seeking to test the Kuypers–Jürgens hypothesis in harbour seals (*Phoca vitulina*).

The comparative approach to vocal control illustrates two important points for biolinguistics. First, it is precisely the use of a broad comparative method (including investigations of dogs, goats, lions, and deer) that allows the exclusion of previous hypotheses that were based mainly on primate vocal anatomy. Second, investigation of bird vocal learning has allowed the first tests of the most plausible hypothesis concerning the neural basis for our sophisticated vocal control, and this test could not have been done in nonhuman primates (which lack complex vocal learning). A number of other tests of this hypothesis remain available, in other distant relatives. Finally, despite intensive exploration of primate vocal production, neuroanatomy and neurophysiology, we know almost nothing about pinnipeds, which provide the most promising model species to further explore the mechanisms underlying complex vocal control in mammals. I believe that this neglect derives, at least in part, from an unconscious assumption that primates are the only group truly relevant to understanding language evolution. I hope, with the examples above, to have demonstrated that this assumption is both incorrect and an active detriment to our understanding of human evolution.

7.2.2 Mitteilungsbedürfnis *(the communicative drive)*

A second crucial component of human language which differentiates it quite sharply from most animal communication systems, particularly that of chimpanzees and other primates, is the use of language to support detailed and open-ended information exchange between individuals. Humans incessantly share their complex, propositional thoughts with one another via language. The thoughts we share include not just our current internal state (anger, pleasure, hunger, fear, etc.) or external factors such as awareness of food or predators (which many other vertebrates do as well), but virtually anything we can think about. We discuss the past and the future. We discuss people and events that are not present, or who perhaps never existed. We posit invisible entities (spirits, gravity, electrons, etc.) and argue about how they influence the visible world. Although we can find some hint of some of these features if we search widely enough (e.g. honeybees inform each other of the location of food, water and shelter that are not visible at the moment), in its entirety this "breadth of communicable topics" appears at present to be absolutely unparalleled in the rest of the animal world (Hockett 1960). Not incidentally, our ability and propensity to communicate about virtually anything we can think about is crucial to culture, science, and technology, and thus to our equally unparalleled success as a species.

Our communicative capacity rests on two different bases. One is the sheer capacity to produce signals of the requisite complexity, and map them onto thoughts. This component is of course tightly tied to both syntax, and the signaling system (phonology and phonetics), and has been much discussed. Another component, however, has less frequently been singled out for attention: our *propensity* to use this capability in honest, informative information exchange. Biologists interested in animal communication have long recognized that there are serious evolutionary problems in getting co-operative signaling systems off the ground. It is quite rare that simply blurting out your knowledge of the world to random others will prove evolutionarily advantageous, and much more frequently the opposite is the case (Axelrod and Hamilton 1981; Krebs and Dawkins 1984; Dunbar 1996; Fitch and Hauser 2002; Fitch 2004). Recent work on chimpanzees has made it clear that ape cognitive skills seem highly biased to perform well in competitive situations, rather than in cooperation (reviewed in Hare and Tomasello 2004), while work on young human children demonstrates just the opposite (Tomasello 1999). These data suggest that, even if chimpanzees *had* the capacity to encode and decode arbitrary thoughts into and from signals, they might simply avoid using this ability except in specialized circumstances (e.g. mothers informing their children).

Humans, of course, have an irrepressible habit of sharing their thoughts with others. I have spent many hours watching chimpanzees at zoos, and am always amazed by the contrast between the mostly silent chimpanzees and the constantly chattering human onlookers. Perhaps this propensity to talk has escaped detailed consideration in the literature on language evolution because English lacks a specific word for this drive to share our thoughts with others. Fortunately, German has the perfect term: *Mitteilungsbedürfnis*. *Mitteilen* means 'to share' and *bedürfnis* means 'a need' or 'drive', but the composite term refers specifically to verbal communication and the basic human drive to talk and share their thoughts and feelings with others.

I suggest that human *Mitteilungsbedürfnis* (MtB) is a crucial component of linguistic communication. Without this pervasive drive to communicate, many of the other components of language, particularly those involving signal creation and parsing, would be far less useful. Because it sharply differentiates us from our nearest living relatives the chimpanzees, and is difficult to explain from the viewpoint of evolutionary theory, the human MtB deserves far more attention than it traditionally receives. The amount of MtB certainly varies, both among individuals and between cultures, and it seems plausible that we could learn much about the neural and genetic nature of this drive by making use of such naturally occurring variation. Are there neural or genetic differences between talkative and taciturn people? I know of no studies addressing this issue.

Regarding the functional evolutionary forces underlying MtB, I have suggested elsewhere that kin selection played a crucial role in driving the evolution of semantic, propositional communication (Fitch 2004, 2007a). That is, this aspect of language initially evolved for communication among kin (particularly among parents and their offspring, but also among extended family groups and all age classes), and kin selection thus provided the evolutionary path to co-operative information sharing. Only later, once the genetic bases for semantics were already in place, would reciprocal altruism have extended the set of potential interlocutors to other unrelated adults. Even today, we have different expectations of our interactions with unrelated individuals (who should be interesting, truthful, informative, on topic, etc.) than we do when communicating with our children. Note that this model of language evolution picks out, as a potential parallel, an animal species often seen to be maximally irrelevant to human language: the honey bee. For while we have no evidence for cooperative communication about non-present objects in any nonhuman primate or mammal, honey bees communicate, in the darkness of the hive, about distant and invisible food, water and shelter on a daily basis. And crucially, honey bees are the classic example of a kin-selected communication system, because all of the worker bees in a hive are sisters, and indeed are each other's closest relatives. Again, we find confirmation of a plausible theory about language evolution in very distantly related organisms. However, while this phylogenetic scenario provides a potential solution to the problem of co-operative communication, we remain in the dark about the neural and genetic mechanisms that are responsible for our species' unusual MtB, and that would allow us to test this hypothesis in our own and other species.

7.2.3 *Mechanisms of syntactic computation*

Finally, the neural computational system underlying syntax has been a major focus of research in contemporary linguistics and neuro-linguistics (Zurif and Caramazza 1976; Caplan 1987; Friederici, Steinhauer, and Pfeifer 2002; Hagoort 2005), but it has received much less adequate treatment from a comparative and evolutionary viewpoint, which has been characterized mainly by divisive and unproductive debate. Much of the debate about "animal syntax" has been characterized by a "line in the sand" approach, where linguists are seen as erecting barriers between human and animal capabilities, which animal researchers then attempt to breach. This unhelpful metaphor dates back at least to Max Müller, an anti-Darwinian Oxford philologist who stated the position very clearly: "language is the Rubicon which divides man from beast, and no animal will ever cross it... the science of language will yet enable us to withstand the extreme theories of the Darwinians, and to draw a hard and fast line between man and brute" (Müller 1861, 1873). By placing language as the key feature of humans, separating them clearly and distinctly from all animals, Müller in effect substituted language for the "esprit," or "soul," that played the key role in earlier religious writings.

A more helpful approach was that of the linguist Charles Hockett, who broke "Language" down into a number of design features, some of which Hockett believed to be unique to human language, and others which were shared (Hockett 1960, 1963). Hockett's approach prefigures the multi-component approach advocated here, and, in some ways, the FLB–FLN distinction. But even this more congenial approach seemed to act mainly as a prod for animal researchers to demonstrate Hockett's errors, and also elicited hostility. Finally, during the 1970s and 1980s, the introduction of generative models of syntax led early researchers to refute the idea that animals lacked syntax by demonstrating that simple rules underlie their vocal production. For example, Hailman and colleagues analyzed the simple sequential rule

underlying the "chick a dee" call of black-capped chickadees, concluding that
the presence of a few finite-state rules along the lines of "chicks must precede
dees" toppled claims of a uniquely human syntax (Hailman, Ficken, and
Ficken 1985, 1987). Although both sides in this long cross-disciplinary battle
probably deserve some blame, the end result has become a tradition where
each side ignores the valid points of the other.

As a result, there remains relatively little that can be said, at a concrete and
quantitative level, about the level and complexity of the rule systems governing
animal communication systems, or how these compare quantitatively with
human language (for an exception see Suzuki, Buck, and Tyack 2006). One
need only read the target article and responses in Kako (1999) to recognize that many of the questions that would be most crucial for making an
objective comparison between animal and human syntactic capacities have
yet to be asked. Kako's commentary points out that no one has even tried
to teach language-trained animals to use some of the features of human
language that do the most work (such as function words: closed-class items
like tense markers, prepositions, and auxiliary verbs); the responses from
three prominent researchers in the animal "language" world suggested that
they weren't interested in doing so. It seems, at least in this domain of
animal-language research, that linguists and animal researchers reached an
impasse.

One way out of this traditional bind is to use the mathematical underpinnings of formal-language theory, which had its roots in Chomsky's early
formal work (Chomsky 1957, 1959b, 1963). Most linguists abandoned work on
this formal foundation relatively quickly, due to the fact that it deals only
with superficial sequences of strings, and not the structural interpretations
of those strings that are central to modern natural-language syntax (Chomsky 1990). However, the theory turned out to be extremely useful in computer science, where it plays an important role today, for example in theorem
proving in parser and programming-language design (e.g. Parkes 2002). This
is now a quite well-developed branch of computer science, and remains an
important factor in computational linguistics (Huybregts 1985; Shieber 1985;
Vijay-Shanker and Weir 1994; Frank 2002; Stabler 2004). But formal language theory has an additional use in the study of animal communication,
where, with few exceptions (Suzuki et al. 2006), formal frameworks have been
eschewed.

Applying this theory to animal "syntax" raises an important difficulty. We
have no way to access the structural assignments an animal might make to a
sequence of sounds or events when looking at just its behavior. Ultimately, as
neuroscience matures, we may be able to examine structural assignment at the

neural level, but at present this is only a dream. Thus, the prime objection to formal-language theory as applied to humans (that it concerns only surface sequence and not structural assignment (Chomsky 1990)) does not apply to animal work. Together with Marc Hauser, I developed a non-verbal "grammar induction" task that can be used with animals (Fitch and Hauser 2004). The technique relies on behavioral measures, like looking time, applicable to a wide variety of species. The essential question is whether a species given a set of strings generated according to some rule can extract that rule, or whether they perhaps generalize to another different rule (or even form no rule at all). Our initial study examined cotton-top tamarins and examined the difference between a simple finite-state rule ("B must follow A," which the monkeys easily mastered) and a simple phrase-structure rule provably beyond the capacity of a finite state grammar ("the number of Bs must match the number of As"). The monkeys were consistently unable to master this latter rule in our experimental procedure. In contrast, humans readily learn both rules (Fitch and Hauser 2004; Perruchet and Rey 2005).

In an important follow-up experiment the same approach was used with starlings, a songbird species with an elaborate vocal repertoire and highly structured songs. These experiments suggested that starlings could, with extensive training, master the phrase-structure rule, and thus induce rules above the level of a finite-state grammar (Gentner et al. 2006). Despite a certain amount of confusion in this literature (particularly regarding the incorrect idea that these grammars will address the issue of recursion or center-embedding (Perruchet and Rey 2005; Gentner et al. 2006; Marcus 2006)), this fusion of experimental techniques from animal cognition with the theoretical grounding of computational linguistics offers one way beyond the impasse reached by previous debates about animal syntax. Work is ongoing at present to test a wider variety of species (including chimpanzees and further bird species), as well as human infants, to determine when the human capacity to recognize these grammars becomes available. Although these are early days, this technique and theoretical framework offers a way in which the syntactic pattern-learning abilities of many different species can be compared, using a mathematically grounded and widely understood hierarchy of complexity. Finally, at least in humans, neuro-imaging work suggests that the same approach can be used to pinpoint brain areas involved in different aspects of human syntax, and suggests that the distinction between finite-state and higher-level phrase-structure grammars may reflect a difference at the neural level as well (Friederici et al. 2006). Again, at present, only one other species appears to offer a promising animal model to explore this distinction further: and it is a songbird, not a primate.

7.2.4 *Summary: Three components to be understood*

I conclude that we must recognize the existence of multiple components of language, rather than treat it as a single monolithic construct. In seeking these sub-components we must attempt to "carve nature at the joints" and find natural divisions of the language faculty. At present we can only guess at what, precisely, these may be. In addition to a large number of widely shared components in the FLB (memory, social intelligence, motor control), there are at least some components which differentiate us from chimpanzees (otherwise chimpanzees would have language). The three components discussed above (which might be thought of as the "Three Ss": speech, syntax, and semantics) seem to represent a consensus view of the minimum number of semi-independent components required at present; there may well be more components required eventually for an adequate model. Although different theorists hold different components to be "most important," all of these are bona fide, well-documented abilities in humans that differentiate us from chimpanzees and other primates, and so need to be explained in an evolutionary account of human language. And in each case, a broad comparative approach, extending beyond primates, has been crucial in recent scientific progress.

7.3 The Tree of Life and Scala Naturae

I hope that the virtues of the broad comparative approach are now clarified. Although my focus in this chapter will be mechanistic and molecular, as discussed in Section 7.4, it is important first to clear away some persistent and widespread misconceptions about the comparative approach, conducted at the behavioral level, before moving on. This is the notion of a *scala naturae*, another pervasive and intuitive metaphor that hinders clear biological thinking (and is probably related to primatocentrism).

Living things on our planet are mind-numbingly diverse. Even familiar animals, like earthworms, butterflies, trout, ducks, cows, and cats show a remarkable variety of form and function. When we begin to consider *all* forms of life, including the plants, fungi, and a simple array of invisible microorganisms, we are faced with a variety that beggars the imagination. The traditional pre-evolutionary way of organizing this diversity is to array all of these organisms on a vast linear scale, from simple and "primitive" to complex and "advanced." This intuitive way of classifying organisms dates back, at least, to the Aristotelian notion of a *scala naturae*, a linear ordering from worms to humans (extended in medieval times to angels, archangels, and beyond). It is usual to place humans at the highest, most "perfect" end of this scale. However, it does not take much humility to recognize that there are many organisms that outclass us, who by rights might be higher on the scale than humans. The eagle's eye, the cheetah's speed, the elephant's strength, or the tortoise's longevity should be the envy of us all. Thus, the logic of a linear scale with humans at the top demands that we arrange things according to some trait at which humans excel. The traditional candidates are one or more mental faculties: man may not be the swiftest or strongest, but he is the most clever of the beasts.

One of the core insights in evolutionary theory is that this way of thinking is fundamentally erroneous, in spite of its intuitive appeal. The basic facts of the matter were clearly recognized by Darwin (1859): because of evolution, and descent with modification, the proper organizing conception of life is a tree, and not a linear scale. Evolution logically entails that all of the descendents living today (that is, members of all the species on the planet at present) have *all* been evolving from that common ancestor for an equal amount of time. Chimpanzees did not stop evolving when the split between them and humans occurred, and there is no reason to expect them to be identical behaviorally, anatomically, or genetically, with our common ancestor. In many cases we have fossil data to back this logical point up. For instance, all living seed plants evolved from a form, the seed ferns, known from fossils (Kenrick and Davis 2004). But no living plant "is" a seed fern: all of them have evolved away from that form which thus no longer exists. The undeniable conclusion is that the overall topological form of life is a tree, not a linear scale from primitive to advanced organisms.

One might object that there are forms that appear to be closer to the original ancestral form than others, and it is certainly true that morphological evolution sometimes occurs at different rates in different lineages. There is enough variation in these rates that the slowest changers are often termed "living fossils" because the living organisms are so similar to fossil forms that are millions (or hundreds of millions) of years old. Examples include horseshoe crabs or lungfish which resemble fossils from the Devonian. Although such forms are a great aid to understanding the ways of life of past forms, they are not identical to them, and in some cases may have diverged greatly in terms of physiology or behavior despite their similarity in form. Thus, biologists studying such living fossils, since Darwin, have recognized the need for caution in assuming any simple-minded identity between living and long-dead organisms. Thus, biologists still rely on the tree as their guiding and organizing metaphor, recognizing that some branches have changed more than others. This insight is a very basic one in modern biology: the only figure in Darwin's *Origin of Species* was a schematic tree of life that illustrates the points just made.

Phylogenetic trees have now become so commonplace in biology that their necessity rarely requires comment (Fitch and Margoliash 1967; Carroll 1988; Pough, Heiser, and McFarland 1996; Brocchieri, 2001).

Unfortunately, this basic insight is far less pervasive among non-biologists, and the metaphor of the *scala naturae* is used, either implicitly or sometimes explicitly, by many scholars untrained in evolutionary biology (including some neuroscientists, psychologists, linguists, philosophers, and anthropologists). Hodos and Campbell recognized the persistence of linear phylogenetic thinking in comparative psychology long ago, in a seminal paper subtitled "Why there is no theory in comparative psychology" (Hodos and Campbell 1969), and offered numerous reasons why this mode of thought is both factually incorrect and positively misleading. The notion that there is an ascending scale of "intelligence" upon which all animals take their allotted place (with humans, of course, at the top of the heap) remains common, despite a formidable array of evidence showing that, no matter how the idea is interpreted, it is wrong (Macphail 1982, 1987). To deny that there is a single scale of mental development is not, of course, to deny the obvious fact that species differ in their mental faculties. The point is that these differently developed faculties cannot be arranged in a simple linear fashion. Categorization based on a linear scale fails, because the shape of phylogeny itself is not a line. Thus, for example, there is steadily increasing consensus that the most intelligent birds show skills, in terms of both physical and social intelligence, closely matching those shown by the highest-performing mammals or primates (e.g. Emery and Clayton 2004). This should not be surprising, since birds have been evolving at the same time as mammals and have faced many of the same cognitive challenges. Birds are not ancestors of mammals in any sense, and there is no reason to expect them to preserve only the simple, primitive characteristics of vertebrates from millions of years ago. Nonetheless, researchers on avian intelligence have had a difficult time, until very recently, convincing others of these facts.

One might fear that abandoning the idea that there are "primitive" organisms robs us of one of our most powerful tools in understanding evolution. Behaviour does not fossilize, and our most powerful tool for understanding the evolution of behaviour must therefore be the study of living forms. But if Darwin is right, and living forms do not actually preserve the primitive behaviours of their extinct ancestors, how are we to know anything at all about these ancestors? Fortunately, biologists today continue to use living forms as their most important tool for understanding the past. The key realization is that although none of today's organisms are *themselves* the ancestral form, we can use comparative study of multiple living descendents to *reconstruct* that long-extinct ancestor. Each living organism is conceptualized as a composite, or mosaic, of features. Some of these are *primitive* in the sense of not having changed from the ancestral state; others are *derived* in the sense that they have changed. Although no single organism may have entirely primitive features, by examining a set of related organisms we can infer which features are primitive and which are not. This, in a nutshell, is the core insight of the modern comparative approach.

Thus, we can derive strong inferences about long-extinct forms from their living descendents. But we cannot choose one living form and assume it is identical to the extinct ancestor. Fortunately, once the power of this insight is appreciated, we can see that the great diversity of life is our most powerful tool for understanding evolution. Even if we have no relevant fossils at all, and all living forms exhibit highly derived traits in one domain or another, we can nonetheless use a broad comparative approach to reconstruct a series of past ancestors, from early single-celled organisms, all the way to any particular terminal branch of the tree of life (be it a beetle, a tree, a chicken, or our own species). In order to accomplish this we need to take the whole tree of life as the potentially relevant field, and then choose the subtree that branches out from a particular ancestor. By carefully examining and comparing all of the living descendents of that ancestor, we can derive inferences about its nature. In some cases, where the number of descendent species is large and well studied, these inferences can be very strong ones. In other cases our data is more partial, and our inferences less certain. In the worst case, we may be capable of only a partial, tentative reconstruction, with many question marks, due to a lack of living species (or knowledge of these species). But today, a very powerful suite of tools are available for comparative analyses, including appropriate statistical techniques (Pagel 1992) and powerful molecular tools for reconstructing phylogenies (Whelan 2001).

To give a sense of the power of a broad and explicit comparative approach, which takes the entire tree of life as its domain, let us consider our ancestors at different time depths. Humans are simultaneously primates, mammals, tetrapods, vertebrates, animals, and eukaryotes. Each of the ever-broader categories includes more and more extant species as our relatives, by mutual descent, from a last common ancestor (LCA) whose nature can be reconstructed by carefully comparing these living species. In some cases, we additionally have fossils to verify and extend these reconstructions (e.g. in the case of early vertebrates or mammals the fossil record is quite good). In other cases, however, the common ancestor has not been identified with any fossils and perhaps never will, but there is nonetheless a huge amount that can be confidently deduced about this ancestor. I will simply sketch out what we know, without giving the detailed evidence for how we know this (for further detail see Cracraft and Donoghue 2004; Dawkins 2004).

The most basic category to which we humans belong is "living thing." Already at this level there is a considerable amount that we share with all other living things at the molecular level, most prominently the genetic code which uses DNA/RNA base-pairs to code for the specific amino acids making up proteins. With a few quite minor exceptions, this code is shared by all living organisms today, meaning that it dates back to at least 3.5 billion years (when the first fossil signs of life can be found). These early living cells would closely resemble what we today call bacteria, although their biochemical nature was probably quite different because the earth at that time had very little oxygen in its atmosphere. Indeed, the generation of oxygen by early plants, and the subsequent oxygenation of the planet's atmosphere, was one of the first and most profound changes wrought by living things.

Another early and important single-celled ancestor was the common ancestor of all eukaryotes. *Eukaryotes* include animals, plants, and fungi, as well as a great diversity of single-celled Protists (amoebae, paramecium, yeast, etc.). All living things except bacteria and the bacteria-like Archaea are thus eukaryotic. Eukaryotes represented a major leap in the complexity of the cell. Most prominently, eukaryotic cells have a circumscribed nucleus housing the genetic material, organized into chromosomes. Eukaryotes also possess various organelles (such as the mitochondria that play a central role in metabolism and energy transformation, or, in plants, the chloroplasts which are the site of photosynthesis). Eukaryotes share a broad suite of traits at the level of cell structure, as well as most basic enzymes and metabolic processes. Thus, all of the main properties of each of the trillions of cells in our body had already evolved at this point and are shared with almost all living eukaryotes (one reason that yeast is such a useful model species for many aspects of human cells). Interestingly, it is now widely accepted that at least some organelles represent an ancient symbiosis between previously independent organisms: a fusion of different "bacterial" cell types. Thus, at the very earliest stages, the topology of the tree of life was actually a weblike net, rather than a well-formed tree *per se*, and the ability of bacteria even today to transfer genes among different "species" also shows that the tree metaphor is imperfect at this level. However, beyond this simple level of cellular organization, and for all multicellular organisms, the tree remains a perfect description of topology.

Another major advance in complexity was the formation of multi-cellular organisms (*metazoans*). Living things had already evolved around 3.5 billion years ago, only roughly one billion years after the Earth itself was born, but metazoans did not appear until perhaps 600 million years ago. Thus, around three quarters of our evolution as living things was spent as a single cell. This fact is perhaps rendered less surprising by the fact that each of us, in our individual ontogeny, also began as a single cell: a fertilized egg. This commonplace fact deserves notice, because at the molecular level many of the genes involved in development date back to these early days. Thus, processes involving intercellular communication, and the differentiation into different cell types, evolved in these early pioneering days of multicellularity. Thus, perhaps surprisingly, genes that play a key role in brain development, like the Hox genes discussed below, already existed and played a role in development in organisms like sponges which have no nervous system at all.

We reach an ancestor whose descendents share a diversity of morphological features when we consider the bilaterians. The *bilaterians* include the great diversity of living animals whose basic body plan is bilaterally symmetrical: the main three groups are insects, crabs, and other arthropods, clams, snails, squid, and other mollusks, and finally fish, birds, dogs, and other vertebrates. This group also includes some clades, like the echinoderms (sea urchins, starfish, crinoids, and their ilk) who are not bilaterally, but radially, symmetrical. At this level, as we will discuss in detail below, there is a surprising amount of conservation of the specific genetic basis for building complex bodies, the eyes and the nervous system. This shared developmental toolkit must therefore have already been present in the common ancestor of bilaterians (sometimes dubbed the *Ur-bilaterian*). This degree of conservation is very surprising given the diversity of body plans that this conserved genetic toolkit creates, and provides the paragon case for deep homology.

Finally we reach the more familiar level of the *vertebrates* (animals with backbones including fish, amphibians, reptiles, mammals, and birds), a point where most proteins are shared at the level of their specific amino-acid sequences, such that clear homologues can be identified for most human genes in fish. Perhaps more importantly, the basic design of the vertebrate brain, including its overall form, basic tissue types, and molecular resources (neurotransmitters and receptors) was already laid down in early ancestral fish. This basic neural chassis has persisted right up to the brain of modern birds or mammals. Although different brain areas expand in active clades like birds and mammals (e.g. the forebrain or telencephalon), these regions are also present in fish, and develop according to the same basic principles. Thus, fish are the most distant relatives that share with us a vertebrate brain that develops and operates according the same principles as our own.

Among mammals, the class of dogs, cats, cows, horses, dolphins, bats, rodents, and primates, shared traits include details of our inner ear, possession of hair (in various amounts), and a novel layered tissue organization in the brain, the *neocortex*. Again, this tissue develops by conserved rules, and the detailed circuitry underlying language in humans has its root in these basic principles.

7.4 Deep Homology at the Molecular Level: Theory and Two Examples

Most of what I have written in this chapter thus far would have made sense to Darwin; it represents a tradition very well-rooted in contemporary biology. The incorrect notion of a line of descent upon which species can be ordered as higher and lower remains as an occasional figure of speech in biology (e.g. "lower mammals"), and as a powerful guiding image for some psychologists, linguists, and anthropologists, it is widely recognized as an erroneous and unhelpful metaphor for those interested in either understanding evolution, or integrating comparative data. This much is already so well established in the biological literature as to represent a mostly unspoken truism, and difficult to find explicitly stated other than textbooks and the older literature (Hodos and Campbell 1969). I have seen biologists simply shake their heads and walk away when they hear their colleagues from other disciplines try to use the *scala naturae* metaphor scientifically at inter-disciplinary conferences and workshops. This much is already well-understood, so I will not belabor it further.

But there is a different reason why a very broad comparative perspective is likely to prove extremely useful in understanding the biology of language: the profound conservatism of the genes involved in development. This new and exciting phenomenon would have been completely foreign to Darwin (who knew nothing of genes). Furthermore, its discovery represented a complete reversal of expectations for biologists when it became clear, in the mid-1980s, that certain genes were so conserved, over a billion years of evolution, that a gene from a mouse could perform "the same" task in a fly. As we shall see below, discussing eye evolution, these findings strike at the very core of the concept of homology, demanding a far more nuanced and mechanistically explicit notion of what it means for two species (or two traits) to be the the same (or different). It is now becoming clear that the most basic and powerful genes involved in development are not the genes that build the proteins making up the cell (things like myosin for muscle, or hemoglobin for blood cells)—these proteins remain virtually identical in function across a wide range of species. Instead, it is the *expression* of genes that appears to play key roles in development and evolution. So far, the crucial genes are typically members of a broad class of genes coding for *transcription factors*—proteins which bind to DNA, and thus affect the expression of other genes.

In the next sections I will briefly recap the discovery of this class of genes, focusing on the extremely conserved homeobox or Hox genes. Then I will discuss the implications of such conservation for our notions of homology, using the example of "paired box" or Pax genes, which play a crucial role in the development of eyes in organisms as diverse as jellyfish, flies, squid, and humans. This is striking because squid and human eyes are a (if not the) textbook case of convergent evolution—the common ancestor of mollusks and vertebrates did not have a complex camera eye. This possibility, that a structure could be evolved independently, but nonetheless be based on the same molecular developmental mechanisms, is the one that I argue will prove crucial for understanding the evolution of language. Because this discussion inevitably entails a certain amount of molecular biology, which I assume will be unfamiliar to many readers, I will describe the stages of discovery in chronological terms which should make the ideas more digestible. I do not, however, intend this as a detailed history, and I apologize that the contributions of many workers and labs go unmentioned.

7.4.1 *Transcription factors and gene regulation*

Because, with few exceptions, every one of the trillions of cells in your body contains all of your DNA, any cell contains DNA which is not always needed for its particular day-to-day function. Thus, the expression of DNA must be regulated in some fashion. In the early days of molecular biology, it was discovered that some genes in bacteria could act as switches that turn other genes on and off. The classic example is the *lac operon*. An operon represents a set of genes controlled by an *operator* (hence the term "operon"). The genes whose expression needs to be controlled are structural genes. For example, in the lac operon the crucial genes code for lactase, an enzyme allowing the bacteria to break down lactose sugar. The operator is a bit of DNA upstream from the lactose genes, to which a special protein can bind and inhibit lactase gene expression, that is, prevent their *transcription* from the DNA code into messenger RNA that will build the corresponding proteins. In the lac operon, the crucial regulatory protein is a *repressor*, coded by a gene that is not part of the operon itself. In its normal state, this repressor protein is tightly bound to operator and blocks downstream expression. As long as the bacterium encounters no lactose, it needs no lactase to digest it, so the repressor stays bound to its DNA and the lactase gene remains unexpressed. When lactose *is* encountered, the lactose itself binds to the repressor, changing the form of the repressor protein so that it unbinds from the DNA. Now the way is clear and the crucial structural protein can be expressed.

The discovery of operons marked a major conceptual breakthrough in understanding gene expression at a mechanistic level, and the discovery of the *lac operon*, reported in 1960, earned François Jacob and Jacques Monod the Nobel Prize in Medicine in 1965. Unfortunately, it gradually became clear that gene expression in non-bacteria such as plants and animals is far more complex than this, and operons are found exclusively in bacteria and some worms. However, the same basic principle—genes that control the expression of other genes via DNA-binding—remains applicable. Proteins that bind to DNA and regulate the expression of other genes are called *transcription factors* (the lactase repressor just discussed is one example of a transcription factor). The term "transcription factor" may occasionally be extended to the genes which code these proteins. There is a crucial distinction to be made between such genes (regulatory genes) and structural genes that build enzymes and proteins. All of the genes we will discuss below are regulatory genes coding for transcription factors deriving from regulatory genes. It is increasingly apparent that much of evolutionary change results from relatively minor changes in the genes that code for transcription factors and/or the bits of DNA to which these factors bind (their "binding sites").

7.4.2 *Deep homology I: Homeotic mutants and Hox genes*

The crucial discoveries regarding the mechanisms underlying development in eukaryotes came initially from studies of the fruit fly *Drosophila melanogaster*. This species (affectionately known as "the fly" by molecular biologists) had become a workhorse species for genetics in the early twentieth century and remains the best understood complex animal, mainly because of an extensive set of mutations affecting diverse aspects of its biology. A special class of mutants had been discovered early on in which whole organs changed their structure to resemble other organs. For example, the *Antennapedia* mutant has well-formed legs attached to its head, in place of its antennae. In the same way, a similar mutant fruit fly has four wings instead of the two wings typical of the entire fly order. In these mutants, the halteres (reduced wings which serve as balancing organs in normal flies) are transformed into full-sized wings. This type of wholesale transformation of one organ into another was termed "homeosis" by William Bateson in 1894, and the general class of mutations were accordingly dubbed *homeotic mutants*. Bateson saw these mutants as posing a serious problem for Darwin's blanket statement that evolution must be gradual, for they represented a massive change in phenotype from one generation to the next. However, most of Bateson's contemporaries agreed with

Darwin's estimation that such nonfunctional mutants, which the Victorians called "monstrosities," were of no import in the evolutionary process.

Nonetheless, fascination with homeotic mutants continued, especially in the genetic world, for they seemed to promise some understanding of the nature of development. Work over a period of twenty years, much of it in the laboratory of Walter Gehring in Basel (Gehring 1994, 1998), focused on Antennapedia mutants, slowly uncovered the genetic basis for these homeotic mutant flies. This work culminated, in 1984, in the simultaneous discovery in two laboratories of the *homeobox*: a short segment of heavily conserved DNA that codes a "homeodomain" protein that binds tightly to certain chunks of DNA. Just as in bacterial operons, eukaryote DNA can be bound by one or more homeodomain proteins which then regulate the expression of nearby genes. The regulated genes may be structural, as in the lac operon, or may be other regulatory genes. In the latter case, we see the outlines of a regulatory network where genes regulate genes that regulate genes, all through the mechanism of DNA-binding proteins. These gene networks appear to be organized in a partly hierarchical fashion, where master control genes high in the hierarchy influence the expression of scores or hundreds of other regulatory genes, which finally control structural genes. The homeobox genes were the first genes to be discovered of this class, and as their number multiplied, they were given the contracted three-letter identifier *Hox* to allow a simple and consistent terminology (Hox-A1, Hox D3, etc.).

The discovery of Hox genes in *Drosophila* would have been momentous, even if it were limited to that fly species. But the big surprise was not that such genes existed. Rather the surprise came when researchers in Gehring's lab decided to look for similar genes in other species, such as the frog species *Xenopus laevis* and in mice. What they found were genes that were not just similar, but *identical,* at the amino acid level of the homeodomain. A striking illustration of this was provided when McGinnis and co-workers in Gehring's lab were able to rescue a mutant fly by injecting the fly embryos with the unmutated genes from vertebrates. A flurry of work around this time quickly established the facts: Hox genes are shared among virtually all animal lineages, and are highly conserved both in the sense of high sequence similarity and in that they play similar roles in development. Even their ordering on the chromosome has been preserved over more than a billion years of separate evolution: It has now become clear that most invertebrates have a single set of Hox genes, laid out in a cluster that is normally expressed sequentially during development and along the major body axis of the embryo. Although vertebrates have extra copies of this cluster (humans, birds, amphibians, and most fish have four clusters, which apparently arose by gene duplication very early in vertebrate phylogeny), the ordering of the genes on the chromosomes has been conserved in each of them.

Thus, organs that are clearly analogs, not homologs (such as the wings of insects and birds), nonetheless share a deeply conserved genetic basis. This basis includes not only the genes themselves and the proteins that they code, but the overall layout of these genes on the chromosome, the order in which they are expressed during development, and their upstream regulators and downstream targets (Carroll, Grenier, and Weatherbee 2005). This level of conservation is clearly *not* the result of convergent evolution, but reflects the preservation of gene clusters that were present in the worm-like common ancestor of vertebrates and flies. Thus, at the genetic level, these structures share a homologous developmental program: a situation that has been dubbed *deep homology* (Shubin, Tabin, and Carroll 1997; Carroll 2008). Organs that evolved convergently (and are thus homoplastic at the surface level) are nonetheless generated by a conserved genetic mechanism (and are thus homologous at the deep, developmental level).

Today, Hox genes are a major focus of research in molecular genetics, and their implications for development and evolution remain a very hot topic (Pearson, Lemons, and McGinnis 2005). The new approach to evolution which has resulted from the discovery of broadly shared genetic mechanisms, called evolutionary–developmental biology or *evo–devo*, has taken the basic insights first derived from Hox genes and applied them to an ever-widening group of organisms and of new types of transcription factors (Hall 1998; Arthur 2002; Carroll 2005a). It is now apparent that minor changes in Hox gene sequences can have major, discontinuous effects on morphology (Ronshaugen, McGinnis, and McGinnis 2002). Furthermore, the time depth of the Hox genes has been pushed back to the very origin of multi-cellular forms: Hox genes exist in sponges and play a role in cell differentiation and proliferation that is functionally related to the role they play in insects or vertebrates (Coutinho et al. 2003). The field is rapidly expanding to the point where it will become difficult for any single individual to read and understand all of the literature on Hox genes, but it is already clear that there are fascinating new twists in the story still to be unraveled (e.g. the existence of micro-RNA genes within Hox gene clusters (Pearson et al. 2005)). It has also become clear that changes in coding sequence (leading to changes in the protein transcribed) are only the tip of the iceberg, and that changes in the non-coding DNA are also crucial, though more challenging to understand (Carroll 2005b). Some of the key data supporting this claim comes from the whole-genome sequencing of birds and fish (Aparicio et al. 1995, Aparicio et al. 2002; International Chicken Genome

Sequencing Consortium 2004), which show non-coding regulatory sequence conservation over a period of 500 million years. The take-home message from all this work is that a quiet revolution has occurred in biology during which it became clear that the genetic programs that determine development are far more universal than anyone would have imagined a few years earlier.

7.4.3 *Deep homology II: Pax genes and the evolution of eyes*

Another remarkable example of deep homology concerns the gene *Pax6*, a member of the "paired box" family of transcription factors that plays an important role in the development of eyes in diverse organisms. Light-sensing organs come in many different forms in the animal kingdom, including the simplest patches of light-sensitive skin on a flatworm, eyes with a simple pin-hole lens and highly complex "camera" eyes, like our own, that include an image-forming lens, a light-controlling diaphragm, and a complex retina upon which the image falls and is converted to action potentials for further neural processing. The complexity of the camera eye might seem intuitively to pose problems for an evolutionary account (it remains a favorite example of irreducible complexity for Creationists); however, Darwin had already shown how the diversity of eyes existing today in various organisms can be arranged in a sequence of increasing complexity, each stage of which is a small but functional improvement on the preceding stage (Darwin 1859). The eye is today seen as an excellent example of the possibility of small transitions leading to an "organ of extreme perfection" (Walls 1942; Nilsson and Pelger 1994; Fernald 2000) and poses no problem for evolutionary theory in the broad sense.

However, recent increases in our understanding of eye evolution at the molecular level do pose interesting challenges for our understanding of homology. There is little question that the striking similarity in anatomy between vertebrate eyes and the camera eye in mollusks such as squid or octopus is the result of convergent evolution. This is because (1) there is no reason to suspect that the common ancestor of mollusks and vertebrates, the wormlike Ur-bilaterian of the late pre-Cambrian, had an image forming eye (if it had, virtually all of the species descended from it *lost* this trait, and only a few retained it); (2) at the level of microanatomy these two organs are very different (for example, the photoreceptors in the squid eye are located in the inner layer of the retina, where they are the first cells upon which light falls, while our own retina, like that of all vertebrates, has the opposite arrangement); (3) the developmental process leading to the lens and iris is completely different in squid and vertebrate. Such considerations have led generations of morphologists to the conclusion that the eye has evolved independently—convergently—in many different taxa.

Thus, it was with considerable surprise that the initial sequencing of the gene responsible for the eyeless mutant fly type, now called Pax6, revealed that precisely the same gene leads to eye deformation when mutated in mice and humans (the mouse "small eye" mutation, and the Aniridia mutation in humans) (Quiring et al. 1994). Furthermore, expression of this gene in Drosophila embryos generates well-formed ectopic (out-of-place) eyes, and such ectopic eyes result when the gene taken from diverse organisms is used (including mice, humans, and squid), which led to the idea that Pax6 is a master control gene for eye formation (Gehring and Ikeo 1999). Although the initial thought was that there was a well-formed eye in the Ur-bilaterian, despite the evidence cited above most scholars now see the situation as more complex and consider Pax6 to be another example of deep homology (Tomarev et al. 1997; van Heyningen and Williamson 2002). It has become clear that Pax6 is a member of a team of several "master" genes involved in eye formation, and that Pax6 also plays a role in the olfactory system and is expressed in a diversity of other locations (Simpson and Price 2002; van Heyningen and Williamson 2002). As for the Hox genes, Pax genes can be traced back to early metazoans: the cubozoan jellyfish *Tripedalia* has combined eye/balancing organs dependent upon PaxB expression (Sun et al. 1997; Piatigorsky and Kozmik 2004). Again, as for Hox genes, a series of gene duplications and subsequent divergence seems to have generated the large family of Pax genes present in mollusks, insects and vertebrates today, but the basic sequence structure as well as the functional role of up- and down-stream genes associated with Pax has been largely preserved.

7.4.4 *Implications of Hox and Pax genes for homology*

The discovery of this extreme conservatism in Hox and Pax genes (and, we now know, many other similar transcription factors) must constitute one of the most surprising discoveries in the entire history of biology. Virtually no one expected that there would be substantial sharing of genes between taxa as disparate as flies, worms, fish, birds, and mammals. Raw sequence similarity approaching identity was surprising enough in such distantly related organisms. Sharing at this detailed level, where whole clusters of genes are shared, along with their ordering on chromosomes and temporal expression pattern, was simply astounding to most biologists. Darwin would have been delighted: what more powerful illustration of the unity of life and the correctness of his core ideas about evolution could be hoped for? Despite their initial surprise, all practicing biologists today accept these findings as facts, and the Hox gene story is already textbook knowledge, taught to beginning biology students. But although the facts of the matter are clear, the discovery of Hox genes raised deep questions about the nature of homology, and demanded that evolutionary theorists revisit the traditional notion of homology from a much more explicit and nuanced perspective (Hall 1994; Shubin et al. 1997; Hall 2003). These questions remain active today.

One uncontroversial revision of homology echoes, at the genetic level, a distinction that had already been made by Darwin as well as his traditional opponent Richard Owen, who coined the term homology (Owen 1846; Panchen 1994). This is the distinction between homology within an organism (so-called segmental of *serial homology*) from that between different species (often simply termed homology). Each of the human ribs or vertebrae is a serial homolog of the others; hands and feet are serial homologs. Each of a centipedes' many legs is also a serial homolog of the others. For Owen a homolog was simply "the same organ under every variety of form and function" leaving "same" up to intuition; as an anti-evolutionist Owen would have strongly opposed the modern term which stipulates "shared by virtue of descent from a common ancestor" as the concept at the core of homology.

In contrast, human hands are also said to be homologous to bat's wings or dolphin's flippers in the second sense of this term. The discovery of Hox genes illustrated a similar distinction at the molecular level. We now know that the regular pattern of gene expression that generate the body segments carrying centipede legs are shared with those generating the vertebrae and ribs in humans and other mammals. These are obviously two quite different things, and the terms paralogous and orthologous have been coined to distinguish these senses. *Paralogous* genes correspond to other genes within the same organism. Thus, if a pair of genes arises by gene duplication they are paralogs. *Orthologous* genes are those that are shared by common descent between different species. Thus, both paralogs and orthologs reflect common descent and subsequent modification, but the branching event for paralogs is a *gene* duplication, while orthologs result from a speciation event. Both orthology and paralogy are important concepts in understanding development and evolution at the molecular level.

It is important to note that these new versions of gene-level homology are not about function. Just as bat's wings and human hands are homologous but have different function, either type of homolog at the genetic level could have the same, or a different, function from the gene(s) with which it is paired (Theissen 2002). Similarity of function never was, and still is not, a prerequisite of homology. However, as we have just seen with the Hox genes, similarity may be conserved over immense time periods, and this is where the combination of a broad comparative approach and the molecular, evo–devo approach to biology and evolution may have important implications for our understanding of language.

7.5 Deep Homology in Language

Returning to the various components comprising the FLB, we would be unsurprised to find that broadly shared components of the language faculty such as memory, auditory perception or motor control are widely shared with other vertebrates (Lieberman 2000). More basic aspects of function at the neural level might be expected to be even more widely shared, given the fact that the neuronal cell type evolved early in metazoan evolution and similar genes have been involved in nervous system patterning since that time (Sun et al. 1997; Piatigorsky and Kozmik 2004). But one might question whether those functions that appear to differentiate language from other primate communication systems—the three Ss described previously—could be profitably considered from a comparative perspective at all, given that they seem unusual, if not unique, to our species. How likely is it that these apparently novel aspects of human nervous function would have a mechanistic basis with other living organisms?

I argue that the data just reviewed suggest that this is not just a real possibility, but quite likely. That is, I will argue that the degree of well-documented genetic conservation in other aspects of development strongly suggests that at least some "novel" aspects of human language will turn out to be based on mechanisms that are widely shared with other organisms far more distantly related to us than chimpanzees. That is, I suggest that distant relatives such as deer, seals, birds, and bats, which lack language, have nonetheless solved similar functional problems by using the same developmental mechanisms, from the genetic toolkit widely shared among (at least) vertebrates. In other words, I am suggesting that deep homology may turn out to be a characteristic of the language faculty, just as it is in body plan development or eye determination.

This may seem a rather wild speculation to some readers. But the well-documented existence of deep homology in the case of Hox and Pax genes would have seemed just as wild to biologists in the 1970s. What is more, for the single language-related gene that we currently know a fair bit about—FoxP2—it is already clear that there is a deep homology with respect to bird song (Haesler et al. 2004; Scharff and Haesler 2005; Wada et al. 2006), as I will discuss below. Thus, although opinions can still vary concerning the likelihood that deep homology will be common, the little presently existing data already force us to recognize it as a reality. Only time will tell if deep homology in the FLB is rife, or a rarity, but the possibility of deep homology for linguistic mechanisms can no longer be ignored. Allow me first to argue the case for deep homology and the FoxP2 gene.

7.5.1 *Deep homology III: FoxP2 and vocal learning*

FoxP2 is a gene involved in human oro-motor control. It is another transcription factor, widely shared among vertebrates. Particularly relevant to my thesis in this chapter, FoxP2 has recently been shown to play a crucial role in song learning in birds. Because this is one of the best-known genes at present, I will keep my review brief: more detailed recent reviews can be found in Marcus and Fisher (2003) and Vargha-Khadem et al. (2005). I will follow the convention that the human version of this gene is denoted with capitals (FOXP2) while the mouse version, shared with many other mammals but different from that in humans is lower-case (FoxP2). FOXP2 first attained prominence with a widely cited paper in *Nature* by Myrna Gopnik. Gopnik studied members of a large family, the KE family, living in London, many of whose members suffer from a severe congenital dysphasia. The genetic basis for this disorder assorted as if caused by a single gene. Gopnik's short paper concluded that the roots of this dysphasia "probably lie in the underlying grammar rather than in a peripheral processing system," and led to the idea that the gene in question was a "grammar gene" (Pinker 1994b). However, detailed work by Faraneh Varga-Khadem and her colleagues reached a different conclusion, namely, that the core deficit is one of oro-motor praxis, with other deficits being subsequent to this (Vargha-Khadem and Passingham 1990; Vargha-Khadem et al. 1995). Meanwhile, intensive genetic work had narrowed the mutation in the KE family down to a small segment of chromosome 7, containing some 70 separate genes. The fortuitous discovery of an unrelated individual with similar symptoms and a chromosomal rearrangement in the middle of this segment finally led to the pinpointing of the crucial gene.

The gene thus located was a member of yet another family of transcription factors encoding a "forkhead box," and thus abbreviated as *Fox* genes (Granadino, Pérez-Sánchez, and Rey-Campos 2000). This extensive family are given letter number codes, as for the Hox genes. The KE mutation was in a novel Fox gene in the P group, and the gene was thus named *FOXP2* (Lai et al. 2001). The mutation in the KE family alters an amino acid that is invariant in all normal versions of this gene, in any species, and thus appears to be a "knockout" of the gene's normal function. Once the gene had been discovered and sequenced, it was relatively easy to compare it with similar genes in other species, which is where things got interesting from an evolutionary viewpoint. When Wolfgang Enard and colleagues in Svante Pääbo's laboratory in Leipzig sequenced the FoxP2 gene in humans, mice, and a variety of primates, they found a surprising degree of conservatism across mammals: all non-human primates sequenced had genes encoding an identical protein sequence (rhesus monkey, chimpanzee, and gorilla were identical, apart from a long, variable sequence of polyglutamine repeats) (Enard et al. 2002). These species differed in only one place from the mouse. However, the human gene is different at two amino acids from that of the chimpanzee or other primates. Furthermore, these changes are universally present in normal humans. By sequencing flanking regions of the gene from various human populations, Enard and colleagues were able to roughly calculate the timing of the selective sweep that led to the fixation of the novel allele among humans to about 120,000 years before explosive growth of the human population began (thus, roughly 200,000 years ago in total). Thus, for the first time in biological history, scientists were able to pinpoint a gene indubitably involved in spoken language, which is both shared among all normal humans and different from that of chimpanzees and other primates.

The discovery of FOXP2 led to a flurry of activity examining the gene in other mammals. It transpires that FoxP2 is, like the Hox and Pax genes, a very heavily conserved transcription factor: when compared with a collection of 1,880 human–mouse gene pairs, FOXP2 is among the 5 percent most-conserved proteins. Nonetheless, humans have endured two substitutions, which are likely to be functionally relevant in that they are within the DNA-binding region of the protein (one of which, interestingly, has also occurred in carnivores (Zhang, Webb, and Podlaha 2002)).

FoxP2 is also present, and has been sequenced, in songbirds, which are of particular interest in that they share the human capacity for complex vocal learning (Zhang et al. 2002; Scharff and Haesler 2005). Although the gene does not appear to differentiate vocal-learning birds from those that lack this capacity, and birds do not share the human substitutions just discussed (Webb and Zhang 2005), FoxP2 nonetheless plays a role in vocal learning (Haesler et al. 2004; Teramitsu et al. 2004). The clearest evidence for this thus far comes from an experiment in which Foxp2 expression is experimentally decreased in young male birds in the midst of song learning, and a significant decrease in the fidelity of the learned song is observed (Haesler et al. 2007). The molecular and neural basis for this effect is beginning to be unraveled in the songbird model, and FoxP2 expression appears to play a role in determining a special class of spiny neurons in Area X, an important region in songbird vocal learning (Rochefort et al. 2007).

There are number of important take-home points regarding FoxP2. It is a transcription factor controlling expression of many other genes, supporting the evo–devo idea that many of the phylogenetic changes we see in phenotypes reflect changes in gene expression (Carroll 2003). It is broadly shared with other vertebrates, existing as a nearly exact homolog in most mammals as well as in birds, and belongs to a family that is even more widely shared among animals (such a fruit flies), indicating that novel functions (vocal learning) can build on ancient foundations. Furthermore, the gene plays a role in song learning in birds (Haesler et al. 2007) consistent with deep homology (homologous developmental mechanisms) in vocal learning (convergently evolved in humans and birds). Finally, the changes in protein-coding in the human version of this gene are very small—an apparently trivial few amino acids. Yet, these small changes have appreciable phenotypic effects: mice which have been genetically engineered to have the human version of the gene show significant neural differences from wild-type mice, including changes in dopamine levels and neuronal morphology, that appear linked to complex motor control (Enard et al. 2009).

It should go without saying the FoxP2 is not "the language gene" (despite pronouncements in the popular press to this effect), and that many more genes will eventually be discovered to play crucial roles in the development of the language faculty. Some interesting new candidates are the genes ASPM and microcephalin, which play an important role in increased brain size of our species (Bond et al. 2002; Zhang 2003; Evans et al. 2004; Kouprina et al. 2004), though not, apparently, in controlling brain-size differences within the species (Woods et al. 2006). Surprisingly, variants of these genes have been found to co-vary with a linguistic trait: the likelihood of tonal languages (specifically the use of pitch to convey lexical or grammatical distinctions), across the globe (Dediu and Ladd, 2007). Although this story remains to be worked out, this correlation raises the possibility of a causal relationship between within-species genetic variation and linguistic variation, which, if true, would violate one of the most basic assumptions in linguistic theory (and human biology more generally): that all normal humans could learn any of the world's languages with precisely equal ease. While still highly speculative, we should have a far better sense of the truth of this radical suggestion within a decade.

Discovery of genes involved in language, so far, has been a haphazard game, mostly dependent on luck. The existence of a large family like the KE family with a large pedigree of affected and unaffected members and a single-gene mutation is highly unusual, and we cannot count on such luck for most of the genes involved in the FLB. I suggest that the fastest route to finding further genes is to consider the following strong hypothesis.

The "Pervasive Deep Homology" Hypothesis

Despite its uniqueness at the phenotypic level, human language (FLB) is generated by mechanisms that are broadly shared, at the genotypic level, with other animals. More specifically, both regulatory genes (Hox, Pax, Fox, etc.) and housekeeping genes (genes building enzymes, neurotransmitters and receptors, cell structures, etc.) involved in language will have clear orthologs in other species. The critical changes in the human genome that underlie the multiple mechanisms of the FLB will be either small tweaks to these orthologous genes at the sequence level (as in FoxP2), or possibly larger changes in paralogous genes, following recent gene duplication events. Finally, the changes in phenotype and function caused by such genotypic changes will have direct parallels in other extant species (though not necessarily in cognitive domains having anything to do with communication), constituting deep homology as already documented for the evolution of eyes, limbs and vocal learning.

As already intimated above, this hypothesis would have seemed absolutely crazy two decades ago, before the discovery of Hox genes, and may strike some as highly implausible even today. This hypothesis is quite strong (in the sense of being readily falsifiable): I have phrased it this way purposefully. But strong and provocative hypotheses play an important role in science, and I think the examples discussed in this chapter make this particular hypothesis not only plausible but, at least for most aspects of the FLB, very likely true. There may well exist aspects of language that are truly unique to humans, and to language, at the phenotypic level (members of the subset of the FLB that my colleagues and I have dubbed the FLN; Hauser et al. 2002), but their specific genetic basis might nonetheless turn out to be shared. That is, traits that are truly unique to human language may nonetheless result from more basic aspects of cell morphology and/or function, or principles of neural development, that are shared, perhaps broadly, with other species. Thus, I will go so far as to suggest that the PDH hypothesis should be treated as the default in biolinguistics, assumed till proven otherwise.

7.6 Conclusions

I have argued that traditional conceptions of the comparative approach and a considerable amount of new molecular data both point in the same direction: we must broaden our conceptions of the nonhuman species that are likely to be useful "model systems" in the study of human language. When we begin to ask questions about genes for language, the distinctions between traditional superficial homology and deep homology will become increasingly important. Hypothetically, we can imagine several situations at the molecular genetic level which cross-cut traditional debates about "continuity" vs. uniqueness, or about catastrophic sudden evolution of a trait vs. gradualistic evolution.

For example, let us accept for the sake of argument the widely held view that language evolved from the pre-existing vocal communication system of some early primate. Although the functional system might have remained the same, the large difference in flexibility and expressiveness of human language might, nonetheless, result from the incorporation into the vocal control system of a gene that played no role in the ancestral communication system. Imagine a gene duplication event, which took a gene previously involved in the neural circuitry underlying breathing, chewing, or memory, and modified it slightly so that it is expressed more during the babbling stage of human childhood. The hypothetical gene would be a paralog of the (still preserved) chewing/breathing/memory gene in humans, and an ortholog of the corresponding gene in chimpanzees, but would nonetheless represent a true novelty in human evolution, and could properly be termed a gene for speech.

In contrast, let us accept for the sake of argument the notion advanced by some linguists that the evolution of syntax was "catastrophic" and sudden, in the sense that, from one generation to the next, a speaker (or population) with only a syntactically simple protolanguage gave rise to offspring (or a new generation) that possessed a syntactically complex one (Bickerton 1990; Berwick 1997). This, too, can be encompassed within a quite similar gene duplication/divergence scenario. In this case, we might imagine a gene previously involved in building neural circuits exclusive to hand motor control, spatial reasoning, social intelligence, or some other suitable precursor function, which was mutated in such a way as to be expressed far more broadly in the brain. The brains thus changed "suddenly" would have syntactic powers that the previous generation did not enjoy. If this hypothetical new allele resulted from a gene-duplication event, rapid selection subsequent to this mutation might have pushed it to evolve further differences from its paralog, honing the syntactic function into a novel adaptation. Then it might rightly be called a novel gene for syntax. On the other hand, if the allele in question still had to serve the old function(s) because there was no preceding gene duplication event, we would have a pleiotropic gene, potentially resistant to further modification or shaping to the needs of syntax, due to the need to preserve the old function.

The point of these exercises is simply to point out that many different and plausible scenarios about language evolution at the behavioral and neural level can be readily encompassed within the new evo–devo paradigm. Ideas that appear diametrically opposed at the functional and behavioural levels, and have traditionally been sharply contrasted in discussions of language evolution, might admit of rather similar explanations at the mechanistic level, in terms of the molecular developmental processes underlying the neural circuits involved. Though different readers may have different intuitions about which of the above scenarios are most likely, I think it is far too early to draw any conclusions, or to reject one or the other as biologically implausible or impossible on evolutionary grounds. In the next ten years, data will be pouring in to help us develop well-grounded empirical hypotheses about possibilities that, today, are entirely speculative. Some of the most important data, most relevant to our eventual understanding of how language works at the neural, genetic and developmental level may come from songbirds, mice, or fruit flies (or even sponges, jellyfish, or yeast). The important lesson to be learned from the last 20 years of molecular and developmental genetics is to be ready to be surprised and open-minded in the face of new data as they come in.

Part II
Variation

8

The Three Design Factors in Evolution and Variation

LYLE JENKINS

8.1 Introduction

From its inception, biolinguistics has been interested in the standard questions that the Nobel Laureate Nikolaas Tinbergen posed many years ago, sometimes known as "Tinbergen's questions." These include questions about biological form (mechanisms) and function, development (ontogeny), and evolution (phylogeny). Early on, Chomsky, in a seminal review of Skinner's theory of behaviorism, which was widely discussed, compared properties of human language with properties of bird song and other animal systems that had been discovered and documented by researchers in animal behavior, including Tinbergen, Lorentz, Thorpe, and many others (Chomsky 1959a).

These questions were also extensively studied in the work of Eric Lenneberg in his *Biological Foundations of Language* (Lenneberg 1967). At the Lenneberg Symposium held in honor of Lenneberg after his death, Chomsky again noted that the Tinbergen questions are central to the study of the biology of language (Chomsky 1976). As work in biolinguistics progressed, these research questions were always either implicitly or explicitly pursued (Chomsky and Lasnik 1993).

8.2 The Three Factors: Genetic Endowment, Environment, and Principles not Specific to the Faculty of Language

As we have already noted, biolinguistics studies language as a biological system and, as such, investigates language in the traditional areas of biology: form/function, development, and evolution (Jenkins 2000). These questions are sometimes called the *what* and *how* questions of biolinguistics (Chomsky 2004b):

1. What is knowledge of language and how is it put to use?
2. How does language develop in the child?
3. How does language evolve in the species?

The biolinguistic perspective is also concerned with the interplay between what Chomsky has termed the "three factors" in language design: (1) genetic endowment, (2) environment, and (3) principles not specific to the faculty of language (Chomsky 2005). It has been suggested that an example of (3) might be computational efficiency. We will suggest another example, namely, viz., principles of symmetry, which are non-domain specific and non-species specific, but which can contribute to the variation seen in biological systems, including language. These kinds of questions about design are sometimes called the *why* questions of biolinguistics; that is, why language is as it is.

Within biolinguistics there are many specific research programs with regard to the study of syntax, semantics, morphology, phonology/phonetics, etc. Where we need to be concrete we will refer to the Minimalist research program, sometimes called Minimalism (Chomsky 1995). Note that within any approach to biolinguistics the theory of the language faculty needs to generate infinitely many expressions that provide instructions to both the sensory-motor and semantic interfaces. Thus there will be an operation that combines structures from lexical items; for example, in English, *loves* and *Mary* can be combined to form *loves Mary* and *John* can be combined with *loves Mary* to form *John loves Mary*. In Minimalism, this operation is called *Merge*. This operation can be applied over and over to generate a discrete infinity of expressions: Peter thinks that Ted said that Bill claimed . . . that John loves Mary. This property is called "recursion" and is postulated to be part of (1), above, our genetic endowment—in this particular case, of the genetic component of the language faculty. To put it another way, recursion is part of our Universal Grammar (see below).

The biolinguistic approach employs a variety of kinds of empirical evidence to study the language faculty. For example, syntactic studies employ introspective evidence (asking native speakers for their judgment about sentences). In addition, studies of language acquisition also observe and elicit responses from children to deduce the stages that language progresses through. Here often strictly controlled situations must be set up and aids such as puppets are employed. Another important approach is comparative linguistics or typology in which structures are compared across languages. The goal in all of these cases is to try to separate those principles of language which are universal or largely universal, as well as to account for the variation present from language to language.

In this connection we point out a common misconception about theoretical linguistics. As we will see, the study of the language faculty draws upon evidence from many areas, such as sign language, pidgin and creole languages, neurology, genetics, and evolution. Nonetheless, some fail to understand that asking a native speaker of Navajo for their judgments in order to construct a theory of grammar is just as much an experiment as is observing a fMRI brain scan while the Navajo speaks that sentence.

This misunderstanding is sometimes couched in the following terms: What do the sentences and abstract structures of theoretical linguistics have to do with biology? The answer is—everything. They are the central object of study of biolinguistics. Ultimately we want to link knowledge of language to nerve circuits in the brain and explain how these circuits grow during development, as well as how they arise during evolution. In the development of many sciences, it was necessary to postulate abstract entities for which only indirect evidence existed. We need only think of Mendel's factors, which were postulated before the role of DNA was understood and of the anti-neutrino which was hypothesized several decades before it was detected.

Note that even language researchers make the mistake of assuming that evidence outside of theoretical linguistics has a privileged status. The psycholinguist Steven Pinker has expressed this by saying that Chomsky is a "paper-and-pencil theoretician who wouldn't know Jabba the Hutt from the Cookie Monster" (Pinker 1994a). Elsewhere he says that "Chomsky's arguments for the innateness of language are based on technical analyses of word and sentence structure, together with some perfunctory remarks on universality and acquisition" (Pinker 1994a). Pinker, on the other hand, thinks that "converging evidence" is crucial, by which he means "facts on children's development, cross-linguistic surveys, genetic language disorders, and so on." The implication here is that Chomsky does not think such evidence is crucial. This kind of thinking resulted in a meaningless debate for years over whether evidence from theoretical linguistics was real or not, as opposed to evidence from psycholinguistics experiments, which was held by some to be psychologically real. This is no more coherent than asking whether Mendel's factors were genetically real or whether the anti-neutrino was physically real.

As an example of how biolinguistics can use evidence from multiple domains, Shapiro et al. provide another example of the application of imaging studies to investigate how linguistic categories like nouns, verbs, and adjectives are organized in the brain. An event-related functional MRI imaging study has found specific brain sites that are activated by either nouns or verbs, but not both (Shapiro et al. 2006). In a series of experiments, subjects were asked to produce nouns and verbs in short phrases as real words (*the ducks, he plays*) as well as pseudowords (*the wugs, he zibs*), both with regular inflections and irregular inflections (*geese, wrote*), including both concrete and abstract words. Specific brain areas were selectively activated for either verb production (left prefrontal cortex and left superior parietal lobule) or for noun production (left anterior fusiform gyrus) across the entire battery of tests. Moreover, the areas were non-overlapping, leading the authors to conclude that these regions "are involved in representing core conceptual properties of nouns and verbs."

Now consider the question of how language develops in the child. One approach with considerable empirical coverage is the Principles-and-Parameters approach which says that the genetic endowment for the language faculty contains general principles such as the principle of recursion discussed earlier and the principle of Structure-Dependence, which says that syntactic rules operate on phrases such as *saw Mary* rather than at the level of lexical items (Chomsky 2007b). These two principles are possibly universal across languages. However, other principles, such as the Head-First principle which determines whether the verb precedes the object, as in English, or follows it, as in Japanese, permit some parametric variation. These parameterized principles make up Universal Grammar.

The idea then is that, as language develops or grows in the child, the principles provided by Universal Grammar have their parameters (if any), specified according to the language environment the child is in. The Head-First principle would be fixed one way in English, and the other way in Japanese. This process has been compared to the process of working one's way through the choices on a menu. Once all the choices have been made and all of the parameters have been fixed, the language has been determined. Thus, both the (near) universality of some features of language and the variation from language to language is accounted for at the same time. In fact, it has been said that under this view, there is really only one language in the world, called *Human*.

An alternative account of parametric variation has been provided by Yang (2004a). In this approach, the child is presumed to have access to all human grammars at once. The job that the child has is to unlearn the languages that are not represented in the language environment. Grammars are "punished" (the probability that it is the correct grammar is lowered) until only the target grammar is left. This is the theory of variational selection and is based on competition between grammars. This theory makes predictions about how long it should take for a parameter to get fixed based on the frequency of occurrence of the relevant sentences that allow the child to determine which way the parameter should be fixed. Yang's analysis provides a nice example of how frequency data from language corpora can provide critical evidence for a theory of language acquisition.

Let us turn to the third question, of how language evolved in the species. In studying this question Hauser, Chomsky, and Fitch emphasized the importance of the comparative approach (Hauser, Chomsky, and Fitch 2002). They distinguish between the faculty of language in the broad sense (FLB) and the faculty of language in the narrow sense (FLN). The basic idea is that before concluding that some property of language is uniquely human, one should study a wide variety of species with a wide variety of methods. And before concluding that some property of language is unique to language, one should consider the possibility that the property is present in some other (cognitive) domain, such as music or mathematics. They tentatively conclude that recursion may be a property of language that is unique to language and, if so, belongs to the faculty of language in the narrow sense (FLN).

An example of the application of the comparative method is the investigation of the computational abilities of non-human primates by Fitch and Hauser, who tested the ability of cotton-top tamarins to process different kinds of grammars (Fitch and Hauser 2004). In another study, Gentner et al. (2006) showed that European starlings, in contrast to tamarins, can recognize acoustic patterns generated by context-free grammars.

Another area where the comparative approach can be useful is in the study of the biological bases of babbling (Aronov, Andalman, and Fee 2008). It has long been known that adult zebra finches require a brain area called HVC (high vocal center) along with several other nuclei for singing. One model of developmental learning proposes that these same areas incorporate the circuits that underlie juvenile song behavior, known as subsong, which is similar to babbling in humans. This view is known as the neuronal group selection theory. It holds that the zebra finch starts off with a large number of motor patterns which compete with one another until a selection process eliminates all the unsuccessful candidates. So it came as a surprise when it was discovered that there is actually a separate circuit for juvenile singing (subsong) that is located in an area called LMAN (lateral magnocellular nucleus of the nidopallium).

To determine this, the HVC was eliminated bilaterally, by electrolytic lesions or by pharmacological inactivation, or else fiber tracts projecting from HVC were transected. However, LMAN was left intact. The juvenile birds were able to continue producing subsong. When the procedure was applied to older birds, they reverted back to subsong-like vocalizations. These observations led to the proposal that distinct specialized circuits underlie juvenile subsong behavior and highly stereotyped adult song behavior.

Another active area of comparative work on language involves the *FOXP2* gene, which codes for a transcription factor, and which has been shown to be involved in deficits in human language, orofacial sequencing, and cognition (Marcus and Fisher 2003; Fisher and Marcus 2006). The homologous gene has also been studied in a number of organisms, including the chimpanzee, the mouse, the zebra finch, the zebrafish, and the medaka fish. The relevant genes have been sequenced, allowing one to compare the differences in gene sequence and to make inferences about the selectional pressures on the gene during evolution.

Although most of the comparative work has focused on FOXP2, other systems affecting language are beginning to be characterized. For example, genetics researchers have also discovered a DNA duplication in a 9-year-old boy with expressive language delay (Patient 1) (Somerville et al. 2005). Although his comprehension of language was at the level of a 7-year-old child, his expression of language was comparable to that of only a 2 1/2-year-old.

The region of DNA duplication in Patient 1 was found to be on chromosome 7, and interestingly, was found to be identical to the region that is deleted in Williams–Beuren syndrome (WBS). Patients with WBS have relatively good expressive language, but are impaired in the area of spatial construction. L. Osborne, one of the researchers on the study, noted that, in contrast, Patient 1 had normal spatial ability, but could form next to no complete words. When asked what animal has long ears and eats carrots, Patient 1 was only able to pronounce the r of the word rabbit but was able to draw the letter on the blackboard and add features such as whiskers.

We now consider the third factor in language design, namely, principles non-specific to language. As already mentioned, Chomsky proposed that computational efficiency might be an example of this factor. I would suggest that symmetry might be considered another such candidate. It has the property that it is non-domain specific as well as non-species specific. It operates across many domains in physics, chemistry and in many biological systems. For example, the notion of symmetry breaking has also proven useful in modeling neural behavior in systems such as singing in songbirds such as canaries (Trevisan et al. 2007). The molecular basis of brain asymmetry is also under active investigation and principles of symmetry breaking have been used to account for the origin of body asymmetry.

Much of current work in syntax on the operation Merge (within the framework of Minimalism) involves building structures that reflect language asymmetries (e.g. the theory of binding of anaphors) (Boeckx 2006; Chomsky 2007b). For work on the "antisymmetry" properties found in the study of word order and hierarchy, see Kayne (1994). For work on asymmetry in morphology, see Di Sciullo and Fong (2005). One might ask whether the principles of symmetry uncovered in internal linguistics investigations of the kind just cited can be accounted for by the principles of symmetry operative in other domains such as physics. Finally, language evolution, language acquisition, and language change are being studied using dynamical systems methods. In this approach a population of speakers, assumed to possess a language-learning mechanism constrained by Universal Grammar, is modeled by a dynamical system called the *language dynamical equation*, which can be studied by such standard techniques as the analysis of symmetry-breaking bifurcations (Niyogi 2004, 2006; Nowak 2006).

8.3 A Neo-Darwinian Critique

In *The Origin of Speech*, Peter MacNeilage argues against what he calls the "generativist view" of Chomsky and in favor of the "neo-Darwinian" view (MacNeilage 2008). But it is not clear how MacNeilage's approach to language differs fundamentally from the view he is criticizing. We should say a few words about the term "generative," which originated in work in formal-language theory. There one says that a grammar generates (specifies) strings, sentences, structures, etc. It is unlikely that MacNeilage has any objection to theories of syntax, phonology, or semantics that try to precisely specify the objects that they are studying.

What he seems to be objecting to is the biolinguistic approach to the study of language (although he does not use the phrase anywhere). But as we have seen, the biolinguistic approach rests solidly on the foundations of standard biology. It is interested in the answers to Tinbergen's questions, as is MacNeilage. The study of evolution in biology has for decades had the findings of Darwin on variation and selection integrated into its core. MacNeilage specifically criticizes Chomsky's views here and we will concentrate on those, although many of these foundational views are shared by many other current approaches to the study of the biology of language (biolinguistics).

MacNeilage asserts that his Neo-Darwinian view of language is different from other biolinguistic approaches as it regards the relationship between nature (organism) and nurture (environment). MacNeilage claims that the (Chomskian) biolinguistic approach has the relationship nature (organism) → nurture (environment). Here the "explanatory burden for language is shouldered almost entirely by the organism—meaning, in this case, the genes." In contrast, the Neo-Darwinian view has the relation: nature (organism) ↔ nurture (environment), where "the organism acts on its environment, and the environment acts on the organism." MacNeilage regards it as a recent discovery that environmental input can cause genes to become active:

A major recent discovery, important enough to have already made it into introductory textbooks (e.g. Gazzaniga and Heatherton 2003), is that environmental input influences the expression of genes; that is, it can cause genes to become active. Thus, just as the genes influence how the organism will act on the environment, the environment will influence how the genes act on the organism.

(MacNeilage 2008: 47)

The problem with MacNeilage's account is that the fact that environment acts on the organism is a truism. Mothers, for example, have always known that if you do not eat, you will not grow. And the general public has also come to understand the importance of the environment in that if you lock your children away in the basement, they will not learn to speak a language, as in the case of Genie.

As for the "major recent discovery" that environmental input can cause genes to become active, this was proven back in the 1950s by the work of Jacob and Monod on the lac operon, when they showed that the presence or absence of lactose in the environment of E. Coli could cause genes to become active or inactive (Stent and Calendar 1978). The mechanisms operative at the DNA level were revealed when Gilbert and Maxam sequenced the lac operator (Gilbert and Maxam 1973). By now, of course, it has become standard fare on TV science programs that there are carcinogenic substances in the environment that can directly damage your genes and cause them to become "active," making cells cancerous. We are perhaps being unfair to the classical geneticists at the beginning of the century who also understood this without knowing the role of DNA in the cell. They understood that mutagenesis of fruit flies somehow damaged the "factors" (their word for genes) along the chromosome, sometimes making them active or inactive. As far as the cognitive domain is concerned, the classical experiments of Hubel and Wiesel demonstrated the effect that the organism has on the environment when they showed the visual deficits that developed when animals were deprived of visual stimuli during a precise critical window.

As much of a stretch as it is to maintain that anyone working in biolinguistics could doubt that the environment acts on the organism, MacNeilage's account of the generative view becomes even less coherent when he zeroes in on a reference in Chomsky to the Fibonacci series. To make sense of it requires reading a long discussion of Plato, Bertrand Russell, Hallet, and Descartes in the introduction ("The Intellectual Context") to the *The Origin of Speech* where MacNeilage places Chomsky in the philosophical tradition of "essentialism" originating with Plato. However, it makes little difference whether you believe this or not, since MacNeilage immediately proceeds to derive absurdities from this idea, such as Tomasello's thesis that generative grammar is "a closed mathematical system," after which MacNeilage goes on to rhetorically ask: "Why, in the light of more than a century of Darwinism, should closed mathematical systems continue to be regarded as solutions to problems of evolution?" MacNeilage, citing Russell, concludes that it must be the belief of generative grammarians that "mathematics could be substituted for empirical observation because it was a superior form of knowledge," resulting in "disaster."

However, ultimately we are not interested in what MacNeilage thinks is in Chomsky's mind (or Plato's), but rather in what Chomsky's approach to language tells us about what is in Nature, namely, human language. And on this score, theories of generative grammar within the biolinguistics approach have more than met Russell's requirement for empirical observation. Generative grammars have been subjected over the years to empirical evidence from studies of adult language, child language, sign language, pidgin and creole language, typology, historical change, comparative neuroanatomy, animal systems, genetics and evolution, to name only a few sources, in addition to others discussed earlier. This is not even conceivable for a closed mathematical system.

Let us return to MacNeilage's comments on the occurrence of Fibonacci numbers in sunflowers. Remember that MacNeilage considers Chomsky a modern essentialist and hence exhibits "essentialistic reluctance to pay any homage to our dominant notion of biological causality." Since Chomsky believes there is "very little to evolutionary theory," he singles out "mathematical forms," "for him, essences," as examples of "unexplained phenomena" such as the polyhedral shapes of some virus shells and the presence of Fibonacci number patterns in some sunflowers. It is difficult to make sense of MacNeilage comments, since they misrepresent the point of the examples Chomsky gave.

The examples can be best understood if we recall what Chomsky has called the three factors in language design: (1) genetic endowment, (2) experience, and (3) principles not specific to the faculty of language. Note that the faculty of language ("language organ") is not the result simply of genetics, but results from an interaction of all three factors, contrary to MacNeilage's claims earlier. Now let us consider the pattern of Fibonacci numbers in the spirals of certain sunflowers. Douady and Couder have shown that these patterns can be created in purely physical systems, for instance with droplets of ferrofluid that are dropped at regular intervals and repel one another in such a way so that Fibonacci patterns are created (Douady and Couder 1992, 1993). They note that as long as the timing of the appearance of the primordia of the sunflower is such that the primordia appear at certain regular intervals, then the mechanical forces acting on them will produce the Fibonacci patterns.

A reasonable hypothesis is that as yet unknown genes control the timing of the appearance of the primordia. Note that, under this scenario, there are no instructions laid down in the genes to specify the Fibonacci patterns. Rather the principles of dynamical systems guarantee that the patterns will appear, given certain assumptions about the forces acting on the primordia. Ian Stewart has called this a "partnership between genetics and physics" (Stewart 1995). Note that the dynamical principles are not explained by Darwinian evolution, as Chomsky noted in the citation given by MacNeilage, although, of course, the genes affecting primordial production can be affected by random mutations in the course of evolution and selection can act on the sunflower. Similar remarks hold for the case of the polyhedral virus shells, where principles of thermodynamic self-organization act in conjunction with genetically specified principles. Note that in the discussion of nature–nurture, MacNeilage claimed that Chomsky denied that "environment can act on the organism," and then when Chomsky gives specific examples where no account can be given totally in terms of genetics, but where environmental factors are required for the explanation, he dismisses these examples as pure mathematical fictions ("essences"). Nor are these examples isolated cases. Genetics and dynamics act hand in hand in a wide variety of systems that have been discovered in recent years such as patterns of hair follicles, cell division in E. coli, cell motility, angelfish patterns, formation of ant cemeteries, etc. However, practitioners in these fields do not call this the study of "essences"; they call it biophysics, molecular biology, and genetics.

8.4 Conclusion

We have seen that in the biolinguistic approach a variety of tools, including comparative linguistics, comparative animal behavior, comparative neuroanatomy, comparative genomics, and dynamical systems, are being successfully brought to bear on the study of the biology of language. Although we do not yet have the answers to the Tinbergian questions for the biology of language, they have provided us with a very fruitful framework for the exploration and mapping out of the language faculty, one of nature's great scientific challenges.

9

Three Factors in Language Variation

CHARLES YANG

9.1 Introduction

How much should we ask of Universal Grammar? Not too little, for there must be a place for our unique ability to acquire a language along with its intricacies and curiosities. But asking for too much will not do either. A theory of Universal Grammar is a statement of human biology, and one needs to be mindful of the limited structural modification that would have been plausible under the extremely brief history of *Homo sapiens* evolution.

In a recent article, Chomsky (2005: 6) outlines three factors that determine the properties of the human language faculty:

(1) a. Genetic endowment, "which interprets part of the environment as linguistic experience . . . and which determines the general course of the development of the language faculty."

    b. Experience, "which leads to variation, within a fairly narrow range, as in the case of other subsystems of the human capacity and the organism generally."

    c. Principles not specific to the faculty of language: "(a) principles of data analysis that might be used in language acquisition and other domains; (b) principles of structural architecture and developmental constraints . . . including principles of efficient computation."

These factors have been frequently invoked to account for linguistic variation—in almost always mutually exclusive ways, perhaps for the understandable reason that innate things need not be learned and vice versa. Rather than dwelling on merits or defects of these efforts—see Yang (2004b) for an assessment—we approach the problem of variation from the angle of acquisition by developing a framework in which all three factors are given a fair billing. The study of child language points to two fairly distinct types of language variation, which appear to invoke two distinct mechanisms of language acquisition.

One kind of variation derives from the innate and invariant system of Universal Grammar (1a). Such a space of variation constitutes the initial state of linguistic knowledge, which traditionally has been considered the "core" linguistic system (Chomsky 1981). The child's task is one of selection from a narrow range of options (e.g. parameter values, constraint rankings) that are realized in its linguistic environment. A prominent line of evidence for the genetic endowment of language comes from the fixed range of linguistic options, some of which are not present in the input data, but which the child nevertheless spontaneously accesses and gradually eliminates during the course of acquisition.

Quite a different type of variation consists of language-specific generalizations which are derived from the linguistic environment—that is, experience (1b). This type of variation can be identified with the periphery of the language faculty (Chomsky 1981: 8): "marked elements and constructions," including "borrowing, historical residues, inventions" and other idiosyncrasies. The child's task, as we shall see, is one of evaluation: decision-making processes that determine the scope of inductive generalizations based on the input yet still "within a fairly narrow range."

We further suggest that the instantiation of language variation by the child learner follows at least certain principles not specific to the faculty of language (1c). The mechanism which selects amongst alternatives in the core parameter system in (1a) is probabilistic in nature and apparently operates in other cognitive and perceptual systems, and had indeed first been proposed in the study of animal learning and behavior. The acquisition of the periphery system in (1b) reflects general principles of efficient computation which manipulate linguistic structures so as to optimize the time course of online processing, very much in the spirit of the evaluation measure in the earlier studies of generative grammar (Chomsky 1965; Chomsky and Halle 1968). Both types of learning mechanism show sensitivity to certain statistical properties of the linguistic data that have been largely ignored in works that ask too much of Universal Grammar but would be difficult to capture under approaches that rely solely on experience.

We take up these matters in turn.

9.2 Variation and Selection

9.2.1 *Return of the parameter*

Saddled with the dual goals of descriptive and explanatory adequacy, the theory of grammar is primed to offer solutions to the problem of language variation and acquisition in a single package. This vision is clearly illustrated by the notion of syntactic parameters (Chomsky 1981). Parameters unify regularities from surface-distant aspects of the grammar both within and across languages, thereby acting as a data-compression device that reduces the space of grammatical hypotheses during learning. The conception of parameters as triggers, and parameter-setting as flipping switches, offers a most direct solution to language acquisition.

There was a time when parameters featured in child language as prominently as in comparative studies. Nina Hyams's (1986) ground-breaking work was the first major effort to directly apply the parameter theory of variation to the problem of acquisition. In recent years, however, parameters have been relegated to the background. The retreat is predictable when broad claims are made that children and adults share the identical grammatical system (Pinker 1984) or that linguistic parameters are set very early (Wexler 1998). Even if we accepted these broad assertions, a responsible account of acquisition would still require the articulation of a learning process: a child born in Beijing will acquire a different grammatical system or parameter setting from a child born in New York City, and it would be nice to know how that happens. Unfortunately, influential models of parameter setting (e.g. Gibson and Wexler 1994, but see Sakas and Fodor 2001) have failed to deliver formal results (Berwick and Niyogi 1996),[1] and it has been difficult to bridge the empirical gap between child language and specific parameter settings in the UG space (Bloom 1993; Valian 1991; Wang et al. 1992; Yang 2002). The explanation of child language, which does differ from adult language, falls upon either performance limitations or discontinuities in the grammatical system, both of which presumably mature with age and general cognitive development—not thanks to parameters.

To return, parameters must provide remedy for both the formal and the empirical problem in child language. The hope, in our view, lies in paying attention to the factors of experience (1b) and the process of learning (1c), which have not been addressed with sufficient clarity in the generative approach to acquisition. The variational learning model (Yang 2002) is an attempt to provide quantitative connections between the linguistic data and the child's grammatical development through the use of parameters. To capture the gradualness of syntactic acquisition, we introduce a probabilistic component to parameter learning, which is schematically illustrated as follows:[2]

---

[1] Baker (2001) and Snyder (2007) both sketched out properties of the parameter space that would make learning more efficient but no specific learning model has been given.

[2] The formal details of the learning model can be found in Yang (2002). We will use the terms of "grammars" and "parameters" interchangeably to denote the space of possible grammars under UG. For analytic results of learnability in a parametric space, see Straus (2008).

(2) For an input sentence s, the child

    a. with probability P_i selects a grammar G_i,

    b. analyzes s with G_i

    c. • if successful, reward G_i by increasing P_i

       • otherwise punish G_i by decreasing P_i

Learning the target grammar involves the process of selection which eliminates grammatical hypotheses not attested in the linguistic environment; indeed, the variational model was inspired by the dynamics of Natural Selection in biological systems (Lewontin 1983). It is obvious that non-target grammars, which all have non-zero probabilities of failing in the target grammar environment, will eventually be driven to extinction. The probabilistic nature of learning allows for alternative grammars—more precisely, parameter values—to co-exist, while the target grammar gradually rises to dominance over time.[3] The reality of co-existing grammars has been discussed elsewhere (Roeper 2000; Yang 2002, 2006; Legate and Yang 2007; and subsequent work) but that line of evidence clearly rests on establishing the fact that parameter setting is not too early, at least not in all cases; if the child is already on target, the appeal to non-target parameter values as an explanatory device would be vacuous. This, then, requires us to develop a framework in which the time course of parameter setting can be quantitatively assessed.

It can be observed that the rise of a grammar under (2) is a function of the probability with which it succeeds under a sample of the input, as well as that of failure by its competitors. The dynamics of learning can be formalized much like the dynamics of selection in the evolutionary system. Specifically, we can quantify the "fitness" of a grammar from the UG Grammar pool as a probability of its failure in a specific linguistic environment:

(3) The *penalty probability* of grammar G_i in a linguistic environment E is[4]

$$c_i = \Pr(G_i \not\rightarrow s \mid s \in E)$$

In the idealized case, the target grammar has zero probability of failing but all other grammars have positive penalty probabilities. Given a sufficient sample of the linguistic data, we can estimate the penalty probabilities of the grammars in competition. Note that such tasks are carried out by the scientist,

---

[3] The appeal to non-target and linguistically possible options to explain child language can be traced back to Jakobson (1968) and more recently Roeper (2000), Crain and Pietroski (2002), Rizzi (2007), etc., though these approaches do not provide an explicit role for either linguistic data or mechanisms of learning.

[4] We write $s \in E$ to indicate that s is an utterance in the environment E, and $G \rightarrow s$ to mean that G can successfully analyze s. Formally, the success of $G \rightarrow s$ can be defined in any suitable way, possibly even including extra-grammatical factors; a narrow definition that we have been using is simply parsability.

rather than the learner; these estimates are used to quantify the development of parameter setting but do not require the tabulation of statistical information by the child. The present case is very much like the measure of fitness of fruit flies by, say, estimating the probability of them producing viable offspring in a laboratory: the fly does not count anything.[5] Consider two grammars, or two alternative values of a parameter: target G_1 and the competitor G_2, with $c_1 = 0$ and $c_2 > 0$. At any time, $p_1 + p_2 = 1$. When G_1 is selected, p_1 of course will always increase. But when G_2 is selected, p_2 may increase if the incoming data is ambiguous between G_1 and G_2 but it must decrease—with p_1 increasing—when unambiguously G_1 data is presented, an event that occurs with the probability of c_2. That is, the rise of the target grammar, as measured by p_1 going to 1, is correlated with the penalty probabilities of its competitor—c_2—which in turn determines the time course of parameter setting. We turn to these predictions presently.

9.2.2 *Frequency and parameter setting*

As a starting point, consider the acquisition of verb raising to tense in French and similar languages. First, what is the crucial linguistic evidence that drives the French child to the [+] of the verb raising parameter? Word order evidence such as (4a), where the position of the finite verb is ambiguous, is compatible with both the [+] and [−] value of the parameter, and thus has no effect on grammar selection. Only data of the type in (4b) can unambiguously drive the learner toward the [+] value.

(4)   a. Jean voit Marie.
        Jean sees Marie.
     b. Jean voit souvent/pas Marie.
        Jean sees often/not   Marie.

The raising of finite verbs in French and similar languages is a very early acquisition. Pierce (1992) reports that in child French as early as 1;8, virtually all verbs preceding *pas* are finite while virtually all verbs following *pas* are non-finite. Bear in mind that children in Pierce's study are still at the two-word stage of syntactic development, which is the earliest stage in which verb raising could be observed from naturalistic production. And this early acquisition is due to the accumulative effects of utterances such as 4b, which

---

[5] In this sense, the use of the probabilistic information here is distinct from statistical learning models such as Saffran et al. (1996), where linguistic hypotheses themselves are derived from the statistical properties of the input data by the learner. See Yang (2004b) for an empirical evaluation of that approach.

amount to an estimated 7 percent of child-directed French sentences.[6] Thus we obtain an empirical benchmark for early parameter setting, that 7 percent of unambiguous input data is sufficient.[7]

If all parameters are manifested at least as frequently as 7 percent of the input, then parameter setting would indeed be early as widely believed. Fortunately that is not case, for otherwise we would not be able to observe parameter setting in action. Let us consider two major cases of syntactic learning: the Verb Second parameter in languages such as German and Dutch and the obligatory use of grammatical subjects in English. Both have been claimed—incorrectly, as we shall see—to be very early acquisitions on a par with the raising of finite verbs in French (Wexler 1998).

In an influential paper, Poeppel and Wexler (1993) make the claim that syntactic parameter setting takes place very early, a claim which partially represents an agreement between the competence-based and the performance-based approach (Pinker 1984; Valian 1991; Bloom 1993; Gerken 1991; cf. Hyams and Wexler 1993) to grammar acquisition: both sides now consider the child's grammatical system to be adult-like. Poeppel and Wexler's study is based on the acquisition of the V2 parameter. They find that in child German, finite verbs overwhelmingly appear in the second, not final, position while non-finite verbs overwhelmingly appear in the final, not second, position.

But this does not warrant their conclusion that the V2 parameter has been set. A finite verb in the second position does not mean it has moved to the "V2" position, particularly if the pre-verbal position is filled with a subject, as the examples from Poeppel and Wexler (1993: 3–4) illustrate below:

(5) a. Ich hab ein dossen Ball.
        I   have a   big   ball
     b. Ich mach das nich.
        I   do   that not

The structural position of the verb here deserves additional consideration. It is entirely possible that the verb has gone only as far as T, and the subject would be situated in the Spec of T, and the clausal structure of the raised verb 5 is not like German but like French. The evidence for V2 can be established only

---

[6] Unless noted through the citation of other references, the frequencies of specific linguistic input from child directed data are obtained from the CHILDES database (MacWhinney 1995). The details can be found in Yang (2002), which was the first generative study of language acquisition that ever used input frequencies in the explanation of child language.

[7] We claim 7 percent to be sufficient but it may not be necessary; an even lower amount may be adequate if the raising of finite verbs is established before the two-word stage, which could be confirmed by comprehension studies such as the preferential looking procedure (Golinkoff, Hirsh-Pasek, Cauley, and Gordon 1987).

when the verb is unambiguously high (e.g. higher than T) and the preverbal position is filled.

To evaluate the setting of the V2 parameter, we must examine finite matrix sentences where the subject is post-verbal. In child-German acquisition, as shown in the quantitative study of Stromswold and Zimmerman (1999), the subject is consistently placed out of the VP shell and is thus no lower than the specifier position of TP. If so, then a finite verb preceding the subject will presumably by in C, or at least in some node higher than T. Now, if the pre-verbal, and thus sentence-initial, position is consistently filled, then we are entitled to claim the early setting of the V2 parameter—or however this property comes to be analyzed. But Poeppel and Wexler's claim is not supported: the pre-verbal position is filled at child language, as shown in Table 9.1, which is based on Haegeman's (1995) Tables 5 and 6 longitudinal study of a Dutch child's declarative sentences. We can see that in the earliest stages, there are close to 50 percent of V1 utterances, in co-existence with V2 patterns, the latter of which gradually increase in frequency.[8] The claim of early V2 setting is therefore not supported.[9] As argued by Lightfoot (1999) and Yang (2002) on independent grounds, the necessary evidence for V2 comes

TABLE 9.1 Longitudinal V1 and V2 patterns. All sentences are finite, and the subjects are post-verbal

Age	V1 sentences	All sentences	V1%
2;4	72	170	43%
2;5	66	132	50%
2;6	147	411	36%
2;7	93	201	46%
2;8	94	292	32%
2;9	98	269	36%
2;10	93	321	28%
2;11	36	259	14%
3;0	56	246	22%
3;1	101	268	37%

[8] The data from 3;1 is probably a sampling oddity: all other months are represented by five to ten recording sessions, but 3;1 had only one.

[9] Poeppel and Wexler's work does show, however, that finite verbs raise to a high position (out of the VP shell), and non-finite verbs stay in the base position, and that the child grammar has an elaborate system of functional projections, thus replicating Pierce's (1989) findings in French acquisition reviewed earlier. Furthermore, we have no quarrel with their more general claim that the child has access to the full grammatical apparatus including functional projections. Indeed, even the V1 patterns displayed in Table 9.1. demonstrate that the structure of the CP is available to the learner.

from utterances with the pre-verbal position occupied by the object; such data only comes at the frequency of 1 percent in child-directed speech, which results in a relatively late acquisition at the 36th–38th month (Clahsen 1986). Now we have established an empirical benchmark for the relatively late setting of a parameter.

The quantitative aspects of parameter setting—specifically, the early and late benchmarks—can be further illustrated by differential development of a single parameter across languages. This leads us to the phenomenon of subject drop by English-learning children, one of the most researched topics in the entire history of language acquisition. Prior to 3;0 (Valian 1991), children learning English leave out a significant number of subjects, and also a small but not insignificant number of objects. However, children learning pro-drop grammars such as Italian and topic-drop grammars such as Chinese are much closer to adult usage frequency from early on. For instance, Valian (1991) reports that Italian children between 2;0-3;0 omit subjects about 70 percent of the time, which is also the rate of pro-drop by Italian adults reported by Bates (1976) among others. In Wang et al. (1992) comparative study of Chinese and American children, they find that 2-year-old American children drop subjects at a frequency of just under 30 percent,[10] which is significantly lower than Chinese children of the same age group—and obviously significantly higher than English speaking adults. By contrast, the difference in subject usage frequency between Chinese children and Chinese adults is not statistically significant.

If the claim of early parameter setting is to be maintained—and that certainly would be fine for Italian and Chinese children—the disparity between adult and child English must be accounted for by non-parametric factors, presumably by either the child's competence or performance deficiencies. Without pursuing the empirical issues of these alternatives, both approaches amount to postulating significant cognitive differences, linguistic or otherwise, between the learners acquiring different languages: that is, English-learning children are more susceptible to competence and/or performance limitations. This of course cannot be ruled out a priori, but requires independent justification.

The variational learning model provides a different view, in which a single model of learning provides direct accounts for the cross-linguistic findings

---

[10] To be precise, 26.8 percent. The literature contains some discrepancies in the rate of subject omission. The criteria used by Wang et al. (1992) seem most appropriate as they excluded subject omissions that would have been acceptable for adult English speakers. Following a similar counting procedure but working with different data sets, Phillips (1995) produced similar estimates of subject-drop by children.

of language development. The time course of parameter setting need not be uniform: Italian and Chinese children do set the parameter correctly early on but English children take longer. And the reason for such differences is due to the amount of data necessary for the setting of the parameter, which could differ across languages. The following data can unambiguously differentiate the grammars for the Chinese-, Italian-, and English-learning children; their frequencies in the child-directed speech are given as well.

(6)   a. [+topic drop, −pro drop] (Chinese): Null objects (11.6%; Wang et al. 1992: Appendix B)

       b. [−topic drop, +pro drop] (Italian): Null subjects in object *wh*-questions (10%)

       c. [−topic drop, −pro drop] (English): expletive subjects (1.2%)

The reasoning behind (6) is as follows. For the Chinese-type grammar, subject omission is a subcase of the more general process of topic drop, which includes object omission as well. Neither the Italian- nor the Chinese-type grammar allows that; hence object omission is the unambiguous indication of the [+] value of the topic drop parameter.[11]

However, topic drop is not without restrictions; such restrictions turn out to differentiate the Chinese-type grammar from the Italian- type.[12] There is a revealing asymmetry in the use of null subjects in topic-drop languages (Yang 2002), which has not received much theoretical consideration. When topicalization takes place in Chinese, subject drop is possible only if the topic does not interfere with the linking between the null subject and the established discourse topic. In other words, subject drop is possible when an adjunct is topicalized (7a), but not when an argument is topicalized (7b). Suppose the old discourse topic is *John*, denoted by *e* as the intended missing subject, whereas the new topic is in italics, having moved from its base position indicated by *t*.

(7)   a. *Mingtian,* [*e* guiji   [*t* hui   xiayu]]. (*e* = John)
          tomorrow, [*e* estimate [*t* will rain]]
          'It is tomorrow that John believes it will rain.'

---

[11] The actual amount of data may be higher: even subject drop would be evidence for the Chinese-type grammar since the lack of agreement is actually inconsistent with the pro-drop grammar.

[12] As is well known, the pro-drop grammar licenses subject omission via verbal morphology. But "rich" morphology, however it is defined, appears to be a necessary though not sufficient condition, as indicated by the case of Icelandic, a language with rich morphology yet obligatory subject. Thus, the mastery of verbal morphology, which Italian- and Spanish-learning children typically excel at from early on (Guasti 2002), is not sufficient for the positive setting of the pro-drop parameter.

  b. *Bill*, [*e* renwei [*t* shi jiandie]]. (*e* = John)
     Bill, [*e* believe [*t* is spy]]
     'It is Bill that John believes is a spy'.

The Italian pro-drop grammar does not have such restrictions. Following Chomsky (1977) and much subsequent work on topicalization and *wh*-movement, the counterpart of (7b) can be identified with an object *wh*-question. In Italian, subject omission is unrestricted as its licensing condition is through agreement and thus has nothing to do with the discourse and information structure. Here again *e* stands for the omitted subject whereas *t* marks the trace of movement.

(8) a. Chi*ᵢ* *e* ha   baciato *t*?
        who*ᵢ* *e* has(3sGm) kissed *t*?
        'Who has he kissed?'

     b. Chi*ᵢ* *e₁* credi   che *e₂* ami   *tᵢ*?
        who*ᵢ* *e₁* think(2sG) that *e₂* loves(3sGf) *tᵢ*?
        'Whom do you think she loves?'

     c. Dove*ₜ* hai   *e* visto Maria *t*?
        where have(2sG) *e* seen Maria *t*?
        'Where have you seen Maria?'

Upon encountering data such as (8), the Chinese-type grammar, if selected by the Italian-learning child, would fail and decrease its probability, whose net effect is to increase the probability of the [+] value of the pro-drop parameter.

  Note that for both the Chinese- and Italian- learning child, the amount of unambiguous data, namely (6a) and (6b), occur at frequencies greater than 7 percent, the benchmark established from the raising of finite verbs in French. We thus account for the early acquisition of subjects in Italian and Chinese children in Valian (1991) and Wang et al. (1992) studies.

  The English-learning child takes longer as the Chinese- type grammar lingers on.[13] The rise of the obligatory subject is facilitated by expletive subjects, but such data appear in low frequency: about 1.2 percent of child-directed English utterances. Using the 1 percent benchmark established on the relatively late acquisition of the V2 parameter (3;0–3;2; Clahsen 1986), we expect English children to move out of the subject-drop stage roughly around the same time, which is indeed the case (Valian 1991). And it is not

---

[13] The Italian-type grammar can be swiftly dismissed by the impoverished English morphology, since sufficient agreement is a necessary condition for pro-drop; see Yang (2002; ch. 4) for additional discussion.

a coincidence that the subject-drop stage ends approximately at the same time as the successful learning of the V2 parameter.

Finally, the variational model puts the parameter back into explanations of child language: learner's deviation from the target form is directly explained through parameters, which are also points of variation across languages. The child's language is a statistical ensemble of target and non-target grammars: deviation from the target, then, may bear trademarks of possible human grammars used continents or millennia away, with which the child cannot have direct contact. In the case of null subjects, we can analyze the English-learning child as probabilistically using the English-type grammar, under which the grammatical subject is always used, in alternation with the Chinese-type grammar, under which subject drop is possible if facilitated by discourse. Thus, the distributional patterns of English child null subjects ought to mirror those of Chinese adult null subjects as shown in (9). Indeed, the asymmetry of subject drop under argument/adjunct topicalization for adult Chinese speakers is almost categorically replicated in child English, as summarized below from Adam's subject-drop stage (file 1–20; Brown 1973):

(9)   a. 95% (114/120) of *wh*-questions with null subjects are adjunct (*how, where*) questions (e.g. "Where *e* go?", "Why *e* working?")

       b. 97.2% (209/215) of object questions (*who, what*) contain subjects (e.g. "What *e* doing?")

Taken together, we have uncovered significant frequency effects in parameter setting. The fact that frequency plays some role in language learning ought to be a truism; language learning is impressively rapid but it does take time. Yet the admission of frequency effects, which can come about only through the admission that experience and learning matter, does not dismiss the importance of the first factor of Universal Grammar (Tomasello 2003; but see Yang 2009). Quite to the contrary, frequency effects in parameter setting presented here actually strengthen the argument for Universal Grammar; frequency effects are effects of the input data that responds to specific linguistic structures. The cases of null subjects and verb second are illustrative because the input data is highly consistent with the target form yet children's errors persist for an extended period of time. To account for such input-output disparities, then, would require the learner to process linguistic data in ways that are quite distant from surface level descriptions. If the space of possible grammars were something like a phrase structure grammar with rules such as "S $\xrightarrow{\alpha}$ NP VP" and "S $\xrightarrow{\beta}$ VP" where $\alpha + \beta = 1$, it is difficult to see how the phenomenon of subject drop is possible with the vast majority of English sentences containing grammatical subjects. However, if the learner were to approach "S $\overset{\alpha}{\to}$ [+topic drop]" and "S $\overset{\beta}{\to}$ [−topic drop]", as proposed in the parameter theory, we can capture the empirical findings of children's null subjects—and null objects as well. Parameters have developmental correlates, but they would only turn up when both the input and the learning process are taken seriously.

9.3 Variation and Evaluation

Selection among a universal set of options is by no means the only mode of language acquisition, and it would be folly to attribute all variation in child language to the genetic component of Universal Grammar. First, and most simply, the size of the search space and the resulting learning time to convergence can increase exponentially with the number of parameters; this may undermine the original conception of parameters as a solution for the problem of explanatory adequacy. One phenomenon, one parameter is not recommended practice for syntax and would not be a wise move for language acquisition either.

Second, it seems highly unlikely that all possibilities of language variation are innately specified; certainly, the acquisition of particular languages does not always exhibit patterns of competition and selection. Variation in the sound system is most obvious. While the development of early speech perception shows characteristics of selectionist learning of phonetic and phonological primitives (Werker and Tees 1983; Kuhl et al. 1992; see Yang 2006 for overview), the specific content of morphology and phonology at any point can be highly unpredictable, partly due to ebbs and flows of language change over time; see Bromberger and Halle (1989). Innate principles or constraints packaged in UG notwithstanding, even the most enthusiastic nativist would hesitate to suggest that the English specific rule for past-tense formation (*-d*) is one of the options, along with, say, the *-é* suffix as in the case of French, waiting to be selected by the child learner. Indeed, the past-tense acquisition appears to have an Eureka moment: when the child suddenly comes to the productive use of the "add *-d*" rule, over-regularization of irregular verbs (e.g. *hold–holded*) starts to take place (Marcus et al. 1992; Pinker 1999).

Close examination of syntactic acquisition reveals that the child is not only drifting smoothly in the land of parameters (Section 9.2) but also taking an occasional great leap forward. A clear example comes from the acquisition of dative constructions, to which we return momentarily. Quantitative analysis of children's speech (Gropen et al. 1989; Snyder and Stromswold 1997; Campbell and Tomasello 2001) has shown that not all constructions are learned alike, or at the same time. For 11 of the 12 children in Snyder and Stromswold's study, the acquisition of double-object construction (*I give John a book*) precedes that of prepositional *to*-construction (*I give a book to John*) by an average of just over 4 months. Prior to that point, children simply reproduce instances of datives present in adult speech. When 3-year-olds productively apply these constructions to novel lexical items as in *pilked the cup to Petey* into *I pilked Petey the cup* (Conwell and Demuth 2007), they must have learned the alternation on the more mundane pairings of *give, lend, send*, and others.

The acquisition of past tense and datives are obviously different: the specific form of the "add -*d*" rule is learned directly from data whereas the candidate verbs for dative constructions are probably provided by innate and universal syntactic and semantic constraints (Pesetsky 1995; Harley 2002; Hale and Keyser 2002; Rappaport Hovav and Levin 2008). But the logical problems faced by the learner are the same. Upon seeing a sample that exemplifies a construction or a rule which may contain exceptions (e.g. irregulars), the learner has to decide whether the observed regularity is a true generalization that extends beyond experience, or one of lexical exceptions that must be stored in memory. For the cases at hand, the answer is positive, but the same decision-making process ought to return a negative answer for the rule "add -*t* & Rime → ɔ" when presented with *bring, buy, catch, seek*, and *think*. In other words, decision-making involves the recognition of the productivity of the language particular processes.

In the rest of this section, we will extend a mathematical model (Yang 2005) that provides the conditions under which a rule becomes productive in the face of exceptions. Even though the empirical motivation for that model is based on morphological learning and processing, there is suggestive evidence that it can extend to the study of syntax as well, as we set out to explain why the acquisition of double objects precedes that of prepositional (*to*) dative construction.

9.3.1 *Optimization and productivity*

Consider how an English child might learn the past-tense rules in her morphology. Suppose she knows only two words *ring-rang* and *sing-sang*; at this point she might be tempted to conjecture a rule "i→a/__ ŋ".[14] The child has

---

[14] One way to do so is to make conservative generalizations over a set of structural descriptions that share the same process of structural change. This is commonly found in inductive learning models in Artificial Intelligence (Mitchell 1982; Sussman and Yip 1997), and its first linguistic application is in Chomsky (1955). How the learner comes to such generalizations is an important issue but one which is of no significant interest to us for present purposes; our key task is to determine the productivity of such generalizations.

every reason to believe this rule to be productive because, at this particular moment, it is completely consistent with the learning data. However, as her vocabulary grows, "i→a/ __ ŋ" will run into more and more exceptions (e.g. *bring–brought, sting–stung, swing–swung*, etc.). Now the learner may decide enough is enough, and the rule will be demoted to the non-productive status: *sing* and *sang* would be memorized as instances of lexical exceptions, which is how English irregular verbs are treated in morphophonology (Halle and Mohanan 1985; Pinker 1999). By contrast, the exceptions to the "add -*d*" rule— about 150 irregular verbs—are apparently not enough to derail its productivity, which is backed up by thousands of regular verbs in English language.

The question is: How much is enough? How many exceptions can a productive rule tolerate? Before we lay out our approach to the problem, let us note that the child learner is superbly adept at recognizing productive processes. For instance, it is well known that English learners over-*regularize* in past-tense acquisition (Marcus et al. 1992; Pinker 1999; Yang 2002), in up to 10 percent of all past-tense uses. It is perhaps less well known that children do not over-*irregularize*: errors such as *bring–brang* are exceedingly rare, only occurring in 0.2 percent of the past-tense production data (Xu and Pinker 1995). In Berko's classic Wug study (1958), 4-year-olds reliably supply regular past tense for novel verbs but only one of 86 children extended *gling* and *bing* to the irregular form of *glang* and *bang*, despite maximum similarity to the *sing–sang* and *ring–rang* irregulars. Children generalize productive rules but do not generalize lexical rules.

Our approach is a throwback to the notion of an evaluation measure, which dates back to the foundations of generative grammar (Chomsky 1955; Chomsky and Halle 1968, in particular p. 172). It provides an evaluation metric, hence a decision procedure, that the learner can deploy to determine whether a linguistic generalization is warranted or not. It is useful to recall that the evaluation measure "is not given a priori [...] Rather, a proposal concerning such a measure is an empirical hypothesis about the nature of language" (Chomsky 1965: 37). A model of productivity, therefore, requires independent motivation. And this is an area where Chomsky's third factor—in particular, principles of efficient computation—may play an important role in the organization of the language faculty. Claims of efficient computation require an independently motivated metric of complexity. To this end, we conjecture that the mental representation of morphological knowledge is driven by the time complexity of online processing: productivity is the result of maintaining an optimal balance between lexical and productive rules.

The combinatorial explosion of morphologically complex languages (Hankamer 1989; Niemi, Laine, and Tuominen 1994; Chan 2008) necessitates a stage-based architecture of processing that produces morphologically complex forms by rule-like processes (Caramazza 1997; Levelt et al. 1999). At the minimum, the stem must be retrieved from the lexicon and then combined with appropriate rules/morphemes to generate the derived form. Both processes appear to be geared toward real-time efficiency, where a telling source of evidence comes from frequency effects. One of the earliest and most robust findings in lexical processing is that high-frequency words are recognized and produced faster than low-frequency words in both visual and auditory tasks (Forster and Chambers 1973; Balota and Chumbley 1984). Within the component of morphological computation, it is well established that the processing of exceptions (e.g. irregulars) is strongly correlated with their frequency (see Pinker and Ullman 2002 for reviews) in generative grammar. When understood in terms of modern computer-science algorithms, formal models of linguistic competence can be directly translated into a performance model (cf. Miller and Chomsky 1963; Berwick and Weinberg 1986); they not only provide accommodation for behavioral results such as frequency effects but also lead to an evaluation measure for productivity.

Generative theories traditionally hold that the organization of morphology is governed by the Elsewhere Condition (Kiparsky 1973; Halle 1990), which requires the application of the most specific rule/form when multiple candidates are possible. This provides a way for representing exceptions together with rule-following items. Algorithmically, the Elsewhere Condition may be implemented as a serial search procedure:[15]

(10)   IF $w = w_1$ THEN ...
      IF $w = w_2$ THEN ...
      ...
      IF $w = w_M$ THEN ...
      apply R

If taken literally, the Elsewhere Condition treats exceptions as a list of if–then statements that must be evaluated and rejected before reaching the rule-following words. For example, suppose $W_{1...m}$ are m irregular verbs of English: to inflect a regular verb, the language user must determine that it is not one of the irregulars, which would have triggered more specific rules/forms, before the application of the "add -*d*" rule. Now the gradient frequency effects in morphological process can be directly captured in the search algorithm. For instance, if the exception clauses (1–m) in 10 are ordered

---

[15] This is again a return to an earlier approach in lexical processing, the serial search model of Forster (1976, 1992). The advantage of this model lies in its ready availability for analytic methods; its empirical coverage is at least as good as other approaches (Murray and Forster 2004).

with respect to their token frequencies of use, then the time required to access a specific entry will directly correlate with its position on the list: more frequent entries will be placed higher on the list and will thus be accessed faster. And the construction of a frequency-ranked list can be achieved by online algorithms that carry minimal computational costs and thus psychological plausibility. For instance, a simple algorithm Move-Front that moves the most recently accessed clause to the beginning of the list can be shown to be no worse than the optimal list by a small constant factor (Rivest 1976).

The key feature of the model in (10) is that productivity does not come for free: a productive rule may induce considerable time complexity in online processing. Specifically, the computation of the rule-following items will have to "wait" until all exceptions are evaluated and rejected. Thus, if a rule has too many irregulars (as measured by type frequency), the overall complexity of morphological computation may be slowed down. An immediate prediction of such a model goes as follows. Take two words, w_e and w_r, the former being an exception to a productive rule R whereas w_r is a rule-following item. The model in 10 entails that w_e will be computed faster than w_r *if* the following conditions are met:

(11)   a. the lexical/stem frequencies of w_e and w_r are matched, *and*

   b. the frequencies of the rules that w_e and w_r make use of, i.e. the sum of the token frequencies of all words that follow these rules, are also matched.[16]

The familiar case of English past tense, unfortunately, is not applicable here. While the irregular verbs are highly frequent, none of the irregular processes comes close to the total frequency of the productive "add -*d*" rule, which collects relatively lower frequency regular verbs but in very high volume (Grabowski and Mindt 1995). To the best of our knowledge, the most appropriate tests can be found in two pockets of German morphology. The first test comes from the German noun plural system. The default rule is to add an -*s* suffix; there are four other classes with varying degrees of productivity (Marcus et al. 1995).[17] Of interest is the decidedly non-productive class that adds the -*er* suffix, which is closely matched with -*s* class in rule frequency (e.g. Sonnenstuhl and Huth 2002). Lexical decision tasks show that when -*er* and -*s*

---

[16] A frequently used rule will be processed faster than a less frequently used one; this effect can be observed in both morphological processing (Sereno and Jongman 1997) and morphological learning (Yang 2002; Mayol and Yang 2008).

[17] The matters are more complicated than the regular vs. irregular dichotomy portrayed in the dual-route approach; see Wiese (1996), Wunderlich (1999) for more refined descriptions of German noun morphology and Yang (2005) for empirical evidence of why at least some of the "irregular" classes must be productive themselves.

suffixing stems are matched in frequency, the *-s* words show considerably slower reaction time (Penke and Krause 2002; Sonnenstuhl and Huth 2002). The other test concerns the formation of past participles in German, where the default rule is to use the *-t* suffix; there is an unpredictable set of irregulars that add *-n*. Despite the low type frequency of *-n* verbs, "add *-t*" and "add *-n*" classes are comparable in rule frequency. In an online production study, Clahsen et al. (2004) find that when stem frequency is controlled for, the regular "add *-t*" class is slower than the irregular classes, at least for words in the higher frequency region which normally constitute the basis for productivity calculation during language acquisition. These pieces of evidence, along with the treatment of frequency effects among exceptions, provide empirical support for the processing model motivated by the Elsewhere Condition (10).

We now turn to the formal properties of the processing model. Consider a rule R that can in principle apply to a set of N lexical items. Of these, M items are exceptions and they are represented in the form of the Elsewhere Condition (10). Let $T(N, M)$ be the expected time of processing if R is productive: in other words, $(N-M)$ items will need to wait until the M exceptions have been searched and rejected. By contrast, if R is not productive, then all N items must be listed as exceptions, again ranked by their frequencies; let $T(N, N)$ be the expected time of processing for a list thus organized. We conjecture:

(12) R is productive if $T(N, M) < T(N, N)$; otherwise R is unproductive.

The reader is referred to Yang (2005) for the mathematical details of the model. In essence, for the $(N-M)$ items, the rule search time is the constant M, the number of exceptions that must be ruled out and waited out. For an item in the set of M exceptions, the rule search time is its rank/position on the list. And the expected time can be expressed as the rule search time weighted by word frequencies. Under the assumption that word frequencies follow the Zipfian distribution, it is possible to show that

(13)   **Theorem:** R is productive if and only if $M < \frac{N}{\ln N}$

That is, the number of exceptions would need to be fairly small compared to the number of rule following items to warrant productivity. Here I will review a simple application of the theorem (13) to provide an explanation for the phenomenon of overregularization.

Following Marcus et al. (1992), let us take the first instance of overregularization as the onset of the productive use of the "add *-d*" rule. (Prior to this point, regular past tense forms produced by children are presumably lexicalized, just like the irregular verbs.) Theorem (13) implies that at this particular juncture, the learner must know a great deal more regular verbs than irregulars. It is difficult to obtain precise measures of the child's vocabulary, let alone at some specific point: the following is what we have managed for Adam, the boy in Brown's (1973) study. The first instance of Adam's over-regularization is at 2;11: *What dat feeled like?* We thus examined his speech from the first transcript recorded at 2;3 to this point. We counted any inflected form of a verb in Adam's production to be part of his vocabulary. There are 211 verbs altogether, among which 143 are regular; the percentage of regular verbs is 68. According to 13, the predicted percentage ought be $\left[211 - \frac{211}{\ln(211)}\right]/211 = 0.81$. Obviously there is a difference between the expected value and the test; this may be a sampling effect, as regular verbs are much lower in token frequency than irregular verbs and more likely to be undersampled, and additional longitudinal studies must be carried out. More important for the present study, the number of regulars overwhelms the irregulars when the "add -*d*" rule becomes productive, which is consistent with the general direction of the theoretical model.

A brief note about the terminology—and the scope of our investigation—before we proceed. The representation in (10) might give the impression that *R* concerns only "Elsewhere" rules, that is, the default rule that could apply across the board. That is not the case. We are broadly interested in the productivity of any rule whose structural description may include a subset of exceptions. Indeed, rules may be nested like Venn diagrams, with the outer rules having broader structural descriptions than inner ones, and each rule may contain listed exceptions.

Nested rules are certainly attested in languages. For instance, it could be said that to the extent that English derivational morphology has a default nominalization process, it is the suffixation of -*ness*; this corresponds to *I* in Figure 9.1. However, there are subclasses that are perfectly productive:

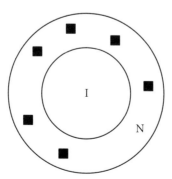

FIGURE 9.1 Rules as nested structures

adjectivals ending /əbəl/ add the suffix *-ity*, which corresponds to *N*, above. Rules in nest structures, of course, may or may not have exceptions: in the present discussion, the inner *-ity* rule under /əbəl/ does not seem to have exceptions but the outer *-ness* rule has plenty (e.g. *grow–growth*, *govern–government*). The German noun plural system appears to be organized in a similar way; see note 17. We assume application of rules will be from inside out, matching the most specific patterns first as dictated by the Elsewhere Condition (10). For instance, nominalization of an adjectival *A* in English goes as follows. The language user first checks if *A* fits the structural description of *I*: if it does, then *I* applies. (If *I* has exceptions, the user will first check if *A* is one of those.) If *A* does not match *I*, it will trickle outward to rule *N*. Again, the language user first checks if *A* is one of the exceptions of *N* first, that is, the black boxes in Figure 9.1. If so, those special forms apply; otherwise *I* will step in.

To derive nested rules and their correct productivity status is a complicated matter. We assume that the learner can inductively derive linguistic descriptions that are appropriate candidates for productivity calculation; a broad range of learning models are applicable here; see note 14. Once these potentially productive rules are in place, the child learner will be in a continuous evaluation process that measures and updates their productivities. For instance, the rule "i→a/__ ŋ" we used earlier for expository purposes might indeed have been productive for a young child but quickly demoted as exceptions to it are accumulated. Likewise, the "add *-d*" rule initially must be unproductive, for the early past-tense vocabulary is likely to consist mostly of irregular verbs, which are far higher in frequency than regulars; its promotion to productive status will have to wait for more regular verbs to register, as we have shown in the case of Adam.

Interestingly, there is one child (Abe; Kuczaj 1976) in the past-tense acquisition who did not show the so-called U-shape learning in his longitudinal data: he started overregularization in his first recording session, at 2;4, which is at least six months before Adam (and Sarah; Marcus et al. 1992). The only possible account for this under the productivity model is that Abe must build up the regular portion of his verb vocabulary much faster. Unfortunately, since Abe started overregularization in the very first transcript, it is impossible to estimate his vocabulary composition as we did for Adam. Yet several strands of evidence together confirm the prediction. Abe turned out to be a fantastic word learner, with a Peabody verbal IQ of 140, using more regular verbs than irregulars already at 2;4, where his peers were using considerably more irregulars than regulars at the same age. Moreover, Abe learned more regulars than irregulars in every subsequent month (Maratsos 2000: Appendix). For his peers, the monthly learning rate for regulars only caught up with that of irregulars at least six months later. In other words, Abe simply reached the productivity threshold a good deal faster than his peers. Such individual level explanations can be achieved only when the learning mechanisms are articulated with sufficient clarity and the learning data are taken seriously as a component in the explanation of child language.

9.3.2 *Evaluating datives*

Does the productivity model, which is grounded in morphological learning and processing, generalize to other arenas of linguistic analysis? By providing quantitative analysis for the acquisition of syntactic rules, we suggest that it can.

While the tension between storage and computation has been the focus of morphological processing since the very beginning (Taft and Forster 1976), there is comparatively less work in this direction for syntactic processing. Fortunately, the important study of Swinney and Cutler (1979) provides experimental results which lend support to the productivity model developed here. Swinney and Cutler conduct a series of experiments investigating the real-time processing complexity of idiomatic expressions such as *He kicked the bucket* compared with fully compositional ones such as *He lifted the bucket*. By controlling for various frequency factors, they find that idioms across a broad range of productivity (Fraser 1970) are processed significantly faster than compositional expressions. Interpreted algorithmically, the output of parsing (i.e. tree-like structures) is shipped off to the semantic interpretation system, which appears to first perform a lexical lookup for stored structures with idiomatic meanings. If that fails, compositional interpretation would ensue, resulting in processing delay. Note that this process would mirror that of morphological processing discussed earlier, suggesting that the Elsewhere Condition may be a general principle running through many domains of linguistic representation and processing.

With this background in mind, let us turn to the acquisition of the double-object construction and the prepositional *to*-dative construction. Earlier analyses have postulated a derivational relationship between these constructions (Baker 1988; Larson 1988), though recent years have seen their treatments as two distinct constructions (Pesetsky 1995; Harley 2002; among others). In addition, there is now broad agreement on the semantic conditioning of these constructions (Goldberg 1995; Hale and Keyser 2002; Beck and Johnson 2004; etc.). Adopting the formulations of Pinker (1989) and Krifka (1999), the double-object dative involves caused possession of the Theme by the Goal, understood in the broad, including metaphorical, sense (14a) whereas the *to* dative must entail caused motion of the theme along a path to Goal (14b):

(14)   a. Double object: NP CAUSES NP$_{theme}$ TO HAVE NP$_{goal}$.

   b. *To* dative: NP CAUSES NP$_{theme}$ TO GO TO NP$_{goal}$.

But it is important to note that these are only necessary conditions on the availability of dative constructions, as language-specific constraints further restrict productivity.[18] Korean, for instance, has extremely limited productivity in these constructions (Jung and Miyagawa 2004). Specifically, Korean exhibits alternations between dative–accusative objects and accusative–accusative objects, with the former patterning with prepositional datives and the latter with double-object datives. The verbs *cwu* ('give'), *kaluch* ('teach') and *cipwul* ('pay') can appear in the double-object construction but verbs such as *ponay* ('send') do not. The child learner of Korean, then, will need to learn that verbs do not productively participate in this construction and memorize the handful of exceptions that do. Similar observations can be made about Yaqui, an Uto-Aztecan language spoken in Sonora, Mexico and Arizona. Jelinek and Carnie (2003) show that although most Yaqui ditransitive verbs have an accusative–dative argument structure, there is a small closed class of verbs that allow their internal arguments to be marked with two accusative cases, which is equivalent to the English double object construction. Finally, there may be additional constraints within a language that further affect syntactic productivity.

The learning of datives, then, seems to involve the following process. UG provides the candidate verb sets such as (14) with specific semantic properties, but the learner still has to learn whether and which of these verbs can participate in constructions such as in (14a) and (14b). In English, the learner must learn that these constructions are productive—and we find recent extensions to novel verbs which fit the semantic criteria, as in *I cc'ed everyone the announcement* and *I texted the apology to John*. The acquisition of datives is thus similar to that of past tense. In the case of past tense, the general rule has counter examples (i.e. irregulars), and the task is to determine when a sufficient number of positive examples have been accumulated to counterbalance the exceptions. In the case of English dative acquisition, the learner also needs to see a sufficient number of attested examples to justify the scope of these

---

[18] Another necessary condition may have to do with availability of a certain prepositional element (P$_{have}$) that encoding possession, as suggested in a decompositional approach to double object constructions (Harley 2002). In fact, one can frame Harley's position as a problem of morphological productivity; that is, whether the head P$_{have}$ can combine with the relevant stems productively.

constructions—that is, to learn that English is not Korean or Yaqui in this aspect of the grammar. In both cases, calibration of linguistic productivity is required.

The empirical evidence from the acquisition of datives supports this view. Gropen et al. (1989) have noted that English dative acquisition is initially conservative with the child closely following the attested constructions in adult speech. The emergence of productivity is indicated by extension of usage to novel items (see Conwell and Demuth 2007), including errors that mirror those of overregularization (e.g. Bowerman 1978) even though the rate of errors is very low (Gropen et al. 1989: 209, 217 and the references cited therein):

(15)   a. Adam: Ursula, fix me a tiger.

      b. Adam: You finished me a lot of rings.

      c. Christy: Don't say me that or you'll make me cry.

      d. Ross: Jay said me no.

      e. Mark: Ross is gonna break into the TV and is gonna spend us
             money. [i.e. cause us to spend money for repair]

      f. Damon: Mattia demonstrated me that yesterday.

Now we are in the position to offer a quantitative account of how—or precisely, when—these constructions are learned. As documented in Snyder and Stromswold (1997), the emergence of the double-object construction is significantly ahead of that of the *to*-dative construction. The application of the productivity model (13) is quite straightforward. We examined a random sample of 86,442 child-directed utterances from the CHILDES database (MacWhinney 1995) that was used for a word-segmentation project (Yang 2004b). We considered only verb stems that appeared at least five times in the input data on the ground that very low-frequency verbs may not be firmly placed in a young learner's vocabulary (see Gropen et al. 1989). From these stems, we generated two sets that could, and indeed do, participate in the double-object and *to*-dative constructions. Then, from these two sets, we counted the number of verbs actually attested at least once in the respective constructions.[19] These verbs are exhaustively listed in 16 and 17, where those in bold are attested for the relevant construction:

(16)   Double-object construction (14a):
      get, tell, make, give, write, bring, tell, read, sing, **find,** hit, **draw, show, buy,** throw, **send, teach, feed,** cook, **buy,** sell, **pay, bake, serve, teach**

---

[19] A verb is considered to have participated in a construction if at least one of its inflectional forms is used in that construction.

(17)   *To*-dative construction (14b):
        tell, **take**, **give**, **said**, write, **bring**, **read**, sing, hit, play, **throw**, pull, push, **show**, shoot, blow, drive, **send**, carry, teach, feed, fly, move, **pay**, serve.

Out of the 25 candidates for the double-object construction, 19 are actually used in the input. By contrast, out of the 25 candidates for the *to*-dative construction, only 10 are attested in the input. Thus, the signal-to-noise ratio for 16 is far higher than that for 17—in fact, if we apply the theorem in 13, we see that the double-object construction has already crossed the threshold of productivity but the *to*-dative construction is nowhere close. Naturally, we expect that as the volume of input data is increased, more and more verbs in 17 will participate in the *to*-dative construction and the threshold of productivity will eventually be met. But the point here is that the tipping point for the double object construction is reached sooner. This pattern of acquisition is ultimately caused by the statistical distribution of usage in the input; it takes a formal model of productivity and learning to map the quantitative measures of the data to syntactic regularities of the grammar.

9.4 Conclusion

We conclude with some brief notes on the connection from language acquisition to the theory of grammar.

The core vs. periphery distinction, like parameters, seems to have fallen out of fashion these days. A current trend in linguistic theorizing aims to dispense with the core parametric system and replace it with a plethora of rules and constructions (Culicover 1999; Newmeyer 2004; Culicover and Jackendoff 2005) which are presumably inductively learned from the data under the guidance of certain principles.[20] One reason for abandoning the core, I suspect, lies in the lack of an articulated theory that draws boundaries from the periphery. Since the periphery is necessary anyway—no one doubts that idioms and irregular verbs must be learned—what's left for the core? Assuming that something like the productivity model presented here is correct, one might ask—and I have indeed been asked—whether that sort of productivity analysis plus some general inductive learning model can carry the learner all the way.

I do not think it is wise to abandon the core, even if we put aside the utility of the parameter system for comparative linguistic descriptions and focus solely on language acquisition instead. From a formal learnability point

---

[20] Which may or may not be specific to language, and may or may not be innate; here opinions differ greatly.

of view, a finite space of parameters or constraints is still our best bet on the logical problem of language acquisition (Nowak, Komarova, and Niyogi 2002) but that is for another day. It is useful to recall the distinction between core and periphery originally drawn by Chomsky (1981):

Marked structures have to be learned on the basis of slender evidence too, so there should be further structure to the system outside of core grammar. We might expect that the structure of these further systems relates to the theory of core grammar by such devices as relaxing certain conditions of core grammar, processes of analogy in some sense to be made precise, and so on, though there will presumably be independent structure as well.   (p. 8)

How do we delimit the domain of core grammar as distinct from marked periphery? In principle, one would hope that evidence from language acquisition would be useful with regard to determining the nature of the boundary or the propriety of the distinction in the first place, since it is predicted that the systems develop in quite different ways.   (p. 9)

Of course, even if the core vs. periphery boundary is difficult to draw, it does not mean that no such boundary exits. Regardless the merit of the specific learning models presented here, the facts from child language do speak to the two distinct components of the grammar that Chomsky alludes to. One type is documented in the quantitative studies of section 9.2. The child spontaneously accesses grammatical options for which she has no external evidence, and the elimination of these options is sensitive to token frequencies of specific linguistic data that are quite far removed from surface level patterns (e.g. expletives for obligatory subjects). The most straightforward interpretation is an internal one: such non-target grammatical options are part of the innate endowment that is invariant across languages and speakers. Quite a distinct kind can be found in Section 9.3, where the substantive form of linguistic knowledge is derived from the external, language particular, environment, which corresponds to the periphery. Acquisition of the periphery is characterized by the conservativeness of the learner at the initial stage: before productive use of the "add -*d*" rule and dative constructions, the child keeps to attested forms only in the input and does not generalize (recall especially the asymmetry in overregularization vs. overirregularization in Section 9.3.1). Moreover, the acquisition of the periphery appears to be a process sensitive to the type frequency of the relevant linguistic experience: hearing "walked" a thousand times will not give the learner the rule of "add -*d*" but hearing a sufficiently diverse range of expressions (*walk–walked, kill–killed, fold–folded*, etc.) will do, even if there are some interfering irregulars that are heard very frequently. And the periphery is not a land of the lawless either. Successful acquisition (of anything) will not be possible with structural principles that govern all components of the grammars. The interdeterminacy of induction is a matter of logic. When deriving a language-specific generalization, the child must be constrained by both linguistic and possible non-linguistic principles of learning: no search for syntactic generalizations over every other word, for example, wherever such generalizations may lie in the linguistic system. The force of the core must radiate through the periphery.

Which leads us to reiterate our position that not asking UG to do too much does not mean asking UG to do too little. The mechanism of learning and the representation of linguistic knowledge are in principle quite different matters, but they must fit well together to yield useful results. An analogy can be made to the separation of data structure and algorithms in computer science: an algorithm (e.g. binary search) operates on any tree but would only turn out good performance when the tree is structured in specific ways. The variational model of learning quite possibly derives from evolutionarily ancient learning and decision making mechanisms in other domains and species (Bush and Mosteller 1951; Atkinson et al. 1965) and similar models have seen applications in other areas of language acquisition (Labov 1994). But it requires particular partitions of the grammar space—rather than making a left or right turn for the rodent in a maze (Gallistel 1990b)—to provide accurate descriptions of children's syntactic development. Likewise, the principle of efficient computation that motivates the productivity model may be a general constraint on cognitive and neural systems, yet its execution is completely derived from the linguistic principle of the Elsewhere Condition, or whatever independent principle from which the Elsewhere Condition derives. A large range of language variation, then, falls under the learner's ability to derive appropriate generalizations from the data; not having to build everything about language in the genetic endowment may produce a concrete program for the study of language in an evolutionary setting (Hauser, Chomsky, and Fitch 2002).

10

Approaching Parameters from Below

CEDRIC BOECKX

10.1 Revisiting Plato's Problem

"Our ignorance of the laws of variation is profound." Darwin's words, taken from the *Origin of Species* (1964: 167), aptly characterize the current state of our knowledge of linguistic variation. At a time when some linguists feel that some *why*-questions concerning the language faculty are ripe for the asking, there is no consensus regarding why linguistic variation should exist at all, let alone why it should take the form that we think it does. There is indeed very little substantive discussion of the issue of linguistic variation in the context of the Minimalist Program. This may come as a surprise to some, as it is fairly common in the literature to introduce the Minimalist Program in the context of the Principles-and-Parameters approach. Specifically, it is fairly common to say that the Minimalist Program grew out of the perceived success of the Principles-and-Parameters approach, which arguably for the first time in the history of the field enabled linguists to resolve in a feasible way the tension between universal and particular aspects of language, and offered a fruitful

The present work benefited from comments from the participants in my advanced syntax seminar at Harvard University in the spring of 2007 and 2009, and in my intensive graduate courses in Vitoria (Basque Country) in the summer of 2007 and Keio University in the summer of 2008, as well as from the audiences at the Biolinguistics Meeting in Venice (June 2007), at the 9th Tokyo Conference on Psycholinguistics (March 2008), and at a talk at University of Massachusetts, Amherst (November 2007). I have been talking to many people about parameters over many years. I cannot thank them all individually here, but I would like to single out Fritz Newmeyer, Norbert Hornstein, Paul Pietroski, Noam Chomsky, Juan Uriagereka, Dennis Ott, Bridget Samuels, Hiroki Narita, Ángel Gallego, Terje Lohndal, Massimo Piattelli-Palmarini, Koji Sugisaki, and Luigi Rizzi.

This work is a very preliminary report. A much more detailed exposition is in preparation (Boeckx, in progress). Portions of this contribution appear as "Did we really solve Plato's Problem (abstractly)?" in the *Proceedings of the 9th Tokyo Conference on Psycholinguistics*, ed. Y. Otsu, 1–25, 2008. Tokyo: Hituzi Syobo. Permission to reuse this material is gratefully acknowledged.

way of thinking about how children acquire their language (Plato's Problem).[1] There is a lot of truth to this statement, but in the absence of important qual- ifications (rarely spelled out in the literature) it can be highly misleading. In particular, it may give the impression that the specific implementation of the Principles-and-Parameters approach explored in the Government–Binding era essentially solves Plato's Problem (abstractly, of course, since no one is under the illusion that GB-theorists got all the details right). This impression must be dispelled, for the idea that a GB-style Principles-and-Parameters architecture provides the right format for a solution to Plato's Problem is, I think, seriously mistaken, on both empirical and conceptual grounds.[2] A Principles-and-Parameters model of the GB style conceived of Universal Grammar as consisting of two main ingredients: principles that were truly universal, manifest in all languages, and, more importantly, principles whose formulations contained open values (parameters) that had to be fixed in the course of language acquisition. Such parametrized principles can be thought of as forming a network that is only partially wired up at the initial state, and that must await a fair amount of data processing to be fully operative. (This is the switchboard metaphor made famous by Jim Higginbotham, adopted in Chomsky 1986: 146.)

This way of thinking about the acquisition process has had undeniable success. It has led to a revival of acquisition studies, and produced some extremely interesting results, in the domains of language development and of comparative syntax. But I think that the traditional way of telling the Principles-and-Parameters story has outlived its usefulness. For one thing, the traditional Principles-and-Parameters model is no longer compatible with the way minimalists think of Universal Grammar. As I will discuss in some detail below, if minimalists are right, there cannot be any parame- trized principle, and the notion of parametric variation must be rethought. Second, it is fair to say that empirically the expectations of the traditional Principles-and-Parameters model have not been met (see Newmeyer 2005). Government–Binding theorists expected a few points of variations each with

---

[1] See Chomsky (2005: 8–9, 2007a: 2–3), Hornstein (2001: 4), Boeckx (2006: 59), among others.

[2] I am certainly not alone in claiming that the traditional Principles-and-Parameters approach is flawed (see Culicover 1999; Jackendoff 2002; Newmeyer, 2005; Goldberg 2006), but unlike the authors just cited, I am not inclined to throw the baby with the bathwater ("if minimalism depends on the success of the Principles-and-Parameters mode, and the latter fails, then. . ."). It is important to bear in mind that the Principles-and-Parameters model is an approach, not a specific theory. The GB way of articulating the Principles-and-Parameters logic was just one possible way. I believe that the Minimalist Program offers us a different, more adequate way of exploring how principles and parameters may interact—a possibility that very few researchers in the Chomskyan tradition seem to appreciate (for a few exceptions that I have been able to find, see Raposo 2002, and Gallego 2008, Hornstein 2009).

lots of automatic repercussions throughout the grammar of individual languages ("macro-parameters"), but they found numerous, ever more fine-grained, independent micro-parameters.

In the limited space allotted to me here, I can focus only on the way in which central Minimalist tenets clash with the traditional Principles-and-Parameters approach. I will have to leave a detailed examination of the alternative offered by the Minimalist Program to another occasion (see Boeckx in progress). As for the empirical shortcomings of the traditional Principles-and-Parameters approach, I urge the reader to take a look at Newmeyer (2005: 77–103) to see some of the major difficulties the standard model faces and to appreciate the empirical task ahead.

10.2 Two Ways of Approaching UG (and Parameters)

To understand the current uneasiness existing between Minimalism and the standard Principles-and-Parameters model it is instructive to go back to an important document of the GB era: Chomsky's introduction to *Lectures on Government and Binding* (Chomsky 1981: 1–16). There Chomsky outlines the Principles-and-Parameters approach that was pursued ever since and that Mark Baker articulated in a very accessible way in his *Atoms of Language* (Baker 2001). Chomsky makes clear that the appeal of the Principles-and-Parameters model is that it provides a compact way of capturing a wide range of differences. As he notes (p. 6), "[i]deally, we hope to find that complexes of properties . . . are reducible to a single parameter, fixed in one or another way." This is clearly the ideal of Parametric Syntax. Elsewhere, Chomsky makes clear that this ideal depends on the richness of UG: "If these parameters are embedded in a theory of UG that is sufficiently rich in structure, then the languages that are determined by fixing their values one way or another will appear to be quite diverse [. . .]" (p. 4). The starting assumption of Government-and-Binding was this: "What we expect to find, then, is a highly structured theory of UG . . ." (p. 3). In a recent paper, Chomsky (2007a: 2) makes this very clear: "At the time of the 1974 discussions, it seemed that FL must be rich, highly structured, and substantially unique."

As Baker (2005) insightfully observes, the traditional Principles-and-Parameters model takes UG to be "overspecified." This is perhaps clearest in Yang's (2002) model, where the acquisition task is reduced to choosing one among all the fully formed languages that UG makes available. In other words, the traditional Principles-and-Parameters model is ultra-selectionist, guided by the slogan that learning (a little) is forgetting (a lot).

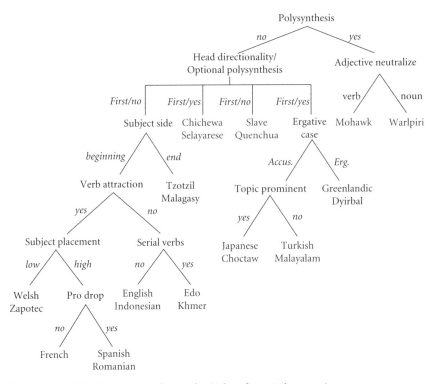

FIGURE 10.1 Baker's Parameter hierarchy (taken from Baker 2003)

Such an approach, relying on a richly structured UG, culminates in Baker's (2001) Parameter hierarchy (see Figure 10.1), a (partial) characterization of the dependencies among parameters (i.e. parametrized principles).

The most obvious question that arises in a Minimalist context, where one seeks to go beyond explanatory adequacy, is, Where does the hierarchy come from? That is, What are the design principles that would make this specific hierarchy emerge? I do not know of any work addressing this issue. I suspect that this is due in part to the fact that Baker's hierarchy makes use of concepts such as topic prominence that have never been rigorously defined in a generative framework. The hierarchy also conceals layers of complexity (well known to practitioners in the field) in the formulation of serial verbs or pro-drop that would undoubtedly render the hierarchy more intricate and elaborate. But the lack of explicit discussion of Baker's hierarchy is also due to the fact that most syntacticians working within the Minimalist Program have shifted their attention away from rich, complex, parametrized principles, and toward the formulation of more basic operations (such as Merge and Agree).

This is part of the shift that Chomsky (2007a: 4) characterizes thus:

Throughout the modern history of generative grammar, the problem of determining the character of FL has been approached "from top down": How much must be attributed to UG to account for language acquisition? The M[inimalist] P[rogram] seeks to approach the problem "from bottom up": How little can be attributed to UG while still accounting for the variety of I-languages attained?

As I write, the research program that approaches UG from below has generated a few interesting hypotheses regarding the nature of basic operations (such as Merge, Agree, and Phasal Spell-Out) that are supposed to capture the essence of the core UG principles identified in the GB era. Such research has (implicitly) abstracted away from the fact that most principles in the GB era were parametrized, and has assumed that things pertaining to linguistic variation will fall into place once we understand the nature of principles. This research strategy was made possible by the perceived success of the traditional Principles-and-Parameters approach as a model solution to Plato's Problem. But it is important to note that the perceived success was not, or at any rate, need not be, dependent on the exact nature of parameters. What enabled the formulation of the Minimalist Program is the perceived possibility of segregating the universal from the particular (suggested by the gradual abandonment of language-specific, construction-specific rules in favor of parametrized principles), not so much the formulation of parametrized principles. In this sense, the traditional Principles-and-Parameters model did not go all the way, as it kept principles and parameters intertwined in the guise of parametrized principles. I think that some syntacticians nevertheless saw in this the possibility that one day principles and parameters could be fully segregated, which in turn warranted certain Minimalist moves. Be that as it may, I believe that recent developments within Minimalism make it possible to entertain the possibility of a truly universal, non-parametric syntax. Perhaps this is what Chomsky had in mind when he formulated the Uniformity hypothesis (Chomsky 2001: 2), given in (1).

(1)   *Uniformity Hypothesis*
      In the absence of compelling evidence to the contrary, assume languages to be uniform, with variety restricted to easily detectable properties of utterances.

Chomsky's formulation is not clear enough, as it fails to make precise what "easily detectable properties of utterances" are. Here I would like to entertain a strong version of the Uniformity hypothesis—call it the Strong Uniformity Thesis (SUT)—which states that narrow syntax is not subject to variation, not even parametric variation. In other words, there is only one syntax, fully uniform, at the heart of the faculty of language, underlying all languages.

(2)   *Strong Uniformity Thesis*
    Principles of narrow syntax are not subject to parametrization; nor are they affected by lexical parameters.

Under the SUT, points of variation (i.e. parameters) would be confined to the margins of narrow syntax, especially the morpho-phonological component (PF).[3]

My reason for pursuing the SUT is that if Minimalist research is taken seriously, there is simply no way for principles of efficient computation to be parametrized. Contrary to what Baker and Collins (2006) seem to assume, it strikes me as implausible to entertain the possibility that a principle like 'Shortest Move' could be active in some languages, but not in others. Put differently, if Minimalist research is on the right track, there can be no parameters within the statements of the general principles that shape natural-language syntax. In other words, narrow syntax solves interface design specifications optimally in the same way in all languages (contra Baker 2008b and Fukui 2006). Modifying Marantz (1995: 380), Minimalism can be seen as the end of parametric syntax. I believe that this conclusion is a natural consequence of the claim at the heart of the generative/biolinguistic enterprise that there is only language, Human, and that this organ/faculty emerged very recently in the species, too recently for multiple solutions to design specifications to have been explored.

10.3 Three Roads to Strong Uniformity

I also believe that the SUT has become more realistic as a result of three recent developments in the Minimalist Program, to which I would like to turn now.

The first development concerns our evolving conception of the lexicon in a Minimalist grammar. Readers familiar with the literature on parameters will no doubt have noted that the SUT is reminiscent of the conjecture first formulated by Hagit Borer, endorsed by Chomsky (1995), according to which "the availability of variation [is restricted] to the possibilities which are offered by one single complement: the inflectional component." (Borer 1984: 3)

---

[3] I remain agnostic concerning the possibility of pragmatic variation of the sort discussed by Svenonius and Ramchand (2007) and Matthewson (2006, 2008). Crucially, if this type of variation exists, it is outside narrow syntax.

But like Chomsky's Uniformity hypothesis mentioned above, Borer's conjecture can be construed in more than one way:[4] What counts as a lexical property? What is the lexicon, and where is it located with respect to other components of the grammar?

Many (including Borer herself) found Borer's conjecture appealing because traditionally the lexicon is viewed as the repository of idiosyncrasies (see Bloomfield 1933; Chomsky 1995). Since the lexicon is clearly the locus of learning, it makes sense to locate parameters there, since parameter settings must be chosen under the influence of the input the child receives. But recently, under the impetus of Hale and Keyser (1993, 2002) research, many aspects of lexical knowledge have been found highly principled, so much so that talk of a l(exical) syntax has appeared feasible. This trend was continued by proponents of Distributed Morphology (Halle and Marantz 1993; Marantz 2000) and by Borer herself (Borer 2005). The net result of this line of research is that much of what we took to be a "messy" pre-syntactic lexical component has now been relegated to post-(narrow) syntactic areas, such as the morpho-phonological component (PF). The pre-syntactic lexicon has been considerably deflated, and very few opportunities remain for it to influence syntactic derivations in dramatic ways. (I return to these few opportunities in Section 10.4.)

Such neo-constructionist or epilexicalist approaches to the lexicon provide the first theoretical development that virtually forces the SUT upon us: once parameters are confined to the lexicon, and much of the lexicon is relegated to post-syntactic components, there is little chance left for (narrow) syntax to be subject to parametric variation.

The second development I would like to highlight is the rise of the Unrestricted Merge model of syntax, beginning with Chomsky (2004a). It has been pointed out on numerous occasions that Minimalism is a research program and that there are multiple ways of exploring it. In what can be called the early Minimalist period (epitomized by Chomsky 1993, 1995), emphasis was laid on the Last Resort character of syntactic operations, as a way to reveal economy principles at work. The most productive way to conceive of syntactic operations being driven by Last Resort operations turned out to be to think of operations taking place to resolve some featural illegitimacy on specific elements (cf. principles like Greed, Attract, and the like). This led to a detailed examination of what features can be found on lexical items, how these could vary, and so on. The number, type, and properties of features became the

---

[4] Borer herself develops a specific implementation of her conjecture in her 1984 book. Ouhalla (1991) and Webelhuth (1991) propose different articulations of the conjecture. All of these proposals must be rethought in the light of the emergence of a Minimalist architecture.

focus of attention in the literature now known as the Cartography approach. It is also at the heart of so-called Crash-proof syntax models. More recently, a few researchers (beginning with Chomsky 2004a) have begun to explore an alternative according to which syntactic operations apply "freely" solely in virtue of elements bearing "edge features." Such an approach vastly overgenerates, and must be supplemented with interface-internal conditions that filter out unwanted combinations (all of which, it must be stressed, are legible). In this way of looking at grammar, the edge feature boils down to the property of being a lexical item. Unlike the features that were used in the early Minimalist period, which varied from lexical item to lexical item, edge features are the common denominator among lexical items; they cannot be the locus of (parametric) variation. In other words, reliance on edge features has insulated narrow syntax from parametric effects. Syntax has become immune to the sort of lexical vagaries and idiosyncrasies that could not be ruled out in the early Minimalist period.[5]

The third development that I want to stress in this section concerns the growing suspicion that the mapping from syntax to sense (SEM) is architecturally privileged over the mapping from syntax to sound/sign (PHON). Until recently, models of grammar treated Phonetic Form (PF) and Logical Form (LF) symmetrically (think of the symmetry of the inverted-Y model), but for a very long time (going back to remarks by traditional grammarians like Jespersen) it has been clear that there is quite a bit of variation at PF, but virtually none at LF. Thus, Chomsky (1998: 123) notes that PHON/PF "yield[s] a variety of morphological systems, perhaps superficially quite different in externalization of a uniform procedure of constructing an LF representation." As Minimalists made progress in understanding the nature of operations internal to narrow syntax, it became clear that these were in some sense designed primarily to meet demands on the sense-side of the grammar (e.g. the elimination of unvalued/uninterpretable features). Chomsky (2008: 136) puts it thus:

It may be that there is a basic asymmetry in the contribution to language design of the two interface systems: the primary contribution to the structure of [the] F[aculty of] L[anguage] may be optimization of the C-I [sense] interface.

In other words, narrow syntax is optimally designed to meet demands from the meaning side, and externalization (PF) is akin to an afterthought, or appendix. Since variation clearly exists on the sound/sign side (an unavoidable consequence of the fact that this is that aspect of language that is used for

---

[5] I should mention one important exception: Gallego (2007) explores variation in phase structure by exploiting Chomsky's (2008) definition of phase- heads as *u*F-bearers, a type of variation that I consider too "deep" or syntactic.

communication and learning, and communication/imitation/reproduction is a more or less imperfect affair), but no evidence exists that it is found at the meaning side, it is not implausible to think of narrow syntax as completely uniform (meeting LF-demands), and not affected (design-wise) or adapted to cope with or code for variation in the guise of (syntactic) parameters. To put it differently, the LF–PF-asymmetry naturally leads one to expect a uniform narrow syntax, designed to meet the uniform demands at the meaning side in an optimal fashion.

I should stress in closing this section that none of the three developments reviewed here provide incontrovertible evidence in favor of the SUT. They simply point to the fact that the SUT emerges as the most natural hypothesis in the context of a Minimalist Program rigorously pursued.

10.4 Parameter Schemata

I pointed out in the previous section that various developments in the Minimalist literature conspire to make the SUT plausible. Architecturally speaking, there is little room left in a Minimalist conception of grammar for lexical parameters to affect narrow syntax. In this section I review a few proposals from the literature I am familiar with that characterize ways in which parameters may affect syntax. Following terminology suggested by Giuseppe Longobardi, I will refer to these as attempts to uncover parameter schemata.[6]

Perhaps the most detailed investigation in this domain comes from Longobardi himself. In a series of works (Longobardi 2003, 2005a; Guardiano and Longobardi 2005; Gianollo, Guardiano, and Longobardi in press), Longobardi argues that languages may differ in the following ways:

(3)   For a given language L,

    a. Is F, F a functional feature, grammaticalized?

---

[6] Works on parameter schemata follow in the steps of GB-syntacticians like Borer (1984), Fukui (1986, 1995), Ouhalla (1991), and Webelhuth (1991), who sought to capture the format of parameters. Such works are sometimes advertised as trying to uncover the nature of possible parameters. But as Howard Lasnik points out (p.c.), one must exercise caution with the phrase "possible parameter." As he notes, in the heyday of GB it was very popular to say that we needed a theory of possible parameters the way we used to need a theory of possible transformations. But the analogy was completely false. We needed a theory of possible transformations because the child had to pick out the right transformations, and if any conceivable formal operation could be a transformation, the task would be hopeless. But in a Principles-and-Parameters model, the child does not have to pick out the right parameters from a set of possible ones. Rather, the child just has to pick out the right *values* for wired-in parameters. So the true analogy would be a theory of possible parameter values. But that, of course, is totally trivial. What we really want to determine is the *actual* parameters. Work on parameter schemata is not about possible parameters, but rather (in the absence of a complete map of all lexical items made available by UG) about what actual parameters may look like (abstractly).

  b. Is F, F a grammaticalized feature, checked by X, X a lexical category?

  c. Is F, F a grammaticalized feature, spread on Y, Y a lexical category?

  d. Is F, F a grammaticalized feature checked by X, strong?

Longobardi (2005a: 410–11) comments on (3) as follows. Question (3a) is meant to capture the fact that in some languages dimensions like definiteness are not marked on functional items like Determiners. Question (3b) boils down to asking whether a given functional head acts as a Probe. Question (3c) asks whether some feature F has an unvalued/uninterpretable variant participating in Agree-relations. Question (3d) is meant to capture that fact that in some languages movement is overt, while in others it is covert. (It is worth pointing out that Longobardi (2005a: 411) leaves open the possibility of a fifth parameter schema pertaining to pronunciation, of the sort familiar with *pro*-drop phenomena.)

    The difference between (3b) and (3c) is not entirely clear to me (for a feature to be a Probe and be checked, it must Agree, hence "spread"), and once eliminated, Longobardi's schema converges with Uriagereka's (1995) characterization of his F-parameter in (4) (posited to capture effects at the left periphery of the clause, distinguishing Germanic from Romance, and also cutting across Romance varieties):

(4) a. Is F present in the language?

    b. Is F strong?

Roberts and Roussou (2002) make a similar proposal when they propose the following parameter format:

(5) a. Does F require PF-support?

    b. Is the support provided via Merge or Move?

Likewise, Borer (2005) puts forth that variation within the functional domain can be attributed only to the mode in which open values are assigned range: either via direct merger of a head, or movement of a head, or by insertion of an adverb, or by Spec–Head agreement.

    As we see, there is a fair amount of consensus about the kind of parameter one finds in UG.[7] The consensus boils down to a nested structure like (6).[8]

---

[7] The emerging consensus provides supports for Fukui's (1995) conjecture that (i) parametric variation outside the lexicon must be limited to ordering restrictions ("linearity"), and (ii) inside the lexicon, only those functional elements that do not play a role at LF (such as AGR-elements) are subject to variation (in the sense that they can be absent from the lexicon of a particular language).

[8] The formulation in (6) requires one to take head movement to be head merger under adjacency in PF (Harley 2004) or (if syntactic) movement to a Specifier position (Matushansky 2006, Vicente 2007).

(6)   Is F present/active in the language? Yes/NO

  If Yes, does F give rise to Movement, or simply Agree (/Merge)?

The nested character of (6) may prove useful in recapturing some of the effects of Baker's (2001) parameter hierarchy. I will not explore this possibility further here, as I am skeptical regarding the adequacy of the first question in (6). I think that all languages make use of the same pool of features, and that one of the ways in which languages differ is how they express the relevant feature F. Specifically, I submit (following Fortuny 2008, and Gallego 2008; see also Bejar 2003) that languages may choose to express f_1 and f_2 separately (analytically) or as a bundle (syncretically). This different way of thinking about the mode of parametrization available has the effect of breaking up the nested dependency expressed in (6). Indeed I claim that the dependent question in (6) must be reformulated independently, namely as: Is F viral? (i.e. does F exhibit a uF variant?). Finally, languages may differ in whether a specific (phase-)head[9] is strong (uF-bearing) or weak (defective). Notice that this way of formulating lexical parameters makes them interdependent; it does not single out one of the parameters as the one on which all others depend. Notice also that the lexical parameters I put forward barely affect narrow syntax. It is the same syntax whether f_1 and f_2 form a bundle or not. It is also the same syntax whether a specific feature F is viral or not. And, finally, it is the same syntax regardless of whether a phase head is weak or strong.[10]

  Of course, there are more ways in which languages may differ, but I contend that all other parametric options arise in the post-syntactic morpho-phonological component, such as whether a head H allows its specifier to be filled by overt material, or whether the head or the tail of a chain can or must be pronounced, or whether a given head H is affixal and requires its expression in the vicinity of another head, or whether a head H precedes or follows its complements. These options arise at the point of Spell-Out, when syntactic structures must be linearized and the demands of (late-inserted) morphemes must be met.

The formulation in (6) is also facilitated by the adoption of the single-cycle syntax model that takes "covert" movement to be either pure Agree or Pre-Spell-Out movement following by pronunciation of a low copy.

  [9] Following Chomsky (2007, 2008), I assume that only phase heads probe. See Boeckx (in progress), Richards (2007), and Gallego (2007) for detailed discussion.

  [10] The only difference will pertain to the timing of transfer, or the amount of structure transferred to the interfaces at a given time (see Boeckx in progress). This should not be characterized as a syntactic parameter as the same issue of timing/amount of transfer arises whenever a lexical choice is made/a numeration is constructed (active v^o vs. passive v^o) in any given language. For a different view on this matter, see Gallego (2007).

10.5 Clustering Effects

The preceding section outlined a very impoverished version of a parametric theory, with parametric options isolated from one another and localized to specific heads. Let me call these nano parameters,[11] to keep them distinct from the more traditional octopus-like macroparameters that GB-research made famous (beginning with Rizzi 1982 and continuing with Baker 1996, 2001, 2008a). Some researchers may find these wholly inadequate, unable as they seem to be to express the clusters of variation that are invariably brought up in the literature on parameters—especially the clusters that seem to align parametric values across independent heads (as the traditional head parameter does).[12] But although such clusters of variation did much to dispel the common impression (endorsed by structuralists) that languages can vary from one another indefinitely, it is fair to say that few of the implicational statements at the heart of traditional Principles-and-Parameters approach have stood the test of time. Some languages indeed appear to display the clusters the theory predicted, but many languages display only a few of the predicted clustering effects; more often than not, languages show no clustering effects whatsoever. (For this reason alone, nano parameters strike me as more adequate empirically.) Newmeyer (2005) is correct in stressing that the rarity of massive clustering effects takes much of the gloss away from the traditional Principles-and-Parameters model.[13] Newmeyer goes on to suggest that clustering effects are just tendencies (probable, but not the only possible languages) to be captured in terms of performance effects, specifically parsing strategies.

I think Newmeyer is correct in taking parametric clusters to be tendencies, not to be accounted for in terms of UG principles. But unlike him, I would like to suggest that these tendencies do not (always)[14] arise due to parsing

[11] I use the term "nano parameter" as opposed to "micro parameter" to stress their low-level, "flat" character. (I would reserve the term micro parameter for points of variation displaying some minimal nested structure such as (6).)

[12] Clusters resulting from the fact that a given head affects the surface appearance of many constructions due to the fact that this head is heavily affected by a variety of derivational options (e.g. INFL in Rizzi's 1982 pro-drop parameter) are much less problematic for the sort of nano parameter I entertain.

[13] It is interesting to note that Nicolis's (2006) re-examination of Rizzi's classical formulation of the pro-drop parameter (with consequences not only for null subjects, but also post-verbal subjects and long-distance subject extraction) ends up with the claim that the only robust correlation is this: if a language allows null referential subjects, it also allows null expletive/non-referential subjects. But this is clearly a lexical correlation (null referential subjects being a (featural) superset of non-referential subjects), expressible at the level of a lexical (nano) parameter, and not a syntactic correlation of the sort one would expect from a traditional (syntactic) parameter and of the sort Rizzi had in mind.

[14] Some tendencies may indeed be due to performance factors. For pertinent discussion, see Rizzi's (2007) treatment of the root-infinitive stage in child language, where it is suggested that

strategies. I propose that some are due to certain biases in the learning process. That is, I would like to suggest that the types of language that parametric clusters describe act as attractors as the child acquires her language, and that only a fair amount of positive counterevidence in the data leads the child to settle on a less homogenous system of parameter settings.[15]

In a nutshell, the guiding intuition I would like to pursue is that clustering results from the child seeking to maximize the similarity across parameter settings, harmonize their values, and thereby economize what must be memorized (via the formation of a generalization across similar parameters). My suggestion goes in the direction of a recent trend expressing a renewed interest in the nature of learning and the interaction between nature and nurture (see Yang 2002, 2004b, 2005; Pearl 2007). As Yang and Pearl have made clear (in a linguistic context; see Gallistel 1990b, 2006 for more general remarks on learning modules), a proper characterization of the learning task requires paying attention to three important components: (i) a defined hypothesis space (for language, UG), (ii) data intake, and (iii) a data-update algorithm.

Yang and Pearl have shown in detail that there are certain data-intake filters or certain learning biases that must be assumed to characterize the language-learning task adequately. For example, Yang shows that the learner must be ready to tolerate a certain amount of noise within limits (which Yang takes to account for a variety of irregular, or semi-regular morphological processes). In a similar vein, Pearl has argued that the child must be ready to filter out potentially ambiguous cues for certain parameter settings. I would like to add to this a bias by which the child strives for parametric value consistency, a Superset bias with which the child processes the data, and which she abandons only if there is too much data contradicting her initial hypothesis.

(7)   *Superset Bias*
       Strive for parametric-value consistency among similar parameters

For example, if the child learns that V precedes its complement and T precedes its complement, she will be inclined to hypothesize that the next head she encounters will also precede its complement, and will only reject her hypothesis if she finds enough positive counterevidence.

---

some parametric values are assumed so as to reduce the computational proceesing load and facilitate production.

[15] I predict that, all else being equal, as the amount of counterevidence decreases, the shape of the language acquire will drift toward the attractors. For relevant discussion on language drift, see Roberts (2007b).

The Superset bias should not look too unfamiliar: something very much like it is at the heart of the evaluation metric in Chomsky and Halle (1968). It may also underlie recurring intuitions in the domain of markedness (see e.g. Hyams 1986: ch. 6) and may help us characterize the notion of default parameter value (which Sugisaki 2007 shows does not fit well with other assumptions in a traditional Principles-and-Parameters setting).

Finally, if it is on the right track, the Superset bias may reveal another economy principle at work in language. But it is too early to speculate in this direction. We must first have a better handle on the range of variation that is allowed. Only then will we be able to study the superset bias with all the care that is required to characterize how much positive counterevidence is necessary for the child to choose a more marked option, etc. The take-home message for now is that if nano parameters are all we are left with in the context of minimalism, clustering effects—when they obtain!—will have to arise from something (or multiple things) external to narrow syntax. It seems to me that the learning process itself constitutes a natural place to look. It will certainly require closer collaboration between theoretical linguists and psycholinguists.

10.6 Concluding Remarks, from a Biolinguistic Perspective

This short paper is very programmatic, and I ask the reader to treat it as such. Many of my suggestions are very tentative, and await much closer empirical investigation than I have been able to provide here. But one thing, I hope, is very clear: the traditional Principles-and-Parameters model does not fit snugly with Minimalist intuitions. If Minimalist ideas are on the right track, the standard take on what would count as a solution to Plato's Problem (parameter setting in the context of an overspecified UG) must be rethought from the ground up.

Although one finds relatively little explicit discussion of parametric variation in the Minimalist literature (other than the convenient appeal to a parameter whenever two languages diverge), I hope to have shown here that one can distill a program for parameters from the Minimalist literature—a Minimalist Program for parametric theory, as it were. It is one that leaves very little room for parameters (i.e. points of variation) to affect narrow syntax. This is not due to the fact that empirically syntactic effects of parameters are rare (the assumption in comparative syntax is that such effects are numerous and pervasive), but rather to the fact that syntactic parameters (i.e. parametrized principles) make no sense within Minimalism.

I believe that the Strong Uniformity Thesis in (2) emerges as a natural consequence of approaching UG from below, and with Galilean lenses. Consider, for example, Chomsky's (2005) claim that three factors enter in the explanation of language design:[16] (i) the genetic endowment (1st factor), (ii) the environment (2nd factor), and (iii) generic good design principles transcending the limits of genetics (3rd factor). The third factor has played a prominent role in Minimalist research, and led to a much less specified view of the genetic endowment specific to language (UG). I have followed this trend here by suggesting that some effects formerly attributed to macroparameters may be due to a very general superset bias (economy guideline) relativized to the thing being learned (language). Invariably, as the importance of the first factor wanes, the interplay between the second and the third factors becomes more critical.

As I have argued elsewhere (see Boeckx 2006: ch. 4), I think that Minimalist guidelines suggest an architecture of grammar that is more plausible biologically speaking that a fully specified, highly specific UG—especially considering the very little time nature had to evolve this remarkable ability that defines our species. If syntax is at the heart of what had to evolve *de novo*, syntactic parameters would have to have been part of this very late evolutionary addition. Although I confess that our intuitions pertaining to what could have evolved very rapidly are not as robust as one would like, I think that Darwin's Problem (the logical problem of language evolution) becomes very hard to approach if a GB-style architecture is assumed. Within GB, there is no obvious answer to why variation exists, and why variation takes the form that it does. But with a considerably leaner vision of the faculty of language, variation becomes almost inevitable. If very little about language is specified genetically, and much of the core of language (narrow syntax) is the result of third factor effects, variation emerges as the direct result of underspecification. It is because so little is specified about language in the genome that the varied, and ever-changing environment gives us variation in the externalized aspects of language. To take an obvious example, it is because Merge is symmetric that both head-first and head-last are possible options. Once a symmetric structure has to be broken by sheer force of the physics of speech, two options are logically available if no restriction has been pre-imposed.[17] (A richer syntax could have specified a rigid head–complement order, as in Kayne 1994.)

This is not to say that we are back to the structuralists' claim that anything goes across languages. Narrow syntax sets the limits of variation (no language

---

[16] See also Lewontin (2000) and Gould (2002) for similar views in a more general biological setting.

[17] A syntactic parameter of the sort proposed by Saito and Fukui (1998) seems redundant in the present context.

will have ternary branching structures if binary branching is a third factor effect; ditto for minimality, the size of phases, etc.), but within these limits, there will be variation. And there will be a lot of it, more than GB-practitioners expected, but probably as much as the detailed empirical work spearheaded by Richard Kayne continues to reveal (for a representative sample, see Manzini and Savoia 2005). Norbert Hornstein has pointed out (Hornstein 2009) that there are many geometrical figures one can draw with a minimal set of tools like a straight edge and a compass, but there are some (e.g. triangles with 20-degree angles) that are impossible. The gappiness of the linguistic morphospace may have to be accounted in exactly these less specified, but no less deterministic terms.

We seem to have reached a stage where the current leading idea about how Darwin's Problem could be solved forces us to reconsider what we took to be our very best bet concerning Plato's Problem. It is true that selectionism has now a distinguished history in biology and that parallelisms between a GB-style, richly-specified UG, and current work in developmental evolutionary biology (evo–devo) are not too hard to find.[18] But one must bear in mind that the role of epigenetic factors in biology is on the rise (see Jablonka and Lamb 2005), and that the selectionism often invoked in evo–devo is in aid of understanding what Gould (1989) called "disparity" (fundamental design differences, as opposed to superficial diversity). One must bear in mind that in the context of language, we are dealing with a single design, a single organ, in a single species. With language, there is no disparity to speak of, only very superficial diversity. Evo–devo seeks to understand the diversity of design by revealing a design of diversity, but there is no diversity of design in language, as 50 years of hard work in generative grammar have revealed. Accordingly, the analogy between UG and the universal genome should not be pushed too far, certainly not in the direction of an overspecified UG, I think.

---

[18] See already Piattelli-Palmarini (1986) and Jerne (1985). Perhaps the clearest parallelism can be found in the context of Sherman's (2007) Universal Genome proposal, where it is argued that descent with modification often takes the form of genetic losses. But there are other, less controversial claims in evo–devo that mirror GB-style analyses. For example, Arthur (2001) lists four ways in which developmental differences among organisms give rise to radically different adult morphologies:

- heterochrony (different timing of gene expression);
- heterotopy (different location of gene expression);
- heterometry (more of the gene product being made);
- heterotypy (change in the nature of the gene product, e.g. switch on different target genes).

It is not hard to find corresponding parameter types, such as:

- is movement overt (pre-Spell-Out) or covert (post-Spell-Out)?
- is the Agr-feature expressed on T or C?
- how many features does H check?/How many elements move to SpecHP?/How many heads are there in the left periphery?
- is H strong or weak?

Inspired by recent developments in Minimalism, I have sketched an approach that I hope captures the outline of the nature of linguistic variation in a more adequate way. The line of argument advocated here provides an answer to why variation exists, and why there is so much of it (but so little in narrow syntax proper). It relates the answer to other current themes in biolinguistics that stress the non-genomic character of nativism, and the formal simplicity of the language organ.

If the approach suggested here is on the right track, narrow syntax shows no sign of design compromise to assimilate variation, and thus provides another piece of evidence in favor of the PF–LF asymmetry recently emphasized by Chomsky. Variation is not structurally encoded (in the form of a parameter hierarchy); instead it is the result of the lack of structural encoding. It arises exactly where we expect it: not where third factors reign (narrow syntax), but where the second factor plays a prominent role (externalization). Nevertheless, variation tends to show signs of optimization in its organization. As a matter of fact, in the present context, parameters emerge as a mini–max solution (as Noam Chomsky and Massimo Piattelli-Palmarini have speculated): an attempt to navigate between the path of least genetic specification (minimal UG) and the path of least instruction (superset bias).

The few suggestions I made in this chapter quickly reveal the vastness of the empirical research program that lies ahead. In many ways, we have not begun to solve Plato's problem (not even abstractly). Since the standard assumption in the field is that there is a lot of syntactic effects out there (the topic of the rich field of comparative syntax), and the main claim of this chapter is that syntactic variation does not exist, many data points will have to be reanalyzed. I suspect that much of what we thought was syntax will turn out to be morpho-phonology (in the same way that the syntactic notion of timing of movement (overt vs. covert) has been replaced by a PF pronunciation algorithm that picks a certain copy in a movement chain). Like GB principles, GB parameters may turn out to be epiphenomena, to be understood as the result of deeper forces.

It is sometimes said that minimalism has not engendered important empirical discoveries (see Pinker and Jackendoff 2005; Koopman 2000). Nothing could be further from the truth, if we bear in mind that the empirical focus of generative grammar and biolinguistics is the language faculty, not specific constructions in languages. If we find efficient design in language, that is a surprising empirical discovery. Likewise, if we find a truly uniform syntax, if indeed it turns out that there is no syntactic variation at all, that too would be a startling empirical discovery, considering that only fifty years ago Martin Joos could write with assurance (Joos 1957) that the range of variation in this realm was virtually infinite.

11

(Bio)linguistic Variation: *Have/be* Alternations in the Present Perfect

M. RITA MANZINI AND LEONARDO M. SAVOIA

11.1 Introduction

According to Chomsky (2000b: 119), "the human language faculty and the (I-)languages that are manifestations of it qualify as natural objects." This approach—that "regards the language faculty as an 'organ of the body' "—has been labeled the "biolinguistic perspective" by Chomsky (2005: 1). Hauser, Chomsky, and Fitch (2002: 1570) base their discussion of the key biological question of evolution on the "biologically and individually grounded" use of the term language "to refer to an internal component of the mind/brain (sometimes called 'internal language' or 'I-language')." They distinguish two conceptions of the faculty of language, one broader (FLB) and one narrower (FLN):

FLB includes FLN combined with at least two other organism-internal systems, which we call "sensory-motor" and "conceptual-intentional . . . A key component of FLN is a computational system (narrow syntax) that generates internal representations and maps them into the sensory-motor interface by the phonological system and into the conceptual-intentional interface by the (formal) semantics system . . . Most, if not all, of FLB is based on mechanisms shared with nonhuman animals . . . FLN—the computational mechanism of recursion—is recently evolved and unique to our species."

(Hauser et al. 2002: 1571)

The conception of the language faculty and of (I-)languages as "natural," "biologically grounded" objects corresponds to specific theories concerning their internal articulation:

the I-language consists of a computational procedure and a lexicon. The lexicon is a collection of items, each a complex of properties (called "features") . . . The computational procedure maps an array of lexical choices into a pair of symbolic objects, phonetic form and LF . . . The elements of these symbolic objects can be called "phonetic" and "semantic" features, respectively, but we should bear in mind that all of this is pure syntax and completely internalist.

(Chomsky 2000b: 120)

The internal articulation of the FLN is crucial to the biolinguistic program, no less than its applications to domains such as language evolution, genetics, and neurology. Here we address some points concerning it; specifically we concentrate on the issue of language variation, starting with the idea that:

the diversity and complexity can be no more than superficial appearance...the search for explanatory adequacy requires that language structure must be invariant.

(Chomsky 2000b: 7)

There is a reason to believe that the computational component is invariant, virtually...language variation appears to reside in the lexicon.

(Chomsky 2000b: 120)

In this perspective, a central aim of our work is to provide empirical support for what we may call the lexical parametrization hypothesis (Wexler and Manzini 1987), making it more precise in which sense it holds. No doubt "one aspect is 'Saussurean arbitrariness,' the arbitrary links between concepts and sounds...However the possible sounds are narrowly constrained, and the concepts may be virtually fixed" (Chomsky 2000b: 120). In the present chapter we address the issue of how the linguistically relevant conceptual space yields different (I-)languages beyond the obvious aspect of Saussurean arbitrariness.

Before proceeding to the empirical core of the argument, we briefly introduce some of the conceptual underpinnings of the framework we adopt, beginning with the thesis that language "is a system that is, as far as we know, essentially uniform. Nobody has found any genetic differences...since its emergence there has not been any significant evolution. It has stayed that way" (Chomsky et al.'s 2002: 147). This view is shared by much current work on human cognitive and linguistic evolution (Lieberman 1991; Jackendoff 2002). The conclusion holds for living languages and for ancient ones (documented and no longer spoken, or merely reconstructed); as argued by Labov (1994), the same mechanisms of (surface) variation and change affect all of them. To take a comparative typology perspective:

no evidence of anything like speciation has been found.... Languages from typologically very different areas have the same latent structural potential...this survey has uncovered no evidence that human language in general has changed since the earliest stage recoverable by the method used here. There is simply diversity, distributed geographically.   (Nichols 1992: 227)

As for this geographically distributed diversity,

a residual zone or a set of residual zones will contain a good deal of the world's possible linguistic diversity in microcosm, and both the existence of internal diversity and its actual profile are stable and obviously very natural situations. Diversity of a particular kind may even be regarded as the state to which a group of languages will naturally revert if left undisturbed...Spread zones, in contrast, are typically highly divergent from one another, but each is internally quite homogeneous...Just which language spreads in a spread zone is a matter of historical accident, which can distort the statistical distribution of linguistic types in an area...   (Nichols 1992: 23)

The set of languages considered in this chapter present the kind of variation that we expect in natural languages in the absence of external constraints. Because of the political and cultural factors that for centuries have kept the Italian peninsula in conditions of great administrative and social fragmentation, dialectal differentiation in Italy has been preserved longer (i.e. up to the present day) than in other areas of Western Europe, including Romance-speaking ones. Thus Italian dialects provide a rich and articulated picture of language variation that contrasts with that of other intensively studied varieties, say, English. The view we take is that it is the linguistic situation of, say, Britain that represents a somehow misleading picture of variation, reflecting not only the internal shaping forces of language development but also external mechanisms of social and political standardization. The variation presented by Albanian, including the major Geg vs. Tosk divide in mainland Albania, and Arbëresh dialects of Southern Italy, has the same general character as that observed in Romance dialects (Manzini and Savoia 2007). In the internalist (i.e. biologically, individually grounded) perspective that we adopt, variation between two or more dialects (linguistic communities) is in fact not qualitatively different from variation within the same dialect (community), or even within the productions of a single speaker. To the extent that speakers alternate, say, between stylistic levels according to the situation of use, they will have a bilingual competence of sorts—which, given the lexical parametrization hypothesis adopted here, can be accounted for as the co-existence of different lexicons with a single computational component (MacSwan 2000).

Suppose then that the lexicon is the locus of linguistic variation—in the presence of a uniform, that is, invariant, computational component, and of an invariant repertory of interface primitives, both phonological and conceptual. Non-trivial questions arise at this point: how can the lexicon vary on the basis of a universal inventory of properties (or "features")? And how come that variation in the lexicon has as its consequence variation in order, agreement, selection, and other relations that are computationally determined? These questions are amply debated in current linguistic theory. Our empirical discussion, concerning *have* and *be* auxiliary selection in Romance and Albanian, aims at supporting certain positions emerging from the debate—as opposed to others, in principle equally possible.

In particular, the answer to the questions that precede is mediated for various scholars by the notion that there is a fundamental distinction between functional and non-functional elements. Thus within the Distributed Morphology framework, Embick (2000: 187) assumes a "distinction between the *functional* and *lexical* vocabularies of a language . . . functional categories merely instantiate sets of abstract syntacticosemantic features" on which the derivational component operates. The actual phonological terminals corresponding to these abstract categories are inserted only after a level of Morphological Structure, where readjustment rules apply (Late Insertion). Leaving empirical considerations aside (Manzini and Savoia 2007, 2010), it is evident that the overall architecture of the grammar implied by this model is considerably more complex than one in which "the formal role of lexical items is not that they are 'inserted' into syntactic derivations, but rather that they establish the correspondence of certain syntactic constituents with phonological and conceptual structures" (Jackendoff 2002: 131).

Kayne's (2005a, 2006b) parametrization model, while avoiding recourse to Late Insertion, is close to Distributed Morphology in assuming that functional items correspond to a universal lexicon of sorts. Lexical and hence grammatical differences are the result of whether the elements of this functional lexicon are overtly realized or "silent." Interestingly, for Kayne (2005a) even variation in the substantive lexicon can be reduced to variation in functional structure, in the sense just defined, as can be seen in his construal of *shallow* as 'LITTLE shallow,' that is, essentially as the specialized lexicalization of *deep* in the context of the silent functional category "little."

Manzini and Savoia (2007) pursue a model under which again there is a unified conception of lexical variation—however, this is of the type traditionally associated with the substantive lexicon: there is a conceptual and grammatical space to be lexicalized and variation results from the different partition of that space. There is no fixed functional lexicon which varies along the axis of overt vs. covert realization—so-called functional space is just like all other conceptual space, and all lexical entries are overt. Thus the distinction between functional, that is, grammatical, contents, and conceptual ones is an external one; as such it is at best useless, while at worst it obscures the real underlying linguistic generalizations.

Our approach typically leads to a redefinition of the categories that play a role in organizing the variation space. Categories considered in the present work will include the person split, transitivity, and voice. We show that in languages where *have* and *be* alternate as auxiliaries of the present perfect, they can do so according to the person split between first/second and third person, according to transitivity, according to voice, or according to two or more of these categories. The relevant categories, or, to be more precise, the primitive notions in terms of which they are defined, are universal; variation reflects the way in which they are (or are not) instantiated in different (sub)lexicons— consisting in the case at hand of the entries for *have* and *be*.

The idea that we have of variation within the so-called functional lexicon is consistent with current conclusions regarding the conceptual space and the different ways in which it surfaces in natural languages. Fodor (1983) and Jackendoff (1994), among others, develop the Chomskyan theme that con- cepts, like other aspects of language, must have an innate basis—largely because of the poverty of stimulus argument. Already Lenneberg (1967) observes that lexical items are the overt marks of a categorization process through which human beings cut out an ontological system from the per- ceptual continuum of the external world. This process of categorization is of course only indirectly connected with the objects of the external world. Jackendoff (1994: 195) notes that the same lexical forms employed to express spatial location and motion (e.g. *The messenger **is in** Istanbul, The messenger **went from** Paris **to** Istanbul, The gang **kept** the messenger **in** Istanbul*) typically also express possession (e.g. *The money **is** Fred's, The inheritance finally **went to** Fred, Fred **kept** the money*), the ascription of properties (e.g. *The light **is** red, The light **went from** green **to** red, The cop **kept** the light red*), etc.

This suggests that thought has a set of precise underlying patterns that are applied to pretty much any semantic field we can think about. Such an underlying "grain" to thought is just the kind of thing we should expect as part of the Universal Grammar of concepts; it's the basic machinery that permits complex thought to be formulated at all.   (Jackendoff 1994: 197)

Dehaene, Izard, Pica, and Spelke (2006) study geometrical concepts in an isolated group of Amazonian people, whose language, Mundurukú, "has few words dedicated to arithmetical, geometrical, or spatial concepts." They conclude that

geometrical knowledge arises in humans independently of instruction, experience with maps or measurement devices, or mastery of *a sophisticated geometrical lan- guage*... There is little doubt that geometrical knowledge can be substantially enriched by cultural inventions such as maps, mathematical tools, or *the geometrical terms of language*... however, the spontaneous understanding of geometrical concepts and maps by this remote human community provides evidence that core geometrical knowledge, like basic arithmetic is a universal constituent of the human mind.

(Dehaene et al. 2006: 385; our italics).

In a similar vein, Hespos and Spelke (2004) study the acquisition of the con- ceptual distinction between " 'tight' and 'loose' fit of one object to another" in

English-speaking children, which is not lexicalized in English, though it is in other languages, like Korean. Their conclusion is that

> like adult Korean speakers but unlike adult English speakers, these infants detected this distinction ... Language learning therefore seems to develop by linking linguistic forms to universal, pre-existing representations of sound and meaning.
>
> (Hespos and Spelke 2004: 453)

In short, the construction blocks that combine into the potentially infinite variety of human lexicons are innate. The lexicons of the different languages are formed on this universal basis, covering slightly different extensions of it and in slightly different ways. The view we advocate here is simply that ways of representing the event such as transitivity or voice are to be thought of as part of this general system. There is no separate functional lexicon—and no separate way of accounting for its variation. We started with the general Chomskyan biolinguistic, or internalist, picture of language, and of its basic components, both broadly and narrowly construed. Variation is crucial to the establishing of this model for the obvious reason that the uniformity thesis, as laid out above, requires a suitably restrictive account of observed cross-linguistic differences. But even more basically, the lexical parametrization hypothesis that we assume means that questions of variation will inevitably bear on the form of the lexicon—one of the crucial components of the I-language.

The other main component of the I-language is "the computational procedure" that "maps an array of lexical choices into a pair of symbolic objects, phonetic form and LF" (Chomsky 2000b, quoted above). As for the latter, Culicover and Jackendoff (2005: 6) aptly characterize a particularly popular conception of the relation of Logical Form (LF) to the syntax (i.e. the computation) as Interface Uniformity—namely "the syntax–semantics interface is maximally simple, in that meaning maps transparently into syntactic structure; and it is maximally uniform, so that the same meaning always maps onto the same syntactic structure." This bias of much current theorizing provides a standardized way of encoding the data, but does not appear to have any strong empirical motivation; nor is the encoding it provides a particularly elegant or transparent one. Conceptually it corresponds to a picture where syntax "includes" interpretation, in the sense that all relevant semantic information finds itself translated into syntactic structure. On the contrary, we agree with Culicover and Jackendoff (2006: 416) on the idea that interpretation is "the product of an autonomous combinatorial capacity independent of and richer than syntax," "largely coextensive with thought," which syntax simply restricts in crucial ways.

Linguistic meanings are but an input to general inferential processes; the linguistic categorization of the conceptual space that lexical items encode does not correspond to "meaning" itself but rather to a restriction of the inferential processes producing it. Sperber and Wilson (1986: 174) provide a particularly compelling discussion of the point that linguistic expressions only denote because of their inferential associations: "Linguistically encoded semantic representations are abstract mental structures which must be inferentially enriched." In such a model the well-known indeterminacy of linguistic meanings becomes a key property of successful communication:

A linguistic device does not have as its direct proper function to make its encoded meaning part of the meaning of the utterances in which it occurs. It has, rather, as its direct proper function to indicate a component of the speaker's meaning that is best evoked by activating the encoded meaning of the linguistic device. It performs this direct function through each token of the device performing the derived proper function of indicating a contextually relevant meaning.   (Origgi and Sperber 2000: 160)

Note that we disagree with Culicover and Jackendoff (2005) on the model of syntax to be adopted. Our analysis depends on a representational version of Minimalism, roughly in the sense of Brody (2003). In such a model, notions of, say, transitivity and voice—hence the selectional restrictions on the complements embedded by *have* and *be*—can be stated directly in terms of LF primitives. Crucially, the LF primitives we employ (argument of, operator–variable, chain, etc.) are independently available within a Minimalist grammar as defined by Chomsky (1995)—with which the approach we take is in this sense compatible. In fact, we would argue that our views on lexical variation and on interpretation are the simplest construal of Chomsky's (2000b) proposals, as summarized above—much simpler than other current approaches, and in this sense closer to the core of minimalism and of the biolinguistic program.

The discussion in this article is based on a set of data which reflect microvariation in a closely connected set of languages (Romance varieties), as well as variation between more distant languages (Romance and Albanian). In Section 11.2, we present the basic evidence. In Section 11.3, we review the notions of person split, transitivity, and voice in terms of which we analyze the data in Section 11.4. Having discussed person-split systems in some detail elsewhere (Manzini and Savoia 2007), we concentrate on auxiliary selection according to transitivity/voice, arguing in particular that object-to-subject movement is insufficient to characterize it. The same conclusion has been reached more than once in the literature—by early work such as Burzio (1986), where *be* selection in Italian is governed by a disjunctive rule, only half of which refers to movement—and by recent work such as

Reinhart and Siloni (2005), where the unaccusative treatment of voice (reflexive etc.) is explicitly argued against. *Contra* Burzio (1986) we maintain that a unified account of auxiliary selection is possible; and *contra* Reinhart and Siloni (2005) we argue that Case cannot be responsible for it. In Section 11.5, we introduce some varieties where the various parameters cross-cut, and in particular selection according to transitivity/voice depends on the person split. In the introductory and concluding sections (Sections 11.1, 11.5.1) we relate our empirical aims and results to general issues, insisting on variation, the lexicon, and the LF interface once again.

11.2 The Evidence

We begin with the well-known evidence concerning standard Italian. As argued by Burzio (1986), auxiliary selection in Italian is sensitive to the distinction between transitive and unergative verbs on the one hand and unaccusatives on the other; the former take *have* as in (1a) and the latter *be*, as in (1b).

(1) a. Ho   lavato   (la camicia).
        I.have   washed   the shirt
        'I have eaten (the cake).'

     b. Sono   arrivato/arrivata.
        I.am   arrived.M/F.
        'I have arrived.'

The most notable complication concerning Italian is that the presence of the *si* element correlates with the selection of *be*, as in (2), independently of the many readings available for *si*, namely reflexive, as in (a), anticausative, as in (b), passive, as in (c), or impersonal, as in (d). Most importantly, quite independently of what one might want to say about the transitivity status of, say, reflexives, there is no doubt that in the impersonal in (d), the auxiliary *be* induced by *si* co-occurs with an overt accusative clitic—in other words, with a transitive frame. The fact that *si* cannot be treated simply as a valency-reducing morpheme (an intransitivizer) is underscored by examples like (d'), where it can be seen that *si* (impersonal again) combines with an intrinsically unaccusative predicate.

(2) a. Gianni si è lavato.
        G.   M is washed
        'Gianni has washed himself.'

   b. Gianni si è svegliato.
      G.   M is woken
      'Gianni has woken up.'

   c. Le camicie si sono lavate   (a   secco).
      the shirts   M are   washed dry
      'The shirts have been dry-cleaned.'

   d. Li   si è mangiati.
      them M is eaten
      'One has eaten them.'

   d'. Si   è arrivati.
       One is arrived
       'One has arrived.'

In (2) we have glossed *si* as M to suggest middle. In fact, the closest morphology to *si* we know of is the so-called middle morphology of languages
like Greek and Albanian. In (3) we show that the non-active morphology of
Albanian has exactly the same range of interpretations as the *si* morphology
of Italian, including reflexive (a), anticausative (b), passive (c), and impersonal (d). Note that crucially in (d) the middle morphology attaches to an
unaccusative verb, exactly as *si* does in Italian.[1]

(3)   Gjirokastër

      a. la-   (h)ɛ- m.
         wash M-   1SG
         'I wash myself.'

      b. zɟu-   (h)ɛ- t.
         wake M-   3SG
         'He wakes up.'

      c. kətɔ kəmiʃə la-   (h)ɛ- n   ŋga ajɔ.
         these shirts wash -M- 3PL by him
         'These shirts are washed by him.'

      d. ŋga   ati   dil- ɛ- t.
         from there exit -M- 3SG
         'One exits from there.'

---

[1] These data originate from original fieldwork of Leonardo Savoia concerning dialectal variation
within the Albanian fold (Manzini and Savoia 2008)—therefore, though they reflect in all relevant
respects the situation of the standard, they are phonetically transcribed. We maintain this transcription
in the interest of providing immediate access to the morphological-level analysis of a not very familiar
language.

The comparison between the middle voice of Albanian and Italian *si* is made particularly direct by the fact that, while in the present the middle voice of Albanian is lexicalized through the specialized inflection in (3), it is lexicalized in the perfective past through a clitic—namely, *u*—which combines with normal active inflections.[2]

(4)   Gjirokastër

    a. u la-   it-   a.
       M wash -PRF -1SG
       'I washed myself.'

    b. u zjɔ-   it.
       M wake -PRF
       'He woke up.'

    c. ata   u zjɔ-   it-ən   ŋga tə tiɛrət.
       they M wake- PRF-3PL by the others
       'They were woken by some people.'

    d. ŋga ati   u dɔð.
       from there M exited
       'One exited from there.'

There is a third way of instantiating middle voice in Albanian—we will come to this directly below. For the time being, returning to the issue at hand, namely the distribution of *have* and *be* in the Italian perfect, the descriptive conclusion is that *be* is found with unaccusatives and with middles. *Have* is restricted to the complementary set: transitives/unergatives and actives. Because of the considerations advanced in describing the data in (2), it appears that the notions of transitivity and activity in Italian cannot be collapsed; surely, example (2d) represents a case of transitive non-active. Indeed it is precisely because of *si* that Burzio (1986) could not provide a unified characterization of *be* selection but ended up with a disjunctive statement.

As indicated at the beginning, here we shall consider the problem of auxiliary selection in a strictly parametric context. Hence, before evaluating whether selection frames for *have* and *be* can be unified in Italian, we shall turn to other parametric settings. One of them is especially well known from Germanic languages like Dutch and German, but is also robustly attested in Romance varieties such as Soazza in (5) and (6). Like Dutch, and like Italian, Soazza has *be* with unaccusatives as in (5a) and *have* with unerga-

[2] Though Greek appears to have a specialized inflection throughout, Manzini, Roussou, and Savoia (in press) show that exactly the same split is present, so that the present is formed by a middle person ending while the perfective past is formed with active person endings attached to a base including a specialized middle suffix—which we take to be akin to the Romance *si*/Albanian *u* clitic.

tives/transitives as in (5b). The interesting point is that exactly the same distribution holds in the presence of *si* morphology, as in (6). Thus the reflexive in (a), the anticausative in (b), the impersonal/passive in (c), which are formed with transitive/unergative verbs, have auxiliary *have*. Only the impersonal in (d), formed with an unaccusative verb, has auxiliary *be*.

(5)   Soazza (Canton Ticino)

   a. som ri'vo/ rivada.
      I am arrived.M/F
      'I have arrived.'

   b. o   dor'mi:t.
      I.have slept
      'I have slept.'

(6)   Soazza

   a. ɛl/la s   a   la'vo/lavada.
      he/she M has washed.M/F
      'He/she has washed himself/herself.'

   b. al s   a   ʒmor'tso al tʃar.
      it M has gone.off the light
      'The light has gone off.'

   c. s   a   sempro dor'mit beŋ.
      M has always slept   well
      'It has always been slept well.'

   d. s   e sempro ri'vo   tart.
      M is always arrived late
      'One has always arrived late.'

Reference to a Romance dialect like Soazza, as opposed to better-known languages like Dutch, allows us to establish a few important points. First, in comparing Italian with Dutch one may be tempted to conclude that the different auxiliary selection with *si* and *zich* respectively is due to their different clitic vs. non-clitic status; the account of Reinhart (2000) and Reinhart and Siloni (2005) is built on this premise. However comparison of sufficiently close languages like Italian and Soazza shows that different auxiliary selection properties can correlate with essentially stable properties of the middle morphology. Thus there is no doubt that the *s* morpheme in (6) has exactly the same clitic prosody, distribution, etc. as its Italian counterpart. Second, Dutch *zich* and Italian *si* also independently differ in that *zich* does not combine with unaccusative verbs to yield the impersonal reading (again we take this to be an independent parameter). But Soazza *s* is of course like Italian *si* in this respect as well—which allows us to show that *s* simply does not influence auxiliary selection: rather, selection is determined by verb class (transitive/unergative vs. unaccusative) in (6) as in (5).

Albanian is in a way the mirror image to Soazza in that it displays no sensitivity to transitivity alternations, but selects *have* and *be* according to voice. The present perfect of Albanian, like that of Romance and Germanic languages, is also formed by the combination of auxiliary and perfect participle. In the active voice the auxiliary is *have* both with transitives and with unaccusatives, as in (7a) vs. (7b). However in the middle—that is, as part of the conjugation that includes the present in (3) and the simple past in (4)—the perfect is formed with *be*. In fact, when *be* is followed by the very same perfect participle found in the active—without the support of either suffixal or clitic material—this yields the set of middle interpretations, namely the reflexive (8a), the anticausative (8b), the passive (8c), and the impersonal (8d).[3]

(7) Gjirokastër

    a. ɛ ka   la-   it- ur.
       it he.has wash PRF PRT
       'He has washed it.'

    b. ka   dalə.
       he.has gone.out
       'He has gone out.'

(8) Gjirokastër

    a. əʃt la- it- ur.
       he.is wash PRF PRT
       'He has washed himself.'

    b. əʃt zɟu- aɾ.
       he.is wake PRT
       'He has woken up.'

    c. kətɔ kəmiʃə jan la-   it-uɾ ŋga ajɔ.
       these shirts are wash-PRF-PRT by him
       'These shirts have been washed by him.'

    d. ŋga ati   eʃt dalə miɾ.
       from there it.is exited well
       'One has exited well from there.'

[3] An otherwise fairly close language like Greek differs in this respect, since both the active and the middle voice are formed with *have*. The difference between the two is conveyed by the perfect participle, which carries middle morphology (Manzini et al. in press). Savoia and Manzini (2007) discuss the relevant dialectal variation within Albanian.

Incidentally, it may be noted that the perfect participle of Albanian never agrees with any of its arguments—though a full agreement paradigm is available to it and emerges in adjectival contexts (Manzini and Savoia 2007). In contrast, Soazza has the same perfect-participle agreement system as standard Italian, even if the auxiliary is *have* as for instance in the reflexive in (5b). In other words, perfect-participle agreement is entirely independent of the selection of *have* or *be*.

Another parametric choice attested by well-known Germanic and Romance languages (say, English or Spanish) is formation of the present perfect with the auxiliary *have* independently of transitivity and voice. In (9) we illustrate this parametric option with a southern Italian dialect which (like Spanish) shows the insensitivity of auxiliary selection to *si*; (unlike Spanish) it provides an example of the independence of participle agreement from auxiliary selection, since unaccusative participles as in (9b) agree with their argument.

(9)   Verbicaro (Calabria)

    a. ajə   laßa:tə (a ˈmakənə).
       I.have washed the car
       'I have washed (the car).'

    b. a   mmuərtə/mmɔrtə.
       s/he.has died.M/F
       'S/he has died.'

    c. s   a   llaßa:tə.
       M he.has washed
       'He has washed himself.'

Another logical possibility, namely, selection of the *be* auxiliary in all of the present perfect, appears to be more rarely instantiated—but can also be found in Romance varieties such as Pescolanciano in (10). While the selection of *be* with the unaccusative in (a) or *si* in (c) may be familiar from Italian, this is a language that also has *be* with transitives, as in (b). Incidentally, it will be seen that the agreement pattern is the one familiar from Italian whereby the feminine morphology in (10b) singles out the internal argument, lexicalized by the accusative clitic.

(10)   Pescolanciano (Abruzzi)

    a. sɔŋgə mənu:tə.
       I.am   come
       'I have come.'

    b. la   suə   ccamata.
       her they.have called.F
       'They have called her.'

c. ts ɛ lava:tə.
　M he.is washed
　'He has washed himself.'

Finally there is another major pattern of *have* vs. *be* split instantiated by Romance languages, since in some varieties auxiliary selection is sensitive to the reference of the EPP argument. The most widely known split opposes the first and second person with *be* to the third person with *have* (Kayne 1993; Cocchi 1995; D'Alessandro and Roberts, forthcoming), as in the paradigm in (11). This classic person split is oblivious to verbal class, as shown in (11), as well as to *si*.[4]

(11)　S. Benedetto del Tronto (Marche)

sɔ	vənu:tə/ vistə	E
ʃi		E
a		A
ʃɛmə		E
ʃɛtə		E
a		A

'I have come/seen' etc.

Note that there is no intrinsic association of *be* with first and second person and of *have* with third person. Thus varieties are found where it is the first and second person that are associated with *have*, while the third person is associated with *be*, as in (12). This parametric choice is less robustly attested, so that in Morcone in (12) it only characterizes the singular, while the plural has *have* in all persons. However, the limitation of the person split to the singular is an independent parameter, since it can also be seen in a dialect like (13), which in the singular has *be* in the first and second person and *have* in the third. Incidentally, the morphophonology of Morcone (with non-neutralized final vowels) lets us see that the participle agreement once more follows exactly the same lines as standard Italian—namely, agreement with unaccusatives (*come*) and lack of agreement with unergatives (*slept*).

(12)　Morcone　　(Campania)

addʒo	menuto/durmuto	A
a		A
ɛ		E
emo	menuti/durmuto	A

---

[4] Note that given the existence of a person split, the reader may reasonably wonder about the full paradigms for the dialects discussed in connection with transitivity/voice. Full paradigms are available from Manzini and Savoia (2005). There is no person split involved in any language mentioned except where it is explicitly noted.

ete		A
ao		A

'I have come/ slept,' etc.

(13) Bisceglie   (Apulia)

sɔ	drəmmi:tə/ vəni:tə	E
si		E
a		A
ɛmm		A
avə:tə		A
onnə		A

'I have slept/come,' etc.

The varieties in (11)–(13) also prompt some general remarks. First, we have seen that though the pattern in (11) may be more robustly attested, the reverse pattern in (12) is equally possible. However, not all parametric choices are reversible. Thus, we are aware of no language where auxiliary selection is the reverse of, say, Soazza, so that *be* is associated with transitive and *have* with unaccusatives. Also, we do not know of any language which patterns in the opposite way to Albanian, selecting *have* with middles and *be* with actives. This lack of reversibility will have to be accounted for as part of the overall parametric picture.

Second, the picture of auxiliary selection according to person provided in (11)–(13) is greatly simplified with respect to the actually observed variation. A fuller picture can be had from the resumptive table in Manzini and Savoia (2007), cf. Loporcaro (2007). Importantly, it is not only auxiliary selection according to person that is subject to this fine variation—rather, transitivity and voice alternations are, too, as briefly discussed in Section 11.4. But, as seen in the study of the person split in Manzini and Savoia (2007), the general principles that inform parametrization are the same whatever the level of detail that one is looking at.

11.3 Analysis

Our study of parametrization in auxiliary selection presupposes a number of assumptions concerning the structure and the interpretation of present perfects. Perhaps the single most important assumption is that the present perfect is not monoclausal, consisting of a verb associated with an auxiliary functional projection—as in the conception of English auxiliaries of Chomsky (1957, 1981, 1995). Rather the embedded participle and the matrix auxiliary define each a separate sentential unit (Kayne 1993).

Motivating this assumption crucially involves looking at the internal structure of the participle. Thus Belletti (1990) notices that standard Italian has
"absolute" participle constructions associated with sentential-level inflectional
properties such as the ability to support an enclitic. If we adopt the theory of
enclisis of Kayne (1989), in which enclisis depends on the high position of the
verb in the sentence, then enclisis on the participle supports the conclusion
that the participial clause has a C layer, hosting the participle itself. As it turns
out, there are Romance varieties which have enclisis on the participle in the
present perfect as well. Piedmontese dialects are an example in point, as in
(14a–b). We take this to be evidence that the participle is a full clause, with the
head verb in C. Quite interestingly, some of the languages that display clitics
attached to the participle in the present perfect also allow them to climb to the
matrix auxiliary, as in (14a′–b′). Note that these behaviors are independent
of auxiliary selection since Forno in (14) has the auxiliary-selection patterns
of standard Italian, namely, *have* with transitives in (14a–a′) and *be* with
unaccusatives, as in (14b–b′).

(14)   Forno Valle Strona   (Piedmont)
    a. l   a   viʃtu   -n.
          he has   seen us
          'He has seen us.'

    a′. a   n   a   viʃt.
          he us   has   seen
          'He has seen us.'

    b. l   ɛ   la'va   -s.
          he is   washed-M
          'He has washed himself.'

    b′. a   s   ɛ   la'va
          he M   is   washed
          'He has washed himself.'

The fact that a biclausal structure such as the one we are outlining can
have monoclausal properties is not an isolated fact about the present perfect,
since it arises in a number of restructuring (Rizzi 1982) and incorporation
(Baker 1988) environments. As in (14), in Rizzi's (1982) restructuring, the
embedded verb can either retain a number of sentential-level properties like
cliticization or these can be subsumed by the selecting modal (or aspectual
etc.) verb. Let us take for granted therefore that auxiliary and perfect participle structures are bisentential and that a restructuring/incorporation process
accounts for their monoclausal properties. The exact nature of restructuring

is an independent question; yet, for the sake of falsifiability, we will briefly outline our main assumptions about it.

According to the literature, the perfect, at least in English, roughly denotes a present state arrived at as a consequence of a concluded event, hence a past by implication. For instance, Parsons (1990) assigns to sentences such as *John has left* a semantics like the following: there is an event *e* of *leaving* whose theme is *John* and the state following $e, CS(e)$ holds at the moment of utterance. It is also well known from the literature (Giorgi and Pianesi 1997) that the English and the French or Italian perfect differ in that the French/Italian perfect can further take on the meaning of a simple perfective past. In any event, the auxiliary verb in the present combined with an embedded perfect participle yields a perfective (and eventually past) reading for the auxiliary–participle expression as a whole. If the argument structure of a predicate includes a (Davidsonian) event argument, we take it that this means that the matrix and embedded events are unified—with the result that the perfective properties of the embedded participles are imputed to the complex predicate resulting from the unification. This is what we call "restructuring".

It is worth mentioning that Albanian dialects provide even stronger evidence than Romance ones that the embedded participle syntactically represents an independent sentence. Thus in the Arbëresh (Italo-Albanian) dialect of Portocannone in (15) the participle can be introduced by the sentential connective ε 'and' and pronominal clitics are associated with the participial clause rather than with the matrix clause, both in the active (a) and in the middle (b) (Manzini and Savoia 2007; Savoia and Manzini 2007). Note that while in Romance dialects like (14) a clitic associated with the participle appears in enclisis (showing that the participle is in a relatively high position, namely C), in Albanian the clitic precedes the participle like any other finite verb. This leads us to conclude that participles and finite verbs occupy exactly the same position in the sentence, namely, I. Incidentally, it will be noted that in this variety the perfect is not formed with the auxiliary *be*, as in the standard, but rather in the Soazza way, that is, with the middle clitic morphology (*u* in this case) combining with the auxiliary *have*—yet another illustration that the parametric combinations that we are studying completely cut across family groupings.

(15)   Portocannone

     a. ai kiʃ ε   ε tʃa- it- ur.
       he had and it break -PRF -PRT
       'He had broken it.'

b. ai kiʃ ɛ   u tʃa- x- ur.
   it had and M break-M-PRT
   'It had broken.'

Beside the conclusion that perfect participles are (ordinary) bi-sentential structures, we share with Kayne (1993) the conclusion that the *have* and *be* auxiliaries are exactly the same verbs that appear in possessive or copular constructions respectively (descriptively as main verbs). The argument is that the coincidence of the different contexts in which the same lexical forms appear is systematic—and cannot therefore be imputed to simple homophony. On the other hand, Kayne (1993) also argues that *have* and *be* are transformationally related. His idea, which is based on the possessive construction, is that *have* is essentially an applicative of *be*, derived through the incorporation of a dative preposition; in other words *have* is *be-to*, essentially as proposed by Benveniste (1966). The problem is that, as far as we can see, there is no Romance dialect, of the many examined, that provides any morphophonological clue in favor of the proposed derivation (not any other language that we know of).[5] Therefore we simply assume that *have* and *be* are two independent lexical entries.

In Kayne (1993), where possessive *have* is derived from copular *be* through the incorporation of a preposition, auxiliary *have* is similarly derived from auxiliary *be* through the incorporation of a (prepositional) complementizer. Whether the latter incorporates or not is determined by the argument of the embedded predicate that moves to the matrix EPP position. On the basis of what precedes, however, *have* and *be* are just what they appear to be— namely the independently known possession and copular verb embedding a participial clause.

There is one major tassel missing in the structural sketch of participles provide above—concerning the EPP argument of the participle. As in all non-finite clauses (including notably infinitivals) the EPP position of the

---

[5] In fact, on the basis of existing morphophonological evidence one may want to argue that on the contrary, *be* is derived from *have*. Thus in (i), *be* and *have* are selected with the unaccusative in (a) and with the unergative in (b), as in standard Italian. The interesting thing is that in the second person and in the first person plural the *be* auxiliary in (a) is actually the result of combining the *s* morpheme with the *have* auxiliary in (b).

(i) Casorezzo (Lombardy)
    a. som/   te se/   l e/   sɛm/   si:/   in   vi'ɲy
       I.am   etc.   come
       'I have come.'
    b. o/   t e/   l a/   ɛm/   i:/   ɛn   dur'mi:
       I.have   etc.   slept
       'I have slept.'

participial clause is not overtly realized—or, we shall say, not lexicalized. According to the theory of empty categories in Chomsky (1981), maintained by Chomsky (1995), the EPP position of non-finite sentences corresponds either to a trace, in other words, a copy, in raising cases or to a base-generated empty category, conventionally PRO, in control cases (obligatory control, or arbitrary control). On the other hand, some authors have sought a unified characterization of these environments in terms of the minimalist notion of trace (copy). Thus, for Hornstein (1999), (obligatory) control as well as raising is derived through movement; raising and control are simply the names for different interpretations of the same syntactic object, namely, a chain. Because this theory seeks to unify only the bound readings of the embedded subject of non-finite sentences, so-called arbitrary PRO is excluded from it—being represented presumably by an empty category again (say, pro).

The third major possibility that has been explored in the literature is that in fact there is no embedded EPP position in non-finite sentences. This stance is explicitly taken by Epstein and Seely (2006) but is also implicit in Manzini and Roussou (2000). It is interesting therefore that both Roussou (2009) and Manzini and Savoia (2009) reject this possibility on the basis of control and raising into finite complements in Greek and Albanian, respectively. Precisely because the latter involve a nominative position, it is evident that control and raising interpretations cannot be linked to the absence of an EPP position—on the contrary, a uniform treatment of control and raising requires the EPP to enforce a subject position in non-finite clauses as well.

We therefore adopt the classical idea that all sentences contain an EPP argument. At this point, it becomes relevant that we also adopt a representational model of grammar, as defined by Brody (2003), in which chain is an interpretive construct as the LF interface—and does not depend on a computationally driven process of movement. As far as we can see, at the LF interface, the reading of a trace (a copy) is that of a variable (bound by its antecedent, i.e. the *wh*-operator in *wh*-movement/chains, etc.). Similarly, the base-generated empty category (i.e. PRO/pro) is generically closed in the arbitrary reading, hence is again a variable (Lebeaux 1984). Therefore we simply assume that in non-finite clauses where the EPP argument is not provided by the morphosyntactic (agreement) structure, it enters the LF interface computation in the form of a variable. In raising and obligatory control, the EPP variable has an antecedent-bound reading; in arbitrary control, it is simply interpreted by generic closure (in the absence of an antecedent).[6]

---

[6] Though reference to the variable construal of the non-finite EPP argument is sufficient for present purposes, this does not mean that PRO/pro and NP-trace are not necessary for independent reasons. Manzini and Savoia (2009) concludes that they are not.

11.3.1 *Background on voice*

Descriptively, in standard Albanian *have* forms the perfect in the active voice, as in (7), and *be* forms the perfect in the middle voice, as in (8); in present terms, this means that *have* selects an active embedded sentence and *be* a middle one. Similarly in Italian (1) the middle voice, as instantiated by *si*, is associated with *be* independently of the transitivity of the verb, while in the active *have* and *be* alternate according to transitivity. The latter is the only alternation present in Soazza in (6) independently of voice. Evidently, explaining these patterns requires a preliminary account of what exactly is meant by the descriptive labels of active and middle or transitive and non-transitive. Note furthermore that the two splits of voice and transitivity cannot be unified, since Albanian and the Romance dialect of Soazza are sensitive to one but not the other.

We shall begin with what appears to be the more complex and therefore problematic of the two notions, that is, voice. While the perfect formation of Albanian has not been studied before to our knowledge (the closest data are those of the Latin perfect; Embick 2000), the lexicalization of the middle by Romance *si* has been frequently studied. At least one of the interpretations associated with the middle morphology—the passive one—is standardly obtained through a transformational process of movement from the object into the subject position (Chomsky 1957, 1965). Therefore, by what Culicover and Jackendoff (2005) call Interface Uniformity, we may want to associate the passive meaning of the middle voice with the same derivation and further extend this derivation to all middle interpretations (Marantz 1984). Despite what may appear to be its theoretical advantages, this approach fails for empirical reasons. In particular, we note that authors that have espoused the unaccusative theory of middle voice have systematically considered languages like French, where the impersonal (non-passive) reading of the middle voice is not found. For a language like Italian, a theory associating *si* with movement from the object to the subject position is directly contradicted by the existence of examples like (2d) where *si* co-occurs with an overtly lexicalized accusative.

A theory such as Burzio (1986), which takes the full range of evidence into account, ends up with an account where each of the main interpretations of *si* individuated in (2) ends up with a separate derivation. Specifically, for Burzio (1986) reflexive *si* bears an anaphoric binding relation to the subject; impersonal *si* bears an expletive relation to it; passive *si* is like impersonal *si*, except that movement takes place from the object to the subject position; and finally anticausative *si* is derived in the lexicon. Needless to say, Burzio's (1986) theory is problematic, insofar as it provides no unification for these various contexts, which are systematically picked up by the same morphology cross-linguistically and thus presumably form a natural class.

Reinhart and Siloni (2005), based on Chierchia (2004), and Reinhart (2000) also introduce as many separate operations on argument structure as the number of basic meanings of *si* distinguished in (2)—namely, reflexive bundling, which bundles the external theta role with some other theta role; saturation/arbitrarization (responsible for passives/impersonals), which saturates the external theta role by existential closure; and decausativization (responsible for anticausatives), which reduces (i.e. suppresses) an external [+cause] theta role. The unification of these various rules by a single morphology is imputed to Case theory. The assumption is that the arity reduction operations just mentioned do not affect the Case properties of the verb, leaving an accusative (or a nominative in arbitrarization contexts) potentially unchecked; "the clitic (or its equivalent) reduces Case" (Reinhart and Siloni 2005: 402).

As far as we can see, both Chierchia (2004) and, consequently, Reinhart (2000) and Reinhart and Siloni (2005) are oblivious to the existence of impersonal unaccusatives as in (2d′). The latter exclude that arbitrarization can be simply construed as reduction of the external theta role, for there is no external theta role to be reduced in (2d′). Furthermore, Reinhart and Siloni (2005) take care to argue that *si* is not an "object clitic"; but their evidence really shows that *si* is not an accusative clitic (for instance not triggering *faire-à* constructions when embedded under a causative). In contrast, Manzini and Savoia (2001, 2007) show that Italian *si* and its Albanian *u* counterpart behave like object clitics with respect to their distribution, their syncretism and suppletivism patterns, and more—also contrasting with subject and other clitics. In other words, any theory that does not treat *si* (or *u*) as an object clitic is forced to state all of the relevant generalizations (distributional, etc.) twice, once for object clitics and once for *si/u*. If *si/u* is a bona fide object clitic, we expect it to be like any other object clitic (with which it patterns) in having not only Case properties, but also denotational and argumental ones. In this respect in fact Reinhart and Siloni (2005) take a step back with respect to Chierchia (1995, 2004), who identifies at least the variable existentially bound in passives/impersonals with the *si* element.

Another clue that Reinhart and Siloni's (2005) theory is on the wrong track when it comes to the status of *si* is that it yields incorrect predictions as to the connection between *si* and auxiliary selection. In order to explain the parameter between Italian, where the middle voice is associated with *be,* and Dutch, where it is associated with *have,* they invoke a distinction between the thematic and structural component of Case. In their account, Dutch *zich* "though referentially defective, occupies the complement position" where it can check structural Case, while Italian *si* cannot, leaving "the structural accusative residue to be checked... The auxiliary *be* is used whenever there is such an accusative residue" (Reinhart and Siloni 2005: 432–3). Leaving aside any other consideration, Soazza shows that the clitic or non-clitic status of the middle morphology is thoroughly irrelevant for the auxiliary selection parameter—thus eliminating a potential argument for treating *si* as anything but the clitic counterpart of *zich*.

In Manzini and Savoia (2007) we take the conclusion that *si* is a bona fide pronoun as our starting point, assuming that as such it (its Albanian counterpart *u*, etc.) fills an argument slot of the predicate. Another premise of our analysis is that the denotation of *si/u* differs from that of other pronominal clitics in that it is indefinite, in other words, a free variable. This is proposed by Chierchia (1995, 2004) for impersonal *si* and by Manzini (1986) for all *si*; the various readings of *si* simply depend on the possible ways to saturate the variable.

The impersonal reading depends on quantificational closure of the *si* variable. In fact we follow Chierchia (1995) in assuming that impersonal *si* can have a generic reading proper (essentially as a universal) and an "episodic" reading (much closer to an existential). Since there is no interaction between the impersonal reading of *si* and the lexicalization of an accusative, we predict the impersonal reading to be able to co-occur with the latter as in (2d). Nor is there any reason why *si* could not yield an impersonal reading if it is inserted as the sole argument of an unaccusative as in (2d′). Remember we noticed above that the arbitrarization rule of Chierchia (2004) and Reinhart and Siloni (2005) (i.e. existential closure of an external argument) could not yield impersonals with unaccusative verbs. If our discussion is on the right track, this problem can be avoided simply by taking arbitrarization to correspond not to an operation on argument structure, which needs to be stated in terms of such primitives as external argument, but to an interpretation at the LF interface, which can apply to any variable not independently closed.

Next, the passive, anticausative, and reflexive readings depend on the closure of the *si/u* variable by the EPP argument. In particular, we take it that the syntactic object (EPP argument, variable) defined by this closure operation is a chain at the LF interface—on the assumption, already mentioned, that variables are the interpretive counterpart of traces. In this respect, though we argued above that movement from the object to the subject position cannot be the basis for the unification of middle voice, we nevertheless retain the idea that its representational counterpart—the notion of chain—accounts for the non-impersonal readings of *si*.

We take the standard properties of chains to hold—namely, that each chain is associated with a single argumental slot and that this argumental slot corresponds to the foot of the chain—hence to an internal argument. These properties are as stipulated in a derivational system as in a representational one, the derivational stipulation being that first Merge of an argument is at a thematic position, and a thematic position must be satisfied by first Merge (Chomsky 1995, *pace* Hornstein 1999). This means that under the bound reading the (EPP argument, *si*) chain is systematically associated with the internal theta role. We agree with Chierchia (2004) and Reinhart and Siloni (2005) that the external argument configurations are responsible for the difference between anticausative, passive, and reflexive reading. Yet it seems to us that they correspond to all and only the logically possible such configurations— and as such they need not be stated but just fall out of logical necessity. Thus in the anticausative the external theta role is not interpreted. In the passive, it is interpreted through existential closure; alternatively, it is interpreted through assignment to an adjunct—that is, the so-called *by*-phrase. It is just a special fact about the middle voice of Romance (and Germanic) that this possibility is excluded—though Chierchia (2004) and Reinhart and Siloni (2005) build it into their system. In Albanian a *by*-phrase can be overtly seen to occur in the middle voice, even when the latter is formed with the *u* clitic, as in (4c).

As for the reflexive, it seems to us that the arguments put forth by Reinhart and Siloni (2005) are not decisive as to whether the external argument is to be imputed to the *si* chain (reflexive). For instance, *ne* cliticization from postverbal subjects is not a reliable test of the internal or external argument status of the latter, depending instead on the presentational (focus) properties of the sentence (Saccon 1992, *pace* Burzio 1986; Belletti and Rizzi 1981; Belletti 1988). Thus under the right conditions we accept *ne*-extraction from the inverted subjects of reflexives (varying pragmatic contextualizations are in fact the better explanation for the variability in grammaticality judgments noted by Reinhart and Siloni (2005) among Italian speakers). Therefore we side with Chierchia (2004) in assuming that reflexives are a subclass of anticausatives, in which agency is imputed to the sole lexicalized argument—by a meaning postulated in Chierchia (2004).

Suppose that these conclusions are on the right track. What ultimately gives rise to all of the different readings of the middle voice is the property of *si* being a variable. As a result of the presence of this variable what these various interpretations have in common is that one of the argumental positions of the predicate remains unassociated (in anticausatives/reflexives) or is interpreted only in that it is existentially closed (passives, impersonal) and/or associated with an argument which is external to the structure of the predicate (the *by*-phrase). Of course, this is not the characterization associated with middle voice by standard generative theory, where this notion is reduced to the promotion from object to subject position (i.e. movement). However, the construal of the notion that we suggest is in a way equally traditional—having to do with the non-closure (or generic closure) of the argument structure of the verb. What is more, the grounds for this switch are entirely empirical, namely that the standard generative construal of the notion middle in terms of object to subject promotion stands no chance of unifying the passive/reflexive reading with the impersonal one, once the full spread of evidence is taken into account.[7]

11.3.2 *Background on transitivity*

It is evident from what precedes that (middle) voice has given rise to considerable discussion, yielding substantially different approaches to its unified characterization. By contrast, the theoretical characterization for the descriptive notion of transitivity would appear to be a settled question on the basis of Burzio (1986) and of the relational grammar work on which it is based. According to Burzio (1986), transitive verbs have both an internal and an external argument—canonically linked to the sister of V position and to the sister of I (EPP) position respectively. Unergatives have only an external argument, canonically linked to the EPP position. Finally, unaccusatives have only an internal argument, which is promoted to the EPP position.

When evaluating this classical approach to transitivity, it should not be forgotten that the core piece of evidence that it is meant to account for is precisely auxiliary selection in Italian. The movement derivation of unaccusative verbs is meant to unify them with middles for the purposes of *be* selection. Yet we have already seen that what is classically taken to be the strongest argument in favor of a uniform movement structure for middles and unaccusatives in reality works against it. For in languages like Albanian it is only middles that combine with *be* to the exclusion of unaccusatives—and the reverse is true in Soazza. Therefore voice and transitivity cannot have an identical characterization.

In the preceding section, we have argued for an LF characterization of middles as predicates with an open variable in their argument structure, either not interpreted or interpreted through quantificational closure. Evidently unaccusatives must not have such an open position since if so, we could not differentiate them from middles. Indeed the classical construal of unaccusatives as predicates with a single argument slot, saturated by the EPP argument, leaves no room for non-interpreted or quantificationally closed slots. Therefore this

---

[7] Note also that a bona fide clitic treatment of *si* is not in itself incompatible with movement from the object to the subject position. Formally, a base-generated *si* could indeed coexist with movement from the object position of the EPP argument, as proposed by Dobrovie-Sorin (1998); further elaborating on this, one could entertain the idea that *si* is base-generated as the head of a so-called big DP, whose Spec is the "doubling" moved DP. It is possible that such extra assumptions prove necessary on grounds not considered here (locality, reconstruction, or other). However, they are not necessary on the evidence considered here.

simple characterization is sufficient to distinguish unaccusatives from middles for present purposes.

The same characterization is also sufficient to distinguish them from transitives and unergatives—for transitives have two arguments, and following Hale and Keyser (1993), Chomsky (1995), unergatives can be treated essentially as concealed transitives, where the internal argument has incorporated into the verb. Thus languages like Soazza appear to be sensitive to whether an embedded participle has a monoargumental frame—i.e. is unaccusative—or has a pluriargumental frame, independently of the status of these argument slots (interpreted as arguments, not interpreted, quantificationally closed).

11.4 Parameters of Auxiliary Selection

We begin our review of auxiliary selection parameters by considering Pescolanciano in (10), where the auxiliary of the present perfect is systematically *be*. In the present perspective, Pescolanciano can very simply be described as a language in which *be* embeds any participial clause—without restrictions of sorts. By contrast, in Verbicaro in (9) it is *have* that embeds any participial clause, without restrictions, yielding a system in which the present perfect is systematically formed with the auxiliary *have*.[8]

Next, we argue that the patterns of auxiliary selection according to person in (11)–(13) can be obtained simply by letting the parameter just formulated—that is the selection of participial clauses by *have* or *be*—interact with the person split between first/second person and third person. The latter is independently motivated by typologically widespread evidence. Thus DeLancey (1981) argues that languages with so-called ergativity splits, that is,

---

[8] Note that here we disregard sentences where *be* is followed by a perfect participle in the *be–en* passive. In Albanian this choice is easily motivated, since in the present perfect *be* is followed by an invariable (non-agreeing) participle, as in (7) and (8), while in the passive it is followed by an agreeing participle, as in (i), presenting both an inflection and a preposed article, exactly as adjectives do. Manzini and Savoia (2008) show that this construction has not only the so-called adjectival passive (i.e. stative) interpretation but also the so-called verbal passive one. Anagnostopoulou (2003) reaches the same conclusion for its Greek counterpart (*pace* Terzi and Wexler 2002).

(i) Gjirokastër
     jan   tə   vɛʃur/'vɛʃura
     they.are   PL   dressed.M/dressed.F
     'They are dressed.'

On the evidence of (7) and (8) vs. (i), the present perfect and the passive involve two different embedding structures (sentential and nominal respectively), possibly also correlating with the fact that the temporal denotation of the sentence is present in (i). It is not impossible that the same holds in Romance, since a contrast between lack of agreement in the present perfect and agreement in the copular construction is marginally found in Romance as well. Thus in the languages in (iia–iia'), the free alternation between *have* and *be* does not have any effect on the perfect participle that maintains its invariable, non-agreeing format. As shown in (iib–iib') on the other hand, in the same languages *be* requires an agreeing adjective in the copular construction.

alternations between the ergative–absolutive case system and the nominative – accusative system, most commonly oppose first and second person to third. Person splits are also pervasive in Romance languages. To restrict ourselves to clitics, extensively discussed by Manzini and Savoia (2007), first- and second-person object clitics differ from third-person ones with respect to their distribution, their morphological make-up (gender and Case distinctions), their agreement properties, and more (for instance the drop phenomenon in Savoia and Manzini, 2010). According to Manzini and Savoia (2007), the person split, in its various manifestations, depends on the fact that the participants in the discourse—the speaker and the hearer (and the sets including them)—are anchored directly at the universe of discourse, independently of their role within the event; on the other hand, non-participants in the discourse depend directly for their characterization on the position assigned to them within the structure of the event.

Let us then cross the *have* vs. *be* parameter defined with respect to Pescolanciano and Verbicaro with the person split—so that *have* and *be* can be sensitive to the reference of the EPP argument. The crossing should in principle yield two systems. In one system *be* is associated with a first- and second-person EPP argument while the third person requires *have*—while in the specular system it is the first and second person that require *have* while the third person is associated with *be*. This means that the unrestricted crossing of the two parameters yields the systems observed, at least in the singular, in S. Benedetto in (11) and Morcone in (12) respectively.

We disregard the further ramifications that the interaction between the person split and auxiliary selection have. Much more intricate patterns can be gleaned from the distribution summarized in the tables of Manzini and Savoia (2007), who discuss them in great detail, in a framework which is compatible in all crucial respects with the present proposals. An illustration is provided by the comparison between S. Benedetto in (11) and Bisceglie in (13)—where the same person split occurs throughout the paradigm in S. Benedetto and only in the singular in Bisceglie. We will return to some finer parameters after discussing transitivity and voice in the next sections.

(ii) Montebello Ionico/Saline Ioniche (Calabria)
  a. ɛra/ɛri/ɛra/ˈɛrumu/ˈɛruvu/ˈɛrunu   durmutu/vinutu
      I.was etc.   slept/come
  a′. aiva/aivi/aiva/aˈivumu/aˈiuvu/aˈivunu   durmutu/vinutu
      I.had etc.   slept/come
      'I had come/slept' etc.
  b. ɛra staŋku
      I.was tired
  b′. ˈɛrumu staŋki
      we.were tired-PL.

11.4.1 *Auxiliary selection according to voice or transitivity*

If our conclusions are correct we should be able to derive the auxiliary selection patterns of Albanian, Soazza, or Italian from the simple statement that *be* selects the properties that characterize middle voice and/or intransitivity (unaccusativity) in the embedded participle—or that *have* selects the complementary properties.

Let us begin with Albanian,[9] and with transitive (i.e. two-place) predicates such as *la-* 'wash'. The question is what properties of the participial sentence determine its combination with the auxiliary *have* in (7a) in the active and with the auxiliary *be* in (8a) or (8c) in the reflexive and passive—all repeated

---

[9] We mentioned above that the closest phenomenon to Albanian perfects considered in the literature are Latin perfects, dealt with in the work of Embick (2000). The latter focuses on so-called deponent verbs, which are associated with a morphologically middle inflection while having an active and in fact transitive construal. We feel entitled to disregard deponents to the extent that we are not aware of the existence of any of them in Albanian—be it as it may, the phenomenon will not be as salient as in Latin. On the other hand, the deponency phenomenon might be present to some extent in any system which has a productive middle voice. Thus traditional grammars of Italian recognize the presence of inherent reflexives—that is, predicates formed with *si* that are presumably unaccusatives and have no transitive counterparts, as in (ia–a′), and predicates formed by *si* that are straight transitives, as in (iib-b′), nor does *si* correspond to an independently attested dative or other argument.

(i) a. *Gianni ha arrabbiato Lucia/   se stesso.
         Gianmi has angered Lucia/   himself
         'John has angered Lucia/himself.'

     a′. Gianni si è arrabbiato.
          Gianni M is angered
          'John has become angry.'

     b. *Gianni lo ha dimenticato a Lucia/se stesso.
         Gianni it has forgotten to Lucia/himself
         'John has made Lucia/ himself forget it.'

     b′. Gianni se lo è dimenticato.
          Gianni M it is forgotten
          'John has forgotten it.'

In effect (i) are the deponents of the Italian middle voice. If Embick (2000) had his way we would have to say that while the middle forms considered in the text are associated with a voice feature, say [pass] associated with the *v* functional projection of the verb, the forms in (i) are associated with a [pass] feature associated with the verb root. The objection that we have to this type of approach is that it at best annotates the relevant differences without explaining anything about them. In other words the middle and deponent construal of [pass] are made to correspond to two different positions—predicting exactly the data this disjunction encodes and none else. At worst, however, Embick's (2000) proposal could result once again in a treatment of *si* that denies what appears to be its completely homogenous behavior as an object clitic.

Therefore, despite the dismissal of such ideas by Embick (2000) we tentatively maintain that (i) as well as the deponent class in Latin (and in Greek) are bona fide instances of middle voice at LF, with the *si* (or its various counterparts) instantiating a variable in the argument structure of the relevant verbs. This can be an internal argument in (ia′) and a second internal argument in (iib′)—despite the lack of non-middle instantiations of such argument structures.

below in (16a–c) respectively, with some added structure. According to the discussion in section 11.2 the participial sentence embeds in all cases an EPP argument with a variable reading; in all cases furthermore this variable is bound by the matrix EPP argument, which is a referential element. Thus, one of the argument slots of *la-* is saturated by argumental material. This leaves the other argument slot. Quite straightforwardly in (16a)—the active—the other argument of *la-* is also filled by an argument—the accusative clitic ε 'him'/'her.' On the other hand in the reflexive in (16b) and in the passive in (16c) the external argument slot is not assigned to an (independent) argument at all, as in the reflexive, or is at best assigned to an adjunct, that is, not a direct argument of the verb, as in the passive. Therefore we may consider that as far as the predicate–argument structure of the embedded verb is concerned, the EPP argument remains unbound. The selection of the participle by *have* in (16a) and by *be* in (16b–c) is sensitive to these properties, in other words descriptively to voice. Anticausatives illustrated in (8b) by a verb with a salient anticausative reading are parallel to that of passives/reflexives.

(16)   Gjirokastër
  a. $[_N \varepsilon$ $[_I$ ka $[x$ $[_I$ laitur $_{(th, th)}$
  b. $[_I$ əʃt $[x$ $[_I$ laitur $_{(th, th)}$
  c. $[_D$ kətə kəmiʃə $[_I$ jan $[x$ $[_I$ laitur$_{(th, th)}$ ŋga ajɔ

Let us then consider the unaccusative predicate *dal-* 'go out' associated with a single argument slot which enters into both (7b) and (8d), repeated in (17a–b) with the relevant structure. In the active (17a) the single argument slot of *dal-* is satisfied by an argument, lexicalized in the matrix EPP position. In the impersonal—i.e. middle—(17b) the same argument slot is not argumentally filled, but is satisfied by quantificational (existential) closure. The minimal pair formed by (17a) and (17b) is again correctly characterized by the preceding discussion of voice, since all of the argument slots of the predicate are closed by arguments in (17a), and not in (17b), where quantificational closure is necessary instead.

(17)   Gjirokastër
  a. $[_I$ ka $[x$ $[_I$ dalə$_{(th)}$
  b. $[∃x$ $[_I$ əʃt $[x$ $[_I$ dalə$_{(th)}$

We can formalize these conclusions as a selectional property of *be* or of *have* as well, since *have* in standard Albanian obviously selects predicates with a closed argument structure, in the sense that no free variables or generically closed ones are instantiated within it, while *be* selects the complementary set.

Let us then turn to the Soazza pattern, which, if the analysis in Section 11.2 is correct, should be accounted for simply by saying that *be* selects mono-argumental predicates. The latter exclude transitives/unergatives, whether in the active or in the middle voice, which will instead combine with *have*. We can verify the model on the rough LFs in (18) and (19). The examples in (18) provide structures for the active (5b) and for the impersonal/passive (6c) of an unergative verb, as well as for the reflexive of a transitive (6a). In accordance with the discussion in Section 11.2, we construe unergatives as two-place predicates with the internal argument incorporated. This is sufficient to determine selection of *have* in the Soazza language, independently of whether the external argument slot is saturated by an argument, as in the active (18a), quantificationally closed, as in the impersonal (18c), or not (independently) interpreted at all, as in the reflexive (18b). In contrast, the schematic structures in (19) concern the active (5a) and the impersonal (5d) of an unaccusative, in other words, by hypothesis of a verb with a single argument slot. Again this property determines the selection of *be* independently of whether this single argument slot is closed by an argument as in the active (19a) or rather closed by existential quantification as in the impersonal (19b).

(18)   Soazza

a. $[_I$ o $[x$ $[_I$ dormit $_{(th, th)}$

b. $[_D$ ɛl $[$ts $[_I$ a $[x$ $[_I$ lavo$_{(th, th)}$

c. $[\exists x$ $[$s $[_I$ a $[x$ $[_I$ dormit$_{(th, th)}$

(19)   Soazza

a. $[_I$ som $[x$ $[_I$ rivo$_{(th)}$

b. $[\exists x$ $[$s $[_I$e $[x$ $[_I$ rivo$_{(th)}$

Finally, in Italian the set of contexts that present *be* with the perfect participle results from the conjunction of the Albanian context (middles) with the Soazza one (unaccusatives). Theoretically, this could mean either that a conjunctive statement is present in the lexicon of Italian or that unaccusatives and middles form a natural (super)class. The latter is of course the line pursued by classical generative theorizing that construes movement as the common characteristics of the two subgroups.

Let us briefly review the adequacy of the conjunctive statement before we consider whether a superclass can be defined. In (20) we provide logical forms for the active transitive (1a) and for its reflexive and passive counterparts (2a) and (2c). It is evident that while the two argument slots of the transitive predicate are satisfied by two arguments in (20a), in (20c) the external argument is existentially closed, while in (20b) it is not assigned—at least not independently of the internal argument. Therefore on the ground of voice we correctly predict that the auxiliary will be *have* in (20a), but *be* in (20b–c). In (21) on the other hand, we report the structures for an unaccusative (monoargumental) predicate, both in the active (1a) and in the impersonal (2d′). In this case the auxiliary is always *be*, for the same reasons as in *Soazza*, independently of whether the argument slot is filled by an argument as in the active (21a) or existentially closed as in the impersonal (21b).

(20) a.   [$_I$ ho   [$_x$ [$_I$ lavato $_{(th, th)}$ le camicie
      b. [$_D$ Gianni   [si [$_I$ è   [$_x$ [$_I$ lavato $_{(th, th)}$
      c. [$_D$ le camicie [si [$_I$ sono   [$_x$ [$_I$ lavate$_{(th, th)}$

(21) a.   [$_I$ sono   [$_x$ [$_I$ arrivato$_{(th)}$
      b. [∃x   [si [$_I$ è   [$_x$ [$_I$ arrivati$_{(th)}$

In keeping with the representational bias of the grammar we are presenting, we propose an LF interface characterization of the superclass formed by unaccusatives and middles. Specifically, we propose that the grammar is sensitive to a categorical distinction between "defective" argument structures, including those with an unbound or generically bound variable (middle), or those with only one argument (unaccusatives) and "non-defective" argument structures (defined as the complement to the above). In this perspective, while Albanian is sensitive to voice, and Soazza is sensitive to transitivity, Italian is sensitive to defectiveness in defining selection frames for auxiliaries.[10]

---

[10] While we have devoted considerable attention to the work of Reinhart and Siloni (2005), we have not commented at all on one of their key proposals: that arity operations apply not only in the syntax, but also in the lexicon. We are entitled to do so by the fact that Reinhart and Siloni (2005) explicitly exclude that this parameter is involved in auxiliary selection. For the sake of completeness, however, we discuss just one of the pieces of evidence they consider, namely whether the middle morphology can be associated with a dative argument slot. For Reinhart and Siloni (2005) the fact that it can in Italian, as in (ia), means that voice is determined in the syntax; the fact that in Albanian it cannot, as in (ib), means that voice would be determined in the lexicon.

(i)   a. Gianni si   lava   i piedi.
         Gianni M   washes the feet
         'John washes his feet.'

      b. Gjirokastër
         a′i   lan   fitirən.
         he   washes face.ACC
         'He washes (his) face.'

It seems to us that as set out by Reinhart and Siloni (2005), the parameter between (i) and (ii) leaves out important facts. Thus in all Romance languages that have so-called indirect reflexives of the type in (i), these forms cannot be plied to a passive reading. There is nothing semantically impossible (or implausible) about saying that "John has his feet washed (by somebody else)"—yet this is an impossible reading of (i). Manzini and Savoia (2007) make the fairly obvious connection between this and the impossibility of forming a *be* passive based on a dative in Italian, hence with the classical parameter as to whether datives count as internal arguments or not.

The present work—like Manzini and Savoia (2005, 2007)—is based on comparison of closely related languages, in which a parameter can be shown to change while other conditions remain stable. The Albanian examples presented here are apparently problematic for this experimental setting in that two parameters vary at once with respect to the Romance languages considered, namely, the auxiliary parameter discussed so far—and the fact that the *be* auxiliary in Albanian alternates with other middle morphology such as the clitic, rather than combining with it as in the Romance examples.[11] The question can therefore legitimately be raised whether these two parameters co-vary.

The answer is negative. Thus there are Romance dialects that have the auxiliary selection pattern of Italian, but alternate between *si* morphology in simple tenses and *be* only (i.e. without *si* or other middle morphology) in the present perfect, reproducing the Albanian pattern. A case in point is the Romansh dialect of Trun. In the present, the reflexive is formed with the *se* clitic as in (22a). On the other hand in the present perfect in (22b) the reflexive can be formed without the *se* clitic, so that the contrast between the middle and the active rests solely on the fact that the middle (22b) has the auxiliary *be*, while the active has the auxiliary *have*. That the transitive active has the auxiliary *have* is established in (22d) with an unergative verb; in turn (22c) shows that in Trun the *be* auxiliary is associated with unaccusatives as well.

Similarly, consider Làconi in (ii). This language is like Italian in allowing indirect reflexives in (iia); furthermore its auxiliary selection pattern generally follows the Italian one, as seen in the fact that ordinary reflexives select *be*, as in (iib). Yet, while in Italian all reflexives select *be*, in Làconi indirect reflexives select *have*, as in (iia). Evidently the latter are treated as 'non-defective' structures under present assumptions—showing again that datives may or may not count as internal arguments.

(ii) Làconi (Sardinia)
   a. s   a   ssamunau   i   mˈmanuzu
      M   has   washed   the hands
      'S/he washed his/her hands.'

   b. s   ɛs   samunəð-a
      M   is   washed-M/F
      'S/he washed him/herself.'

If there is a syntactic parameter of the kind hinted at here, concerning the internal argument status of datives, then (i) could be just one of its manifestations—allowing or not allowing middle morphology to associate with the dative slot.

[11] There is a third morphological instantiation of middle voice in Albanian, namely, the specialized inflection in (2). A discussion of how this lexicalization relates to the ones considered here can be found in Manzini and Savoia (2008) and Manzini, Roussou, and Savoia (in press).

(22)   Trun (Grisons)

 a. ɛl/ɛlts se lava/lavan.
  he/they M washes/wash
  'He washes himself/They wash themselves.'

 b. ɛl/ɛlts ai/ain (se) lavaus/lavai.
  he/they is/are M washed/washed.PL
  'He has washed himself/They have washed themselves.'

 c. jau sʊn veɲɪus/veɲiða.
  I am come/come.F
  'I have come.'

 d. jau ai durmiu.
  I have slept
  'I have slept.'

The fact that here we have insisted on a unified account for reflexives and impersonal/passives in language like Italian or Albanian does not imply that they will necessarily have a unified lexicalization cross-linguistically. In particular, we know that many Romance languages, like French, as well as the Germanic languages, have separate lexicalization for the bound middle readings (*se* in French, *sich* in German, etc.) and for the impersonal readings (*on* in French, *man* in German, i.e. 'man, people'); in other words, the middle voice reduces to the bound readings. The same is true in several Romansh dialects, as illustrated in (23) with a Surselva dialect closely related to Trun (where the impersonal is *ins* 'one'). This means that the middle voice reduces to (22b) displaying the relevant pattern of Albanian.[12]

(23)   Mustér (Grisons)

 a. ins dɔʀma bain lɒu.
  one sleeps well there
  'One sleeps well there.'

 b. kwɛl vɛz-ins adina pɛʀ la vias.
  that.one sees-one always in the street
  'One always sees him on the street.'

11.4.2 *Irreversibility*

One major fact introduced in Section 11.1 has not been yet accounted for by the previous discussion, namely, that auxiliary selection according to voice and/or

---

[12] More relevant Romance evidence can be found in n. 17.

transitivity is non-reversible. A relevant observation in this respect is that in all Romance and Albanian dialects the *be* auxiliary of the perfect is also the copula and as such embeds nominal predicates.[13] Following a fairly standard analysis of copular *be* (Moro 1997) we take it that it yields raising structures. In other words, *be* selects a predication as its complement and no external argument. This forces the subject of the embedded predication to serve as the matrix EPP argument. Thus in Italian (24) the EPP argument of the copula corresponds to the thematic argument of the embedded predicate 'happy.'

(24)   Sono contento.
       I.am happy
       'I am happy.'

In turn, the raising analysis of *be* implies that it is defective in the sense defined in connection with (20) and (21)—possibly an unaccusative verb. As for *have*, in both Romance and Albanian varieties it is independently attested as a possession verb and as a necessity modal, as in Italian (25).

(25)   a. Ho   tre figli.
          I.have three children
          'I have three children.'

       b. Ho   da fare questo.
          I.have to do   this
          'I have to do it.'

Have as a possession verb is fairly uncontroversially a transitive predicate. In turn, the modal reading of *have*[14] can be construed by analogy with that of the necessity modals in other Romance languages, for example, *dovere* in standard Italian. Independently of the present theory of auxiliaries as main verbs, the relevant modals of Italian are widely assumed to be main verbs subject to restructuring (Rizzi 1982, *pace* Cinque 2006). In particular, the deontic reading is taken to depend on the fact that the necessity modal behaves as a control verb. In other words, it selects a full sentence—and eventually an external argument controlling the EPP argument of the embedded sentence. Thus in all readings, *have* can be characterized as a non-defective (transitive active) predicate.

Given this much background, the non-reversibility of the auxiliary selection patterns according to transitivity and/or voice can be described by saying

---

[13] The evidence is complicated somewhat by the fact that several Romance languages, e.g. Spanish, southern Italian dialects, have the type *estar* (Spanish) lit: 'to stay' in what in English (or Italian) are copular contexts; however, other copular contexts have *be*. The relevant distinction appears to be the one between stage-level predicates (*estar*) vs. individual-level ones (*be*).

[14] In several Romance varieties, e.g. again Spanish, southern Italian dialects, the possession verb is the type *tener* (Spanish) lit: 'to hold'; however, *have* is attested as the necessity modal.

that the defective *be* is constrained to select defective (i.e. intransitive and/or middle) predicates; conversely, the transitive active *have* is constrained to select transitive and/or active predicates. In other words, the non-reversibility of the selection pattern corresponds to a fairly obvious uniformity requirement on the argumental structures of auxiliary and embedded predicates. This constraint is implicit in current accounts though for some reason it is not made explicit (at least as far as we can tell).

11.5 The Fine Nature of Parametrization

Our main aim in this chapter is to draw some general conclusions about the nature of parameters within the biolinguistic framework—based on the (fairly) detailed case study advanced in the previous sections. Before doing so, however, we want to address further the fact that while the present discussion possibly captures all of the fundamental parameters in auxiliary selection in the present perfect, the observed parametrization is actually much more finely grained.[15]

---

[15] To our knowledge, the finer parametrization of auxiliary selection has been discussed relatively little in the literature (but see Loporcaro 2007)—with a notable exception, which concerns the alternation between *have* and *be* according to transitivity. Sorace (2000) concludes that only a core class of unaccusative verbs takes auxiliary *be* in all languages, namely change-of-location verbs like *to come*; correspondingly, there is a core class of verbs that are not overtly transitive that take *have*—in her terms controlled (non-motional) process verbs like such as *to work*. With these verbs furthermore the choice of auxiliary *be* is stable within each given language. With other verbs auxiliary selection varies across languages and correspondingly there is a greater or lesser amount of variation within each given language (i.e. for each given speaker). One of the best understood factors that determines auxiliary alternations is telicity; thus Hoekstra and Mulder (1990) argue that telic construal of manner of motion verbs results in *be* selection, while atelic construals result in *have* selection in Dutch. Yet Sorace (2000) points out that Italian follows this pattern much less systematically than Dutch and that in French the auxiliary is systematically *have*. Similarly, change-of-state verbs tendentially associate with *be* in a language like Italian but with *have* in a language such as French. Furthermore, Cennamo and Sorace (2007) extend this fine-grained description to Paduan.

Legendre (2007) takes up again the evidence of Sorace (2000), providing a hierarchy of several verbal properties (displacement, telicity, etc.) ranked as a function of the property of blocking *have*; the auxiliary selection pattern of a language is a result of the ranking of the constraint *E (blocking *be*) within this hierarchy. Kayne (2008) takes an altogether different approach, proposing that the difference between Italian and French reduces to the different treatment of a class of verbs that he takes to be formed with a silent causative head. He argues that in French the perfect participle of this causative verb (like its overt counterpart) does not agree; on the further assumption that *be* requires an agreeing participle, this forces selection of *have* with the relevant class of verbs. In Italian, causative participles agree and *be* is selected with the same verbs.

Despite all of the empirical evidence displayed by Sorace (2000) and Legendre (2007) in favor of a hierarchy-based/Optimality-Theory approach to auxiliary selection (in split intransitive contexts), the entire bias of this chapter favors the same kind of categorial split between two given languages (i.e. competences) that Kayne (2008) also adopts. At the same time, one of the running themes of the present discussion of the facts is that auxiliary selection and perfect participle agreement are independent phenomena (Manzini and Savoia 2005, 2007). Leaving aside the fact that as far as we can see the non-agreement of causative participles in French by Kayne (2008) is not explained, a key observation is

A look at the tables of Manzini and Savoia (2007) reveals many possible sub-patterns in auxiliary selection according to person, discussed in some detail there. One such pattern in particular is worth reporting upon in the present context. In some dialects certain persons are associated with both *have* and *be*—which alternate not freely, but according to transitivity and voice, in other words, essentially according to the pattern of standard Italian. This person split, in which only certain persons have auxiliary selection according to transitivity and voice, is found both in languages where the other persons have *be*, such as *Colledimacine* in (26), and in languages where other persons have *have*, as in *Aliano* in (27). Specifically in *Colledimacine* it is the third person

that the relevant implication between *be* and perfect participle agreement would hold only of Romance languages. But even in Romance languages it is far from obvious that the generalization holds, since in *Montebello Ionico/Saline Ioniche*, *have* and *be* appear to be in free variation while the participle remains non-agreeing, as in n. 8 And second, should not the same implication hold in Germanic languages (Kayne 2008: n. 24) or in Albanian?

Within the framework defined by the present chapter, the simplest hypothesis as to the parameter between Italian and French would be that Kayne's "anticausatives" are construed as monadic (unaccusative) predicates in Italian, while in French they count as diadic (i.e. concealed transitives). We see no objections to the speakers learning this type of information about argumental frames—and we know that there is no necessary connection between the shape of an event and the transitivity properties of a predicate depicting it—compare to *arrive* and its transitive ("applicative") counterpart *reach* (Italian *giungere* vs. *raggiungere*).

In all fairness to Kayne (2008), there is a set of Romance examples that provide a clear connection between agreement and auxiliary selection (not known to Kayne, as far as we can tell). Consider a language like Làconi in (i), which in simple tenses has the verb agreeing with the definite postverbal subject in (ia) but not with the indefinite postverbal subject in (ia′). In the present perfect, the non-agreeing indefinite determines the selection of *have*, irrespective of transitivity and voice, as (ib), though agreeing unaccusatives and middles are associated with *be*, as in (ib′) in a way entirely comparable to Italian.

(i) Làconi

    a. iŋ kuɖˈɖei   drommi   ppipˈpiuzu.
        there   sleeps   children
        'Children sleep there.'

    a′. iŋ kuɖˈɖei   dromminti   is   pipˈpiuzu.
        there   sleep   the   children
        'The children sleep there.'

    b. a   ßenˈniu   una   ˈvemmina/ˈvemminaza
        has   come   a   woman/women
        'There came a woman/women.'

    b′. funti   enˈniuzu/enˈnias   kussas   ˈfeminaza/kussuz ˈomminizi
        are   come.ᴍ/come.ꜰ   these   women/these men
        'These men/women came.'

What we would have to say about these examples is that *have* with postverbal indefinites, as in (i), reflects a treatment of these structures as transitive (or in present terms, non-defective)—which would in turn imply that the postverbal subject and the EPP position are in some relevant respects independent arguments. Manzini and Savoia (2005) develop precisely this intuition—which implies that the EPP position (hence the verb inflection) and the postverbal argument are not in an agreement relation.

that is sensitive to transitivity and voice, as shown in (the relevant forms of) (26a) vs. (26c); similarly, in *Aliano* the same sensitivity is displayed by the third person singular, as in (27b) vs. (27c). The first and second person have *be* in *Colledimacine*, as in (26a) and (26b), and *have* in Aliano, as in (27a)—where *have* in fact characterizes the plural in general (including the third person). Similar patterns have been described in the literature by Loporcaro (1999, 2007) and La Fauci and Loporcaro (1989).

(26)   Colledimacine (Abruzzi)

     a. so/ʃi/e/   semmə/se:tə/e   mənu:tə.
       I.am/you.are/he.is/ we.are/you.are/they.are come
       'I have come' etc.

     b. ə   so/ʃi/   semmə/se:tə   cama:tə
       him I.am/you.are/ we.are/you.are called
       'I/you/we have called him.'

     c.   a   cama:tə
       him he.has/they.have called
       'He has/they have called him.'

(27)   Aliano(Lucania)

     a. ɛddʒə/(γ)ei/ɛmmə/avesə/ɛnə   vənutə/durmutə.
       I.have/you.have/we.have/you.have/they.have come/slept.
       'I have come/slept' etc.

     b. ɛ   vvənutə.
       he.is come
       'He has come.'

     c. a   durmutə.
       he.has slept
       'He has slept.'

It will be noticed that in both of the examples set in (26) and (27) it is the third person (singular) that displays auxiliary selection to transitivity and voice, while the first and second person do not display such sensitivity and are associated with a single auxiliary. As it turns out, at least the data provided by Manzini and Savoia 2005, 2007) support the conclusion that this selection pattern cannot be reversed. In particular there are dialects where auxiliary selection according to transitivity and voice is observed in other persons in addition to the third, for instance Vastogirardi (discussed by Manzini and Savoia (2007)) where it occurs in the first singular as well. Crucially, however, we know of no language where a first or second person has auxiliary selection according to transitivity and voice to the exclusion of the third person.

In Section 11.3 we argued that first and second person can obtain their reference directly through anchoring at the universe of discourse, while for person, reference is established necessarily through anchoring at the event. This means that in auxiliary selection systems with person split, it can be the case that third-person elements are the only ones to display sensitivity to the event structure of the predicate—hence to transitivity and voice. In the same systems, discourse-anchored first- and second-person elements will be insensitive to this distinction—or will be sensitive to it only to the extent that the third person is too. This proposal confirms that the third person cannot simply be characterized in negative terms, as excluding speaker and hearer reference (Benveniste 1966). Rather, third-person reference is characterized in positive terms by its necessarily anchoring at the event.

The systems in (26) and (27) also illustrate an important point about parameters in general, namely, that complex surface patterns are obtained through the combination of more elementary patterns, attested in isolation in other systems. As far as we can see, this conclusion has not been strongly pursued before in the literature, which has been concerned with a different kind of simplification, whereby the setting of one parameter implies the setting of several others. In turn, the irreversibility of the parametric choices discussed in connection with (26) and (27) configures an implication between two parameters. For, what we are saying is that if selection of *have* and *be* is sensitive to the person of the embedded EPP argument, then "uniform" selection (cf. Section 11.4.2) must involve the third person—configuring an implication from person split to uniform selection. Note, however, that in this case the parametric choices that display an implicational relation to one another do so with respect to a lexical domain in which each of them independently applies. Thus, we do not expect an implication to exist, say, from perfect participle agreement to auxiliary selection (Kayne 2008) or from auxiliary selection to the null subject parameter (D'Alessandro and Roberts (2008), since these implications involve two parameters applying in different lexical domains and connected only by derivational processes (or their representational counterparts). The overall finding of our work on parametrization in Romance and Albanian dialects is that such non-local implications do not in fact hold.[16]

---

[16] The implications quoted are just the two most recent proposals we are aware of in the relevant empirical domain. We discuss Kayne (2008) in n. 15. As for D'Alessandro and Roberts (forthcoming), they propose that "If a language has person-driven auxiliary selection, that language must be a null-subject language."

However, the evidence presented below concerning Molina di Ledro in (28) and Briga in n. 17 shows that northern Italian dialects have person splits in auxiliary selection, though they are subject clitic languages. Two responses are possible to this objection; both of them seem problematic to us. First, subject-clitic languages could be null subject (Rizzi 1986); but note that French has never been taken

Nothing in what precedes implies that the interaction of the person split with auxiliary selection according to transitivity and voice results in the alternation between persons that are sensitive to the latter and persons that are not. It is perfectly conceivable that the person split results in different persons being sensitive to voice or to transitivity or to both. The languages in (28) and (29) are good cases in point. Thus in the reflexive Molina di Ledro presents a classical person split with *be* in the first and second person and *have* in the third person. As expected on the basis of the general reversibility of person split patterns, Buonabitacolo exemplifies the reverse association of *be* with the third-person singular and *have* with the other persons (the first and second-person singular and the plural). However both, in Molina di Ledro and in Buonabitacolo, unaccusatives associate with *be* throughout the paradigm, as in the (b) examples, and transitives with *have*, as in the (c) examples.

(28)   Molina di Ledro (Veneto)

a.		me	so	la'va	A
	te	te	se		A
	el/la	s	a		E
		ne	sume	la've	A
		ve	se		A
	i/le	s	a		E
	CIS	REFL	AUX	washed	

'I have washed myself' etc.

b. l/ i   ɛ   vi'ɲu.
   CIS   AUX   come-M/F
   'I have come' etc.

c. o   miɣa   dur'mi.
   I.have   not   slept
   'I have not slept.'

(29)   Buonabitacolo (Campania)

a.	m	addʒa	lavato	A
	t	a		A
	s	ɛ		E
	ɲtʃ	amma	lavati	A

---

to be. Manzini and Savoia (2007) argue that the overall variation picture within Romance establishes the continuity between French and northern Italian. A second answer could be that the generalization only holds for auxiliary selection according to person of the simple type in Section 11.2, excluding alternations according to both person and transitivity/voice. In fact, nothing in D'Alessandro and Roberts leads us to believe that they take their theory to apply to languages like Molina or Briga. But if so, this is a further problem for it.

v	aita		A
s	anna		E
REFL	AUX	washed	

'I have washed myself' etc.

b. so/si/simmo/siti   vvənuto/vənuti.
   Aux   come/come-PL
   'I have come,' etc.

c. iddu   a   camatu   a 'patitu.
   he   has   called   to your father
   'He called your father.'

In terms of the parametrization picture laid out in this chapter, Molina di Ledro can be described as a language where the third person has the same auxiliary selection system as Soazza, that is, according to transitivity only, while the first and second person have the auxiliary selection system of Italian, according to transitivity and voice. The result is *be* in the first and second person of the middle (reflexive)—as in Italian—and *have* in the third person. Buonabitacolo has the reverse pattern. In other words, it is the third person that displays the standard Italian system, with sensitivity to both transitivity and voice, and therefore *be* in the middle (reflexive), while the first and second person have the Soazza paradigm, with sensitivity only to transitivity and hence *have* in the middle (reflexive). This also makes it clear that the resumptive table in Manzini and Savoia (2007) is itself a very partial record of person splits in auxiliary selection, which should be enriched for instance with data of the type in (28) and (29).[17]

11.5.1 *Some conclusions*

The review of the phenomena of auxiliary selection that precedes argues that there is a very limited range of descriptive categories that get into the definition of superficially very articulated parametric systems. These include the split

---

[17] An interesting Romance sub-pattern combines the person split of the type in (28) and (29) with the *be* only morphology for the middle described in the text for Trun in (22). Thus Briga, exactly like Molina di Ledro in (28) alternates between *be* in the first and second person and *have* in the third person as in (ib) in the present perfect reflexive. At the same time, exactly as in Trun in (24), or in Albanian, *be* in (ia) appears without any clitic middle morphology, though *have* combines with it, as in (ib).

(i) Briga (Piedmont)
   a. sum/t ɛ/ sumen/ si   la'va/lavai.
       I.am/you are/we.are/you.are   washed/washed.PL
       'I/you/we have washed.'
   b. s   a/aŋ   la'va/lavai.
       M   he.has/they.have   washed/washed.PL
       'He has washed/they have washed.'

between event-anchored and discourse-anchored referents, the split between active and middle voice, and the split between transitive and unaccusative predicates. As we (implicitly) construed it in the previous discussion, the task of linguistic theorizing is to specify to which primitives of Universal Grammar these descriptive categories belong. In fact, fine parametrization results from the interaction of these primitives. As for the transitivity split, we proposed that what is involved is simply the n-adicity of the predicate—the basic split being between monadic and poliadic. As for voice, we concluded that the unification of reflexives and passives with impersonals requires reference to a notion of free/generic variable in the argument structure.[18]

We were at pains to illustrate the reasons why we conclude that transitivity and voice alternations cannot be characterized in terms of movement from object to subject position, either separately or together. Faced with any set of empirical difficulties, such as those encountered in applying the classic movement analysis of passive to the middle voice of Italian or Albanian, there are in principle two ways forward. One is to add stipulations to the theory so as to fit the new evidence. The other is to make a new start. In the case of middle voice, we are satisfied that the extensive literature of the last decades has shown that no simple manipulation of the movement theory of passive suffices to capture the facts. Therefore there are reasons why the alternative we are offering should be seriously considered. In providing such an alternative, we of course lay ourselves open not only to criticisms based on empirical shortcomings, but also to criticisms on grounds of explanatory adequacy. However, the primitives that we employ, namely, the notions of selection, LF variable, generic binding, predicate–argument structure, and so on, are (as far as we can tell) all independently included into minimalist theories, to whose fold we take the present theory to belong.

---

[18] In the body of the chapter we considered in some detail only notions of transitivity and voice, but the person split would have deserved an equally thorough treatment. Very briefly, the kinds of facts that we are thinking of when we use labels like event- or discourse-anchored are, for instance, the generalization mentioned (and not explained) above, whereby in conditions of person split, there cannot be sensitivity to voice and transitivity on the part of the first and second person to the exclusion of the third. Facts like this lead Manzini and Savoia (2005, 2007) to conclude that what is at stake is not so much the referential properties of first/second person vs. third person as the way in which they interact with their anchoring in argument structure. Yet the deeper level of explanation (in terms of the real primitives of the computational component/LF interface) remains to be explored. The natural line to follow is to connect the anchoring properties to the referential ones. Thus Manzini (2008) explores the possibility that what is at stake is the anaphoric properties of the third person (which can function as a variable) vs. the purely deictic properties of the first and second person. For instance, if we think of the argument slots associated with a given predicate as variables (Adger and Ramchand (2005), we could assume that third-person referents provide (quantificational) binders for these variables, while the mechanism for hooking first and second person at the argument structure must of necessity follow some other route.

The reason why we went into so much detail with these matters is strictly connected with the general conclusions we want to draw from them about the nature of parametrization. A core pursuit of linguistic theory is to define the categorial distinctions of UG. Languages vary as to whether these categories are or are not instantiated (and how) in their lexicon. These categorial distinctions are the true "atoms" of language (Baker 2001); on the one hand they are part of the universal competence, on the other hand they enter into the differentiation of the various language-particular grammars. If what precedes is correct, what appear to be complex syntactic patterns of auxiliary selection reduce to the lexical, selection properties of *have* and *be*. For the sublexicon consisting of *have* and *be*, the relevant categories are "defectiveness" for standard Italian, transitivity for Soazza, voice for Albanian, and the person split for Verbicaro, Morcone, Bisceglie; both defectiveness and the person split are relevant for Colledimacine, Aliano, Molina di Ledro, Buonabitacolo.

One issue that we left completely out of the present discussion is that some parameter values or clusters appear to be favored over others. Thus the data we have would seem to indicate that there is a considerable imbalance between systems with *be* in the first and second person and *have* in the third (which are relatively many, and relatively stable) and the reverse systems (which are fewer, but also very much subject to internal variation). We take these facts to be outside the scope of the present discussion—in other words, we think it is legitimate to separate the question as to which parameter values and clusters are instantiated at all from the question of which of them appear to be favored over others. Generalizations in the typological and functionalist tradition seem to us to typically target this latter level of explanation. In fact, they might provide precisely the type of external explanation that parametric preferences require; by the same token, internalist frameworks would seem to be ill-advised to try to mimic them, to the extent that such a thing is possible at all. The irreversible parameter values that we found do not amount to vast implications between structural properties of languages, as typological, functional generalizations typically do. Rather, our implications range over restricted subsets of lexical properties, which represent the true primitives of parametrization.

The distinction between microparametric and macroparametric approaches to variation has been discussed so often that the contours of the debate have become somewhat blurred. It is evident that to the extent that the primitives of variation are macrocategories like transitivity or voice, we could equally describe our approach as macroparametric, though the fact that the unit of variation can be as small as a single lexical item qualifies it as microparametric. What is clear is that the empirical evidence at our disposal appears to be entirely incompatible with macroparameters in the sense of

Baker (2001)—that is, structural parameters with cascading effects over much of grammar. If there is a tendency for certain parameter values to cluster together, its explanation appears to be essentially external to linguistics, in the sense in which typological or functional explanations are.

As anticipated in Section 11.1, none of our findings imply that the distinction between lexical and functional categories has any import for variation. Thus all syntactic structures can be projected from lexical terminals, and there is neither a specialized morphological component, nor specialized lexicalization principles applying to abstract functional nodes. The mechanisms that determine variation in so-called functional categories (such as those relevant for the selection of perfect participles by *have* and *be*) are the same responsible for variation in the substantive lexicon (including natural kinds, spatial relations, and similar universals connected with general cognition). The argument developed here in favor of this hypothesis is essentially an economy one; since the lexical–functional divide is not necessary, it can be dispensed with.

In fact, any theory maintaining a functional–lexical divide must define where the boundary between the two is, which is a far from trivial task. The domain of spatial relations and of events involving them is a case in point. Spatial relations are covered among others by prepositions (or particles in their intransitive use). In particular, prepositions/particles can combine with elementary verbs to lexicalize events with a spatial component; for instance, English has *put down* (*the book*), northern regional Italian has *mettere giù* (*il libro*). At the same time Tuscan and literary Italian has a verb *posare* 'put down'; and the examples could be multiplied (*go in* and *enter* in English etc.). Particles in Germanic languages (but also in Romance, for instance in northern Italian dialects) also admit of aspectual interpretations. If on the basis of these interpretations and of the role they play in Case systems, we treat prepositions/particles as part of the functional lexicon, what should we infer about spatial primitives? Are they functional? If so, how is their relation to *posare*, *enter*, etc.—that is, canonical lexical verbs—expressed?

The answer envisaged by authors such as Kayne (2006b) is that apparent variation in the substantive lexicon reduces to variation in the pronunciation of functional categories; hence the substrings lexicalized by what would traditionally be thought of as lexical categories consist in reality of a number of functional specifications, which may surface in some languages and not in others, or surface to different extents in different languages. In this way, the functional lexicon effectively spreads over considerable portions of the substantive lexicon; at the limit, one may want to say that lexical categories are but an epiphenomenon of abstract functional structure.

Since the proposal we are putting forward is that lexicons are but ways of partitioning an abstract categorial space, we are closer to alternative theories than it may at first appear. At the same time, we consider it significant that we take the step of calling the lexical–functional divide into question, while they typically do not. To begin with, the different approaches make different predictions in data domains which they both address. Thus we have specifically referred to Kayne (2006a, 2006b) and Distributed Morphology in that we can directly compare our respective approaches to fine variation in clitic structures (Manzini and Savoia 2007). We have argued elsewhere (Manzini and Savoia 2010, Savoia and Manzini 2010) that we believe our model to be preferable on grounds of descriptive as well as explanatory adequacy.

The lexical–functional issue seems to us particularly worthy of note because it concerns at heart the distinction between the narrow and broad language faculties (FLN and FLB in Section 11.1). Let us assume that there is a universal inventory of concepts and that the lexicon represents a way of realizing it. In theories where the inventories are in fact two, one for functional categories, and one for non-functional ones, it seems to us that implicitly or explicitly the functional and non-functional lexicon are apportioned to the language faculty narrowly construed and broadly construed, respectively. The reduction of the divide that we are proposing has implications not only for the more technical aspects of the theory of grammar reviewed so far, but also opens the possibility that the universal conceptual repertory that language-particular lexicons partition is part of the broadly construed language faculty in its entirety. In fact, to limit ourselves to the grammatically relevant categories investigated here, we see no reason why notions such as transitivity and voice (i.e. effectively valency reduction of some sort) should not constitute categorizations in a general cognition domain. In other words, what we are saying is that the existence of a functional lexicon associated with the FLN is not a matter of logical or factual necessity—and as such it should be open to scrutiny.

Given the position that we tentatively take on the matter—that eliminating the divide does not imply any empirical problem, and on the contrary allows for a certain simplification of the architecture of language—we may wonder why such a distinction is so prominent in linguistics. The neuropsychological literature provides much evidence, both based on recent brain imaging techniques and on more traditional language disorders and acquisition studies that different brain areas are implicated by different conceptual clusters. The prediction is that

manipulable objects such as tools are strongly linked to motor behavior and therefore their representational networks should comprise a significant amount of neurons in motor contexts. Animals, which are most of the time (visually) perceived rather than manipulated, should be represented by networks that partly reside in visual cortex. (Bastiaansen et al. 2008)

Conversely, "assemblies representing function words remain limited to the perisylvian cortex and strongly left-lateralized in typical right-handers" (Pulvermüller 1999: 260–1). This appears to underlie in particular the differential treatment of different sublexicons by aphasic patients (anomics, agrammatics, etc.). Granting such results, it seems to us the conclusion is not necessary that there is a functional lexicon associated with the computational system of natural language and distinguished on these grounds from a contentive lexicon. Another possibility is that

there is a continuum of meaning complexity between the "simple" concrete content words that have clearly defined entities they can refer to… more abstract items that may or may not be used to refer to objects and actions and function words… According to the present proposal, the important criterion is the strength of the correlation between the occurrences of a given word form and a class of non-linguistic stimuli or actions.   (Pulvermüller 1999: 261)

In other words, it is not so much the functional lexicon that has a special status within the architecture of the mind–brain, but, rather, certain contents as opposed to others.

Once freed from the burden of highly articulated inventories and hierarchies of functional categories, we can entertain a simpler syntax, much in the sense of Culicover and Jackendoff (2005). Nor do we believe that levels of representations of the type proposed by Culicover and Jackendoff (2005), including rich notions such as grammatical functions, linking rules, etc., are required by such a simpler syntax. For the grammar implemented here for auxiliary selection is a representational version of current minimalist theories.

The relation of the syntax, and more precisely its LF component, to interpretation, as outlined once again in Section 11.1, is crucial in our view to understanding the role of language variation in the overall economy of the faculty of language. If our construal of syntax and its relation to interpretation is correct, the syntax restricts interpretation, but does not "contain" it (Culicover and Jackendoff 2006). Thus the boundary between syntax and interpretation is a loose one, allowing for a number of different matchings of syntactic form to (inferentially determined) meaning. The looseness of this relation seems to be an essential design feature of the faculty of language, in the sense that it permits the invariant constructs of syntax to cover varying meanings. Lexical items are at the core of language variation simply because they represent the core unit of this loose interface between syntax and interpretation. In this sense, variation is not an accidental property of the faculty of language—nor are the characteristics of variation that we have tried to outline in this study. Rather, they represent pretty much a by-product of the general architecture of the language faculty.

12

The Biolinguistic Program and Historical Reconstruction

GIUSEPPE LONGOBARDI AND
CRISTINA GUARDIANO

12.1 Introduction

The contribution of formal syntactic theories to modern linguistics is still widely regarded as focused on synchronic generalizations rather than on classical evolutionary problems. This chapter sums up the results of an ongoing research project, which suggest that theoretical syntax may provide unexpected evidence for phylogenetic issues typical of the historical–comparative paradigm. The level of analysis tentatively used in the research is not that of surface patterns, but that of the more abstract grammatical parameters investigated since Chomsky (1981). On these grounds, we will contend that formal grammar, along the model of molecular genetics, can be construed as a potential contribution to the study of the human past; and that, in turn, the reality of parameter systems, as cognitive theories of grammatical variation and its implicational structure, receives radically new support precisely from their success with historical issues.

12.2 Classification and Historical Explanation in Biology and Linguistics

12.2.1 *Biology and linguistics*

Since the nineteenth century, evolutionary biology and historical linguistics have followed parallel paths, attempting to classify human populations and languages, respectively, into genealogically significant families, thus explaining

This chapter exactly reproduces an article published in *Lingua* 119 (11): 1679–1706, special issue *The Forests behind the Trees*, ed. by John Nerbonne and Franz Manni, under the title "Evidence for Syntax as a Signal of Historical Relatedness."

the distribution of their resemblances and reconstructing the origins of their diversity.

Such shared interest in historically connected lineages has long suggested the opportunity of also sharing some procedures of comparison and reconstruction.[1] In particular, both disciplines have been confronted with the problem of identifying and adequately evaluating relevant patterns of similarities/differences.

12.2.2 *Biological classifications*

The most traditional classifications of species, or populations within a species, are based on externally accessible evidence, the so-called morphological characters (e.g. anthropometric traits in the case of human populations, such as shape and size of body and skull, color of skin, hair, eyes, etc.). Such features are not completely adequate taxonomic characters, because they are often highly unstable through time, as subject to strong evolutionary selection on the part of the environment.

Phylogenetic, hence typically *historical*, investigation underwent a revolution over the past few decades, on the grounds of purely *theoretical* progress in biology—namely, the rise of molecular genetics. The newly available molecular evidence has one great advantage: it is less subject to change driven by natural selection and, therefore, is more likely to retain genealogical information.[2]

Furthermore, genetic polymorphisms—that is, the *comparanda* of molecular classifications—exhibit a very useful formal property: they are drawn from a finite and universal list of discrete biological options. The practical benefit of this property for taxonomic purposes will become apparent when we discuss analogous aspects of linguistic evidence.

12.2.3 *Linguistic classifications*

As in biological classifications, phylogenetic relatedness among languages has also been traditionally investigated on the most externally accessible elements, which are, in this case, sets of words and morphemes (roots, affixes, or inflections); we will term such entities "lexical" in a broad sense, as they are saliently characterized by Saussurean arbitrariness (nearly infinite possibilities of pairing sound and meaning for each language). Precisely for this reason,

---

[1] Even abstracting away from the more complex question of possibly matching results: compare Cavalli-Sforza et al. (1988), Barbujani and Sokal (1990).

[2] "... the major breakthrough in the study of human variation has been the introduction of genetic markers, which are strictly inherited and basically immune to the problem of rapid changes induced by the environment" (Cavalli-Sforza, Menozzi, and Piazza 1994: 18).

lexical items, when resembling each other in form and meaning, seem able to provide the best probative evidence for relatedness. Linguistic classification was only rarely supported through the comparison of entities less accessible to superficial observation and apparently less arbitrarily variable across languages, such as grammatical principles, in particular syntactic rules.[3]

Basically, two methods of identifying genealogical relatedness have been proposed in linguistics, both based on lexical comparison in the sense defined above: the classical comparative method and Greenberg's mass or multilateral comparison. Their respective advantages and drawbacks are discussed directly.

12.2.3.1 *The classical comparative method*   Phylogenetic linguistics has two basic goals: establishing a relative taxonomy among three or more languages and establishing absolute historical relatedness between two (or more) languages. Therefore, the main problems for comparative methods in linguistics are that of measuring language distance/similarity and that of identifying a sufficient number of similarities so improbable as to go beyond chance and call for historical explanation (prove some form of relatedness).

The classical comparative method can yield neat conclusions on language relatedness, which are immune from the need of serious mathematical evaluation, as they are based on few highly improbable phenomena, like agreements in irregular morphology and, especially, recurrent (optimally "regular") sound correspondences. Such phenomena patently provide what Nichols (1996: 48) terms individual-identifying evidence, that is to say phenomena whose "probability of multiple independent occurrence among the world's languages is so low that for practical purposes it can be regarded as unique and individual," essentially the equivalent of a haplotype in evolutionary genetics.[4] In principle, even a single well-attested regular sound correspondence could provide such evidence, defining a language family (a haplogroup) with certainty.

This way, the classical comparative method has largely solved the problem of identifying *comparanda* safe from chance similarity (i.e. it has provided reliable cognation judgments), without having to resort to especially sophisticated measurements. Therefore, the method, undoubtedly one of the

---

[3] Syntax will be understood here, again in a broad sense, as a set of generalizations combining words and their meanings into well-formed and interpretable sentences.

[4] Such evidence should then characterize a unique individual protolanguage, rather than a set of languages or a language type. The statistical threshold for individual-identifying was obtained by Nichols (1996), multiplying the probability of the occurrence of individual languages, calculated in the order of 0.001, with a conventional level of statistical significance, considered to be 0.05 or 0.01, reaching a probability between 1 in 20,000 and 1 in 100,000. She assumes then that "a probability of occurrence of one in a hundred thousand or less is individual-identifying at a statistically significant level, and a probability of one in ten thousand is at least interesting and borderline useful" (ibid., p. 49).

greatest achievements of the human sciences, has the major epistemological advantage of providing a sharp and much-needed demarcation criterion between science and pseudo-science in etymology and historical linguistics.

The other side of the coin is that it is limited by the very conditions warranting its success as a demarcation criterion: it necessarily narrows the scope of inquiry to sets of languages and chronological spans in which such improbable (hence, necessarily rare) phenomena as recurrent correspondences ("sound laws") are recognizable. It has offered spectacular a posteriori proofs of the relatedness of language families whose state of cognation was relatively easy to suspect already before the systematic application of the method itself. In contrast, it has not been equally useful as a heuristic, nor as a proof, for long-distance grouping of such families into deeper stocks, nor (perhaps precisely because it does not need to care for sophisticated measurements to prove relatedness) has it always been effective in identifying lower taxa—that is, family-internal articulation.

12.2.3.2 *Mass comparison*   The most notable attempt to overcome this practical limit, aiming at more far-reaching, long-range taxonomic conclusions, is Joseph Greenberg's (1987, 2000, among other works) highly controversial multilateral or mass comparison.

The method is still based on lexical data, but does not rely on the criterion of exact sound correspondences to identify cognate sets: Greenberg notices that exceptionless sound laws and rigorous reconstruction procedures were discovered only after the best-assessed language families, such as Uralic or Indo-European, had been identified. Greenberg's proposal is that the lack of exact sound correspondences—that is, the reliance on mere phonetic and semantic resemblance—can be compensated by comparing lists of words not just in pairs of languages, but across larger sets at the same time. This should reduce the risk of mistaking accidental similarity for etymological cognacy: for, if the probability of chance agreement between two languages on a certain item is $1/n$, the probability of the same agreement in three languages is $(1/n)^2$, in four it is $(1/n)^3$, etc.

Similarly, Greenberg has claimed that reconstruction of protolanguages and of precise diachronic steps is not a necessary prerequisite to hypothesize phylogenetic taxonomies, and that consideration of synchronic similarities/differences may be sufficient.

The method has the advantage that, given a sufficiently universal list of meanings, it can in principle be applied to any set of languages, no matter how remote, and not just to those which exhibit recognizable sound correspondences.

The critical disadvantage of Greenberg's method is that it fails to provide, let alone justify, any precise measure of similarity in sound and meaning. This has two serious consequences. First, it is hard to establish mathematically accurate relative taxonomies, no less than with the classical comparative method. Second, although Greenberg's method, unlike the classical one, should crucially be warranted by explicit non-trivial probabilistic calculations, in fact it is unable to specify the amount and degree of similarities beyond which resemblance becomes non-accidental (individual-identifying in Nichols's terms) and proves absolute relatedness. The relevant probabilistic questions, often of hardly manageable complexity, have been mostly raised by other scholars and in general have received answers which do not support Greenberg's position.[5]

Thus, epistemologically, mass comparison does not yield so sharp a demarcation criterion as one founded on recurrent sound laws: it remains unclear how it may be safe from chance similarity.

To conclude:

(1) a. The classical comparative method has severe restrictions of applicability.

   b. Mass comparison has been unable to yield satisfactory proof of absolute historical relatedness.

   c. Neither method has proved particularly apt to provide exact measuring of taxonomic distances (also see Section 12.4.3.2).

12.2.4 *Phylogenetic issues and theoretical linguistics*

In view of the skeptical and sometimes harshly critical replies to Greenberg's proposals, we can safely conclude that the twentieth century has hardly seen any major widely accepted progress in comparative methods based on the lexicon, in particular as heuristics for novel genealogical conclusions.[6] It is natural, then, to begin to look at linguistic domains beyond the lexicon, as especially suggested by Nichols (1992), Heggarty (2000), and McMahon (2005).

As noted, in biology the impasse resulting from the limits of morphological traits as taxonomic characters was overcome by accessing more sophisticated evidence provided by independent theoretical developments of the discipline. *Mutatis mutandis*, analogous theoretical progress has been made in linguistics since the 1950s with the rise of typological and formal approaches to syntax

---

[5] Cf. Ringe (1992, 1996); also cf. discussions in Joseph and Salmons (1998), among others.

[6] Many linguists concerned with phylogenetic issues would subscribe to Nichols's (1996: 65) claim: "What linguistics needs now are heuristic measures that will be valid in situations where comparativists cannot expect to have reliable intuitions, measures that will detect relatedness at time depths at which face-value individual-identifying evidence has disappeared and the standard comparative method cannot apply."

(Chomsky 1955, 1957; Greenberg 1963). In particular, the theory of Principles-and-Parameters, developed since Chomsky (1981) within the general framework of cognitive science, has tried to tie together insights from both approaches about grammatical universals and variation. As a result, theoretical syntax—studying the mind as a system of computation of abstract symbolic entities—has not only made available a new level of evidence, but also one including culturally variable data, most suitable for comparison and classification.[7]

On the analogy of the theoretically induced progress in biological classifications, we think it natural in linguistics to ask if syntax can now serve genealogical purposes better than lexical methods.

12.3 Lexical Comparison and Grammatical Typology

12.3.1 *Humboldt's problem*

Asking this question means challenging a tacit assumption in much linguistic practice, namely, that the classification of languages based on lexical arbitrariness (which is assumed to be genealogically relevant) and that based on syntactic properties (alleged to be only typologically significant[8]) are essentially orthogonal (see Section 12.4.1).[9] Thus, we will state our guiding issue as follows:

(2)   Are syntactic and lexical classifications of languages significantly isomorphic?

Since the very inspiration for raising this question is rooted in Wilhelm von Humboldt's original distinction between several possible levels of language classification, we will conventionally, and rather anachronistically, refer to (2) as "Humboldt's problem."[10] Humboldt's problem admits in principle of two basic answers:

(3)   a. Syntax and lexicon provide analogous taxonomic results.

b. Syntax provides taxonomic results radically at odds with those of the lexicon.

---

[7] See the remarks on this point in Roberts (2007b).

[8] In fact, with the inspiring exceptions of the mentioned Nichols (1992) and Dunn et al. (2005). Cf. the remarks in Sections 12.3.2 and 12.4.4 for the difference in level of abstraction between the evidence used in these works and in the present research.

[9] For a recent statement cf. Newmeyer (2005: 102): "... parameter settings do not 'correspond' in the way that cognates do. We can reconstruct *pater* [*patrem*? L&G] as the ancestor of *père* and *padre* because the similarities of form and meaning that have been passed down for 2,000 years allow us to conclude that in some relevant sense they are all the 'same' form. Nothing like that can be concluded from the fact that two languages, related or not, share the same value for, say the Ergativity Parameter."

[10] Cf. von Humboldt (1827, 1836 *passim*). Also see Morpurgo Davies (1996: 163 ff.) for discussion.

For clarity we take (3a) to mean that, given two genealogical trees for the same set of languages, built on lexical and syntactic evidence respectively, at least a clear majority of sub-portions of the two trees will overlap. Now, if this is the case, three logical possibilities arise:

(4) a. Syntax provides weaker insights, that is, the same taxonomic results, but only up to a shallower level of chronological depth (climbing back the past, the threshold of uncertainty is reached "more quickly").[11]

  b. Syntax and lexicon provide the same tree.

  c. Syntax provides stronger insights, that is, more ancient taxa can be safely identified (the threshold of uncertainty is reached "later," that is, further back in the past).

We will address Humboldt's problem by devising and empirically evaluating a comparison method based on the renovated insights and data provided by syntactic theory over the past twenty years.

12.3.2 *On the notion of grammar*

A clarification is in order, at this point, with respect to the notions of *grammar* and *syntax* adopted here and the various concepts of grammatical evidence used in other phylogenetic studies. In Greenberg (1987) grammatical elements taken into consideration for taxonomic purposes are essentially inflectional and derivational morphemes; Greenberg states that "the separation of lexical evidence and grammatical evidence is of course to some extent arbitrary" (Greenberg 1987: 271): this is obvious since his so-called grammatical elements are, in fact, just closed-class lexical items, whose probative value in comparisons relies on the usual idiosyncratic sound–meaning relationships. Similarly, in Nichols (1996) "grammatical evidence" is, in fact, morphological material, again characterized by the arbitrary pairing of sound and meaning.

Nichols's (1992) pioneering work and, more recently, Dunn et al. (2005), instead remarkably apply phylogenetic concerns and methods to "language structure": for instance, in the latter study, what is considered is "sound system and grammar" (Dunn et al. 2005: 2072), encoded in a data matrix of 125 binary features identified as 'features that would typically be described in a published sketch grammar' (ibid. 2073). The description of linguistic characters in the supporting online material shows that several features are actually generalizations spanning different lexical items (thus grammatical in

---

[11] Even in this case the pursuit of syntactic comparison might be useful for deciding in controversial cases of dialectal classification.

our sense) and that a subset deals with syntactic properties. Therefore, such results, along with Nichols's (1992) original insights, are an encouraging basis for the enterprise presented in this chapter.[12] However, our inquiry still differs, in several cases, from theirs as for the exact nature of the evidence involved: we will try to explore the historical significance not of surface generalizations, but of syntactic parameters, which should encode the rich implicational relations supposedly connecting distinct observable phenomena at the level of abstract cognitive structures.[13]

12.4 Syntax as Historical Evidence?

12.4.1 *Syntactic comparison*

Syntax has indeed never been central to the discovery of genealogical relatedness among languages. For instance, relationships among Indo-European varieties have hardly ever been supported exclusively or prevailingly by syntactic evidence. Apparently, there are two main reasons for this:

(5)   a. It is difficult to identify precise syntactic *comparanda*.

     b. Syntax is not as variable as the lexicon, hence similarities are less probative.

Objection (5b) has to do with probabilistic considerations addressed in Section 12.6.2. Here we will be concerned with (5a).

As observed by Watkins (1976), in order to establish syntactic correspondences among languages, one must adopt the same strict requirements which characterize the comparative method in other modules, that is, one must compare items clearly falling into equivalence classes. Some surface syntactic patterns occasionally provide sufficient correspondences of form and meaning, as suggested by Watkins himself; however, these phenomena are often not so systematic as to allow for measuring distances and for supporting relatedness hypotheses.

In agreement with Roberts (1998), we suggest that Principles-and-Parameters theory does in principle provide the required systematic *comparanda*, namely parameter values.

The possibility of an efficient lexically blind system of (morpho-)syntactic comparison, precisely the Parametric Comparison Method (henceforth,

---

[12] Nichols (1992) is a precursor of this work also for her explicit proposal of regarding structural comparison as a population science. For a first mathematical attempt at founding historical syntax in this sense, see Niyogi and Berwick (1996).

[13] For a first attempt of comparison between the results provided by lexical, phonetic, and syntactic data on the same geolinguistic domain, now also see Spruit (2008).

PCM), was first suggested in Longobardi (2003), then in Guardiano and Longobardi (2005).

12.4.2 *Some basic properties of parametric data*

In Principles-and-Parameters theory, parameters are conceived of as a set of open choices between presumably binary values, predefined by our invariant language faculty, Universal Grammar (UG), and closed by each language learner on the basis of his/her environmental linguistic evidence ("triggers," in Clark and Roberts's 1993 terms, or "cues" in Lightfoot's 1991b sense). Therefore, setting the value of a parameter is an operation of selection rather than instruction, in the perspicuous terminology adopted by Piattelli-Palmarini (1989) pursuing the biological analogy. Open parameters would define the space of variation of biologically acquirable human grammars, closed parameters specify each of these grammars. Thus, grammar acquisition should reduce, for a substantial part, to parameter setting, and the core grammar of every natural language can in principle be represented by a string of binary symbols (e.g. a succession of 0,1 or +,−; cf. Clark and Roberts 1993), each coding the value of a parameter of UG.[14] Such strings can easily be collated and used to define exact correspondence sets.

12.4.3 *Potential advantages of the PCM*

12.4.3.1 *Formal properties*   Thus, parameters, like genetic markers of molecular biology, form a universal list of discrete options. Because of these properties, PCM may share one of the useful formal features of molecular genetic tools and is likely to enjoy some advantages over other linguistic taxonomic methods. In particular, it combines the two strengths of the classical comparative method and of multilateral comparison.

Like the latter and unlike the former, it is in principle applicable to any set of languages, no matter how different: since parameters are drawn from a universal list, PCM only needs to collate their values in the languages under comparison. It does not need to search for highly improbable phenomena (individual-identifying agreements between such languages, such as e.g. sound correspondences) and rely on their existence as a prerequisite to being applied.

Like the classical method, though by completely different means, PCM overcomes the intrinsic uncertainty about the appropriate identification of

---

[14] In the current minimalist view of language variation, parameters are ideally regarded as properties of functional heads, essentially following Borer (1984). See Newmeyer (2005: 53–69) for a survey of the history of the parametric approach since its appearance in the 1980s, and Boeckx and Piattelli-Palmarini (2005) for the best epistemological presentation of the roots of the Minimalist Program.

comparanda which undermines mass comparison. For, owing again to the universal character of parameters, in PCM there cannot be any doubt about what is to be compared with what. As, in genetics, a blood group, for instance, must be compared to the same blood group in another population, and not to other genetic polymorphisms, so the value of a parameter in a language must and can be collated with the value of exactly the same parameter in other languages. Of course, agreement in one binary parameter proves nothing by itself (as opposed to the probative value of even a single regular sound law of the classical method); but, unlike Greenberg's resemblances, parameters, owing to their discrete nature, lend themselves to precise calculations: the probability of agreements in large numbers of parameters chosen from exactly predefined sets can, in principle, be objectively computed.

12.4.3.2 *Measuring syntax and lexicon*   The other key factor of progress in evolutionary biology, beyond a new domain of taxonomic characters, was precisely the introduction of objective mathematical procedures. Their application guarantees the replicability of experiments under controlled variable conditions, so allowing one to test the impact of every minimal variation and progressive enrichment of the input data.[15]

In linguistics, the statistical treatment of data and the use of quantitative methods have successfully been proposed in such fields as sociolinguistics, dialectology, and corpus linguistics. These methods and, more specifically, the computational tools devised in biology to automatically generate genealogical trees, begin now to be exploited in historical linguistics.[16]

Most quantitative experiments in phylogenetic linguistics have exclusively or prevailingly focused on lexical databases.[17] Given the poor role of syntax in traditional comparative linguistics, this is understandable. Nonetheless, parametric comparison lends itself to such procedures much better than lexical comparison. For the fact that the values of a parameter are discrete settings (in principle binary ones, hence equidistant) enables the PCM to also overcome the common failure of the two lexical methods: it can provide exact measuring of how close or distant two languages are, allowing for mathematically grounded taxonomies. Parametric comparisons, indeed, yield clear-cut

---

[15] Furthermore, as stressed by Koyré (1961), in the history of science, the search for accuracy of measurement and a precise mathematical structure of the data has often been an a priori methodological decision, eventually rewarded by its empirical success.

[16] See for instance Lohr (1998), Ringe, Warnow, and Taylor (2002), McMahon and McMahon (2003, 2005), Nerbonne and Kretzschmar (2003), the papers collected in Clackson, Forster, and Renfrew (2004) and those in *Transactions of the Philological Society* 103: 2 (2005).

[17] See for instance Embleton (1986), Boyd et al. (1997), Gray and Atkinson (2003), Warnow et al. (2004), McMahon (2005). As remarked, Dunn et al. (2005) and Spruit (2008) use some syntactic data within their structural evidence.

answers: two languages may have either identical or opposite values for a given parameter.[18] The lexicon is different: in a given language any meaning may be arbitrarily coded by a huge and hardly definable set of minimally different phonological expressions. In such a virtual continuum of possibilities it is hard to specify how similar a word must be to the word of another language to begin to count as *relevantly* similar, not to speak of making probabilistic evaluations about the individual-identifying value of whole sets of resemblances.

Further problems with the use of lexical data as a reliable input for quantitative phylogenetic treatments are related to the frequent vagueness of cognacy judgments and to the unstable relation between form and meaning, and are especially acute when the comparanda are not drawn from limited closed-class paradigms (e.g. inflectional categories, cf. Nichols 1996 for some discussion).[19] Briefly, there are at least four common sources of vagueness (mathematical uncertainty):

(6) a. partial correspondence of form (e.g. Italian *prendo*, English *get*);

b. partial correspondence and non-discreteness in meaning comparisons (e.g. the classical case of German *Hund* vs. English *dog/hound*);

c. correspondence of form without correspondence of meaning (English *clean*, German *klein*);

d. similarity of meaning shifts with no correspondence of form (e.g. Italian *fegato*, Greek συκώτι).

Parameters neutralize even such difficulties virtually by definition, since they do not encode a form–meaning relation and, for the reasons discussed above, formal correspondences are exact, in principle, within any language set whatsoever, even between pairs of languages so dissimilar (e.g. Wolof and Norwegian) that no serious cognacy judgment can be imagined on their core vocabularies.

12.4.3.3 *Substantive properties*   Parameters are promising characters for phylogenetic linguistics in at least two other respects.

Like many genetic polymorphisms, they are virtually immune from natural selection and, in general, from environmental factors: e.g. lexical items can be borrowed along with the borrowing of the object they designate, or adapted in meaning to new material and social environments; nothing of the sort seems to happen with abstract syntactic properties.[20]

---

[18] Unless that parameter is made irrelevant for one of the languages by the interaction with independent properties; cf. Section 12.4.4, below.

[19] For a summary of the debate, see McMahon and McMahon (2005).

[20] On syntactic borrowing in general, cf. Thomason and Kaufman (1988).

Furthermore, parameter values appear to be unconsciously and rather uniformly set by all speakers of the same community in the course of acquisition, therefore they are largely unaffected by deliberate individual change, which, according to Cavalli-Sforza (2000), may influence the history of other culturally transmitted properties;[21] therefore, parameters promise to be better indicators of general historical trends than many cultural features.

12.4.4 *The implicational structure of linguistic diversity*

A problem for accurate quantitative treatments might be, however, that observable syntactic properties are often not independent of each other. The difficulty can be controlled for. Two levels of considerations are in order, one related to the classical concept of parameter, since Chomsky's first proposals at the end of the 1970s, the other to more recent empirical and theoretical work.

As for the first point, parametric hypotheses already intrinsically encode a good deal of the implicational structure of language diversity, in the very formulation of many parameters: as a matter of fact, Principles-and-Parameters theory, inspired by Greenberg's discovery of implicational universals, regards parameters as abstract differences often responsible for wider typological clusters of surface co-variation, often through an intricate deductive structure. In this sense, the concept of parametric data is not to be simplistically identified with that of syntactic pattern.

A parameter will be such only if all the grammatical properties supposed to follow from it typologically co-vary; conversely, it will be satisfactorily defined only if no other property significantly co-varies with them. This is a necessary, though not sufficient, condition to ensure that we focus on cognitive structures (i.e. components of I-language, in Chomsky's 1986 terms), not just on generalizations over surface extensions of such structures (parts of E-language). In fact, patterns such as the traditional N–Gen/Gen–N, for instance, have already proved at best epiphenomenal at the parametric level: there exist several unrelated types of both constructions and, most importantly, they follow from the combinations of more abstract and independent parameters.[22] Thus, they might even turn out to be misleading if used to

---

[21] Cavalli-Sforza (2000: 176): "There is a fundamental difference between biological and cultural mutation. Cultural 'mutations' may result from random events, and thus be very similar to genetic mutations, but cultural changes are more often intentional or directed toward a very specific goal, while biological mutations are blind to their potential benefit. At the level of mutation, cultural evolution can be directed while genetic change cannot."

[22] Cf. at least Longobardi (2001b), Crisma (in press), on this topic.

arithmetically assess areal or genetic relatedness, or just typological similarity, although we will not address this issue in the present experimentation.[23]

The second pervasive implicational aspect of parametric systems, potentially challenging independence of characters, has been highlighted in Baker (2001) and by the present research: one particular value of a certain parameter, but not the other, often entails the irrelevance of another parameter. Therefore, the latter parameter will not be set at all and will represent completely implied information in the language, deducible from the setting of the former. These entailments affect both single parameters and entire formal classes of parameters, termed *schemata* in Longobardi (2005a). Unsettable parameters in this sense will have to be appropriately disregarded for assessing degrees of relatedness. The symbolism we adopt to represent this aspect of such databases will be presented in Section 12.5.3. In Section 12.6.1, we will discuss how it can be encoded in the measuring of distances in a way to tentatively neutralize its negative effects on successive computations.

12.5 The empirical domain

12.5.1 *The choice of the parameters*

A crucial step in this research line is the choice of the parameters to be compared: a completely random choice or one based on external criteria (for instance, choosing those which have been studied in some recent literature) runs the risk of accidentally producing unbalanced results; two languages might look alike or different precisely on that subset by pure chance, rather like Spanish *mucho, día, haber* and English *much, day, have*. In principle, the only way to avoid introducing spurious variables into the experiment would be pursuing exhaustiveness, in other words, considering all parameters. On the other side, at this stage, a practical choice must be made: UG parameters number at least in the hundreds, although we are too far from being able to make precise estimates.

A viable approach, in our view, is trying to be exhaustive relatively to a limited subdomain, possibly intrinsically well defined within syntactic theory itself (and sufficiently vast to hopefully be representative). Here, the only fully arbitrary choice is selecting the module. This should also help us to better avoid a risk pointed out by Nichols for lexical mass comparison: randomly choosing *comparanda* from a larger sample poses serious probabilistic problems, as "a set of elements has much greater individual-identifying value when

---

[23] A good parametric theory could actually contribute to solving the problem noted in Nerbonne (2007), namely that sometimes it is hard to decide *how many* surface properties typologically cluster together.

taken as a closed set rather than when taken as a group of trials in a larger sample" (Nichols 1996: 62).

The suggested approach is actually the historical application of the general strategy proposed in Longobardi (2003) under the label "Modularized Global Parametrization" (MGP).

12.5.2 *Modularized Global Parametrization*

In order to realistically investigate the properties of parameters, either theoretically or historically, it is important to study a sufficiently broad set of them in a congruous number of languages. Most cross-linguistic analyses within the generative framework have instead been devoted to single or few parameters investigated within a narrow number of languages at a time.[24] MGP has been proposed precisely with the goal of overcoming the drawbacks of this situation. Such a strategy aims to attain at the same time the depth of analysis required by parametric hypotheses and sufficient crosslinguistic coverage. In particular, a sound parametric testing ground should involve:

(7)   a. a sufficient number of parameters, possibly subject to reciprocal interactions, but relatively isolated from interaction with parameters external to the set;

   b. a sufficient number of languages;

   c. a sufficiently fine-grained analysis of the data.[25]

In MGP these goals can be neared at the acceptable cost of narrowing the study to a single syntactic module and trying to be as exhaustive in that module as allowed by our best current linguistic understanding.

The MGP strategy in principle requires the elaboration of a complex tool consisting of:

(8)   a. a set of parameters, as exhaustive as possible, for the module chosen;

   b. a set of UG principles defining the scope and interactions of such parameters;

   c. a set of triggers for parameter values;

   d. an algorithm for parameter setting.

In the execution of MGP used for the present genealogical experiment, the module chosen is the nominal domain, more technically the internal syntax of

---

[24] Cf. Newmeyer (2005: 50 ff.): "researchers have not attempted a comprehensive treatment of parameters and their settings." Also cf. Chomsky (1995: 7): "the P&P model is in part a bold speculation rather than a specific hypothesis." Notice, however, the exception of Baker (2001), who discusses a system of hierarchical relations among parameters connected to polysynthesis.

[25] Descriptions in terms of, say, Dixon's (1998) Basic Linguistic Theory are normally insufficient to determine the setting of parametric values.

the Determiner Phrase (DP). The DP, besides presumably meeting condition (7a), has a further advantage for historical purposes: it is less rich than the clausal domain in informational structure, an area often regarded as a typical source of diachronic reanalysis. Let us consider to what extent the database collected conforms to MGP requirements.

12.5.3 *Database*

12.5.3.1 *Parameters*   As for (8a), 63 binary parameters have been identified within the DP domain, listed in the first column of Table A (see Figure 1 in the appendix). Parameters have been tentatively selected on the basis both of existing proposals and of novel empirical investigation over the collected database. As a matter of fact, many parameters of Table A represent current assumptions within generative or typological literature, sometimes with slight – and mostly irrelevant for our purposes – variants in their formulation.[26]

Values for the 63 parameters have been hypothesized in 23 contemporary and 5 ancient languages, each represented as a vertical string of values in a column of Table A. The 28 languages were chosen from the Indo-European ones with six exceptions. They are the following: Italian (It), Salentino[27] (Sal), Spanish (Sp), French (Fr), Portuguese (Ptg), Rumanian (Rum), Latin (Lat), Classical Greek (ClG), New Testament Greek (NTG), Grico[28] (Gri), Modern Greek (Grk), Gothic (Got), Old English (OE), Modern English (E), German (D), Norwegian (Nor), Bulgarian (Blg), Serbo-Croatian (SC), Russian (Rus), Irish (Ir), Welsh (Wel), Hebrew (Heb), Arabic (Ar), Wolof (Wo), Hungarian (Hu), Finnish (Fin), Hindi (Hi), and Basque (Bas).

The basic alternative states of each parameter are encoded as + and − in Table A. It is important to bear in mind that such symbols have no ontological, but just oppositional value. All parameters in Table A exhibit at least one contrast in value over our language sample (see the rows corresponding to each parameter), with the exception of parameters 1, 2, and 24, which however define characteristics known to clearly distinguish other languages presently under investigation, but not yet comprised in the sample.

As a general guiding criterion, we decided to build a cross-linguistic morpho-syntactic difference into Table A as a parameter if and only if it appeared to entail any of three types of surface phenomena: the position of a category, the variable form of a category depending on the syntactic context,

---

[26] See for example Bernstein (2001), Longobardi (2001b), and Plank (2003) as basic overviews of the literature in the two approaches.

[27] The Italo-Romance variety spoken in the provinces of Brindisi and Lecce (represented here by the dialect of Cellino San Marco).

[28] A Greek variety spoken South of Lecce (represented here by the dialect of Calimera).

or the presence of obligatory formal expression for a semantic distinction (i.e. the obligatory valuing of an interpretable feature). Thus, we did not encode as a parameter differences in pure morpho-phonological representation which, as far as we know, do not produce, even indirectly, any of the three manifestations above (e.g. the presence or absence of gender marking on adjectives).

Within the chosen DP module, further subdomains can be distinguished: the status of various features, such as person, number, gender (param. 1–6), definiteness (roughly 7–16), countability and related concepts (17–24), and their impact on the syntax–semantic mapping; the grammar of genitive case (25–31); the properties of adjectival and relative modification (32–41); the position of the head noun with respect to various elements of the DP and the different kinds of movement it undergoes (42–50); the behavior of demonstratives and other determiners, and its consequences (51–55 and, in a sense, 60–63); the syntax of possessive pronouns (56–59).

12.5.3.2 *Principles and implications*   With respect to (8b), what we are able to explicitly provide, within the limits of this work, is a set of theorems which derive from the relevant UG principles and express partial implications among parameter values. It is often the case that setting a parameter A on one value leaves the choice for a parameter B open, but setting A on the other value necessarily determines the value of B as well.

Now, similarities or differences among languages must not be overstated by considering completely redundant information. In order to encode the irrelevance of such settings, that is, their dependence on the value of another parameter, a 0 has been used in these cases in Table A; the implication giving rise to 0 has been indicated next to the name of the implied parameter in the first column, in the form of (conjunctions or disjunctions of) valued implying parameters, identified by their progressive number. For example "+5, −17, or +18" in the label of parameter 19 means that 19 can only be valued when 5 is set on + and either 17 is set on − or 18 is on +; otherwise 19 will receive a 0.

Sometimes implications are virtually analytical in the formulation of a parameter: for instance, every time a given parameter refers to the behavior of, say, the feature definiteness (e.g. parameters 12, 14, 15, ...), its setting becomes irrelevant in languages where such a feature is not grammaticalized, that is, if the language does not display a + value for parameter 7.

Some other times, instead, implications are formulated on the basis of empirically observed correlations: for instance, following Greenberg's Universal 36, it is assumed that a language will grammaticalize gender (value + for parameter 3) only if it grammaticalizes number (value + for parameter 2):

as a consequence, languages not displaying positive evidence for the feature number will receive a 0 for (the absence of) grammaticalization of gender; the implication will be signaled in the label of parameter 3 as "+2."

Such implications as carefully made explicit in Table A are, for practical purposes, the most important consequences of UG principles on the variation domain under study. A fuller treatment of the theory and observations presupposed by our parameters could only be contained in a dedicated monograph.

12.5.3.3 *Triggers*   As for (8c), for each parameter a set of potential triggers has been identified and used to build up a questionnaire for data collection, using English as a metalanguage. In defining the notion of trigger, we follow Clark and Roberts (1993: 317): "A sentence σ expresses a parameter p_i just in case a grammar must have p_i set to some definite value in order to assign a well-formed representation to σ." Such a sentence (or phrase) σ is thus a trigger for parameter p_i. The structural representations of the literal translation(s) of the utterances contained in our questionnaire should be able to set the relevant parameter to a specific value in a given language. Two languages have been set to opposite values of a parameter only if their triggers for that parameter in the questionnaire differ in structural representation in at least one case. The contents of the questionnaire, called Trigger List, will be made available on the project's website, in construction at www.units.it/linglab, along with the answers provided by our informants: for modern languages, each value assigned in Table A and not warranted by reliable literature has been checked with at least one linguistically trained native speaker.[29]

12.5.3.4 *Parameter setting*   With respect to (8d), again, a realistic approach would require the explicit statement of the conditions under which a parameter is set to + or to −, together with an acquisitionally plausible order of setting. Again, it is impossible to pursue such a task in the limits of the present research. The current list of parameters in Table A simply reflects the practical ordering condition that a parameter always follows other parameters on which its setting depends.

12.6 Elaboration of Data

12.6.1 *Coefficients and distances*

The information collected in Table A can now be elaborated in numerical terms. The first operation is to compute the number of identities and

---

[29] The parameter values assigned to the ancient languages in our sample rely on specific research done on written corpora, such as Crisma (1997, in press) for Old English (eleventh-century prose), Guardiano (2003) for Classical (fourth century BC) and New Testament Greek, Gianollo (2005) for Latin (first century BC–first century CE), and on further personal work by the authors.

differences in the parameter settings of each pair of languages. Such computations are represented in the form of ordered pairs of positive (or zero) integers $< i;d >$, called *coefficients*. Table A contains a robust number of 0s. As noted, 0s cannot be taken into account for measuring relatedness; therefore, even if only one of the languages of a pair has a 0 for a certain parameter, that correspondence is not counted at all for that pair. Also a few empirically uncertain states, indicated in Table A by a "?," are counted like 0s for the purposes of these computations. For these reasons, the sum of i and d in a coefficient does not necessarily equal 63, and rarely is it the same for different language pairs.

As such, coefficients are not a practical measure to rank the distances instantiated by different pairs of languages and answer questions like "Are Italian and French closer than English and German?" Therefore, coefficients must be reduced to a monadic figure, suitable for a uniform ranking of distances.

The simplest distance between any two strings of binary characters is the *Hamming distance* (Hamming 1950), which amounts to the number of differences between the two strings. Yet it is conceptually (and even empirically) wrong to reduce our coefficients to the number of differences (or alternatively to that of identities), because, as they are computed over non-uniform totals, both figures contain relevant information. The computation of $i - d$ (call it *algebraic coefficient*) is misleading too, as the result obscures the respective weight of identities and differences.

Thus, we adopted another form of reduction of coefficients into a single figure, which will be called a *normalized Hamming distance*. It results from dividing the number of differences by the sum of identities and differences of each pair, thus making the differences proportional to the actually compared parameters (i.e. $d/(i + d)$).[30] Two languages with identical settings for all valued parameters will then have distance 0, two with opposite settings for all valued parameters will have distance 1, all other cases falling in between. Such a distance turns out to be conceptually and empirically more satisfactory, even if not yet completely adequate in at least the theoretical case of pairs of languages with no differences at all, for which the distances so computed uniformly equal 0, irrespectively of the number of identities: the distance between two languages exhibiting, for example, 45 identities and 0 differences and that between two other languages exhibiting 15 identities and 0 differences would be identical.[31] Nonetheless, in practice, already very satisfactory reconstructions are attainable by means of the normalized Hamming distance

---

[30] This distance is essentially equivalent to a so-called Jaccard distance (Jaccard 1901).

[31] Dubious is also the more common case of pairs with a high number of identities and a very limited (though non-null) number of differences: for example, the distance between two languages

(cf. Section 12.7).[32] Table B (see Figure 2 in the appendix) contains both the coefficients and the normalized Hamming distances for the 378 pairs generated by the 28 languages of Table A.

12.6.2 *Probability of chance agreement*

The probability of two languages coinciding by chance in the value of a specific binary parameter (ideally assuming both values to be unmarked, i.e. equiprobable[33]) is 1/2, which, as such, has no probative value at all. The probative value becomes more significant as the number of *comparanda* increases: indeed, 63 binary independent parameters generate 2^{63} languages. The probability for two languages to coincide in all the values of 63 chosen parameters is $1/2^{63}$, which is highly significant. However, in the real world, we expect most language pairs to agree in but a subset of the parameters compared. Therefore, one must calculate the probabilistic significance of such partial agreements. Sticking to the usual assumption that parameters are binary, a rough formula to begin computing the probability of partial agreement is the following: suppose n is the total number of relevant parameters in the sample and h the number of disagreeing (or agreeing, for that matter) parameters; the probability of such an event will be

$$(9) \quad P = \frac{\binom{n}{h}}{2^n} = \frac{\frac{n!}{h! \, (n-h)!}}{2^n},$$

where $n!$ is the product of the first n integer numbers, and similarly for $h!$ and $(n-h)!$. So, for example, in the case of 44 agreements (i.e. identities), 6 divergences (i.e. differences), and 13 irrelevant comparisons out of 63 independent parameters (or of 6 agreements and 44 divergences, which has the same probabilistic value, but is unattested in our domain for principled reasons, cf. Section 12.7.1), the probability of this event will be computed in the following two steps:

with 44 identities and two differences is twice the distance between two languages with 45 identities and one difference, probably running counter the historical linguist's intuition.

[32] It is hoped that the exploration of other distance metrics, such as those elaborated by dialectometry for lexical data since Séguy (1971) and Goebl (1982), might even improve on the present results (see also Spruit 2008). On this topic, see also Cavalli-Sforza and Wang (1986).

[33] Assuming equiprobability—that is, neglecting markedness—is an obviously false, but very useful, idealization: since no solid theory of markedness exists to date, it would be risky to assign impressionistic weights to the various parameter values. On the contrary, if parametric comparison turns out to be empirically successful already under the idealization of equiprobability, it will be surprising for an eventually more realistic approach, assigning correct weights to different parameter values, to fail to match, or improve on, this result.

(10)

a. $\binom{50}{6} = \dfrac{50 \times 49 \times 48 \times 47 \times 46 \times 45}{6 \times 5 \times 4 \times 3 \times 2} = \dfrac{11\ 441\ 304\ 000}{720} = 15\ 890\ 700$

b. $\dfrac{15\ 890\ 700}{2^{50}} = \dfrac{15\ 890\ 700}{1\ 125\ 899\ 906\ 842\ 620} = \dfrac{1}{70\ 852\ 757} = 0.000000014113777$

12.7 Evaluation of Results

Table D (Figures 3a and 3b in the appendix) lists the 378 pairs in increasing order of distance; for each pair, the table also reports the probability of chance agreement and indeed the normalized Hamming distance, in parallel columns. Conceptual and empirical criteria of adequacy have been applied to Table D: the empirical criteria evaluate the correlation of our results with independently known historical variables, such as lexically based taxonomies; the conceptual ones are independent of any specific historical evidence, thus they allow one, in principle, to ascertain the degree of potential failure of the system irrespectively of contextual information.

12.7.1 Conceptual tests

In order for our results to be probative, they must present both a significant and a plausible distribution of differences and similarities between languages. Hence, a first obvious conceptual test is the following:

(11)   The pairs in Table D should be scattered across different degrees of similarity.

For, if all or most pairs were concentrated around the same distance, say 0.5, no significant taxonomic conclusion would be available in syntax.

Since the coefficients range from <40;1> (distance 0.024) to <13;18> (distance 0.64), assuming many intermediate values, we believe that such a criterion is satisfied.

The second conceptual test is related to Nichols's (1996) notion of *individual-identifying* evidence:

(12)   The probability of chance resemblance for the most similar languages must attain individual-identifying levels.

The probabilistic threshold in order for a value to begin to be individual-identifying, defined by Nichols (see n. 4), lies around $1/(2 \times 10^4)$. Among the

378 pairs of Table A3, 116 show probabilities ranging from less than $1/(3 \times 10^{12})$ to $1/(2 \times 10^4)$, that is, low enough to satisfy Nichols's requirement.

The third conceptual test is based on an assumption formally stated for the first time in Guardiano and Longobardi (2005) as the Anti-Babelic Principle:

(13)   *Anti-Babelic Principle*
       Similarities among languages can be due either to historical causes (common origin or, at least, secondary convergence) or to chance; differences can only be due to chance[34] (no one ever made languages diverge on purpose).

The Anti-Babelic Principle should have long been an obvious founding postulate of historical linguistics. However, it has been formulated just so recently because it may have measurable effects only in domains of discrete variation drawn from a universal list, such as parametric syntax, hardly in an infinitely variable field like the lexicon.

The Principle's main consequence for our model is that negative algebraic coefficients must essentially be due to chance. In a system of binary equiprobable differences, the Anti-Babelic Principle predicts that two completely unrelated languages should exhibit a distance closer to 0.5 than to 1.

For example, such coefficients as <46;5> and <5;46> would have the same (negligible) probability of being due to chance (1/958,596,125), therefore both would call for an explanation. However, historical explanations can be advocated only for the former, not for the latter. Thus, in a realistic system of parametric comparison, negative coefficients like <5;46> or, more generally, pairs where the differences largely exceed the identities should not exist.

According to the Anti-Babelic Principle, we expect pairs of languages known to be related to exhibit coefficients of a clear form $i>d$, while other pairs should tend toward $i = d$, that is, a distance of 0.5. An extremely encouraging result of our data is that among the 378 pairs of languages in Table D only 7 (i.e. 1.85%) display a negative coefficient, with distances between 0.51 and 0.64, and chance probability between 1/7 and 1/16.

12.7.2 *Empirical tests*

12.7.2.1 *Distribution of distances*   An obvious methodological procedure to evaluate the reliability of the results produced by new taxonomic methods

---

[34] This statement needs obvious qualification for the case where a language moved away from the bulk of properties of its family as a consequence of contact with external varieties: see n. 37 for an example. However, this simplistic formulation is sufficient to make the crucial point of the present argument.

is comparing them with independently established phylogenetic relations.[35] Thus, to test the validity of PCM, the relations between pairs in Table D were compared with those arrived at by traditional taxonomies, usually based on quantitatively unanalyzed, but abundant and sometimes precise, lexical, and phonological data. The knowledge of the different degrees of historical relatedness among the 28 languages of Table A gives us the possibility to define three main types of relations:

(14)   a. *Strong* relations: a relation between a pair of languages is strong if and only if one of the languages derives from the other or both derive from a common ancestor within a time span of (presumably) at most ± 4000 years.[36]

       b. *Looser* relations: a relation between a pair of languages is looser if and only if it is not strong but both languages derive from a safely established common ancestor (e.g. Proto Indo-European).

       c. *Weak* relations: a relation between a pair of languages is weak if and only if the pair does not instantiate an independently safely assessed genealogical relation.

The pairs falling into each type are signaled by progressive order of dark shading in Table D: those belonging to the first type are not shaded; those belonging to the second type are shaded in pale gray; those of the third type are variously shaded (relations involving Semitic, Uralic, and IE among each other in darker gray, relations involving Wolof and Basque in black). The distribution of shades in Table D is immediately suggestive, as most strong pairs cluster in the topmost part of the table, while weak relations tend to occur from the middle to the bottom. In more detail:

(15)   a. Out of the 378 pairs in Table D, 48 instantiate strong relations. Thirty-nine out of 48 occur among the top 50 of the table (which also include two pairs which are independently known to have undergone lexically conspicuous interference: It–Gri, Sal–Gri), and 46 within the first 93 pairs. Furthermore, such 46 strong relations show values of chance probability lower than $1/(2 \times 10^4)$, that is, they all satisfy

---

[35] As suggested by e.g. McMahon and McMahon (2005).

[36] Among the strong relations, we have included those between Finnish and Hungarian and between Arabic and Hebrew. The decision on the latter is based on the fact that the variety of Arabic analyzed is the Standard one, still somewhat based on Classical Arabic from the first millennium of the Christian era, while that representing Modern Hebrew draws from the Biblical language (12th–6th cent. BC). The relationship of all the ancient varieties of the sample with one another were considered strong, with the exception of Old English, thus tentatively locating Proto Indo-European within the fourth millennium BC.

the requirement proposed by Nichols for a value to be considered individual-identifying (see n. 4).[37]

b. Of the 145 weak relations, none occurs in the topmost 112 positions and 90 occur among the last 100 pairs. Only one reaches a (low) individual-identifying level of similarity.

The results obtained through PCM largely overlap with those suggested by traditional lexical comparative practice: this leads us to the preliminary conclusion that a positive answer to Humboldt's problem is likely to be possible.

12.7.2.2 *Phylogenetic algorithms*   A second empirical test for the PCM consists in the elaboration of phylogenetic hypotheses through computational algorithms. As remarked above, such methods have been devised by computational evolutionary biology and have been increasingly applied to linguistic data over the last fifteen years, all relying on lexical and/or phonological evidence, for example the list of words in Dyen, Kruskal, and Black's (1992) Indo-European database.[38] Figure 12.1 represents a first attempt to generate a computational phylogeny using purely syntactic data, that is, our parametric distances of Table D, as an input: to generate the tree we relied on a distance-based program, Kitsch, contained in Felsenstein's PHYLIP package (Felsenstein 2004a, 2004b). The database was subjected to bootstrapping through 1,000 re-samplings.[39]

Kitsch—like all similar phylogenetic algorithms—imposes some conditions on the output not necessarily appropriate to our linguistic data: it produces only binary-branching trees and treats all taxonomic units as leaves (i.e. with no acknowledgment of possible mother–daughter relationships among the languages of the sample). Such properties may in principle represent sources of possible grouping problems; yet, the tree generated from our syntactic distances meets most of our expectations, again based on the genealogical hypotheses traditionally established.

Basque, one of the most commonly proposed isolates, is the first outlier; second comes Wolof (indeed, no long-distance hypothesis has ever attempted to closely connect the West Atlantic family to any of the European or Mediterranean languages); both are solidly recognized as external to a node coinciding

[37] The only two strong relations occurring relatively low in Table D (actually below the 145th position) both involve the oldest language of a subfamily and the modern variety of that subfamily known to have undergone the sharpest effects of interference (ClGr–Grico, Got–E).

[38] For an overview of some applications of computational cladistics to linguistic phylogenies, see Wang (1994) and McMahon and McMahon (2005).

[39] See Rigon (2009) for further experiments.

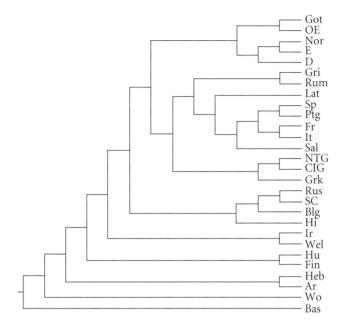

FIGURE 12.1 Bootstrapped tree from Table D (Kitsch, 1,000 resamplings, all languages)

with a *lato sensu* Nostratic grouping, a split suggested, though hardly proven, by long-distance comparativists.

Then the next outmost bifurcation singles out the (West) Semitic sub-group.[40] The Uralic (Finno-Ugric) family is correctly singled out as well, as opposed to the Indo-European unity. Within the latter cluster, the branching is overwhelmingly the expected one, at least at the taxonomic levels on which there is independent general agreement: the Celtic, Slavic, Germanic, and (homeland) Greek families are correctly detected, as well as some relative similarity of Slavic and Indic (the ə varieties). Within the Romance group, a Western Romance unity as opposed to Rumanian is captured, with Latin occurring intermediately, as well as the plausible unity of the two Iberian varieties.

The internal articulation of the Germanic group resulting from the computational elaboration is apparently questionable if compared to the traditionally accepted reconstruction, according to which a West Germanic unity—Old English, English, and German—would be expected as opposed to Gothic (East Germanic) and Norwegian (North Germanic). However, two plausible factors may affect the output: the position of English, paired with Norwegian, might

---

[40] The remnant cluster happens to coincide with Greenberg's (2000) proposed Eurasiatic family.

correctly reveal actual historical events, like the Scandinavian influence on English and the Norman conquest, whose traces are very obviously manifested also in the vocabulary of modern English, keeping it more removed from Old English and German; then, the two ancient varieties, chronologically closer to the common source, will naturally attract each other, and indirectly affect the position of German.

Such results show anyway that parametric comparison brings to light various types of definitely historical information, though it is hard, at this stage, to single out genetic from areal sources of similarities. Future empirical research in the PCM might identify parameters whose values are easy to borrow from genetically stable ones. Some hints are already available: for example, Bulgarian and Rumanian are likely to have come to share as an areal feature their + for parameter 12, which produces the peculiar noun–article constructions; but they continue to be well-behaved Slavic and Romance languages, respectively, with opposite values for parameter 45. It is also possible to argue that this persistence in 45 makes the two languages very different in other subtler surface properties, which go beyond the simplest noun–article phrases; incidentally, such differences would normally escape non-parametric, less formal analyses, somewhat overstating the impression of interference. Other diachronically stable parameters might be similarly identified.

Still, two clear errors are visible in the topology of the tree. The first affects the node merging Russian and Serbo-Croatian together and excluding Bulgarian, thus failing to recognize the plausible south Slavic unity; it is possible that our parameter sample accidentally underrepresents the difference between Serbo-Croatian and Russian. It remains to be seen if the result would still hold under an extension of parametric comparison to non-nominal domains and/or if this discrepancy can be partly imputed to areal influences, again, affecting Bulgarian as an effect of substrate or membership in the Balkan *Sprachbund*.

Factors of areal influence obviously explain the other mistake: the appearance of Grico within the Romance family (actually clustering with the Balkan Romance language), rather than in a node with homeland Greek. Needless to say, any pure tree-like representation is insufficient to formalize admixture of this sort.[41]

As noted in n. 37, at least two of the controversial points (involving the relations between Classical Greek and Grico, and Gothic and English) might be due to the combined effect of time-span and admixture with external

---

[41] This representational problem may perhaps be avoided through the use of network algorithms (as suggested among others by McMahon and McMahon 2005).

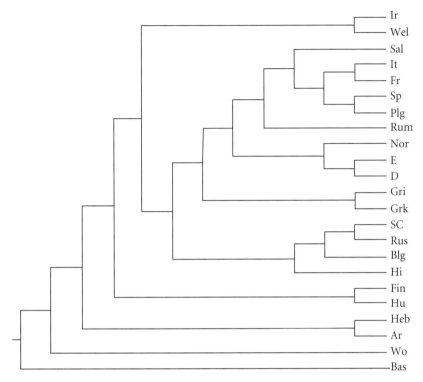

FIGURE 12.2 Bootstrapped tree from Table D (Kitsch, 1000 resamplings, modern languages)

varieties. Furthermore, it must be recalled that a program like Kitsch is devised to best classify coeval entities. Therefore, a further experiment was attempted: another tree was drawn using Kitsch, under the same conditions, though leaving out the non-contemporary languages of the sample (see Figure 12.2). Here the results are sharply improved, with Grico recognized as clustering with Greek, and English with German.

Given PCM's sensitivity to some salient contact effects, it is significant that, in spite of the strong similarities in DP syntax pointed out in the literature,[42] no particular support arises for the hypothesis of prehistoric Semitic substrate influence on Insular Celtic, explicitly raised by Vennemann (2002).[43] Even singling out from Table A data on absolute relatedness, the relations between the two Celtic and the two Semitic languages fall far short of the

---

[42] See e.g Rouveret (1994), Duffield (1996), and Roberts (2005: 94).
[43] See Roberts (2004) for the suggestive proposal of the using PCM to address this question.

threshold of individual-identifying probability (ranging from Irish–Hebrew 1/865, dist. 0.256, to Welsh–Arabic and Irish–Arabic 1/55, dist. 0.33).

Apart from a few problems, the computational elaboration of parametric data with Kitsch yields a phylogeny of the whole sample (out of the 53!! possible rooted bifurcating ones),[44] which is largely in agreement with the commonly accepted reconstructions of traditional historical linguistics. This result, notwithstanding the relatively small number of traits compared, supports the effectiveness of the PCM and its potential for quantitative historical linguistics. Notice that, perhaps surprisingly, the fact that it has been achieved simply on the basis of distances among attested languages without hypotheses about ancestral states, turns out to support, in a completely different context, one of Greenberg's methodological claims, namely, that reasonably successful phylogeny can apparently dispense with preliminary reconstruction of proto-languages and intermediate stages. After all, as pointed out by E. Stabler (p. c.), the situation is not different from what is often found in evolutionary biology.

12.8 Lexical and Syntactic Phylogenies

12.8.1 *Distances and trees*

In order to compare parametric and lexical phylogenetic results more precisely (of course with the provisos of Section 12.4.3.2 on the accuracy limits of lexical figures), we performed a further experiment. In the lexical database used by McMahon and McMahon (2005), there are 15 languages also represented in our syntactic database (i.e. the modern standard Indo-European languages); thus, it is possible—using the same taxonomic units (that is, completely overlapping samples of languages)—to minimally compare genealogical trees produced through the same algorithm from two different inputs, the lexical distances and the parametric ones.

In order to bridge the quantitative mismatch between the number of lexical characters (Swadesh's lists with 200 words with cognacy judgments ultimately derived from Dyen, Kruskal, and Black 1992) used by McMahon and McMahon and that of our syntactic characters (the 63 parameters of Table D), distances have all been calculated using the formula of the normalized Hamming distance ($d/(i + d)$); the matrices represented in Figure 4 in the appendix reveal that, even under such normalization, syntactic distances are considerably smaller than the lexical ones, most of which show clear "Babelic"

---

[44] See Felsenstein (2004a: 19–36), Cavalli-Sforza et al. (1994: 32). $n!!$ is the semifactorial of n, in this case the product of all odd integers up to 53.

values (that is higher than 0.5): this suggests that syntactic differentiation proceeds more slowly than lexical differentiation from the same common source.[45]

Analogous results are produced by Kitsch and shown in Figures 12.3 (tree from lexical distances) and 12.4 (tree from parametric distances). The topologies of the two trees largely overlap, with just minimal rearrangements

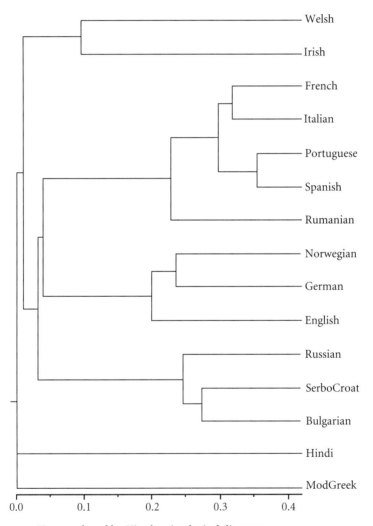

FIGURE 12.3 Tree produced by Kitsch using lexical distances

[45] Anyway, no pair of languages shows a syntactic distance bigger than their lexical distance.

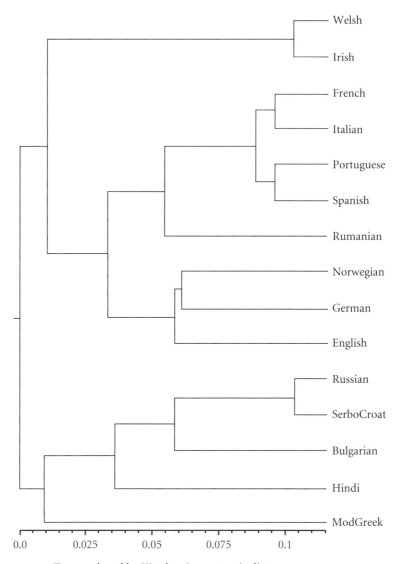

FIGURE 12.4 Tree produced by Kitsch using syntactic distances

basically revolving around the position and structure of the Slavic group. However, it is relevant to notice that in the outputs of Kitsch—as in those of most phylogenetic algorithms—branch length signals the amount of evolution that occurred between two nodes (cf. Felsenstein 2004a); thus, in the light of the information provided by the distances, we expect the branches of the lexical tree to be longer than those of the syntactic one. Although the editing of the two tree images has reduced them to the same size for reasons of space, the ruler placed below the two trees signals the actual original proportion of branch length from the root to the leaves. Figures 12.3 and 12.4, in which trees are not bootstrapped for better comparability, confirm our expectation. The distance from the root to the leaves suggested by Kitsch is almost four times bigger for the lexical tree. Thus, this further quantitative experiment substantiates the hypothesis that syntax is more conservative than the lexicon.[46]

12.8.2 *Syntax and distant relationships*

This conclusion is also supported by Figure 12.5, displaying a scatter plot of lexical distances versus syntactic distances for all possible pairs of languages

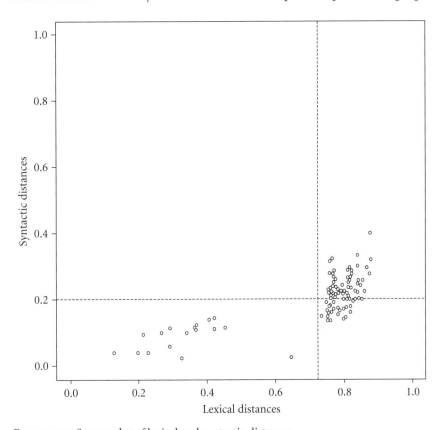

FIGURE 12.5 Scatter plot of lexical and syntactic distances

[46] This is precisely the expectation of diachronic theories in the spirit of Keenan's notion of inertia: cf. Keenan (1994, 2000, 2002) and Longobardi (2001a).

in Figure 4 in the appendix: each pair is represented by a circle whose co-ordinates are given by the two distances.

The vertical (horizontal) dashed line denotes the mean of lexical (syntactic) distances. Two clouds of points are clearly discernible in the scatter plot: one in the bottom-left part of the graphic, containing pairs with both distances smaller than the respective mean, the other in the right part of the graphic, containing pairs with lexical distance bigger than the mean.

The first group or cloud contains all and only the pairs where both languages belong to the same Indo-European subfamily, that is, strong relations (non-shaded in Figures 3a and 3b), while in the second group only pairs where the two languages do not belong to the same subgroup are found. In the first cloud, the increase of the two distances is essentially proportional. Only one clear outlier is visible, on the rightmost part of the bottom-left area, namely the pair formed by Irish and Welsh, which have a relatively small syntactic distance and a relatively big lexical one.[47]

The second cloud is more compact, that is, points are closer to each other. In particular, lexical distances show little variability, whereas crucially a greater degree of variability continues to be exhibited by syntactic distances.

The visual impression can be confirmed by measuring variability with the aid of standard deviation: 0.035 for lexical distances versus 0.051 for syntactic distances. Alternatively, variability can be measured with respect to the mean distance by means of the coefficient of variation (ratio of the standard deviation to the mean). This gives 0.044 for lexical distances, and 0.22 for syntactic distances, clearly emphasizing that syntactic distances are much more capable of discriminating among languages which are far from each other. On the other hand, the first cloud suggests an inverted configuration; indeed, the standard deviations are 0.12 for lexical distances and 0.041 for syntactic distances. However, the coefficients of variation are here 0.36 for the lexical distances and 0.47 for the syntactic distances, showing that relative variability is still greater with syntactic distances, also for languages which are close to one another.

The moral seems to be, then, again that syntactic divergence from a common ancestor is slower; but also and most noticeably that syntax continues to be a good indicator of relative taxonomy among sets of distant languages whose vocabularies display too few cognates to make solid clusters identifiable. In principle, long-distance relationships could thus be hinted at, even if not proved by individual-identifying evidence, by syntactic properties better than by lexical ones.

---

[47] I. Roberts (p.c.) suggests this may reflect the wealth of Latin loanwords in Welsh.

12.9 Humboldt's Problem: Answers

The evidence provided by PCM shows that the taxonomies obtained through syntax and vocabulary closely resemble each other: thus, the diachronic persistence of syntactic properties is sufficiently robust to allow for plausible genealogical reconstructions. Positive answers to Humboldt's problem then appear at hand: testing the phylogenetic hypotheses based on syntactic characters against those known from traditional comparison warrants answer (4b). Furthermore, in light of the preliminary results described in Section 12.8, there seems to be no reason to exclude the possibility that the eventually correct answer to Humboldt's problem will be (4c).

The impression of historical irrelevance of syntax is likely to be an artifact of the poor number and quality of grammatical variables traditionally considered, and fades away when a sufficiently large set of formally analyzed syntactic polymorphisms is taken into account.

Thus, the belief in the orthogonality of grammatical typology and historical taxonomy is recalled into question by a new level of evidence—parametric syntax—and the search for a systematic and mathematically accurate description of the facts.

The same two factors, as pointed out, have caused a major breakthrough in contemporary natural sciences: the choice of a more sophisticated domain of entities, though more remote from common sense and observation, such as genetic markers, has indeed provided biologists with a better object of evolutionary investigation, as well as with the opportunity of a more articulated mathematical representation of the data. It is suggestive to think of formal syntactic data as potentially playing the same role in historical linguistics.

12.10 Conclusions: Parametric Syntax as Cognitive Anthropology

PCM is a new method to classify languages on the basis of syntactic characters, whose results lend themselves particularly well to mathematical and computational evaluation. It exploits parametric theories to formally measure grammatical diversity and suggests that the taxonomies so derived are likely to have not only typological value, but also some historical (genealogical) significance (see also Nerbonne 2007: 4). Such first results of PCM may point to three sorts of consequences: for theoretical linguistics, historical linguistics, and neighboring disciplines, respectively. First, the historical success of PCM indirectly provides evidence of an unprecedented type for Principles-and-Parameters models of grammatical variation, on which the method is based.

Second, PCM suggests the possibility of a full historical paradigm in formal syntax beyond the simple description of scattered cases of diachronic syntactic change. Through parametric linguistics, successfully applied to relatedness issues, historical concerns may be re-established as central in the study of language and in the wider paradigm of modern cognitive science. A crucial breakthrough in nineteenth-century science was the development of a whole scientific paradigm instantiated by the classical comparative method and by historical linguistics in general. This success was warranted precisely by phylogenetic discoveries: as a matter of fact, hardly any serious theory of etymology and of phonological change would have been conceivable if the sound shape of the lexicon evolved in so chaotic a way as to display no salient cues on the genealogical relations of languages. Similarly, we think that no serious historical paradigm in syntax could be warranted if grammatical characters evolved in so chaotic a way as to provide no hints on language relatedness.

Finally, PCM promises to make a new tool for the investigation of our linguistic past, which we hope is able to overcome the limits of the classical comparative method and the issues raised by Greenberg's more questionable mass comparison: in this sense, it might eventually join traditional comparative linguistics, archeology, and genetics in the New Synthesis approach to the study of human history and prehistory.[48]

Acknowledgments

Some preliminary results of this research have been presented to audiences at the XIV Colloquium in Generative Grammar, 2004, Porto; TiLT, 2004, Budapest; DiGS 8, 2004, Yale; Workshop on the Structure of Parametric Variation, 2005, Newcastle; The Fifth Asian GLOW, 2005, Delhi; Digital Humanities Conference, 2006, Paris; Conference on Biolinguistics: Language Evolution and Variation, 2007, Venice; BCI Summer School, 2007, Trieste; Workshop on Formal models of linguistic diversity, 2007, Trieste; XXXII SIG Conference, 2007, Verona; Workshop on Bantu, Chinese, and Romance nouns and noun phrases, 2007, London; the XVIII International Congress of Linguists, 2008, Seoul. They were also made the object of individual presentations in Paris, Potsdam, Rome, Los Angeles, and Cambridge (Mass.). We are grateful to all audiences.

We want to thank, for discussion and comments at various stages of this project, Luca Bortolussi, Luca Cavalli-Sforza, Lucio Crisma, Francesco Guardiano, John Nerbonne, Andrea Novelletto, Andrea Sgarro, Marco René Spruit, Ed Stabler, and two anonymous referees. Special gratitude for

[48] See Cavalli-Sforza (2000) and Renfrew (1987).

invaluable help and advice is due to Paola Crisma, Gabriele Rigon, and Serena Danesi. Paola Crisma has also designed the basic structure of the website allowing a revealing and efficient encoding of the parametric data. Gabriele Rigon assisted us with most of the computational experiments.

Part of this research was accomplished while either author was visiting the Linguistics Department at UCLA, to which we are very grateful.

We are extremely indebted to our informants and consultants, who agreed to complete a Trigger List for us and/or to discuss the most intricate issues concerning the languages already included or others in the process of analysis: Birgit Alber, Manuela Ambar, Marcello Aprile, Rocco Aprile, Zlatko Anguelov, Judy Bernstein, Željko Bošković, Ana Castro, Ariel Cohen, Ricardo Etxepare, Franco Fanciullo, Abdelkader Fassi Fehri, Judit Gervain, Manuel Leonetti, Io Manolessou, Lanko Marušic, Matti Miestamo, Maria Polinsky, Sanja Roić, Alain Rouveret, Paweł Rutkowski, Roumyana Slabakova, Donca Steriade, Maryam Sy, Øystein Vangsnes, Akira Watanabe, Marit Westergaard, and David Willis. Of course, any errors are ours and we accept all responsibility for the parametric analysis of data.

Appendix

TABLE A	It	Sal	Sp	Fr	Ptg	Ru	Lat	ClG	NTG	Gri	Grk	Got	OE	E	D	Nor	Blg	SC	Rus	Ir	Wel	Heb	Ar	Wo	Hu	Fin	Hi	Ba
(1) ± gramm. person -1	+	+	+	+	+	+	+	+	+	+	+	+	+	+	+	+	+	+	+	+	+	+	+	+	+	+	+	+
(2) ± gramm. number -1	+	+	+	+	+	+	+	+	+	+	+	+	+	+	+	+	+	+	+	+	+	+	+	+	+	+	+	+
(3) ± gramm. gender +2	+	+	+	+	+	+	+	+	+	+	+	+	+	-	+	+	+	+	+	+	+	+	+	+	-	-	+	+
(4) ± variable person on D +1	+	+	+	+	+	-	-	+	+	+	+	?	?	?	+	+	+	-	-	?	?	+	+	-	+	+	+	+
(5) ± feature spread to N +2	+	+	+	+	+	+	+	+	+	+	+	+	+	-	+	+	+	+	+	+	?	+	+	0	-	-	+	-
(6) ± numb. on N (BNs) +5	+	+	+	+	+	+	+	+	+	+	+	+	+	+	+	+	+	+	+	+	+	+	+	0	+	+	+	0
(7) ± gramm. partial def	+	+	+	+	+	-	-	+	+	+	+	-	-	+	+	+	+	-	-	+	+	+	+	+	-	-	-	-
(8) ± gramm. def +7	+	+	+	+	+	0	0	+	+	+	+	0	+	+	+	+	+	0	0	+	+	+	+	+	0	0	0	0
(9) ± free null partitive Q +6	-	-	+	+	+	0	0	-	-	+	+	0	-	-	+	+	-	0	0	-	-	-	-	-	0	0	0	0
(10) ± gramm. dist. art. -5 or -6 or +7	-	-	-	-	-	0	0	-	-	-	-	0	-	-	-	-	+	0	0	-	-	-	-	-	0	0	0	0
(11) ± gramm. top. art. -10	-	-	-	-	-	0	0	-	-	-	-	0	-	-	-	-	0	0	0	-	-	-	-	-	0	0	0	0
(12) ± def checking N +7	+	+	-	-	-	0	0	-	-	-	-	0	-	-	-	-	+	0	0	-	+	-	-	-	0	0	0	0
(13) ± def spread to N +12	0	0	0	0	0	0	0	0	0	0	0	0	0	0	0	0	+	0	0	0	+	0	0	-	0	0	0	0
(14) ± def on attrib. +7, -12	-	-	+	+	+	0	0	+	+	+	+	0	+	-	+	+	0	0	0	-	0	+	+	+	0	0	0	0
(15) ± def on relatives +7	-	-	-	-	-	0	0	-	-	-	-	0	-	-	-	-	+	0	0	-	-	+	+	+	0	0	0	0
(16) ± D-controlled infl. on N +5	-	-	-	-	-	-	+	-	-	-	-	-	-	-	-	-	0	-	-	-	+	-	-	0	-	-	-	0
(17) ± gramm. cardinal nouns	+	+	+	+	+	+	+	+	+	+	+	+	+	+	+	+	+	+	+	+	+	+	+	+	+	+	+	+
(18) ± gramm. cardinal adjectives +17	0	0	0	0	0	0	+	0	0	0	+	0	+	+	+	+	+	+	+	?	+	+	+	?	+	+	+	-
(19) ± plural spread from cardinals +5, -17 or -18	+	+	+	+	+	+	+	+	+	+	+	+	+	+	+	+	+	+	+	+	+	+	+	0	+	+	+	0
(20) ± gramm. mass-to-count	+	+	+	+	+	+	+	+	+	+	+	+	+	+	+	+	+	+	+	+	+	+	+	+	+	+	+	+
(21) ± N-to-predicate incorporation	-	-	-	-	-	-	-	-	-	-	+	0	-	-	-	-	-	-	-	+	-	-	-	+	-	-	+	?
(22) ± gramm. partial count -5 or -6 or +7, -21	+	+	+	+	+	0	0	+	+	+	0	0	+	+	+	+	+	0	0	0	+	+	+	0	+	+	+	0
(23) ± gramm. count +22	+	+	+	+	+	0	0	+	+	+	0	0	+	+	+	+	+	0	0	0	+	+	+	0	+	+	+	0
(24) ± count checking N +21 or +22	+	+	+	+	+	0	0	+	+	+	+	0	+	+	+	+	+	0	0	+	+	+	+	+	+	+	+	0
(25) ± prepositional Gen	-	-	+	+	+	-	-	-	-	+	+	-	-	-	-	+	+	-	-	+	+	+	+	+	-	-	-	-
(26) ± free inflected Gen -25	0	0	0	0	0	+	+	+	+	-	-	+	+	+	+	-	-	+	+	-	-	-	-	-	+	+	+	+
(27) ± GenO +25 or +26	0	0	0	0	0	+	+	+	+	+	+	+	+	+	+	+	+	+	+	+	+	+	+	+	+	+	+	+
(28) ± GenS +25 or +26	0	0	0	0	0	+	+	+	+	-	-	+	+	+	+	+	-	+	+	-	-	-	-	-	+	+	+	+
(29) ± postpositional Gen +27 or +28	0	0	0	0	0	-	-	-	-	-	-	+	+	+	+	+	-	-	-	-	-	-	-	-	+	+	+	+
(30) ± Gen over DemP	-	-	-	-	-	-	-	-	-	-	-	0	0	-	-	-	-	-	-	-	-	-	-	-	-	-	-	?
(31) ± poss checking N	+	+	+	+	+	-	-	-	-	-	+	-	-	-	-	-	+	-	-	+	+	+	+	-	-	-	-	-
(32) ± structured APs	+	+	+	+	+	+	+	+	+	+	+	+	+	+	+	+	+	+	+	+	+	+	+	+	+	+	+	+
(33) ± feature spread to structured A Ps +32	+	+	+	+	+	+	+	+	+	+	+	+	+	-	+	+	+	+	+	-	-	+	+	0	-	-	+	-
(34) ± feature spread to pred. A Ps	+	+	+	+	+	+	+	+	+	+	+	+	+	-	+	+	+	+	+	-	-	+	+	-	-	-	+	-
(35) ± numb. on A +6, +33 or +34	+	+	+	+	+	+	+	+	+	+	+	+	+	-	+	+	+	+	+	-	-	+	+	0	-	-	+	0
(36) ± D-controlled infl. on A +33	-	-	-	-	-	+	+	-	-	+	+	+	+	-	+	+	-	+	+	-	-	-	-	0	-	-	-	0
(37) ± DemP over relatives	+	+	+	+	+	+	+	+	+	?	?	+	+	+	+	+	+	+	+	+	+	-	-	?	+	+	+	+
(38) ± free A Ps in Mod +32	+	+	+	+	+	-	-	+	+	+	+	-	-	-	-	-	+	-	-	+	+	+	+	+	-	-	?	-
(39) ± A Ps in Mod -38	0	0	0	0	0	+	+	0	0	0	0	+	+	+	+	+	0	+	+	0	0	0	0	0	+	+	?	+
(40) ± overt Mod° -32 or +38 or +39	+	+	+	+	+	-	-	+	+	+	+	-	-	-	-	-	+	-	-	+	+	+	+	+	-	-	?	-
(41) ± adjectival Gen	-	-	-	-	-	+	+	+	+	+	+	+	+	+	+	+	-	+	+	-	-	-	-	-	+	+	+	+
(42) ± N-raising with pied-piping	-	-	-	-	-	-	-	-	-	-	-	-	-	-	-	-	-	-	-	-	-	-	-	-	-	-	-	-
(43) ± N over ext.arg. -42	+	+	+	+	+	-	-	+	+	+	+	-	-	-	-	-	+	-	-	+	+	+	+	+	-	-	-	-
(44) ± N over GenO +26 or +27, -30, +43	0	0	0	0	0	-	-	+	+	+	+	-	-	-	-	-	+	-	-	+	+	+	+	0	-	-	-	0
(45) ± N over As +32, (-26 or -27, +43) or +44	+	+	+	+	+	-	-	+	+	+	+	-	-	-	-	-	+	-	-	+	+	+	+	0	-	-	?	0
(46) ± N over M2 As +45	0	0	0	0	0	-	-	+	+	+	+	-	-	-	-	-	+	-	-	+	+	+	+	0	-	-	?	0
(47) ± N over M1 As +46	0	0	0	0	0	-	-	+	+	?	+	-	-	-	-	-	+	-	-	+	+	+	+	0	-	-	?	0
(48) ± N over high As +47	0	0	0	0	0	-	-	+	+	+	+	-	-	-	-	-	-	-	-	+	+	-	-	0	-	-	+	0
(49) ± N over cardinals +42 or +48	-	-	-	-	-	-	-	+	+	-	-	-	-	-	-	-	-	-	-	-	-	-	-	0	-	-	+	0
(50) ± strong D (person) +1, +8 or +28	+	+	+	+	+	+	+	+	+	?	+	-	-	+	+	+	+	+	+	?	?	+	+	+	+	+	?	?
(51) ± NP over D	-	-	-	-	-	+	+	-	-	-	-	+	+	-	-	-	-	+	+	?	?	-	-	+	+	+	?	?
(52) ± strong deixis	+	+	+	+	+	+	+	+	+	+	+	+	+	+	+	+	+	+	+	+	+	+	+	+	+	+	+	+
(53) ± strong anaphoricity +52	+	+	+	+	+	+	+	+	+	+	+	+	+	+	+	+	+	+	+	+	+	+	+	+	+	+	-	+
(54) ± DP over Dem -51, +52	+	+	+	+	+	0	0	+	+	+	+	0	0	+	+	+	+	0	0	?	?	+	+	0	-	-	?	?
(55) ± D checking Dem -5 or -6 or +7, +52	+	+	-	-	-	0	0	-	-	-	-	0	0	-	-	-	+	0	0	-	0	-	?	0	-	-	0	0
(56) ± D-checking poss -5 or +8, +50 or -28	-	-	-	?	-	+	+	-	-	-	-	0	0	-	-	-	+	0	0	-	0	-	-	0	-	-	0	0
(57) ± feature spread on poss +35 or +34 or +33	0	+	+	+	+	+	+	-	-	-	+	0	0	-	-	-	+	0	0	?	0	+	+	0	-	?	+	0
(58) ± feature spread on postp. Gen +29, +57	0	0	0	0	0	0	0	0	0	0	0	+	+	-	-	-	0	0	0	0	0	0	0	0	+	?	+	0
(59) ± enclitic possessives	-	-	-	-	-	-	-	-	-	-	+	-	-	-	-	+	+	-	-	+	+	+	+	0	-	?	-	+
(60) ± Consisten. Princ. +51 or (44 or ... or 47, +A-Compl)	+	+	0	0	0	+	+	+	+	+	+	-	-	0	0	0	+	+	+	?	?	+	+	?	+	+	0	?
(61) ± null-N-licensing art -5 or -6 or -12, +50 or +51	0	-	0	0	0	0	0	0	0	0	-	0	0	0	0	0	0	0	0	0	0	0	0	0	0	0	0	0
(62) ± obl.def.inh. +7,-22, (-25,+26) or +27,-42 or +45 or -50	0	0	0	0	0	0	0	0	0	0	0	0	0	0	0	0	0	0	0	0	0	?	0	0	?	?	0	0
(63) ± gramm. geogr. art. -5 or +6 or +7, -22 or -23 or +45	+	+	+	+	+	0	0	+	+	+	+	0	0	+	+	+	+	0	0	0	+	+	+	0	+	+	+	0

	It	Sal	Sp	Fr	Ptg	Rum	Lat	CIG	NTG	Gri	Grk	Got	OE	E	D	Nor	Blg	SC	Rus	Ir	Wel	Heb	Ar	Wo	Hu	Fin	Hi	Bas
It		49; 3	48; 5	49; 2	50; 2	45; 5	28; 3	36; 8	38; 5	45; 5	40; 10	33; 8	38; 9	38; 6	40; 7	37; 7	38; 8	28; 8	29; 8	32; 8	28; 9	34; 10	31; 14	21; 12	32; 12	24; 11	26; 8	18; 17
Sal	0,0577		44; 8	45; 5	46; 5	42; 7	27; 4	34; 10	36; 11	44; 6	38; 11	31; 10	35; 11	35; 8	38; 8	35; 8	36; 9	27; 8	28; 8	32; 9	28; 10	32; 13	29; 17	22; 11	30; 13	23; 11	26; 8	18; 17
Sp	0,0943	0,1538		46; 5	50; 2	43; 7	29; 2	37; 7	38; 9	40; 10	40; 10	34; 7	37; 10	36; 8	38; 9	35; 9	38; 8	26; 10	27; 10	33; 7	29; 8	32; 12	32; 13	20; 13	31; 13	22; 13	24; 10	19; 16
Fr	0,0392	0,1000	0,0980		47; 3	41; 7	25; 4	32; 10	34; 11	41; 7	36; 12	30; 9	35; 10	36; 7	37; 8	34; 8	34; 10	25; 9	26; 9	30; 8	27; 9	30; 12	27; 16	22; 11	29; 13	22; 11	23; 9	17; 18
Ptg	0,0385	0,0980	0,0385	0,0600		43; 6	28; 3	35; 8	37; 9	42; 7	38; 11	33; 8	38; 9	38; 6	40; 7	37; 7	38; 7	28; 8	29; 8	32; 7	28; 8	33; 10	30; 14	21; 11	33; 11	24; 11	26; 8	19; 15
Rum	0,1000	0,1429	0,1400	0,1458	0,1224		28; 3	35; 7	38; 8	45; 6	39; 10	35; 6	39; 9	35; 9	40; 8	39; 8	39; 8	29; 9	30; 9	31; 10	27; 11	33; 10	29; 14	20; 13	35; 11	29; 9	29; 7	21; 15
Lat	0,0968	0,1290	0,0645	0,1379	0,0968	0,0968		31; 2	29; 4	25; 7	28; 5	29; 4	31; 6	21; 7	24; 7	24; 6	24; 4	26; 6	27; 6	20; 6	16; 7	20; 8	21; 8	12; 10	20; 10	23; 9	25; 5	13; 9
CIG	0,1818	0,2273	0,1591	0,2381	0,1860	0,1667	0,0606		43; 2	35; 10	40; 5	34; 5	31; 11	26; 12	29; 12	29; 10	35; 10	24; 9	25; 9	26; 9	22; 10	29; 12	31; 11	15; 16	26; 13	21; 12	23; 8	15; 15
NTG	0,1915	0,2340	0,1915	0,2444	0,1957	0,1739	0,1212	0,0444		41; 8	46; 3	40; 4	37; 10	27; 14	34; 11	30; 11	34; 8	31; 8	32; 8	31; 9	27; 10	31; 13	32; 13	21; 13	30; 13	24; 12	26; 8	16; 17
Gri	0,1000	0,1200	0,2000	0,1458	0,1860	0,1176	0,2188	0,2222	0,1633		45; 6	34; 9	40; 9	34; 10	41; 8	35; 10	35; 10	31; 7	32; 7	36; 6	31; 8	33; 12	28; 17	25; 10	35; 11	29; 9	28; 8	21; 15
Grk	0,2000	0,2245	0,2000	0,2500	0,1915	0,2041	0,1515	0,1111	0,0612	0,1176		39; 5	38; 12	30; 15	36; 13	32; 13	36; 9	31; 8	32; 8	31; 9	26; 11	32; 12	34; 11	21; 15	32; 13	25; 13	26; 10	19; 17
Got	0,1951	0,2439	0,1707	0,2308	0,1951	0,1463	0,1212	0,1282	0,0909	0,2093	0,1136		39; 5	28; 10	36; 6	31; 7	29; 8	30; 7	31; 7	28; 9	25; 9	28; 10	28; 11	19; 12	30; 11	25; 11	27; 7	15; 12
OE	0,1915	0,2391	0,2128	0,2222	0,1915	0,1875	0,2121	0,2619	0,2128	0,1837	0,2400	0,1136		37; 8	44; 5	37; 8	35; 9	34; 6	36; 5	33; 8	30; 9	32; 12	28; 16	26; 9	35; 10	30; 9	29; 6	21; 12
E	0,1364	0,1860	0,1818	0,1628	0,1364	0,2045	0,2500	0,3158	0,3415	0,2273	0,3333	0,2632	0,1778		40; 5	38; 5	31; 10	23; 11	24; 11	26; 9	26; 9	30; 10	24; 16	18; 14	32; 10	21; 13	23; 8	19; 13
D	0,1489	0,1739	0,1915	0,1778	0,1489	0,1667	0,2258	0,2927	0,2444	0,1633	0,2653	0,1429	0,1020	0,1111		41; 5	33; 11	29; 9	30; 9	33; 7	31; 6	30; 12	25; 17	23; 10	35; 10	27; 11	28; 7	18; 15
Nor	0,1591	0,1860	0,2045	0,1905	0,1591	0,1702	0,2000	0,2564	0,2683	0,2222	0,2889	0,1842	0,1778	0,1163	0,1087		32; 11	25; 10	26; 10	28; 8	25; 8	28; 12	25; 15	17; 13	32; 10	25; 11	27; 7	18; 14
Blg	0,1739	0,2000	0,1739	0,2273	0,1739	0,1702	0,1429	0,2051	0,1905	0,2222	0,2000	0,2162	0,2045	0,2439	0,2500	0,2558		31; 4	31; 4	27; 10	23; 10	33; 8	27; 13	17; 15	28; 13	21; 12	24; 7	16; 16
SC	0,2222	0,2286	0,2778	0,2647	0,2222	0,2368	0,1875	0,2727	0,1622	0,1842	0,2051	0,1892	0,1500	0,3235	0,2368	0,2857	0,1143		40; 1	25; 7	23; 7	26; 9	20; 14	19; 8	25; 12	29; 10	29; 5	15; 13
Rus	0,2162	0,2222	0,2703	0,2571	0,2162	0,2308	0,1818	0,2647	0,1579	0,1795	0,2000	0,1842	0,1220	0,3143	0,2308	0,2778	0,1143	0,0244		25; 7	22; 8	25; 10	22; 13	19; 8	25; 13	30; 10	30; 5	15; 13
Ir	0,2000	0,2195	0,1750	0,2105	0,1795	0,2439	0,2308	0,2571	0,2250	0,1429	0,2250	0,2432	0,1951	0,2571	0,1750	0,2222	0,2703	0,2188	0,2188		39; 1	29; 10	26; 12	20; 10	27; 9	23; 8	19; 9	11; 15
Wel	0,2432	0,2632	0,2162	0,2500	0,2222	0,2895	0,3043	0,3125	0,2703	0,2973	0,2727	0,2647	0,2308	0,2571	0,1622	0,2424	0,3030	0,2333	0,2667	0,0250		27; 10	24; 12	18; 11	24; 10	19; 10	15; 10	9; 16
Heb	0,2273	0,2889	0,2727	0,2857	0,2326	0,2326	0,2857	0,2927	0,2955	0,2727	0,2727	0,2632	0,2727	0,2500	0,2857	0,3000	0,1951	0,2571	0,2857	0,2564	0,2703		40; 7	16; 16	30; 10	25; 9	19; 11	17; 16
Ar	0,3111	0,3696	0,2889	0,3721	0,3182	0,3256	0,2759	0,2619	0,2889	0,3778	0,2444	0,2821	0,3636	0,4000	0,4048	0,3750	0,3250	0,4118	0,3714	0,3158	0,3333	0,1489		14; 19	26; 14	22; 12	16; 15	15; 19
Wo	0,3636	0,3333	0,3939	0,3333	0,3438	0,3939	0,4545	0,5161	0,3824	0,2857	0,4167	0,3871	0,2571	0,4375	0,3030	0,4333	0,4688	0,2963	0,2963	0,3333	0,3793	0,5000	0,5758		22; 10	17; 9	16; 8	15; 13
Hu	0,2727	0,3023	0,2955	0,3095	0,2500	0,2391	0,3333	0,3333	0,3023	0,2391	0,2889	0,2683	0,2222	0,2381	0,2222	0,2381	0,3171	0,3243	0,3421	0,2500	0,2941	0,2500	0,3500	0,3125		26; 14	16; 15	20; 12
Fin	0,3143	0,3235	0,3714	0,3333	0,3143	0,2368	0,2813	0,3636	0,3333	0,2368	0,3421	0,3056	0,2308	0,3824	0,2895	0,3056	0,3636	0,2564	0,2500	0,2581	0,3448	0,2647	0,3529	0,3462	0,1622		25; 9	19; 9
Hi	0,2353	0,2353	0,2941	0,2813	0,2353	0,1944	0,1667	0,2581	0,2353	0,2222	0,2778	0,2059	0,1714	0,2581	0,2000	0,2059	0,2258	0,1471	0,1429	0,3214	0,4000	0,3667	0,4839	0,3333	0,2571	0,2647		18; 8
Bas	0,4857	0,4857	0,4571	0,5143	0,4412	0,4167	0,4091	0,5000	0,5152	0,4167	0,4722	0,4444	0,3636	0,4063	0,4545	0,4375	0,5000	0,4643	0,4643	0,5769	0,6400	0,4848	0,5588	0,4643	0,3750	0,3214	0,3077	
	It	Sal	Sp	Fr	Ptg	Rum	Lat	CIG	NTG	Gri	Grk	Got	OE	E	D	Nor	Blg	SC	Rus	Ir	Wel	Heb	Ar	Wo	Hu	Fin	Hi	Bas

FIGURE 2 Table B

Pairs	Ch. Prob.	NHD
SC, Rus	1/53634713550	0,0244
Ir, Wel	1/27487790694	0,0250
It, Ptg	1/3396379809480	0,0385
Sp, Ptg	1/3396379809480	0,0385
It, Fr	1/1766117500930	0,0392
ClG, NTG	1/35539769787	0,0444
It, Sal	1/203782788569	0,0577
Fr, Ptg	1/57443872798	0,0600
Lat, ClG	1/16268816	0,0606
NTG, Grk	1/30555251488	0,0612
Sp, Lat	1/4618244	0,0645
NTG, Got	1/129591576	0,0909
It, Sp	1/3138741449	0,0943
It, Lat	1/477749	0,0968
Ptg, Lat	1/477749	0,0968
Rum, Lat	1/477749	0,0968
Sal, Ptg	1/958596125	0,0980
Sp, Fr	1/958596125	0,0980
It, Rum	1/531395678	0,1000
Sal, Fr	1/531395678	0,1000
It, Gri	1/531395678	0,1000
OE, D	1/295219821	0,1020
D, Nor	1/51335793	0,1087
ClG, Grk	1/28798128	0,1111
E, D	1/28798128	0,1111
Got, OE	1/16198947	0,1136
Grk, Got	1/16198947	0,1136
Blg, SC	1/656221	0,1143
Blg, Rus	1/656221	0,1143
E, Nor	1/9137868	0,1163
Gri, Grk	1/125034277	0,1176
Rum, Gri	1/125034277	0,1176
Sal, Gri	1/70852757	0,1200
Lat, NTG	1/209920	0,1212
Lat, Got	1/209920	0,1212
OE, Rus	1/2934386	0,1220
Ptg, Rum	1/40257248	0,1224
ClG, Got	1/954840	0,1282
Sal, Lat	1/68250	0,1290
It, E	1/2492146	0,1364
Ptg, E	1/2492146	0,1364
Fr, Lat	1/22604	0,1379
Sp, Rum	1/11127030	0,1400
Sal, Rum	1/6553506	0,1429
Ptg, Gri	1/6553506	0,1429
Got, D	1/838396	0,1429
Gri, Ir	1/838396	0,1429
Rus, Hi	1/105842	0,1429
Lat, Blg	1/13110	0,1429
Fr, Rum	1/3822878	0,1458
Fr, Gri	1/3822878	0,1458
Rum, Got	1/489064	0,1463
SC, Hi	1/61741	0,1471
It, D	1/2237782	0,1489
Ptg, D	1/2237782	0,1489
Heb, Ar	1/2237782	0,1489
OE, SC	1/286452	0,1500
Lat, Grk	1/36193	0,1515
Sal, Sp	1/5984547	0,1538
Ptg, Blg	1/775334	0,1556
NTG, Rus	1/99569	0,1579
It, Nor	1/459079	0,1591
Sp, ClG	1/459079	0,1591
Ptg, Nor	1/459079	0,1591
NTG, SC	1/59119	0,1622
D, Wel	1/59119	0,1622
Hu, Fin	1/59119	0,1622
Fr, E	1/272966	0,1628
NTG, Gri	1/1248287	0,1633
Gri, D	1/1248287	0,1633
Rum, D	1/745927	0,1667
Rum, ClG	1/163021	0,1667
Lat, Hi	1/7535	0,1667
Rum, Nor	1/447556	0,1702
Rum, Blg	1/447556	0,1702
Sp, Got	1/97813	0,1707
OE, Hi	1/21168	0,1714
It, Blg	1/269681	0,1739
Sal, D	1/269681	0,1739
Sp, Blg	1/269681	0,1739
Rum, NTG	1/269681	0,1739
Sp, Ir	1/58975	0,1750
D, Ir	1/58975	0,1750
OE, E	1/163228	0,1778
OE, Nor	1/163228	0,1778
Fr, D	1/163228	0,1778
Ptg, Ir	1/35743	0,1795
Gri, Rus	1/35743	0,1795
It, ClG	1/99260	0,1818
Sp, E	1/99260	0,1818
Lat, Rus	1/7756	0,1818
Gri, OE	1/274014	0,1837
Got, Nor	1/21781	0,1842
Gri, SC	1/21781	0,1842
Got, Rus	1/21781	0,1842
Sal, E	1/60659	0,1860
Sal, Nor	1/60659	0,1860
Ptg, ClG	1/60659	0,1860
Rum, OE	1/167834	0,1875
Lat, SC	1/4740	0,1875
Got, SC	1/13349	0,1892
Fr, Nor	1/37262	0,1905
NTG, Blg	1/37262	0,1905
It, NTG	1/103282	0,1915
It, OE	1/103282	0,1915
Sp, NTG	1/103282	0,1915
Sp, D	1/103282	0,1915
Ptg, OE	1/103282	0,1915
Rum, Hi	1/8232	0,1944
It, Got	1/23015	0,1951
Ptg, Got	1/23015	0,1951
OE, Ir	1/23015	0,1951
Blg, Heb	1/23015	0,1951
Ptg, NTG	1/63872	0,1957
It, Grk	1/109606	0,2000
Sp, Gri	1/109606	0,2000
Sp, Grk	1/109606	0,2000
Sal, Blg	1/39704	0,2000
Grk, Blg	1/39704	0,2000
It, Ir	1/14297	0,2000
Grk, Rus	1/14297	0,2000
D, Hi	1/5110	0,2000
Lat, Nor	1/1808	0,2000
Rum, Grk	1/68504	0,2041
Sp, Nor	1/24815	0,2045
Rum, E	1/24815	0,2045
OE, Blg	1/24815	0,2045
ClG, Blg	1/8936	0,2051
Gri, Wel	1/8936	0,2051
Grk, SC	1/8936	0,2051
Got, Hi	1/3194	0,2059
Nor, Hi	1/3194	0,2059
Gri, Got	1/15598	0,2093
Fr, Ir	1/5621	0,2105
Lat, OE	1/2011	0,2121
Sp, OE	1/27180	0,2128
NTG, OE	1/27180	0,2128
It, Rus	1/3560	0,2162
Sp, Wel	1/3560	0,2162
Ptg, Rus	1/3560	0,2162
Got, Blg	1/3560	0,2162
Lat, Gri	1/1276	0,2188
SC, Ir	1/1276	0,2188
Rus, Ir	1/1276	0,2188
Sal, Ir	1/6277	0,2195
ClG, Gri	1/11029	0,2222
Fr, OE	1/11029	0,2222
Gri, Nor	1/11029	0,2222
Gri, Blg	1/11029	0,2222
OE, Hu	1/11029	0,2222
D, Hu	1/11029	0,2222
It, SC	1/2271	0,2222
Sal, Rus	1/2271	0,2222
Ptg, SC	1/2271	0,2222
Ptg, Wel	1/2271	0,2222
Gri, Hi	1/2271	0,2222
Nor, Ir	1/2271	0,2222
Sal, Grk	1/19322	0,2245
Ptg, Grk	1/19322	0,2245
NTG, Ir	1/4021	0,2250
Grk, Ir	1/4021	0,2250
Lat, D	1/817	0,2258
Blg, Hi	1/817	0,2258
Sal, ClG	1/7090	0,2273
Fr, Blg	1/7090	0,2273
Gri, E	1/7090	0,2273
It, Heb	1/7090	0,2273
Sal, SC	1/1460	0,2286
Fr, Got	1/2594	0,2308
Rum, Rus	1/2594	0,2308
OE, Wel	1/2594	0,2308
D, Rus	1/2594	0,2308
OE, Fin	1/2594	0,2308
Lat, Ir	1/291	0,2308
Ptg, Heb	1/4588	0,2326
Rum, Heb	1/4588	0,2326
SC, Wel	1/527	0,2333
Sal, NTG	1/8080	0,2340
It, Hi	1/946	0,2353
Sal, Hi	1/946	0,2353
Ptg, Hi	1/946	0,2353
NTG, Hi	1/946	0,2353
Rum, SC	1/1686	0,2368
D, SC	1/1686	0,2368
Rum, Fin	1/1686	0,2368
Gri, Fin	1/1686	0,2368
Fr, ClG	1/2989	0,2381
E, Hu	1/2989	0,2381
Nor, Hu	1/2989	0,2381
Sal, OE	1/5275	0,2391
Rum, Hu	1/5275	0,2391

(continued)

FIGURE 3A Table D

ri, Hu	1/5275	0,2391	Got, Ho	1/696	0,2683	Fr, Hu	1/172	0,3095	Gri, Ar	1/32	0,3778
rk, OE	1/9274	0,2400	Sp, Rus	1/395	0,2703	It, Ar	1/211	0,3111	Wel, Wo	1/16	0,3793
or, Wel	1/619	0,2424	NTG, Wel	1/395	0,2703	ClG, Wel	1/67	0,3125	E, Fin	1/19	0,3824
t, Wel	1/1105	0,2432	Blg, Ir	1/395	0,2703	Wo, Hu	1/67	0,3125	NTG, Wo	1/19	0,3824
Got, Ir	1/1105	0,2432	Wel, Heb	1/395	0,2703	E, Rus	1/82	0,3143	Got, Wo	1/15	0,3871
al, Got	1/1961	0,2439	It, Hu	1/834	0,2727	It, Fin	1/82	0,3143	Sp, Wo	1/15	0,3939
um, Ir	1/1961	0,2439	Sp, Heb	1/834	0,2727	Ptg, Fin	1/82	0,3143	Rum, Wo	1/15	0,3939
E, Blg	1/1961	0,2439	Grk, Heb	1/834	0,2727	ClG, E	1/102	0,3158	E, Ar	1/17	0,4000
r, NTG	1/3466	0,2444	OE, Heb	1/834	0,2727	Ir, Ar	1/102	0,3158	Wel, Hi	1/10	0,4000
TG, D	1/3466	0,2444	ClG, SC	1/223	0,2727	Blg, Hu	1/125	0,3171	D, Ar	1/17	0,4048
rk, Ar	1/3466	0,2444	Lat, Ar	1/125	0,2759	Ptg, Ar	1/153	0,3182	E, Bas	1/12	0,4063
r, Grk	1/4040	0,2500	Sp, SC	1/270	0,2778	Ir, Hi	1/39	0,3214	Lat, Bas	1/8	0,4091
D, Blg	1/2294	0,2500	Grk, Hi	1/270	0,2778	Fin, Bas	1/39	0,3214	SC, Ar	1/12	0,4118
tg, Hu	1/2294	0,2500	Nor, Rus	1/270	0,2778	E, SC	1/60	0,3235	Rum, Bas	1/12	0,4167
, Heb	1/1297	0,2500	Fr, Hi	1/153	0,2813	Sal, Fin	1/60	0,3235	Gri, Bas	1/12	0,4167
us, Fin	1/1297	0,2500	Lat, Fin	1/153	0,2813	SC, Hu	1/74	0,3243	Grk, Wo	1/12	0,4167
eb, Hu	1/1297	0,2500	Got, Ar	1/328	0,2821	Blg, Ar	1/91	0,3250	Nor, Wo	1/9	0,4333
r, Wel	1/730	0,2500	Fr, Heb	1/398	0,2857	Rum, Ar	1/112	0,3256	E, Wo	1/9	0,4375
r, Hu	1/730	0,2500	D, Heb	1/398	0,2857	Grk, E	1/102	0,3333	Nor, Bas	1/9	0,4375
at, E	1/227	0,2500	Nor, SC	1/187	0,2857	ClG, Hu	1/68	0,3333	Ptg, Bas	1/9	0,4412
or, Blg	1/1529	0,2558	Rus, Heb	1/187	0,2857	NTG, Fin	1/55	0,3333	Got, Bas	1/8	0,4444
G, Nor	1/865	0,2564	Gri, Wo	1/187	0,2857	Wel, Ar	1/55	0,3333	D, Bas	1/8	0,4545
C, Fin	1/865	0,2564	Lat, Heb	1/6	0,2857	Sal, Wo	1/44	0,3333	Lat, Wo	1/6	0,4545
, Heb	1/865	0,2564	Grk, Nor	1/482	0,2889	Fr, Wo	1/44	0,3333	Sp, Bas	1/8	0,4571
r, Rus	1/487	0,2571	Sal, Heb	1/482	0,2889	Fr, Fin	1/44	0,3333	SC, Bas	1/7	0,4643
lG, Ir	1/487	0,2571	Sp, Ar	1/482	0,2889	Lat, Hu	1/36	0,3333	Rus, Bas	1/7	0,4643
E, Ir	1/487	0,2571	NTG, Ar	1/482	0,2889	Ir, Wo	1/36	0,3333	Wo, Bas	1/7	0,4643
, Wel	1/487	0,2571	Grk, Hu	1/482	0,2889	Wo, Hi	1/23	0,3333	Blg, Wo	1/8	0,4688
u, Hi	1/487	0,2571	Rum, Wel	1/228	0,2895	NTG, E	1/62	0,3415	Grk, Bas	1/8	0,4722
, Heb	1/487	0,2571	D, Fin	1/228	0,2895	Grk, Fin	1/51	0,3421	Ar, Hi	1/7	0,4839
E, Wo	1/487	0,2571	ClG, D	1/278	0,2927	Rus, Hu	1/51	0,3421	Heb, Bas	1/7	0,4848
lG, Hi	1/272	0,2581	ClG, Heb	1/278	0,2927	Ptg, Wo	1/33	0,3438	It, Bas	1/8	0,4857
E, Hi	1/272	0,2581	Sp, Hi	1/131	0,2941	Wel, Fin	1/27	0,3448	Sal, Bas	1/8	0,4857
r, Fin	1/272	0,2581	Wel, Hu	1/131	0,2941	Wo, Fin	1/21	0,3462	Blg, Bas	1/7	0,5000
G, OE	1/1027	0,2619	Sp, Hu	1/339	0,2955	Ar, Hu	1/47	0,3500	Heb, Wo	1/7	0,5000
lG, Ar	1/1027	0,2619	NTG, Heb	1/339	0,2955	Ar, Fin	1/31	0,3529	ClG, Bas	1/7	0,5000
ot, E	1/581	0,2632	SC, Wo	1/60	0,2963	OE, Ar	1/42	0,3636	Fr, Bas	1/8	0,5143
l, Wel	1/581	0,2632	Rus, Wo	1/60	0,2963	ClG, Fin	1/24	0,3636	NTG, Bas	1/7	0,5152
t, Heb	1/581	0,2632	Grk, Wel	1/161	0,2973	Blg, Fin	1/24	0,3636	ClG, Wo	1/7	0,5161
r, SC	1/328	0,2647	Nor, Heb	1/197	0,3000	It, Wo	1/24	0,3636	Ar, Bas	1/9	0,5588
G, Rus	1/328	0,2647	Sal, Hu	1/240	0,3023	OE, Bas	1/24	0,3636	Ar, Wo	1/10	0,5758
t, Wel	1/328	0,2647	NTG, Hu	1/240	0,3023	Heb, Hi	1/20	0,3667	Ir, Bas	1/9	0,5769
in, Hi	1/328	0,2647	Blg, Wel	1/93	0,3030	Sal, Ar	1/40	0,3696	Wel, Bas	1/16	0,6400
eb, Fin	1/328	0,2647	D, Wo	1/93	0,3030	Sp, Fin	1/23	0,3714			
rk, D	1/2144	0,2653	Lat, Wel	1/34	0,3043	Rus, Ar	1/23	0,3714			
us, Wel	1/183	0,2667	Got, Fin	1/114	0,3056	Fr, Ar	1/33	0,3721			
ri, Heb	1/1223	0,2667	Nor, Fin	1/114	0,3056	Nor, Ar	1/27	0,3750			
G, Nor	1/696	0,2683	Hi, Bas	1/43	0,3077	Hu, Bas	1/19	0,3750			

FIGURE 3B Table D continued

	It	Sp	Fr	Ptg	Rum	Grk	E	D	Nor	Blg	SC	Rus	Ir	Wel	Hin	
It	0,0000	0,2120	0,1970	0,2270	0,3400	0,8220	0,7530	0,7350	0,7540	0,7690	0,7550	0,7610	0,8000	0,7930	0,8180	It
Sp	0,0943	0,0000	0,2660	0,1260	0,4060	0,8330	0,7600	0,7470	0,7610	0,7820	0,7680	0,7690	0,8050	0,8130	0,8190	Sp
Fr	0,0392	0,0980	0,0000	0,2910	0,4210	0,8430	0,7640	0,7560	0,7700	0,7910	0,7720	0,7780	0,8120	0,8100	0,8240	Fr
Ptg	0,0385	0,0385	0,0600	0,0000	0,3710	0,8330	0,7600	0,7530	0,7610	0,7810	0,7660	0,7730	0,8170	0,8040	0,8130	Ptg
Rum	0,1000	0,1400	0,1458	0,1224	0,0000	0,8430	0,7730	0,7510	0,7860	0,7980	0,7780	0,7810	0,8370	0,8120	0,8270	Rum
Grk	0,2000	0,2000	0,2500	0,2245	0,2041	0,0000	0,8380	0,8120	0,8210	0,8110	0,8210	0,8320	0,8590	0,8670	0,8740	Grk
E	0,1364	0,1818	0,1628	0,1364	0,2045	0,3333	0,0000	0,4220	0,4520	0,7720	0,7660	0,7580	0,8170	0,8410	0,8540	E
D	0,1489	0,1915	0,1778	0,1489	0,1667	0,2653	0,1111	0,0000	0,3670	0,7690	0,7640	0,7550	0,8060	0,8200	0,8530	D
Nor	0,1591	0,2045	0,1905	0,1591	0,1702	0,2889	0,1163	0,1087	0,0000	0,7730	0,7720	0,7580	0,8360	0,8490	0,8520	Nor
Blg	0,1739	0,1739	0,2273	0,1556	0,1702	0,2000	0,2439	0,2500	0,2558	0,0000	0,2910	0,3650	0,8180	0,8380	0,8010	Blg
SC	0,2222	0,2778	0,2647	0,2222	0,2368	0,2051	0,3235	0,2368	0,2857	0,1143	0,0000	0,3250	0,7960	0,8210	0,8050	SC
Rus	0,2162	0,2703	0,2571	0,2162	0,2308	0,2000	0,3143	0,2308	0,2778	0,1143	0,0244	0,0000	0,7820	0,8180	0,8000	Rus
Ir	0,2000	0,1750	0,2105	0,1795	0,2439	0,2250	0,2571	0,1750	0,2222	0,2703	0,2188	0,2188	0,0000	0,6450	0,8780	Ir
Wel	0,2432	0,2162	0,2500	0,2222	0,2895	0,2973	0,2571	0,1622	0,2424	0,3030	0,2333	0,2667	0,0250	0,0000	0,8760	Wel
Hin	0,2353	0,2941	0,2813	0,2353	0,1944	0,2778	0,2581	0,2000	0,2059	0,2258	0,1471	0,1429	0,3214	0,4000	0,0000	Hin
	It	Sp	Fr	Ptg	Rum	Grk	E	D	Nor	Blg	SC	Rus	Ir	Wel	Hin	

Syntactic distances

Figure 4 Lexical and syntactic distances among fifteen IE languages

13

A Biolinguistic Approach to Variation

ANNA MARIA DI SCIULLO

According to Chomsky (2005), variation is the result of experience, given the genetic endowment and independent principles reducing complexity. Variation is not endogenous to the faculty of language (FL); it requires exposition to linguistic data, as for language acquisition. If variation is exogenous to FL, no additional machinery is needed to derive variation other than that which is part of FL. In the Principles-and-Parameters approach (P&P) (Chomsky 1979, 1981, and related works), parameters of variation are binary choices left open in the principles of Universal Grammar (UG). In the Minimalist Program (Chomsky 1995 and related works), these choices are left unspecified, variation following from the interaction of the derivational system with factors reducing complexity (Holmberg 2009, Boeckx, in this volume). Thus, while FL provides features (valued and unvalued) and asymmetric feature-valuing operations, the range of variation allowed by the underspecification of FL is constrained by external factors. Why would parameters take the form of valued/unvalued features? Why would feature-valuing operations derive language diversity? And why would variation constrained by principles external to FL? From a biolinguistic perspective language is part of human biology, there might be properties shared by language and biology that could bring further light to these questions.

  In this chapter, I focus on the linearization of affixes, clitics, and DPs, and I explore the hypothesis that asymmetry provides a link between variation in language and variation in biology.[1] First, I relate linguistic parameters to

This research was supported by the SSHRC to the Major Collaborative Research Initiative on Interface Asymmetries, grant 214-2003-1003, and by a grant from the FQRSC to the Dynamic Interface project. I would like to thank Robert Berwick, Noam Chomsky, and Lyle Jenkins for discussions on previous versions of this chapter.

[1] Broadly speaking, asymmetric relations are analogous to the "if→then" logical relation where A implies B, but B does not imply A. Domain-specific definitions are needed, however, to distinguish for

"biological parameters." Second, I relate the directionality of language change to the directionality of phylogenetic variation in body plans. Finally, I raise the question of why asymmetry would be central in language variation.

13.1 Parameters

13.1.1 *Linguistic parameters*

In P&P, UG specifies a set of principles common to all languages and a set of parameters of variation. The parameters are fixed binary choices related to the principles of UG.[2] For example, the Head-directionality parameter leaves the choice to fix the position of the head of a syntactic constituent to the initial or the final position, (1), (2).

(1)   *X-bar Theory* Xmax → Spec–Xbar
                  Xbar → X–Compl

(2)   *Head-directionality parameter*
      Head position is initial or final.

   The setting of parameter (2) covers the broad syntactic difference between head-initial languages such as English and Italian and head-final languages such as Japanese (Chomsky 1981; Radford 1997; Baker 2003a, b, among other works). Language acquisition, too, like language variation and change, is thought to be the result of parameter setting. Given UG, language grows in contact with experience, and the language children develop will be a function of the setting of the parameters of UG. Since human language is an object of the natural world, it will change through time, and there will be variation in the language children develop with respect to the language of their caretakers and the populations to which they are exposed. Moreover, a grammatical theory, in conjunction with an acquisition model, is expected to be able to distinguish more likely patterns of language change from less likely ones (Lightfoot 1991a, 1998, 1999; Clark and Roberts 1993; Pintzuk, Tsoulas, and Warner 2000; Roberts and Roussou 2003; among other works).

   The Principles-and-Parameters model provides a way to derive observable macro differences between languages. For example, parametric syntax

example asymmetry in syntax (asymmetric c-command (Kayne 1994; Moro 2000), proper inclusion relation (Di Sciullo 2005; Di Sciullo and Isac 2008a, b)) from asymmetry in biology (fluctuating asymmetry, directional asymmetry; Palmer 1994, 1996), and in set theory (symmetry, asymmetry, antisymmetry, reflexivity).

   [2] See also Rizzi (1982); Borer (1984); Berwick and Weinberg (1986); Niyogi and Berwick (1996, 2009); Baker (1996); Guardiano and Longobardi (2005, ?); Longobardi and Guardiano (in this volume); Manzini and Savoia (in this volume).

opened the possibility of deriving Greenberg's universals from more abstract principles, and more generally to derive cross-linguistic differences in word order from abstract properties of the grammar (see Kayne 1994, 2000, 2005a, b; Cinque 2005). P&P covers micro-variation as well. For example, in Guardiano (2003) the syntactic behavior of demonstratives in different languages and dialects follows from the settings of a small set of syntactic parameters. Demonstratives (Dem) are universally generated in a "low area" of the nominal domain DP (D Gen1 Adjs Dem Gen2 NP), and the cross-linguistic differences in the position of Dem are the consequence of the setting of the following parameters:

(3)   Parameter 1: *Strong deixis* (*Dem* moves to Spec of DP to check *deixis*)
       Parameter 2: *Strong locality* (*Dem* moves to Spec of DP to check *deixis* and *locality*)
       Parameter 3: *DP over Dem* (*Dem* moves to the Spec of DP, DP moves to its left periphery)
       Parameter 4: *D(person)-licensing Dem* (*Dem* and the article never co-occur in Spec of DP)

   Parametric syntax also has consequences for phylogeny. Guardiano and Longobardi (2005, **?**) and Longobardi and Guardiano (in this volume) argue that parametric syntax serves phylogenetic purposes better than lexical methods (Gray and Atkinson 2003; Pagel, Atkinson, and Meade 2007). By using abstract syntactic markers such as parameters in phylogeny, languages and dialects can be shown to be more closely related than what it might appear from the classifications based on lexical items. In the parametric-syntax approach to phylogenetic language classification, the syntactic data can be seen as being similar to genetic markers. Moreover, the parametric comparison method displays the advantages of population genetics by comparing values (alleles) of parameters (syntactic polymorphisms) in different grammars, assuming that the parameters are drawn from a finite universal list of discrete biological options.

   A step forward brought about by the Minimalist Program is the reduction of GB principles to more basic properties of the computational system. For example, (1) is derived by Merge, and thus it is dispensed with. Furthermore, the FL does not specify the values of the parameters. Thus, (2) is also dispensed with. Merge derives binary branching structures; the position of the head of a constituent with respect to its complement is left unspecified, and follows from principles reducing derivational complexity. FL says nothing about the order of a head and its complement. Since the properties of perception and articulation make it impossible to pronounce and perceive a head and its complement at the same time, they must be linearly ordered. There are exactly two options: precede and follow.

In the feature-driven approach to parametric variation (Chomsky 2000a), micro-variations, such as the ones described in (3), rely on the values of the features available in the grammars; feature valuation derives language diversity. Viewed as binary choices (a choice between a valued or an unvalued formal feature for a category), parameters do not add to the complexity of the language design. They use what FL makes available, namely features, valued and unvalued, and feature-valuing operations. Thus, in this framework, setting a parameter's value has consequences for the triggering or the non-triggering of an operation of FL. Why should language diversity be implemented in these terms?

Let me start by underlying that feature-valuing is brought about by asymmetric Merge.[3] According to Di Sciullo and Isac (2008a), Merge is asymmetric in the sense that it applies to a pair of elements in the Numeration whose sets of features are in a proper inclusion relation.[4] This asymmetry holds for External Merge and for Internal Merge (move), as specified in (4). The example in (5) provides the feature specifications for lexical and functional categories; the partial derivation tree in (6b) is derived by Merge on the basis of the Numeration in (6a).

(4)   a. *Asymmetry of External Merge*
       External Merge is an operation that applies to a pair of elements in the Numeration whose categorial features are in a proper inclusion relation.

       b. *Asymmetry of Internal Merge*
       Internal Merge is an operation that applies to a pair of elements in the workspace whose (total set of) features are in a proper inclusion relation.   (Di Sciullo and Isac 2008a: 270 (17))

(5)   a. Nouns: [N]; Indefinite D: [Num], [uN]; Definite D: [D] [uNum]; wh-D: [D]
       [uNum] [wh]; Unergative V: [V]; Transitive V: [V] [uD]; Unaccusative V: [V],

---

[3] See Chomsky (1995), Zwart (2006), and Di Sciullo and Isac (2008a) on the asymmetry of Merge. In Chomsky (2005), Merge is defined as follows: Target two syntactic objects α and β, form a new object $\Gamma\{\alpha, \beta\}$, the label LB of $\Gamma(LB(\Gamma)) = LB(\alpha)$ or $LB(\beta)$.

[4] The proper-inclusion requirement derives the order of application of Merge. It also provides an account for the differences between possible and impossible sub-extractions. See Di Sciullo and Isac (2008b).

[uD]; *v*: [*v*] [uV] [uD], [uTense]; Unaccusative *v*: [*v*], [uV] [uTense];

b. Tense: [Tense], [u*v*], [uD] [EPP] [uClauseType:]; C₁: [D], Clause-Type],
[uTense]; C: [D], [ClauseType], [uTense], [*wh*]

(6)   a. {C, T, {D, Num, N, *v*, V, D, Num, N}}

b.

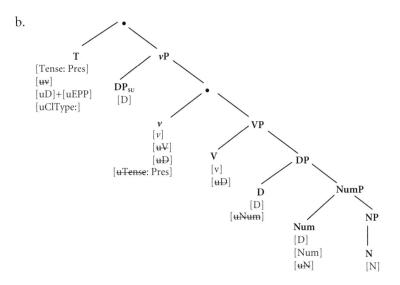

Why should variation be brought about by feature-valuing? Beyond the fact that feature-valuing is part of Merge. Considering this question from a biolinguistic perspective, it might be the case that the asymmetry of Merge and the subsequent feature-checking operation triggered by the need to eliminate unvalued features, namely, the Principle of Full Interpretation of Chomsky (1995), would find its roots in biology.

13.1.2 *Biological parameters*

As there have been advances in our understanding of language variation since P&P, there have also been advances in evolutionary developmental biology that made it possible to further understand variation in biology. Brought together, these findings are interesting for the biolinguistic enterprise, which asks why-questions (why these principles, not others), and pursues the biolinguistic issues that arise only when these questions are posed and at least partially answered.[5]

The biolinguistic approach to language variation opens a new domain of inquiry where why-questions can be addressed by taking into consideration the properties of biological variation. Approaching language variation from the biolinguistic perspective may lead to an understanding of this phenomenon that goes beyond explanatory adequacy. Interestingly, works in evolutionary developmental biology, including Gehring and Ikeo (1999), Montell (2008), Gehring (2005), and Palmer (1994, 1996, 2004a, 2004b, 2009), point to the central role of asymmetry in biological variation and change.

That asymmetry is part of biological variation is not surprising, since more than a decade's detailed research has led to general consensus that asymmetry is responsible for how cells move and divide. For example, Montell (2008) notes that asymmetry explains morphogenetic dynamics. She writes: "It is probably generally the case that signalling pathways…function to localize mechanical forces asymmetrically within cells. By definition, an asymmetry in force will cause dynamics." (Montell, 2008: 1505).

From a biolinguistic perspective, one important question is whether parameters have biological correlates. If they do, the understanding of the "biological parameters" may have consequences for the understanding of the linguistic parameters. Interestingly, the dynamics of certain gene products responsible for biological diversity may lead to a deeper understanding of language diversity. Namely, we know from evolutionary developmental biology that core aspects of biological variation could be attributed to the properties of master genes such as in the Homeobox (HOX) system. HOX genes can be selectively switched on and off in evolution, giving rise to differences and similarities among and within species (humans and mice), see also Berwick and Chomsky (in this volume), Berwick (in this volume), and Fitch (in this volume). For example, Gehring discovered much of the HOX system related to the Pac-6 eye formation genes, giving rise to the variation of mammalian and non-mammalian eye types (Gehring and Ikeo 1999; Gehring 2005)—see Figure 13.1. Dyer et al. (2003, 2009) showed that a single change in the mammalian retinal cell distinguishes primates with diurnal vision from mammalians with nocturnal vision.

According to Gehring and Ikeo (1999), in the evolution of the eye's morphogenetic pathway, the regulatory HOX genes act at the top of a deductive

[5] See Lenneberg (1967); Jenkins (2000, 2004); Hauser, Chomsky, and Fitch (2002); Boeckx and Piattelli-Palmarini (2005); Di Sciullo (2007); Di Sciullo et al. (2010); Piattelli-Palmarini and Uriagereka (2004, 2008); among other works on biolinguistics.

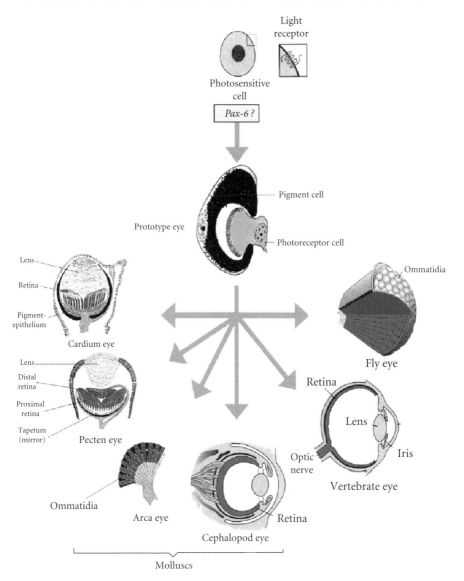

FIGURE 13.1 Hypothetical evolution of photosensitive cells containing Rhodopsin as a light receptor and monophyletic evolution of the various eye types. The eye prototype consisting of a photoreceptor cell and a pigment cell is assembled under the control of Pax-6 (after Gehring and Ikeo 1999)

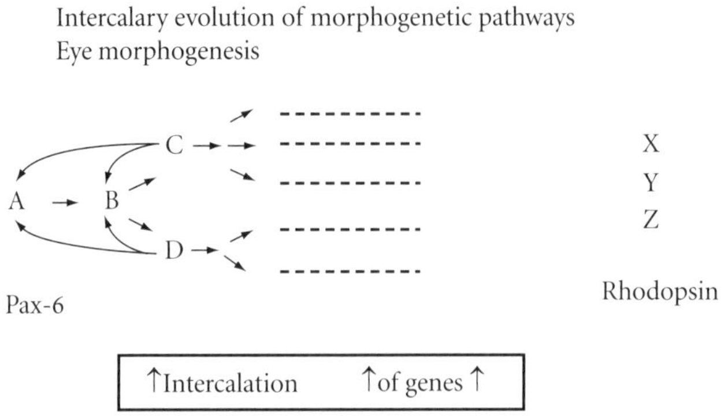

Intercalary evolution of morphogenetic pathways
Eye morphogenesis

FIGURE 13.2 Models for the evolution of biosynthetic and morphogenetic pathways. Intercalary evolution of the eye's morphogenetic pathway (after Gehring and Ikeo 1999)

cascade, leading to a set of dependent changes (if X, then Y) rather than being the product of independent parameters. See Figure 13.2, in which the dynamics of change for eye morphogenesis is asymmetric in the sense that it is based on implicational relations.

If the notion of linguistic parameter has a biological correlate, this networked arrangement of if–then "triggers" suggests that language variation may follow a similar asymmetric logic. The dynamics of HOX genes could very well be part of the biological basis of parameters. This hypothesis opens the possibility to link, via asymmetry, variation in language to variation in biology.

13.1.3 *Variation in language and biology*

It is possible to view the asymmetric if–then logic of biological parameters as part of the feature-driven approach to language variation as well, where the choice of an unvalued functional feature triggers an operation valuing it. The dynamics of the feature-driven approach to language variation would then present germane properties with the dynamics of biological parameters. In this perspective, the asymmetric if–then logic of biological parameters could contribute to our understanding of why linguistic diversity is feature-driven.

The feature-driven approach to language variation covers fine-grained variation in the distribution of syntactic constituents, for example the variation in the position of demonstratives in DPs, where the displacement of a demonstrative is triggered by the unvalued functional feature, [uDem], of the higher functional category. The feature-driven approach to language variation also covers the variation observed in morphological structures, differentiating for example so-called strong suffixing languages, such as Turkish, from strong prefixing languages, such as Yekhee. The examples in (7) and (8) illustrate the variation.[6] Needless to say, broad classifications based on distributional properties are problematic from a biolinguistic perspective, since they offer no principles from which the facts would be derived, and thus no basis to address questions that could lead to a further understanding of why certain principles and not others are at play in variation.

(7) a. Yekhee   c. Turkish
        émà-wò   yavaşç-a
        able drink   slow-ly
        'drinkable'   'slowly'

      b. à- gùè   d. uyku-da
        at sleep   sleep at
        'asleep'   'a sleep'

(8) a. Yekhee   c. Turkish
        akpa, ikpa   kitap, kitap-lar
        'cup', 'cups'   'book', 'books'

      b. ukpo, ikpo   d. öküz, öküz-ler
        'cloth', 'cloths' 'ox', 'oxen'

Furthermore, besides the fact that such classifications of languages do not provide any explanation for the cross-linguistic variation in the linearization of affixes, they are also descriptively inadequate. For example, they fail to cover the cases where certain affixes follow the root in strong prefixing languages such as Yekhee, as in (9a,b) with aspectual affixes linearized to the right of the root, and cases where certain affixes precede the root in strong suffixing languages such as Turkish, as in (9c–f), where the *wh-* and *th-*affixes precede the root.[7]

(9) a. Yekhee   c. Turkish
        dè nà pùe   ne-rede
        fall repeatedly complete   'where'
        'finished falling'   d. ne-vakit

---

[6] Yekhee is a North Central Edoid SVO language from the Niger-Congo family (Bendor-Samuel and Hartell 1989; Elugbe 1989). Turkish is an SOV language of the Turkic family (Sebüktekin 1971; Kornfilt 2004). In this language, vowel harmony is root rightwards (Baković 2000).

[7] See also Di Sciullo and Fong (2005) on the bipartite structure of *wh-* and *th-*words in English and Romance languages, as well as Di Sciullo and Banksira (2009) on the bipartite structure of *wh-*words in Ethiopian Semitic languages.

b. gbà nò nè   'when'
tie repeatedly up   e. bu-rada
'finished tying'   'here'
                         f. şu-rada
                            'there'

Moreover, these facts would not follow straightforwardly if the Head-directionality parameter, in (2) above, would be extended under the word-level. While Yekhee is an SVO language, like English, the position of the categorial head in English word structure is generally final, while it is generally initial in Yekhee. The setting of the Head-directionality parameter would then have to be domain dependent, which would weaken the principled account for the variation.

In contrast, the feature-driven approach to variation targets abstract properties of linguistic elements, namely the valued/unvalued features of functional categories. In this approach, language diversity follows from feature-valuing, and is restricted by external factors reducing complexity. Assuming that the structure of words is binary-branching and is derived by a general operation such as Merge, which recursively combines affixes and roots, this leaves only two possibilities: an affix either precedes or follows a root. Given the reductionist methodology of the Minimalist Program, there is no need for a head directionality parameter under the word level either.

13.1.4 *Factors reducing derivational complexity*

Di Sciullo (2004, 2005) proposes that cross-linguistic variation in the linearization of affixes with respect to roots is feature driven and proceeds by phases in the morpho-phonological component (PF). The difference between Yekhee and Turkish is reduced to the presence or absence of an unvalued feature at the edge (Specifier) of a morphological phase. This is motivated in Yekhee, where each affix is associated with a tone. A valued tone feature is located at the edge of a morphological phase, and the affix heading the phase is not ordered to the right of the root, as in (10). In Turkish, there is an unvalued feature at the edge of a morphological phase, as in (11), and feature valuing leads to the ordering of the affix to the right of the root.[8]

(10)   [[F] [af [root]]]

(11)   [[uF] [af [root]]]

---

[8] Different implementations are available for affix–root linearization. One option is to derive the PF orderings by applying Internal Merge in the derivation to PF. Another option is to flip the constituents. See Di Sciullo (1999, 2005) for discussion, as well as Williams (2003) and Wurmbrand (2003) on the post-syntactic Flip operation.

Thus, according to this approach, the variation in the linearization of affixes takes place in the PF component, and it relies on the properties of the computational system, feature-valuing and derivation-by-phase. The phase is part of the factors reducing derivational complexity (Uriagereka 1999; Chomsky 2001, 2005, 2008; Legate 2003; Boeckx and Grohmann 2007; Gallego 2006; Grohmann 2009). It does so by reducing the search space for the application of the operations of FL.

Complexity-reducing mechanisms related to the presence or absence of PF features at the edge of morphological phases are needed independently for linearization. The computational results reported in Di Sciullo and Fong (2005) using the LR Shift-reduce parsing framework indicate that derivational complexity increases in parsing complex words, such as *formalize*, (13), where multiple PF-empty edge (Specifier) positions are located to the left of the head, instead of to the right.

(13)   a.

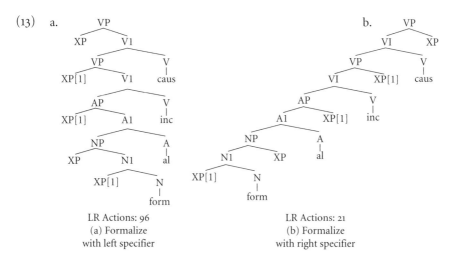

LR Actions: 96
(a) Formalize
with left specifier

LR Actions: 21
(b) Formalize
with right specifier

The table in (14) shows that there is a considerable difference both in terms of the number of LR actions performed and the stack depth required to process an example like *formalize*, analyzed as *form-al-i(z)-e*. The simple explanation is that the LR machine has to be able to predict an arbitrary number of empty argument positions before it can shift or "read" the first item, namely *form*, in (13a). Contrast this with the situation in (13b), where Specifiers are generated on the right side only. Here, the LR machine needs only to generate a single empty argument position before a shift can take place. Hence only 21 actions and a stack depth of two are required in this case, compared to 96 and a stack depth of five.

(14)

		LR actions	
Word	Items	Left Specifier	Right Specifier
form	1	8	6
read-able	2	19	11
simple(e)-i(f)-y	3	47	16
form-al-i(z)-e	4	96	21
form-al-i(z)-(e) able	5	172	26

These results suggest that factors reducing complexity do play a role in the derivation of morphological expressions. General principles of computational efficiency, external to the language faculty, would apply in the linearization of affixes and roots. This comes as no surprise, since general laws, falling into the class of Chomsky's (2005) "third factor," play a role in language design.

13.1.5 *Summary*

According to the feature-driven approach to language variation, language diversity is the consequence of the choice of a valued or unvalued functional feature, asymmetric feature-valuing, and factors reducing derivational complexity. In this perspective, the setting of a parameter requires exposure to linguistic data, but the derivation of linguistic diversity relies on the properties made available by the faculty of language and independent principles reducing derivational complexity.

Thus, from a biolinguistic perspective, our understanding of the dynamics of HOX genes, and in particular the asymmetric logic of the biological triggers, may lead to a better understanding of linguistic parameters and the role of asymmetric Merge and feature-valuing in the derivation of linguistic diversity. Linguistic variation can be linked to what we know of variation in biology, and it is likely that a further understanding of the role of asymmetry in the dynamics of HOX genes will deepen our understanding of language variation.

In the next section we relate the directionality of language evolution to the phylogenetic variation in the evolution of animal body plans. The discussion of the role of asymmetry in language evolution and change brings additional support to the hypothesis that asymmetry may very well be a link between variation in language and variation in biology.

13.2 Directionality of Language Change and Phylogenetic Patterns of Variance

There is extensive evidence that linguistic change is directional (Lightfoot 1991b; 1998, 1999; Kiparsky 1996; Andersen 2001; Haspelmath 1999; Roberts and Roussou 1999, 2003, among other works). For example, the trajectory of lexicalization is directional and not bi-directional. Condovardi and Kiparski (2001) show that this is the case in the evolution of clitic placement in Greek, as they provide evidence that the syntactic combinations tend to become grammaticalized as lexical, but not the reverse. The schema in (15) traces the directionality of the change from Medieval Greek, to Kozami, to Standard Modern Greek (SMG) and Western Greek (W.Gr).

(15)   Homeric Greek

      ↓   rise to TnsP

    Classical ⟶ Pontic

    "Proto-Pontic"

      ↓   rise to ΣP

    Medieval/Type A ⟶ Kozami type ⟶ SMG, W.Gk

          Xmax ⟶ Xo   Xo ⟶ Affix

                           (Condovardi and Kiparski 2001: 63)

From a biolinguistic perspective, while change, like variation more generally, is brought about by the environment, questions arise whether the directionality of language change has a biological correlate, and whether factors reducing complexity also play a role in diachronic change.

Interestingly, recent works in evolutionary developmental biology show that directionality is observed in the evolution of the form of body plans. Palmer (1996, 2004a) identifies phylogenetic patterns of variance in the evolution of bilateral asymmetric species. He analyzes biological evolution and variation in terms of "directional asymmetry" and "fluctuating asymmetry," and he shows by extensive description of the evolution of different species that the evolution and variation within species follows the ordered stages in (16), where > stands for the precedence relation.[9]

(16) Symmetry > anti-symmetry > asymmetry

---

[9] In evolutionary developmental biology, with random/fluctuating asymmetry or anti-symmetry, right- and left-handed forms are equally frequent in a species. With fixed asymmetry or directional asymmetry, only right- or only left-handed forms are observed.

In the symmetric stage, there is no left or right difference in the organism (e.g. amoeba). The following—anti-symmetric—stage presents random prominence of the right or the left side of the organism (e.g. fiddler crab). In the last—asymmetric—stage prominence is observed only to the right or only to the left of the organism. The three stages in the evolution and change going from symmetry to asymmetry, through an intermediate anti-symmetric stage, are illustrated in Figure 13.3 with male phallostethid fishes. This evolutionary sequence covers the phylogenetic variational patterns observed in the dextral/sinistral forms of certain animals and plants, whose development moves from a symmetric amoeboid stage to an asymmetric one, via an intermediate antisymmetric stage, where either the organism's left or right side predominates. Because of its simplicity, the binary-switch nature of the left–right asymmetry permits meaningful comparisons among many different organisms.

Phylogenetic analyses of asymmetry variation (fluctuating asymmetry, directional asymmetry), inheritance, and molecular mechanisms reveal unexpected insights into how development evolves. These analyses have novel extensions to human language. It is possible to view certain aspects of language variation in light of the natural evolution of bipartite organisms, given that

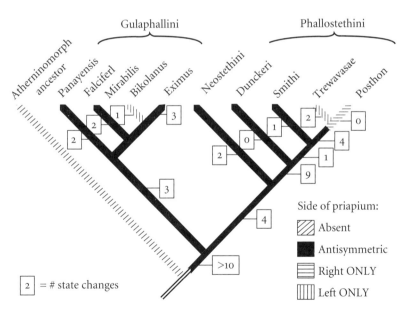

FIGURE 13.3 Phylogenetic variation in the side of the asymmetrical priapium in male phallostethid fishes (after Palmer 1996), illustrating the evolutionary changes in asymmetry stage expected for a post-larval developing trait

language expressions form hierarchical binary branching trees, with right–left asymmetries at each sub-tree.

(17)   a.   Y   b.   Y

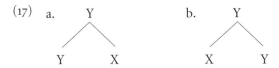

             Y   X   X   Y

If this is correct, language evolution can be approached in an innovative way by identifying phylogenetic patterns of variance in the linearization of constituents. Assuming an emergent view of language (Berwick and Chomsky in this volume; Berwick in this volume) and the hypothesis that asymmetry emerged with language (Di Sciullo 2005), there would be no symmetric stage, like the amoeba stage, in language evolution. Anti-symmetric stages can be observed across languages as well as within languages, and language evolution and change with respect to the linearization of constituents could be reduced to the two following stages:

(18)   Anti-symmetry > asymmetry

Language evolution includes stages where two options for the linearization of constituents are available, followed by stages where only one option is available. The evolutionary dynamics leading to directional asymmetry in phylogenetic patterns of variance may bring further understanding of language evolution and change. In this perspective, I hypothesize that anti-symmetry breaking (fluctuating > directional asymmetry/anti-symmetry > asymmetry) is part of the dynamics of language change. I will point to specific aspects of language acquisition and language change that support this hypothesis.

13.2.1 *Acquisition*

Assuming that the elements of linguistic variation are those that determine the growth of language in the individual (Chomsky 2005, 2007a), anti-symmetry breaking is part of language acquisition, as can be observed, for example, in the acquisition of compounds.

New compounds can be coined in any language. Children produce new compound forms quite early, around age 2 or 3 (see Clark and Barron 1988; Nicoladis 2007, among other works), sometimes with meanings that they are unlikely to have heard before, and always without any formal instruction. Interestingly, around 3, English children consistently produce compounds of the type V-N instead of N-V, then they go through an intermediate stage where both V-N (e.g. *pull-er-wagon*) and N-V (e.g. *wagon-pull-er*) are possible, before they reach a stage where only one of the two options survives (*wagon-pull-er*). This change can be understood as being the consequence of anti-symmetry breaking, since an anti-symmetric stage, where the noun in some case follows and in other cases precedes the verb, precedes an asymmetric stage, where the noun precedes the verb:

(19)   V N or N V > N V

While the order of the constituents in compounds is derived by morphological merger and feature-valuing (Di Sciullo 2005, 2009; Roeper 1996), data from language development provide evidence that anti-symmetry breaking is part of the dynamics of language acquisition. Thus, an explanation for these facts can be provided within the biolinguistic program, which asks why-questions and seeks possible answers in the properties of the evolution and the development of biological organisms, which are, like human language, objects of the natural world.

13.2.2 *Change in the linearization of the genitive DPs*

According to the anti-symmetry breaking hypothesis, language evolution includes stages where a given constituent may be linearized to the right or to the left of a head (anti-symmetric stage), whereas in a latter stage of that language only one option is available (asymmetric stage). The historical change in the linearization of syntactic constituents brings support to this hypothesis. This can be illustrated by the change in the position of DPs within the nominal domain in the history of Greek (Stávrou and Terzi 2005; Horrock 1997; Tsimpli 1995). If an anti-symmetric stage precedes an asymmetric one, we expect to find DPs to be linearized to the left or to the right of a nominal head in earlier stages of Greek, whereas only one option would survive in later stages. This is indeed the case for genitive DPs (Gentheme) in Modern Greek (Lascaratou 1998; Alexiadou 1999). Alexiadou (2002) discusses the change in the word-order patterns of Greek nominalizations that took place from the Classical Greek (CG) period to the Modern Greek (MG) period. In MG nominals, agents can only be introduced in the form of a prepositional phrase following the head noun, while they could appear pre-nominally bearing the genitive case in CG. Crucially for our purpose, the theme genitive—that is the object genitive—could precede or follow the head nominal in CG, (20), whereas it immediately follows the head in MG, (21), as described in Alexiadou (2002: 91).

(20)   a. Det-(Gen$_{agent}$)-N$_{process}$-Gen$_{theme}$ (CG)

   b. Det-Gen$_{theme}$-N$_{process}$

(21)   Det-N$_{process}$-Gen$_{theme}$ (PP$_{agent}$) (MG)

Alexiadou attributes the unavailability of prenominal genitive DPs in MG to the properties of the nominal functional projection within process nominals and to other related changes in the nominal system of Greek. This change in the linearization of DPs shows that in the evolution of Greek an anti-symmetric stage where the genitive object DPs may precede or follow a nominal head, preceded an asymmetric stage, where only post-nominal genitive objects are possible. The difference in the linearization of genitive object DPs in the history of Greek can be analyzed as following from a change in the value of functional features, with the consequent effects of the asymmetric feature-valuing mechanism. The question arises why anti-symmetry breaking is observed and its possible relatedness to anti-symmetry breaking in the natural world. In particular, the phylogenetic patterns of variance discussed by Palmer may bring new light to our understanding of diachronic changes.

Furthermore, anti-symmetry breaking may also be part of the factors reducing derivational complexity, which would eliminate through historical evolution and change choice points for linearization—in this specific case, the choice of linearizing a DP to the right or to the left of a nominal head. The complexity brought about by two possible linearizations of a genitive DP in CG, anti-symmetric linearization, is reduced in MG to asymmetric linearization only. Anti-symmetry breaking can be viewed as part of the factors reducing the complexity brought about by a choice point in the derivation. In this perspective, anti-symmetry breaking would not drive the derivation, as in Moro (2000), but would be part of what Chomsky (2005) calls "the third factor" in the language design, computational factors external to FL, which contribute to make language tractable by the external systems.

13.2.3 *Change in the linearization of possessive clitics*

The change in the linearization of possessive clitics in MG and Greek dialects is another example of the anti-symmetry > asymmetry historical pattern of variance and of the role of the anti-symmetry breaking mechanism in language change.

In MG, the weak forms of the genitive case of personal pronouns serve as possessive pronouns (Mackridge 1985). Possessive clitics manifest person and number distinctions (sing.: mu_1, Su_2, $tu_{3\,MASC}$, NEUT, $tis_{3.\,FEM}$; plural: mas_1, sas_2, tus_3), have gender morphology only at the third person, and show no agreement in phi-features with the possessed object. Modern Greek also uses complex possessive expressions with an emphatic possessive adjective *diko* 'own' (Alexiadou 2005). The possessive adjective agrees in phi features with the possessed object. Modern Greek has no other possessive adjective than *diko*, contrary to CG, which does have possessive adjectives preceding and following nominal heads. In MG, the basic position of possessive clitics is post-nominal, as in (22a), from Alexiadou and Stávrou (2000). However, possessive clitics may occupy the pre-nominal position in the presence of an adjective, (23), and must occupy this position in the presence of *diko*, (24).

(22)   Modern Greek
     a. to vivlio-tu   b. to vivlio tu fititi
        the book-his   the book GEN student. GEN
        'his book'   'the student's book'

(23)   Modern Greek
     a. to oreo vivlio-mu   b. to oreo-mu vivlio
        the nice book-my   the nice-my book
        'my nice book'   'my nice book'

(24)   Modern Greek
     a. to diko-mu vivlio   b. *to diko vivlio-mu
        the own-my book   the own book my
        'my own book'   'my own book'

Interestingly, in Grico (GR), a Modern Greek dialect spoken in southern Italy,[10] while the weak forms of the genitive case of personal pronouns also serve as possessive pronouns, as in MG, possessive clitics are only post-nominal, with or without the presence of the emphatic adjective *diko*; see (25) and (26).[11]

(25)   Grico
     a. o spiti-mu   c. o spiti-tu
        the house my   the house his
        'my house'   'his house'
     b. *o mu-spiti   d. *o tu-spiti

---

[10] Two small Grico-speaking communities survive today in the Italian regions of Calabria (east of the province of Reggio Calabria) and Puglia (peninsula of Salento and Aspromonte).

[11] I thank Dimitra Melissaropoulou for the GR data and Natalia Pavlou for the CyG data.

(26)   Grico
     a. o spiti diko-mmu   c. o spiti diko-ttu
          the house mine-my   the house his-his
          'my own house'   'his own house'
     b. *o diko-mmu spiti   d. *o diko-ttu spiti

The variation in the linearization of possessive clitics in MG and in GR can be analyzed as the presence or the absence of [uF] in the feature specification of functional heads within the DP, which minimally includes the projections in (27). Possessive clitics would be generated in FPPoss; feature-driven Internal Merge would apply in the derivation of the different orders. Alternatively, if the ordering of clitics is post-syntactic, and more generally if syntax (narrow syntax) is immune to variation, differences in the linearization of possessive clitics can be seen as being triggered by unvalued morpho-phonological features in the PF derivation.

(27)   [DP [AP [FPPoss [NP]]]]

I will not discuss these alternatives here, but rather focus on the fact that the difference in the linearization of possessive clitics in MG and in GR can be further understood in a biolinguistic perspective, as another case of anti-symmetry breaking, and anti-symmetry > asymmetry pattern of variance. Dialects include remnants of ancient languages, and they nevertheless provide novel developments of the languages. Thus, a dialect may preserve the anti-symmetric stage of the more ancient language from which it evolved, and it may also evolve to an asymmetric stage. However, once the asymmetric stage is reached, the anti-symmetry breaking hypothesis predicts that a language may no longer evolve into the preceding anti-symmetric stage.

Thus, in GR, the possessive pronoun follows the head noun and may not precede it, whether the emphatic adjective *diko* is part of the derivation or not. A similar situation is observed in Cypriot Greek (CyG), a MG dialect spoken in Cyprus. In CyG, bare possessive clitics are post-nominal only (see 28a,b), contrary to MG (23). However, when possession is expressed with emphatic *diko*, the possessive clitic is pre-nominal only, (29), as is the case in MG (24).

(28)   Cypriot Greek
     a. to spiti-mu   b. to spiti-tu
          the house-my   the house-his
          'my house'   'his house'
          *to mu-spiti   *to tu-spiri

(29)   Cypriot Greek
    a. to diko-mu spiti   c. to diko-tu spiti
       the own-my house   the own-his house
       'my own house'   'his own house'
    b. *to spiti diko-mu   d. *to spiti diko-tu

Anti-symmetric linearization is thus observed in MG with bare posses-sive clitics, which may be linearized to the right or to the left of a nominal head. However, only directional asymmetric linearization is observed in MG dialects, GR and CyG, where bare possessive clitics may only linearize to the right of a nominal head.

Further evidence for anti-symmetry breaking and the anti-symmetry > asymmetry pattern of variance in language change comes from the differ-ence in the linearization of possessive clitics in Italian and dialects spoken in Abruzzo. While possessive adjectives may be linearized to the right or to the left of a noun in Italian, (see 30),[12] only directional asymmetric linearization is observed in certain western and eastern dialects of Italian, where the pos-sessive clitic may follow the noun, but may not precede it. This is the case for Marcilian varieties (MA) spoken in western Abruzzo (data from Pescasseroli (Saltarelli 2008)),[13] as well as for Fallese (FA) and Ariellese (AR), two varieties of Eastern Abruzzese.

(30)   Italian
    a. la sorella mia   b. la mia sorella
       the sister my   the my sister
       'my sister'   'my sister'

(31)   Marcilian
    a. sorda-me   b. *(la) me sorda
       sister-my   (the) mine sister
       'my sister'   'my sister'
    b. *(la) me sorda

(32)   Fallese   Ariellese
    a. la casa-mè   c. la casa-mé
       the house-my   the house-my
       'my house'   'my house'
    b. *la mè casa   d. *la mé casa

---

[12] This is also the case in the Virgilian tradition, e.g. *quoniam sic videtur filii* parente suos *agnoscere ... ille petit ut* suos parentes *ostendisset.* (Ziolkowski and Putnam 2008: 686).

[13] Possessive clitics are morphologically restricted to personal pronouns; they are prosodically enclitics (Rohlfs 1966; Maiden and Parry 1997).

The difference in the linearization of possessive clitics differentiating MG and IT from their dialectal variants, GR and CyG in the case of MG, FA, and AR in the case of IT, can be derived by asymmetric feature-valuing and is yet another example of anti-symmetry breaking where an anti-symmetric stage precedes an asymmetric stage.

13.2.4 *Summary*

Language change is directional—why is this the case? The fluctuating–directional asymmetry characterizing the variation in the evolution of the shape of bipartite asymmetric animals and plants brings new light to the directionality of language evolution and change. The trajectory of the change in the linearization of linguistic constituents from an anti-symmetric stage, where linearization may take place either to the right or to the left of a head, to an asymmetric stage, where only one option survives, is predicted not to be invertible.

Evidence from language acquisition as well as from language change in the linearization of linguistic constituents brings support to the anti-symmetry-breaking hypothesis. These findings bring language variation and change closer to variation and evolution in biology. Moreover, anti-symmetry breaking can be thought of as being part of the factors reducing the complexity brought about by the presence of choice points in the derivations.

13.3 Conclusion and a Further Question

In this chapter I explored some relations between variation in language and variation in biology. Because language is grounded in biology and variation is central in biology, the understanding of biological variation is likely to shed light on linguistic diversity. First, I discussed the notion of parameter in linguistic theory and in biology, and suggested that they share asymmetric dynamical properties. Second, I considered the change in the linearization of linguistic constituents from the perspective of patterns of phylogenetic variation identified in evolutionary developmental biology. I suggested that the directionality of language change in the linearization of constituents observable in language change through time, as well as in the course of language acquisition, could be further understood as an effect of anti-symmetry breaking, which in turn could very well be part of the factors reducing complexity.

Why should asymmetry be central? It might be the case that asymmetry ensures stability to FL, when symmetry is brought about by experience. This does not discard the possibility that symmetry could be available in communication systems in place before the emergence of language. In biology, an asymmetric system might arise from a symmetric precursor, and if this asymmetric system is more robust, it will be genetically fixed in the genome. The stability brought about by asymmetric relations can be seen as a core element in the emergence and evolution of FL. The biolinguistic approach to language variation opens the possibility to go beyond explanatory adequacy, and to ask why parametric variation is derived in FL via asymmetric relations, why anti-symmetry breaking is part of language change, and to relate via asymmetry variation in language to variation in biology. Further understanding of diversity in language and in biology will contribute to the understanding of language as a biological object and of language variation as an instance of variation in biology.

Part III
Computation

14

Antisymmetry and the Lexicon

RICHARD S. KAYNE

In this chapter, I will try to show that what we think of as the noun–verb distinction can be understood as a consequence of antisymmetry, in the sense of Kayne (1994). I will also make some remarks (in the first two sections) concerning counterparts of the human language faculty in other species. Properties of nouns will, from this perspective, lead me to suggest that sentential complements (and derived nominals) involve relative clause structures.

14.1 Recursion

Hauser, Chomsky, and Fitch, (2002: 1578) consider the "hypothesis that recursion evolved to solve other computational problems such as navigation, number quantification" and consider that it is "possible that other animals have such abilities."

Assume, then, that recursion is not unique to humans but that the FLN (faculty of language narrowly understood) in their sense is. We can ask what other more specific property or properties of the FLN might keep it from appearing in other species. Or, put the other way round, what is it about non-human species that makes the FLN unavailable to them? Some possible properties more specific than recursion that might be conjectured to characterize non-human species (as opposed to humans) are as follows.

1. It might be that in non-human species recursion is available with spell-out to Phonological Form (PF), but there is no compositional interpretation available, that is no mapping to Logical Form (LF) (and correspondingly no notion of idiom).
2. It might be that external merge is available, but no internal merge.

This chapter (with a different title) originated as a talk given in June 2007 at the conference "Biolinguistics: Language Evolution and Variation" (University of Venice).

3. Counterparts of language in non-human species might allow branching of arbitrary degree, rather than just binary branching.

4. Recursion might be available, but without any notion of phase, in which case, if Kayne (2006b) is on the right track, non-human species might lack the possibility of having pronounceable elements be unpronounced in certain contexts.

5. Counterparts of human language in non-human species might more generally have no silent elements at all, including in particular elements that are invariably silent. (For example, there might be no contentful pauses in birdsong.)

6. It might be that parametric differences are absent within any given non-human species (assuming a sufficiently clear way to individuate species). For example, there might be no parametric differences in birdsong (within a given species) comparable to the parametric differences present in human language. (Related to this is the question why parametric variation exists in humans (and why only certain kinds); for some discussion, see Baker (2001: ch. 7).)

14.2 Antisymmetry

The antisymmetry property that Kayne (1994) attributed to the human language faculty might or might not have counterparts in other species.

Informally speaking, a relatively weaker interpretation of antisymmetry has it that no two human languages can be mirror images of one another, that is no pair of languages can have the property that one is the exact mirror image of the other (in the sense that each grammatical sentence of one has a grammatical counterpart in the other that is its mirror image, counting by morphemes, say). Put another way, take some human language, English for instance, and construct mirror-image English by taking the mirror image of each grammatical English sentence and "putting it into" mirror-image English. Though perfectly easy to imagine, such a mirror image of English is not a possible human language (if antisymmetry is correct).

Correspondingly (in part), one could ask whether a given species of bird could have two songs that are mirror images of one another. Again informally speaking, a stronger interpretation of antisymmetry has it that if some subtree (with both hierarchical structure and precedence relations specified) is well-formed in some human language, then its mirror image is well-formed in no human language. The similar question for birdsong would be: can two subparts of songs (in a given species) be mirror images of one another, with hierarchy preserved?

These questions can also be asked in a cross-species fashion. Taking bird-song as an example, could a whole song from one species be the mirror image of a whole song from another species? Taking hierarchical structure specifically into account, could a well-formed subpart of a song from one species have its mirror image be well-formed in some other species?

A conjecture would be that antisymmetry holds both within and, in the above sense, across species. (Whatever the exact extent to which it holds, we would need to further ask why it holds.)[1]

Assuming antisymmetry to be related to sequence in time, one can ask to what extent sequence in time is a PF interface property, as opposed to holding more fundamentally of internal "thought" (in which case linearization/precedence would not need to be restricted to PF/Spell-out).

14.3 Antisymmetry and Anti-optionality

In the early years of generative syntax, transformations were commonly taken to divide into optional transformations and obligatory ones.[2] Starting in the 1980s, Chomsky, for example in his "last resort" proposal (see Chomsky 1986, 1995), began to move away from the idea that transformations/movement operations were free to vary between optional and obligatory, toward the idea that derivations do not countenance (a certain kind of) optionality. Antisymmetry can itself be (informally) thought of as reflecting a particular dimension along which the human language faculty rejects optionality—in the case of (temporal) order (for a given hierarchical arrangement).

Important to the present chapter is a question involving the optionality of projection, thinking of Chomsky (2005: 14), who emphasized the (widely-agreed-upon) fact that when a head is merged with a phrase it is the head that projects—there is no choice/option. In agreement with Chomsky, I take this lack of optionality to be desirable.

Chomsky's discussion left open the question of initial derivational steps in which one head is merged with another. Contrary to the case of head–phrase merger, where the identity of the projecting element is plausibly fixed by general principle, it seems at first glance that in head–head merger the language faculty must countenance optionality, allowing either of the two heads to project.

---

[1] Asking a cross-species question of the sort mentioned amounts to asking a question concerning what the brains of different species might have in common, and what the limitations might be on what such brains can do.

[2] See e.g. Kayne (1975); on clitic movement, cf. also Kayne (2000: ch. 9).

This problem with respect to projection recalls the one that seemed to arise for antisymmetry if one tried to reconcile antisymmetry (in particular the LCA-based formulation of it from Kayne 1994) with Chomsky's (1995: ch. 4) bare phrase-structure proposal. The linear-correspondence axiom (LCA) approach, while deriving various other properties of X-bar theory, took over intact from X-bar theory the idea that one could have non-branching projections, something that bare phrase structure prohibits (see Chomsky 1995: 246). Non-branching projections were necessary for the LCA to work properly precisely in the case of what bare phrase structure would now call the merger of two heads, insofar as two sister nodes both of which are pure heads would involve no asymmetric c-command and would therefore, according to the LCA, not be properly linearized.

A solution to the challenge of reconciling the LCA with bare phrase structure was proposed by Guimarães (2000), who suggested that the language faculty should be taken to allow what he called Self-Merge, where some head x is merged with itself, yielding {x}. Let me follow more closely Chomsky's (2005: 16) formulation (from a different context) of a similar idea. Without saying that x can merge with x (which leads to questions about how to distinguish occurrences of x and what to say about three or more xs merging all at once), let us say only that one option for merge, taken to be set-formation, is the direct formation of the singleton set {x}.[3]

From an LCA perspective, this works informally as follows.[4] Whereas having heads y and x as sisters yields a linearization problem (since neither y nor x asymmetrically c-commands the other), having y the sister of {x} does not. In this configuration, y asymmetrically c-commands x (and so y will be ordered before x). (I am assuming that c-command has the property that a head c-commands each member of the set it merges with.)

14.4 Antisymmetry of Projection

Another way to put the Guimarães (2000) type proposal is to say that anti-symmetry compels the language faculty to have recourse to singleton-set

---

[3] It seems unlikely that {x} (or Guimarães's (self-merge) could be the source of what is called morphological reduplication. Gulli (2003) has proposed that syntactic reduplication is found only in remnant movement configurations, where neither copy c-commands the other. A plausible conjecture is that exactly the same holds of what we think of as morphological reduplication.

Alongside {x}, there seems to be no need for {{x}}, which would be unavailable in principle if every merge operation must directly involve a head.

[4] Full integration of the LCA with bare phrase structure will require reformulating the LCA without recourse to non-terminals.

formation in the relevant case.[5] From this perspective, we can now say that antisymmetry, by inducing singleton-set formation, has simultaneously provided a solution to the head–head projection problem (even though that problem had nothing to do with linearization/pronunciation),[6] tying it to various other ramifications of antisymmetry (see also Kayne 2005b: ch. 9).

The problem, again, was that merging distinct heads y and x seemed to lead to an option with respect to projection—either y could project or x could, with distinct results. But merging y with {x} reduces to the general case of merging a head with a phrase (set), for which there is no ambiguity of projection (it is always the head, here y, that projects).[7] Put another way, a language faculty that respects antisymmetry is not, given Guimarães's (2000) proposal, subject to the optionality of projection problem.

If it should turn out that antisymmetry itself is ultimately derivable from some more general (and precise) notion of antioptionality—one compatible with the presence in the language faculty of certain instances of optionality, such as parameter setting and the optionality involved in choosing items to be drawn into the numeration from the lexicon and into the derivation from the numeration (or into the derivation directly from the lexicon)—, then the title of this chapter would be appropriately changed to "Antioptionality and the Lexicon," without, I think, affecting the core claim to be made beginning with the next section, namely, that the existence in the language faculty of a noun–verb distinction is a consequence of antisymmetry (or, then, antioptionality) rather than an intrinsic property of anything called the lexicon.

14.5 The Closed–Class vs. Open–Class Distinction

From the preceding discussion, we can see that in a given derivation, some lexical items x will appear as part of {x}, others (the ys) will not. That is, some lexical items will be involved in singleton-set formation, others will not.

It is commonplace that some categories are open, in the sense of (having a large number of members and) allowing (further) expansion, while others are not. Why should this be? Why are there closed categories at all? Let me

---

[5] I agree with Guimarães that neither Chomsky's (1995: 337) nor Moro's (2000) attempt (see also Babyonyshev 2004) to use obligatory movement of one of the two heads in "[y x]" to solve the problem is sufficiently general.

[6] Bare phrase structure alone, without antisymmetry, would not have solved the problem.

[7] If, in merging a head y and a phrase XP, it was the phrase that projected, we would have y as the specifier of the head of XP, which is excluded by antisymmetry—Kayne (1994: sect. 3.7). Note that just as the solution to the optionality problem for head–head merger is that the merger of two distinct heads is in fact never possible, there is a sense in which two phrases never merge directly with one another, but only via the intermediary of the head of one.

suggest an answer based in part on Chomsky's (2001: 15) proposal that unvalued (uninterpretable) features have to be valued immediately upon entering the derivation,[8] and in part on the idea that the set of parameters is fixed. Assume, crucially for what follows, that singleton-set formation is part of the derivation; together with Chomsky's proposal, this would then yield the conclusion:

(1)   If x participates in singleton-set formation (yielding {x}), then x cannot have an unvalued feature.

This is so, since the initial derivational step that forms {x} will have no way of valuing such a feature, given that that derivational step involves no y distinct from x. Thus Chomsky's requirement can be met only if x has no features in need of valuation.

Collins (2005: 117) suggests that parametric variation is limited to uninterpretable features, which is very close to:

(2)   Parametric variation is a property of unvalued features only.
      If this holds, then combining it with (1) yields:

(3)   If x participates in singleton-set formation, then x is not the locus of parametric variation.
      Strengthening (1) would lead to:

(4)   If y remains bare (i.e. does not participate in singleton-set formation), then y must have an unvalued feature.
      A parallel strengthening of (2) would give (cf. Kayne (2005b: 285)):

(5)   All unvalued features are associated with parametric variation.
      Assume further that parameters are hard-wired:

(6)   Parameters (though not their values) are fixed by the language faculty, that is they constitute a closed set.

Now by (4) + (5), a bare y must be associated with parametric variation. Therefore, by (6), the set of such y must be closed, in other words, the category that y belongs to must constitute a closed class. (This constitutes an answer to the question raised toward the beginning of this section, with the next question being why (6) should hold.)

By standard assumption, the lexicon as a whole is not closed. If so, it follows from the present perspective—which has lexical elements necessarily being

---

[8] An open question is whether the existence of a distinction between valued and unvalued features could itself follow from antisymmetry/anti-optionality. (The reverse seems less likely.) On the possibility that unvalued features could be reinterpreted as a subtype of doubling, see Kayne and Pollock (2008).

either of the y type or of the x type—that the category that x belongs to must constitute an open class.

14.6 Nouns and Verbs

The antisymmetry-driven picture of the lexicon we have arrived at is that there are lexical items of category x and lexical items of category y, with the following properties:[9]

(7)   x: open class, singleton-set formation, initially valued features, not locus of parametric variation.

(8)   y: closed class, no singleton-set formation, initially unvalued features, locus of parametric variation.

Part of my proposal is:

 (9)   An x is what we call a noun.[10]

That is, nouns match the properties listed in (7).
    Related to these, we might have:

(10)   An element can "denote" only if it enters the derivation with no unvalued features.

From this it would follow, given (7) and (8) (cf. in particular Baker's 2003b: 118 kind-denotation:[11])

---

[9] If a non-human species lacked antisymmetry, then it should lack the x vs. y distinction—necessarily so if antisymmetry is the only possible source of this bifurcation.

[10] From this perspective there may be no need for a category-creating *n* such as in Marantz (to appear). (The text discussion uses "noun" where one might want to speak of "nominal root.") On gender and on Harris's (1991) notion of word marker, both of which I will be leaving aside (perhaps wrongly), see also Ferrari (2005).

If classifiers are nouns, then parametric variation involving classifiers must be reinterpreted in terms of properties of other heads that are non-nominal, and similarly for measure nouns and for parametric variation with *at the age of five* (cf. Kayne (2005b: ch. 10).

[11] Also, Déprez (2005) and Vergnaud and Zubizarreta (1992).
Parallel to (10) and linked to Baker (2003b: 95) would be:

(i) An element can have *criteria of identity* only if it enters the derivation with no unvalued features.

As Terje Lohndal (p.c.) points out, the absence of unvalued features on nouns is incompatible with Pesetsky and Torrego (2004). It may rather be that Case morphemes are always a subtype of adposition, with the widespread absence of visible nominative (cf. Bittner and Hale 1996) then linked to the widespread absence of PP subjects.

Note that Pesetsky and Torrego's proposal shows that in the absence of antisymmetry/anti-optionality nothing in the theory of uninterpretable features by itself leads to a fundamental noun–verb distinction of the sort proposed here.

(11)   The only lexical elements that can denote are nouns.[12]

Paired with (9) is the following proposal:

(12)   A y is what we call a non-noun.

Falling under "non-noun" are at least verbs (and aspectual heads), with the apparent paradox that verbs are normally thought to belong to an open class.

That paradox needs to be rethought, however, in light of Hale and Keyser (1993: 55) proposal concerning *laugh* and similar items. For Hale and Keyser,[13] English *laugh* is a noun that in some sentences co-occurs with a light verb that is unpronounced, giving the (misleading) impression that *laugh* in English can also be a verb. Strictly speaking, though, *laugh* is invariably a noun, even when it incorporates (in some sense of the term) into a (silent) light verb (for example, by adjoining to the light verb,[14] or perhaps by moving to some Spec position related to the light verb).[15] Put another way, if Hale and Keyser (1993: 55) are right, which I take them to be, *laugh* must be subtracted from the set of English verbs.

Without addressing any of the various challenges that arise for the Hale and Keyser proposal,[16] let me jump to the following claim:

(13)   All verbs are light verbs.

This amounts to the conjecture that if we pursue the Hale and Keyser approach consistently, we will see that most of what we call verbs are really like *laugh*, actually involving a noun and a silent light verb (or more than one silent light verb).[17] If this is correct, we are led to the following conclusion:

(14)   The class of verbs is closed.

The paradox under discussion then disappears and we can maintain the conclusion that the antisymmetry-driven distinction between (7) and (8) is what

----

[12] One might ask whether it is x or {x} that denotes.

[13] Hale and Keyser (2002: 98) move away from that position.

[14] On incorporation, cf. Baker (1988).

[15] Cf. Kayne (2005b: ch. 9, n. 5). In bare phrase structure, there is no way for a noun to derivationally "become" a verb.

[16] For a proposal concerning cognate objects that is compatible with a strong form of the Hale and Keyser position, see Real Puigdollers (2007).

[17] In languages like English, "incorporation" can also involve phrases, as in:

(i)   Don't Monday-morning-quarterback him so much.

Other instances involve adjectives:

(ii)   You need to thin the soup.

If *download* is phrasal (cf. Koopman 2000), then English also has phrasal incorporation into a nominal structure, in.

(iii)   the downloading of the program.

underlies the distinction that we are used to calling the noun–verb distinction. In other words, a basic property of (what we think of as) the lexicon is called into being by a property (antisymmetry) of the language faculty that is not intrinsically a property of the lexicon.

14.7 Other Categories

Questions arise about other traditional categories. Take adpositions, for example. If there is a core x – y (noun–non-noun) distinction, then, if an adposition is simplex it must be either of category x or of category y, in other words, either nominal or not. It seems virtually certain that, as many authors have suggested, some adpositions are (simplex and) nominal.[18] Adpositions that are not nominal, that is, not of the x type, must be of the y type. Determiners might be uniformly of one type, or perhaps some determiners are x and others y;[19] the same goes for other categories. Another possibility is that some categories that look simplex actually are not. For example, Amritavalli and Jayaseelan (2003) have suggested that adjectives might cross-linguistically be analyzed as resulting from the incorporation of a noun to a (silent) Case morpheme.[20]

14.8 Lexical Specialization

The question arises as to whether lexical items are necessarily specialized relative to the x vs. y distinction. Could there be a lexical item with the property that in some derivations it acts as an x and in other derivations as a y? The antisymmetry/antioptionality perspective that I have been taking suggests not. Two more specific considerations that point in the same direction are as follows. First, given the open- vs. closed-class distinction that matches x vs. y, it is clear that not all items of type x could alternatively act as type y, otherwise the set y would not be closed. The question remains whether a closed subset of x could have the property of appearing as y in some derivations. This second question can be made more concrete by thinking of a particular x, say *thing*. Could *thing* act as a y (non-noun) in some derivations? The answer would seem to be a clear no. The most plausible conclusion, then, is that the x's and the y's constitute disjoint sets of lexical items.

---

[18] With a reduced amount of functional structure above them, as compared with ordinary nouns— cf. Collins (2006a).

[19] This question is relevant only for those determiners that are monomorphemic. Leu (2008) argues that most are in fact phrasal.

[20] As opposed to Baker's (2003b) approach to adjectives. Case morphemes are probably a subtype of adposition.

Although not found with *thing*, there are of course sentences (in English) such as (15):

(15)   John impersonated Bill.

But these (like many others) will have an incorporation-type derivation, including the presence of a (silent) light verb and in this case a prepositional element *im-*, in addition to *person*, which can therefore be taken to be an x here, as in general.[21]

Similarly, there are (in English) even some cases in which light verbs might be thought to act as nouns:[22]

(16)   You should give it a go/*be/*have.

But a plausible alternative is that *go* here is a y embedded in a structure much of which is silent, perhaps partially parallel to what is seen overtly in (17):

(17)   We gave them the go-ahead.

which is in turn similar to the control sentence with obviously verbal *go*:

(18)   We gave them permission to go ahead.

Similar considerations hold for cases like (19) alongside (20):

(19)   Neither the haves nor the have-nots will be happy about this.

(20)   Neither those who have nor those who do not have ...

The conclusion that the x's and the y's must be disjoint in a given language leads to the question of cross-linguistic consistency. If some lexical item is an x in one language, must its counterpart in the next language also be an x?[23] The Hale and Keyser (1993: 55) discussion of English *laugh* and its Basque counterpart lends itself to thinking that the answer is yes, that lexical items do distribute consistently across languages as far as the noun–verb distinction goes.[24] I agree with a strong version of this (but will not pursue the question).

---

[21] The contrast in the following sentences is well known:
  (i) They rang/*ringed us up.
  (ii) The soldiers ringed/*rang the city.
It may be that both involve denominal verbs (i.e. noun and light verb), with the difference due to the fact that (ii) has a (complex) locative structure that the first does not have.

[22] Beyond the scope of this chapter is the question (which cuts across the silent vs. pronounced dimension) how best to distinguish one light verb from the next, one consideration being that light verbs themselves are not (all) simplex.

[23] The identification of lexical counterparts across languages (with silent elements playing an important role) is central to comparative syntax. For relevant discussion, see Cinque (1999) and Kayne 2005b: ch. 12).

[24] In the present framework, it is clear that every language must have a distinction between y and x (between non-noun and noun). This agrees with Baker's (2003b: 169) argument that all languages have nouns. How best to express the difference between English and Basque with respect to *laugh* is left an open question.

14.9 Nouns Do Not Project

The complement of a head is the phrase that the head initially merges with. When y merges with {x}, {x} is the complement of y. However, elements of type x cannot themselves have a complement, since when they enter the derivation they invariably undergo singleton-set formation, rather than merging with a phrase or set. (As in the previous section, x's and y's have disjoint properties.) In more familiar terms, this yields the conclusion that nouns must not have complements.

Can x ever have a specifier? This amounts to asking whether {x} can merge with some phrase in such a way that x projects (is the label of the resulting larger phrase). Relevant here (and perhaps also to the question of complements) is our earlier conclusion in (1) that x cannot have any unvalued feature. If an unvalued feature is necessary to the derivational coming into being of a specifier, then x can have no specifier. I will take this to be valid.[25] Let me therefore add this difference concerning projection to the set of differences between x and y given earlier in (7) and (8), which yields:

(21)   x: open class, singleton-set formation, initially valued features, not locus of parametric variation, no complement or specifier

(22)   y: closed class, no singleton-set formation, initially unvalued features, locus of parametric variation, complement and specifier possible.[26]

14.10 A Consequence of Nouns Not Projecting: *The fact that …*

If nouns never project,[27] then in:

(23)   the fact that they're here

that they're here cannot be a complement (or specifier) of *fact* if *fact* is a noun (an x).[28] Since it is unlikely that *fact* is a verb (a y), there appears at first glance

---

[25] This agrees with Baker (2003b: 23) on verbs vs. nouns.

[26] And perhaps obligatory, though I will not pursue that here, and similarly for the question whether {x} can itself be the specifier of another head.

[27] Ghomeshi (1996: 63) takes this position for Persian.

[28] Little would change in the text discussion if *fact* turned out to be phrasal, as suggested perhaps by its German counterpart *Tatsache* ('deed', 'thing'), though that might perhaps help with the potential gender problem (depending on one's analysis of complementizer *that/dass*) of *die Tatsache, dass/*die sie intelligent ist* ('the fact that she intelligent is') brought to my attention by Luka Szucsich, which recalls French *quelque chose de beau/*belle* ('some thing of beautiful').

to be a problem. The solution, I think, involves taking (23) to be a relative clause structure.[29]

There are, needless to say, differences as compared with more familiar relative clauses:

(24)   *the fact which they're here

(25)   the fact which they mentioned

If (23) contains a relative clause, why is *which* not possible? An answer is to be found in the realm of *way*, which occurs in ordinary relative clauses like (26):

(26)   the way in which they solved the problem

Way also appears in:

(27)   the way (that) they solved it

which is uncontroversially a relative-clause structure with the preposition *in* unpronounced, as it can (optionally) be elsewhere:

(28)   They solved it (in) this way.

What is notable is that when *in* is unpronounced, *which* is impossible despite being possible in (26):[30]

(29)   *the way which they solved it

The suggestion, now, is that (24) is impossible for the same reason as (29). If so, then (24) is not incompatible with a relative-clause analysis of (23), since (29) shows that *which* is not automatically available in English, even when the head of the relative is inanimate.

It is unlikely that Stowell's (1981: ch. 3, sect. 7) appositive proposal for finite clauses in derived nominals could (if correct) be generalized to *fact*, given:

(i)   a.   The (very/mere) fact that they lied is scandalous.
       b.   *?The (*very/*mere) fact, (namely) that they lied, is scandalous.

Also

(ii)   a.   His claim to the effect that he's innocent is hard to believe.
       b.   The fact (*to the effect) that he is innocent is well known.

as well as

(iii) a.   ?That man we deplore the fact that she's in love with.
       b.   *That man the fact is (that) she's in love with.

Example (iiia) recalls the extraction out of relatives discussed by Taraldsen (1981) and Chung and McCloskey (1983).

[29] For related discussion, see Kayne (in press). Partially similar proposals can be found in Aboh (2005) and Arsenijević (2007).

[30] The absence of a following lexical noun, in combination with the non-pronunciation of *in*, seems to be at issue, to judge by (i):

(i)   (There are many known ways of solving this equation) ??In which did they solve it this time?

(ii)   *Which did they solve it this time?

Linking (23) vs. (24) to (27) vs. (29) rests in part on the proposal that the former pair has in common with the latter the presence of silent *in*, that is, that (23)/(24) is to (30) as (27)/(29) is to (28):

(30)   They're here, in fact.

In other words, (23) contains a relative clause in which what has been relativized is the object of the (silent) *in* of (30).[31] That *which* is not possible in (24) reflects a broader incompatibility between *which* and silent *in*, as shown by (29).

A further apparent problem lies with the unacceptability of (31) and the contrast between it and (26).

(31)   *the fact in which they're here

A possible solution would involve relating this contrast to others having nothing to do with relatives, for example (32) and (33):

(32)   In what/?which way did they solve it this time?

(33)   *In what/which fact are they here this time

That is, to the substantially greater restrictions on determiners found with *fact*,[32] as also seen in:

(34)   We solved it in another way.

(35)   *We're here, in another fact.

and arguably in (36) and (37):

---

[31] Or possibly that of:

(i)   They're in fact here.
       (with no pauses around *in fact*) or of:

(ii)   In fact, they're here.

[32] Also greater than with nouns like *rumor*:

(i)   There's a rumor/*fact that John is ill.
       which also differ from *fact* with respect to:

(ii)   the rumor/*fact according to which John is ill

(iii) the rumor/*fact to the effect that John is ill
       Possibly, (iii) is to be linked to (iv):

(iv)   John is ill, in effect.
       though one will need to understand:

(v)   John is indeed ill.

(vi)   *the deed that John is ill

Example (ii) and the following show (along with relativization based on *in fact*) that there is no general prohibition against relativizing (high) adjuncts:

(vii) the scandal as a result of which they resigned
(viii) the reason why they resigned

(36)   In ways, they're right.

(37)   In fact(*s), they're right.

which may correlate in turn with:

(38)   (?)the ways that they're right

(39)   the fact(*s) that she's right and (that) he's wrong

The contrast between (24) and (25), which I have been arguing is compatible with the idea that both are relative clause structures, has a counterpart in (40) and (41):[33]

(40)   The fact ?(that) they're here is irrelevant.

(41)   The fact (that) they mentioned is irrelevant.

Having no relative marker at all is difficult in the first, as opposed to the second. That (40) is marginal may, however, be related to the marginality of (42), which clearly involves a(n extraposed) relative clause, in which case (40), too, is compatible with the idea that *the fact that…* always contains a relative clause.

(42)   The very person walked in ?(that) they used to know in high school.

The two subtypes of relative clause found with *fact* (one based on adjunct-like *in fact*, the other not) also differ with respect to *one*:

(43)   the fact that they're right and the fact/*one that you're wrong

(44)   the fact that they mentioned and the fact/one that you mentioned

As earlier, we find that the *in fact*-based relative has a counterpart with (clear cases of) relative clauses based on *way*:

(45)   the way that they solved it and the way/*one that you solved it

The restriction in question depends in part on the preposition not being pronounced (in both (43) and (45)), in a way that recalls (29):

(46)   They solved it this way and you solved it that way/*one.

(47)   They solved it in this way and you solved it in that way/?one.

Luigi Rizzi (p.c.) points out that what from my perspective are two cases of relative clauses with *fact* differ in Italian in that the one that I take to

---

[33] Cf. perhaps the *som* ('as') vs. at(t) ('that') contrast found in Scandinavian languages, which needs to be elucidated.

be related to *in fact* allows subjunctive, while the other does not. Let me give polarity-like examples from (my) English that I think mimic the Italian contrast (cf. perhaps the *ever* of *Why ever did they run away?*):

(48)   The fact that they could ever have run away disturbs me.

(49)   *The fact that they could ever have mentioned disturbs me.

It may be that "ordinary" relatives like the one with *mention* always have a (sometimes silent) demonstrative, as opposed to the *in fact*-based relative, which does not, and that the *ever* of (48) (along with subjunctive in Italian) is incompatible with relatives whose head has a demonstrative.

   In conclusion of this section, then, a relative-clause analysis of (23) is more plausible than it might initially seem to be. If so, then (23) is compatible with the idea that nouns do not have complements.[34]

14.11 Derived Nominals

If *removal* is a noun, then there might appear to be a problem with (50) insofar as *the evidence* looks like the complement of *removal*.

(50)   the removal *(of) the evidence

One response could be to deny that *the evidence* is a complement by arguing, for example, that if it were, there should not be any need for *of* (one would then call the inability of nouns to assign (accusative) Case a stipulation). Yet if *the evidence* is not a complement of remov(al), how does one express the obvious parallelism with (51)?:

(51)   They removed the evidence.

A second approach, of a familiar and plausible type, is to factor out *-al* and to say that *the evidence* is indeed a complement in (50), but not exactly of *removal*. Rather it is a complement of *remov-* (cf. Pesetsky 1995: 131) Since *remov-* is presumably not a noun, the potential problem disappears. But it comes back in a different form, if one asks about *-al* itself. If *-al* were a y (a non-noun), then there would be no problem, except that if neither *remov-* nor *-al* is nominal, the presence of the initial *the* in (50) becomes hard to understand, along with the presence of *of* and the possibility of having an adjective:

(52)   the sudden removal of the evidence

---

[34] Stowell's (1981) appositive idea (or den Dikken's 2006: 244 updated version of it) would, if extended to *fact*, also be compatible with *fact* not taking complements. See however n. 29.

If *-al* in our terms is an x (a noun) (cf. Williams 1981), the presence of *the sudden* here becomes more straightforward, but the original problem returns as soon as one asks what the relation is between *-al* and *remov- the evidence*. If, as seems plausible, *-al* is merged directly with *remov- the evidence*, then the (suffixal) noun *-al* has a complement, contrary to present expectations.

The alternative is to take *-al* (and similar nominalizing elements) to have an analysis partially similar to what was proposed above for *fact*. Suffixal *-al* will be merged as the object of a silent preposition and then relativized.[35] (Thinking of Lees's 1963 discussion of the interpretation of derived nominals, *-al* could (sometimes) be a suffixal counterpart of *fact* or of *way*.) The suffixal character of *-al* will translate into the requirement that the relative be a non-finite small clause of a certain sort and into the need for *remov-* to raise past *-al* (making (50) have something in common with internally-headed relatives). The derivation might (very sketchily) look like this:

(53)   remov- the evidence P -al $\longrightarrow$ Case-related movement
the evidence$_i$ remov- t$_i$ P -al $\longrightarrow$ relativization of *-al*, pied-piping P
[P -al]$_j$ the evidence$_i$ remov- t$_i$ t$_j$ $\longrightarrow$ remnant movement
[remov- t$_i$ t$_j$]$_k$ [P -al]$_j$ the evidence$_i$ t$_k$

From this perspective, *of* in (50) occurs between the "head" of the relative, which is *-al* and the relative clause proper, which begins with *the evidence*. (There is no complementizer or relative pronoun in this kind of non-finite relative.) Expanding (53) to include merger of *of* yields (54):[36]

(54)   remov- the evidence P -al $\longrightarrow$ Case-related movement
the evidence$_i$ remov- t$_i$ P -al $\longrightarrow$ merger of *of*
of the evidence$_i$ remov- t$_i$ P -al $\longrightarrow$ relativization
[P -al]$_j$ of the evidence$_i$ remov- t$_i$ t$_j$ $\longrightarrow$ remnant movement
[remov- t$_i$ t$_j$]$_k$ [P -al]$_j$ of the evidence$_i$ t$_k$

Having relativization move a phrase to the left of (into the Spec of) *of* also seems called for (in a partially similar case) by the parallelism (cf. (43) and (45)) between (55) and (56)/(57):

---

[35] Cf. Collins (2006b). The text discussion is in the spirit of the head-raising approach to relatives. Conceivably it is *-al* that is adpositional, in which case its object would be silent FACT or WAY or some other comparable noun.

[36] Since extraction from relatives is not in general impossible—cf. Taraldsen (1981), Chung and McCloskey (1983)—the existence of (i):

(i)   the evidence that we condemned the removal of is not entirely surprising, though the extraction in (i) may be facilitated by the application of Case-related movement.

(55)   the way/*one they solved the equation

(56)   that way/*one of solving it

(57)   the other way/*one of solving it.

This supports the idea that the *of* of (56)/(57) introduces a (non-finite) relative. Similar to (56)/(57), with an interesting twist, is:

(58)   You have a funny way/*one of wording your letters.

This example misses, in the gerund clause, the manner adverb that *word* normally requires, and which we can take here to have been relativized. That *way* has actually been raised into the pre-*of* position in (58) is supported by (59):[37]

(59)   *You have a funny way.

whose unacceptability, compared with the acceptability of (58), can be attributed to *way* in (59) having no source, since there is no relative clause present. Note in addition:

(60)   You have a different way of wording each type of letter, don't you?

in which *different* readily scopes under embedded *each*, most straightforwardly as the result of a reconstruction effect keyed to the original position of (*a*) *different way* within the gerundial relative, much as in the infinitival relative example:

(61)   You have a different book to offer each of the students, don't you?

where again *different* readily scopes under the *each* embedded in the relative.

14.12 Restrictions on Derived Nominals

When related to verbs in English that take a direct object plus a prepositional object, derived nominals show divided behavior. There is a broad contrast between cases in which the P is *from* or *to* and cases in which it is *with* or *of*:

(62)   the removal of the money from the children

(63)   the gift of the money to the children
          as opposed to:[38]

---

[37] One will ultimately need to fit in (i):

(i)   You have a funny way about you.

[38] Cf. Kayne (1981b: sect. 4). I have found one speaker who accepts these, along with the example of n. 43. What the parametric difference is remains to be elucidated.

(64)   *the deprivation of the children of their money

(65)   *the provision of the children with money.

For me, these different kinds of PP behave differently under PP-preposing, too, in particular of the non-contrastive (and non-*wh*) kind:[39]

(66)   ?From so many poor children, they've stolen so much money!

(67)   ?To so many poor children, they've given so much money!

as opposed to:

(68)   *Of so much money, they've deprived so many people!

(69)   *With so much money, they've provided so many people!

The hypothesis that derived nominals are derived as in (53)/(54) fits these facts as follows. Transposing (54) to *the removal of the money* (without the *from*-phrase for the time being) gives (70):

(70)   remov- the money P -al → Case-related movement
       the money$_i$ remov- t$_i$ P -al → merger of *of*
       of the money$_i$ remov- t$_i$ P -al → relativization
       [P -al]$_j$ of the money$_i$ remov- t$_i$ t$_j$ → remnant movement
       [remov- t$_i$ t$_j$]$_k$ [P -al]$_j$ of the money$_i$ t$_k$

To have *from the children* in (62) end up after *the money* in a way compatible with the application of remnant movement as the final step in (70), *from the children* must be scrambled at an early stage:[40]

(71)   remov- the money from the children P -al → scrambling
       [from the children]$_k$ remov- the money t$_k$ P -al → Case-related
       movement
       [the money]$_i$ [from the children]$_k$ remov- t$_i$ t$_k$ P -al → merger of *of*
       of [the money]$_i$ [from the children]$_k$ remov- t$_i$ t$_k$ P -al →
       relativization
       [P -al]$_j$ of [the money]$_i$ [from the children]$_k$ remov- t$_i$ t$_k$ t$_j$ →
       remnant movement
       [remov- t$_i$ t$_k$ t$_j$]$_m$ [P -al]$_j$ of [the money]$_i$ [from the children]$_k$ t$_m$

---

[39] Hinterhölzl (2006) shows that contrastive/stressed scrambling in German is freer than non-contrastive/non-stressed scrambling.

[40] If Kayne (2000: ch. 14; 2005b: ch. 5, 7) is on the right track, the first line of this derivation itself has a non-trivial derivational history that must ultimately be integrated with the present proposal.

If the scrambling in this derivation is of the same type as the movement operative in (66), then that makes it possible to relate the (surprising) deviance of (64)/(65) to that of (68)/(69), by virtue of the movement in question not being applicable to certain types of PP.[41]

Derived nominals are also impossible with double objects:

(72)   *the gift of the children (of) a book

The indirect object might be incompatible with the Case associated with *of*, and/or the second object might have a problem with Case-licensing. Instead, or in addition, scrambling of the second object might be at issue.[42]

Assume that the Case-related movement in (71) is limited to DPs. Then in (73):

(73)   the discussion with the children

with the children must (in order to sidestep the subsequent application of remnant movement that places *discuss-* to the left of *-ion*) have moved past *discuss-* via scrambling (parallel to *from the children* in (71)):

(74)   discuss- with the children P -ion → scrambling
         [with the children]$_i$ discuss- t_i P -ion → relativization
         [P -ion]$_j$ [with the children]$_i$ discuss- t_i t_j → remnant movement
         [discuss- t_i t_j]$_k$ [P -ion]$_j$ [with the children]$_i$ t_k

This point generalizes to all cases of derived nominals followed by a PP other than '*of* + direct object'.

The proposal that scrambling is necessarily involved in derived nominals like (73) leads to the expectation that phrases that do not scramble will be excluded from derived nominals. This may provide an account of (75):[43]

(75)   *your appearance to have made a mistake

in terms of the non-scramble-ability of raising infinitives in German mentioned by Hinterhölzl (2006: 16), which has a (somewhat faint) reflex in English, where preposing a control infinitive is less bad than preposing a raising infinitive:[44]

---

[41] There is a link here to Kayne and Pollock (2001: sect. 13).

[42] Note that some English (not mine) allows (some) DPs like (i) (cf. Jespersen 1970: sect. 8.4):
(i) the giving of children books
       Cf. also Wik (1973: 136).

[43] Which would make unnecessary Kayne's (1981b) use of government or Pesetsky's (1991, 1995) zero-affix approach, neither of which appear to carry over to the scrambling facts.

[44] As opposed to clefts (to some extent), focalization, and topicalization in Italian—see Cinque (2006: 41, 48).

(76)   ?the kind of mistake to avoid which he always tries

(77)   *the kind of mistake to have made which he definitely appears

Example (78) is like (77), despite the well-formedness of (79):

(78)   *the kind of mistake to have made which he is definitely believed

(79)   He is definitely believed to have made that kind of mistake.

Example (80), then, is like (75):[45]

(80)   *his belief to have made a mistake

The verb *claim* is unusual in English in allowing both control and raising:

(81)   He claims to be a genius.

(82)   He is claimed to be a genius.

Preposing/scrambling distinguishes them:

(83)   ??the kind of genius to be which he has never claimed

(84)   *the kind of genius to be which he has never been claimed

As expected now, there is also a difference in derived nominals (see (85)), which can have the control interpretation of (81) but not the raising interpretation of (82).

(85)   his claim to be a genius

The parallelism between derived nominals and scrambling/preposing may extend to (86) and (87):

(86)   his eagerness to introduce you to people

(87)   *his easiness to introduce to people[46]

given the (arguably parallel) contrast between (88) and (89):

(88)   ?those people, to introduce you to whom he would certainly be eager

(89)   *those people, to introduce to whom he would certainly be easy

---

[45] Also:

(i)   He is considered intelligent.

(ii)   *his consideration intelligent

    suggesting that small clauses cannot scramble in the necessary way, with the details to be worked out.

[46] Some speakers accept such examples with *-ness* (though not with other suffixes); cf. Pesetsky (1991: 101).

14.13 More on the Absence of Complements to Nouns

One will ultimately need to address, of course, the entire range of examples given by Chomsky (1970: 196) in favor of his idea that nouns take complements just as verbs do. Another type of example that might lend itself to a relative clause analysis would seem to be (90), insofar as there is a close relation to (91).

(90) the reason for his departure

(91) the reason for which he departed

In the case of (92) one can think of (93):

(92) the weather in England

(93) the weather that is found in England

with the possibility of leaving *found* unpronounced in turn related to the hypothesis that (94) is really (95).

(94) They are in Paris.

(95) they are FOUND in Paris

Example (95) might give us a handle on (96) via (97):

(96) *They became in Paris.

(97) Such things were/*became found in Paris.

combined with the fact that in French a normal way of expressing (94) is with the verb 'find'

(98) Ils se trouvent à Paris. ('They REFL find in Paris')

In the realm of possessives, Kayne (1993: sect. 1.2, 1994: 86) proposed that (99)

(99) a friend of yours

does not have (*of*) *yours* as a complement of *friend*, but rather that (*a*) *friend* moves into the specifier position of *of*, starting from a position following *yours*, and similarly for *the sister of that linguist* and other instances involving *of*. Possessives such as *you(r)* in (99) may originate in a (non-adpositional) specifier position above and outside the projection of the noun (*friend*) or as the object of a (silent) adposition;[47] in either case the noun *friend* itself will have no complement.

[47] See Szabolcsi (1983, 1994) and den Dikken (1997). The presence of a special possessive morpheme in Hungarian (cf. perhaps English *'s*) may reflect the possessor being neither the complement nor the

In the same vein, there may be a close relation between (100) and the relative clause structure in (101):

(100)   the way to Paris

(101)   the way in which to go to Paris

In this case (100) will contain a silent GO of the sort shown to be needed elsewhere by van Riemsdijk (2002).

There may also be a close relation between (102) and (103)

(102)   He's in the habit of refusing.

(103)   He refuses out of habit.

In other words, *the habit of refusing* may involve relativization starting from (104) with the *of* in (102) akin to that of (56)/(57), as well as to that of (105), which is itself a relative clause structure based on *in fact* (i.e. on "IN fact"), essentially parallel to (23) and (56)/(57).

(104)   refusing OUT OF habit

(105)   the very fact of his refusing

Although English readily allows DPs of the form (106), these are plausibly reduced relatives, perhaps of the sort discussed by Emonds (1976: 167).

(106)   the book on the table

In summary of this section and the two before it, the antisymmetry/anti-optionality-based approach pursued here leads to the expectation that nouns, unlike verbs, will not have complements. If so, reanalyses of Chomsky's (1970: 196) examples of the sort just suggested should turn out to be on the right track.[48]

14.14 More on Possessives

The question of possessives broached at (99) is indirectly relevant to the question of derived nominals mentioned at (50). Like *removal* is *assassination*, as in:

specifier of the possessee, parallel to the idea that the agent is neither the complement nor the specifier of the lexical verb (as opposed to being the specifier of little v, as in much recent work).

I take this parallelism to extend to "obligatoriness." Just as agents are sometimes obligatory, e.g. with *destroy* (on passives, see Collins 2005), so, sometimes, are possessors, e.g. with *for John's sake*, as discussed by Barker (2005), despite *John* not being either complement or specifier (cf. (21)) of *sake*.

[48] The pervasiveness of relatives from the text viewpoint recalls Koopman (2003, 2005), as does Kihm's (2000) revival of the idea that possessives originate in relatives.

(107)   They were witness to the assassination of the prime minister.

where we can take *-ion* to play the role of *-al*, and attribute to (107) a derivation like that given in (53)/(54). Seemingly very close to (107) is (108):

(108)   They were witness to the murder of the prime minister.

which differs in that there is no visible suffix comparable to *-ion/-al*. Let us, then, take there to be an unpronounced one, as in:

(109)   … murder -ION of…

That an unpronounced derivational suffix of this sort is not automatically available is suggested by the contrast between (108) and (110) (and similarly if either of the *the*s is replaced by *a* or if *the prime minister* is replaced by *him*).

(110)   *They were witness to the punch of the prime minister.

With *punch*, as opposed to *murder*, an object interpretation of the DP following *of* seems impossible. (Irrelevantly to the present discussion, a subject interpretation of a lexical DP following *of* is to some extent possible.) Like *punch*, and unlike *murder*, are *slap*, *kick*, *pinch*, *tug*, *shove*, *push*, *kiss*, and *hug*, all of which lack a visible suffix.

Recalling that *-al* plays a key role in the derivation (53)/(54), a natural proposal is that (110) is excluded precisely because *punch* (and similarly for *slap*, etc.) could not co-occur with a silent counterpart of *-al* (even if *punch* were verbal). Without any counterpart of *-al*, the relative clause type derivation given in (53)/(54) could not go through in the case of (110). By standard assumption, in the absence of relativization a bare verb phrase cannot be embedded directly under *the* either. That leaves the option of taking *the prime minister* in (110) to be the complement of nominal *punch*. But that option, too, is excluded, if nouns take no complements.

The availability, in the object interpretation, of (111) suggests that *-ing* can play the role of *-al* or *-ion*.

(111)   They were witness to the punching of the prime minister.

Similar to (108) vs. (110) is the contrast between (112) and (113):

(112)   The desire to win is widespread.

(113)   *The want to win is widespread.

The latter can be excluded parallel to (110) if *want*, like *punch*, can have no silent suffix of the *-al/-ion* sort.[49] If it cannot, then no derivation of the relative

---

[49] As opposed to with a (partially) different sense of *want*, here similar to *lack*.

(i) for want of a good idea

clause sort is available. Nor can *to win* be the complement (or specifier) of nominal *want*, since by hypothesis nouns take no complements (or specifiers). The admissibility of (112), with *desire*, indicates that *desire* is like *murder* in allowing a silent counterpart of *-al/-ion*. (Like *want* are *love* and *like*.)[50] Although why *murder*, *desire*, etc. allow a silent suffix and the others not remains to be understood, it seems plausible to interpret (110) and (113) as direct reflections of the inability of nouns to take complements.

A problem may appear to arise if we bring together this discussion of (110) with a version of the Hale–Keyser approach to sentences like (114):

(114)   Somebody punched the prime minister.

According to that approach, (114) must have a silent light verb to which the noun *punch* has incorporated. Yet (110) shows that nominal *punch* takes no complement. Where, then, does *the prime minister* in (114) come from? A reasonable answer, thinking of (115) with an overt light verb, is that *the prime minister* originates as the possessor of *punch* (in a way licensed by the presence of *give*, which must have no silent counterpart in (110)), in which case it is not an argument of *punch*, much as in the discussion of (99).

(115)   Somebody gave the prime minister a punch.

14.15 Sentential Complements

Ordinary sentential complements, as in (116), appear not to fall under the present discussion.

(116)   They think (that) everything is fine.

Recall however Rosenbaum's (1967) hypothesis that all sentential complements (in English, but his hypothesis is readily generalized to all languages) are associated with *it*, which is sometimes deleted (in present terms, is sometimes silent) and sometimes not, as in (117):

(117)   They'll see to it that everything is in place.

If *it* is a noun, then Rosenbaum's hypothesis brings ordinary sentential complementation close to structures with *the fact that…*, which must

---

[50] Cf. Pesetsky (1991: 99). Note also (i) and (ii):

(i)   His attempt/*try to solve the problem failed.

(ii)   Their hatred/*hate of losing is well known.

Pesetsky (1991) contains a great deal of relevant material that will need to be integrated; similarly for Szabolcsi (1994: Part II).

be relative-clause structures, as in Section 14.10, in which case senten-tial complementation in general must rest on (partly invisible) relative clauses.[51]

If *it* is a determiner, as in Postal (1966), then this does not follow, unless there is necessarily present, in addition to *it*, a silent noun. If there is, then, again, all sentential complementation must involve relative clauses (in all languages).[52]

14.16 Conclusion

The noun–verb distinction may not be a primitive property of the language faculty, but may rather be underlain by antisymmetry/anti-optionality. The execution of this idea as developed here leads to the characterization of nouns as having neither complements nor specifiers. That in turn leads to the conclusion that *the fact that* . . . , derived nominals, and sentential comple-mentation are varieties of relative clause structures.

---

[51] Cf. also Kayne (in press) and Manzini (2007). Both take complementizers in the classic sense of the term not to exist, though in different ways.

[52] On the misleading appearance of what look like sentential complements, see also Caponi-gro and Polinsky (2008). On the absence of complements to nouns in Malayalam, see Jayaseelan (1988).

Notable here is the colloquial (i) (cf. Legate 2002):

(i)   They were saying (like) as how everything was fine.

with *how* arguably a relative pronoun and *as* arguably close to the *as* found in non-standard relatives like (cf. Herrmann 2005):

(ii)   the man as they were talking to

The status of root clauses will depend (in part) on the status of Ross's (1970) performative hypothesis.

Rosenbaum's hypothesis elicits the question why the language faculty would impose the pres-ence of *it* and/or a silent noun. Kayne (1982) suggested, with verbs, adjectives, and preposi-tions in mind, that arguments must be nominal. If that is correct, that might provide the reason.

Infinitives and gerunds that are arguments seem to lie somewhere between derived nominals and the finite complements illustrated in this section (i.e. they must be subtypes of relative clauses). How exactly to integrate them into the present analysis is left open here.

15

What Kind of Computing Device is the Human Language Faculty?

HOWARD LASNIK

The generative power of various models of grammar, a significant topic of investigation in the early days of generative grammar, has entered recent discussions in a variety of ways. The following quote is one instance among many, from a variety of perspectives:

> The capacity to generate a limitless range of meaningful expressions from a finite set of elements differentiates human language from other animal communication systems. Rule systems capable of generating an infinite set of outputs ("grammars") vary in generative power. The weakest possess only local organizational principles, with regularities limited to neighboring units. We used a familiarization/discrimination paradigm to demonstrate that monkeys can spontaneously master such grammars. However, human language entails more sophisticated grammars, incorporating hierarchical structure. Monkeys tested with the same methods, syllables, and sequence lengths were unable to master a grammar at this higher, "phrase structure grammar" level.   Fitch and Hauser (2004)

15.1 Markovian and Non-Markovian Properties in Lower-Level Syntax

I begin with some simple examples of finite-state languages (the first finite, the second infinite), from Chomsky (1957), and graphic representations of the finite-state Markov processes generating them:

(1)   The old man comes/The old men come

(2)

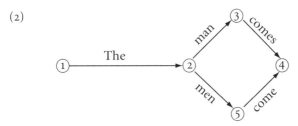

(3)   The man comes/The old man comes/The old old man comes/...

(4)

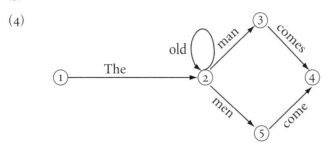

Alongside these, Chomsky presents some non-finite state context-free languages. I present these, and context free ("Σ, F") grammars generating them. (In Chomsky's terminology, Σ is a finite set of initial strings and F a finite set of rewriting rules, each rewriting a single symbol.)

(5)   *ab, aabb, aaabbb,* ... , and in general, all sentences consisting of n occurrences of *a* followed by n occurrences of *b* and only these

(6)   Σ : S
          F: S → aSb
             S → ab

(7)   *aa, bb, abba, baab, aaaa, bbbb, aabbaa, abbbba,* ... , and in general, all sentences consisting of a string *X* followed by the "mirror image" of *X* (i.e., *X* in reverse), and only these

(8)   Σ : S
          F: S → aSa
             S → bSb
             S → aa
             S → bb

Chomsky argues that (portions of) English cannot be described by finite-state grammars:

(9)   a. If S_1, then S_2
          b. Either S_3, or S_4
          c. The man who said that S_5, is arriving today

As Chomsky observes, the crucial property of these examples is not merely that there can be a string of unlimited length between the dependent items (if-then, either-or, man-is). There can also be a string of unlimited length between *the* and *man* in the finite state language (4). Rather, there is recursion between the dependent items.

In [(9)a], we cannot have "or" in place of "then"; in [(9)b], we cannot have "then" in place of "or"; in [(9)c], we cannot have "are" instead of "is". In each of these cases there is a dependency between words on opposite sides of the comma (i.e., "if"-"then", "either"-"or", "man"-"is"). But between the interdependent words, in each case, we can insert a declarative sentence S_1, S_3, S_5, and this declarative sentence may in fact be one of [(9a–c)]... It is clear, then, that in English we can find a sequence $a + S_1 + b$, where there is a dependency between a and b, and we can select as S_1 another sequence containing $c + S_2 + d$, where there is a dependency between c and d, then select as S_2 another sequence of this form, etc. A set of sentences that is constructed in this way... will have all of the mirror image properties of [(7)] which exclude [(7)] from the set of finite state languages.   (Chomsky 1957: 22)

Morris Halle (1968 class lecture) presents another example:

(10)   anti^n missile^{n+1} (n *anti*'s followed by n+1 *missile*'s)

(11) $\Sigma : W$
          $F : W \rightarrow$ anti W missile
              $W \rightarrow$ missile

Σ, F grammars are wonderfully capable of handling languages with the properties of those in (5), (7), and (10). Further, they can easily generate all finite state (E) languages as well.

(12)

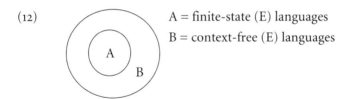

A = finite-state (E) languages

B = context-free (E) languages

The fundamental descriptive advantage of PS grammars compared to finite-state grammars is that PS grammars can pair up things that are indefinitely far apart, and separated by dependencies without limit. The way they do it is by introducing symbols that are never physically manifested: the non-terminal symbols. That is, they automatically introduce structure, as graphically represented in the tree diagram of a sentence from language (5):

(13)

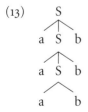

I return to this important consideration.

There is actually a certain irony that arises at this point. While languages abstractly like (5) and (7) were presented by Chomsky as motivating the move from finite state description to Σ, F description, he did not actually use the crucial relevant properties of Σ, F grammars in his linguistic work at the time. The relevant property is, of course, unbounded self-embedding. However, the theory of Chomsky (1955), assumed in Chomsky (1957), has no "recursion in the base." Instead, it is the transformational component that accounts for the infinitude of language. This point is only hinted at in Chomsky (1957: 80), but had been fully developed in Chomsky (1955: 518, 526).

One of the major benefits of Σ, F description is that, unlike finite-state description, it automatically and unavoidably provides sentences with structure. This is overwhelmingly positive since, alongside infinitude, constituent structure is the most fundamental and universal property of human languages. But there are rare exceptions, as discussed by Chomsky (1961: 15) and Chomsky and Miller (1963: 298). One of the most striking ones is what Chomsky called "true coordination" as in (3), repeated here.

(14)   The man comes/The old man comes/The old old man comes/ . . .

Chomsky states, for this and for certain other cases, "Immediate constituent analysis has been sharply and, I think, correctly criticized as in general imposing too much structure on sentences." That is, there is no evident syntactic, semantic, or phonological motivation for a structure in which, say, each *old* modifies the remaining sequence of *old*s plus *man*, as in (15), or some such. (with irrelevant details omitted).

(15)

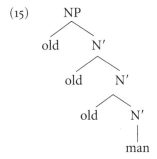

Preferable might be something like:

(16)

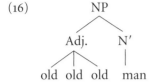

Chomsky mentions a similar case:

(17)   the man was old, tired, tall . . . , but friendly

He says

The only correct P-marker would assign no internal structure at all within the sequence
of coordinated items. But a constituent structure grammar can accommodate this
possibility only with an infinite number of rules; that is, it must necessarily impose
further structure, in quite an arbitrary way.   (Chomsky, 1961: 15)

Chomsky (1963: 298) present a very similar argument:

a constituent-structure grammar necessarily imposes too rich an analysis on sentences because of features inherent in the way P-markers are defined for such
sentences.

With respect to an example identical to (17) in all relevant respects, they
say:

In order to generate such strings, a constituent-structure grammar must either impose
some arbitrary structure (e.g., using a right recursive rule), in which case an incorrect structural description is generated, or it must contain an infinite number of
rules. Clearly, in the case of true coordination, by the very meaning of the term,
no internal structure should be assigned at all within the sequence of coordinate
items.

The conclusion of Chomsky and of Chomsky and Miller: we need to
go beyond the power of Σ, F description to adequately describe natural
languages. In particular, the model is augmented by a transformational
component.

    Chomsky (1955) had, of course, already shown in great detail how trans-
formations can provide natural accounts of phenomena that can only be
described in cumbersome and unrevealing ways (if at all) by Σ, F grammars.
But he had little to say there about the "too much structure" problem we
are now considering. Chomsky (1961) and Chomsky and Miller (1963) don't
have a lot to say either, beyond the implication that transformations will
solve the problem. That is, we need to move up the power hierarchy. In
fact, as already mentioned, Chomsky (1955) had already claimed that there

is no recursion in the Σ, F component, the transformational component (in particular generalized transformations (GTs)) being responsible in toto for infinitude.

Chomsky discussed several aspects of the coordination process, though without actually giving a precise formulation of the relevant transformation(s). It is interesting to note that all the examples discussed in Chomsky (1955) involve coordination of two items, as in (18).

(18)   John was sad and tired

For such cases, it is relatively straightforward to formulate an appropriate generalized transformation, even if, as claimed by Chomsky (1961: 134), GTs are strictly binary (an idea that is important in Chomsky's recent work, as in this quote, "arguably restriction of computational resources limits n for Merge to two," from Chomsky (2008)). As an example, he gives "John is old and sad" from "John is old" "John is sad," with resulting structure (19).

(19)

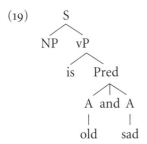

Chomsky and Miller also seem to assume binarity, at least in one place in their discussion:

The basic recursive devices in the grammar are the generalized transformations that produce a string from a *pair* [emphasis mine] of underlying strings.

(Chomsky and Miller 1963: 304)

It is not entirely clear what is supposed to happen when we have multiple items coordinated, as in the phenomena principally under discussion here, or for example in (20):

(20)   old and sad and tired

One possibility is that we would preserve the structure of "old and sad" in (19) and create a higher structure incorporating "and tired."

(21)

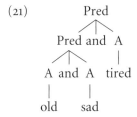

Or, somewhat revising (19):

(22)

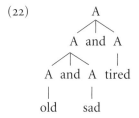

Another possibility is a right branching analogue:

(23)

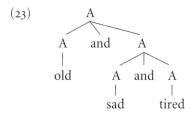

But any of these would run afoul of Chomsky's argument: in general, we do not want that extra structure.

Yet another possibility, one that would yield the desired "flatness," arises if we relax the binarity requirement. Chomsky and Miller seemingly countenance this possibility in at least one place in their discussion:

> We now add to the grammar a set of operations called *grammatical transforma-tions*, each of which maps an *n*-tuple [emphasis mine] of *P*-markers (*m*) into a new *P*-marker. (Chomsky and Miller 1963: 299)

Then a GT could be formulated to coordinate three items (alongside the GT coordinating two items). But, as already noted, there is no limit on the number of items that can be coordinated—Chomsky's original point. So this solution merely replaces one untenable situation with another: in place of an infinite number of phrase structure rules, one for each number of coordinated items, we have an infinite number of generalized transformations.

Thus, moving up the power hierarchy ultimately does not help in this instance. In a manner of speaking, what we really want to do is move *down* the hierarchy. Finite-state Markov processes give flat objects, as they impose no structure. But that is not quite the answer either. While it would work fine for coordination of terminal symbols, phrases can also be coordinated, and, again, with no upper bound. Alongside (24), we find (25).

(24)   John and Bill and Fred and ...

(25)   The old man and the young man and the boy and ...

We need a sort of higher order flatness.

Chomsky and Miller (1963: 298) consider, but reject, an extension of constituent structure grammar to yield such flatness. Their extension is, as far as I can tell, equivalent to the so-called Kleene-* device of Kleene (1956). The specific instance they give is:

(26)   Predicate → Adj^n and Adj (n ≥ 1)

Chomsky and Miller indicate that there are "many difficulties involved in formulating this notion so that descriptive adequacy may be maintained. . . ." But they do not elaborate on this point. It would surely be interesting to explore this, but that project will have to wait for further research.

15.2 Markovian and Non-Markovian Properties in Higher-Level Syntax

15.2.1 *Trace deletion: Subjacency vs. ECP (Chomsky 1991, Chomsky and Lasnik 1993)*

Markovian vs. non-Markovian properties have also been discussed with respect to transformational derivations. Typically, transformational derivations were assumed to be Markovian: the determination of applicability of a transformation to a given derived phrase marker depended solely on the formulation of the transformation and that current derived phrase marker. In passing, I note that even in the earliest transformational generative work there were occasional exceptions. For example, Chomsky (1957) indicated of his *wh*-transformation that it is conditional on his subject–auxiliary inversion one. This was to exclude sentences such as (27), with no inversion in a matrix *wh*-question (a puzzle that persists to this day).

(27)   *Who you will see [cf. Who will you see]

On this account, at the point of application of the *wh* transformation, the prior history of the derivation must be checked to ascertain that the Aux-fronting transformation had already applied. For the most part, though, such "conditional dependence" was avoided, and sometimes explicitly rejected. However, aspects of non-Markovianism continued to crop up occasionally. I turn to two such occasions now.

Chomsky, extending an account by Lasnik and Saito (1984) and Lasnik and Saito (1992) of observations of Huang (1981/82), notes an asymmetry in Subjacency (island-)violating movement. Long movement of an argument is generally much less degraded than corresponding movement of an adjunct:

(28)   ??Who do you wonder [$_{CP}$ whether [$_{IP}$ John said [$_{CP}$ t' [$_{IP}$ t solved the problem]]]]?

(29)   *How do you wonder [$_{CP}$ whether [$_{IP}$ John said [$_{CP}$ t' [$_{IP}$ Mary solved the problem t]]]]?

Chomsky's account of this asymmetry is in terms of the theory of economy. I briefly summarize the relevant concepts here. First, the level of LF must satisfy the principle of Full Interpretation (FI). This principle, introduced in Chomsky (1986), is parallel to economy of derivation. Just as economy of derivation demands that there be no superfluous steps in derivations, FI requires that there be no superfluous symbols in representations. In particular, every element in an LF representation must be "legitimate." The legitimate LF objects are (30a) and (30b):

(30)   a. Uniform chains (all of whose members are in A-positions; A$'$-positions; or X^0-positions)

   b. Operator-variable pairs.

By economy, the deletion operation is possible only to turn an illegitimate LF object into a legitimate one. Deletion in the chain (*Who*, t', t) in (28) is permissible since the chain is neither uniform (*Who* and t' are in A$'$-positions, t in an A-position) nor is it an operator–variable *pair*. Thus the trace t', which was the result of excessively long movement, can be deleted, yielding an operator-variable pair. More generally, in the case of successive-cyclic A$'$-movement of an argument, an intermediate trace (starred or otherwise) can (in fact must) be deleted in LF, voiding an Empty Category Principle (ECP) violation when the trace to be deleted is starred. On the other hand, long movement as in (29), repeated as (31), will be an ECP violation, since the movement chain in this instance is uniformly A$'$, so economy prevents the deletion of t', the offending trace:

(31) *How do you wonder [CP whether [IP John said [CP *t′* [IP Mary solved
       the problem *t*]]]]?   (*)

Not a great analysis, perhaps, but it has one advantage over existing alternatives: it evidently gets the facts right. The interesting problem that it raises
is that inspection of both the ultimate representation and specific points in
the transformational derivation is necessary to correctly determine the status
of the examples. This is in seeming violation of the usually assumed strictly
Markovian nature of transformational derivations.

15.2.2 *Island-violation amelioration*

This situation discussed in Section 15.2.1 is remarkably reminiscent of one first
discussed by Ross (1969). Ross shows that a particular deletion operation,
which he dubs Sluicing, has a palliative effect on island violations. Example
(32) illustrates Sluicing, and the following examples—all from Ross 1969—
illustrate island violations and their (partial) repair. The judgments are Ross's.

(32) I believe that he bit someone, but they don't know who (I believe that
       he bit).

(33) a. *I believe the claim that he bit someone, but they don't know who I
          believe the claim that he bit. [Complex NP Constraint, noun com-
          plement]

      b. (??) I believe the claim that he bit someone, but they don't know
         who.

(34) a. *Irv and someone were dancing together, but I don't know who Irv
          and were dancing together. [Coordinate Structure Constraint]

      b. (??) Irv and someone were dancing together, but I don't know who.

(35) a. *She kissed a man who bit one of my friends, but Tom doesn't realize
          which one of my friends she kissed a man who bit. [Complex NP
          Constraint, relative clause]

      b. (??)She kissed a man who bit one of my friends, but Tom doesn't
         realize which one of my friends.

(36) a. *That he'll hire someone is possible, but I won't divulge who that
          he'll hire is possible. [Sentential Subject Constraint]

      b. (??)That he'll hire someone is possible, but I won't divulge who.

   Ross argues that the phenomenon of island-violation repair provides "evidence of the strongest sort that the theoretical power of [global] derivational

constraints is needed in linguistic theory" (Ross 1969: 277) [that is, that derivations are non-Markovian].

(37) If a node is moved out of its island, an ungrammatical sentence will
result. If the island-forming node does not appear in surface structure,
violations of lesser severity will (in general) ensue.   (Ross 1969: 277)

Chomsky (1972a) rejects this kind of global derivational constraint, and
suggests that * (# in Chomsky's presentation) is assigned to an island when
it is crossed by a movement operation (the complex NP in (39)).[1] An output
condition forbidding * in surface structures accounts for the deviance of
standard island violations. If a later operation (Sluicing in this case) deletes
a category containing the *-marked item, the derivation is salvaged.

(38)   a. (*)I don't know which children he has plans to send to college.

        b. He has plans to send some of his children to college, but I don't know
            which ones.

(39)   I don't know CP

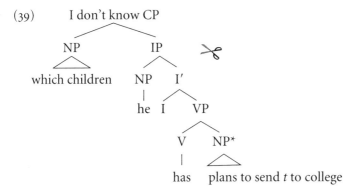

As Lakoff (1972) points out, though, on Ross's judgments substantial globality
still remains (as in the Subjacency vs. ECP phenomenon discussed above).
For Ross, the examples are improved, but still deviant. Neither the step in
the derivation causing the violation nor the ultimate structure suffices to
determine the status of the examples. Both must be inspected.

Chomsky (1972a) briefly addresses this point in his footnote 13, saying

What is at issue is only whether in determining (degree of) deviance, we refer to the
presence of # only in the surface structure or, alternatively, to its presence anywhere in
the derivation as a feature of the category X that is deleted. Thus the issue is one that
belongs to the theory of interpretation of deviant structures.

---

[1] See also Baker and Brame (1972), and, for an opposing view, Lakoff (1970, 1972).

Of course, the theory of interpretation of deviant structures might be exactly what is at issue. How interpretation of structures (deviant or otherwise) interfaces with the syntactic derivation is the fundamental architectural question under investigation here, and in much current work. Strictly cyclic interpretation of the multiple spell-out sort is strictly Markovian, one of its major virtues, but, evidently, a significant source of difficulty as well. How this will play out remains to be seen.

16

Clauses, Propositions, and Phases

RICHARD K. LARSON

The Minimalist Program of Chomsky, (2000a, 2001) conceives the human grammatical faculty as an austere computational device (C_{HL}) spanning articulatory–perceptual (π) and conceptual–intentional (λ) systems, with properties largely determined by this architecture:

$$\pi \leftarrow C_{HL} \rightarrow \lambda$$

Specifically, π and λ are taken impose legibility requirements on C_{HL} insofar as only certain kinds of objects can be "read" at the interface. C_{HL} representations are assumed to be wholly characterized by these interface constraints: they are all and only what they need to be in order to be read by π and λ. Conceptually, therefore, C_{HL} constitutes something like the minimal bridge between π and λ.

The Minimalist view carries with it the clear expectation that one will find significant properties of linguistic representations, and perhaps of the architecture itself, that can be traced back to π or λ. In this chapter, I suggest that semantic intensionality and its representation in syntax are a promising place to seek such properties. More precisely, I argue the following three central points.

- Natural language seems to project the semantic property of **intensionality** uniquely into the syntactic domain of **clausal complement**, although this can be concealed by grammatical phenomena to some extent.
- Children's mastery of intensionality appears to be crucially tied to mastery of clausal complementation, which also correlates with the development of the child's theory of mind (de Villiers (1995a, b).

Parts of this chapter were presented at the 2000 Rutgers Semantics Workshop and the 2007 USC joint Linguistics and Philosophy Colloquium series, as well as the 2007 Biolinguistics Conference in Santo Domingo. I am grateful to audiences at those events for helpful comments and discussion. I am particularly indebted to Scott Soames for clarifying discussion on the last sections.

- The correlation between intensionality and clausal complementation ("sententialism") plausibly reflects an interface constraint: roughly, that λ inputs propositions from C_{HL} only when these presented in appropriate form.

As I show, these results suggest an attractive view of the current syntactic notion of "phase" quite different from the current one in terms of grammar-extrinsic notions like memory and processing load. Phases can be seen as the point where the language faculty computes propositions for the psychological faculty. I begin by considering some basic points about intensionality and its expression in grammar.

16.1 Intensionality and Grammar

Typical transitive sentences are well known to manifest the following semantic properties: (i) substitution of identically referring object DPs preserves truth; thus if Max met Boris Karloff then it follows that he met William Pratt, given these names refer to the same individual (1a);[1] (ii) presence of a non-referring/non-denoting object yields falsity—thus (1b) must be false given that there are no unicorns; and finally, (iii) indefinite objects must be understood "specifically:" if Max met someone, there must be someone that Max met (1c).

(1)   a. i. Max met [DP Boris Karloff].
         ii. Max met [DP William Pratt].

      b.   Max met [DP a unicorn].

      c.   Max met [DP someone].

The same observations apply to typical intransitives, ditransitives and PP-complement predicates as well (2a–c):

(2)   a. [DP Boris Karloff]/[DP William Pratt] sneezed/arrived.

      b. Max gave [DP a unicorn] to Mary.

      c. Max talked to [DP someone].

By contrast, as Frege (1893) famously observed, in clausal complement constructions these properties are all suspended. Substitution of co-referring DPs in the complement need not preserve truth (3a); presence of a non-referring/non-denoting term need not induce falsity (3b); and indefinites can be understood "non-specifically": Max can believe that someone is

---

[1] "Boris Karloff" is the stage name taken by Mr. William Pratt, who starred in a number of well-known horror films from the 1930s including *Frankenstein*, *The Mummy*, and *The Black Cat*.

approaching without there being a particular person about whom Max has a belief (3c).

(3)   a. i. Max believed [$_{CP}$ that [$_{DP}$ Boris Karloff] was approaching]].
       ii. Max believed [$_{CP}$ that [$_{DP}$ William Pratt] was approaching]].

       b.   Max believed [$_{CP}$ that [$_{DP}$ a unicorn] was approaching]].

       c.   Max believed [$_{CP}$ that [$_{DP}$ someone] was approaching]].

These properties are manifest not only with verbs like *believe*, but in fact across the whole range of predicates selecting a cognitive agent and a complement clause, including adjectives, as in (4):

(4)   a. It was apparent/desirable to Max [$_{CP}$that[$_{DP}$BK]/[$_{DP}$WP] was approaching]].

       b. It was apparent/desirable to Max [$_{CP}$that[$_{DP}$a unicorn] was approaching]].

       c. It was apparent/desirable to Max [$_{CP}$that[$_{DP}$someone] was approaching]].

These results give rise to an interesting hypothesis about intensionality and its expression in grammar, namely that semantic intensionality arises exactly in the context of clausal complementation:

Sententialist Hypothesis:
Semantic intensionality ↔ Clausal complementation

This correlation seems natural from a general point of view. Intuitively, in examples like (3) and (4), our explanation for why substitution can fail, why non-denoting terms need not induce falsity, and why indefinites can be read nonspecifically, turns on how individuals represent the world to themselves. In explaining how (3a.i) and (3a.ii) might have different truth-conditions, for example, we might appeal to the fact that Max knows the individual in question only under the name *Boris Karloff*, not *William Pratt*. Hence representing his belief with a clause involving *William Pratt* gets something wrong: it presents the world in a way that Max would not represent it to himself, etc. The category that represents states of the world, either truly or falsely, is uncontroversially the clause. Hence intensionality has its natural home in the clause.

As attractive as this correlation may appear to be between semantics (intensionality) and grammar (clausal status), it nonetheless appears vulnerable to a range of counterexamples. Specifically there are predicates like *want*, *need*, *imagine*, *expect*, and *look for*, which resemble transitives in their surface grammar, but nonetheless show all the earmarks of intensionality:

(5) a. Max wanted/imagined/needed/looked-for [DPBK]/[DPWP].

  b. Max   wanted/imagined/needed/looked-for   [DPa unicorn]/[DP   an assistant].

Thus it seems that Max can want Boris Karloff without wanting William Pratt. It seems he can need a unicorn, even if there are none to be had. And it seems that he can look for an assistant, without there be any particular individual that he is seeking. Because of their combination of properties, predicates like these are often referred to as Intensional Transitive Verbs (ITVs).

  Interestingly, beginning with McCawley (1974) and Ross (1976), a number of authors have argued that in examples like (5a, b) appearances are deceiving—that the latter are in fact covert clausal complement constructions despite their superficial transitive syntax. Suggestive evidence for this view, coming from temporal modification, was observed by Kajita (cited in Ross 1976). Note first that in clausal complement constructions like (6), the sentence-final temporal adverb *next week* is ambiguous depending on whether it is understood as modifying *need/want* or *have*. This ambiguity can be understood as a structural one, reflecting whether the adverb is attached in the matrix clause (7a), or the embedded clause (7b):[2]

(6) Max will need/want to have a bicycle **next week**.   (ambiguous)

(7) a. Max will need/want [PRO to have a bicycle] next week
  b. Max will need/want [PRO to have a bicycle next week]

Observe now that the intensional transitive counterpart of (6), namely (8), shows the very same ambiguity:

(8) Max will need/want a bicycle next week.   (ambiguous)

Given the parallel ambiguity in (6) and (8), it is sensible to propose a parallel structural analysis. Thus (8) should involve a covert clausal complement, with a silent version of the verb *have*, again affording two possible structural attachment sites for the adverb (9a, b). Note carefully that the ambiguity in question is not one generally available with transitives. The example in (10) shows no such ambiguity, for instance.

---

[2] Here PRO is a silent (unpronounced) pronoun with the approximate content of *himself* (cf. *Max wants himself to have a bicycle next week*).

(9)   a. [Max will need/want [$_{CP}$ PRO HAVE a bicycle tomorrow]].

    b. [Max will need/want [$_{CP}$ PRO HAVE a bicycle] tomorrow]].

(10)   Max will ride/repair a bicycle tomorrow.   (unambiguous)

Accordingly, it seems reasonable to attribute the possibility of ambiguity with *want/need* to a special structural possibility open to so-called intensional transitive verbs—one associated with clausal complementation.

16.2 Cross-Linguistic Expression of Intensionality

The Sententialist Hypothesis, coupled with the possibility of covert clausal complementation, suggests an interesting general prediction, namely, that the superficial objects of ITVs should not pattern like the objects of ordinary TVs. We should find differences suggesting a hidden clause. More specifically, we should find that patterns observed with ITVs should correlate with the possibilities for covert clausal complementation in a given language. Below I consider a number of brief case studies suggesting that this prediction may be on the right track.

16.2.1 *Case study:* Want *and verbs of volition*

On the view suggested above, the analysis of (11a) is as in (11b), with elliptical subject and null V:

(11)   a. Polly wants a cracker.

    b. Polly wants [PRO TO HAVE a cracker].

On this analysis, *want* is strictly clause-taking. Surface transitivity arises through null *HAVE*, which takes the surface object as its object. This proposal makes two interesting predictions:

- (11b) will be able to appear as (11a) only in languages allowing null *HAVE*.
- (11b) will surface as (11a) only if the expression of possession follows the pattern of *have*.

Let us consider these predictions in the light of facts from Eskimo and Japanese.

16.2.1.1 *Affixal want in Inuktitut (Johns 1999).*   Languages of the Inuit family are polysynthetic: predicates of complex clauses collapse together into a single word-like element. Thus in (12) the concept of "want-to-sleep" is expressed with a complex lexical form.

(12)   a.   Labrador Inuit
      *sugusik   sini-**guma**-juk.*
      child(ABS) sleep-want-INTR.PART.3S
      'The child wants to sleep.'

    b.   Quainirmiut Inuit
      nutaraq   hini-**guaq**-tuq.
      child(ABS) sleep-want-INTR.PART.3S
      'The child wants to sleep.'

According to Woodbury (1977), Smith (1982), and Baker (1988) (among others), such sentences are underlyingly bi-clausal, bound morphemes occupying the head positions occupied in non-polysynthetic languages; for example (12b) would be as in (13):

(13)

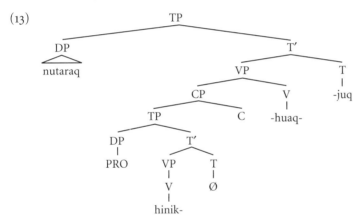

The polysynthetic character of these languages appears to follow (at least in part) from the status of elements like *-guma-* and *-huaq-* as affixes/clitics, that is, as phonologically dependent elements that must be supported by some non-null V form, similarly to the behavior of tense in English (see Baker 1996).

Now, interestingly, although Inuit allows (the equivalent of) "want to have DP" (14a, b), it does not allow (the equivalent of) "want DP":

(14)   a.   Labrador
      savi-**t**-**guma**-vunga.
      knife-get-want-INTR.INDIC.1S
      'I want to get a knife.'

    b. Quainirmiut
       pana-**taa**-**ruaq**-tunga.
       knife-get-want-INTR.PART.1S
       'I WANT TO GET A KNIFE.'

(15) a. Labrador
       *savi-**guma**-vunga.
       knife-get-want-INTR.INDIC.1S
       'I want a knife.'

    b. Quainirmiut
       *pana-**ruaq**-tunga.
       knife-get-want-INTR.PART.1S
       'I want a knife.'

Why this restriction? Why should Inuit be restricted in this way? Under the Sententialist Hypothesis, the polysynthetic nature of the languages suggests a clue. Suppose the affixes -*guma*- and -*huaq*- mean 'want', and as such are strictly clause-taking. To derive the equivalent of *want*-DP, they would need to affix to null *HAVE*. But as affixes, -*guma*- and -*huaq*- require non-null phonological support; bound elements cannot be supported by a null stem (Lasnik 1981). It would follow, then, that the only way to express 'want to have' would be via an overt lexical V affix as in (14a, b); (15a, b) would be disallowed. This is exactly what we observe.

16.2.1.2 *Volitional Vs in Japanese*   The usual case-marking pattern in Japanese is that subjects are marked with with -*ga*, and objects are marked with -*o* (16). However, with Japanese volitional Vs, subjects are marked with -*ga*, and the object is *ga*-marked too. *O*-marking is disfavored (17):

(16) Japanese
     Taroo-**ga**   pizza-**o**   tabetta.
     Taroo-NOM pizza-ACC ate
     'Taroo ate a/the pizza.'

(17) a. Taroo-ga   **okane -ga**/*?-**o** hoshii.
       Taroo-NOM money   -NOM/-ACC want
       'Taroo wants money.'

    b. Taroo-ga   **konpyuutaa -ga** /*?-**o**   hitsuyoo-da.
       Taroo-NOM computer   -NOM/-ACC need-COP
       'Taroo needs a/the computer.'

Why this case pattern? Why do objects of verbs counterpart to *want* and *need* show with nominative marking? Endo, Kitagawa, and Yoon (1999) make the interesting proposal that the data in (17) reflect the case pattern of a hidden clause.

The languages of the world standardly express possession through two basic patterns (Benveniste 1960; Freeze 1992). One is a transitive *have*-type construction. English and German exemplify this pattern; see (18). The second, and typologically more common, pattern is an intransitive, copular *be*-type construction; Hungarian and a minority dialect of German exemplify this possibility; see (19):

(18)   Transitive *have*-type construction

    a. John has a hat

    b. German
        Ich   habe einen Hut.
        I(NOM) have a(ACC) hat
        'I have a hat.'

(19)   Copular *be*-type construction

    a. Hungarian
        Péter-nek   van egy ernyö-je.
        Peter-DAT be an umbrella-3s
        'Peter has/owns an umbrella.'

    b. Péter-nél van egy ernyö.
        Peter-LOC be an umbrella
        'Peter has an umbrella with him.'

    c. German
        Mir   ist der   Hut.
        I(DAT)   be the(NOM) hat
        'I have a hat.'

The two patterns for expressing possession differ not only in choice of main verb (*have* vs. *be*) but also in case-marking. The *have*-type construction marks the possessor with nominative and the possessed with accusative as in (20a), whereas in the *be*-construction, the possessor shows up as a PP or in an oblique case, while the possessed is marked with nominative (20b). The two different structures for possession admit two possibilities for a bi-clausal construction expressing "want-to-have"; see (21):

(20)   a. *Have*-type: DP-**NOM** *have* DP-**ACC**

    b. *Be*-type DP-**OBL** *be* DP-**NOM**

(21)   a. DP *wants* [PRO-NOM *to have* DP-ACC]   (*have*-type)

    b. DP *wants* [PRO-OBL *to be* DP-NOM]   (*be*-type)

Observe now that if *be* can be covert, just like *have*, the result will surface as an apparent transitive construction with nominative case-marking on the object:

    DP *wants* [PRO-OBL *TO BE* **DP-NOM**]

Japanese, like German, has both a *have*-type possession construction (*motteiru*) and a *be*-type (*aru*) (22a, b). And both possession constructions can appear overtly under *hoshii* 'want' and *hitsuyoo* 'need' (23a, b):

(22) a. Taroo-wa konpyuutaa-**o** motteiru. (*have*-type)
       Taroo-TOP computer-ACC have
       'Taroo has a computer.'

     b. Taroo-**ni**-wa   konpyuutaa-**ga** aru. (*be*-type)
       Taroo-DAT-TOP computer-ACC be
       'Taroo has a computer.'

(23) a. Watashi-ga Taroo-ga   konpyuutaa *-**ga**/-**o**   motte hoshii.
       I-NOM   Taroo-NOM computer -NOM/-ACC have   want
       'I want Taroo to have a computer.'

     b. Watashi-ga Taroo-ni   konpyuutaa -**ga**/*-**o**   atte hoshii.
       I-NOM   Taroo-DAT computer -NOM/-ACC be   want
       'I want Taroo to have a computer.'

Endo et al. (1999) propose that the Japanese case pattern in (17a, b) (repeated below as (24a, b)) reflects a silent version of the *be* possession-type:

(24) a. Taroo-ga   [PRO-DAT **okane-ga**   ARU] hoshii.
       Taroo-NOM PRO-DAT   money-NOM be   want
       'Taroo wants money.'

     b. Taroo-ga   [PRO-DAT **konpyuutaa-ga** ARU] hitsuyoo-da.
       Taroo-NOM PRO-DAT   computer-NOM be   need-COP
       'Taroo needs a/the computer.'

Thus if they are correct, case-marking with Japanese volitional verbs provides evidence for hidden clausal complementation.

16.2.2 *Case study:* fear *and psych-verbs*

In the case of English volitional verbs like *want* and *need*, the hidden-clause analyzes the surface object as the underlying object of an embedded verb *HAVE* (25a, b).

(25) a. John needs **a vampire**.

b. John needs [PRO TO HAVE **a vampire**].

Consider now so-called psychological (or psych-)predicates such as *fear*, *admire*, and *love*. These also show familiar intensionality effects in examples like (26); thus (26a) can apparently differ in truth conditions depending on choice of name; likewise (26b) can be true despite there being no vampires. Nonetheless, an analysis of the surface object as an underlying object does not seem correct. We would be much more inclined to understand (27a), for example, along lines like (27b), where the surface object is an underlying subject of some implicit action predicate (*attack, bite,* etc.):

(26)   a. Mary fears [$_{DP}$ **Boris Karloff**]/[$_{DP}$ **William Pratt**].

b. Mary fears [$_{DP}$ **vampires**].

(27)   a. Mary fears sharks.

b. Mary fears [that sharks will attack her/bite her/do something to her].

This point leads to the general expectation that when we have a surface transitive construction involving a psych-V ($\Psi - V$) (see 28a), the surface object (DP2) should be the underlying subject of a covert predicate (PRED), as in (28b):

(28)   a. DP1 $\Psi - V$ DP2

b. DP1 $\Psi - V$ [DP2 PRED]

Thus the "object" in construction (28a) might betray its embedded status by showing unexpected subject properties. There is interesting evidence from Chinese that appears to illustrate this case.

Chinese has psych-verbs like English *fear*, which show an equivalent surface transitive structure (29).

(29)   Zhangsan **haipa** Lisi.
       Zhangsan fear   Lisi
       'Zhangsan fears Lisi.'

But these constructions show an interesting peculiarity. As Cheung and Larson (2006, 2007) observe, both English and Chinese freely passivize normal transitive verbs, for example, canonical verbs of contact (30a, b). However, whereas English *fear* undergoes passive (31a), Chinese *haipa* does not (31b). This result is in fact quite general for Chinese psych-verbs of the *fear*-class; these verbs do not passivize.

(30)   a. Chinese
        Lisi   da-le   Zhangsan.
        Lisi   hit-ASP Zhangsan
        'Lisi hit Zhangsan.'

     b. Zhangsan bei Lisi da-le
        Zhangsan BEI Lisi hit-ASP
        'Zhangsan was hit by Lisi.'

(31)   a. Lisa is feared by John.

     b. *Lisi bei Zhangsan haipa.
        Lisi   BEI Zhangsan fear
        'Lisi is feared by Zhangsan.'

These facts raise a very simple question: why do Chinese and English differ in this way? Why do Chinese *fear*-type psych-verbs resist passive? Interestingly, Huang (1999) has argued that the operation of passive in Chinese involves a very different structure than that of English. Briefly, English passives raise a DP directly to subject position. Thus in (32a) the underlying object *John* is raised to surface subject position. By contrast, Chinese passives involve a construction in which the subject is base-generated in object position and an empty operator raises from the position of the passivized DP and establishes a predication relation with the subject. Thus in (32b) *Zhangsan* is base-generated in subject position and an operator raises from the object position of *da-le* 'hit'. A predication relation is subsequently established between *Zhangsan* and *OP*, linking them. This analysis of Chinese passive is thus analogous to the standard account of English constructions involving *tough* and *easy*, which also involve a gap bound to an empty operator (32c):

(32)   a. John was hit __ by Mary

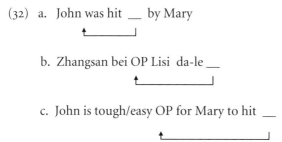

     b. Zhangsan bei OP Lisi da-le __

     c. John is tough/easy OP for Mary to hit __

In effect, Chinese passives involve a *tough*-predicate, *bei*, that is devoid of independent meaning.

    This difference in passivization strategies is significant because the movement of empty-operators in *tough*-constructions (*tough*-movement) is well known to be more sensitive than passive (Cinque 1990). For example, subjects of reduced clauses are passivizable in English, but are not as readily *tough-moveable* (33)–(35). Chinese shows similar restrictions on *bei*-passivization with subjects of reduced clauses (36) and (37):

(33) a. Mary believes/considers John to be intelligent.

　　　b. John is believed/considered __ to be intelligent.

　　　c. *?John is tough/easy to believe/consider __ to be intelligent.

(34) a. Mary saw John talking to Alice.

　　　b. John was seen __ talking to Alice.

　　　c. *John was tough/easy to see __ talking to Alice.

(35) a. Mary made John wear a tux.

　　　b. John was made __ to wear a tux.

　　　c. *John is tough/easy to make __ to wear a tux.

(36) a. Lisis kanjian [Zhangsan jin-le   najia canguanr].
　　　　Lisi saw   Zhangsan enter-ASP that restaurant
　　　　'Zhangsan saw Lisi entering the restaurant.'

　　　b. *Zhangsan bei Lisi kanjian [__ jin-le najia canguanr].
　　　　Zhangsan BEI Lisi see   enter-ASP that restaurant
　　　　'Zhangsan was seen by Lisi entering the restaurant.'

(37) a. Zhangsan rang [Lisi likai].
　　　　Zhangsan let   Lisi leave
　　　　'Zhangsan let Lisi leave.'

　　　b. *Zhangsan bei Lisi rang [__likai].
　　　　Zhangsan BEI Lisi let   leave
　　　　'Zhangsan was allowed by Lisi to leave.'

Cheung and Larson (2006, 2007) further observe that Chinese psych-verbs of the *fear*-class uniformly permit a reduced clause complement (38). In this respect they differ from other psych-verbs—for example, those of the *frighten*-class (39):

(38) a. Zhangsan haipa [Lisi da ta].
　　　　Zhangsan fear   Lisi hit he
　　　　'Zhangsan feared that Lisi would hit him.'

　　　b. Pingping haipa [nazhi gou yao ta].
　　　　Pingping fear   that   dog bite her
　　　　'Pingping feared that the dog would bite her/him.'

(39)   a. Zhangsan gandong Lisi.
           Zhangsan touch   Lisi
           'Zhangsan touched/moved Lisi.'

        b. *Zhangsan gandong [Lisi ku]
           Zhangsan touch   Lisi cry
           'Zhangsan was touched that Lisi cried.'/'Zhangsan moved Lisi to
           tears.'

The hypothesis that Cheung and Larson (2006, 2007) offer is the following: Chinese psych-verbs resist passivization because they are underlyingly
reduced clausal structures, even in their surface "transitive" form. The ill-
formedness in (40a) and (41a) thus has the same source, namely, (40b)
and (41b):

(40)   a. *Lisi bei Zhangsan haipa da ta].
           Lisi BEI Zhangsan fear   hit him
           'Zhangsan fears that Lisi will bite him.'

        b. *Lisi bei [OP Zhangsan haipa [__ da ta]
                      ┗_____┛

(41)   a. *Lisi bei Zhangsan haipa.
           Lisi BEI Zhangsan fear
           'Lisi is feared by Zhangsan.'

        b. *Lisi bei [OP Zhangsan haipa [__PRED]
                      ┗_____┛

If Cheung and Larson (2006, 2007) are correct, these cases thus illustrate
the situation of the surface object of an intensional transitive verb showing
unexpected "subject properties"—in this case with respect to extraction under
passive.

16.2.3 *Case study:* believe-in *and existence*

As a final case study in concealed complementation, consider verbs of belief.
English exhibits two forms of *believe* in which the verbal complement is apparently non-clausal. One is a simple transitive construction (42a); the second is
a PP-complement structure involving the preposition *in* (43a). The difference
in syntactic structure, though apparently small, carries a substantial difference
in meaning. The simple transitive (42a) is extensional, and when it appears
with a human object, its semantics involves deferred reference to some speech

act (cf. (42b)).[3] By contrast, the verb–preposition combination *believe-in* is intensional (43a), with a semantics notionally similar to a clausal counterpart expressing an existence-belief (43b).

(42) a. Gwen **believes** the tooth fairy.   (false; there is no such being!)

   b. Gwen **believes** what the tooth fairy says/said.

(43) a. Gwen **believes in** the tooth fairy.

   b. Gwen **believes** that the tooth fairy **exists**.

The presence of *in* in (43a) and its correlation with an understood "exists" appears to be non-accidental. It is a remarkable fact that many other world languages appear to use a specifically locative element (P or case-marker) for the equivalent of the *believe-in*. Thus Hungarian uses the locative postposition *-ben* 'in' in exactly the same context (44a). German employs the locative preposition *an* 'at'. Russian uses the locative element *v* (44c). And Korean uses a postposition containing a form *-ey* that was historically a locative (44d).

(44) a. Hungarian
      Péter   hisz   Isten-**ben**.
      Peter   believe   God-in(LOC)
      'Peter believes in God.'

   b. German
      Max   glaubt   **an**   Gott
      Max   believes at(LOC)   God
      'Max believes in God.'

   c. Russian
      Olga   verit   **v**   Deda-Moroza.
      Olga   believes in (LOC)
      'Olga believes in Santa Claus.'

   d. Korean
      Nay-ka Jesus-**ey**tayhay mit-nun-ta.
      I-NOM Jesus-about   believe-PRES-DECL
      'I believe in Jesus.' (*ey* in *eytayhay* is originally a locative)

Hungarian displays the link between locativity and existence in an even more revealing way. Hungarian finite clausal complements to *believe* expressing existence claims are introduced by a special complementizer *abban* that includes

---

[3] Transitive *believe* seems to select nominals denoting speech events or parts of them:

(i) John believed **those words/Mary's words/Jim's allegations/Bill's claims**. Thus in the case where the object is a person, the latter is understood in terms of something they said, claimed, alleged, etc.

a locative element. This is not the case with the non-existential complement (45b).

(45)   a. Hungarian

Péter hisz   **abban** hogy Isten létezik.
Peter believe in-that COMP God exists

'Peter believes that God exists.'

b. Péter hiszi   hogy Petra okos.
Peter believe COMP Petra smart

'Peter believes that Petra is smart.'

Again, these simple facts raise some equally simple, but intriguing questions.
Intensionality with *believe* appears to be tied to existence propositions; how
and why is correlated with the appearance of locative elements—prepositions,
postpositions, complementizers, and particles? What is the link among these
things?

In fact, it is a familiar typological generalization that existential and locative constructions consistently pattern alike across the world's languages. The
Hindi example in (46) is typical. The locative construction (46a) and the
existential (46b) are distinguished only by word order.[4]

(46)   a. mai bhaarat-mee thaa.
I   India-in   COP-SG.MASC.PAST
'I was in India.'

b. kamree-mee aadmii hai.
room-in   man   COP-SG.MASC.PRES
'There is a man in the room.'

Generative semanticists argued that existential sentences derived from locatives (Fillmore 1968; Lyons 1967), and indeed the existential *be* copula does
not normally occur in English without a locative or temporal complement (cf.
*John is *(in Rome)*). Attention to such facts has regularly led to the proposal
that existentials are underlyingly a form of locative.[5]

Suppose this basic viewpoint is correct: that existentials are a form of
locative. Then a tempting hypothesis is that the locative element in (43a),
(44a–d) and (45) is a grammatical reflex of the status of these constructions
as existentials, whether covert or explicit. More specifically, observe that the
preposition *in* occurs in a nominalized version of existential sentences (47a,

---

[4] These examples are drawn from Freeze (1992).

[5] Kahn (1966) argues that location in space is in fact the basic picture of existence for Greek
philosophy: "whatever is, is somewhere; whatever is nowhere, is nothing (p. 258)."

b); the verbal form *exist* is matched by the nominalized form *be-in-existence*. This possibility is also observed with *believe*, as shown in (48):

(47)   a.   i.   Three copies of this manuscript **exist**.
            ii.   There **exist** three copies of this manuscript..
       b.   i.   Three copies of this manuscript **are in existence**.
            ii.   There **are** three copies of this manuscript **in existence**.

(48)   a.   Gwen **believes in** the tooth fairy.

       b.   Gwen **believes** the tooth fairy to **exist**.

       c.   Gwen **believes** the tooth fairy (to be) **in existence**.

Then one concrete idea might be to analyze the *in* of (48a) as the *in* of (48c), dislocated by movement; in other words, to derive (48a) from (48c) by raising of *in* to a functional position F. On this picture, PP-complement *believe* would take as its complement an existential "small clause" containing *in*. Along with covert *BE*, we would thus also have its null nominal counterpart *EXISTENCE* (49):

(49)

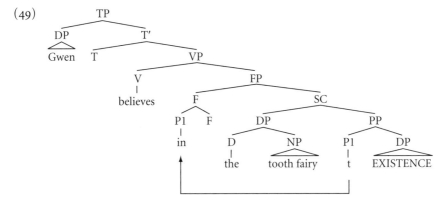

This proposal is simply one (very tentative) execution of an analysis relating (43a) to (43b). But it is sufficient to illustrate how such an account might go, which takes the PP-complement form of *believe* to conceal a clausal complement structure.

16.3 Development of Intensionality[6]

The facts surveyed above suggest that intensionality is tied to clausal complementation insofar as where we find the first we find the second. There is interesting evidence from developmental psychology which

---

[6] I am particularly indebted in this section to the illuminating discussion in Segal (1998).

seems to show a version of this correlation in the opposite direction as well—specifically that a child's grasp of intensionality is part of the general development of its "theory of mind," and that the latter in turn hinges on the development of linguistic structures associated with clausal complementation.

One apparent milestone in children's cognitive development is the point at which they grasp that other humans have minds capable of entertaining thoughts different than their own, including false thoughts (Perner 1991; Wellman 1990). This capacity typically appears around age 3–4, as revealed by performance on so-called false-belief tests. In a typical test paradigm, a child is told a story and given accompanying questions like the following:

(50)   Jill puts her doll in a drawer, and goes out to play. While Jill is outside, and cannot see, Jack comes in and moves the doll to a box.

    Questions: (i) Where does Jill think her doll is?
                      (ii) Where will Jill look first?

Before 3–4 years of age, children identify the box—the doll's genuine location—as the place that Jill will look. They apparently fail to separate Jill's beliefs from their own, and hence answer that Jill will look where they know the doll to be. By contrast, after 3–4 years, they identify the drawer, the site where Jill left it, as the place she will look. They have apparently grasped that Jill may have a false representation, which is different from their own correct understanding of the situation. This cognitive achievement appears to be part of a broader transition involving the understanding of misrepresentation, including pictures that represent falsely, etc.

De Villiers and Fitneva (1996) offer interesting evidence that development of intensionality in children is tied to understanding of false belief. They record experiments in which preschoolers were presented stories and accompanying test questions like this:

(51)   Mother put candy in a silver box as a birthday present for her daughter Sarah. Mother placed the box on the table. Sarah walked into the room and saw the silver box. She thought: "I wonder what that silver box is?"

    Questions: (i) Does Sarah know the silver box is on the table?
                      (ii) Does Sarah know the candy is on the table?

De Villiers and Fitneva (1996) report that children who fail the false-belief test also permit substitution and treat *know* as transparent. In other words, they answer "yes" to both of the test questions, allowing free substitution of the co-referring terms *the silver box* and *the candy*. By contrast, children who pass the false-belief test disallow substitution and treat *know* as referentially opaque. That is, they answer "yes" to the first question (since the little girl sees the box and observes that it is silver), but "no" to the second question (since the little girl does not know the silver box is also the candy). Tager-Flusberg (2000) conducted a similar experiment with autistic and mentally retarded subjects and obtained similar results: those subjects who failed false belief tests also treated propositional attitude verb contexts as transparent/nonintensional.

Intriguingly, children who fail false belief tests also seem to show a weak grasp of clausal complement grammar, appearing to treat complement questions as if unembedded. Thus de Villiers, Roeper, and Vainikka (1990), Roeper and de Villiers (1994), and de Villiers (1998) report that children in this stage very typically respond to questions like (52a) as if the question being posed were the unembedded (52b). More exactly, in a situation where the things that Mary bought and the things she said they bought are different, they answer with the things actually purchased:

(52) a. What did Mary say she bought?

 b. What did Mary buy?

A similar result is reported by Tager-Flusberg (1997) in reference to the false-belief story and question shown in (53):

(53) Mommy told Johnny that she would make hamburgers for dinner. Johnny goes out to play. Mommy changes the menu and cooks spaghetti instead.
 Question: Does Johnny know what Mommy made for dinner?

Tager-Flusberg (1997) reports that five of eight children who failed the false-belief test answered "spaghetti" to the test question. In other words, they appeared to treat the latter as if it contained the unembedded, independent interrogative *What did Mommy make for dinner?*

These results suggest a correlation between mastery of clausal complement grammar and development of "theory of mind" as revealed by false-belief test results. Nonetheless, in and of themselves they do not show a direct dependence between the phenomena. They are, for example, compatible with a maturationalist view in which general cognitive development, unfolding at the appropriate time, separately underwrites both of these achievements: understanding of embedding grammar and understanding of other minds.

Interestingly, there is evidence to suggest this broad maturationalist view, however natural, is not correct, and that linguistic development is in some way the key factor responsible for "triggering" theory of mind. Gale et al. (1996), Tager-Flusberg (2000), and de Villiers (2000) investigate the development of theory of mind in oral deaf children of average-to-high intelligence, exhibiting normal social function. By standard tests, these subjects were at the normal stage of cognitive development for their age; however, due to their profound deafness, their language development was severely delayed (2–3 yrs). Gale et al. and de Villiers found that their subjects' theory of mind development, as measured by performance on false belief tests, was correspondingly delayed. Apparently, the connection between linguistic development and theory of mind is more direct than a general, maturational view would suggest.

Summarizing our results in this section, the following broad picture emerges. At approximately 3 years of age, children do not grasp sentence embedding, they do not pass false-belief tests, and they do not show knowledge of referential opacity/intensionality. At 3–4 years, embedding of clausal complements develops and theory of mind also appears; children can now ascribe false or incomplete beliefs to others, and they understand opacity in complements of attitude Vs. The linguistic development seems to constitute a precondition of the theory of mind development; if the former is delayed, including by factors specifically involving language development, the latter is delayed correspondingly.

These results strongly suggest that grammar—specifically clausal complementation—is in some way "enabling" children's theory of mind. An attractive proposal, due to Segal (1998), is that it does so by providing the psychological faculty (the "Ψ faculty") with an appropriate kind of representation to compute with—a representation for propositions that is "legible" at the interface between grammar and cognition, and which was previously unavailable. Note that if this suggestion is on the right track, then we seem to be on our way toward a general explanation for sententialism. If what is solved by the child's mastery of clausal complementation is the problem of providing legible representations for propositions, and propositional representation is itself required for theory of mind and understanding of intensionality/referential opacity, then sententialism will nearly follow. The key question will simply be whether the Ψ faculty can acquire propositional representations only this way, through calculation on clausal input, or whether other means are available. It seems to me that, to a large extent, the answer to this question depends on one's theory of propositions—the objects denoted by clauses embedded under propositional attitude predicates. In the final section I sketch a theory of propositions that I believe fits well into the sententialist picture and the general minimalist picture of grammar.

16.4 Interpreted Logical Forms and Phases

The semantics of propositional-attitude constructions is an extremely rich and complex area, with a variety of competing theories. Following initial proposals by Higginbotham (1986) and Segal (1989), Larson and Ludlow (1993) argue that to accommodate the full range of opacity/intensionality effects observed in propositional-attitude report sentences, semantics must deploy structured objects which encode the full space of linguistic features of a clause—phonological, syntactic, and semantic.

16.4.1 *Interpreted Logical Forms*

It is a fact familiar since Frege (1893) that substitution of distinct co-referring proper names in a clausal embedding context can fail to preserve truth; see (54). However, Larson and Ludlow (1993) point out that this is really just the tip of an iceberg. The same result holds true with what would be typically regarded as a single lexical item pronounced with different regional accents; see (55). The truth of propositional-attitude reports is thus sensitive to phonological variation at the sub-lexical level:

(54) a. Kelly believes [**Judy Garland** sang *Somewhere over the Rainbow*].

  b. Kelly believes [**Frances Gumm** sang *Somewhere over the Rainbow*].

(55) a. Jack believes [**Harvard** is a fine school].

  b. Jack believes [[harvərd] is a fine school].

  c. Jack believes [[ha:vad] is a fine school].

A similar observation can be made regarding sensitivity to syntactic structure in propositional attitude reports. Evidently, gross differences in constituency can produce truth-conditional differences. The truth conditions of (56a) can diverge according to whether the embedded VP is understood with *the whole year* as the object of *study* (56b), or as a modifier of an intransitive version of the verb, as in (56c):

(56)   a. Kathy believes [Max **studied the whole year**].

     b. Kathy believes [Max [$_{VP}$[$_{VP}$ studied][the whole year]]].

     c. Kathy believes [Max [$_{VP}$ studied [the whole year]]].

However, sensitivity to syntactic constituent structure extends down further, to the structure of morphemes. Thus the truth conditions of (57a) can differ according to whether *unlockable* is parsed as (57b) or (57c). In the first case Alice believes that the door cannot be locked; in the second, she believes that it can be unlocked (57c):

(57)   a. Alice believes [that door is **unlockable**].

     b. Alice believes [that door is [un-[lockable]]].

     c. Alice believes [that door is [[unlock]-able]].

Likewise, representational distinctions encoding so-called binding relations appear relevant. The truth conditions of (58a) can differ according to whether Mary believes John is the only individual who loves John's mother, or the only individual who loves his/her own mother, see (58b). These differences are typically encoded with numerical indices:

(58)   a. Mary believes [**only John** loves **his** mother].

     b. Mary believes [[only John$_i$]$_j$ t$_j$ loves his$_i$ mother].

     c. Mary believes [[only John$_I$]$_j$ t$_j$ loves his$_j$ mother].

Finally, attitude report semantics appear to be sensitive to semantics, including the real reference of terms. The truth of (59a) can plainly depend on whom the pronoun *she* refers to:

(59)   a. Kelly believes that [**she** sang *Somewhere over the Rainbow*].

     b. Context: *she* refers Judy Garland.

     c. Context: *she* refers Patti Page.

Standard theories of pronominal interpretation associate pronouns with a referent in a context, and within a given context, a given pronoun (however indexed) can refer to any individual. On this view, the relevant truth conditions for (59a) cannot be made in terms of syntactic distinctions in the complement clause. Arguably, what is needed to distinguish the two cases for (59a) is the reference of the pronoun itself: *she* interpreted as Judy Garland vs. *she* interpreted as Patti Page. If so, then semantic features are relevant as well.

Larson and Ludlow (1993) propose to capture these points within a formal theory in which the objects denoted by embedded clauses are Interpreted

Logical Forms (ILFs): phrase markers annotated with semantic values, whose nodes (including lexical items) bear the full set of phonological (segmental and prosodic), syntactic, and semantic features assigned to them by the grammar. Structures (60a) and (60b) are (simplified versions of) the ILFs for the embedded clauses in (54a, b). Here each node of the syntactic representation is associated with the value it receives under a standard truth theory. Note that although the semantic value of the subject expressions is identical (both refer to the individual Judy Garland, denoted by the constant j), the names differ. Accordingly, these constitute distinct ILFs—distinct propositional objects—and standing in the belief relation to one is different from standing in the belief relation to the other.

(60) a.

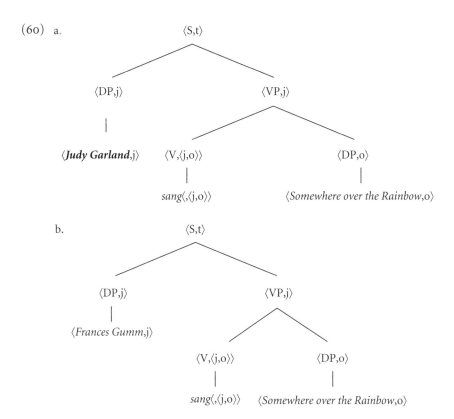

Similarly, (60a, b) are ILFs for the embedded clause in (59a). Here the syntactic form of the subject expressions is identical (*she*), but the referent differs (Judy Garland vs. Patti Page), hence these also constitute distinct ILFs and distinct propositional objects:

(61) a.

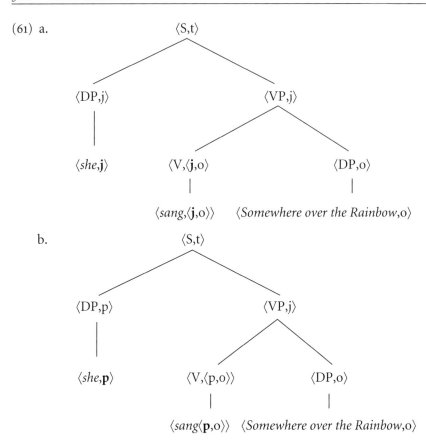

The ILF theory thus accounts for the range of distinctions that propositional attitude semantics appears to demand, by making every feature of the linguistic expression part of the propositional representation itself.

16.4.2 *Phases*

In Larson and Ludlow (1993), ILFs are computed at truth-value denoting nodes (CP and VP) in the complement of propositional-attitude predicates, a move largely dictated by technical considerations. ILFs are deployed as part of the general project of constructing a truth theory for natural language, and a truth theory assigns only truth conditions to sentences. Expressions receive definite values only in the context of their occurring in a sentence that is assumed to be true. It follows that an algorithm for constructing ILFs, which associates expressions with definite values, naturally begins at nodes that are truth-value denoting.

The computation has an additional property worth drawing attention to. Consider the truth conditions assigned to an iterated attitude report—one with more than one level of clausal embedding; see (62).

(62)   *Bill thinks Max believes Judy Garland sang Somewhere over the Rainbow is true iff Bill thinks*

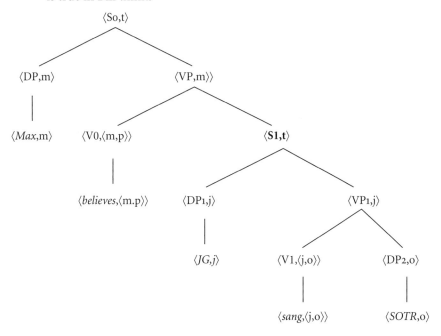

where = p ⟨S₁,t⟩

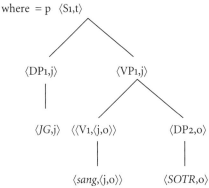

Under the Larson and Ludlow (1993) algorithm, the ILF for the most deeply embedded clause (*Judy Garland sang Somewhere over the Rainbow*) becomes the value (p) for the most deeply embedded attitude verb (*believes*). Although this lowest portion of structure also figures in the calculation of the ILF for the larger embedded clause (*Max believes Judy Garland sang Somewhere over the Rainbow*), the individual ILF corresponding to it has essentially been collected up and stored in the value of the second argument of *believes*. The nodes for all the embedded clauses in the tree get collected up and stored in this way, as values for higher predicates.

Strikingly, current syntactic theory offers a picture of syntactic computation that is highly reminiscent of the one just given. Chomsky (2000a, 2001) proposes that the human language computational device (C_{HL}) constructs syntactic representations in stages, or *phases*, defined as points in syntactic computation where structure-building is obliged to interact with the two interfaces: π (articulatory–perceptual) and λ (conceptual–intentional). Specifically, the syntactic heads C and v (described as "propositional nodes") are identified as phase points. When these nodes are reached, their complements are said to be "sent to the interfaces" for interpretation. After interpretation this complement material is treated as stored and unavailable for further syntactic computation—it becomes "impenetrable."

In the Minimalist picture, the specific properties of phases do not actually follow conceptually from the architecture of grammar $\pi \leftarrow C_{HL} \rightarrow \lambda$, and are in fact simply stipulated. No reason is offered for why CP and vP should be phases—there is no conceptual reason given for why propositional nodes should be accorded special computational status. Indeed the existence of phases themselves does not follow from anything conceptual insofar as no grammar-internal reasons drive the derivation to interact with π and λ at pre-final stages of computation. Motivation for phases is standardly ascribed to grammar-external processing requirements, including memory limitations, and ease-of-computation, etc. (see Chomsky 2000a, 2001). As an alternative proposal, consider a view that connects phases integrally to the $\pi \leftarrow C_{HL} \rightarrow \lambda$ architecture. Specifically:

Phases constitute the point where C_{HL} computes potential "propositions" (understood as ILFs) for the Ψ faculty, a part of λ.

Presumably on any acquisition theory within the Minimalist picture, mastery of clausal complementation will involve the child dealing with phase architecture. We have seen that grasp of theory of mind and intensionality seems to attend the successful negotiation of this stage: that once children have the former, they appear to have the latter as well. It is attractive, from the standpoint of ILF theory and the remarks made above, to attempt to relate these things. We might thus propose that the general phasal architecture identified by the Minimalist program emerges as part of how complementation is integrated into the linguistic system. Specifically children interpret clausal complements by building ILFs for them, and π and λ are accessed as part of building a representation that encodes the full PF/LF properties of a proposition. In effect, if computation must build propositional objects for λ, then the latter must access interpretation to get the full range of features such objects demand. Furthermore π and λ must be accessed at nodes where all features can be assigned to expressions: propositional nodes.

16.5 Summary

To summarize our results, we have seen that in natural language the presence of semantic intensionality appears to be associated with presence of a clausal complement, whether the latter is overt or covert. We have also seen that the development of semantic intensionality appears to correlate with development of clausal complementation, insofar as the latter appears to trigger or enable the child's theory of mind, which itself seems to be necessary for grasp of intensionality/referential opacity. The hypothesis we explored (due to Segal 1998) is that clausal complementation enables the theory of mind by providing the representations with which the Ψ faculty computes. In addition, we explored a particular theory of such representations, namely, Interpreted Logical Form—linguistically structured representations that are computed at propositional nodes. Under this picture, Sententialism can plausibly be seen to reflect an interface constraint: once enabled, the Ψ faculty requires propositional representations as input. And propositional representations are computed at clausal nodes, since they are the point where ILFs can be defined. As we saw, this proposal suggests an alternative view of phases as points in derivation where potential propositions are computed for the Ψ faculty.

This general picture, if correct, would lend strong general support to Sententialism, and make the connection between intensionality and clausal complementation a principled one. Intensionality would arise with clausal complementation, not simply as an empirical fact (which seems to be true in any case), but from the very way the architecture of is C_{HL} is designed.

17

Reflections on the *Optimal Solution*: On the Syntactic Representation of Indexicality

ALESSANDRA GIORGI

17.1 Introduction

In his paper "Three Factors in Language Design" (2005), mostly devoted to the definition and the scope of the biolinguistic program, Chomsky points out that (p. 4): "A core problem of the study of the faculty of language is to discover the mechanisms that limit outcomes to optimal types." According to the Strong Minimalist Thesis (Chomsky 2001, 2005), the Faculty of Language (FL) is perfectly designed. Language is an optimal solution to the interface conditions that it must satisfy. One of the issues arising in this framework concerns the nature of language variation, a traditional domain of inquiry in linguistics. Language variation—whatever its origin might be, lexical, syntactical or phonological—is one of the most popular areas of investigation by linguists from all backgrounds, generative ones included. In the Minimalist perspective, however, it ends up being considered as a residue, as an imperfection of the optimal system, lying outside Narrow Syntax. On the other hand, exactly under this very same perspective, one is also forced to assume that no particular language is, generally speaking, more optimal than any other, and that therefore each language expresses a different optimal way to satisfy the interface conditions: those imposed by the sensory–motor system (S-M) and by the conceptual–intentional system (C-I).

These considerations might be particularly relevant when applied to those categories that are central to the computational system, as for instance the category Tense (T). T plays an important role at both interfaces, triggering agreement with the subject in many languages—at the S-M interface—and being the crucial locus for the temporal interpretation of the utterance—at the C-I interface. Note that, in both cases, T functions as a bridge toward the context. On the one hand, it identifies the subject, which, roughly speaking, can be the speaker, the hearer, or neither. Hence, it locates the event with respect to the speech-act participants. On the other hand, in the C-I system it locates the events with respect to each other and, in particular, with respect to the utterance event.

In this chapter I will consider this issue, analyzing some cases having to do with the interpretation of tenses, or, better to say, with the temporal location of events. Typologically, languages differ widely as to the way of expressing temporal relations. Some languages—for instance Italian and Rumanian, to mention just two—have a rich and complex morphological system encoding various temporal relations. Others—such as English—have quite a simpler system, explicitly encoding only a subset of the distinctions encoded in Italian or Rumanian. Finally, some languages—for instance Chinese—have no temporal morphemes at all.[1]

On the other hand, however, in all languages—independently of the existence of temporal morphemes—sentences express a temporal ordering of events. Events must be located along the temporal dimension, be the language Italian, Rumanian, English, or Chinese, as remarked by many scholars.[2] Hence, languages behave uniformly as far as the requirements they satisfy, even if they accomplish this in very different ways. Here I will address the question more closely, trying to better define the optimal solution for the temporal interpretation of utterances.[3]

17.2 The Role of Indexicality: Temporal Relations in English

In a grammatical sentence, the eventuality—where this term refers to both processes and states—must be temporally located, or, using a more technical term, anchored. The default anchor of the main clause eventuality is the

---

[1] On Chinese, see among others Smith and Erbaugh (2005), Smith (2007), and Lin (2003, 2006).

[2] In the syntactic domain the first scholar who presumably formally addressed this question was Enç (1987).

[3] In some languages, such as Latin, it is possible to have main clauses without a morphological verbal form. Still, they are temporally interpreted, and the value assigned to them is present. Consider for instance sentence (i):

(i)   Caesar imperator.
      Lit.: 'Caesar emperor.'

This sentence expresses the meaning *Caesar is the emperor*. In this chapter, I will also leave aside the discussion concerning the so-called a-temporal sentences, such as *two plus two is four*. Let me only point out that a literal notion of a-temporality, however, is highly questionable and that these sentences are obviously temporally anchored as any other. See for instance Barwise and Perry (1983).

utterance event, that is, the *here and now* defined on the basis of the temporal and spatial coordinates of the speaker.[4]

In this section I will consider the distribution of finite verbal forms in English. In this language the main clause obligatorily expresses tense:[5]

(1) John is happy
         BE-pres

(2) John ate a sandwich
         EAT-past

(3) John will   call Mary tomorrow
         modal(fut) CALL

The morphological tense realized on the verb is interpreted as locating the event in the present, in the past, or in the future with respect to the utterance event itself—that is, with respect to the temporal location of the speaker.[6]

In English, the temporal location of the speaker is relevant for the temporal location of events embedded in complement clauses as well. Consider for instance the following sentence:

(4) John said that Mary is pregnant

For this sentence to be felicitous, the embedded state must hold at the time John spoke and at the time of the utterance. In other words, the embedded present tense must be located twice: once with respect to the main clause subject's (John's) temporal location and once with respect to the speaker's temporal location, that is, *now*. This property goes under the name of Double Access Reading and is obligatory in English to the extent that the following sentence is infelicitous:

(5) #Two years ago, John said that Mary is pregnant.

---

[4] On the relevance of the spatial coordinate of the speaker for the temporal location of events, see Ritter and Wiltschko (2005, 2008). They show that in some Salish languages the relevant notion to this end is spatial, in terms of *here* and *there*, and not of *now* and *then*. In what follows, however, I will consider only systems based on the temporal location of the speaker.

[5] I will not consider here the distribution of the English subjunctive because it is a non-productive form, appearing only in quite learned language in very few contexts. See Portner (1997) for an interesting discussion of such cases.

[6] Several scholars addressed this point adopting slightly different perspectives. See among others Ogihara (1996), Stowell (1996), Zagona (1999), Giorgi and Pianesi (2001), Higginbotham (2001), Schlenker (2003), Guéron (2004).

Since we know that human pregnancy lasts much less than two years, in this case it is not possible for Mary to be pregnant both at the time John spoke and at the time of the utterance.[7]

If the embedded form is a past, English exhibits two different patterns, one for stative predicates and progressive verbal forms, and one for eventive predicates. Consider the following cases:

(6)   John said that Mary was pregnant.

(7)   John said that Mary was eating a sandwich.

(8)   John said that Mary ate a sandwich.

In examples (6) and (7), the embedded state/event can be taken to be ongoing at the time of the saying by John, in that it is interpreted as simultaneous with the main event. In example (8), the embedded event is interpreted as preceding the saying. In all three cases, the eating is located before the utterance time. The difference between (6) and (7) on the one side, and (9) on the other, is due to aspectual properties. I come back to these distinctions when I address the properties of the Italian temporal system.[8]

Note also that in no case, including example (4) above, can the embedded event be interpreted as a pure indexical. In other words, in (4) the pregnancy cannot be ongoing now, while lying in the future with respect to the main predicate. Analogously, in (6)–(8) the eating cannot be past only with respect to *now*, while future with respect to the saying. In other words, sentence (4) cannot be a faithful report of the following discourse by John:

(9)   "Mary will be pregnant."

Similarly, sentences (6)–(8) cannot be a faithful report of the following one:

(10)   "Mary will eat a sandwich."

If the events in question are located with respect to each other as in (11), then the only verbal form available in English is the so-called future-in-the-past, as shown in examples (12) and (13):

(11)   saying_____state/event_____*now*

(12)   John said that Mary would be pregnant.

(13)   John said that Mary would eat a sandwich.

---

[7] There are two main accounts for this phenomenon. The *de re* approach, originally developed by Abush (1997), and the Generalized Double Access Reading proposal, discussed in Higginbotham (1995, 2001) and Giorgi and Pianesi (2000, 2001). Here I will not provide a discussion of the various theoretical proposals, but see Section 17.3 for further details.

[8] For a discussion, see Giorgi and Pianesi (1997, 2001).

By means of this periphrasis, the speaker can locate the embedded event in the future with respect to the saying, but not necessarily in the future with respect to *now*, that is, with respect to her own temporal location.

On the other hand, an event, or a state, expressed by means of the English *will* future is obligatorily located both in the future of the subject—that is, *John*—and in the future of the speaker as well:

(14)   John said that Mary will be pregnant.

(15)   John said that Mary will eat a sandwich.

Interestingly, both the *would* and the *will* future forms might be a faithful report of the future-oriented discourse by John mentioned above in (9) and (10). This consideration is important because it shows that indirect discourse—the reporting of somebody else's speech—cannot be thought of as something merely derivable from the direct speech by means of grammatical conversion rules. The choice between the *would* and the *will* future, in fact, depends not only on John's original speech, but also on the speaker's temporal location with respect to the reported state/event. Therefore, the material circumstances of the reporting itself—that is, the context of the specific utterance—are relevant for the choice of the embedded morphosyntactic form.

Note also that the *would* future verbal form is not available in main assertions *qua* future. Consider the following example:

(16)   #Mary would eat a sandwich.

This sentence can only convey a *modal* meaning—something like: Mary would eat a sandwich if she could—and cannot be used to express the meaning that in the future Mary is going to eat a sandwich, as, on the contrary, is possible in the following case:

(17)   Mary will eat a sandwich.

Concluding these brief remarks about English, it is possible to say that embedded verbal forms do not have the same meaning as in main clauses. The lack of the mere indexical reading is an argument in this direction, as shown by the interpretation of the embedded present tense and of the embedded past forms. Moreover, the properties of the embedded future forms show that the location of the speaker is a necessary ingredient in the choice of the subordinate verbal form and that even in English there is at least one verbal form—the *would* future—that can only appear in embedded contexts.

17.3 A Theoretical Proposal

Giorgi and Pianesi (2001) and Giorgi (2010) proposed an account for this paradigm, dubbed Generalized Double Access Reading (DAR). According to this perspective, all verbal forms appearing in embedded contexts—with the exception of the *would* future, which I discuss below—must be evaluated twice: once with respect to the main event, and once with respect to the utterance event. Both the temporal location of the superordinate subject and the location of the speaker are relevant to the interpretation.

The anchoring of the embedded event to the superordinate predicate is taken to be universally obligatory, as already proposed for instance in Enç (1987) and Higginbotham (1995). In main clauses the superordinate event is the utterance event itself.

Giorgi and Pianesi's novel idea is the proposal concerning the anchoring to the speaker's temporal coordinate, giving rise to the DAR. This anchoring is obligatory with certain verbal forms in languages like English and Italian, whereas it is not in languages such as Rumanian and Chinese. In what follows, I will discuss these languages in turn, showing in what ways they differ.

17.3.1 *A brief overview of Italian sequence of tense*

17.3.1.1 *The imperfect*   Italian indicative verbal forms are like the corresponding English ones with respect to the enforcing of the DAR:[9]

(18)   Gianni ha detto che Maria è incinta.
       'Gianni said that Maria is pregnant.'

(19)   #Due anni fa, Gianni ha detto che Maria è incinta.
       'Two years ago, Gianni said that Maria is pregnant.'

The discussion of sentences (18) and (19) is analogous to the one given above for the corresponding English ones. The DAR is obligatory in Italian, to the extent of ruling out (19), on the basis of what we know about human pregnancy.

Analogously, the embedded past and future forms do not exhibit significant differences with respect to the English ones:

---

[9] In examples (18) and (19) the main past form—*ha detto*—is translated in English as a simple past. The form in question is literally a present perfect, being formed by the present tense of auxiliary *avere* 'have' and the past participle of the verb. The simple past is *disse* 'said', but this form is only very rarely used in spoken language in central and northern Italy. In southern Italy, the situation is exactly the opposite, the simple past being the form of choice in most cases. Here I adopt my own variant of Italian and will not discuss the matter any further, even if the subject is not as simple as it might seem at first sight. See also Giorgi and Pianesi (1997: ch. 3).

(20)   Gianni ha detto che Maria ha mangiato un panino.
       Gianni said that Maria ate(PAST IND) a sandwich

(21)   Gianni ha detto che Maria mangerà un panino.
       Gianni said that Maria will eat(FUT IND) a sandwich

In sentence (20) the embedded event must be interpreted as preceding both the saying and the utterance time, and the embedded event in sentence (21) must be understood as following both the saying and the utterance time. Finally, even in Italian it is impossible to have a purely indexical interpretation for embedded tenses, as discussed above with respect to English.

An interesting difference between Italian and English concerns stative predicates. The Italian equivalent of example (6) is the following:

(22)   Gianni ha detto che Maria era incinta.
       Gianni said that Maria was(IMPF) pregnant

In this case, the embedded verbal form is an imperfect indicative. A simple past or a present perfect—according to the variant of Italian adopted by the speakers—would sound odd:[10]

(23)   #Gianni ha detto che Maria fu/è stata incinta
       Gianni said that Maria was(SIMPLE PAST/PRES PERF) pregnant

The reason for the oddness is mostly due to the aspectual properties of the imperfect verbal form.[11] Here, I will not go into this discussion because it lies too far away from the central topic of this chapter. The important point to be stressed here is that the simultaneity of the embedded state with the main predicate, expressed by means of the English verbal form *was,* must be rendered in Italian with the imperfect *era* and cannot correspond to the past forms *fu* or *è stato.* Analogously, the progressive periphrasis appearing in the English example (7) corresponds to the Italian progressive periphrasis with imperfect morphology:

(24)   Gianni ha detto che Maria stava magiando un panino.
       Gianni said that Maria was(IMPF) eating a sandwich

----

[10] On regional variation in Italian concerning the use of the past tenses, see n. 9.

[11] As discussed at length in Giorgi and Pianesi (1997, 2001, 2004a), aspectual properties deeply affect the anchoring procedures. Note also that the simple past and the present perfect are aspectually perfective. Perfectivity can sometimes be combined with stativity, as for instance in the following case, yielding however the so called life-time effect (Mittwoch 1982):

(i)   Napoleone fu/è stato un grand'uomo.
       Napoleon was(SIMPLE PAST/PRESENT PERFECT) a great man

The implication conveyed by this sentence, because of the presence of a perfective, is that the subject is dead.

The past morphology would be totally unavailable, as is in general the case with the progressive periphrasis in Italian:[12]

(25)   Gianni ha detto che Maria *stette/*è stata mangiando un panino.
       Gianni said that Maria was(PAST/PRES PERF) eating a sandwich

Again, the presence of the imperfect in Italian enables the embedded state/event to be interpreted as simultaneous with the main one, whereas this option is not available with the simple past/present perfect, as happens with the English example (8).

A first conclusion might therefore be that the English past collapses both functions—the past and the imperfect—and that aspectual properties of the event to which they are attached select then for the one or for the other. Only the imperfect function, however, is able to give rise to the simultaneous reading of the embedded event. Consider in fact the following additional piece of evidence:

(26)   Gianni ha detto che Maria mangiava un panino.
       Gianni said that Maria ate(IMPF) a sandwich

In example (26) the embedded event appears with imperfect morphology—in this case I intentionally did not use a progressive periphrasis—and is interpreted as temporally simultaneous with the superordinate predicate.

The proposal could therefore be that the English past tense is ambiguous between a perfective past and an imperfective, Italian-like, one, but the latter is available only with stative and stative-like (progressive) predicates.

17.3.1.2 *The subjunctive*   In Italian finite clauses the embedded verbal forms come in two varieties: indicative mood and subjunctive mood. The bipartition of the embedded verbal forms is common to many Romance and non-Romance languages, such as Spanish, Catalan, Rumanian, Portuguese, Greek, Icelandic, and German. In all the Romance languages (one form or the other of) the indicative appears embedded under (non-negated) verbs of saying, whereas the subjunctive typically appears under verbs of wishing, even if with some exceptions.[13] But beside these core cases, even among Romance languages there are several differences as far as the contexts requiring one mood or the other are concerned. In Germanic languages, for instance, the subjunctive appears also under verbs of saying, making the general picture even more complex.[14]

---

[12] On the progressive in Italian, see among others Bonomi (1997), Zucchi (1997), Bertinetto (2000).

[13] For instance in Rumanian, the subjunctive does not appear with factive–emotive predicates. See among others Terzi (1992), Quer (1998), and Farkas (2003).

[14] For a discussion of the indicative–subjunctive alternation, see among others Giorgi and Pianesi (1997), Roussou (1999), Manzini (2000), and Schlenker (2005a). See also n. 13.

In this chapter I do not describe or discuss the reasons why the indicative or the subjunctive mood must or can appear in the various contexts. I will propose the following generalization:

(27)   In complement clauses of Italian the indicative appears if the superordinate verb is a speech act verb.

As far as complement clauses go, this generalization works quite well for Italian. Psychological predicates such as *pensare* 'think', *credere* 'believe', *sperare* 'hope', and *desiderare* 'wish', select an embedded subjunctive, whereas predicates such as *dire* 'say', *affermare* 'affirm', and *dichiarare* declare, select an indicative. Consider the basic distribution and interpretation of the subjunctive verbal forms in Italian:

(28)   Gianni crede che Maria sia/*fosse felice.
        Gianni believes that Maria is(PRES SUBJ/*PAST SUBJ) happy

(29)   Gianni credeva che Maria fosse/*sia felice.
        Gianni believed that Maria was(PAST SUBJ/*PRES SUBJ) happy

The embedded verbal form in examples (28) and (29) is interpreted as simultaneous with the main one. Note that in (28) the main verb appears in the present tense, and the embedded verb has present-subjunctive morphology. Analogously, in example (29) the main verb has past-tense morphology and the embedded one features a past subjunctive. The opposite choices would not be possible, as shown by the ungrammatical options given earlier. Subjunctive morphology, in other words, manifests itself as an agreement phenomenon between the morphological tense of the superordinate verb and the embedded one. As an argument in favor of this hypothesis, consider the following example:

(30)   Gianni pensava che Maria partisse ieri/oggi/domani.
        Gianni thought that Maria left(PAST SUBJ) yesterday/today/tomorrow

The embedded verbal form is a past subjunctive. The example shows that the temporal interpretation of the leaving event is not constrained by any indexical adverb. All indexical expressions are in fact compatible with it, so that the leaving can actually be located either in the past, in the present, or in the future with respect to the utterance event. The only requirement to be satisfied is temporal agreement with the main verbal form—present under present and past under past—as shown in the examples given above.

It is possible to express anteriority with respect to the main predicate, but this is obtained derivatively by means of the compound subjunctive forms:

(31)   Gianni crede che Maria abbia telefonato.
       Gianni believes that Maria has(PRES SUBJ) called

(32)   Gianni credeva che Maria avesse telefonato.
       Gianni believed that Maria had(PAST SUBJ) called

The past participle *telefonato* 'called', expressing the resultant state—that is, the state resulting from a preceding event – is taken to hold at the time of the believing. This configuration yields as a result a past interpretation without the intervention of a past morpheme. Note again that the auxiliary agrees with the main verbal form: present subjunctive under a present, past subjunctive under a past. Naturally enough, no DAR arises with the subjunctive, given the purely morphological nature of the temporal morphemes.

   Consider however the following case, discussed in Giorgi and Pianesi (2004b) and Giorgi (2010):

(33)   Gianni ha ipotizzato che Maria fosse incinta.
       Gianni hypothesized that Maria were(PAST SUBJ) pregnant

(34)   Gianni ha ipotizzato che Maria sia incinta.
       Gianni hypothesized that Maria is(PRES SUBJ) pregnant

Ipotizzare 'hypothesize' is a predicate which can be interpreted either as a purely psychological predicate or as a communication one, similar to the English *guess*.[15] As a psychological predicate, it selects the subjunctive, but it is anomalous, permitting a non-agreeing configuration—present under past—as the one in (34). Interestingly, the configuration in (34) forces the DAR interpretation, analogously to the indicative cases analyzed above. Sentence (34) in fact crucially implies that the pregnancy of Maria both held in the past, at the time Gianni hypothesized about it, and *now*.

   The presence of the DAR effect in (34) shows that the DAR cannot be simply due to the presence of a certain verbal form in the embedded clause—that is, the indicative. In the next section I address this issue, which is central to the point investigated in this paper.

17.3.2 *Toward a syntax of indexicality*

17.3.2.1 *The complementizer and the DAR*   As is well known—see among others Scorretti (1994), Poletto (1995, 2000, 2001)—in Italian the complementizer

---

[15]   Thanks to J. Higginbotham for pointing this out to me.

can be omitted when introducing (certain) subjunctive clauses, but it can never be deleted when introducing indicative ones.[16]

Giorgi and Pianesi (2004b) and Giorgi (2010) observed that the possibility of deleting the complementizer correlates with the cases in which the DAR is enforced. This generalization can be stated as follows:

(35)   In Italian the DAR interpretation and Complementizer Deletion never co-occur

This proposal accounts for the following contrast:

(36)   Gianni ha detto *(che) Maria è incinta.
        Gianni said (that) Maria is(IND) pregnant (DAR)

(37)   Gianni credeva (che) Maria fosse incinta.
        Gianni believed (that) Maria was(SUBJ) pregnant (non-DAR)

More interestingly, it also accounts for the contrast found with *ipotizzare* 'hypothesize':[17]

(38)   Gianni ha ipotizzato (che) Maria fosse incinta.
        Gianni hypothesized (that) Maria were(PAST SUBJ) pregnant (non-DAR)

(39)   Gianni ha ipotizzato *(che) Maria sia incinta.
        Gianni hypothesized (that) Maria is(PRES SUBJ) pregnant (DAR)

As illustrated above, when the verb *ipotizzare* selects a subordinate subjunctive, it permits CD, as in (38). On the contrary, in the DAR case—that is, the present under past configuration in example (39)—the complementizer must obligatorily appear.

Giorgi (2010) proposed that the non-deletable C position is the locus for the realization in the syntax of the speaker's temporal coordinate. The complementizer introducing the subjunctive has different properties and does not occupy the same position in the projection. It does not bear any reference to the speaker and can be omitted. To put it intuitively: it does not convey any

---

[16] The Florentine dialect seems to admit CD even in certain indicative contexts, such as those embedded under the predicate *dire* 'say'. According to my informants, however, it seems that there are some usage restrictions, rendering the phenomenon not totally identical to the other CD cases; recall in fact that CD in Italian is totally optional. These properties of the Florentine dialect therefore require further study.

[17] Sentence (39) therefore seems to violate the generalization according to which the subjunctive morpheme does not express tense, but only morphological agreement. It can be shown however that the violation is only apparent. In this case, the present tense is not licensed by the superordinate verbal form, but by the speaker's coordinate itself, hence *now*. On the precise working out of this proposal, see Giorgi (2010).

information relevant to the interpretation and therefore, in a way, it can be dispensed with.

In this perspective, the absence of the complementizer in English is to be considered as the realization of a null-complementizer, exhibiting the properties of the indicative-like complementizer in Italian. Notice in fact that the presence or absence of *that* does not have any effect on the DAR non-DAR interpretation of the following sentence:

(40)   John said (that) Mary is pregnant

In example (40), the complementizer can be omitted even if the sentence is interpreted according to the DAR. This result actually fits with what is already known on the subject. As pointed out originally by Kayne (1981a), in fact, the null complementizer is not an available option in Italian.[18]

So far, therefore, it can be said that in Italian the DAR is enforced due to the presence of a high complementizer position, constituting the *trait d'union* between the syntax and the context. In this Italian and English are identical—modulo the existence of the null complementizer in English. In Italian there is a further option, due to the presence in the system of the subjunctive, a form resistant to the DAR interpretation, unless appearing in a communication context, such as the one created by *ipotizzare*.

17.3.2.2 *The Italian imperfect and the English past*   What about the Italian imperfect and the English (stative) past? We saw above, in fact, that these forms are immune from the DAR. Note also that the Italian imperfect, with respect to C, patterns with the indicative and not with the subjunctive:

(41)   Gianni ha detto *(che) Maria era incinta.
       Gianni said (that) Maria was(IMPF) pregnant

Giorgi (2010) proposed that the normal indicative verbal forms—present, past, and future—always enforce the DAR, being introduced by the leftmost complementizer in the C-layer, containing the representation of the speaker's temporal coordinate. The subjunctive does so only when it co-occurs with communication predicates—such as *ipotizzare*. In all the other cases, the subjunctive complementizer does not contain any reference to the speaker's temporal coordinate. Finally, the imperfect is an indicative form, and is introduced by the leftmost undeletable complementizer. Hence, it should exhibit DAR effects, contrary to facts.

Note that the imperfect, in general across Romance languages, has often been dubbed as an anaphoric temporal form. This is because it can appear in

---

[18]   For a recent account in the minimalist framework, see Bošković and Lasnik (2003) and references cited there.

main assertions, but it must be introduced by some temporal topic. In other words: it cannot be used out of the blue; a temporal reference must be given in the previous discourse or in the context. Consider for instance the following examples:

(42)   #Gianni mangiava un panino.
       Gianni was eating(IMPF) a sandwich

(43)   Ieri alle 5, Gianni mangiava un panino.
       Yesterday at 5, Gianni was eating(IMPF) a sandwich

In order to be acceptable, the sentence must be introduced by a temporal topic, as in (43). Looking at the facts from another perspective, discussed in Giorgi (2010), the imperfect cannot be anchored to the utterance time as the indicative past, as opposed to the indicative past forms. One way of capturing this observation could be to say that the imperfect cannot be anchored to the utterance event because it bears the feature [*anti-speaker*]. For this reason, it cannot be directly anchored to the speaker's temporal coordinate, but can be located with respect to it only *indirectly*, as happens when a temporal locution such as *yesterday at 5* appears.

By virtue of its anti-feature, the imperfect, even if it appears in clauses introduced by the high indicative-like complementizer, does not locate the event with respect to the speaker's coordinate, but only with respect to the superordinate event, yielding a simultaneous reading.[19] Interestingly, it is exactly because of this property that the imperfect appears in the contexts embedded under *dream* predicates, as discussed in Giorgi and Pianesi (2001, 2004b). Giorgi and Pianesi argued that dream contexts are special because the tense is not anchored. The clause embedded under the *dream* predicate expresses the content of the dream without locating it in the past, present, or future of the speaker (nor is the embedded event located with respect to the subject either). Other verbal forms of the indicative, such as the present perfect or the simple past, do not yield grammatical results. Consider the following examples:

(44)   Gianni ha sognato che c'era un terremoto.
       Gianni dreamed that there was(IMPF) an earthquake

(45)   *Gianni ha sognato che c'è stato/ci fu un terremoto.

---

[19] When the embedded clause is introduced by a temporal topic, as might be expected, the imperfect gives rise to a simultaneous interpretation with respect to the temporal topic:

(i)   Gianni ha detto che ieri alle 5 Maria mangiava un panino.
      Gianni said that *yesterday at 5* Maria was eating a sandwich

For further discussion, see Giorgi (2010).

Gianni dreamed that there has been(PRES PERF/PAST) an earthquake
(ok if *evidential dream*)

The imperfect is the form used to express the content of the dream. If some
other indicative form is used, the result is—at best—that of *evidential dream*,
a dream in other words, which, according to the speaker, reveals reality, as
pointed out in the gloss.

The point of interest here is that the form appearing in *dream* contexts in
English is the simple past. Consider the following examples:

(46)   John said that Mary left.
        (The leaving is located in John's past and in the speaker's past)

(47)   John dreamed that Mary left
        (*The leaving is located in John's past and in the speaker's past. The
        leaving is just the *content* of the dream)

There is a contrast between the ordinary subordinate contexts, for instance
those embedded under a verb of *saying* as in (46), and the contexts created by
dream. In the former case, the temporal interpretation of the embedded event
must be past both with respect to the subject of the superordinate verb and
with respect to the speaker's temporal location. This does not make any sense
inside a *dream* context: there is no way in which the leaving event in example
(47) might be said to be located in the past with respect to the dreaming event
and in the past of the speaker.

With respect to the phenomena illustrated here, it can be concluded therefore that the English past corresponds both to the Italian simple past and to
the Italian imperfect. Hence it can be said to be a real past tense, instantiating
a preceding relation between two arguments. In some contexts, however,
it behaves as an *anti-speaker* form, corresponding to the Italian imperfect.
Which of the two values will be selected depends on two factors: the nature of
the superordinate predicate—for instance, *say* vs. *dream*—and the aspectual
value of the embedded predicate: – stative vs. eventive.[20]

Concluding this discussion, it is possible to say that English and Italian are both DAR languages. In Italian the clauses exhibiting the DAR are
always introduced by the leftmost undeletable complementizer. Subjunctive
clauses are usually introduced by a lower, deletable complementizer. The
indicative–subjunctive distinction mostly coincides with the DAR–non-DAR

---

[20] In Giorgi (2010: ch. 5) the same hypothesis is proposed to explain the verbal pattern in free
indirect discourse in Italian and English. In English, in literary FID contexts we find an overwhelming
presence of past forms, whereas in Italian these almost always correspond to imperfect verbal forms.
The idea would be that even in this case, the English past is an imperfect in disguise. Note also that
in the literature on the topic, mostly about the English texts, the presence of a past form creates
considerable problems. The proposal developed here therefore also solves a problem in that domain.

interpretation of embedded clauses. In some cases, the presence of the left-most high complementizer does not give rise to the DAR; in these cases, an imperfect verbal form appears. The proposal is that the imperfect, due to its anti-speaker feature, neutralizes the effect of the presence of the speaker's temporal coordinate in C.[21]

In English there is no indicative–subjunctive distinction, but the past tense collapses both the function of a "real" past form, and that of an Italian-like imperfect. I have argued that the absence of DAR effects with statives and progressives is due to the possibility for statives to select this option, whereas this is not possible, for independent reasons, with eventive predicates.[22]

Hence, it looks as if languages have two ways to encode the DAR–non-DAR dimension: (a) presence of the leftmost C-position vs. its absence—basically, encoded in the indicative–subjunctive distinction; (b) the past–imperfective distinction, where both tenses are introduced by the leftmost C position. Italian has both possibilities, whereas English can only exploit the second one.

In the following section, I will briefly discuss Rumanian and Chinese. Rumanian is a non-DAR language, exhibiting the indicative–subjunctive distinction. Chinese does not have any tense or mood morphology associated with the verbs and is a non-DAR language. The cross-linguistic variation can be summarized as in Table 17.1. This kind of variation seems at first sight quite puzzling. It is not clear at all why, with respect to the DAR, Rumanian patterns with Chinese and not with Italian, and conversely, languages with poorer morphology, such as English and Chinese, do not pattern alike.

My proposal, as sketched in the introduction, is that morphological variation is only a superficial clue and that what really matters is the pattern observed at the C-I interface.

TABLE 17.1 The distribution of subjunctive and DAR across languages

	Subjunctive	Double Access Reading
Italian	+	+
Rumanian	+	−
English	−	+
Chinese	−	−

[21] For a detailed discussion, see Giorgi and Pianesi (2004b) and Giorgi (2010).

[22] Giorgi and Pianesi (2001) argue that English statives can be made simultaneous with a superordinate event. Due to the punctuality constraint, English eventives, on the contrary, cannot. Simplifying, the reasoning runs as follows: English eventive predicates are always inherently perfective—that is, they are bounded eventive sequences. The superordinate, anchoring event is seen as a (mereological) point. A perfective verbal form can never be made simultaneous with a superordinate event because a bounded sequence cannot coincide with a (mereological) point (the *punctuality constraint*).

17.4 Toward a Generalization: Some Remarks on Rumanian and Chinese

17.4.1 *Rumanian*

As mentioned above, Rumanian is a non-DAR language. Consider the following Rumanian examples:[23]

(48)   Maria e insarcinata.
         Maria is(PRES IND) pregnant

(49)   Acum 2 ani Gianni a spus ca Maria e insarcinata.
         Two years ago John said that Maria is(PRES IND) pregnant

The present tense is the form used in main sentences to express simultaneity with the utterance time, as shown in example (48). In Rumanian, however, a sentence such as (49) has the same meaning as sentence (50) in English:

(50)   Two years ago, John said that Mary was pregnant

In sentence (49), as in sentence (50) in English, Mary's pregnancy holds at the time of the saying, but does not have to hold at utterance time. Recall in fact, as discussed above, that the temporal[24] specification *two years ago* is totally incompatible with an embedded present tense in DAR languages, such as English and Italian:[25]

(51)   *Two years ago, John said that Mary is pregnant.

(52)   *Due anni fa Gianni ha detto che Maria è incinta.

In other words, on the one side Rumanian is like English and Italian in that a present tense in a main clause is interpreted indexically. On the other, in Rumanian the indexical component disappears when the present tense is in a complement clause.

Rumanian also has the indicative–subjunctive distinction. Typically, the subjunctive appears under control verbs in the place of the English and Italian infinitive, as in the following example (from Farkas 2003, ex. 4):

---

[23] I wish to thank all my Rumanian students, in Venice with our Erasmus program, who participated in the course of "Theoretical Linguistics" in the academic years 2006–7 and 2007–8, for discussing with me these and related data. In particular, I thank Iulia Zegrean for her kindness in answering all my questions about the data. Every misusage of the evidence is obviously exclusively my fault.

[24] The subjunctive in Rumanian also appears in a periphrastic construction to express future and as an imperative.

[25] Recall that states might be persistent, and therefore they might be holding *now*, even if the language is not a DAR language. This effect does not mean anything: the crucial test must always be provided by a sentence like the one in (51).

(53)   Maria vrea sa-i raspunda.
       Maria wants SUBJ PRT-clitic answer(SUBJ)
       'Maria wants to answer him.'

Interestingly, the subjunctive does not appear in factive-emotive contexts; see among others Farkas (2003). This suggests that the indicative–subjunctive distinction encodes partially different properties with respect to the Italian subjunctive. On the other hand, like Italian, Rumanian admits Complementizer Deletion with the subjunctive. The subjunctive verbal form in Rumanian is introduced by a syntactically low particle *sa*. Such a particle is syntactically lower than the complementizer *ca*. *Sa* is in most cases the only element distinguishing the indicative verbal form from the subjunctive one—with the exception of the third-person singular—and is therefore the distinctive property of the subjunctive in Rumanian.[26]

The complementizer *ca* cannot be deleted with the indicative, but it is in general omitted with the subjunctive. Consider in this respect examples (54) and (55):

(54)   Jon a spus *(ca) Maria e insarcinata.
       Jon said *(that) Maria is(PRES IND) pregnant

(55)   Maria vrea (*ca) sa-i raspunda.
       Maria wants (*that) *sa*-him answer(SUBJ)
       'Maria wants to answer him.'

In example (54) the complementizer cannot be omitted, whereas in (55) it cannot be present.

However, if the subjunctive clause has a lexical subject, the complementizer *ca* is again obligatorily realized:

(56)   Maria vrea *(ca) Jon sa-i raspunda
       Maria wants *(that) Jon *sa*-him answer(SUBJ)
       Maria wants *(that) Jon answers him

The presence of *ca* in (56) shows that in principle in Rumanian the high complementizer position is available even with the subjunctive.[27]

In these pages I do not intend to provide an exhaustive analysis of the Rumanian mood system because it lies outside the scope of this work, but

---

[26] In Italian the personal endings of the subjunctive present differ in at least four persons out of six, depending on the verbal declension. In Rumanian, moreover, there is no subjunctive imperfect—that is, there is only one simple subjunctive form.

[27] For a discussion, see Aboh (2004: ch. 5). On this topic, see also Terzi (1992), Dobrovie-Sorin (1994), Motapanyane (1995).

I will discuss some generalizations and propose some possible lines of future research on the topic.

I illustrated above with respect to Italian that the DAR/ non-DAR– interpretation largely coincides with the indicative–subjunctive distinction. In particular, in indicative clauses, the high complementizer encoding the speaker's coordinates is present, whereas in (most) subjunctive clauses such a complementizer is not realized. To some extent, this accounts for the indicative–subjunctive bipartition of clauses in Italian from a syntactic point of view: in indicative embedded clauses the speaker is represented at phase level in the C-layer, whereas in subjunctive clauses the speaker is not there.

The problem raised by these considerations with respect to Rumanian is the following. Given that it is a non-DAR language, the functional reasons for the distinction between a complementizer encoding the speaker's coordinates— the indicative-like complementizer—and a deletable complementizer, not encoding this information—that is, the subjunctive-like complementizer— disappear. Non-DAR clauses do not require anchoring of the embedded verbal form to the speaker's temporal coordinate, hence, in Rumanian there is no reason to hypothesize a complementizer encoding the speaker's temporal location, as opposed to one that does not.[28]

Pursuing this line of reasoning, one might suggest that the indicative– subjunctive distinction has a different role in the grammar of Rumanian with respect to the role it has in the grammar of Italian. This might seem a reasonable suggestion, given the empirical observation concerning the absence of infinitival control structures in this language. In the same vein, one might propose that the absence of DAR in Rumanian points to the absence of the complementizer encoding the speaker's temporal coordinates. Hence, a possible line of investigation could be the analysis of the properties of the complementizer, in order to ascertain if it is significantly differ from the Italian one.

This line of research, however, might not be the most promising one. The possibility of deleting the complementizer in fact looks very close to Italian CD—or, at least, closer to the Italian-like deletion phenomena, than to the English null complementizer pattern, since it follows the indicative–subjunctive divide. Hence, one might suggest that CD phenomena in Rumanian are to be traced back to the presence or absence of the speaker's temporal and spatial coordinates in the left periphery of the clause, as in Italian. So far, however, I do not have positive empirical arguments to offer

---

[28] Interestingly, d'Hulst et al. (2003) discussed the lack of the future-in-the-past in Rumanian. Again, since this language never anchors the embedded event to the speaker's coordinate, the necessity of a distinction between the equivalents of a *will* future and a *would* future disappears.

in favor of this view, but, on the other hand, there are no counter-arguments that I can see.

More importantly, it might be desirable to claim that the possibility of encoding the speaker's coordinate in the leftmost position in the C-layer is a universal one, as argued in Giorgi (2010). In this way, the interface between syntax and context would be univocally represented by grammar. In the next section I will argue that the analysis of Chinese might provide an argument in favor of the second perspective.

17.4.2 *Long-distance anaphors and the speaker's coordinates*

17.4.2.1 *Long-distance anaphors in Italian*   In this section I will briefly analyze the properties of Chinese with respect to the interface with the context. As I just illustrated above, Italian has a rich verbal morphology encoding tense and mood distinctions, as well as aspectual properties. Chinese, in contrast, is a language almost without morphology and with no tense and mood distinctions detectable on the verb, but only aspectual ones. Temporal interpretation is taken to be derivative on lexical and aspectual properties.[29]

Given this state of affairs, one might think that it is impossible to test the relevance of the hypothesis proposed here with respect to Chinese. The issues related to the presence of the speaker's temporal coordinate in the C-layer of the embedded clause in fact seem to be irrelevant, or at least not testable, due to the lack of tense and mood distinctions.

However, in Italian, beside the facts related to the DAR, there is another set of phenomena sensitive to the presence of the indicative–subjunctive distinction, namely, the distribution of long-distance anaphors, henceforth LDAs.

As is well known, LDAs are cross-linguistically permitted to get over a clause featuring a subjunctive, or infinitive, verbal form, but are blocked by an indicative one. That is, simplifying somehow, the antecedent of an LDA cannot lie outside the first clause containing an indicative, but can lie outside a clause containing a subjunctive. This phenomenon was observed both in the Germanic, for instance in Icelandic, and in the Romance domain, for instance in Italian.[30]

To illustrate this point, consider the following examples:

(57)   Quel dittatore$_i$ spera che i notiziari televisivi parlino a lungo delle proprie$_i$ gesta.
       That dictator hopes that TV news programs will talk(SUBJ) for a long time about self's deed

---

[29] See Lin (2006) and Smith (2007).
[30] See, among the others, Giorgi (1984) and Thráinsson (1991).

(58) Quel dittatore_i ha detto che il primo ministro_j era convinto che i notiziari televisi avessero parlato a lungo delle proprie_{j/*i} gesta.

That dictator said that the Prime Minister was(IND) convinced that the TV news program had(SUBJ) talked a lot about self's deeds

(59) *Quel dittatore_i ha detto che i notiziari televisivi hanno parlato a lungo delle proprie_i gesta.

That dictator said that the TV news programs talked(IND) for a long time about self's deeds

(60) *Quel dittatore_i ha detto che i notiziari televisivi parleranno a lungo delle proprie_i gesta.

That dictator said that the TV news programs will(IND) talk a lot about self's deeds

This paradigm shows that for the anaphor to be long-distance bound, the main verb of the embedded clause must be a subjunctive. In particular, the ungrammaticality of (59) and (60) shows that an indicative prevents the anaphor from looking any further for an antecedent, whereas the grammaticality of (57) and (58) shows that a subjunctive is transparent to this purpose. LDAs also exhibit a series of further properties, which I will not take into account in this brief discussion; for instance, they are usually subject-oriented.

The point to be stressed here is that the indicative mood actually has a blocking effect on the long-distance anaphor, defining the domain in which it has to look for an antecedent.

Interestingly, the blocking effect I just described is not limited to sentences featuring an indicative verbal form, but it also extends to some types of subjunctive clause. I showed above that the speaker's coordinate is represented in the left periphery of the clause also in some subjunctive contexts, which, as expected, give rise to the DAR, as for instance the *ipotizzare* cases described in exx. (33)–(34) and (37)–(38). The prediction is therefore that on these cases long distance binding should be blocked, as happens with the indicative mood in sentences (59) and (60). Consider to this end the following examples:

(61) Quel dittatore_i ha ipotizzato che il primo ministro venda illegalmente i propri_{?*i} tesori.

That dictator hypothesized that the prime minister illegally sells(PRES SUBJ) self's treasures

(62) Quel dittatore_i ha ipotizzato che il primo ministro vendesse illegalmente i propri_i tesori.

That dictator hypothesized that the prime minister illegally sold(PAST SUBJ) self's treasures

In example (61) a present subjunctive is embedded under a main past, whereas in example (62) the usual past-under-past configuration obtains. The superordinate subject is much more available as an antecedent in example (62) than in example (61), where the sentence is preferentially interpreted with *propri* 'self's' referring to *il primo ministro* 'the prime minister'. This contrast, even if subtle, certainly goes in the expected direction and cannot be accounted for by invoking the indicative/subjunctive distinction discussed above.

An account for these cases can be provided along the following lines. Sentence (61) is a DAR sentence—that is, a sentence in which the embedded eventuality has to be located both with respect to the temporal coordinates of the superordinate subject, *that dictator*, and to the temporal coordinates of the speaker. Therefore, in order to reach its expected antecedent, the anaphor should cross a clause endowed with the speaker's coordinate. In the indicative clauses given above—see exx. (59) and (60)—the LDA should do the same, whereas this would not happen in the "normal" subjunctive cases illustrated in examples (57) and (58).

Given this pattern, the alternative hypothesis to explain the whole of the cases given above can be the following: the blocking of the anaphor is due to the presence of the speaker's coordinate in the left periphery of the clause, and not to the presence of the indicative mood *per se*.[31] In other words, an LDA could look for an antecedent beyond its own clause only if the speaker's coordinates are not represented in its left-periphery, hence the anaphor *proprio* can take a superordinate, long distance, subject as an antecedent.[32]

Consider also that, in line with what I said above, the indicative imperfect is not transparent to LD binding—that is, it does not admit a long-distance anaphor to be bound outside its domain, showing that it is in this respect a well-behaved indicative. Consider in this light the following sentences:

(63)   Quel dittatore$_i$ ha detto che i libri di storia parlavano spesso delle proprie$_{*i}$ gesta.
        That dictator said that the books of history often spoke (IMP) about self's deeds

(64)   Quel dittatore$_i$ ha detto che i libri di storia hanno parlato spesso delle proprie$_{*i}$ gesta.
        That dictator said that the books of history often spoke (PAST IND) about self's deeds

---

[31] For a detailed discussion of long-distance binding see Giorgi (2006, 2007).

[32] As a side note, the intermediate subject, *il primo ministro* is available as an antecedent in both cases.

(65)   Quel dittatore$_i$ sperava che i libri di storia parlassero spesso delle proprie$_i$ gesta.

That dictator hoped that the books of history often spoke (SUBJ) about self's deeds

The imperfect verbal form in example (63) patterns with the past indicative in example (64), and both contrast with the subjunctive in sentence (65). Only in example (65), in fact, can the LDA be bound outside the minimal clause containing it.

The important conclusion following from this evidence, which will be useful in the subsequent discussion, is that with the imperfect no DAR effects are detectable—due to its peculiar feature endowment. With respect to the distribution of LDAs, however, the effects due to the presence of the speaker's temporal coordinates become visible again. In other words, even if it does not show up with the DAR, the imperfect does encode reference to indexicality in the C-layer.

17.4.2.2 *Long-distance anaphors in Chinese*   In Chinese there are no DAR effects, as remarked in the previous sections, but LDAs are fairly common.[33]

In Chinese there is no subjunctive–indicative divide, given that there is no mood distinction at all. I showed in the preceding discussion that the presence of the speaker's coordinates could be detected even in absence of DAR effects, by means of the analysis of the distribution of LDAs. One might wonder, therefore, if there is any blocking effect in Chinese as well, in spite of the absence of indexical morphology associated with the verb.

It is a well-known fact that in Chinese the binding domain of a LDA is indeed bounded by intervening items, which however do not have a *verbal* nature, but (mostly) a nominal one. In other words, the blocking items are not connected with the category verb, but in most cases connected with the category noun. For instance, in Chinese an intervening first- or second-person pronoun prevents the anaphor from being bound by the subject of the superordinate clause. Consider the following example:

(66)   Zhangsan$_i$ danxin wo/ni$_j$ hui piping ziji$_{*i/j}$.

(Huang and Liu 2001: ex. 11a)

Zhangsan is worried that I/you might criticize myself/yourself/*him

In this example, the anaphor *ziji* cannot refer to the higher third person noun *Zhangsan*. This example contrasts with the following one:

---

[33] In Italian, LDAs are not very common in spoken language and for some speakers they are not totally natural. In Chinese, in contrast, LDAs are very common in all linguistic registers. It is not clear to me what the difference between the two languages is and I will not consider this issue any further.

(67)   Wo$_i$ danxin Zhangsan$_j$ hui piping ziji$_{i/j}$.

(Huang and Liu 2001: ex. 11b)

I am worried that Zhangsan will criticize me/himself

As discussed by the authors, in Chinese the blocking effect is asymmetrical in that an intervening third-person noun phrase does not have the same effect and the LDA *ziji* can refer back to *wo* (I).[34]

They also show that the blocking effect induced by a first or second person pronoun persists even if the pronoun in question does not occur in a position where it may count as a potential antecedent. Consider to this end the following example:

(68)   Zhangsan$_i$ gaosu wo$_j$ Lisi$_k$ hen ziji$_{*i/*j/k}$.

(Huang and Liu 2001: ex. 8a)

Zhangsan told me that Lisi hated self

In this example, *wo*—the first-person pronoun—is not a potential antecedent, given that it does not appear in subject position. In spite of this, the binding domain of the LDA is limited to the embedded clause and the superordinate subject, *Zhangsan*, is not a possible antecedent.

The relevant question at this point concerns the nature of the blocking effect in Chinese. Which property distinguishes first- and second-person pronouns from third persons? An interesting insight comes from some examples by Huang and Liu (2001) that are not easily amenable to the theoretical accounts formerly proposed.[35]

They observe that some third-person NPs can act as blockers, when they are identified by means of deixis, as illustrated by the following example:

(69)   Zhangsan$_i$ shuo DEICTIC-ta$_k$ qipian-le ziji$_{*i/k}$.   (Huang and Liu 2001: ex. 12)

Zhangsan said that DEICTIC-she/he cheated himself/herself

The word DEICTIC here stands for the ostensive gesture pointing at a person present in the context. When this is the case, the superordinate subject *Zhangsan* is not available as an antecedent, and the anaphor must necessarily have an antecedent in the embedded domain. In the example given above, the antecedent is the deictically identified noun.

---

[34] Huang and Liu (2001) point out that some sentences with an intervening third-person antecedent might be controversial. Some speakers might find it hard to pass over a third-person intervening subject. Their own judgment, however, is that the sentences with an intervening third person, like the one provided in the text, are fully acceptable.

[35] On the movement theory of LDAs, see Cole and Wang (1996). Huang and Liu (2001) themselves adopt a revised version of such a theory.

Another interesting observation comes from the analysis of the effects on LD binding of items, which are not even clearly nominal ones, that is, explicit temporal locutions. As I pointed out above, Chinese does not have temporal morphemes, only aspectual ones. Temporal locutions can be used to the purpose of defining the sequence of events, that is, the ordering of the events with respect to each other.

Consider the following examples:

(70)   ? Zhangsan$_i$ kuanjiang-guo houlai sha si ziji$_i$ de naxie ren$_j$.

(Huang and Liu: ex. 107)

Zhangsan has praised those persons who **later** killed him

(71)   * Zhangsan$_i$ shang xingqi zanmei-le jin zao piping ziji$_i$ de nei-ge ren.

(Huang and Liu: ex. 109)

Zhangsan praised last week the person who criticized self **this morning**

Later is an anaphoric temporal item, given that it must refer back to a time already given in the sentence. The expression *this morning,* on the other hand, is an indexical locution, and as such its location depends on the temporal coordinate of the speaker. Interestingly, the indexical temporal expression seems to act as a blocker for the LDA, so that the superordinate subject *Zhangsan* in (71) is not available as an antecedent. In contrast, in (70) the anaphor can refer back to it.[36]

Given this evidence, it is possible to formulate a generalization. The blocking effect in Chinese seems to be induced by items which crucially rely for their interpretation on indexicality—that is, on the context defined on the basis of the speaker's temporal and spatial coordinates. First- and second-person pronouns; deictically identified noun phrases; indexical temporal locutions— they all share this property. If this is correct, then Italian and Chinese would not differ at the relevant level of abstraction, in that in both languages the distribution of LDA would be affected by the presence in the sentence of indexical items.

The morphosyntactic properties of Italian are such that indexicality is prototypically encoded, as far as the syntax goes, in the verbal system—as for instance by means of the distinction between indicative and subjunctive. In Chinese, indexicality cannot be encoded in the same way, but the relevant effects are visible with all indexically related items.[37] In other words, the

---

[36] Huang and Liu (2001) actually mark this example as "?" for unclear reasons. It is nevertheless a significant contrast.

[37] See Giorgi (2010) for a discussion of indexically related nominal expressions in Italian. As I said in the text, the prototypical encoding in Italian is on the verbal system, but other indexical items, such as first- and second-person pronouns, also show a milder blocking effect with LDAs.

presence of the speaker's coordinates shows up in different ways, due to the fact that the languages in question differ with respect to their morphosyntactic properties. In Chinese, because the lack of verbal morphology, the presence of speaker's coordinates does not show up in DAR phenomena, as in Italian, but their effects on LD binding are exactly the same.

17.5 Conclusions

The evidence discussed in this chapter points to the conclusion that, in all the languages considered here, the speaker's temporal and spatial coordinates are encoded in the syntax and have detectable effects on the interface conditions imposed by conceptual–intentional system. This requirement might therefore reasonably be taken to be universal and to be part of Narrow Syntax.

It is even possible to speculate that precisely this property is at the bottom of the phase nature of the complementizer projection. In fact, the location of events with respect to indexicality, or their lack of location with respect to it, might be taken to be the universal and basic property that clauses have to satisfy. In this perspective, therefore, it can be concluded that all languages are optimal, independently from the specific morphosyntactic implementation they exhibit, because they all interface with the C-I system and with the context in the same way once the appropriate level of abstraction is established.

18

Emergence of a Systemic Semantics through Minimal and Underspecified Codes

WOLFRAM HINZEN

18.1 Introduction

In this chapter I will revisit and rehearse some claims of an architectural nature that conflict with standard Minimalism in linguistic theory, with a view to bringing into sharper focus what I am calling an explanatory theory of semantics. I also want to make some further steps towards this project, by assessing which generic competencies allowing a systematic mode of thought are plausibly available in the absence of linguistic communication. This will make clearer which elements of semantics in a human sense such competencies do not entail.

From all the components or aspects of the language faculty, the semantic component is arguably still the most obscure, at least if we look at it from a naturalistic or biolinguistic perspective. Theories of semantics since Frege have largely not adopted this perspective and been driven by rather different theoretical concerns. For Frege himself, logic was a normative enterprise, not a naturalistic one, and natural language was a functional device for representing the logical structure and contents of thoughts, in radically imperfect ways. Being "internal" to the organism or its "mind" here equated with "subjective," whereas (propositional) meaning was meant to be "objective," and a naturalistic basis for objectivity could not be seen. Hence such meaning had to be associated with mind-external and language-independent "propositions": abstract Platonic objects that have their truth conditions essentially, whereas everything else that one might want to endow with meaning (like natural language) had those truth conditions only 'derivatively'. If there was any stability in theorizing about semantics in the twentieth century at all, it was this externalist drive in the analysis of meaning, which is hard to square with the internalist viewpoint that the biolinguistic program has adopted.

Frege's Platonism was hardly to the taste of twentieth-century philosophers of mind, in an era that was largely dominated by the reductionist viewpoint of metaphysical physicalism. According to this view, only the physical is real. Hence meanings, which do not exactly wear their physical identity on their sleeves, are not, as such, real—or, rather, if and to the extent that they are, they need to "supervene" on the physical, as was (and is) commonly proposed (e.g. Fodor 1990). If, moreover, externalism holds, the meanings will have to be fixed by external relations to the physical world rather than by organism-internal conditions. Thus the most prominent paradigm in the theory of semantics became the reference theory of meaning. According to this theory, what fixes the meaning of any linguistic entity is the reference relation. The meaning of a word is its referent, and for a word to mean something is for there to be this particular relation in place, between the word as such—analyzed physicalistically as a "noise" or physical shape—and the physical object that is its referent. If meaning reduces to this relation and the relata are physical objects, physicalism is maintained and the metaphysical problem that meanings pose has disappeared.

Yet, the explanatory problems have not even begun to be addressed. Thus we precisely wish to know, for each syntactic unit, how the reference relation gets into place. It is exactly the reference relation that we need to explain—and analyze empirically first so we know what there is to explain (Hinzen 2006). One might wonder, for example, how an externalist viewpoint that identifies meaning with reference could illuminate the semantic difference between Latin *currere* 'run' and *cursus* 'the/a run', two words that, in virtue of their grammatical form, provide two different perspectives on what can be the same external thing or event.

As things stand, the project of describing human uses of words for referential purposes in purely physical terms, using the vocabulary of causation, "learning," or "reinforcement," has not reached a level of an explanatory and predictive theorizing. Despite the methodological flaws in this project as identified in Chomsky (1959a), in philosophical theories of semantics the attitude prevails that the reference relation can be used to an explanatory purpose, and it is not primarily the underlying grammatical structure of a linguistic expression that needs to be invoked in order to explain how we use a word to refer to things in the uniquely human ways that we do. Against this consensus, some voices have contended that reference in the above sense does not exist in human language at all (Chomsky 1959a, 2000b). It has been argued that a reference relation qua direct relationship between words and mind-independent things that are extensionally and physically identified is a suitable model of non-human animal reference only (Mukherji 2010). Arguably what is most striking about human reference is that it is physically unconstrained. Physical realization in this world is clearly no constraint for what we can decide to use language to refer to. The notion of a referential expression in the linguistic sense (e.g. Longobardi 2005a) makes no reference to physical existence. It seems fair to say that while the theory of reference has formed almost an axiomatic basis for much of the philosophy of language and the philosophy of mind, it has not been systematically investigated empirically or experimentally tested.

Within the logic paradigm, of which the philosophy of language is a part, this was not required: it was not the point of what Frege and Russell had conceived as the project of a philosophical logic. But within biolinguistics it is the very point. Dealing with semantics formally, as in the Montagovian tradition, and replacing the notion of reference with the formal notion of a semantic value, is a way of abstracting from the empirical and explanatory problems involved. Observations about the various truth conditions of expression—like the famous ambiguity in *The king of France is not bald*, which motivated Russell's theory of descriptions—form the heart of this tradition. But these are merely data for a genuine theory of semantics; the formalization of such intuitions in first-order predicate logic or lambda calculus is not yet the explanation we seek.

An explanatory approach to human semantics is what we need and lack. The perceived failures of the theory of reference have created a lacuna which no other theory of meaning has so far been able to fill. Theories of semantics are about a domain in nature that we do not understand.

18.2 What Needs to be Explained

What we need to explain in this domain is what is not "virtually conceptually necessary" in human semantics, in the sense of Chomsky (1995): that is, what is not a feature that the system has to have in order to be usable at all. The problem here is that almost none of the features that human semantics has are necessary ones in this sense. I will argue that this applies to the systematicity and compositionality of semantics, but even more so to an aspect of semantics that has to be crucially distinguished from this, namely reference and truth.

It remains a rather striking fact that no human being, pathologies aside, only knows 17 sentences, or 17,000, or 17 million. Clearly this is for a similar reason as that no normal human being, roughly beyond the age of four, only knows 17 natural numbers, or 17,000, or 17 million. Knowledge of meaning in language, like knowledge of number, is highly systemic, despite the massive contextuality that every single linguistic expression equally exhibits.

One way of putting this observation is that knowledge of meaning in language has an algebraic character: it is based on abstract rules stated over variables (Marcus 2001). Knowledge of the relation between x and z expressed in the equation $x + 2 = z$ is not based on any knowledge of specific relations between 2 and 4, say, or between 11 and 13. Knowledge of the equation is knowledge of a relation that obtains between an infinity of possible values that the relevant variables can take—crucially including values that have never appeared in our experience, and that we therefore cannot have learned anything about. In the same way, children know that the stem *lov*- conjoined with the inflection *-ed* yields the past tense of the relevant stem: lov- + -ed = Past. But they would also know that the same rule could be applied to an entirely novel possible word *brig*, whose past-tense form would be *brigged*, as long as the novel input is classed as a value of the relevant variable stem.

The abstract and algebraic character of natural language semantics has as such nothing to do with how language relates to the world, and hence it has nothing to do with reference or truth either. *John loves Mary*, say, means what it does because it involves a relation between variables, one of which plays the role of the Agent (lover), the other of which that of the Patient (beloved), in such a way that whatever pair of NPs we insert in these positions (which are specific phrase-structural configurations in the underlying structure of the expression in question) will result in the same algebraic relation between love, a lover, and a beloved, be it *Mary loves John*, *The police love Christmas*, *Martians love humans*, or another of an infinity of possible expressions instantiating the same equation. The variables in question and the relations stated over them exist in a human brain—and as far as we know in no other brain or part of physical reality: algebraicity is a formal property of expressions as processed by minds (and/or brains), and hence does not entail truth or reference, if these are viewed as outer relations, in any way, as far as I can see.

From this we predict, correctly, that real-world reference, in the sense of referential acts actually picking out something physically real, plays no direct role for the systematicity of language. And indeed, how we compose concepts in accordance with algebraic relations is not constrained by what is true in the world or which objects exist. The combinatorial machinery will operate blindly as before, without noticing whether some concept it retrieves from memory is a fictional concept or not ("blue house" vs. "pink unicorn"). No grammatical process is known to either operate or not, depending on whether the lexical item or phrase it applies to depicts something fictional or not. This is why we can "build" possible worlds as much as we can depict the actual one, and in either case proceed with equal ease, using, from a linguistic point of view, the exact same mechanisms and combinatorial principles. In sum, language is insensitive to the difference that existence makes and it leaves ontology behind.[1]

A second sense in which systematicity and the compositionality of meaning that goes with it has nothing to do with reference or truth transpires when we look at adjunct structures. Consider (1).

(1)   a. [a man who is] young, handsome, smart, fair, tall, . . .

      b. [walk] slowly, thoughtfully, in the garden, alone, . . .

Both (1a) and (1b) are undoubtedly compositional, but while (1a) as a whole can be used referentially (namely, to refer to a man under this description), the modificational parts of either (1a) or (1b) (which consist of a series of modifiers of the bracketed constituents) cannot be so used. The purpose of a modifier precisely is to modify an object of reference rather than to refer to one. Referring and modifying are two different intentional activities to which grammars are sensitive, and they correspond to different construction types: the former to noun phrases and sentences (if one includes truth among reference), the latter to adjunctions. But, and this is the crucial point, compositionality, an aspect of systematicity, is not affected by this difference. Again, therefore, referential uses of compositional structures go beyond what compositionality as such entails. In theory, or logically, there could be a creature that could only generate adjunct structures, hence have a compositional mind, while arguments (which are syntactically more complex, involving verbs, Theta theory, and Case assignment) remain a mystery to it.

Note, moreover, that in a very perspicuous sense, a phrase that has a referential use, like *a man who is* . . . presupposes the compositional structure *man who is* . . . as an inherent part of it, while the reverse is not true. One can generate the latter expression without generating the former, which involves one extra operation, correlating with quantificational reference. In this sense, intentionality and reference are not only different from compositionality but presuppose it asymmetrically (Uriagereka 2008): intentionality in the human sense presupposes a compositional mind, while, at least logically, a mind

---

[1] No human language, to my knowledge, has any morphological marker of existence in the way that it may have markers of animacy, tense, or social status.

merely able to compose concepts is not necessarily one that can also refer or make judgments.

A prominent current hypothesis on the origin of language (Spelke 2003) helps to explain a mind of the former (compositional) type, not the latter (intentional), which is more discontinuous with pre-linguistic animal cognition. There is a form of reference in the absence of compositionality in the animal world, but this is functional reference, which, unlike intentional reference in humans, is situation-specific and stimulus-controlled (there tends to be a direct causal link between the vocal signal and the external object that acts as a stimulus for the call), context-independent (more information about the context need not be known to understand the signal's meaning), and non-intentional (the caller need not have had any intentions to communicate anything, nor have a representation of the intentions of his recipients) (Hauser 2000). Intentional reference in non-linguistic beings, by contrast, in either their gestures or their vocal communications, is scarce, if existent at all (Hauser, Chomsky, and Fitch et al. 2002; Terrace 2005; Hauser 2008). However, that their thought exhibits systematicity and relational competence is not as implausible (see Section 18.4). Hence, once again, systematicity and reference are distinguishable aspects of a human semantics, which need to be independently explained; a systemic (or compositional) semantics is not as such a referential (or intentional) one.

Just as nouns do not change their meaning in line with whether they are instantiated in the world or not, sentences do not change their meaning depending on whether they are true or false. Meaning is governed by different principles than whether or not we actually "hit our target" (what we say is true). Truth is for sentences what existence is for noun phrases. The factual truth or falsehood of a sentence is a matter not intrinsic but extraneous to language. None of this means that this extraneous and relational aspect of language as such would have existed, had language not existed. The existence of truth as such could fall out from constraints on linguistic form; and we will later suggest it does. Indeed, we have already seen that intentional acts of language use need the right grammar to support them, using the right layers of syntactic complexity. So the question I want to bring into focus is really the question of how we move from a compositional mind to an intentional one—and what kinds of structures are involved in this transition. An answer to this question would go some way toward pursuing an explanatory approach to human semantics, since one will thereby have illuminated one of its design primitives.

Some architectural commitments in current Minimalism may prevent progress on this front, which is what I argue next.

18.3 Minimalism and the Semantic Component

Minimalism has involved a tentative view of the nature of the semantic component that is implicit in how the Strong Minimalist Thesis (SMT) and hence the research program of Minimalism itself is pursued. According to this thesis, the design of the language faculty is a result of conditions imposed on this faculty by outside, non-linguistic cognitive systems. These will interface with the language system once it is "inserted" into the brain of a pre-linguistic hominid, and the optimal design hypothesis that the SMT explores entails that what kind of representations arrive at these interfaces is a direct result of external conditions imposed on them. Put differently, what the syntax qua computational system of language produces has to match what is independently there, in the hypothesized pre-linguistic conceptual–intentional (C-I) systems. The semantics, in short, imposes, demands, or requires, and the syntax satisfies. To whatever extent it does so optimally and with maximal efficiency, the SMT is vindicated and language finds a principled explanation.

This is what I want to characterize as a "matching complexity" model of grammar. There is a task set for the system, as it were, to which the language engineer then provided an optimal solution. The solution is rationalized by the task. A tight coupling between input and output is thereby assumed; structures are specified for a particular function. Evolution, though, does not design solutions for specific tasks. What evolves is adaptability, the ability to use given resources that have a generic character to new tasks, and to scale up given solutions when new adaptive challenges arise (Wagner 2005). Just as we do not want a grammar architecture in which we engineer a special rule system for every new construction that we encounter, we should not assume that syntax evolved to match any specific and preset task.

The matching complexity model, since it begins from the task to be accomplished, will also invite the assumption that there is a rich innate endowment to match the complexity in question. One way of reading the Minimalist Program, and especially its formulation in Chomsky (2007a), is quite in conflict with this: here the innateness of language (the UG component) is programmatically minimized, and the scope of domain-general explanatory principles is maximized. We might think of this program as beginning from minimal codes (structures generated by Merge, say) that are as such entirely unspecified for the output achieved by them. The most minimal principles prove rich enough. This program is not consistent with the idea of setting an output that is to be matched. Indeed, as I will here contend, there is no independent task or output to be matched; the task accomplished by grammar arises with grammar itself: syntax formats human thought rather than expressing it, unlike what Chomsky, with the rationalist tradition, has assumed since his earliest writings.[2]

Syntax, therefore, is not task-specific either, as there was no task before syntax was there. Syntax provides underspecified codes.

By adopting the matching complexity model, Minimalism has effectively adopted the axiomatic assumptions of its functionalist opponents.[3] Thus, Pinker and Jackendoff (2005) argue that language evolved for the communication (expression) of complex propositions. Blatantly, this research program presupposes what is to be explained—that we think propositionally, in the format of language: the task is there, in order for the grammar to match it. The opposite idea, that thought is not independently there, or is only there with a different format, is not systematically considered here—any more than in recent Minimalist thinking on the evolution of language (Hauser et al. 2002).[4] With the above suggestion, however, certain circularities in the standard formulation of the SMT can be avoided.

These can be exemplified through three hypotheses currently explored in the context of vindicating the SMT. One departs from the fact that C-I incorporates a dual semantics: (i) extended argument structure and (ii) discourse properties. The rationalization of the design of grammar then is pursued along the following lines (Chomsky 2008): language "seeks to satisfy the duality in the optimal way, EM [external Merge] serving one function and IM [internal Merge] the other, avoiding additional means to express these properties." Therefore, Chomsky concludes, this particular aspect of grammar has found a principled explanation. It is clear, however, that insofar as no evidence from comparative cognition is provided for the independent and systematic availability of the duality of semantics, these explanations lack force.

---

[2] It is the founding assumption of Port Royal grammarians that human grammar is merely an arbitrary and more or less efficient way of expressing independently given thoughts, which are structured, not by grammar, but logic:

La Grammaire est l'Art de parler./ Parler, est expliquer ses pensées par des signes, que les hommes ont inventez à ce dessein./ On a trouvé que les plus commodes de ces signes, estoient les sons & les voix. Arnauld and Lancelot 1662 (1676/1966)

In short, language is an arbitrary system, based on convenient conventions whose essential function is the material rendering of immaterial thoughts.

[3] My thanks to Elisabeth Leiss for conversations on this topic.

[4] The idea of not assuming task-specificity is clearly there in this framework, though. Thus, as Chomsky (2008) points out, the simplification of the computational system to iterated Merge "incorporates the effects of three of the EST/Y-model compositional cycles, while eliminating d- and s-structure." As we might put this: it so happens that a maximally simple, domain-general, and non-task specific operation gives us all the other effects for free, which the earlier constructs specifically coded for.

Chomsky also states that the "C-I interface requires the A/A′ distinction . . . if expressive potential is to be adequately utilized." The syntax provides just that: via the device of inheritance. Therefore, again, this aspect of syntax has found a principled explanation. Here the same criticism can be made, as it can in the third example: Chomsky (2004a) argues that the workings of C-I involve an operation of predicate composition. Therefore the syntax has to provide it (through the process of adjunction to a category), and we understand why adjunction, in addition to standard Merge, exists. These explanations do not capture the generative principles that give rise to the phenomena in question, no matter whether we locate them on the linguistic or non-linguistic side of the semantic interface. Clearly, they may not arise from external conditions imposed on language at all.

Perhaps the most basic question to be asked here is why non-linguistic thought should obey a propositional format in the first place. Where it is argued that it is part of the function of a syntactic phase (Chomsky 2007a) to compute a propositional unit, it is assumed that the C-I systems are propositionally structured. But persistent problems in observing sentential organization in chimpanzee communication, either in the wild or under conditions of heavy training and tutoring (Terrace 2005), point against this conclusion. This is not to say, in the light of our earlier distinction between compositionality and reference, that a certain systematicity of thought (Fodor and Pylyshyn 1988) is not something that can be brought on in the non-human primate mind, especially when it is scaffolded by a public medium of shared and stable signs, and I return to this in the next section.

Note here that, since thought, if it exists as an independent module or domain, is generative as much as language is, there needs to be a computational engine that powers its generativity. That in turn requires thoughts to be internally structured, which in turn raises the question of whether these internal structures of thought could potentially be radically different from those that we see in linguistic expressions.[5] Note however that the relations that structure thought are of a logical nature: predication or modification, for example. While it is entirely conceivable that physical relations can differ from possible world to possible world (e.g. causation could be a different relation in a world with a different physics), it is harder to see how logical relations can possibly differ, if they exist at all. Hence if these relations structure thought, and we know anyhow that they structure language (clearly, they are present in syntax and are subject matters of syntactic theory), then the two systems

---

[5] Thoughts would not have a linguistic structural format in, say, possible world semantics, where a thought (proposition) simply is a set-theoretic abstraction. But as this is a formal model only, it does not help in the task of explaining the specific format that human thought has taken in evolution.

cannot fundamentally differ in the structures they exhibit. Put differently, thought can be syntactically studied: syntactic theory is a cognitive theory.[6]

Consider the discrete infinity of human thought in this respect. What achieves this particular aspect in the linguistic case is the part–whole constituency structure of the underlying syntactic representations of sentences. Could there be a radically different solution to the same problem in the case of thought? This is hard to see, especially if, in line with the explanatory aims of Minimalism, we have minimalized the computational system of language to such an extent that it only exhibits those features that any system exhibiting the basic features of language has to have. How could thought, as a generative system exhibiting discrete infinity, lack those features?

An idea quite foreign to SMT as currently viewed, therefore, namely that language formats thought as opposed to expressing it, deserves a hearing. This idea has been as natural to the first tradition of Universal Grammar in Europe, Modistic grammar around 1300, as the rationalist idea of language as a medium for conveying thought has become natural to us. The earlier generative tradition in the twentieth century has, given its emphasis on modularity in the sense of Fodor (1983), thoroughly emphasized the independence of thought and language, so as to provide evidence for the status of the latter as an autonomous module with a strong innate basis (e.g. Yamada 1990). But case studies such as Yamada's are no doubt controversial, and we have seen already that a central aspect of Minimalism is the attempt to maximize the use of domain-general and generic principles in explaining the language faculty. The older ideas of modularity do not fit naturally with how the field has developed. In general, the more we make semantics modular and separate its generativity from that of syntax, as in Jackendoff (2002), the less we can use the form of language to explain the contingent features of its semantics. The more syntax is part of the etiology of specifically human thought, on the other hand, and in fact provides its format, the more the opposite is true.

Which stance we take on this issue is important, as a rich view of what the C-I systems as such entail will typically go along with a deflationary view of what the syntax contributes. On the view of Hauser et al. (2002) and Chomsky (2007a, 2008), what it contributes is not phrase structures, categories, or propositions, but only recursion plus the mapping of hierarchical recursive structures to the phonetic and semantic interfaces. If I am right, however, that syntax gives us C-I as we know it, rather than answering any conditions it imposes, there is, strictly speaking, no such thing as a mapping to the semantic interface. Hence we are moving from the standard architectural

---

[6] It helps with cognitive history as well, as Longobardi and Guardiano demonstrate (this volume).

model (2a), where there is an independent semantic component, to the model (2b), where there is none. The path of computation departing from the lexicon, LEX, is inherently the path of generating meanings rather than interfacing with them.

(2) a.

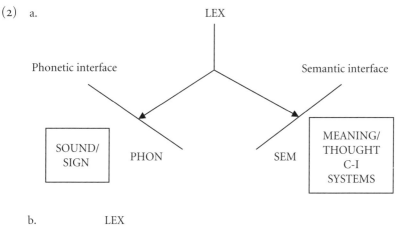

b.

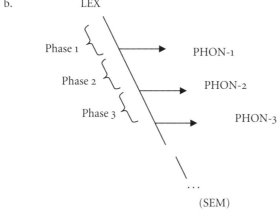

If syntax intrinsically generates semantic contents, or the structure of content, it does not make much sense to think of it as mediating sound and meaning either. Accordingly, one prediction is that there should not be any semantically uninterpretable features in syntax, and syntax should not be a mechanism for eliminating them. Everything in syntax should be inherently semantically interpretable; else it should belong to PHON. There is evidence that this might be the case (Kayne this volume; Sigurðsson 2009). An interesting example for a paradigmatically uninterpretable feature in syntax, in particular, is abstract Case. As Leiss (2000) argues along with a rich tradition in German linguistics going back to J. Grimm, Case closely interacts with verbal Aspect in the determination of *definiteness*: this quantificational function of Case may well be its central function.

If we go down this route, compositionality is another principle that may have to be rethought. It is traditionally stated as a constraint on how a structure of meaningless symbols is mapped onto semantic contents (referents). If there is no independent semantic component, syntax is not autonomous, and syntactic structure-building is the construction of an inherently interpretable structure, compositionality cannot depend on the mapping of such structures to anything (unless that is an identity-mapping). All that compositionality of language will mean is that the interpretation of complex expressions depends on the interpretation of their parts, which is precisely Chomsky's (2007a) formulation of the principle, and which does not depend on a syntax–semantics duality in terms of composition operations.[7] That is, while the syntax composes and constituent structure is visible to the performance systems and exploited for interpretational purposes, there may not be independent composition operations in the semantics at all (see further Hinzen 2009a).

That the part–whole structure of an expression matters at the semantic interface, as Chomsky's formulation suggests, is consistent with the fact that a part (constituent) of an expression in turn also depends for the way it functions on the wholes in which it occurs. We will see in Section 18.5 that this is indeed the case: how a given sentence is interpreted strongly depends on whether it is subordinated or not, for example. In a similar way, the normal functioning of the human hand depends on each of the fingers. Clearly, these are independently identifiable units, and there is a sense in which a hand is composed of fingers (or a body of a head and a torso, etc.). But what a finger is cannot be determined without reference to a hand. Intensional dependencies of parts on wholes in this sense are excluded by standard formulations of compositionality in philosophy, which always depend on the assumption of the existence of two independent generative systems, one in syntax and one in semantics.

Thus, in particular, Fodor and Pylyshyn's classic (1988: 16) stance makes it mandatory that the "objects to which the content A&B is ascribed (i.e. tokens of the expression A&B) literally contain, as proper parts, objects to which the content A is ascribed (viz. tokens of the expression A)." "Content" here distributes over the syntactic parts of an expression, and it is something external to an expression (or its instances on an occasion)—as it must be, in line with the physicalist assumptions of the model, which views elements

---

[7] As Chomsky (2007a) puts it: "A Merge-based system will be compositional in general character: the interpretation of larger units at the interfaces will depend on the interpretation of their parts."

of syntax as physical tokens of abstract types, and hence cannot ascribe any intrinsic content to such physical entities. The availability of the content A moreover has nothing to do with A's figuring in a specific composite structure such as A&B. On the line developed here, there is no physicalist ontology and there is no language- and mind-independent content. There is only linguistic form, which by hypothesis patterns in semantically meaningful ways as used by performance systems. I will return to compositionality in Section 18.5.

For now I conclude that we may want to rethink the SMT, replacing a matching complexity model that depends on fixed tasks already set with a model that puts grammar itself into the driver's seat of the evolution of human thought. That project in part depends on which generic cognitive abilities in non-humans we can count on for purposes of generating a propositional semantics.

18.4 Emergent Systematicity through Minimal and Relational Codes

In human semantics, sentences essentially state relations between objects or between objects and their properties that are subject to objective verification in some sense (*Alf is bigger than Bart, Peter loves Mary, This is round*). Beyond a basic and generic capacity for relational competence, the development of a language clearly further depends on the executive power to combine and recombine the elements of relational structures so as to change their serial order, while preserving their hierarchical structure. Are relational and hierarchical competencies of this sort beyond the reach of the simian mind, under suitable conditions of training?

One would hope not: the evolutionary transition to a linguistic semantics becomes a mystery if the pre-linguistic simian mind was entirely incapable of coding information in such a relational format, as has been claimed (Tomasello and Call 1997; McPhail 1998; Conway and Christiansen 2001). Thus, suppose the simian mind is an association-forming engine only, based on experience-dependent statistical relations between individual objects. On what might the objective nature of a linguistic semantics—a system of sharable codes grounded in non-arbitrary (non-subjective) features of an environment—be based? There had better be a basis for developing such codes privately, in order for them to be then externalizable in a communication system. As McGonigle and Chalmers (2007) point out, this may require suitable conditions not available in the wild, where the environment may not pose the challenges to which we subject human babies by immersing them in a linguistic environment.

In this section I will point to evidence that this conclusion may indeed be correct. If so, there is a basis for the idea of grounding the systematicity of semantics in something like a private grammar, which is recognizably like the syntax of human languages. This would establish that systematic forms of semantics go along with or involve correlating forms of syntactic sophistication, rather than providing any conditions for them. The objectivity of the thoughts in question arises with the relational codes that bring them into place.

As research by McGonigle and Chalmers has shown, squirrel monkeys are able to code size and brightness stimuli relationally (for a review of this line of research over three decades, see McGonigle and Chalmers 2007). Comparing their way of doing so with a group of monkeys required to code them on an absolute basis revealed the superior adaptive value of the more abstract relational encoding. The relational codes in question are irreducible to a set of discrete associative stimulus–response connections based on absolute size. A relational code such as bigger/biggest in principle allows the encoding of novel stimuli not encountered before, and different in terms of absolute size; hence it generalizes freely over the training set in ways that Marcus (2001) identifies as a criterion for the "algebraic mind." A pivotal example of this sort of competence is transitive inference. McGonigle and Chalmers (1977) adapted a transitivity test designed for very young children for use in animals, and showed a capacity in the animals for dealing with the transitivity of binary choices in a set of four pairs of tins (A or B; B or C; C or D; D or E, with transitive test cases such as B or D), coded as different in ways that did not allow any easy perceptual solutions to the choice problem so that relational solutions had to be employed. Given all this it seems that at least under suitable conditions of extensive training and tutoring, monkeys achieve systematicity in the broad Fodor–Pylyshyn (1988) sense.

The culmination of this research was to demonstrate the simian's ability not only to merely code in terms of such relations as "biggest" or "smallest," but also in terms of a connected system of multiple rules operated concurrently, involving more complex codes such as "second biggest" and rules such as "if red, then biggest" (McGonigle and Chalmers 2007). The requirement here is the assignment of an ordinal value to each object in a set based on its systematic relations to other objects, whatever the objects are. Five rules such as the above were handled concurrently, with the limits to the number of rules arguably more indicative of the limits of the experimental design than the generativity of the simian minds involved. Again, where a new set of stimuli is used in which absolute size values are changed, ordinal values could be conserved, attesting to the abstractness of the codes involved.

That a form of semantic systematicity is attained here, and that it is unboundedly generative as revealed in longitudinal learning trajectories, seems hard to deny. Crucially, moreover, this system gets into place gradually, begining from a minimal dimension of difference, of which there is some underlying representation, which then gives rise gradually to a relational structure on to which arbitrary color values of stimuli can be mapped as instructions to perform particular tasks. This is the sort of conclusion we expect, on a model like the above, where hardwired innateness is traded for generic processes and codes that are available and adaptable as experience provides the occasions.

Of the essence of language, however, is not only the power to order or employ relational and transferable codes, but to do so on the basis of "chunking," where stimuli are grouped on the basis of categories—a device of economy. In short, the productivity and flexibility that comes with language depends on hierarchical control. Again, this can be tested outside the linguistic domain, as in a serialization task that depends on the execution of a rule such as "all the Xs come before the Ys" and "all Ys come before the Zs." Competence in designing such a task goes beyond the earlier levels of cognitive achievement and is the basis for recombination, as when linear order is changed while hierarchical structure is maintained. Hierarchical control can further involve the nesting of one dimension of difference within another, as when all blue circles come before all blue squares while red squares come before green circles.

In a culmination of their developmentalist program started in the 1970s, and against a consensus captured by, for instance, Spinozzi et al. (1999), McGonigle, Chalmers and Dickinson (2003) trained *cebus appella* monkeys to touch icons on a touchscreen so as to reveal levels of hierarchical control. Again, not so as to reveal the spontaneous ability of such levels of control (as an innate ability), but their availability over a learning trajectory of several years where such levels of control can emerge (for evidence for such multiple hierarchical classification in the wild, though, see Bergman et al. 2003). Being presented first with three shapes and learning to put them in a particular order (e.g. squares before triangles before circles), the monkeys gradually expanded sequences by increasing the numbers of items within each category (two squares before two triangles before two circles; three squares before three triangles before three circles, etc.), including one condition in which, within each category, there was an imposed condition of increased size (smallest square, then second-smallest square, biggest square, smallest triangle, second-smallest triangle, biggest triangle, etc.), so that there is order at several hierarchical levels, both within and between categories. This brings us back to the model of the syntax–semantics interface I criticized in Section 18.3. Where the view of the C-I systems is so inflated, syntax can be deflated so as not to provide any relevant constraints on semantic interpretation at all. But a syntax thus deflated will also deprive syntax of explaining the forms of semantics that we get. In a final condition, nine items were serialized in one single sequence of increasing size, with category transitions twice on the way. McGonigle and Chalmers (2007) argue that it is quite impossible to model such performance with a finite-state device entrained through simple associations.

Arguably, then, semantic systematicity depending on the development of a suitable internal syntax of relational codes is available to non-humans under suitable conditions of environmental challenge and training. The same seems to apply to a basic capacity to map stimuli onto binary relational codes (a form of Merge, under a specific binary relation), as well as impressive levels of hierarchical, if not recursive, executive control. None of this takes us all the way to intentionality and reference in the human sense, but it provides a systematic basis for it.

18.5 From a Relational to an Intentional Code

Coding stimuli relationally, then, leads to representations that are objective and allow for verification: truth, therefore, is on the horizon of evolution here. The human sentence invokes a more specific categorial anatomy and relational resources. These provide for a unique *Gestalt* that as such in no way follows from a basic ability to employ relational codes, and is possibly also conditioned by the way we happen to externalize such codes in a language and employ it to a communicative use. Which primitives are involved?

Take a merely thematic structure like (3) unspecified for Tense, Aspect, or even category (i.e. let destruct be a lexical root):

(3)   [$_{VP}$ Caesar [destruct [Syracuse]]]

It picks out an event with a fully specified thematic structure, yet leaves completely open how we refer to it. Logically, (3) specifies a relational predicate, with an internal compositional structure, but does not include a predication in the sense of a localization in either time or discourse. In short, whatever happens in lexically projected argument structures (thematic structures) does not help with reference.

Once predicates are available, they can be combined conjunctively, as in (4), again with no referential possibilities or predication of some logical subject arising. Clearly, a square circle is not any particular circle: it is merely the conceptual and compositional specification of a condition that an object satisfies if it is square and a circle (4b), irrespective of whether there are any:

(4)   a. square circle

    b. λx [SQUARE (x) & CIRCLE (x)]

Neo-Davidsonians such as Higginbotham (1985) have argued that a sentence, equally, is the compositional specification of a condition that an object satisfies just in case it satisfies a number of predicates, such as CAUSE and OPEN in (5b), which the Neo-Davidsonian finds in the underlying syntactic structure of an expression such as (5a).[8]

(5)   a. John opened the door.

    b. λe [CAUSE (John, e) & OPEN (the door, e)].

In essence, thus, a sentence is a conjunction of predicates, which is the kind of semantics appropriate to adjuncts (Chomsky 2004a: 117). In contemporary versions of Neo-Davidsonianism (Pietroski 2005), arguments are even more fully assimilated to adjuncts, all arguments being predicates of events conjoined conjunctively. Adjunction, a flat, concatenative operation, thus becomes the core operation of grammar.

Since adjunction to a category leaves that category exactly as it was before (Chomsky 2004a), and nothing changes in the phrase structure or level of projection, adjunction is too weak a relational primitive around which a grammar can be constructed. Again it will not help with reference and intentionality, for which the conjunction of predicates is not what is needed.

The symmetric nature of adjunction is particularly worrisome, given that intentional aspects of language use all correlate with crucial asymmetries in syntax: topic vs. comment, subject vs. predicate, reference vs. description, functional vs. lexical, etc. Even with adjuncts, in fact, we see elements of hierarchy and asymmetry arising where adjuncts of semantically different types are stacked. The order of adverbs is relevant. For example, (6b) is less natural than (6a) (cf. Cinque 1999):

(6)   a. I was evidently once married.

    b. ?I was once evidently married.

---

[8] At least the Neo-Davidsonian has to assume that there is something in the syntax that allows us to map it to the logical form in (5b).

Thus, adverbial modifiers target specific layers in the functional hierarchy of the clause: they are not merely conjoined, and their combination is not symmetric. But such asymmetries of meaning have nothing to do with reference and truth either. What we need to understand for this is the special behavior of the functional layers of projection lines emanating from lexical heads within their respective cycles of generation. Consider the differences between (7a–c), in comparison to the thematic structure (3):

(7)   a. [NP Caesar's destruction of Syracuse].

     b. [TP Caesar destroyed Syracuse].

     c. [CP (That) Caesar destroyed Syracuse].

None of these differ from (3) in regard to their conceptual–thematic (eventive) content: clearly, the very same event or predicate, conceptually and compositionally speaking, is involved. All three differ from (3), rather, in that this same content is viewed under three different *referential perspectives*. In (7a), we could say that we refer to the event itself; in (7b) we refer to the time (in the past) at which the event takes place; in (7c) it is the proposition as such. As the event itself stays the same, therefore, our referential perspective on it changes. What we are looking at is the emergence of a *grammatical* over a mere lexical semantics: grammar, through the functional layers of lexical projections, provides the perspectives in question, which nothing in the external world or in non-linguistic cognition seems to determine. Generally speaking, the intentional structure of an expression gets more and more intricate (involving elements of Aspect, Tense, and Force), as syntactic complexity (projection levels) increases. To refer, clearly, we have to follow the footpaths of the (extended) projections that lexical heads project up to their outer limits.

Truth, interestingly, arises where these layered sentential projections come to their very end, and nothing projects any further (Arsenijević and Hinzen 2009). No truth-bearing proposition can be expressed by anything short of the full hierarchy of the human clause,[9] and there is nothing more in language that can systematically happen beyond this point, if compositional and recursive operations is what we mean. Truth, in short, not only emerges at a late stage in the build-up of hierarchical, structural complexity, but at the last one: once an expression has been evaluated for truth, nothing can really happen to it any more: a move in the language game has been made.[10] The

---

[9] Naturally there are syntactically reduced forms of assertions such as *You idiot!* and *Good cook, your mother*. However, as Potts and Roeper(2006) plausibly argue, the former is not equivalent semantically to a propositional claim; and the latter functions semantically in different ways as well.

[10] This is discussed in much more detail, and with qualifications, in Hinzen (2009b).

assertion that took place is now moved into the discourse, it becomes part of the common ground, and it cannot be taken back.[11]

Adding more relational predicates to a given derivation and composing them with others already existing does not allow us to understand what happens at this point of a derivation. Predication as the application of a predicate to a logical subject also does not help: it is a relation which we find in embedded Small Clauses as well, for example, which are not evaluated for truth and carry no assertoric force, as in (8):

(8)   She found [John dead].

Nor does finite Tense suffice, which again we find in embedded clauses as well, hence in the absence of any truth values or alethic force assigned, as in (9), where the truth value of the whole sentence in no way depends on that of its embedded part, and that part must in fact not be evaluated for truth (creating particular difficulties for children prior to the age of four: see de Villiers 2005):

(9)   [Mom said [she bought oranges]].

The question of what truth adds, and in what sense this is something different from merely another relational predicate, is thus a pressing one. All we have seen so far is that truth appears to be an outer limit to structure building: it is how far structures in human language stretch. Yet, this in itself tells us something.

What I will do in the remainder of this chapter is to present a proposal I have made elsewhere on what, in fact, it might tell us about the origin of human truth (see Hinzen 2009b). The basic idea is that the linguistic system appears to be fundamentally bounded by truth, this being the intrinsic function of truth as a specific form of semantic evaluation in human language. Before the truth value is assigned, only predicative relations are being composed. Adding the truth predicate is not to do anything new at all in terms of semantic content, and does not contribute any further descriptive information, exactly as philosophers have observed when they noted that to assert (10a) is semantically no more and no less than to assert (10b) (Quine 1968):

(10)   a. It is true that snow is white.
       b. Snow is white.

[11] Even conceptually, it is unclear what could come next here. The truth, once established or asserted, for instance cannot then again be tensed. It is one of the oldest intuitions in philosophical reflections, dating back to Parmenides, that the truth is not tensed: if some truth holds at any one time, it holds at all times. If am typing now, it will be true forever that I am typing now (it will not have become false tomorrow, say).

Truth as a form of semantic evaluation thus equates with leaving the derivational workspace in which predicates are being composed. Truth and compositionality inversely relate. Compositionality is thus not, as anticipated in
Section 18.3, a process in semantics that runs in parallel to a compositional
process in syntax: composition of predicates happens in the syntax, and it
is what syntax does. Semantics, in the form of an evaluation for truth, is
the end to that. While, from an abstract point of view, recursive structure
building in language can go on forever, it cannot and does not, in reality, where
recursive growth is constrained by use: semantic access to the derivation stops
the recursive growth in question.

This brings us back to the model of the syntax–semantics interface I criticized in Section 18.3. Where the view of the C-I systems is so inflated, syntax
can be deflated so as not to provide any relevant constraints on semantic
interpretation at all. But a syntax thus deflated will also deprive syntax of
explaining the forms of semantics that we get. A syntactic tree as modeled in
Minimalism grows forever—a residue of the autonomy of syntax. There is no
intrinsic limit to Merge as minimalistically conceived: it iterates unboundedly.
Hence all restrictions must come from the outside, an unexplained semantic
component. Yet, just as ageing and death in organic growth are built into the
cell and are more rarely externally caused through accident or murder, limits
to recursive growth in language may be intrinsic and built-in as well. If so, no
external conditions need to be invoked.

Indeed, what we see is that every single projection line emanating from a
lexical head (even if "extended" in the sense of Grimshaw 1990) is radically
finite and in fact quite short: there is no recursion—no recurrence of the
same category in the same—inside a single phase. In each derivational phase
(Chomsky 2008), moreover, semantic evaluation is withheld while descriptive
complexity is being built up and the phase boundary is not yet reached.
When it is, referential evaluation takes place, and the phase is canceled: the
phase is transferred out of the derivational workspace, with only its head
and left periphery staying behind, so as to *save* the derivation.[12] Thus there
is in this sense no recursion beyond the phase either: the phase as such is
gone the moment it could recursively embed (Arsenijević and Hinzen 2009).
Even saving the derivation in this fashion and letting some recursion happen,
depends on choosing either the nominal or the eventive phase (based on the

---

[12] Here I am following Arsenijević's (2007) model that each phase corresponds to a *completely
referential expression*. Talking is about updating a given set of discourse referents by new information,
or to set up new ones: delivering discourse referents to the discourse interface and updating them with
new information is what phases in syntax do. Referents come in three types, depending on the phase in
question: they can be objects-in-space (DP), events-in-time (v^*P), or propositions-in-discourse (CP).

head *v*). If the choice falls on whatever head initiates the final C-phase (say, T), the moment of referential evaluation for truth at the phase boundary may be final (depending on the feature specification of C), and the derivation will stop.

Recursion thus does not come for free: in the domain of language it is wrought, and it arises only with the help of the phase, and by saving a derivation from cancellation. Semantic evaluation remains the mystery it is if syntax is as unbounded as current conceptions of Merge suggest. If it is intrinsically bounded, and there is strictly no unboundedness in syntax at all, we may begin to understand what it is for a linguistic expression to be evaluated for truth.

Given the mechanisms of phasal Transfer and phase-level interpretation together with the function of truth as a stop to compositionality and recursion, it is entirely expected that no truth-values should be assigned at intermediate phase boundaries, as noted for (9) above. The same fact is systematically unexpected on the common view in formal semantics that semantics is compositional and the basic semantic value that a sentence carries, no matter whether embedded or not, is a truth value. On this view, opacity and intensionality become anomalies. Why should a perfectly normal syntactic unit, on this view, once it becomes an embedded constituent of a larger whole, not function as it normally does, and refer to whatever extensional semantic value it usually has? Unsurprisingly, therefore, sentences like (9) have caused fundamental consternation ever since Frege and various formal devices have been employed to heal this grave deficiency of language: its intensionality.

The most radical therapy is due to Davidson (2001), for whom there is no intensionality; (9) is in fact two paratactically conjoined sentences. Yet subordination and the lack of symmetry in combined constituents is what characterizes syntax most centrally. Could it really be that we really have to deny the semantic significance of hypotaxis—deny syntax, in effect—in order to get the semantics right? Curing intensionality by effectively denying syntax and its interpretive effects is, on the model of syntax above, like killing a patient whose only deficiency is age. Intensionality is what the way that recursion is implemented in language straightforwardly entails: a structure that is transferred for interpretation becomes opaque and inaccessible for interpretation.

A systematic semantics, then, may emerge from relational codes: predicates that can be conjoined and applied. But this will not have much to do with intentionality and truth. For truth is the opposite of that; it is a limitation imposed on recursive growth. The phase in its various guises as nominal, verbal, and clausal is the one irreducible *Gestalt* that neither syntax qua Merge nor semantics will explain.

To put this differently, if syntax is Merge, syntax cannot be the answer to the emergence of a systematic semantics. But it must be, as a systematic semantics cannot arise in its absence: this is as true of the relational competence in monkeys as of the referential competence in humans. Rather than constraining syntax from the outside as in the SMT and reducing it to Merge, we should take our cues from syntax as it is empirically given, namely as a radically finite system. In one of its sub-systems, the adjunctive one, it involves the operation of combining predicates. Even here no combinations are fully symmetric, and as part–whole structures in argument structures arise, symmetry disappears entirely, and intensionality appears, disturbing the smooth path of semantic composition. With phases added, compositionality appears as even more restricted (it is bound to the phase), until the final moment in a derivation, where the truth value is assigned, and composition stops entirely.

If a syntactic object that occurs embedded—becomes a part of a whole—does not function as it does when it occurs in isolation, this is a prima facie break with compositionality as traditionally defined, as syntactic constituents will not then have their semantic values context-independently. If, beyond that, the truth value of a whole sentence does not depend on the truth value of its parts, and the parts cannot in fact have any truth values assigned to them, compositionality as a general principle for the fixation of meaning in recursive structures fails.

18.6 Conclusions

A systemic semantics emerges where organisms can map experiential input to an internal system of relational codes that scaffold a form of representation that can bring out an objective content in the organism's experience. Semantics can be compositional in limited ways within such an internal relational scheme, which is likely to stabilize further and get even more systematic once externalized in a public symbolic medium. None of this, I have argued, yet explains the specific character of the computational dynamics in language that gives rise to its characteristic intentional uses, as when expressions are evaluated for reference and truth. These, I have argued, can be rationalized as bounding elements to the system—intrinsic and built-in limits to what kind of structures can be built. Merge is not "free," but tied to these limits. Just as some biologists have argued that the organism with its life cycle is an irreducible unit of biological description (Brandon 1988; Goodwin 1994), the phase in syntax may be such an irreducible unit too. My suggestion has been that the attempt to reduce higher-order units such as the phase or the sentence to the basic operation Merge is a reductionist and ultimately nominalist perspective, which may point linguistic research in the wrong direction. Nor is it a remedy for such austerity in syntax to implausibly assume a richly articulated semantics on the other side of the interface, where no specific syntactic format will support it.

19

Bridging the Gap between Brain and Syntax: A Case for a Role of the Phonological Loop

CARLO CECCHETTO AND COSTANZA PAPAGNO

19.1 Introduction

It is commonly accepted that language comprehension relies on memory resources. This conclusion is forced by the observation that a characteristic (possibly, a defining) property of natural languages is that they involve long-distance dependencies, which are illustrated by the following examples:

(1) The paper that we submitted to the second volume of the *Biolinguistics* series argues for an involvement of Short-Term Memory (STM) in language comprehension.

(2) Which paper did a former colleague of yours willingly submit to this volume?

(3) No author denied that the next volume of the *Biolinguistics* series would publish his paper.

In (1) the matrix subject (*the paper*) is separated by the matrix predicate (*argues for...*) by the center-embedded relative clause; in (2) the *wh* phrase *which paper* must be related to the argument position of the verb *submit*; and (3) admits a reading in which the pronoun *his* is semantically dependent on the negative quantifier *no author*. These dependencies are analyzed in different ways in the linguistic literature, but they all have in common that they extend across intervening linguistic material, so the link between the two categories is non-local.

Given the emphasis that generative models (starting from Chomsky 1957) have given to what is called today the displacement property of natural languages, a typical case of which is the long distance dependency illustrated in

(2), it is perhaps surprising that, up to recent years, linguistic models did not explicitly thematize the question of which computational resources (including memory resources) are actually involved in language production and comprehension. This topic has been more intensively investigated by psycholinguists studying language processing and by neuropsychologists studying patients with STM (and/or language) disorders. However, things are changing, starting from the version of the Minimalist Program proposed in Chomsky (1995). Current models of linguistic competence do not ignore the question of the computational resources and the gap between purely linguistic models and psycholinguistic and neuropsychological models is getting smaller.

In this scenario, we believe that it is important to re-address the question of the STM resources that are involved in language comprehension. A better understanding of this issue is important for different reasons. On the one hand, clarifying this question would allow generative models to become more and more psychologically plausible. On the other hand, this question has potential consequences in clinical practice, because identifying the role of verbal STM in language is important for patients' rehabilitation. We start by presenting the start-of-the-art of the psychological research on verbal STM, then we critically examine the relevant literature.

This chapter is organized as follows: in Section 19.2 we summarize the main features of the most established model of Working Memory (WM, Baddeley and Hitch 1974). In Section 19.3 we report research investigating whether memory resources measured by a popular test, the reading span, are involved in language processing. In this section we also introduce the so-called separate-sentence-interpretation-resource theory, according to which memory resources used in sentence processing constitute a separate module within WM and are not measured by any standard procedure testing verbal memory. Section 19.4 reports results from the available literature on the issue of whether the Phonological Loop, a component of Baddeley and Hitch's model, is involved in syntactic parsing. Section 19.5 discusses evidence from languages in the visuo-spatial modality. In Section 19.6, which concludes the chapter, the evidence discussed in previous sections is summarized and it is proposed that (contra the separate-sentence-interpretation-resource theory) the Phonological Loop does assist sentence processing. Possible consequences for theoretical linguistic models and for brain activation studies are drawn.

19.2 Baddeley and Hitch's Model of Working Memory

Working memory is defined as the limited-capacity system where information is stored for a short period of time and manipulated during an ongoing cognitive activity. According to the most established model (see Baddeley and Hitch 1974; Baddeley 2007), working memory has three components:

(i)   a Phonological Loop (that is the phonological short-term memory), which maintains verbally coded information;

(ii) a Visuo-Spatial Sketchpad, which maintains and manipulates visuo-spatial information;

(iii) the Central Executive, a supervisory system which regulates the flow of information within WM, retrieves information from other memory systems such as long-term memory and processes information during a (possibly combined) cognitive task.

Recently, a fourth component, the episodic buffer (Baddeley 2000), has been added. This system is assumed to form an interface between the three WM subsystems and long-term memory. The Phonological Loop is directly relevant for our discussion in this chapter.

19.2.1 *The Phonological Loop*

Short-term memory capacity is defined as span: the highest number of unrelated verbal items (digits, letters, words, etc.) that a subject is able to repeat in the same order immediately after presentation. The earliest quantification of phonological STM was by Miller (1956), who noticed that the memory span of young adults was around seven elements, regardless whether the elements were digits, letters, words, or other units. However, later research revealed that span does depend on the category of chunks used (e.g. in English, span is around seven for digits, six for letters, and five for words). Individual span is influenced by two variables, phonological similarity and word length, which support a distinction within the Phonological Loop between two components: a phonological short-term store (STS), within which memory traces fade after about 2 seconds, and an articulatory process of rehearsal, capable of refreshing the memory trace, preventing its decay (Baddeley 1990). Rehearsal does not need to be overt (it can be sub-vocal).

By phonological similarity is meant that, in immediate serial recall, performance level is higher for lists of phonologically dissimilar stimuli. Lists of sequences of words like *pit, day, cow, sup*, are remembered better than strings of phonologically similar words, such as *man, cat, map, can* (Conrad 1964; Conrad and Hull 1964). The standard interpretation is that similar words are more likely to be forgotten because the normal degradation of a phonological representation within the phonological store is more disruptive when two words are similar (the probability of losing a phonological feature that discriminates one item from the other members of the memory set will be greatest when the number of discriminating features is smallest). So the phonological similarity effect suggests that verbal information held in the phonological STS is coded phonologically.

Word-length effect refers to the fact that span for short words, like *day and pen*, is higher than span for longer ones, such as *opportunity and constitutional* (Baddeley, Thomson, and Buchanan 1975; Baddeley, Lewis, and Vallar 1984). Articulatory Rehearsal has been assumed to be responsible for the word length effect (Baddeley and Hitch 1974), since words that take longer to be articulated require longer rehearsal and this maximizes the possibility that the memory trace fade before it is rehearsed. Confirmation for a role of articulatory rehearsal in Phonological Loop comes from the observation that, when subjects occupy their articulatory apparatus with an irrelevant activity, for example, by repeating *ta ta ta*, their memory span is reduced. This is explained by assuming that rehearsal is prevented in this situation.

A final piece of background information is that there is evidence (see Vallar and Papagno 2002) that, when material is presented visually (printed words or nameable pictures), the articulatory system is needed to recode it in phonological form, while auditory presented material gains automatic access to the phonological STS.

Two discrete regions in the left hemisphere—the inferior parietal lobule and the premotor cortex—seem to be the anatomical correlates of the phonological STS and the rehearsal process, respectively (see Vallar and Papagno 2002 for a review, but also Romero, Walsh, and Papagno 2006 for a critical discussion).

Given the considerable body of evidence that confirms the existence of the Phonological Loop, an obvious possibility is that when language comprehension requires mnestic resources, for example because a long-distance dependency must be processed, the Phonological Loop is involved. This hypothesis has been explored, but before reviewing this literature, we need to introduce some information on the Central Executive of Baddeley and Hitch's model.

19.2.2 *The Central Executive*

The Central Executive operates by allocating resources to its slave systems, the Phonological Loop and the Visuo-Spatial Sketchpad, and by coordinating cognitive processes when more than one task must be done at the same time.

Sentence comprehension is a complex task, since it requires manipulation of information at various levels (lexical, phonological, morphological, syntactic, and semantic). So it seems plausible that it requires the intervention of the Central Executive. Individual measure of WM capacity can be tested by a variety of tasks. One which is commonly used is Daneman and Carpenter's (1980) "reading span" task, in which subjects are required to read aloud increasingly longer sequences of sentences and to recall the final word of all the sentences in each sequence. A subject's WM capacity is defined as the longest list length at which he or she is able to recall the sentence-final words on the majority of trials.

Several researchers have investigated if individual differences in WM, measured by the reading span task and by similar tests, correlate with efficiency of sentence interpretation, the expectation being that they should do if resources measured by WM span are actually involved in sentence comprehension.

19.3 Is Working Memory Span Predictive of Sentence-Comprehension Skills?

As we anticipated, one possibility is that memory resources measured either by simple STM span or by complex WM span can in fact be used in sentence comprehension. However, a different hypothesis has been proposed and it is very influential in the field. This hypothesis is called by its proponents "separate-sentence-interpretation-resource theory" (see Caplan and Waters 1999 for an articulated presentation) and claims that the memory system called on in interpretive processing at the sentence level constitutes a separate subsystem within verbal WM. This sub-system would be distinct from the Phonological Loop and would use resources that are not measured by the reading span task. In terms of Baddeley and Hitch's model, the memory system actually used in sentence comprehension would be a specialized part of the Central Executive.

Support for this fractionated view of WM comes mainly from negative results, showing that impairment of the Phonological Loop and of the Central Executive does not result in shortfall in sentence comprehension. Similarly, the separate-sentence-interpretation-resource theory would be supported if an imposed load on the Central Executive and/or on the Phonological Loop (for example, when subjects are required to process a sentence and concurrently hold a sequence of items) does not reduce comprehension accuracy in normal subjects. In this section, we will first comment on the existing literature on the correlation between WM span and sentence comprehension. We will then focus on the role of the Phonological Loop (Section 19.4).

19.3.1 *The correlation between WM span and sentence comprehension*

The typical experiment that aims at investigating a correlation between WM and proficiency in sentence comprehension is a group study in which subjects are divided according to their WM span in several groups, as high-, medium-, and low-span subjects. It is then investigated if reading times or accuracy in a series of tests that measure syntactic comprehension vary for the different groups of subjects. For example, King and Just (1991) presented results suggesting that low-span subjects—WM span being measured by the reading span task of Daneman and Carpenter (1980)—have a longer reading time than high-span subjects. Furthermore, low-span subjects read even more slowly at specific points of the sentence that are known to be demanding for memory resources, for example their reading time at the embedded verb *attacked* was longer in sentence (4) than in sentence (5):

(4)   The reporter who the senator attacked admitted the error.

(5)   The reporter who attacked the senator admitted the error.

This is in agreement with models of parsing (see Gibson 1998; Grodner and Gibson 2005) that identify the embedded verb in object relatives as a point of integration particularly demanding for memory resources (but see De Vincenzi 1991 and Frazier and Flores d'Arcais 1989 for an alternative theory of parsing). These results may be explained by the hypothesis that language processing relies on the pool of resources measured by WM span (Just and Carpenter 1992). Similar results emerge from the work of Miyake, Carpenter, and Just (1994), who report interactions between span group and sentence type in a series of experiments, in which low-, medium-, and high-span subjects were required to indicate the agent of reaction or answer questions about sentences that required syntactic analysis.

    However, these results, aiming at showing a correlation between syntactic comprehension and WM span have been seriously challenged, most notably by Caplan and Waters (1999), who claim that the original experiments suffer from several drawbacks. Furthermore, they reran these experiments but found no significant correlation between WM span and level of performance. Although the absence of correlation may be due to lack of power, as extensively argued by Miyake, Emerson, and Friedman (1999) in their reply to Caplan and Waters (1999), it is fair to say that there is not any compelling evidence that memory resources measured by WM spans are actually used in language comprehension.

    We suspect that the impossibility to firmly establish a correlation may not be due only to limitations of the experimental setting but might reflect a more basic problem. Indeed, the idea that, since language is a complex activity that can be divided into several largely simultaneous sub-tasks, working memory span should be predictive of linguistic performance is prima facie attractive, but the use of WM tests might conceal a serious misunderstanding. WM tests, like the reading span, measure conscious coordination of complex abilities, like keeping in mind the last word of the previous sentence(s) while reading the next one. However, language processing is based on unconscious and automatic processes, so absence of a correlation between language comprehension skills and level of performance in tests that measure the coordination of conscious higher level cognitive abilities is not particularly surprising.

19.3.2 *Sentence comprehension in subjects with reduced WM resources*

A different type of research, which does not suffer from a similar drawback, is comparing language-comprehension skills of groups of subjects that are known to be impaired in their WM capacities. For example, patients with Alzheimer's dementia (AD) suffer impairment of the Central Executive, resulting in reduced performance in tasks involving executive functions. For this reason, several studies (see Rochon, Waters, and Caplan 2000 and references cited there) have compared the performance of these patients and of control subjects in sentence comprehension, the expectation of the separate-sentence-interpretation-resource theory being that AD patients should not be impaired in syntactic processing. In a similar vein, other studies have compared comprehension skills of elderly and younger subjects, since WM declines with age (cf. Waters and Caplan 2005).

Many of these studies have been run by Caplan and colleagues, who used the same set of sentences in different experimental conditions. We report these sentences, since we will need to analytically discuss some of them:

(6) ACTIVE
     The elephant kicked the lion.

(7) ACTIVE WITH COORDINATED OBJECT
     The horse chased the dog and the cow.

(8) TRUNCATED PASSIVE
     The horse was touched.

(9) PASSIVE
     The dog was followed by the pig.

(10) CLEFT OBJECT
     It was the dog that the horse passed.

(11) DATIVE
     The elephant pulled the dog to the horse.

(12)   SUBJECT RELATIVE IN RIGHT PERIPHERAL POSITION
       The horse kicked the elephant that touched the dog.

(13)   VERB PHRASE COORDINATION
       The dog passed the horse and touched the elephant.

(14)   OBJECT RELATIVE IN CENTER-EMBEDDED POSITION
       The lion that the horse touched passed the pig.

In an experiment by Rochon et al. (2000), AD patients and control subjects had to match these sentences with a picture (or a video) that depicted them. AD patients' performance differed from that of controls only for the last three types of sentence, namely (12), (13), and (14). Since these sentences are the only ones that contain two propositions (a proposition being defined as a set of thematic roles relatives to the verb), Rochon et al. conclude that AD patients show a number of proposition effects, namely they have problems in matching two propositions with a single picture (or video). This effect, according to Rochon et al., is post-interpretative since picture matching takes place when on-line processing has already ended. Accordingly, they claim that their results would support the separate-sentence-interpretation-resource theory, since smaller capacity in WM has impact only post-interpretatively.

However, as observed by Papagno et al. (2007), Rochon et al.'s conclusion is dubious. Examples (12), (13) and (14), the sentences in which AD patients fail, are syntactically complex and are likely to be demanding for memory resources. This is not controversial for relative clauses like (12) and (14), since relative clauses contain a long-distance dependency (the link between the relative operator and its trace). Sentences with a center-embedded relative clause like (14) are the prototypical case of hard-to-process structures, as repeatedly and extensively shown in a literature that goes back to Miller and Chomsky (1963). The claim that (13) too is syntactically complex and demanding for memory requires some motivation. Indeed, in (13) the subject noun phrase (*the dog*) is in a predication relation with two different verb phrases (*passed the horse* and *touched the elephant*). Crucially, the relation between the subject and the VP *touched the elephant* takes place at long distance. More technically, given the subject VP internal hypothesis (see Koopman and Sportiche 1991), a minimally adequate syntactic analysis of a sentence like (13) involves a case of across-the-board extraction from the specifier of the two coordinated VPs (see 15). In this sense, (13) would be structurally similar in the relevant sense to a sentence like (16), in which across-the-board *wh*-extraction has taken place. Therefore, it appears very likely that (13) too is demanding for memory resources, since it contains a different type of long distance dependency.

(15)   [$_{IP}$ the dog ... [$_{VP}$*t* passed the horse] and [$_{VP}$*t* touched the elephant] ...].

(16)   Which movie did you watch *t* and appreciate *t*?

So, the fact that AD patients fail in (12), (13), and (14) suggests an interpretation which differs from Rochon et al.'s: AD patients might show an impairment in processing long distance dependencies, due to their WM limitations. Rochon et al. consider but reject this hypothesis, because control and AD patients perform at the same level with sentence pairs that differ in syntactic complexity, for example active (6) and passive (9) sentences. However, passive sentences, although arguably more complex than active ones, may not be demanding enough for AD patients. Technically, passive sentences do contain an A-dependency, but this is shorter than A-bar dependencies found in relative clauses. Furthermore, even (some) aphasic patients can handle passives (cf. Caramazza et al. 2001). So, the same level of accuracy of AD patients and controls in sentence types (6) and (9) might be due to a ceiling effect.

    In order to decide between the two alternative interpretations, one should test AD patients with a sentence that expresses two propositions but is structurally simple. One obvious possibility is the coordination of two independent sentences, for example (17):

(17)   The elephant pulled the dog and the horse passed the pig.

If Rochon et al.'s interpretation is correct and AD patients show a two-proposition effect, they should perform poorly on sentences like (17). If AD patients, due to their WM limitations, cannot handle a long-distance dependency, they should perform like controls with (17) since it does not contain any. Strikingly, sentences like (17) are not included in the experimental set by Rochon et al. (2000), so this question needs further investigation. Studies with AD patients are presently under way in our lab. Preliminary results (see Chitò 2006) show that, while patients are always worse than controls in sentence comprehension, except for active sentences, digit span correlates only with performance on center-embedded sentences. Interestingly, there is no correlation between digit span and the Italian equivalent of sentences like (17), which we did include in our experimental set.

    It seems fair to conclude this section by saying that data from patients with executive deficits do not offer any conclusive evidence that the Central

Executive is directly involved in processing syntactic structures. However, they do not show that language comprehension relies on a separate set of memory resources either.

This does not mean that the discussion about the separate-sentence-interpretation-resource theory must be left unresolved, though. In particular, up to now we have been discussing possible correlations between WM span and language comprehension skills. However, simpler STM tasks, like word or digit span, involve largely automatized lower level abilities that might be used in language comprehension. It is therefore possible that a correlation between digit or word span and syntactic abilities holds, even in the absence of a correlation between WM span and syntactic abilities. In fact, some developmental studies support this.

Booth, MacWhinney, and Harasaki (2000) found that digit span, but not working-memory span, interacted with both on-line and off-line comprehension of relative clauses: high-digit-span children had longer reading and listening time and were more accurate than low digit span children. Similar results have been recently obtained by Arosio, Adeni, and Guasti (2009) with Italian children. We will critically review some studies investigating the role of STM in the next section.

19.4 Is the Phonological Loop involved in Sentence Comprehension?

The investigation of the role (if any) of the Phonological Loop in syntactic processing has followed two main directions. The first direction is examining patients with a selective STM deficit and a consequently low span, the expectation being that they should be impaired in comprehension of sentences that contain long distance dependencies only if the syntactic parser relies on the Phonological Loop.

The second direction is examining the effects of a concurrent digit or word span load on syntactic processing in healthy subjects, the rationale being that, if there is a single set of resources for both STM and language comprehension, engaging these resources with a STM task should make syntactic processing less efficient. Let us start reporting the second direction of research.

19.4.1 *The effect of concurrent memory loads on language comprehension*

Several studies have found an effect of concurrent memory load on off-line tasks, like accuracy in responses made by participants after the entire sentence has been presented. For example, Baddeley and Hitch (1974) reported that passive sentences were more disrupted than active sentences when a six-digit load task interfered with picture matching these sentences (but see Caplan and Waters 1999 for a critique of this experimental setting).

Waters, Caplan, and Hildebrandt (1987) reported interaction between syntactic complexity and digit load in a plausibility judgment task, but the interaction was significant only in the analysis of results by subjects, making it harder to assess the reliability of this result.

We know of one study measuring the effect of digit load on on-line syntactic processing (Waters, Caplan, and Yampolsky 2003). Subjects were presented with a list of numbers to remember while reading sentences that were segmented into phrases; they had to press a button to hear each following phrase. After reading the last phrase, subjects had to judge if the sentence was plausible and then they had to repeat the list of numbers. Reaction times were recorded for each phrase in which the sentence was segmented. Pairs of sentences that differ only for syntactic complexity were used, for example (18) and (19) (double slashes indicate how the sentences were segmented into different phrases):

(18)   The cabin // that // warmed // the scout // contained // the firewood.

(19)   The cabin // that // the scout // warmed // contained // the firewood.

Waters et al. (2003) found that total listening times in a five-digit load condition were longer than those in a three-digit load condition and that those in the three- and five-digit load conditions were longer than those in a no-load condition. So, it appears that concurrent digit loads do have an effect on on-line language processing, prima facie disproving the separate-sentence-interpretation-resource theory. However, the authors give a different interpretation by capitalizing on one aspect of their result. They measured listening times for the verb form *warmed* and found that they were longer in the object relative (19) than in subject relative (18). This is expected adopting Gibson's (1998) model of parsing, which identifies the position of the verb in sentences like (19) as a point of integration which is particularly demanding for memory resources. However, Waters et al. also found that the difference in reading times of the verb *warm* did not increase under conditions of load. This suggests that the extra load introduced by an object relative does not burden the same set of memory resources occupied by the digit span.

From this experiment it would therefore emerge that some aspects of language processing rely on the Phonological Loop. This explains the overall longer reading under conditions of load. However, other aspects of language processing, like establishing long-distance dependencies in relative clauses, would use a different pool of resources. Waters et al. (2003) identify this pool with the specialized part of the Central Executive that, according to them, is devoted uniquely to syntactic processing. So, they interpret their results as supporting the separate-sentence-interpretation-resource theory. Note, however, that the specialized part of the Central Executive postulated by the separate-sentence-interpretation-resource theory, at least in this case, would have a very restricted area of application. Since listening times do get longer in the digit load condition, the Phonological Loop must play a role in on-line parsing. Therefore only *some* aspects of parsing (like linking a relative operator to its trace) would be left to the memory system specialized for syntax postulated by the separate-sentence-interpretation-resource theory.

19.4.2 *Single case studies of patients with an STM impairment*

A second line of direction is investigating whether subjects with an impaired Phonological Loop are also impaired in comprehension of sentences that contain long distance dependencies. Caramazza et al. (1981) and Friedrich, Glenn, and Martin (1984) reported verbal STM and sentence comprehension of two conduction aphasics with a very reduced digit and word span. Both patients showed deficits in syntactic comprehension for reversible active and passive sentences and for center-embedded subject and object relative clause sentences.

Vallar and Baddeley (1984) reported sentence comprehension of a patient, PV, with a selective deficit of the phonological STS. Patient PV performed well on a "syntactic" battery, but this did not include syntactically complex structures like center-embedded relative clauses, and, instead, mainly focused on aspects of lexical meaning (*down/up, over/under*). Furthermore, PV displayed comprehension problems when tested on anomaly detection in long sentences where word order was critical, such as *The world divides the equator in two hemispheres: the northern and the southern.* Vallar and Baddeley claimed that this might be due to the fact that PV cannot maintain exact word order information for sentences that exceeded her "sentence repetition span of six words." PV's inability to detect semantic anomalies might be due to impaired syntactic analysis (confusion in thematic role assignment). Alternatively, PV's performance might be a post-interpretative effect, if anomaly detection is a cognitive task that requires reactivation of the degraded phonological representation of the sentence when on-line interpretation is over. This second interpretation is consistent with the view that STM never contributes to on-line sentence processing. Lacking a complete assessment of PV's ability to parse complex syntactic sentences, it's difficult to choose between these two hypotheses.

Patient EA, with a verbal STM impairment, and reported by Martin (1987), did have difficulty in comprehending center-embedded relative clauses, but only when the embedded clause was either a passive or an object relative. This suggests a role of the Phonological Loop, at least for these very complex structures. Martin (2006), reviewing this case, suggests that EA's degraded performance, rather than being an outcome of her phonological storage deficit per se, might be due to the interaction of her syntactic processing deficit and her STM deficit.

The role of rehearsal in syntactic comprehension has been investigated in two patients, BO (Waters, Caplan, and Hildebrandt 1991), who had a vascular lesion in the left internal capsule, and MC, who suffered the surgical removal of a low-grade glioma involving the posterior part of the second and third left frontal gyri, extending to the insula (Papagno et al. 2007). Both had a very low span. BO, whose span was two to three items, showed apraxia of speech (a disorder of motor programs necessary to speak). This patient did not show word-length and phonological-similarity effects with visual presentation. This pattern is similar to the one seen in unaffected people under articulatory suppression; accordingly, the authors assume the inability to use the articulatory rehearsal component of WM (although a limited impairment of the phonological STS cannot be excluded, as discussed by the authors). BO's syntactic comprehension skills were assessed on a battery of 41 types of sentence. Comprehension was checked by using an enactment task, in which BO had to reproduce the event described in the sentence she was exposed to by manipulating some toys the experimenter had displayed in front of her.

Overall, BO's performance with auditory presentation was judged as quite good, which led Waters et al. (1991) to state in the abstract of their paper that "articulatory rehearsal is not needed for the assignment of syntactic structures." In the general discussion they affirm that data from BO are incompatible with Caramazza et al.'s (1981) claim that the Phonological Loop is involved in the operation of the parser. This interpretation of BO's performance became standard in the literature. For example, Martin (2006) in a review article, summarizes Waters et al.'s (1991) results by saying that

whereas patient BO had very restricted span and failed to show normal phonological similarity and word length effects on memory span, she showed excellent comprehension of a variety of long and syntactically complex sentences.... Thus, BO most likely also represents a case with restricted phonological storage capacity together with excellent comprehension of syntax.

However, this may not be a totally accurate description of BO's results, since her performance with some complex structures like object relatives was at chance level with written sentence presentation and fell to 25 percent correct when she was given a limited viewing (15 seconds or less). In fact, Waters et al. (1991: 116) notice that BO "did perform poorly on subject-object and object-object sentences" and this "may reflect the high local memory load imposed by object relativization form." They also claim that BO's pattern with object relativized sentences "might be because STM is involved in the comprehension of the sentences with object relativization."

In summary, although the performance by BO is generally pretty good, she failed in some structures that are known to be demanding for memory resources, and this indicates that the Phonological Loop is involved in processing *some* complex structures (despite the common wisdom about BO that got established in the following literature).

The second patient, MC, had a digit span of 2.25 and a word span of 2. She did not show any semantic impairment. Several different tasks of sentence comprehension were administered. In one task, MC's comprehension of several sentences types, including (20)–(29), was checked by using a picture matching task:

(20)   ACTIVE
      La mamma insegue il bambino. ('Mummy chases the child.')

(21)   ACTIVE WITH COORDINATED OBJECT
      Il bambino insegue il cane e il gatto. ('The child chases the dog and the cat.')

(22)   PASSIVE
      Il cane viene guardato dal bambino. ('The dog is watched by the child.')

(23)   DATIVE
      La mamma dà la torta al bambino. ('Mummy gives the cake to the child.')

(24)   SUBJECT RELATIVES IN RIGHT PERIPHERAL POSITION
      Il bambino insegue il cane che morde il gatto. ('The child chases the dog which bites the cat.')

(25)   OBJECT RELATIVES IN RIGHT PERIPHERAL POSITION
      La mamma guarda il cane che il bambino accarezza. ('Mummy looks at the dog which the child caresses.')

(26)   SUBJECT RELATIVES IN THE CENTER-EMBEDDED POSITION
      Il cane che insegue il gatto guarda il nonno. ('The dog which chases the cat looks at grampa.')

(27)   OBJECT RELATIVES IN THE CENTER-EMBEDDED POSITION
Il gatto che il bambino accarezza beve il latte. ('The cat which the child caresses drinks milk.')

(28)   OBJECT CLEFT
È il cane che il bambino insegue. ('It is the dog that the child chases.')

(29)   SENTENTIAL COORDINATION
La bambina mangia la torta e il bambino beve il latte. ('The girl eats the cake and the boy drinks the milk.')

MC significantly differed from controls in four types of sentence, namely center-embedded structures (26–27), object cleft (28), and object relative sentences in right-peripheral position (25). In the latter type, her performance was not so dramatically affected but was nonetheless worse than controls. For the remaining sentence types, MC matched controls. This pattern suggests that MC's syntactic comprehension of complex structures *is* impaired, since she did worse exactly when structures became more complex for parsing (object relatives are standardly taken to be more demanding than subject relatives and, similarly, center-embedded relatives are more complex than right peripheral ones). Interestingly, MC and controls did not differ with sentences like (29), that are a simple case of coordination but contain two propositions. This excludes the hypothesis that MC shows a two-propositions effect instead of an effect of syntactic complexity, as proposed by Rochon et al. (2000) for AD patients. MC performed well with passives, but this structure, as discussed above, may not be demanding enough, as shown by the fact that some aphasics can handle it.

MC was also tested in an on-line task (self pace listening), which showed converging results, since her reaction times were significantly slower than those of controls in the same types of sentence (center-embedded and relatives in right peripheral position).[1]

Therefore, it is clear that syntactic comprehension proves to be impaired in STM patients if they are tested with sentences with the appropriate level of syntactic complexity. It is not surprising that PV (Vallar and Baddeley 1984) was reported as normal (78/80) in syntactic comprehension, since a test was

---

[1] Martin and colleagues (Martin and Romani 1994; Hanten and Martin 2001; Martin and He 2004) have argued that span tasks tap both phonological and semantic retention and that, while the phonological component of span tasks is independent of the capacity involved in sentence processing, the semantic component plays a (limited) role in sentence comprehension. To test a possible role of so-called semantic STM, MC was administered the Italian counterpart of Martin and Romani's (1994) Sentence Anomaly Task but she did not differ from controls in the relevant respect. Therefore, MC's impaired performance must depend on the phonological component of the span task.

used that did not systematically check for variables of syntactic complexity like center-embedding and dependency length. Similarly, MC scored 76/80 in this same test.

19.5 Evidence from Sign Languages

Sign languages offer some insight into the role of the Phonological Loop in sentence processing. It is known that signs are retained in a sign-based code parallel to the speech-based code for spoken language (Klima and Bellugi 1979). Furthermore, evidence has been accumulating that there is a close equivalence of structure between STM for signed and spoken languages. Wilson and Emmorey (1997, 1998) found a sign-phonological similarity effect and showed that lists of short signs were better recalled than lists of long signs. This indicated the presence of a sign-length effect analogous to the word-length effect for speech, suggesting the presence of parallel articulatory processes for sign and spoken languages.

However, span for auditorily presented English words is higher than span for ASL signs (Bellugi, Klima, and Siple 1975) and the same gap has been observed for other pairs of sign-spoken languages (Logan, Mayberry, and Fletcher 1996, Geraci et al. 2008).

The reduced span for signs introduces the question of how sign languages can be full-fledged grammatical systems (as 40 years of research have shown) if they depend on a limited STM. There are two possibilities. The first is that the separate-sentence-interpretation-resource theory is correct and the capacity measured by sign span is *not* involved in sign language processing (Boutla et al. 2004).

An alternative interpretation, suggested by linguistic evidence, is that sign languages have an internal organization that reduces the load on verbal STM. First, it is well known that sign languages use space to give a series of grammatical information (agreement, tense, aspect, etc.) which many spoken languages express using morphological affixation and/or function words. Even some content words, like adverbs, may be expressed without introducing a separate sign (for example, a change in the rhythm of articulation of the verb is functionally equivalent to a manner adverb). Second, Cecchetto, Geraci, and Zucchi (2006) observed that sign languages like Italian Sign Language (LIS) and American Sign Language (ASL) do not tolerate even one single level of center-embedding. For example, in these languages relative clauses are translated by constructions similar to those found in spoken languages like Hindi, in which the (cor)relative clause always precedes the matrix one. Furthermore, whereas in LIS the canonical order is SOV, this order becomes impossible if the object is a subordinate clause, plausibly because this would be a case of center-embedding (the subordinate clause is either left or right dislocated in LIS, giving rise to OSV or SVO order). These facts, taken together, conspire to make the typical sign-language sentence short in terms of the lexical items it contains. Sign-language clauses are also easy to process since clauses are always one after the other in a row and are never interspersed. In principle, these grammatical characteristics and the fact that STM for signs has a reduced capacity may be coincidental. However, if other sign languages share with LIS and ASL exactly those grammatical properties that seem perfectly suited to reduce the load on verbal STM, the claim that sign languages are structured to cope with a reduced STM becomes more and more plausible and the separate-sentence-interpretation-resource theory becomes more and more unlikely.

19.6 Conclusion

In this chapter we have been exploring two alternative hypotheses. According to a first view, humans have a set of memory resources that can be devoted to all verbal tasks, ranging from span to automatic syntactic processing. According to the second view, the separate-sentence-interpretation-resource theory, the memory system used in processing constitutes a separate subsystem within verbal WM.

We have first sharpened the question, by pointing out that the first hypothesis admits two declinations. The resources allegedly used in sentence processing might be either those measured by WM span like the reading span or by simpler tasks (digit or word span). The difference is crucial since the former case would suggest a specific role of the Central Executive, while in the latter case the Phonological Loop would be involved. We have argued that, despite some initial indication, it is not clear whether resources measured by WM span are involved in sentence processing. Studies involving AD patients, according to us, do not lead to a clear conclusion on the role of the Central Executive either.

The case for a role of the Phonological Loop in language processing is better supported, but caution is needed in this case as well. The clearest evidence comes from patients with a pathologically low span who cannot handle sentences that impose a heavy load on memory, MC being a particularly clear-cut case.

However, as we have seen, MC performs equally well with sentence pairs that vary for their level of syntactic complexity (active and passive sentences, for example). These sentences may contain non-local dependencies that impose a burden on memory, although a more limited burden than do sentences on which MC systematically fails. For example, a passive sentence contains a link between the internal argument position of the transitive verb and the derived subject position. This link is shorter than A-bar dependencies contained in relatives, but it is non-local nonetheless. How can patients with a severely impaired Phonological Loop process these non-local dependencies? There are basically two possibilities. Either a weak version of the separate-sentence-interpretation-resource theory is right and a separate subsystem within verbal WM operates just with these short dependencies (while the Phonological Loop is called into action by longer dependencies). Alternatively, it must be the case that also a severely impaired Phonological Loop has sufficient resources for processing passive sentences and structures of comparable complexity. Several considerations favor the second alternative. First, *entia non sunt multiplicanda praeter necessitatem*, so the postulation of a distinct sub-system is justified only if it is necessary to explain the available data. Second, hypothesizing a parser in which two separate memory systems operate at the same time (at least with certain types of structures) introduces the issue of how these two sub-systems are coordinated.

Third, at least for patients like BO and MC, whose articulatory rehearsal is impaired, the Phonological Loop might sustain moderately complex structures, because the relevant phonological information does not decay. This may seem prima facie problematic, considering that patients like BO and MC have a word span of 2 or 3, but they can process sentences containing dependencies extending over this span. However, there is evidence that immediate memory for sentential material (sentence span) is typically substantially greater than span for unrelated words (Brener 1940; Baddeley et al. 1987). A suggested hypothesis is an interactive process whereby a basic phonological core is amplified by contributions from long-term memory, where lexical items are stored. In particular, the recall advantage of sentences over unrelated words presumably stems from the capacity to bind together individual words into meaningful chunks, whose maintenance is partially supported by the semantically based long-term memory. This explains why patients whose phonologically based span is grossly restricted are less severely impaired with sentential material (for example, Vallar and Baddeley's patient PV had a span of 2 or 3 but a sentence span of 6, and a gap between span and sentence span is also found in healthy subjects).

We therefore propose that simple non-local dependencies, like the chain between a subject and its trace in passive sentences, may be short enough to be managed by a degraded Phonological Loop since span may be increased by creating meaningful chunks that are retained with some support from semantically based memory.[2] If this hypothesis is correct, a separate memory sub-system dedicated to syntactic processing can be dispensed with. Importantly, if this picture is on the right track, we can answer a serious objection against the role of the Phonological Loop in syntactic processing, raised by Waters et al. (1991). They claim that the Phonological Loop cannot be used in first-pass language comprehension because "rehearsal processes—especially articulatory based rehearsal—are too slow to be used in on-line comprehension. Accessing lexical forms, word meaning, and morphological form, and the construction of syntactic structure, propositional meanings, and discourse representations are processes that normally occur within 250 milliseconds" after the presentation of the relevant auditory stimulus. This, as Waters et al. (1991) claim, is far too fast for rehearsal processes to be useful. This objection applies only to models that assume an intervention of rehearsal also in simple sentences. Data from BO and MC shows that rehearsal is relevant only for long dependencies. On the other hand, the high speed at which processing applies prevents the trace in the phonological STS to decay, even in cases of non-local (but not too long) dependencies like passives. A review of data available in normal subjects' sentence comprehension during articulatory suppression or unattended speech (Gathercole and Baddeley 1993) suggests that it is the subvocal rehearsal used to maintain the phonological representations that is consulted during complex language processing, rather than the phonological record of the sentence.

We conclude by indicating two possible lines of research that move in two different directions, namely, towards experimental techniques investigating brain activity and towards linguistic models.

Focusing on techniques investigating brain activity is motivated by a possible objection against conclusions uniquely based on association between STM impairment and comprehension deficits in patients. The concern is that the co-occurrence of STM impairment and language comprehension deficits may be not causally related (with the former triggering the latter) but can simply reflect the fact that, since the brain areas controlling both types of function are adjacent, the damage might cover both areas.

As reported in Section 19.2.1, the anatomical correlates of the Phonological Loop have been identified as two discrete regions in the left hemisphere, namely, BA 44 (articulatory rehearsal) and BA 40 (phonological STS). If

---

[2] In principle, this hypothesis can be tested. For example, it predicts that subjects with a STM deficit who do not show any impairment with ordinary passives should be impaired if passive sentences are composed of pseudo-words (*the vonk was fustered by the snup*).

the Phonological Loop is involved in syntactic processing, damage to these areas should reduce performance in sentence comprehension. Since repetitive Transcranial Magnetic Stimulation (rTMS) can temporarily disrupt cortical activity, we are currently running an rTMS experiment. Subjects are required to match sentences of varying complexity to pictures, under TMS stimulation of BA 40, BA 44 and in a control condition, so that each subject is his/her own control. In principle, this type of experiment, in addition to confirming the role of the Phonological Loop, might allow us to disentangle the role of articulatory rehearsal and of the phonological STS. Initial results confirm a role of the Phonological Loop in sentence processing (see Romero et al. 2008). Accordingly, an fMRI study (Cooke et al. 2001) showed a core region of left posterior superior temporal cortex during all sentence conditions and a recruitment of left inferior frontal cortex clearly associated with sentences that featured both an object-relative clause and a long antecedent-gap link-age, suggesting that this region supports the cognitive resources required to maintain long-distance syntactic dependencies during the comprehension of grammatically complex sentences.

Finally, let us consider the relevance of the debate about the role of the Phonological Loop in the light of current linguistic models. Chomsky (2001) has proposed a highly derivational model ("the theory of phases"), which is motivated by empirical considerations as well as by a conceptual need, namely that the active memory at each step of the derivation be required to contain a very limited set of items. In the theory of phases, the access to the lexicon is a one-time selection of a lexical array. To reduce the computational burden, it is also assumed that the initial lexical array (LA) enters the derivation in different steps. In each step, a subarray of the lexical array is put in active memory. Crucially, the derivation must exhaust one subarray, by forming a certain syntactic object, before returning to the lexical array to extract another subarray. A phase is defined as the syntactic object which is formed when a subarray is exhausted. Under this model, some movement types (A-movement, like passive and raising) are phase-internal, while other move-ment types (*wh*-movement, for example) are cross-phasal. The latter move-ment is more complex, since an intermediate step in the periphery of each intervening phase is required.

Chomsky's theory of phases is a model of linguistic competence, not a psycholinguistic model, so caution is needed when one tries to posit a direct mapping between the theory of phases and the Phonological Loop model. However, the fact that one explicit motivation of the theory of phases is reduc-ing the load on WM is an invitation to fill (or reduce) the gap between purely linguistic models and neuropsychological models of WM. If phases have a psychological reality, in principle one should be able to indicate the functional counterpart of the phase in the Phonological Loop model. Our best guess, after our survey in this chapter, is that the phase space may be determined by the number of items that can be retained in the phonological STS without the intervention of rehearsal. Future research will say if this conjecture is on the right track.

20

All you Need is Merge: Biology, Computation, and Language from the Bottom Up

ROBERT C. BERWICK

Overture

In recent years, there has been a resurgence of activity surrounding biolinguistics along with a parallel, renewed interest in the connections between language and evolution. To be sure, from one standpoint it has often been said, quite correctly, that linguistic science just *is* biology: the study, however abstract, of a particular, apparently species-specific human trait: knowledge of language. But beyond this immediate point, how might linguistics and biology, especially evolutionary biology, inform one another? How does one go about making a proper evolutionary argument? What can genomics and evolutionary biology tell us now about language, and what might be out of reach, now, or out of reach forever, and why? To answer such questions, this chapter attempts to clear up some possible misunderstandings about evolutionary thinking that one might dub "vulgar Darwinism"—that is, the popular versions of evolutionary theory that sometimes find their way into analyses about language and evolution. The bottom line is that proper evolutionary explanations are often much more difficult to execute than one might think, and that language is a particularly difficult, even uniquely difficult, case to crack. Like linguistics, there is a substantial body of knowledge and theory grounding modern evolutionary analysis, with subtleties that are often missed, even by biologists themselves.

I would like to thank Noam Chomsky, Guglielmo Cinque, Anna Maria Di Sciullo, Morris Halle, Richie Kayne, Andrea Moro, Massimo Piattelli-Palmarini, and Juan Uriagereka for many helpful discussions that sharpened the thoughts in this chapter. Anna Maria Di Sciullo deserves special thanks for fostering and organizing a conference of science and beauty that made such work possible. Any remaining flaws remain the evolutionary deficits of the author, sometimes known as "genetic load."

For example, much excitement has followed from the full genome sequencing of our nearest living relative, the chimpanzee, with other primate genomes to come. However, the special problem of evolutionary inference given close but sparsely populated neighboring species suggests this may tell us very little about human cognitive faculties such as language. The well-known example of a putative "language gene," *FOXP2*, is a prime example: as we shall show, if we re-examine the data from Enard et al. (2002) more carefully, the differences between us and chimps, or for that matter, the more recent similarity between us and Neandertals (Krause, Lalueza-Fox et al. 2007) could be due to chance alone.[1] Where then can we look for insight? The most recent research by Halle in language metrical systems combined with Chomsky's most recent model of syntax may provide a possible and so far unexplored connection to birdsong.

As this chapter immodestly dons the mantle of an opera, it divides into two Acts. Act I opens by outlining the requirements of evolutionary explanations in biology generally and the special problems faced by evolutionary explanations of human language in particular. As we shall see, if one had to choose some trait for evolutionary study, one would be hard pressed to find a trait more challenging than language. Evolution by natural selection can be a potent force, but it is a weak dynamical one, acting over long time frames and easily confounded with demographic effects such as rapid population growth. It therefore becomes difficult to draw inferences about forces in the past given only observations about the present, particularly in the case of humans, who by all accounts passed through just such a population "bottleneck," expanding from a base estimated at 4,000–10,000 individuals and then growing exponentially just at the presumptive time when language emerged and we started on the long trek out of Africa. Moreover, the task becomes even more challenging when the "data points" upon which comparative evolutionary analysis builds are sparse—too few neighboring species compared to other vocal learners like birds. To understand these challenges, Act I lays out the bare bones of evolutionary dynamical theory—the "auto mechanics" required to understand the inferential issues of evolutionary analysis.

Act I concludes with an application of this evolutionary auto mechanics to the recent "banner case" for the genetic, evolutionary analysis of human language, the *FOXP2* transcription factor gene. *FOXP2* has gained much currency in recent years as a putative genomic component that assists in the

---

[1] We follow convention here by writing the names for human genes in italic uppercase, with their corresponding protein products in plain uppercase as in *FOXP2* and FOXP2, with the corresponding non-human genes and protein products written with just initial capitals as *FoxP2* and FoxP2.

construction of the language faculty, if not the language gene itself, and so has been used as a probe for the genomic dissimilarity between us and primates; for detecting the signal of natural selection and perhaps establishing the "starting point" of human language; and even, after extraordinary technical effort, for the evolutionary comparison between modern humans and Neandertals (Fisher et al. 1998; Enard et al. 2002; Krause, Lalueza-Fox et al. 2007). However, on re-analyzing the original Enard et al. (2002) data in light of the extremely small differences that were found between *Homo sapiens* and *Mus musculus* (us and mice)—just two DNA letters, two nucleotides changing just two amino acids—taken together with the special difficulties of evolutionary analysis, Act I concludes that we cannot confidently say that this is a gene 'selected for' language, or even that it was selected for at all. Nor can one say with much confidence that there was a selective sweep that drove this gene to fixation or when it occurred. The differences may well be due to chance alone.

If this is correct, then how does *FOXP2* fit into the picture of language evolution? Act II returns to *FOXP2*, by way of songbirds, to see whether we can face the gap between internal syntax and the external stream of words, the sensor motor interface. Berwick and Chomsky (this volume) argue that there are many reasons to suppose that *FoxP2* operates quite generally in vocalizing species as part of a system for building an externalization procedure, that is, as part of the sensori-motor system mapping between syntax proper (hierarchical structure generated by Merge) and the output vocal tract or manual gesture articulations. Externalization flattens the hierarchical structures generated by internal syntax by projecting them into a temporally linear succession of articulatory commands (words can only come out one at a time, left-to-right, as it were). Further, Di Sciullo (this volume) already notes that Merge operates at the level of morphology. Taken together, these ideas suggest that one might unpack the syntax–sensori-motor interface even further, into successive stages (perhaps operating in parallel): first moving from syntax, where left-to-right precedence is not expressed; then to morphology, where precedence is expressed. Going one step further, we note that the precedence relation is itself unordered; without further stipulation, a precedence relation does not state whether it is left-to-right or right-to-left. Thus, some additional step of externalization imposes this constraint in order to reach some final, viable, string of temporally ordered motor commands.

In particular, we illustrate this layered analysis of the sensori-motor interface by analyzing metrical stress along the lines of Halle (1997). We show that the Halle system operates very much like Merge, but with one key twist: there can be, obviously, no lexical features, just marks denoted by asterisks, corresponding roughly to consonant–vowel pairs. Following the Halle approach, by a successive sequence of merge operations (projection and selection of heads, as in syntax), we arrive at all and only the possible natural metrical patterns. This is, in effect, pure syntax, with no lexical features and no associated semantics; without features, there is no possibility of internal merge and the movement that we see in ordinary syntax.

We can now raise a key comparative evolutionary question: where else in the biological world might one find metrical structure, but without any lexical information? Act II's proposed answer is: songbirds. Songbirds too produce metrical patterns, but necessarily without lexical information or semantics. Act II then suggests, quite speculatively, that here is precisely where a connection can be made between language, or more precisely the externalization process of language, and FoxP2: recent studies have shown that songbirds (finches) too have altered *FoxP2* DNA sequences (though importantly *not* the same DNA letters or nucleotides as in humans) and that *FoxP2* disruption also disturbs song learning and its patterning (Teramitsu et al. 2004; Haesler et al. 2007; Vernes et al. 2007). Then, by analyzing birdsong in a novel way, following Coen (2006) to extract its "songemes," we can suggest that birdsong too has a metrical structure—in fact exactly that described by the Halle theory as applied to human language. On this view, songbird metrical structure may give us the right kind of comparative, evolutionary insight into at least the externalization process associated with language. Whether this is enough to tell us about Merge itself remains an open question.

20.1 Act I: The Incredible Lightness of Being an Evolutionary Argument

20.1.1 *The challenge for evolutionary explanations and the origin of human language*

Nowhere is the evolutionary explanatory challenge more pointed than in the case of human language. It is practically the polar opposite of a straightforward case such as sickle-cell anemia, where just a single DNA nucleotide change, a DNA letter (adenine to thymine, A to T), leads to a corresponding amino-acid change in the hemoglobin molecule (glutamic acid to valine, this normal amino acid being hydrophobic and thus twisting away from water, the second hydrophilic and thus attracted to water). This single change bends the hemoglobin molecule, in turn visibly crimping the red blood cells—a visibly damaged phenotype or form that shows.

But what is the phenotype, the form that shows, in the case of language? Experts cannot even come to an agreement on this most basic of evolutionary questions, whose answer would be the standard starting point for further analysis. Indeed, as noted in the most recent survey article in *Nature* (2008), the link between complex behaviors such as psychiatric conditions and underlying genetics is poorly understood in general. As Harvard neurobiologist and geneticist Steve Hyman remarks, "We are just too ignorant of the underlying neurobiology to make guesses about candidate genes" (Abbott 2008: 157). So how to proceed? Berwick and Chomsky (this volume) observe that one conventional assumption, "language as communication," leads to difficulties. Alternatively, they adopt the position of Hauser, Chomsky, and Fitch (2002), and construe language as the faculty of language in the narrow sense (FLN), in effect, recursive syntax. In this chapter we shall for the most part simply adopt the FLN view, putting to one side many legitimate questions about this assumption, focusing instead on the evolutionary problematic that remains.

We begin the discussion with language evolution re-described as hypotheses about characters and character states (made explicit with cladograms, that is, branching diagrams of which species held traits in common, and when certain novel traits appeared), but we immediately run into a problem: we have no close living relatives among species, so comparative analysis, the mainstay of the evolutionary program, becomes extremely difficult. Using this representation and the terminology of cladistics invites a discussion of when selectionism provides good explanations for observed traits, in this case, the FLN, and when selectionism is limited.

To explain differences in traits accounted for by adaptation (or natural selection), typically in evolutionary theory we choose exemplars that are as close as possible; to explain adaptationist similarities we choose exemplars that are as far apart as possible. Why is this so? In the best case, what an evolutionary biologist would like to find are examples of what is called "convergent evolution"—multiple, independent solutions to the same functional biological problem. The classic case is that of two forelimbs evolving into wings, as in bats and birds. From this fact we can deduce that four limbs were the ancestral, basal vertebrate state, because both mice, known relatives of bats, and crocodiles, relatives of birds, have four limbs; indeed so do many other vertebrates, providing us with the 'cladogram' depicted in Figure 20.1. Logically this picture says that since all the ancestors of bats and birds had four ordinary limbs, then the two front limbs of bats and birds must have evolved into wings independently, for functional, that is, adaptive reasons. A glance at the similarity in aerodynamic shape of the limbs also calls attention to this adaptive argument, with form following function.

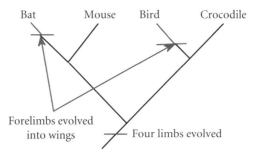

FIGURE 20.1 Multiple independent inventions of wing development from forelimbs established by a cladogram

These two occurrences of wing evolution are therefore multiple *independent* apomorphies. Like independent natural experiments, they offer evidence of convergent evolution where the same evolutionary problem was solved in the same way at different times, powerful evidence that similar functional constraints were at work.[2] In contrast, consider the possible evolutionary explanations for why people and crocodiles share the same number of limbs, four. We might say that four limbs were selected for in both people and crocodiles, for the usual Darwinian reasons. But this would not be a sound explanation. A more satisfying answer is that both species have four limbs not because of some convergent selectional pressure, but because their parents, grandparents, and so forth all had four limbs, back to the common tetrapod ancestor of both. The four-limb solution was not "invented" independently by humans and crocodiles; it is true simply in virtue of shared common descent. Indeed, running the timeline backwards, the reason why we are all tetrapods seems to be a contingent fact about survival during the so-called Cambrian explosion: there were other species with other limb numbers, but all of these five- and seven-limbed alternative species went extinct, for reasons still unclear, but seemingly contingent (Gould 1989).

Returning to comparative evolutionary analysis and language, the point is that it is far easier to run an adaptationist (or selectionist) argument for a trait like wings if one knows, first, whether that trait was simply passed on from a common ancestor or not; and second, whether such a trait has ever

[2] Another example is that of Old World vipers vs. New World pit vipers (*Viperinae* vs. *Crotalinae*). Their last common ancestors are quite ancient (hence the Old World vs. New World split), so we can conveniently use the geographic division to note that the New World vipers must have snake relatives with whom they share common ancestors that are not held in common with the Old World vipers. As with bats and birds, it seems that there are both New World and Old World vipers that have developed "eye lashes" and an arboreal habit. So this must again be an independent development in both lines, just like wings in bats and birds.

evolved independently in remote lineages—independently in the sense that the two species could not possibly have shared the trait in question. Turning now to language, we can immediately see the difficulties. The problem with relatives and near neighbors is that it can be too difficult tell about differences by looking at neighbors—they are too similar and it can be impossible to tell whether a trait is common simply due to common ancestry. This seems to be the case with us, and, say, chimpanzees. In contrast, looking at a very close neighbor without a certain trait usually tells us nothing. From this point of view, a focus on whether chimps, apes, or cotton-top tamarins have some competence similar to us is doomed from the start. Further, if language, or rather the FLN, is indeed a trait unique to the human lineage, a unique, independent autapomorphy, we cannot as easily unfurl the bat wing/bird wing selectionist argument, at least not in the same straightforward way. And there seem to have been no independent inventions of language in the FLN sense of Hauser, Chomsky, and Fitch (2002)—that is, syntax with a recursive operator, which Chomsky calls Merge.

Figures 20.2 through 20.4 depict this explanatory challenge graphically, illustrating the relative sparsity of primate species and the relevant trait of

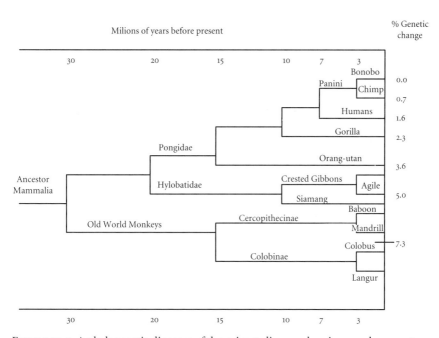

FIGURE 20.2 A phylogenetic diagram of the primate lineage showing rough percentage genetic change among extant groups

vocal learning ability as compared to the same situation in birds. Figure 20.2 exhibits a conventional phylogenetic diagram of the rough genetic distance among living primate lineages. Figure 20.2's horizontal axis runs time backwards from the present, right to left, while the vertical axis measures the percentage genetic difference. (We return to focus on the chimpanzee–human differences in a later section.) Which of these species are true vocal learners, apart from humans, remains unclear (cf. the recent reports on gibbons and gibbon syntax by Clarke, Reichard, and Zuberbühler 2006; and the apparent lack of the FLN in cotton-top tamarins, as described in Fitch and Hauser 2004). Whatever the outcome of this ongoing research, the point is that there are only a handful of primate vocal learners/nonlearners to compare, and so, as Lewontin (1998) observes, "it is difficult to connect the dots sensibly."

We can contrast this phylogenetic situation to that in birds, partly shown in Figure 20.3, as redrawn from Zhang, Webb, and Podlaha (2002) and Jarvis (2004), which displays the much richer patterning of vocal learners and

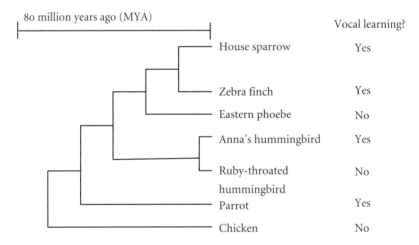

FIGURE 20.3 (Redrawn after Zhang, Webb, and Podlaha 2002; Jarvis 2004.) The pattern of vocal learning–non-learning traits in songbirds is considerably denser with respect to species than in the case of primates. For example, two very closely related species of hummingbirds (*Trochiliformes*), one Anna's hummingbird, the other, the Ruby-throated hummingbird, differ: Anna's hummingbird does vocal learning while the Ruby-throated hummingbird does not. On the other hand, a lineage that has a more distant most recent common ancestor to the hummingbirds, the parrots (*Psitterciformes*) do exhibit vocal learning. This kind of pattern is much more suitable for comparative evolutionary analysis: we can at least raise the question as to whether vocal learning is an independent autapomorphy or not

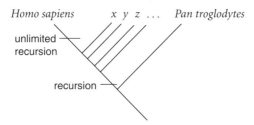

FIGURE 20.4 Notional (and fictional) cladogram with the trait of recursion marked as appearing at some point after the split with chimpanzees (*Pan troglodytes*). Here $x, y, z, \ldots$ denote a range of intermediate fossil species, which might or might not have had the trait of recursion or not (*Orrorin tugenensis, Australopithecus ramidus, Ardipithecus ramidus, Australopithecus anamensis, Australopithecus afarensis, Homo antiquus, Australopithecus bahrelghazali, Kenyanthropus platyops, Australopithecus africanus, Australopithecus garhi, Paraustralopithecus aethiopicus, Australopithecus aethiopicus, Paranthropus robustus, Australopithecus robustus, Australopithecus walkeri, Zinjanthropus boisei, Australopithecus boisei, Paranthropus crassidens, Australopithecus crassidens, Homo antiquus praegens, Australopithecus praegens, Homo habilis, Homo louisleakeyi, Pithecanthropus rudolfensis, Homo rudolfensis, Homo microcranous, Homo ergaster, Pithecanthropus erectus, Homo erectus, Homo antecessor, Homo heidelbergensis, Homo rhodesiensis, Homo helmei, Homo neanderthalensis, Homo sapiens,* and others to be described.)

non-learners in the avian lineage (many thousands of species are not shown in the diagram). This is the type of trait dispersion that is more closely tailored for comparative evolutionary study.

Finally, in Figure 20.4 we sketch a purely notional (and fictional) cladogram illustrating what one might hope to find in the case of the human-language FLN trait (here noted as "recursion"). The split between recursion and unlimited recursion is marked here as a representative example of what one would ideally like to find in the case of comparative evolutionary analysis where a trait appears on a lineage, as with vocal learning in birds; it is completely fictional.

Unfortunately, Figure 20.4 is more than speculative: it is almost certainly incorrect. As far as we know, the FLN is unique to the human lineage. If this is so, then what one can say about a unique autapomorphy is anything at all, or nothing at all. And saying nothing is much more compact. Note that this does *not* mean that one cannot run an adaptationist argument in such situations; just that it is more difficult. Of course, this has never stopped anyone in the evolution-and-language business, possibly including this author, since one can spin any kind of story whatsoever, and compelling story-telling is something our species does best.

Turning to a second major conceptual challenge of evolutionary theory's explanatory "problematic," there is the question of how to infer the operation of selective forces in the past, given that we have only data about the here-and-now. Once again we must face general issues as well as those particular to human language that make this inference more difficult than has sometimes been realized.

The general difficulties with evolutionary inference center on the distinctive character of evolution by natural selection: its time course and speed; its strength; and the possibility of interference from causes other than selection. Though demonstrably effective, as Darwin himself noted, natural selection operates over very long time scales. Typically, the selective advantage of even a highly beneficial gene variant is slight compared to the original, on the order of a tenth of one percent—that is, just one additional surviving gene variant out of one thousand. Further, the force of natural selection is easily overwhelmed by most other forces that can also alter gene frequencies— for example, demographic effects like migration. As Dobzhansky and other founders of the evolutionary Modern Synthesis of the 1930s realized, as few as one or two migrants per generation between populations can block two populations from drifting apart (one of the reasons for invoking 'reproductive isolation' as the definition of a species, despite its numerable problematic aspects). The upshot of these constraints is that the natural selection simply does not operate on a human time scale: we cannot see it happening on the wing, as it were, but are reduced to taking static snapshots of an ultimately long-term dynamical process, as Lewontin (2002) notes. Equation (1) below illustrates this in the simplest possible case of one gene having two variants, or alleles, with frequencies p and $(1 - p)$:

$$\Delta p = \frac{p(1 - p)}{2\bar{w}} \frac{d\bar{w}}{dp} \tag{1}$$

From this equation we can immediately see that the amount of evolutionary change—the change in frequency of gene variant delta p—is directly proportional to the product of two terms: first, the variance of the gene variants in the standing population, $p(1 - p)$, at a particular time; second, the derivative (slope) of the natural logarithm of mean fitness with respect to the frequency p. Viewed this way, the equation has a natural geometric interpretation of evolution as "hill climbing" via gradient ascent through an adaptive landscape while always increasing mean fitness, in Sewall Wright's (1932) famous picture, a precise form of some of the popular recent verbal expositions of this notion. The first term corresponds to the step size taken each generation, while the second term is the slope and direction of the ascent—which way the climb is headed. (It is quite crucial to emphasize that equation (1) and its topographic interpretation holds only in the simplest possible case, with just two variants of a single gene, no interacting genes, and no interactions of fitness with frequency; as soon as such more realistic complications are introduced, the smooth rise to a single adaptive peak does not follow.)

Supposing now that a new gene variant starts out at some low frequency, say with p nearly 0, then evolutionary change will initially be very, very tiny; then it will gather steam, becoming greatest (steepest slope) when p and $(1 - p)$ are both at their half-way points, 0.5; after this, evolutionary change again levels off, asymptotically approaching zero as p fixes at frequency 1.0 and the variation in the population between the two gene types goes to 0.[3] Variance is thus the jet fuel that evolution burns—no variation, no evolution. The overall shape of the curve is sigmoid (a logistic equation), with an inflection point exactly at the middle. So unless one happens to catch change occurring at roughly the 50–50 midpoint, it will in general be difficult to see evolution in action. Further complications to this model may be introduced by adding the stochastic effects of finite population size, as is familiar, but we put to one side this important topic here.

An equation like the one above gives us a way of computing the evolutionary dynamics of what *will* happen going *forwards* in time, from some known starting point. However, this is not the inferential situation in which we find ourselves. Instead, we are only given some array of data—on frequencies of traits, genes, what have you—in the here and now. Our goal is to determine what the forces were in the past, including selection, migration, and so forth, that, starting from some unknown initial state at some point in the past, conspired to yield a trajectory with this observed end-state data. But as Lewontin (2002) observes, this is very nearly an ill-posed or under-determined problem with three unknowns and essentially just one equation: we cannot know the initial state; we do not know the forces that have operated over some (generally unknown) period of time—that is what we aim to solve. We know only the end-state. There is a standard escape to this problem in evolutionary inference, as Lewontin notes:

Either we assume that we know the forces, in which case we can make probability statements about the initial conditions, or else we assume that we know the initial conditions, in which case we can make estimates of the forces that have led to the

---

[3] This over-simplified continuous form equation assumes an arbitrarily large population, so the frequency of p never actually reaches zero. In a more realistic form, with finite demographics, at some point p actually will go to zero.

present. We cannot do both. There is one solution to this dilemma. If the evolutionary process has gone on for a sufficiently long time with no changes in the forces, then there is an equilibrium probability distribution of the present states, the so-called steady-state distribution, that is reached irrespective of the original state of the population. What this means … [is that] all the effects of the initial state have disappeared. So, if we can observe many genetic variations all of which can be assumed to be the result of the same forces, then the distribution of those variations can be used to estimate those forces.   (Lewontin 2002: 5)

20.1.2 *Case study: The problem with FOXP2 and the evolutionary explanation of language*

The recent and much publicized research on the *FOXP2* transcription factor gene serves as an excellent case study of the difficulties of evolutionary analysis, revealing the problems with backwards inference from observed present conditions, sensitivity to equilibrium assumptions, and conclusions drawn given a relatively small number of differences amongst a thinly populated species space. Apparently there are just two amino acid differences in this gene between *Homo sapiens* and Neanderthals.

Taken together with the apparent connection between defects in this gene and language disorders, the evolutionary analysis of *FoxP2* in other species and humans has sometimes been implicated as part of the push to language. We shall see that argument here is tendentious, both statistically and biologically, because when there are so few differences at such a far remove from a phenotype, and so much intervening time, it may simply be impossible to tell whether the gene in question was "selected for" or not, or when this selection happened, if at all. There are so many modeling parameters it resembles weather forecasting: assumptions have to be made regarding population size and changes, generation times, and selection coefficients, among others. This is well known in the evolutionary literature, but the consequences of changing the assumptions—a sensitivity analysis—are sometimes not explored. That is what we shall do here. The results point to a much weaker connection between *FoxP2* and language. While the evolutionary analysis remains cloudy, it may be that if we look at this gene in a different light, as part of the genomic machinery connected to externalization and serial motor coordination, then we can revive its analysis as a probe into language and evolution, a matter we take up in Act II, below.

To begin, let us quickly sketch the basics of the *FOXP2* story, its connection to language disorders, and its comparative evolutionary genetic analysis, omitting many details that may be found in several excellent summaries; we follow the presentation in Marcus and Fisher (2003). They describe the connection between *FOXP2* and language this way (original references in the text have been omitted for clarity):

The first direct evidence of a specific gene that influences speech and language acquisition has come not from complex traits, but from an unusual autosomal dominant form of communication disorder that is caused by mutation of the forkhead box P2 (*FOXP2*) gene....The consequences of *FOXP2* disruption differ from typical SLI [Specific Language Impairment, RCB] in that they include prominent difficulties in learning and producing sequences of movements that involve the mouth and lower part of the face. Affected individuals have problems with speech articulation (developmental verbal dyspraxia or DVD), which are accompanied by wide-ranging deficits in many aspects of language and grammar. Crucially, although general intelligence varies among individuals who carry the same *FOXP2* mutation, speech and language deficits are always evident, even for children with normal non-verbal intelligence. Moreover, the associated problems with processing language and grammar are not exclusively tied to speech—they are evident in the written domain and occur for comprehension as well as expression....The link between *FOXP2* and disordered language was initially identified through genetic studies of a large three-generational family (known as KE), in which affected members carry a heterozygous missense mutation that alters the DNA-binding domain of the FOXP2 protein. The KE substitution markedly affects the function of the encoded protein (J. Nicôd, S.C. Vernes, F.M. Elahi, A.M. Coupe, L.E. Bird and S.E.F., unpublished observations). *FOXP2* mutations are not a predominant cause of language impairment; however, a second heterozygous point mutation in *FOXP2* was recently identified that co-segregates with speech and language deficits in another family. This nonsense mutation severely truncates the protein, deleting essential functional motifs, including protein–protein interaction domains, the DNA-binding domain and suspected nuclear localization signals. Independent chromosomal aberrations (including translocations and deletions) that disrupt *FOXP2* are associated with speech and language deficits.   (Marcus and Fisher 2003: 5–6)

Turning now to evolutionary analysis, the crucial data has been provided by a phylogeny based on a comparative study of certain *FoxP2* regions from individuals of five different primate species along with an outgroup comparison to the mouse, as illustrated in Figure 20.5, redrawn after Enard et al. (2002). The crucial evolutionary distinction to focus on is the difference between what are called synonymous and nonsynonymous amino acid substitutions in these gene regions. A synonymous substitution is a change in one of the triplet DNA codon bases (Adenine, Cytosine, Thymine, Guanine) that does not alter the corresponding amino acid that is coded for—this is because the DNA triplet code is redundant, usually with several distinct triplets or "codons," especially those varying only in the third position, "spelling out" or specifying the same amino acid. Because a nonsynonymous change does not alter the corresponding amino acid comprising the protein coded for by

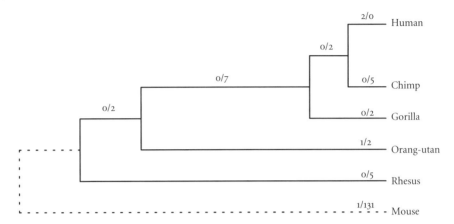

FIGURE 20.5 (Redrawn after Enard et al. 2002.) The phylogenetic relationship of *FoxP2* exonic regions for five primate species (human, chimpanzee, gorilla, orang-utan, and rhesus macaque) along with a comparison outgroup of *Mus musculus* (mouse). The upper/lower numbers denote the number of nonsynonymous (amino-acid changing)/synonymous (non-amino-acid changing or silent) substitutions along that branch of the lineage, respectively. For example, there are two nonsynonymous substitutions on the line leading from the least common ancestor of *Homo sapiens* and *Pan troglodytes* to *Homo*, at positions 303 and 325, and zero synonymous substitutions. The two changes were Threonine to Asparginine at amino acid position 303 in exon 7 and Asparginine to Serine at position 325. There are one nonsynonymous substitution and 131 synonymous substitutions on the line leading from the common ancestor of the primate clade and *Mus musculus* to *Mus*. See the main text for the results of computing a McDonald—Kreitman statistical test for detecting selection given these data, which turns out to be statistically indistinguishable from chance

the *FoxP2* gene, it is assumed to be functionally silent and so not subject to direct natural selection. (Like many assumptions in biology, this one may actually not hold, but we put this issue to one side here.) For example, the amino acid Threonine (Thr) is spelled out by the DNA codon A–C–{T,C,A,G}. Therefore, any possible change to the third position to the DNA will not alter the corresponding amino acid. For example, a single nucleotide point mutation in the third codon position, from ACT to ACG will not result in any change in the corresponding protein coded for—it will remain Threonine. The amino acid Serine is redundant in the third position as well: it is spelled out by T–{T, C, A, G}. Serine has a further redundancy: it is also spelled out by the triplets AGT and AGC. To repeat, such changes are therefore assumed not to matter for selection, because they do not alter protein function.

In contrast, the amino acid Asparagine (Asn) is spelled out by the codons A–A–{T, C}, so any change in the third position from T or C to A or G will be *nonsynonymous* because it will result in a DNA codon that spells out a *different* amino acid from the original, namely, Lysine. Since such a change, a point mutation results in a new amino acid that may have functional consequences, it is assumed to be subject to selection. Note that both synonymous and nonsynonymous changes arise stochastically as the result of random mutational processes. By comparing synonymous to nonsynonymous changes, evolutionary biologists have developed a range of statistics to see whether natural selection has been operating, subject to certain assumptions.

The Enard et al. (2002) evolutionary study sequenced the genomic regions of exons 4–7 of *FoxP2* in five extant primate species (see Figure 20.5), along with mouse (*Mus musculus*), in order to carry out a comparative evolutionary analysis of exactly this sort. Enard et al. found that there were just two key nonsynonymous amino acid differences between non-human primates, mouse, and human: humans, but not the other species, have the DNA codon AAC specifying the amino acid Asn at position 303 in exon 7 of the gene, and DNA codon AGC specifying Serine (Ser) at amino acid position 325, just a bit further along down the gene. The corresponding DNA codons in chimpanzee *Pan troglodytes* and *Mus* are both ACC, specifying the amino acid Threonine (Thr), and AAT, specifying the amino acid Asparginine (recall that Asp is redundantly specified by several different triplet codons). This evidence suggests that the ancestral codon state was AGT, and a single nucleotide mutation in the second position from A(denine) to G(uanine) changed this to AGC, and so altered the amino acid coded for at position 303, a nonsynonymous change; similarly, that ACC was ancestral and mutated to AGC via a single nucleotide change from C(ytoseine) to G(uanine), changing the amino acid at position 325. (Neither of these changes are those involved in the KE-family disruption, which are due to other defects in *FOXP2*.)

We should also note that this analysis assumes by convention that just a single nucleotide change has occurred here, say from A to G—an assumption of parsimony. Of course it could also have been possible that the A mutated to G, then back to A, then to G, and so on, along the line leading from the common ancestor of mouse and human to human. One simply cannot know for certain; it is merely simplest to assume that there was but one such change. Lewontin (1989) notes this is true simply because, first, "any nucleotide position has only four possible states, so that although two sequences may be *observed* to be identical at some position, they may be separated by numerous evolutionary changes but have converged to the same state," and, second, "each state is, at least mutationally, accessible from each other state so sequences of evolutionary states are not well ordered" (1989: 15). Lewontin then points out that how to correctly estimate the number of nucleotide substitutions along an evolutionary lineage can radically differ, depending upon whether amino acid substitutions (nonsynonymous changes) are completely unconstrained, strongly constrained, or somewhere between these two extremes. In the case of *FoxP2*, there is a (perhaps tacit) assumption that amino acid substitutions have a strong functional impact, but it is not clear that this was taken into account (note that except in the case of mouse, we have very little evidence of a large number of synonymous substitutions as compared to nonsynonymous substitutions for any of the primate species, the hallmark of strong functional constraints on amino acid substitutions, as Lewontin notes.)

Putting such questions to one side for the moment, let us examine the phylogenetic diagram in Figure 20.5 more carefully. Time runs left to right. The horizontal line after each branch point between two species is labeled with two numbers, one above the other. The top one denotes the number of *nonsynonymous* amino acid changes in exons 4–7 after the branch point, the bottom denotes the number of *synonymous* amino acid changes in exons 4–7. So for example, in the Enard et al. sequencing data there is one nonsynonymous amino acid change in mouse and 131 synonymous substitutions after the common ancestor between all the other primates and mouse. Similarly, since the split between chimpanzees and human, seen there have been two nonsynonymous amino acid changes in humans, and there are apparently zero synonymous substitutions, for a set of individuals drawn from a wide variety of geographic regions.

From this data, Enard et al. drew a number of striking evolutionary inferences. Perhaps most importantly, they computed a number of standard statistical tests to detect natural selection, suggesting that there was a "selective sweep" in the case of *FOXP2*—that is, strong positive selection for specific *FOXP2* changes along the evolutionary line that led to humans, as well as an estimate of the time when that sweep occurred, perhaps 50,000–100,000 years BCE.

But are these strong conclusions justified? There seem to be at least three main difficulties:

1. The tests that were used to detect selection at the two crucial amino acid differences between us and primates adopted the standard assumption of 'stochastic equilibrium' as described above. A re-analysis using the only statistical test known that is *not* sensitive to such an assumption (McDonald

and Kreitman 1991; Kreitman 2000), details given below, reveals no statistically significant positive selection.

2. The simulation study Enard et al. used to estimate the time when this putative selection acted also made certain biological assumptions about the strength of natural selection, generation times, and particular computational assumptions regarding numerical accuracy. When we alter these, for example, changing selection to a more naturally occurring value, then the sweep disappears.

3. Even supposing that *FOXP2* was "selected for," it remains unclear exactly *what* function it might have been selected for: initially it might not have been selected for its role in serial motor control, always an issue for a transcription factor gene that regulates other genes. At this point we simply cannot say.

Let us take up these points one by one. First, consider the assumption of stochastic equilibrium. From the data in Figure 20.5 one can compute a two-way contingency table, the McDonald–Kreitman statistical test for detecting selection. The idea is to compare the number of synonymous and nonsynonymous amino acid substitutions *within* species and also *between* species, for example, both *within* humans and *between* humans and, in this case, mouse. By doing a comparison both within and across species groups and looking at the ratios, the intuition is that any stochastic ripple that could affect one column would also proportionately affect the other (roughly because all historical events that could have jiggled both groups' numbers would have affected both in equal proportion; for further explanation, see McDonald and Kreitman 1991). This is the only test for selection we currently have that does not rely on the assumption of stochastic equilibrium (Kreitman 2000). There is a price paid for this robustness: the test is known to be very conservative, that is, it errs on the side of rejecting true positives. Thus, if one has a McDonald—Kreitman test that says that selection has occurred at some statistically significant level (say $p = 0.05$ or 0.01) then one can be fairly confident that selection has indeed taken place. Of course, the converse is not true; but as we have noted, all the stronger tests are subject to the slings and arrows of the equilibrium assumption.

What about the case at hand? There are $1 + 2 = 3$ between-species nonsynonymous amino acid differences between *Homo* and *Mus*, and $131 - 3 = 128$ between-species synonymous differences. Enard et al. found 47 within-species *Homo* synonymous amino acid differences across the different individuals they sampled, and 0 nonsynonymous differences. This yields the two-way contingency table in Figure 20.6, for which we can use Fisher's exact test to

	Human	Mouse
Synonymous amino acid substitutions	47	128
Nonsynonymous amino acid substitutions	0	3

FIGURE 20.6 A McDonald–Kreitman (two-way contingency table) test on the between- and within-group synonymous/nonsynonymous *FoxP2* exonic data from Enard et al. (2002). A calculation of the probability of such a pattern appearing solely by chance using Fisher's exact test finds that the probability that this array of counts could be due to chance alone to be in effect 1.0, i.e., near certainty. Thus it is highly statistically insignificant (*p* value effect in 1.0, i.e., at chance level)

find the precise probability that this distribution of numbers could be due to chance alone, which happens to be very nearly 1.0. The reason for this negative result is that there are so few nonsynonymous differences between *Homo* and mouse (or chimpanzee), and no nonsynonymous variation at all within *Homo*.

Second, the simulation study Enard et al. used to estimate the time when this putative selection acted also made certain biological assumptions about the strength of natural selection, generation times, and particular computational assumptions regarding numerical accuracy. In particular, Enard et al. found that a selection coefficient of 0.01 (1%) yielded a statistically significant selective sweep under their model, but importantly, note that when this value is reduced to a value that has more often been found in field studies of selection, $\frac{1}{2}$ to $\frac{1}{10}$ of a percent, then the sweep disappears: in fact, these more biologically realistic values about the strength of selection (as Enard et al. themselves note) do not lead to the same statistically reliable results.

Third, even supposing that *FOXP2* was selected for, it remains unclear exactly *what* function it might have been selected for: initially it might not have been selected for its role in serial motor control, always an issue for a transcription factor gene that regulates other genes. We simply do not know. While *FOXP2* clearly operates in modern human neural development, and its disruption affects motor learning and language in human and other species, as confirmed by an increasing number of studies (e.g. Teramitsu et al. 2004; Haesler et al. 2007), it is also presumptively involved in the formation of the digestive gut epithelial lining. Crucially, the key amino-acid change proposed as being under strong positive selection, at position 325, also seems common to all *Carnivora* (see Figure 20.7). If so, then the human *FOXP2* changes might well have been due to dietary modifications related to the move from trees to savannah, with the related neural effects a concomitant effect, in this sense a kind of hitchhiking. The causal sequence remains unclear.[4]

Summarizing, what should we conclude about the evolution of human language and the observed evolutionary changes in *FOXP2*? If anything, this re-analysis serves as a cautionary example of the challenges of evolutionary inference when there are so few differences between closely related species. Some confirming evidence for this conclusion comes from the first comparison of the human genome and the draft chimp genome, as reported by the Chimpanzee Sequencing Consortium in *Nature*, 2005. This study compared 13,454 "matching" (orthologous) human–chimp genes, and found evidence for accelerated evolution in the human lineage for only 585 genes, all but a handful related to the expected categories of immunity, olfaction (humans lost their sense of smell), and reproduction (e.g. spermatogenesis).

The Consortium also carried out comparisons of these genes and others in mouse and rat with respect to synonymous vs. nonsynonymous substitution reported in their Supplementary Data (details were omitted in the main text). In contrast to other studies, *FOXP2* did not stand out: the ratio of synonymous/nonsynonymous substitutions for *FOXP2* in human was 0.81, a ratio one expects to see when there is no selection going on.[5] Again, this is not a surprising result; it is simply what happens when we look for differences by examining species that are too close, or, as the Consortium put it in the case of *FOXP2*: "given the small number of changes involved, additional data will be required" (2005: 79). The *FOXP2* changes could have been due to chance alone. What can be done about this situation? Act II suggests the obvious course: look at species that are farther away. Since there is increasing evidence that the

---

[4] A final, more minor point is that Enard et al. provide some evidence that they suggest points to a *functional* reason why the amino acid under possible positive selection might have changed in the manner it did: a computer simulation indicating that this change prompts an alteration in the gene product's binding site. Repeating their analysis with three other tools confirms this. However, there is one problem: in other species that have also been argued to have accelerated *FoxP2* evolution (bats, birds), this particular amino acid is *not* changed. Rather, the changes occur at other positions in the DNA sequence of *FoxP2*, and when one carries out the same computer simulations, there appears to be no comparable functional change in these other species. I conclude that this functional evidence is weak at best.

[5] For comparison, the Consortium's ratios for mouse and rat were both 0.15, a number indicative of so-called negative or purifying selection. The chimpanzee ratio could not be tested, as the Consortium actually found zero substitutions of either sort.

Order	Species	Site 303	Site 325
Galliformes	Chicken	Thr	Asn
Tubulidentata	Aardvark	Thr	Asn
Artiodactyl	Pig	Thr	Asn
	Cow	Thr	Asn
Cetacea	Whale	Thr	Asn
Perissodactyla	Zebra	Thr	Asn
	Tapir	Thr	Asn
Carnivora	Cat	Thr	**Ser**
	Dog	Thr	**Ser**
	Wolf	Thr	**Ser**
	Wolverine	Thr	**Ser**
	Bear	Thr	**Ser**
	Fox	Thr	**Ser**
	Sea lion	Thr	**Ser**
Chiroptera	Bat	Thr	Asn
Rodentia	Mouse	Thr	Asn
Lagomorphs	Rabbit	Thr	Asn
Insectivora	Mole	Thr	Asn
Primates	Lemur	Thr	Asn
	Tamarin	Thr	Asn
	Rhesus	Thr	Asn
	Gorilla	Thr	Asn
	Chimp	Thr	Asn
	Bonobo	Thr	Asn

FIGURE 20.7 (Excerpted and redrawn from Zhang et al. 2002, Figure 3.) The bounded box highlights species where position 325 of the *FoxP2* transcription factor gene codes for the amino acid Serine (Ser) rather than Asparginine (Asn), the same putative change under selective pressure in *Homo* according to Enard et al. (2002). Note that this encompasses the entire order *Carnivora*, as reported by Zhang et al.

transcription factor protein FoxP2 assists in neural development, including the development of serial motor coordination, specifically in vocal external-ization and imitation in birds, then perhaps we can rescue the FoxP2 story by resurrecting it in another guise—not as the hallmark of recursive syntax, but as part of how serial motor externalization (and possibly vocal imitation) are linked. If so, then *FOXP2* would not speak so much to the origin of the core of human language, recursive syntax, but to how language is externalized. Act II examines this possibility in more detail, by considering the metrical structure of language.

20.2 Act II: Merge from the Bottom Up—The Return of the FOX?

According to the Minimalist Program, we can envision the entire computa-tional system associated with language as having two main interfaces with the other cognitive/computational systems external to language proper: the first the conceptual–intentional interface, roughly, the interface between syntax and the systems of thought, belief, reasoning, and the like; the second the sensori–motor and articulatory–perceptual interfaces comprising the connec-tion between syntax and its external form (either its perception, via parsing, or its production as, for example, the articulatory gestures of spoken language or sign language). The central operation of this central computational language system, or "CS" as it is dubbed by Reinhart (2006), is the single operation Merge.

Act I reviewed some of the existing comparative evolutionary evidence and arguments available that might shed light on the natural selection for Merge, finding these lacking, primarily due to the autapomorphic (species-specific) nature of Merge and issues with primates being "too close" to humans and too sparsely populated in species space. Act II attempts to remedy these problems by taking a highly speculative and quite radical position: instead of studying species that are quite close to humans, like chimpanzees or other primates, perhaps one can find an analog in another domain, in a species at some remove from humans so that the problem of accidental convergence does not arise. Act II argues that such an analog might be found in the process by which the metrical structure of sentences—their rhythmic character—is formed, and that this process may well be shared with songbirds. If this approach is on the right track, then one could use comparative evolutionary analysis in birds as a window into similar processes in humans. In particular, Act II adopts the Halle–Idsardi model of metrical stress assignment, as refined in Fabb and Halle (2006), as its theory of metrical stress assignment. It shows how this model, essentially a form of counting, applies to human metrical patterns, and then extends that analysis to songbirds using a novel method for extracting syllables posited by Coen (2006). The end result is a skeletal form of Merge: it operates without formal lexical features of the sort found in syntax proper, combining only the asterisks that Fabb and Halle associate with basic syllables. In this sense, it is pure syntax—literally a skeleton—with the combination-and-selection character of Merge (or formerly X-bar theory), but without any other features at all of the sort usually associated with lexical entries. But this is just what one would like for comparative purposes, since presumably songbirds lack precisely these formal syntactic features as well. Birds have songs, but no semantics or lexical items in the conventional sense. Primates face the opposite problem: they seem to have a conceptual–intentional system, perhaps even lexical items ("words") according to much evidence accumulated over the past several decades, but seemingly lack the Merge operation itself (otherwise, they would indeed have the capabilities of human language). Only humans have lexical items and Merge, yielding a fully recursive syntax.

To proceed, we first consider how the Halle system for the assignment of metrical stress or rhythmic structure to syllables works. We then apply it to the songbird case. Finally, we show how this really does amount to a reduced form of Merge.

To begin, we sketch the Halle system, drawing directly from the exposition in Fabb and Halle (2006). The process works by the repeated counting and grouping of syllables, denoted simply as asterisks, according to an ordered set of rules, forming as output a metrical grid whose periodic structure reflects whether a syllable will be stressed or unstressed. An example taken from Fabb and Halle (2006) will serve to illustrate. Suppose we have the English line, *Tell me not in mournful numbers* (from the poem by Longfellow). Fabb and Halle present an ordered list of seven rules (their 12a–g) that accomplishes this. We can mark out the syllables as follows, assuming the following associated metrical structure where a slash marks a syllable likely to have strong stress, while an "x" marks a syllable likely to have weak stress or no stress, where we have inserted dashes for readability:

```
 /   x   /  x  /    x   /  x
Tell me not in mourn-ful num-bers
```

Fabb and Halle's rules associate an initial set of asterisks ("gridline 0") with the syllables in this line, and then their ordered rules operate to produce a vertical grid that matches this rhythm. Initially the asterisk marking, one per syllable, is given by their first rule, (12a), "Project each syllable as an asterisk on gridline 0," as follows:

Tell me not in mourn-ful num-bers
  *   *   * *   *   *   *   *

Next, Fabb and Halle's rule (12b) groups these asterisks into pairs by inserting left parentheses, left to right, obtaining what Fabb and Halle call 'the gridline 0 feet' (we have again inserted dashes for readability):

Tell me not in mourn-ful num-bers
(* * (* *   (*   *   (* *   gridline 0

We now apply rule (12c): the leftmost asterisk in the next group is projected to the next gridline (gridline 1):

Tell me not in mourn-ful num-bers
(* * (* * (*   * (*   *   gridline 0
 *   *   *   *   gridline 1

We now apply their rule (12d) on gridline 1, moving now from right to left every two asterisks and inserting a right parenthesis to obtain a new grouping:

Tell me not in mourn-ful num-bers
(* * (* *   (*   * (*   *   gridline 0
 *   *) *   *)   gridline 1

We next apply their rule (12e): the rightmost asterisk on gridline 1 is projected to form the next gridline, gridline 2:

Tell me not in mourn-ful num-bers
(*   * (* *   (*   * (*   *   gridline 0
 *   *)   *   *)   gridline 1
       *   *   gridline 2

We now re-apply rule (12d) (rule (12f)) to gridline 3:

Tell me not in mourn-ful num-bers
(*   * (* *   (*   * (*   *   gridline 0
 *   *)   *   *)   gridline 1
       *   *   *)   gridline 2

Finally, we apply the rightmost projection rule one more time, their (12g), obtaining gridline 3 and the final result (since there is only one asterisk remaining and no more rules can apply):

```
Tell me  not  in mourn-ful num-bers
(*    *   (*   *      (*     *     (*    *    gridline 0
 *            *)              *             *)       gridline 1
              *                             *)       gridline 2
                                            *        gridline 3
```

If we now match up the grid positions with the most asterisks, we see that they correspond to the observed rhythmic pattern of the line as desired:

```
/    x   /   x    /    x   /    x
Tell me  not  in mourn-ful num-bers
(*    *   (*   *      (*     *     (*    *    gridline 0
 *            *)              *             *)       gridline 1
              *                             *)       gridline 2
                                            *        gridline 3
/    x   /   x    /    x   /    x
```

Of course, this is just one line of words from a single language, while there are many metrical patterns and many languages. According to Fabb and Halle's analysis, all of the various valid metrical patterns of human languages may be defined by parameterizing their procedure above as a list of binary choices for each of the gridlines. We list their parameters as follows (0/1 numbers denote our binary encoding of the parameter values):

1. Insert either left or right parentheses (0/1).
2. Insert parentheses at every binary/ternary asterisk (0/1).
3. Start inserting parentheses at either the left/right edge of the grid (0/1).
4. Project a "head" (an asterisk at the next gridline) by selecting either the leftmost or the rightmost asterisk of a group delimited by parentheses and placing an asterisk above this one on a new line above the existing line (0/1).
5. Start the process at either the first or the second syllable (0/1).

In the Longfellow example, we can see for instance that the parameterization applied to the first line of the grid was to (a) insert left parentheses; (b) insert binary; (c) start at the left; (d) project left; (e) start at the first syllable. Thus as a bit-vector this parameterization would be simply [0 0 0 0 0]. Note that at the second gridline, we reversed direction, and inserted right parentheses starting from the right, promoting the rightmost asterisk to the next gridline, for instance, parameterization [1 0 1 1 0]. Crucially, Fabb and Halle note that certain parameterizations will lead to invalid metrical structures, that is, those that do not seemingly correspond to the particular rhythmic structure of this example. For instance, as they note, if instead the system moved from right to left at gridline 0, the resulting grouping and projection of a head would result in an improper pattern, where the first syllables of *mournful* and *numbers* would not be placed on gridline 1, to be eventually stressed, which is incorrect:

```
/   x  /  x   /   x  /   x
Tell me not in mourn-ful num-bers
*   *) *  *)   *   *)  *   *)  gridline 0
    *      *        *       *   gridline 1
```

Though the Fabb and Halle system is presented in a form that uses the vocabulary of selection, projection, and heads (as in X-bar theory), we may recall that in the Minimalist Program, this vocabulary has been replaced by the (largely minimally necessary) properties of Merge. We can illustrate this by comparing an example from the older X-bar system in syntax, and then a corresponding example from the Fabb–Halle gridline system. In the systems antedating Merge, we would say that a verb phrase *saw Mary* is comprised of the element *saw* (putting to one side tense, etc.), and the DP *Mary*. As is familiar from X-bar theory, the +V lexical item *saw* has been selected as the head of the phrase, and then projected to the next level, that of a constituent (the verb phrase), with all its features copied to this position, leading to the familiar hierarchical structure depicted below on the left. Indeed, some would go so far as to say that all the features of *saw* are copied to this position, leading to the second figure below on the right, where we place *saw* at the root node of the hierarchical structure formed by the combination of *saw* and the DP:

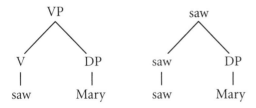

Of course, all this means is that *saw* and the DP have been grouped together, just as in the Fabb and Halle system, with *saw* selected as the head of the phrase and projected, as is familiar. Applying this to the asterisk-based system, we can write the Fabb and Halle notation as on the left, and its equivalent in X-bar form in the notation on the right.

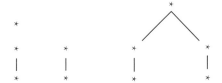

It is easy to see that the Fabb–Halle system operates formally precisely like the familiar X-bar system, but with one crucial difference: there are no lexical features whatsoever, that is, features like +V associated with lexical entries, no agreement features, and the like. There are simply the marks as we have shown them in the diagram, which have no features. Nonetheless, the rest of the formal apparatus remains the same and operates geometrically as before: in both cases, one of the items is selected to be the head of the next line, and whatever features it has (in this case, the empty set, there being no features) are copied to that level.

A Merge-based account operates similarly. In its simplest form, Merge takes two objects, here just asterisks, and combines (i.e. groups) them into a single new object, selecting one as the head to be the label of the grouped object. But this again simply describes the basic operation of the Fabb–Halle selection-and-grid-projection procedure. Fabb and Halle's system differs only insofar as the label contains simply a single vacuous feature, namely, just an asterisk (and so probe–goal agreement applies vacuously). We might therefore regard it as the simplest (and degenerate) kind of system that exhibits the most basic property of grouping, that is, Merge. Indeed, Chomsky (2007a) notes that Merge operating even more degenerately on just a single featureless item would yield counting (the number system), but without grouping. Thus the proposal advanced here is in this sense the simplest nontrivial extension of the Chomsky (2007a) proposal, showing that metrical stress assignment, too, falls under the Merge model.

If this is on the right track, then we can ask the next question: this computational system, like syntax, must interface to the outside world via some externalization process. The final output from the Syntax–SM externalization process is assumed to have at least two properties: first, it must be linear (rather than hierarchical), that is, the syntactic objects passed from syntax are flattened so that the relation of precedence is imposed (a topic pursued in great depth in Kayne 1994); second, it is ordered left-to-right, in virtue of the necessary time course of sound and articulators operating in the real world. We unpack the externalization mapping into two steps that correspond to each of these properties: (1) impose precedence (what comes next to what, in the

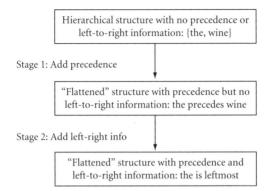

Figure 20.8 Externalization as a two-stage process

linear order projection); (2) take the precedence-ordered object and determine whether it is to be output left-to-right or right-to-left. (See Figure 20.8)

Minimally, this requires adding two new relations: (1) precedence, that is, whether one element comes before or after another (the minimal relation needed for any linear ordering); and (2) global order (whether the resulting sequence output right-to-left or left-to-right; note for example, that the grid-lines can be read in either order so there is indeed a choice). The output result is a series of high-to-low stress assignments. This suggests that much of the Fabb and Halle system might be forced by conditions at the external interface, leaving only binary Merge as its central operative principle, the best possible result.[6]

Since the Fabb–Halle system is based solely on counting syllable marks (asterisks) and their groupings, one might inquire as to whether the observable externalization of such a system of metrical patterns can be found in the

[6] We leave for future research this possible redundancy in the Fabb–Halle parameterization that might follow from this externalization procedure and its imposition of both precedence and left-to-right relations. Examining the Fabb–Halle parameters (1)–(5) it may be noted that many are left-to-right symmetrical: one can insert either left or right parentheses; one can proceed either from the left- or right-hand side; one starts inserting parentheses (counting) at either the right or left edge; etc. If, however, there is no "right" or "left" at some earlier internal stage of grouping that is simply Merge before externalization, then these parameters cannot be distinguished and may be collapsed together. This suggests that the system might be simplified by breaking it down into a two-stage process: stage 1, Merge of items with no lexical features; stage 2, externalization and thereby imposition of "left" and "right" parentheses (precedence) as well as externalization in left-to-right or right-to-left order, a condition imposed by the interface. If so, then the interface condition forces all of the parameterizations in (1)–(5) above, leaving just binary Merge. (We put to one side here the question about reducing Fabb and Halle's ternary counting, which might be derivative from binary Merge plus adjacency: on this account, the notion "ternary" is a binary grouping, supplied by Merge, plus the addition at either the right- or left-hand edge, of a singleton. It remains to work out the details of this reduction.)

vocalizations in other species. If so, perhaps we can use this as evolutionary insight into at least part of the language system. The answer here seems to be yes, at least for a preliminary set of cases. Consider birdsong, in particular a species that does vocal learning and where FoxP2 is also known to be involved, zebra finches, *Taeniopygia guttata*. The first issue that arises is what counts as a "syllable." The avian biologist's traditional division of a finch song into syllables would delimit them by silences—the start of a syllable is a period of silence, and similarly its end is marked by a period of silence. However, this does not correspond to what would be a linguist's analysis.

We can more properly approach the linguistic representation by applying a method developed by Coen (2006) to find what he calls "songemes." Coen processes a finch song by means of peak-power filtering, which produces a more nuanced division into regions of high and low intensities, rather than just regions of silence/no silence. This becomes a presumptive proxy for songemes: each looks like a hill—a rise followed by a drop in peak power. We can partition these as illustrated in Figure 20.9, from Coen (2006), where the blue vertical lines indicate the songeme boundaries, and the yellow curve highlights the peaks and valleys of the resulting metrical structure.

For example, we now consider in more detail the interval in Figure 20.9 from approximately 600 msec to 850 msec. In this case one can recover a pattern of peaks and valleys that amounts to roughly the following sequence of High–high–Low–low regularities, a metrical structure close, though not identical, to the Longfellow structure, H–L–H–L–H–L ... We have analyzed several dozen finch songs available from the datasets in Coen's thesis, and they all fall under the Halle-type analysis, using parameters (1)–(5), usually trochaic or iambic in format: a Merge-type grouping system, followed by linear externalization, if the previous analysis is correct.[7]

From an evolutionary standpoint, this result, if correct, leads to the following connection. There has been recent accumulated evidence that interference with FoxP2 in these birds (via the knock-down of the *FoxP2* genes) disrupts syllable structure (on the production side, that is, either directly on motor externalization, or through some more complicated feedback cycle in terms of vocal learning and imitation); syllables are over-extended, doubled, or absent. Put more generally, syllabic metrical structure becomes defective (Haesler et al. 2007). While it is impossible to say in any detail exactly what aspect of the machinery has been disrupted, this result is consistent with the view that the human FOXP2 transcription factor, more generally the FoxP2

---

[7] Very preliminary analysis of humpback whale and other cetacean songs such as bluenose dolphins, for example, as in Suzuki, Buck, and Tyack (2006), yield similar results, as do subsonic elephant songs and ultrasonic mouse song.

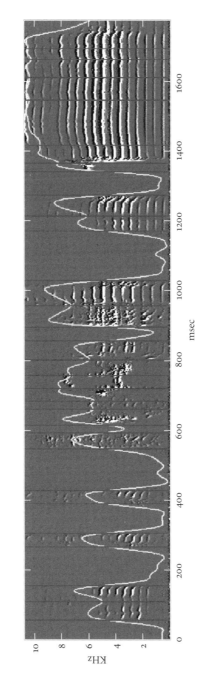

FIGURE 20.9 A partitioning of a zebra finch song by means of a peak-power filtering. Note the hills and valleys. Vertical lines at maxima and minima divide the song into a more nuanced pattern of high and low intensities. (Courtesy of Michael Coen, from Coen 2006, figure 5.14.) Time is on the *x*-axis; frequency in kHZ on the *y*-axis

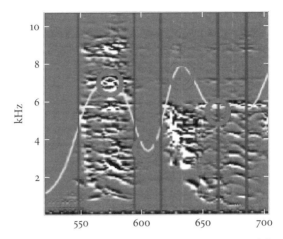

FIGURE 20.10 The high–low "metrical structure" of one section of the finch birdsong from Figure 20.9

vertebrate transcription factor, is largely part of a secondary externalization process. However, there remains one (highly speculative) connection back to the internal system and Merge: if it is true that rhythmic structure is initially Merge-generated, without a lexicon, and then linearized at the S–M interface, then it might be that this computational ability shared by both birds and humans, and possibly the entire vertebrate lineage. Of course, it might also be true that this is an independent apomorphy, invented separately by both birds and humans to solve the interface problem for rhythmic structure. Only a much more detailed investigation of metrical structure in birds, as well as mammals, could begin to answer this; there are many open questions, among them whether the Merge-like complexity of the Halle system is required at all to describe or explain rhythmic structure and how this structure varies between vocal learners and non-learners. For example, if it is required only for vocal imitative learning, as suggested in Haesler et al. (2007), then it would surface only in the case of vocal learners. It also might well be true that this interface solution is entirely a third-factor constraint that has nothing whatsoever to do with Merge; it is simply a common solution to a similar functional problem, as in the similar aerodynamic shape of bird and bat wings. So while this "zero feature" Merge computational ability might be antecedently present in other, distantly related species, it raises both opportunities and puzzles: opportunities for evolutionary investigation in that it does not encounter the problems with comparisons to other primates, but puzzles in that as Chomsky (2007a) notes, unary feature-less Merge leads to arithmetic and counting. If so, why do we not observe the same arithmetical ability in birds as in humans? We leave all these as open questions, noting however that Chomsky (2007a) asserts that unbounded Merge is associated with what he calls "undeletable edge features," rather than a totally feature-free lexicon as in the assumptions regarding rhythmic structure.

20.3 The Big Bang and a Venetian Fairy Tale: All You Need is Merge

This chapter has advanced three main points about the connection between evolution and language. First, it advocated caution: one can no more do armchair evolutionary theory than one can do armchair linguistics. Many folk intuitions about evolution and the ease of inferring that natural selection has operated in one or another scenario may simply be wrong, even for experts. In particular, echoing Lewontin (1998) but in the new domain of comparative genomics, inference in the sparse space of primate species is exceedingly difficult.

Second, it argued that where the FoxP2 transcription factor seems to be operating is in the domain of the S–M interface, but with a hint of Merge behind it, in particular, suggesting that the Fabb and Halle system for building metrical structure just *is* Merge, operating without lexical features and under the constraints of the external S–M interface system.

Third, and perhaps the most fanciful point of all, hence a Venetian fairy tale: it is suggested that if the story about metrical structure is correct, it allows us to rescue the FoxP2 story in a dramatic, though perhaps fanciful way to account for the Big Bang or apparently saltational appearance of human language. In line with what this chapter has indicated, Chomsky (2007a) has sometimes advanced the view that what it took to get us language was in fact a small change, "at the minimum, some rewiring of the brain, presumably a small mutation or a by-product of some other change, provided Merge and undeletable E[edge] F[eatures] (unbounded Merge), yielding an infinite range of expressions." It may be possible to say more than this. Chimpanzees, and possibly other primates, got conceptual atoms. Birds got rhythm. But only people combined both, getting undeletable features, *and* Merge. And from this, came language: Merge is all you need.

References

Abbott, A. (2008). 'The Brains of the Family', *Nature* 454: 155–7.

Aboh, E. (2004). *The Morphosyntax of Complement-Head Sequences*. Oxford: Oxford University Press.

——(2005). 'Deriving Relative and Factive Constructions in Kwa', in L. Brugè, G. Giusti, N. Munaro, W. Schweikert, and G. Turano (eds.), *Contributions to the Thirtieth Incontro di Grammatica Generativa*. Venice: Libreria Editrice Cafoscarina, 265–85.

Abush, D. (1997). 'Sequence of Tense and Temporal De Re', *Linguistics and Philosophy* 20: 1–50.

Adger, D., and Ramchand, G. (2005). 'Merge and Move: *Wh*-dependencies Revisited'. *Linguistic Inquiry* 36: 161–93.

Ahouse, J., and Berwick, R. C. (1998). 'Darwin on the Mind', *Boston Review of Books* April/May.

Akam, M. (1989). 'Making Stripes Inelegantly', *Nature* 341: 282–3.

Alexiadou, A. (1999). 'On the Properties of Some Greek Word Order Patterns', in A. Alexiadou, G. Horrocks, and M. Stávrou (eds.), *Studies in Greek Syntax*. Dordrecht: Kluwer Academic, 45–65.

——(2002). 'Word Order Patterns in Greek Nominals: Aspects of Diachronic Change', *ZAS Papers in Linguistics* 27: 91–107.

——(2005). 'A Possessive Adjective in Greek DP', in D. Theophanopoulou-Kontou, M. Stávrou, A. Terzi, and D. Alexiadou (eds.). *Advances in Greek Generative Syntax: In Honor of Dimitra Theophanopoulou-Kontou*. Amsterdam/Philadelphia: John Benjamins, 127–52.

——and Stávrou, M. (2000). 'Adjective-Clitic Combinations in the Greek DP', in B. Gerlach and J. Grijzenhout (eds.), *Clitics in Phonology, Morphology and Syntax*. Amsterdam/Philadelphia: John Benjamins, 63–84.

Alon, U. (2007). 'Simplicity in Biology', *Nature* 446: 497.

Amritavalli, R., and Jayaseelan, K. A. (2003). 'The Genesis of Syntactic Categories and Parametric Variation', in H.-J. Yoon (ed.), *Generative Grammar in a Broader Perspective: Proceedings of the 4th GLOW in Asia 2003*. Seoul: Hankook.

Amundson, R. (2005). *The Changing Role of the Embryo in Evolutionary Thought: Roots of Evo–devo*. Cambridge: Cambridge University Press.

Anagnostopoulou, E. (2003). 'Participles and Voice', in A. Alexiadou, M. Rathert, and A. von Stechow (eds.), *Perfect Explorations*. Berlin/New York: Mouton de Gruyter, 1–36.

Andersen, H. (ed.) (2001). *Actualization: Linguistic Change in Progress*. Amsterdam/Philadelphia: John Benjamins.

Anderson, S. R. (2004). *Doctor Dolittle's Delusion: Animals and the Uniqueness of Human Language*. New Haven, Conn: Yale University Press.

Aparicio, S., Chapman, J., Stupka, E., Putnam, N., Chia, J., Dehal, P., Christoffels, A., Rash, S., Hoon, S., and Smit, A. (2002). 'Whole-genome Shotgun Assembly and Analysis of the Genome of Fugu Rubripes', *Science* 297: 1301–10.

——Morrison, A., Gould, A., Gilthorpe, J., Chaudhuri, C., Rigby, P., Krumlauf, R., and Brenner, S. (1995). 'Detecting Conserved Regulatory Elements with the Model Genome of the Japanese Puffer Fish, Fugu Rubripes', *Proceedings of the National Academy of Sciences* 92: 1684–8.

Aristotle. (350 BC). *The History of Animals of Aristotle, and His Treatise on Physiognomy* [translated by Thomas, T (2004). Somerset: The Prometheus Trust].

Arnauld, A., and Lancelot, E. (1966). *Grammaire générale et raisonnée de Port-Royal*. Édition critique présentée par Herbert E. Brekle. Stuttgart-Bad Cannstatt: Frommann [Facsimile reprint of the 3rd ed. (1676). Paris : Pierre Le Petit].

Aronov, D., Andalman, A. S., and Fee, M. S. (2008). 'A Specialized Forebrain Circuit for Vocal Babbling in the Juvenile Songbird', *Science* 320(5876): 630–4.

Arosio, F., Adeni, F., and Guasti, M. T. (2009). 'Children's Processing of Relative Clauses Based on Different Disambiguating Information'. Ms., University of Milan-Bicocca.

Arsenijević, B. (2007). 'Clausal Complementation as Relativization'. Ms., University of Amsterdam.

——and Hinzen, W. (2009). 'On the Origins of Recursion in Human Grammar'. Ms., University of Amsterdam.

Arthur, W. (2001). *Biased Embryos and Evolution*. Cambridge: Cambridge University Press.

——(2002). 'The Emerging Conceptual Framework of Evolutionary Developmental Biology', *Nature* 415: 757–64.

Atkinson, R., Bowever, G., and Crothers, E. (1965). *An Introduction to Mathematical Learning Theory*. New York: John Wiley & Sons.

Axelrod, R., and Hamilton, W. D. (1981). 'The Evolution of Cooperation', *Science* 211: 1390–6.

Babyonyshev, M. (2004). 'Deriving the Restrictions on Pronominal Complements of Nouns', in J.-Y. Kim, Y. A. Lander, and B. H. Partee (eds.), *Possessives and Beyond: Semantics and Syntax*. Amherst: GLSA Publications, 263–77.

Baddeley, A. D. (1990). 'The Development of the Concept of Working Memory: Implications and Contributions of Neuropsychology', in G. Vallar and T. Shallice (eds.), *Neuropsychological Impairments of Short-term Memory*. Cambridge: Cambridge University Press, 54–73.

——(2000). 'The Episodic Buffer: A New Component of Working Memory?', *Trends in Cognitive Sciences* 4: 417–23.

——(2007). *Working Memory, Thought, and Action*. Oxford: Oxford University Press.

——and Hitch, G. (1974). 'Working Memory', in G. A. Bower (ed.), *Recent Advances in Learning and Motivation*, vol. 8. New York: Academic Press, 47–90.

Baddeley, A. D., Lewis, V., and Vallar, G. (1984). 'Exploring the Articulatory Loop', *Quarterly Journal of Experimental Psychology* 36: 233–52.

——Thomson, N., and Buchanan, M. (1975). 'Word Length and the Structure of Short-term Memory', *Journal of Verbal Learning and Verbal Behavior* 14: 575–89.

——Vallar, G., and Wilson, B. A. (1987). 'Sentence Comprehension and Phonological Memory: Some Neuropsychological Evidence', in M. Coltheart (ed.), *Attention and Performance XII: The Psychology of Reading*. London: Lawrence Erlbaum, 509–29.

Baker, C. L., and Brame, M. (1972). 'Global Rules: A Rejoinder', *Language* 48: 51–75.

Baker, M. C. (1988). *Incorporation: A Theory of Grammatical Function Changing*. Chicago: University of Chicago Press.

——(1996). *The Polysynthesis Parameter*. Oxford: Oxford University Press.

——(2001). *The Atoms of Language: The Mind's Hidden Rules of Grammar*. New York: Basic Books.

——(2003a). 'Linguistic Differences and Language Design', *Trends in Cognitive Sciences* 7: 349–53.

——(2003b). *Lexical Categories. Verbs, Nouns, and Adjectives*. Cambridge: Cambridge University Press.

——(2005). 'Mapping the Terrain of Language Learning', *Language Learning and Language Development* 1: 93–124.

——(2008a). *The Syntax of Agreement and Concord*. Cambridge: Cambridge University Press.

——(2008b). 'The Macroparameter in a Microparametric World', in T. Biberauer (ed.), *The Limits of Syntactic Variation*, Amsterdam: John Benjamins, 351–74.

——and Collins, C. (2006). 'Linkers and the Internal Structure of *v*P', *Natural Language and Linguistic Theory* 24: 307–54.

Baković, E. (2000). *Harmony, Dominance and Control*. Ph.D. dissertation, Rugigers University.

Balari, S., Benítez-Burraco, A., Camps, M., Longa, V. M., Lorenzo, G. & Uriagereka, J. (2008), '¿Homo loquens neanderthalensis? En torno a las capacidas simbólicas y lingüísticas del Neandertal'. Munibe (Antropología-Arkeología) 59, pp. 3–24.

Balota, D., and Chumbley, J. (1984). 'Are Lexical Decisions a Good Measure of Lexical Access? The Role of Frequency in the Neglected Decision Stage', *Journal of Experimental Psychology: Human Perception and Performance* 10: 340–57.

Barbujani, G., and Sokal, R. R. (1990). 'Zones of Sharp Genetic Change in Europe Are Also Linguistic Boundaries', *Proceedings of the National Academy of Science* 87(5): 1816–19.

Barker, C. (2005). 'Possessive Weak Definites', in J.-Y. Kim, Y. A. Lander, and B. H. Partee (eds.), *Possessives and Beyond: Semantics and Syntax*. Amherst: GLSA Publications, 89–113.

Barry, J. G., Yasin, I., and Bishop, D. V. M. (2007). 'Heritable Risk Factors Associated with Language Impairments', *Genes, Brain & Behavior* 6(1): 66–76.

Barwise, J., and Perry, J. (1983). *Situations and Attitudes*. Cambridge, MA: MIT Press.

Bastiaansen, M., Oostenbergh, R., Jensen, O., and Hagoort, P. (2008). 'I See What You Mean: Theta-power Increases Are Involved in the Retrieval of Lexical Semantic Information', *Brain and Language* 106: 15–28.

Bates, E. (1976). *Language and Context: The Acquisition of Pragmatics*. New York: Academic Press.

Bateson, W. (1909). 'Heredity and Variation in Modern Lights', in A. C. Seward (ed.), *Darwin and Modern Science: Essays in Commemoration of the Centenary of the Birth of Charles Darwin and of the Fiftieth Anniversary of the Publication of the Origin of Species*. Cambridge: Cambridge University Press, 85–101.

Bazett, H. C., and Penfield, W. G. (1922). 'A Study of the Sherrington Decerebrate Animal in the Chronic as well as the Acute Condition', *Brain* 45: 185–265.

Beadle, G. W., and Beadle, M. (1966). *The Language of Life: An Introduction to the Science of Genetics*. Garden City: Doubleday.

Beck, S., and Johnson, K. (2004). 'Double Objects Again', *Linguistic Inquiry* 35(1): 97–124.

Bejan, A. (2000). *Shape and Structure from Engineering to Nature*. Cambridge: Cambridge University Press.

—— and Marden, J. H. (2006). 'Unifying Constructal Theory for Scale Effects in Running, Swimming and Flying', *Journal of Experimental Biology* 209: 238–48.

Bejar, S. (2003). *Phi-Syntax*. Ph.D. dissertation, University of Toronto.

Belletti, A. (1988). 'The Case of Unaccusatives', *Linguistic Inquiry* 19: 1–35.

—— (1990). *Generalized Verb Movement*. Turin: Rosenberg and Sellier.

—— and Rizzi, L. (1981). 'The Syntax of *ne*: Some Theoretical Implications', *The Linguistic Review* 1(2): 117–54.

Bellugi, U., Klima, E. S., and Siple, P. (1975). 'Remembering in Signs', *Cognition* 3: 93–125.

Bendor-Samuel, J. T., and Hartell, R. L. (eds.) (1989). *The Niger-Congo Languages: A Classification and Description of Africa's Largest Language Family*. Lanham: University Press of America.

Benítez-Burraco, A. (2007). *Genes del Lenguaje: Implicaciones Ontogenéticas, Filogenéticas y Cognitivas*. Ph.D. dissertation, University of Oviedo.

—— (2009). *Genes y lenguaje: aspectos ontogenéticos filogenéticos y congnitivos*. Barcelona: Reverté.

—— Longa, V., Lorenzo. G., and Uriagereka, J. (2008). 'Así Habló (o tal vez no) el Neandertal', *Teorema*, 27(1): 73–83.

Benveniste, É. (1960). '*Être* et *avoir* dans leur fonctions linguistiques', in É. Benveniste (ed.), *Problèmes de Linguistique Générale*. Paris: Gallimard.

—— (1966). *Problèmes de Linguistique Générale*. Paris: Gallimard.

Bergman, T. J., Beehner, J. C., Cheney, D. L., and Seyfarth, R. M. (2003). 'Hierarchical Classification by Rank in Kinship in Baboons', *Science* 302(5648): 1234–6.

Berko, J. (1958). 'The Child's Learning of English Morphology', *Word* 14: 150–77.

Bernstein, J. (2001). 'The DP Hypothesis: Identifying Clausal Properties in the Nominal Domain', in M. Baltin and C. Collins (eds.), *The Handbook of Contemporary Syntactic Theory*. Oxford: Blackwell, 536–61.

Bertinetto, P. M. (2000). 'The Progressive in Romance as Compared with English', in O. Dahl (ed.), *Tense and Aspect in the Languages of Europe*. Berlin/New York: Mouton de Gruyter, 559–604.

Berwick, R. C. (1997). 'Syntax Facit Saltum: Computation and the Genotype and Phenotype of Language', *Journal of Neurolinguistics* 10: 231–49.

—— and Epstein, S. D. (1995). 'Merge: The Categorial Imperative', *Proceedings of the 5th AMAST Conference*. Enschede: University of Twente.

—— and Niyogi, P. (1996). 'Learning From Triggers', *Linguistic Inquiry* 27: 605–22.

—— and Weinberg, A. (1986). *The Grammatical Basis of Linguistic Performance*. Cambridge, MA: MIT Press.

Bickerton, D. (1990). *Language and Species*. Chicago: Chicago University Press.

Bird, A. T. (1995). 'Gene Number, Noise Reduction and Biological Complexity', *Trends in Genetics* 11(3): 94–100.

Bishop, D. V. M. (2002). 'Putting Language Genes in Perspective', *Trends in Genetics* 18(2): 57–9.

—— and Snowling, M. J. (2004). 'Developmental Dyslexia and Specific Language Impairment: Same or Different?', *Psychological Bulletin* 130(6): 858–86.

Bittner, M., and Hale, K. (1996). 'The Structural Determination of Case and Agreement', *Linguistic Inquiry* 27(11): 1–68.

Blencowe, B. J. (2006). 'Alternative Splicing: New Insights from Global Analyses', *Cell* 126(14): 37–47.

Blevins, J. (2004). *Evolutionary Phonology: The Emergence of Sound Patterns*. Cambridge: Cambridge University Press.

Bloom, P. (1993). 'Grammatical Continuity in Language Development: The Case of Subjectless Sentences', *Linguistic Inquiry* 24(44): 721–34.

—— (2000). *How Children Learn the Meanings of Words*. Cambridge, MA: MIT Press.

Bloomfield, L. (1933). *Language*. New York: Holt, Rinehart and Winston.

Boeckx, C. (2006). *Linguistic Minimalism: Origins, Concepts, Methods, and Aims*. Oxford: Oxford University Press.

—— (2008). *Bare Syntax*. Oxford: Oxford University Press.

—— (2009). 'On the nature of Merge', in *Of Minds and Language: A Basque Encounter with Noam Chomsky*, J. Uriagereka, M. Piattelli-Palmarini, P. Sal-aburu (eds.) Oxford: Oxford University Press, 44–57.

—— (2010). 'Lingustic minimalism', in *Oxford Handbook of Linguistic Analysis*, B. Heine and H. Narrog (eds.) Oxford: Oxford University Press, 485–505.

—— (in progress). 'Elementary Syntactic Structures'. Ms., Institució Catalana de Recerca i Estudis Avançats/Universitat Autònoma de Barcelona.

—— and Grohmann, K. (2007). Putting Phases in Perspective'. *Syntax* 10: 204–22.

—— and Piattelli-Palmarini, M. (2005). 'Language as a Natural Object, Linguistics as a Natural Science', *The Linguistic Review* 22(2–4): 447–66.

Bond, J., Roberts, E., Mochida, G. H., Hampshire, D. J., Scott, S., Askham, J. M., Springell, K., Mahadevan, M., Crow, Y. J., Markham, A. F., Walsh, C. A., and Woods, C. G. (2002). 'ASPM is a Major Determinant of Cerebral Cortical Size', *Nature Genetics* 32: 316–20.

Bonomi, A. (1997). 'The Progressive and the Structure of Events', *Journal of Semantics* 14: 173–205.

Booth, J. R., MacWhinney, B., and Harasaki, Y. (2000). 'Developmental Differences in Visual and Auditory Processing of Complex Sentences', *Child Development* 71(4): 981–1003.

Borer, H. (1984). *Parametric Syntax: Case Studies in Semitic and Romance Languages*. Dordrecht: Foris.

—— (2005). *Structuring Sense*, (vols. 1, 2). Oxford: Oxford University Press.

Bošković, Ž., and Lasnik, H. (2003). 'On the Distribution of Null Complementizers', *Linguistic Inquiry* 34: 527–46.

Boutla, M., Supalla, T., Newport, E. L., and Bavelier, D. (2004). 'Short-term Memory Span: Insights from Sign Language', *Nature Neuroscience* 7: 997–1002.

Bowerman, M. (1978). 'Systematizing Semantic Knowledge: Changes over Time in the Child's Organization of Word Meaning', *Child Development* 49(4): 977–87.

Boyd, R., Bogerhoff-Mulder, M., Durham, W. H., and Richerson, P. J. (1997). 'Are Cultural Phylogenies Possible?', in P. Weingart, S. D. Mitchell, P. J. Richerson, and S. Maasen (eds.), *Human by Nature: Between Biology and the Social Sciences*. Mahwah, NJ: Lawrence Erlbaum, 355–86.

Brandon, R. N. (1988). 'Levels of Selection', in D. Hull and M. Ruse (eds.), *The Philosophy of Biology*. Oxford: Oxford University Press, 176–97.

Brener R. (1940). 'An Experimental Investigation of Memory Span', *Journal of Experimental Psychology* 26: 467–83.

Brocchieri, L. (2001). 'Phylogenetic Inferences from Molecular Sequences: Review and Critique', *Theoretical Population Biology* 59: 27–40.

Brody, M. (2003). *Towards an Elegant Syntax*. London: Routledge.

Bromberger, S., and Halle, M. (1989). 'Why Phonology is Different', *Linguistic Inquiry* 20(1): 51–70.

Brown, R. (1973). *A First Language*. Cambridge, MA: Harvard University Press.

Burling, R. (1993). 'Primate Calls, Human Language, and Nonverbal Communication', *Current Anthropology* 34(1): 25–53.

Burzio, L. (1986). *Italian Syntax*. Dordrecht: Kluwer Academic.

Bush, R., and Mosteller, F. (1951). 'A Mathematical Model for Simple Learning', *Psychological Review* 68: 313–23.

Calvin, W. H., and Bickerton, D. (2000). *Lingua Ex Machina: Reconciling Darwin and Chomsky With the Human Brain*. Cambridge, MA: MIT Press.

Campbell, A., and Tomasello, M. (2001). 'The Acquisition of English Dative Construction', *Applied Psycholinguistics* 22: 253–67.

Camper, P. (1779). 'Account of the Organs of Speech of the Orang Outang', *Philosophical Transactions of the Royal Society of London* 69: 139–59.

Camps, M., and Uriagereka, J. (2006). 'The Gordian Knot of Linguistic Fossils', in J. Rossello, and J. Martin (eds.), *The Biolinguistic Turn*. Barcelona: Promociones y Publicaciones Universitarias, 34–65.

Caplan, D. (1987). *Neurolinguistics and Linguistic Aphasiology*. New York: McGraw Hill.

—— and Waters, G. S. (1999). 'Verbal Short-term Memory and Sentence Comprehension', *Behavioral and Brain Sciences* 22: 77–126.

Caponigro, I., and Polinsky, M. (2008). 'Almost Everything is Relative in the Caucasus', *Semantics and Linguistic Theory* 18: 38–55.

Caramazza, A. (1997). 'How Many Levels of Processing are there in Lexical Access?', *Cognitive Neuropsychology* 14(1): 177–208.

—— Basili, A. G., Koller, J. J., and Berndt, R. S. (1981). 'An Investigation of Repetition and Language Processing in a Case of Conduction Aphasia', *Brain and Language* 14(2): 235–71.

—— Capitani, E., Rey, A., and Berndt, R. S. (2001). 'Agrammatic Broca's Aphasia is Not Associated with a Single Pattern of Comprehension Performance', *Brain and Language* 76: 158–84.

Carlson, C. S., Eberle, M. A., Kruglyak, L., and Nickerson, D. A. (2004). 'Mapping Complex Disease Loci in Whole-genome Association Studies', *Nature* 429(6990): 446–52.

Carroll, R. L. (1988). *Vertebrate Paleontology and Evolution*. New York: W. H. Freeman.

Carroll, S. B., Grenier, J. K., and Weatherbee, S. D. (2001). *From DNA to Diversity: Molecular Genetics and the Evolution of Animal Design*. Malden, MA: Blackwell Scientific.

—— (2003). 'Genetics and the Making of *Homo sapiens*', *Nature* 422: 849–57.

—— (2005a). *Endless Forms Most Beautiful: The New Science of Evo-devo and the Making of the Animal Kingdom*. New York: W. W. Norton & Co.

—— (2005b). 'Evolution at Two Levels: On Genes and Form', *PLoS Biology* 3: e245.

—— (2008). 'Evo-Deyo and an Expanding Evolutionary Synthesis: A Genetic Theory of Morphological Evolution', *Cell* 134: 25–36.

Carruthers, P. (2006). *The Architecture of the Mind*. Oxford: Oxford University Press.

Carstairs-McCarthy, A. (1999). *The Origins of Complex Language*. Oxford: Oxford University Press.

Cavalli-Sforza, L. L. (2000). *Genes, Peoples, and Languages*. Berkeley: University of California Press.

—— Menozzi, P., and Piazza, A. (1994). *The History and Geography of Human Genes*. Princeton: Princeton University Press.

—— Piazza, A., Menozzi, P., and Mountain, J. (1988). 'Reconstruction of Human Evolution: Bringing Together Genetic, Archeological and Linguistic Data', *Proceedings of the National Academy of Science* 85: 6002–6.

—— and Wang, W. S. Y. (1986). 'Spatial Distance and Lexical Replacement', *Language* 62: 38–55.

Cecchetto, C., Geraci, C., and Zucchi, S. (2006). 'Strategies of Relativization in Italian Sign Language', *Natural Language and Linguistic Theory* 25: 945–75.

Cennamo, M., and Sorace, A. (2007). 'Auxiliary Selection and Split Intransitivity in Paduan: Variation and Lexical-Aspectual Constraints', in R. Aranovich (ed.), *Split Auxiliary Systems*. Amsterdam/Philadelphia: John Benjamins.

Chan, E. (2008). *Distributional and Structural Basis on Morphological Learning*. Ph.D. dissertation, University of Pennsylvania.

Chen, B. L., Hall, D. H., and Chklovskii, D. B. (2006). 'Wiring Optimization Can Relate Neuronal Structure and Function', *Proceedings of the National Academy of Sciences* 103(12): 4723–8.

Cheney, D. L., and Seyfarth, R. M. (1990). *How Monkeys See the World*. Chicago: University of Chicago Press.

—— —— (2007). *Baboon Metaphysics: The Evolution of a Social Mind*. Chicago: University of Chicago Press.

Cheung, C., and Larson, R. (2006). 'Chinese Psych Verbs and Covert Clausal Complementation', paper presented at the Chicago Workshop on Chinese Linguistics, Chicago.

—— —— (2007). 'Psych Verbs in Mandarin Chinese', paper presented at the joint meetings of International Association of Chinese Linguistics, Chicago, IL.

Chierchia, G. (1995). 'Impersonal Subjects', in E. Bach, E. Jellinek, A. Kratz, and B. H. Partee (eds.), *Quantification in Natural Languages*. Dordrecht: Kluwer Academic Publishers, 107–43.

—— (2004). 'A Semantics for Unaccusatives and its Syntactic Consequences', in A. Alexiadou, E. Anagnostopoulou, and M. Everaert (eds.), *The Unaccusativity Puzzle*. Oxford: Oxford University Press, 22–59.

Chimpanzee Sequencing Consortium (2005). 'Initial Sequencing of the Chimpanzee Genome and Comparison with the Human Genome', *Nature* 437: 69–87.

Chitò, E. (2006). *Comprensione di Frasi e Memoria di Lavoro in Pazienti con Probabile Malattia di Alzheimer*. Ph.D. dissertation, University of Milan-Bicocca.

Chomsky, N. (1955). 'The Logical Structure of Linguistic Theory'. Ms., Harvard University, and MIT, Cambridge, MA. [Revised 1956 version published in part by Plenum, New York, 1975; University of Chicago Press, Chicago, 1985].

—— (1957). *Syntactic Structures*. The Hague: Mouton.

—— (1959a). 'A Review of B. F. Skinner's *Verbal Behavior*', *Language* 35(1): 26–58.

—— (1959b). 'On Certain Formal Properties of Grammars', *Information and Control* 2: 137–67.

—— (1961). 'On the Notion "Rule of Grammar"', in R. Jakobson (ed.), *Structure of Language and its Mathematical Aspects*. Providence: American Mathematical Society, 6–24. [Reprinted in J. A. Fodor and J. J. Katz (eds.). (1964). *The Structure of Language: Readings in the Philosophy of Language*. Englewood Cliffs: Prentice-Hall, 119–36].

Chomsky, N. (1963). 'Formal Properties of Grammars', in R. D. Luce, R. R. Bush, and E. Galanter (eds.), *Handbook of Mathematical Psychology*. New York: John Wiley & Sons, 323–418.

—— (1965). *Aspects of the Theory of Syntax*. Cambridge, MA: MIT Press.

—— (1966). *Cartesian Linguistics*. New York: Harper and Row. [Third edition, with introduction by James McGilvray. (2009). Cambridge: Cambridge University Press.]

—— (1970). 'Remarks on Nominalization', in R. A. Jacobs and P. S. Rosenbaum (eds.), *Readings in English Transformational Grammar*. Waltham: Ginn, 184–221.

—— (1972a). 'Some Empirical Issues in the Theory of Transformational Grammar', in P. S. Peters (eds.), *Goals of Linguistic Theory*. Englewood Cliffs: Prentice-Hall Inc, 63–130.

—— (1972b). *Language and Mind*. New York: Harcourt Brace Jovanovich.

—— (1975). *Reflections on Language*. New York: Pantheon.

—— (1976). 'On the Biological Basis of Language Capacities', in R. W. Rieber (ed.), *The Neuropsychology of Language: Essays in Honor of Eric Lenneberg*. New York: Plenum Press, 1–24.

—— (1977). 'On Wh-Movement', in P. Culicover, T. Wasow, and A. Akmajian (eds.), *Formal Syntax*. New York: Academic Press, 71–132.

—— (1979). 'The Pisa Lectures'. Ms., MIT.

—— (1980). *Rules and Representations*. New York: Columbia University Press.

—— (1981). *Lectures on Government and Binding: The Pisa Lectures*. Dordrecht: Foris.

—— (1986). *Knowledge of Language*. New York: Praeger.

—— (1990). 'On Formalization and Formal Linguistics', *Natural Language and Linguistic Theory* 8: 143–7.

—— (1991). 'Some Notes on Economy of Derivation and Representation', in R. Freidin (ed.), *Principles and Parameters in Comparative Grammar*. Cambridge, MA: MIT Press, 417–54. [Reprinted in Chomsky, N. (1995). *The Minimalist Program*. Cambridge, MA: MIT Press, 129–66].

—— (1993). 'A Minimalist Program for Linguistic Theory', in K. Hale and S. J. Keyser (eds.), *The View from Building 20*, Cambridge, MA: MIT Press, 1–52.

—— (1994). 'Bare Phrase Structure', *MIT Occasional Papers in Linguistics* 5. [Reprinted in G. Webelhuth (ed.) (1995), *Government and Binding Theory and the Minimalist Program*, Oxford: Blackwell, 383–439.]

—— (1995). *The Minimalist Program*. Cambridge, MA: MIT Press.

—— (1998). 'Some Observations on Economy in Generative Grammar', in P. Barbosa, D. Fox, M. McGinnis, and D. Pesetsky (eds.), *Is the Best Good Enough?* Cambridge, MA: MIT Press, 115–29.

—— (2000a). 'Minimalist Inquiries: The Framework', in R. Martin, D. Michaels, and J. Uriagereka (eds.), *Step by Step: Essays on Minimalist Syntax in Honor of Howard Lasnik*. Cambridge, MA: MIT Press, 89–155.

—— (2000b). *New Horizons in the Study of Language and Mind*. Cambridge: Cambridge University Press.

—— (2001). 'Derivation by Phase', in M. Kenstowicz (ed.), *Ken Hale: A Life in Language*. Cambridge, MA: MIT Press, 1–52.

—— (2002). *On Nature and Language.* Cambridge: Cambridge University Press.

—— (2004a). 'Beyond Explanatory Adequacy', in A. Belletti (ed.), *Structures and Beyond.* Oxford: Oxford University Press, 104–31.

—— (2004b). *The Generative Enterprise Revisited: Discussions with Riny Huybregts, Henk van Riemsdijk, Naoki Fukui and Mihoko Zushi.* Berlin/New York: Mouton de Gruyter.

—— (2005). 'Three Factors in Language Design', *Linguistic Inquiry* 36(1): 1–22.

—— (2007a). 'Approaching UG from below', in U. Sauerland and M. Gaertner (eds.), *Interfaces + Recursion = Language? Chomsky's Minimalism and the View from Syntax-semantics.* Berlin/New York: Mouton de Gruyter, 1–30.

—— (2007b). 'Biolinguistic Explorations: Design, Development, Evolution', *International Journal of Philosophical Studies* 15(1): 1–21.

—— (2007c). 'Some Simple Evo-devo Theories about Language: How Might They Be True of Language?', paper presented at the Conference on Language, Stony Brook University. [A version published in R. Larson, V. Déprez, and H. Yamakido (eds.), *The evolution of human language* Cambridge: Cambridge University Press, 45–62.]

—— (2008). 'On Phases', in R. Freidin, C. Otero, and M. L. Zubizarreta (eds.), *Foundational Issues in Linguistic Theory*, Cambridge, MA: MIT Press, 133–66.

—— and Halle, M. (1968). *The Sound Pattern of English.* New York: Harper.

—— and Lasnik, H. (1993). 'Principles and Parameters Theory', in J. Jacobs, A. van Stechow, W. Sternefeld, and T. Vennemann (eds.), *Syntax: An International Handbook of Contemporary Research.* Berlin: Walter de Gruyter, 506–69. [Reprinted in Chomsky, N. (1995). *The Minimalist Program.* Cambridge, MA: MIT Press, 13–127].

—— and Miller, G. A. (1963). 'Introduction to the Formal Analysis of Natural Languages', in Duncan R. Luce, Robert R. Bush, and Eugene Galanter (eds.), *Handbook of Mathematical Psychology 2.* New York: John Wiley & Sons, 269–321.

Christensen, K. R. (2008). 'Interfaces, Syntactic Movement, and Neural Activation: A New Perspective on the Implementation of Language in the Brain', *Journal of Neurolinguistics* 21(2): 73–103.

Chung, S., and McCloskey, J. (1983). 'On the Interpretation of Certain Island Facts in GPSG', *Linguistic Inquiry* 14: 704–13.

Cinque, G. (1990). *Types of A-bar Dependencies.* Cambridge, MA: MIT Press.

—— (1999). *Adverbs and Functional Heads: A Cross-linguistic Perspective.* New York : Oxford University Press.

—— (2005). 'Deriving Greenberg's Universal 20 and Its Exceptions', *Linguistic Inquiry* 36(3): 315–32.

—— (2006). *Restructuring and Functional Heads: The Cartography of Syntactic Structures.* Oxford: Oxford University Press.

Clackson, J., Forster, P., and Renfrew, C. (eds.) (2004). *Phylogenetic Methods and the Prehistory of Languages.* Cambridge: McDonald Institute for Archaeological Research.

Clahsen, H. (1986). 'Verbal Inflections in German Child Language: Acquisition of Agreement Markings and the Functions They Encode', *Linguistics* 24: 79–121.

Clahsen, H., Hadler, M., and Weyerts, H. (2004). 'Speeded Production of Inflected Words in Children and Adults', *Journal of Child Language* 31: 683–712.

Clark, E. V., and Barron, B. J. S. (1988). 'A Thrower-Button or a Button-Thrower? Children's Judgments of Grammatical and Ungrammatical Compound Nouns', *Linguistics* 26: 3–19.

Clark, R., and Roberts, I. (1993). 'A Computational Model of Language Learnability and Language Change', *Linguistic Inquiry* 24: 299–345.

Clarke E., Reichard, U. H., and Zuberbühler, K. (2006). 'The Syntax and Meaning of Wild Gibbon Songs', *PLoS ONE* 1(1): e73.

Cocchi, G. (1995). *La selezione dell'ausiliare*. Padova: Unipress.

Coen, M. (2006). *Multimodal Dynamics: Self-Supervised Learning in Perceptual and Motor Systems*. Ph.D. dissertation, MIT.

Cole, P., and Wang, C. (1996). 'Antecedents and Blockers of Long-Distance Reflexives', *Linguistic Inquiry* 27: 357–90.

Collins, C. (2005). 'A Smuggling Approach to the Passive in English', *Syntax* 8: 81–120.

—— (2006a). 'Home Sweet Home'. Ms., New York University.

—— (2006b). 'A Note on Derivational Morphology'. Ms., New York University.

Colosimo, P. F., Hosemann, K. E., Balabhadra, S., Villareal J. G., Dickson, M., Grimwood, J., Schmutz, J., Myers, R. M., Schluter, D., and Kingsley, D. M. (2005). 'Widespread Parallel Evolution in Sticklebacks by Repeated Fixation of Ectodysplasin Alleles', *Science* 307(5717): 1928–33.

—— Peichel, C. L., Nereng, K., Blackman, B. K., Shapiro, M. D., Schluter, D., and Kingsley, D. M. (2004). 'The Genetic Architecture of Parallel Armor Plate Reduction in Threespine Sticklebacks', *PLoS Biology* 2: 635–41.

Condovardi, C., and Kiparski, P. (2001). 'Clitics and Clause Structure', *Journal of Greek Linguistics* 2: 1–40.

Conrad, R. (1964). 'Acoustic Confusions in Immediate Memory', *British Journal of Psychology* 55: 75–84.

—— and Hull, A. J. (1964). 'Information, Acoustic Confusions and Memory Span', *British Journal of Psychology* 55: 429–32.

Conway, C. M., and Christiansen, M. H. (2001). 'Sequential Learning in Non-human Primates', *Trends in Cognitive Sciences* 5(12): 539–46.

Conwell, E., and Demuth, K. (2007). 'Early Syntactic Productivity: Evidence from Dative Shift', *Cognition* 103(2): 163–79.

Cooke, A., Zurif, E. B., DeVita, C., Alsop, D., Koenig, P., Detre, J., Gee, J., Piñango, M., Balogh, J., and Grossman, M. (2001). 'Neural Basis for Sentence Comprehension: Grammatical and Short-term Memory Components', *Human Brain Mapping* 15: 80–94.

Coutinho, C. C., Fonseca, R. N., Mansurea, J. J. C., and Borojevic, R. (2003). 'Early Steps in the Evolution of Multicellularity: Deep Structural and Functional Homologies among Homeobox Genes in Sponges and Higher Metazoans', *Mechanisms of Development* 120: 429–40.

Cracraft, J., and Donoghue, M. J. (eds.) (2004). *Assembling the Tree of Life*. Oxford: Oxford University Press.

Crain, S., and Pietroski, P. (2002). 'Why Language Acquisition is a Snap', *Linguistic Review* 19: 163–83.

Crisma, P. (1997). *L'Articolo nella prosa inglese antica e la teoria degli articoli nulli*. Ph.D. dissertation, University of Padova.

——(in press). 'Triggering Syntactic Change: The History of English Genitives', in D. Jonas, J. Whitman and A. Garrett (eds.), *Grammatical Change: Origin, Nature, Outcomes*. Oxford: Oxford University Press.

Culicover, P. (1999). *Syntactic Nuts: Hard Cases, Syntactic Theory, and Language Acquisition*. Oxford: Oxford University Press.

——and Jackendoff, R. (2005). *Simpler Syntax*. Oxford: Oxford University Press.

————(2006). 'The Simpler Syntax Hypothesis', *Trends in Cognitive Sciences* 10: 413–18.

D'Alessandro, R., and Roberts, I. (2008). 'Movement and Agreement in Italian Past Participles and Defective Phases', *Linguistic Inquiry* 39(3): 477–91.

————(forthcoming). 'Past Participle Agreement in Abruzzese: Split Auxiliary Selection and the Null-Subject Parameter'. *Natural Language and Linguistic Theory*.

Daneman, M., and Carpenter, P. A. (1980). 'Individual Differences in Working Memory and Reading', *Journal of Verbal Learning and Verbal Behavior* 19: 450–66.

Darwin, C. (1859). *On the Origin of Species*. London: John Murray.

——(1868). *Variation of Plants and Animals under Domestication*. London: John Murray.

——(1871). *The Descent of Man and Selection in Relation to Sex*. London: John Murray.

——(1964). *On the Origin of Species* (Facsimile of 1st ed. 1859). Cambridge, MA: Harvard University Press.

Davidson, D. (2001). *Inquiries into Truth and Interpretation* (2nd edition). New York: Oxford University Press.

Davidson, E. H. (2006). *The Regulatory Genome: Gene Regulatory Networks in Development and Evolution*. London/San Diego: Elsevier.

——and Erwin, D. H. (2006). 'Gene Regulatory Networks and the Evolution of Animal Body Plans', *Science* 311(5762): 796–800.

Dawkins, R. (1982). *The Extended Phenotype*. Oxford: Oxford University Press.

——(1996). *Climbing Mount Improbable*. New York: W. W. Norton & Co.

——(2004). *The Ancestor's Tale*. New York: W. W. Norton & Co.

de Villers-Sidani, E., Chang, E. F., Shaowen, B., and Merzenich, M. M. (2007). 'Critical Period Window for Spectral Tuning Defined in the Primary Auditory Cortex (1) in the Rat', *The Journal of Neuroscience* 27(1): 180–9.

de Villiers, J. (1995a). 'Questioning Minds and Answering Machines', in D. MacLaughlin and S. McEwen (eds.), *Proceedings of the Boston University Conference on Language Development*. Somerville, MA: Cascadilla Press, 20–36.

——(1995b). 'Steps in the Mastery of Sentence Complements', paper presented at the Symposium on Language and the Theory of Mind, Society for Research in Child Development, Indianapolis, IN.

——(1998). 'Mind Matters', in P. Rose (ed.), *Professorial Passions*. Northampton, MA: Smith College Press.

de Villiers, J. (2000). 'Language and Theory of Mind: What are the Developmental Relationships?', in S. Baron-Cohen, H. Tager-Flusberg, and D. Cohen (eds.), *Understanding Other Minds: Perspectives from Developmental Cognitive Neuroscience*. Oxford: Oxford University Press, 83–123.

—— (2005). 'Can Language Acquisition Give Children a Point of View?', in J. W. Astington and J. A. Baird (eds.), *Why Language Matters for Theory of Mind*. Oxford: Oxford University Press, 186–219.

—— and de Villiers, P. (2001). 'Linguistic Determinism and the Understanding of False Belief', in P. Mitchell (ed.), *Children's Reasoning and the Mind*. NY: Psychology Press.

—— and Fitneva, S. A. (1996). 'On the Role of Language in the Development of Propositional Attitudes', paper presented at the VIIth International Congress for the Study of Child Language, Istanbul, Turkey.

—— Roeper, T., and Vainikka, A. (1990). 'The Acquisition of Long Distance Rules', in L. Frazier and J. de Villiers (eds.), *Language: Processing and Acquisition*. Dordrecht: Kluwer Academic Publishers, 257–97.

De Vincenzi, M. (1991). *Syntactic Parsing Strategies in Italian*. Dordrecht: Kluwer Academic Publishers.

Dediu, D., and Ladd, D. R. (2007). 'Linguistic Tone is Related to the Population Frequency of the Adaptive Haplogroups of Two Brain Size Genes, *ASPM* and *Microcephalin*', *Proceedings of the National Academy of Sciences* 104: 10944–10949.

Dehaene, S., Izard, V., Pica, P., and Spelke, E. (2006). 'Core Knowledge of Geometry in an Amazonian Indigene Group', *Science* 311: 381–4.

DeLancey, S. (1981). 'An Interpretation of Split Ergativity and Related Patterns', *Language* 57(3): 626–57.

Dennett, D. (1995). *Darwin's Dangerous Idea: Evolution and the Meanings of Life*. New York: Simon and Schuster.

—— (1996). *Kinds of Minds*. New York: Basic Books.

Déprez, V. (2005). 'Morphological Number, Semantic Number and Bare Nouns', *Lingua* 115: 857–83.

d'Hulst, Y., Coene, M., Avram L., and Tasmowski, L. (2003). 'Verbal Morphology and Tense Anchoring in Romanian', in J. Guéron and L. Tasmosky (eds.), *Tense and Point of View*. Paris: Université Paris X, 167–84.

Di Sciullo, A. M. (1999). 'FLIP to PF', paper presented at the Classics, Modern Languages, and Linguistics Department. Concordia University.

—— (2000). 'Parsing Asymmetries', *Proceedings of the Second International Conference on Natural Language Processing*. London: Springer Verlag, 1–15.

—— (2004). 'Morphological Phases', in H.-J. Yoon (ed.), *Generative Grammar in a Broader Perspective. The 4th GLOW in Asia* 2003. Seoul: The Korean Generative Grammar Circle & Cognitive Science, 113–37.

—— (2005). *Asymmetry in Morphology*. Cambridge, MA: MIT Press.

—— (2007). 'A Remark on Natural Language and Natural Language Processing from a Biolinguistic Perspective', in H. Fujita and D. Pisanelli (eds.), *Frontiers in Artificial Intelligence and Applications*. Amsterdam: IOS Press, 126–44.

—— (2009). 'Why Are Compounds Part of Natural Languages: A View From Asymmetry Theory', in R. Lieber and P. Štekauer (eds.), *Handbook of Compounds*. Oxford: Oxford University Press, 145–77.

—— and Banksira, D. P. (2009). 'On *wh*-words of Ethiopian Semitic Languages', in C. Häbert (ed.), *Afroasiatic Studies in Memory of Robert Hetzron. Proceedings of the 35th Annual Meeting of the North American Conference on Afroasiatic Linguistics (NACAL 35)*, Newcastle upon Tyne: Cambridge Scholars Publishing, 245–55.

—— and Fong, S. (2005). 'Morpho-Syntax Parsing', in A. M. Di Sciullo (ed.), *UG and External Systems*. Amsterdam/Philadelphia: John Benjamins, 247–8.

—— and Isac, D. (2008a). 'The Asymmetry of Merge', *Biolinguistics* 2(4): 260–90.

—— —— (2008b). 'Mouvement Chains at the Interfaces', *Canadian Journal of Linguistics, Special Issue on Interfaces* 53(2/3): 181–217.

—— Piattelli-Palmarini, M., Hauser, M., Wexler, K., Berwick, R. C., Boeckx, C., Jenkins, L., Uriagereka, J., Stromswold, K., Cheng, L., Harley, H., Wedel, A., McGilvray, J., van Gelderen, E., and Bever, T. (2010). 'The Biological Nature of Language'. *Biolinguistics* 4: 4–34.

Didelot, G., Molinari, F., Tchénio, P., Comas, D., Milhiet, E., Munnich, A., Colleaux, L., and Preat, T. (2006). 'Tequila, a Neurotrypsin Ortholog, Regulates Long-term Memory Formation in Drosophila', *Science* 313(11): 851–3.

Dikken, M. den (1997). 'The Syntax of Possession and the Verb "have" ', *Lingua* 101: 129–50.

—— (2006). *Relators and Linkers: The Syntax of Predication, Predicate Inversion, and Copulas*. Cambridge, MA: MIT Press.

Dixon, R. M. W. (1998). *The Rise and Fall of Languages*. Cambridge: Cambridge University Press.

Dobrovie-Sorin, C. (1994). *The Syntax of Romanian*. Berlin/New York: Mouton de Gruyter.

—— (1998). 'Impersonal *se* Constructions in Romance and the Passivization of Unergatives', *Linguistic Inquiry* 29: 399–437.

Dobzhansky, T. (1973). 'Nothing in Biology Makes Sense Except in the Light of Evolution', *American Biology Teacher* 35: 125–9.

Dogil, G., Ackermann, H., Grodd, W., Haider, H., Kamp, H., Mayer, J., Riecker, A., and Wildgruber, D. (2002). 'The Speaking Brain: A Tutorial Introduction to fMRI Experiments in the Production of Speech, Prosody and Syntax', *Journal of Neurolinguistics* 15(1): 59–90.

Douady, S., and Couder, Y. (1992). 'Phyllotaxis as a Physical Self-Organized Growth Process', *Physical Review Letters* 68(13): 2098–2101.

—— —— (1993). 'Phyllotaxis as a Physical Self-Organized Growth Process', in J. M. Garcia-Ruiz, E. Louis, P. Meakin, and L. M. Sander (eds.), *Growth Patterns in Physical Sciences and Biology*. New York: Plenum Press, 341–52.

DuBrul, E. L. (1977). 'Origins of the Speech Apparatus and its Reconstruction in Fossils', *Brain and Language* 4: 365–81.

Duffield, N. (1996). 'On Structural Invariance and Lexical diversity in VSO Languages: Arguments from Irish Noun Phrases', in R. Borsley and I. Roberts (eds.), *The Syntax of the Celtic Languages: A Comparative Perspective*. Cambridge: Cambridge University Press, 314–40.

Dunbar, R. (1996). *Grooming, Gossip and the Evolution of Language*. Cambridge, MA: Harvard University Press.

Dunn, M., Terril, A., Reesink, G., Foley, R. A., and Levinson, S. C. (2005). 'Structural Phylogenetics and the Reconstruction of Ancient Language History', *Science* 309(5743): 2072–5.

Dyen, I., Kruskal, J., and Black, P. (1992). 'An Indoeuropean Classification: A Lexicostatistical Experiment', *Transactions of the American Philosophical Society* 82(5).

Dyer, M. A., Livesey, F. J., Cepko, C. L., and Oliver, G. (2003). 'Prox1 Function Controls Progenitor Cell Proliferation and Horizontal Cell Genesis in the Mammalian Retina', *Nature Genetics* 34: 53–8.

—— Martins, R., da Silva Filho, M., Cepko, C. L., and Finlay, B. L. (2009). 'Developmental Sources of Conservation and Variation in the Evolution of the Primate *Eye*', *Proceedings of the National Academy of Sciences*, 106(22): 8963–8.

Elugbe, B. O. (1989). 'Edoid', in J. Bendor-Samuel and R. L. Hartell (eds.), *The Niger-Congo Languages: A Classification and Description of Africa's Largest Language Family*. Lanham: University Press of America, 291–304.

Embick, D. (2000). 'Features, Syntax and Categories in the Latin Perfect', *Linguistic Inquiry* 31: 185–230.

Embleton, S. M. (1986). *Statistics in Historical Linguistics*. Bochum: Brockmeyer.

Emery, N. J., and Clayton, N. S. (2004). 'The Mentality of Crows: Convergent Evolution of Intelligence in Corvids and Apes', *Science* 306: 1903–7.

Emonds, J. E. (1976). *A Transformational Approach to English Syntax. Root, Structure-Preserving and Local Transformations*. New York: Academic Press.

Enard, W., Przeworski, M., Fisher, S. E., Lai, C. S. L., Wiebe, V., Kitano, T., Monaco, A. P., and Pääbo, S. (2002). 'Molecular Evolution of *FOXP2*, a Gene Involved in Speech and Language', *Nature* 418: 869–72.

—— Gehre, S., Hammerschmidt, K., and 53 others, (2009). 'A Humanized Version of Foxp2 Affects Cortico-basal Ganglia Circuits in Mice', *Cell* 137, 961–71.

Enç, M. (1987). 'Anchoring Conditions for Tense', *Linguistic Inquiry* 18: 633–57.

Endo, Y., Kitagawa, Y., and J. Yoon (1999). 'Smaller Clauses'. Proceedings of 6th GLOW in Asia, Nagoya, Japan.

Epstein, S. D. (1999). 'Un-principled Syntax and Derivational Relations', in S. D. Epstein and N. Hornstein *Working Minimalism*, 317–45 Cambridge, MA: MIT Press.

—— and Seely, T. D. (2006). *Derivations in Minimalism*, Cambridge: Cambridge University Press.

Evans, P. D., Anderson, J. R., Vallender, E. J., Gilbert, S. L., Malcom, C. M., Dorus, S., and Lahn, B. T. (2004). 'Adaptive Evolution of ASPM, a Major Determinant of Cerebral Cortical Size in Humans', *Human Molecular Genetics* 13(5): 489–94.

Fabb, N., and Halle, M. (2006). 'Telling the Numbers: A Unified Account of Syllabotonic English and Syllabic French and Polish Verse', *Research in Language* 4: 5–30.

Falcaro, M., Pickles, A., Newbury, D. F., Addis, L., Banfield, E., Fisher, S. E., Monaco, A. P., Simkin, Z., Conti-Ramsden, G., and SLI Consortium. (2008). 'Genetic and Phenotypic Effects of Phonological Short-term Memory and Grammatical Morphology in Specific Language Impairment', *Genes, Brain and Behavior* 7: 393–402.

Farkas, D. (2003). 'Assertion, Belief and Mood Choice', paper presented at the *European Summer School in Logic, Language and Information (ESSLLI)*, Vienna.

Feigenson, L., and Halberda, J. (2004). 'Infants Chunk Object Arrays into Sets of Individuals', *Cognition* 91: 173–90.

Felsenstein, J. (2004a). *Inferring Phylogenies.* Sunderland, MA: Sinauer.

——(2004b). *PHYLIP (Phylogeny Inference Package)* version 3.6b. Distributed by the author. Department of Genome Sciences, University of Washington, Seattle.

Fernald, R. D. (2000). 'Evolution of Eyes', *Current Opinion in Neurobiology* 10: 444–50.

Ferrari, F. (2005). *A Syntactic Analysis of the Nominal Systems of Italian and Luganda. How Nouns Can Be Formed in the Syntax.* Ph.D. dissertation, New York University.

Fiez, J. A., Petersen, S. E., Cheney, M. K., and Raichle, M. E. (1992). 'Impaired Nonmotor Learning and Error Detection Associated with Cerebellar Damage: A Single Case Study', *Brain* 115: 155–78.

Fillmore, C. (1968). 'The Case for Case', in E. Bach and R. Harms (eds.), *Universals in Linguistic Theory.* New York: Holt, Rinehart and Winston, 1–90.

Fisher, S. E., Lai, C. S. L., and Monaco, A. P. (2003). 'Deciphering the genetic basis of speech and language disorder's', *Annual Review of Neuroscience* 26: 57–80.

——and Marcus, G. F. (2006). 'The Eloquent Ape: Genes, Brains and the Evolution of Language', *Nature Genetics* 7: 9–20.

——Vargha-Khadem, F., Watkins, K. E., Monaco, A. P., and Pembrey, M. E. (1998). 'Localisation of a Gene Implicated in a Severe Speech and Language Disorder', *Nature Genetics* 18: 168–70.

Fitch, W. M. and Margoliash, E. (1967). 'Construction of Phylogenetic Trees', *Science* 155(760): 279–84.

Fitch, W. T. (2000). 'The Phonetic Potential of Nonhuman Vocal Tracts: Comparative Cineradiographic Observations of Vocalizing Animals', *Phonetica* 57: 205–18.

——(2004). 'Kin Selection and "Mother Tongues": A Neglected Component in Language Evolution', in D. K. Oller and U. Griebel (eds.), *Evolution of Communication Systems: A Comparative Approach.* Cambridge, MA: MIT Press, 275–96.

——(2005). 'The Evolution of Language: A Comparative Review', *Biology and Philosophy* 20: 193–230.

——(2007a). 'Evolving Meaning: The Roles of Kin Selection, Allomothering and Paternal Care in Language Evolution', in C. Lyon, C. Nehaniv, and A. Cangelosi (eds.), *Emergence of Communication and Language.* New York: Springer, 29–51.

Fitch, W. T. (2007b). 'The Evolution of Language: A Comparative Perspective', in G. Gaskell (ed.), *Oxford Handbook of Psycholinguistics*. Oxford: Oxford University Press, 787–804.

——(2008). 'Nano-intentionality: A Defense of Intrinsic Intentionality', *Biology and Philosophy* 23: 157–77.

——(2010). *The Evolution of Language*. Cambridge: Cambridge University Press.

——and Hauser, M. D. (2002). 'Unpacking "Honesty": Vertebrate Vocal Production and the Evolution of Acoustic Signals', in A. M. Simmons, R. F. Fay, and A. N. Popper (eds.), *Acoustic Communication*. New York: Springer, 65–137.

————(2004). 'Computational Constraints on Syntactic Processing in a Nonhuman Primate', *Science* 303: 377–80.

————and Chomsky, N. (2005). 'The Evolution of the Language Faculty: Clarifications and Implications', *Cognition* 97: 179–210.

——and Reby, D. (2001). 'The Descended Larynx is not Uniquely Human', *Proceedings of the Royal Society of London* B268: 1669–75.

Fodor, J. A. (1975). *The Language of Thought*. Cambridge, MA: Harvard University Press.

——(1983). *The Modularity of Mind*. Cambridge, MA: MIT Press.

——(1990). *A Theory of Content*. Cambridge, MA: MIT Press.

——(1998). *Concepts: Where Cognitive Science Went Wrong*. Oxford: Oxford University Press.

——(2003). *Hume Variations*. Oxford: Oxford University Press.

——(2008). 'Against Darwinism', *Mind and Language* 23: 1–24.

——and Pylyshyn, Z. (1988). 'Connectionism and Cognitive Architecture: A Critical Analysis', *Cognition* 28: 3–71.

——Bever, T., and Garrett, M. (1974). *The Psychology of Language*. New York: Mc-Graw-Hill.

Fong, S. (1990). *Computational Properties of Principle-based Grammatical Theories*. Ph.D. dissertation, MIT.

Forster, K. (1976). 'Accessing the Mental Lexicon', in R. Wales and E. Walker (eds.), *New Approaches to Language Mechanisms*. Amsterdam: North Holland, 257–87.

——(1992). 'Memory-Addressing Mechanisms and Lexical Access', in R. Frost and L. Katz (eds.). *Orthography, Phonology, Morphology, and Meaning*. Amsterdam: Elsevier. 413–34.

——and Chambers, S. M. (1973). 'Lexical Access and Naming Time', *Journal of Verbal Learning and Verbal Behavior* 12: 627–35.

Fortuny, J. (2008). *The Emergence of Order in Syntax*. Amsterdam/Philadelphia: John Benjamins.

Frank, R. (2002). *Phrase Structure Composition and Syntactic Dependencies*. Cambridge, MA: MIT Press.

Fraser, B. (1970). 'Idioms in Transformational Grammar', *Foundations of Language* 6: 22–43.

Frazier, L., and Flores d'Arcais, G. (1989). 'Filler-driven Parsing: A Study of Gap-Filling in Dutch', *Journal of Memory and Language* 28: 331–44.

Freeze, R. (1992). 'Existentials and Other Locatives', *Language* 68: 553–95.

Frege, G. (1893). *Grundgesetze der Arithmetik*. Jena: Verlag Hermann Pohle, vol i. [Partial translation as *The Basic Laws of Arithmetic* by M. Furth, Berkeley: University of California Press, 1964].

Frey, R., and Riede, T. (2003). 'Sexual Dimorphism of the Larynx of the Mongolian Gazelle (*Procapra gutturosa* Pallas, 1777) (Mammalia, Artiodactyla, Bovidae)', *Zoologischer Anzeiger* 242: 33–62.

Friederici, A. D., Bahlmann, J., Heim, S., Schubotz, R. I., and Anwander, A. (2006). 'The Brain Differentiates Human and Non-human Grammars: Functional Localization and Structural Connectivity', *Proceedings of the National Academy of Sciences* 103: 2458–63.

——Steinhauer, K., and Pfeifer, E. (2002). 'Brain Signatures of Artificial Language Processing: Evidence Challenging the Critical Period Hypothesis', *Proceedings of the National Academy of Sciences* 99: 529–34.

Friedrich, F., Glenn, C., and Martin, O. S. M. (1984). 'Interruption of Phonological Coding in Conduction Aphasia', *Brain and Language* 22: 266–91.

Fujita, E., Tanabe, Y., Shiota, A., Ueda, M., Suwa, K., Momoi, M. Y., and Momoi, T. (2008). 'Ultrasonic Vocalization Impairment of Foxp2 (R552H) Knockin Mice Related to Speech-language Disorder and Abnormality of Purkinje Cells', *Proceedings of the National Academy of Sciences* 105(8): 3117–22.

Fujita, K. (2002). 'Review of *Biolinguistics* by L. Jenkins (2000)', *Gengo Kenkyu* 121: 165–78.

Fukui, N. (1986). *A Theory of Category Projection and its Applications*. Ph.D. dissertation, MIT.

—— (1995). 'The Principles and Parameters Approach: A Comparative Syntax of English and Japanese', in M. Shibatani and T. Bynon (eds.), *Approaches to Language Typology*. Oxford: Oxford University Press, 327–72.

—— (2006). *Theoretical Comparative Syntax*. London: Routledge.

Galaburda, A. M., LoTurco, J. Ramus, F., Fitch, R. H., and Rosen, G. D. (2006). 'From Genes to Behavior in Developmental Dyslexia', *Nature Neuroscience* 9(10): 1213–17.

Gale, E., de Villiers, J., de Villiers, P., and Pyers, J. (1996). 'Language and Theory of Mind in Oral Deaf Children', in A. Stringfellow, D. Cahana-Amitay, E. Hughes, and A. Zukowski (eds.), *Proceedings of the 20th Annual Boston University Conference on Language Development*. Somerville: Cascadilla Press, 213–24.

Gallego, Á. J. (2006). 'Phase Effects in Iberian Romance', in N. Sagarra, and A. J. Torbio (eds.), *Selected proceedings of the 9th Hispanic Linguistics Symposium*. Somerville: Cascadilla Press, 43–55.

—— (2007). *Phase Theory and Parametric variation*. Ph.D. dissertation, Universitat Autònoma de Barcelona.

Gallego, Á. J. (2008). 'Phases and Variation. Exploring the Second Factor of the Language Faculty'. Ms., Universitat Autònoma de Barcelona.

Gallistel, C. G. (1990a). 'Introduction', in C. G. Gallistel (ed.), 'Animal Communication'. *Cognition* 37: 1–2.

—— (1990b). *The Organization of Learning*. Cambridge, MA: MIT Press.

—— (2006). 'Learning Organs'. Ms., Rutgers University.

—— (2007). 'L'Apprentissage de Matières Distinctes Exige des Organes Distincts', in J. Bricmont and J. Franck (eds.), *Cahier Chomsky*, 181–7. Paris: L'Herne.

Gathercole, S. E., and Baddeley, A. D. (1993). *Working Memory and Language*. Hove: Psychology Press.

Gazzaniga, M. S., and Heatherton, T. F. (2003). *Psychological Sciences: Mind, Brain and Behavior*. New York: W. W. Norton & Co.

Gebhart, A. L., Petersen, S. E., Thach, W. T. (2002). 'Role of the Posterolateral Cerebellum in Language', *Annals of the New York Academy of Sciences* 978: 318–33.

Gehring, W. J. (1994). 'A History of the Homeobox', in D. Duboule (ed.), *Guidebook to the Homeobox Genes*. Oxford: Oxford University Press, 1–10.

—— (1998). *Master Control Genes in Development and Evolution: The Homeobox Story*. New Haven: Yale University Press.

—— (2005). 'New Perspectives on Eye Development and the Evolution of Eyes and Photoreceptors', *Journal of Heredity* 96(3): 171–84.

—— and Ikeo, K. (1999). 'Pax 6. Mastering Eye Morphogenesis and Eye Evolution', *Trends in Genetics* 15: 371–7.

Gentner, T. Q., Fenn, K. M., Margoliash, D., and Nusbaum, H. C. (2006). 'Recursive Syntactic Pattern Learning by Songbirds', *Nature* 440: 1204–7.

Geraci, C., Gozzi, M., Papagno, C., and Cecchetto, C. (2008). 'How Grammar Can Cope With Limited Short-term Memory: Simultaneity and Seriality in Sign Languages', *Cognition* 106(2): 780–804.

Gerken, L. A. (1991). 'The Metrical Basis for Children's Subjectless Sentences', *Journal of Memory and Language* 30: 431–51.

Ghomeshi, J. (1996). *Projection and Inflection: A Study of Persian Phrase Structure*. Ph.D. dissertation, University of Toronto.

Gianollo, C. (2005). *Constituent Structure and Parametric Resetting in the Latin DP: A Diachronic Study*. Ph.D. dissertation, Università di Pisa.

—— Guardiano, C., and Longobardi, G. (in press). 'Historial Implications of a Formal Theory of Syntactic Variation', in D. Jonas and S. Anderson. (eds.), *Proceedings of DIGS VIII*. Oxford: Oxford University Press.

Gibson, E. (1998). 'Linguistic Complexity: Locality of Syntactic Dependencies', *Cognition*, 68: 1–76.

—— and Wexler, K. (1994). 'Triggers', *Linguistic Inquiry* 25: 355–407.

Gilbert, W., and A. Maxam (1973). 'The Nucleotide Sequence of the *lac* Operator', *Proceedings of the National Academy of Science* 70(12): 3581–4.

Gillespie, J. H. (1984). 'Molecular Evolution over the Mutational Landscape', *Evolution* 38: 1116–29.

—— (1991). *Population Genetics: A Concise Guide.* (2nd ed.). Baltimore: Johns Hopkins University Press.

Giorgi, A. (1984). 'Toward a Theory of Long Distance Anaphors: A GB Approach', *The Linguistic Review* 3: 307–61.

—— (2006). 'From Temporal Anchoring to Long Distance Anaphors', *Natural Language and Linguistic Theory* 24(4): 1009–47.

—— (2007). 'On the Nature of Long Distance Anaphors', *Linguistic Inquiry* 38(2): 321–42.

—— (2010). *About the Speaker: Toward a Syntax of Indexicality.* Oxford: Oxford University Press.

—— and Pianesi, F. (1997). *Tense and Aspect: From Semantics to Morphosyntax.* New York: Oxford University Press.

—— and Pianesi, F. (2000). 'Sequence of Tense Phenomena in Italian: A Morphosyntactic Analysis', *Probus* 12: 1–32.

—— —— (2001). 'Tense, Attitudes and Subjects', in R. Hastings, B. Jackson, and Z. Zvolenszky (eds.), *Proceedings of SALT-11.* Cornell University.

—— —— (2004a). 'The Temporal Perspective of the Speaker and the Subject: From Semantics to Morphosyntax', in J. Guéron and J. Lecarme (eds.), *The Syntax of Time.* Cambridge, MA: MIT Press, 129–52.

—— —— (2004b). 'Complementizer Deletion in Italian', in L. Rizzi (ed.), *The Structure of CP and IP.* New York: Oxford University Press, 190–210.

Givón, T. (2002). *Bio-Linguistics: The Santa Barbara Lectures.* Amsterdam/ Philadelphia: John Benjamins.

Gleitman, L.R., Cassidy, K., Nappa, R., Papafragou, A., and Trueswell. J. C. (2005). 'Hard Words', *Language Learning and Development* 1: 23–64.

Goebl, H. (1982). *Dialektometrie: Prinzipien und Methoden des Einsatzes der Numerischen Taxonomie im Bereich der Dialektgeographie.* Vienna: Österreichische Akademie der Wissenschaften.

Goldberg, A. (1995). *Constructions.* Chicago: University of Chicago Press.

—— (2006). *Constructions at Work.* Oxford: Oxford University Press.

Golinkoff, R., Hirsh-Pasek, K., Cauley, K., and Gordon, L. (1987). 'The Eyes Have It: Lexical and Syntactic Comprehension in a New Paradigm', *Journal of Child Language* 14: 23–46.

Goodwin, B. (1994). *How the Leopard Changed its Spots.* London: Weidenfeld & Nicolson.

Gopnik, M. (1990). 'Feature-Blind Grammar and Dysphasia', *Nature* 344: 715.

—— and Crago, M. (1991). 'Familial Aggregation of a Developmental Language Disorder', *Cognition* 39: 1–50.

Gould, S. J. (1977). *Ontogeny and Phylogeny.* Cambridge, MA: Harvard University Press.

—— (1989). *Wonderful Life.* New York: W. W. Norton & Co.

—— (2002). *The Structure of Evolutionary Theory.* Cambridge, MA: Harvard University Press.

Gould, S. J. and Vrba, E. S. (1982). 'Exaptation: A Missing Term in the Science of Form', *Paleobiology* 1: 4–15.

Grabowski, E., and Mindt, D. (1995). 'A Corpus-based Learning of Irregular Verbs in English', *Computers in English Linguistics* 19: 5–22.

Granadino, B., Pérez-Sánchez, C., and Rey-Campos, J. (2000). 'Fork Head Transcription Factors', *Current Genomics* 1(4), 353–82.

Gray, R. D., and Atkinson, Q. D. (2003). 'Language-Tree Divergence Times Support the Anatolian Theory of Indo-European Origin', *Nature* 426: 435–9.

Greenberg, J. (1963). 'Some Universals of Grammar with Particular Reference to the Order of Meaningful Elements', in J. Greenberg (ed.), *Universals of Language*. Cambridge, MA: MIT Press, 73–113.

—— (1987). *Language in the Americas*. Stanford: Standford University Press.

—— (2000). *Indoeuropean and its Closest Relatives: The Eurasiatic Language Family*. Stanford: Standford University Press.

Grimshaw, J. (1990). 'Extended Projection'. Ms. Brandeis University.

Grodner, D., and Gibson, E. (2005). 'Consequences of the Serial Nature of Linguistic Input', *Cognitive Science* 29: 261–90.

Grodzinsky, Y. (2000). 'The Neurology of Syntax: Language use without Broca's Area', *Behavioral and Brain Sciences* 23: 1–71.

—— and Amunts, K. (eds.) (2006). *Broca's Region*. New York, Oxford University Press.

Grohmann, K. (ed.) (2009). *Inter-Phases*. Oxford: Oxford University Press.

Gropen, J., Pinker, S., Hollander, M., Goldberg, R., and Wilson, R. (1989). 'The Learnability and Acquisition of the Dative Alternation in English', *Language* 65(2): 203–57.

Groszer, M., Keays, D., Deacon, R., de Bono, J., Prasad-Mulcare, S., Gaub, S., Baum, M., French, D., Nicod, J., Coventry, J., Enard, W., Fray, M., Brown, S., Nolan, P., Pääbo, S., Channon, K., Costa, R., Eilers, J., Ehret, G., Rawlins, N., and Fisher, S. E. (2008). 'Impaired Synaptic Plasticity and Motor Learning in Mice with a Point Mutation Implicated in Human Speech Deficits', *Current Biology* 18: 354–62.

Guardiano, C. (2003). *Struttura e storia del sintagma nominale nel greco antico: Ipotesi parametriche*. Ph.D. dissertation, University of Pisa.

—— and Longobardi, G. (2005). 'Parametric Comparison and Language Taxonomy', in M. Batllori, M. L. Hernanz, C. Picallo, and F. Roca (eds.), *Grammaticalization and Parametric Variation*. Oxford: Oxford University Press, 149–74.

Guasti, M. (2002). *Language Acquisition: The Growth of Grammar*. Cambridge, MA: MIT Press.

Guéron, J. (2004). 'Tense Construal and the Argument Structure of Auxiliaries', in J. Guéron and J. Lecarme (eds.), *The Syntax of Time*. Cambridge, MA: MIT Press, 299–328.

Guimarães, M. (2000). 'In Defense of Vacuous Projections in Bare Phrase Structure', in M. Guimarães, L. Meroni, C. Rodrigues, and I. San Martin (eds.), *University of Maryland Working Papers in Linguistics* 9: 90–115.

Gulli, A. (2003). *Reduplication in Syntax*. Ph.D. dissertation, City University of New York.

Haegeman, L. (1995). 'Root Infinitives, Tense, and Truncated Structures', *Language Acquisition* 4: 205–55.

Haesler, S., Rochefort, C., Geogi, B., Licznerski, P., Osten, P., and Scharff, C. (2007). 'Incomplete and Inaccurate Vocal Imitation after Knockdown of FoxP2 in Songbird Basal Ganglia Nucleus Area X', *PLoS Biology* 5(12): e321.

—— Wada, K., Nshdejan, A., Morrisey, E. E., Lints, T., Jarvis, E. D., and Scharff, C. (2004). 'FoxP2 Expression in Avian Vocal Learners and Non-learners', *The Journal of Neuroscience* 24(13): 3164–75.

Hagoort, P. (2005). 'On Broca, Brain, and Binding: A New Framework', *Trends in Cognitive Sciences* 9: 416–23.

Hailman, J. P., Ficken, M. S., and Ficken, R. W. (1985). 'The "chick-a-dee" Calls of *Parus Atricapillus*: A Recombinant System of Animal Communication Compared with Written English', *Semiotica* 56: 191–224.

—— —— —— (1987). 'Constraints on the Structure of Combinatorial "chick-a-dee" Calls', *Ethology* 75: 62–80.

Haldane J. B. S. (1927). 'A Mathematical Theory of Natural and Artificial Selection', *Proceedings of the Cambridge Philosophical Society* 23, *Part V. Selection and Mutation*: 838–44.

Hale, K., and Keyser, S. J. (1993). 'On Argument Structure and the Lexical Expression of Syntactic Relations', in K. Hale and S. J. Keyser (eds.), *The View from Building 20* Cambridge, MA: MIT Press, 53–110.

—— —— (2002). *Prolegomenon to a Theory of Argument Structure*. Cambridge, MA: MIT Press.

Hall, B. K. (1998). *Evolutionary Developmental Biology*. London: Chapman & Hall.

—— (2003). 'Descent with Modification: The Unity Underlying Homology and Homoplasy as Seen Through an Analysis of Development and Evolution', *Biological Reviews* 78: 409–33.

—— (ed.). (1994). *Homology: The Hierarchical Basis of Comparative Biology*. San Diego: Academic Press.

Halle, M. (1990). 'An Approach to Morphology', *Proceedings of the Northeast Linguistic Society* 20: 150–84.

—— (1997). 'On Stress and Accent in Indo-European', *Language* 73: 275–313.

—— and Marantz, A. (1993). 'Distributed Morphology and the Pieces of Inflection', in K. Hale and S. J. Keyser (eds.), *The View from Building 20*. Cambridge, MA: MIT Press, 111–76.

—— and Mohanan, K.-P. (1985). Segmental Phonology of Modern English. *Linguistic Inquiry* 16: 57–116.

Hamming, R. W. (1950). 'Error Detecting and Error Correcting Codes', *Bell System Technical Journal* 26(2): 147–60.

Hankamer, J. (1989). 'Lexical Representation and Processes', in W. Marslen-Wilson (ed.), *Morphological Parsing and the Lexicon*. Cambridge, MA: MIT Press.

Hanten, G., and Martin, R. (2001). 'A Developmental Short-term Memory Deficit: A Case Study', *Brain and Cognition* 45: 164–88.

Hare, B., and Tomasello, M. (2004). 'Chimpanzees are More Skillful in Competitive than Cooperative Cognitive Tasks', *Animal Behavior* 68: 571–81.

Harley, H. (2002). 'Possession and the Double Object Construction', *Language Variation Yearbook* 2: 29–68.

—— (2004). 'Merge, Conflation, and Head Movement: The First Sister Principle Revisited', *Proceedings of North East Linguistic Society 34*. Amherst: University of Massachusetts, GLSA, 239–54.

Harris, J. W. (1991). 'The Exponence of Gender in Spanish', *Linguistic Inquiry* 22: 27–62.

Harris, Z. (1951). *Methods in Structural Linguistics*. Chicago: University of Chicago Press.

Haspelmath, M. (1999). 'External Possession in a European Areal Perspective', in D. Payne and I. Barshi (eds.), *External Possession*. Amsterdam/Philadelphia: John Benjamins, 109–35.

Hauser, M. D. (1996). *Animal Communication*. Cambridge, MA: MIT Press.

—— (2000). *Wild Minds*. New York: Holt, Rinehart and Winston.

—— (2005). 'Our Chimpanzee Mind', *Nature* 437(1): 60–3.

Hauser, M. D. (2008). 'Humaniqueness', paper presented at American Association for the Advancement of Science, Boston. [A version published in *Nature* as 'The Possibility of Impossible Cultures', *Nature* 460: 190–6.]

—— Chomsky, N. and Fitch, W. T. (2002). 'The Faculty of Language: What Is It, Who Has It, and How Did It Evolve?', *Science* 298: 1569–79.

Hayes, C. (1951). *The Ape in Our House*. New York: Harper.

Heggarty, P. A. (2000). 'Quantifying Change Over Time in Phonetics', in C. Renfrew, A. McMahon, and L. Trask (eds.), *Time-Depth in Historical Linguistics-2*, Cambridge: MacDonald Institute for Archaeological Research, 531–62.

Herrmann, T. (2005). 'Relative Clauses in English Dialects of the British Isles', in B. Kortmann, T. Herrmann, L. Pietsch, and S. Wagner (eds.), *A Comparative Grammar of British English Dialects. Agreement, Gender, Relative Clauses*. Berlin/New York: Mouton de Gruyter, 21–123.

Hespos, S. J., and Spelke, E. S. (2004). 'Conceptual Precursors to Language', *Nature* 430: 453–6.

Higginbotham, J. (1985). 'On Semantics', *Linguistic Inquiry* 16: 547–93.

—— (1986). 'Linguistic Theory and Davidson's Program in Semantics', in E. Lepore (ed.), *Truth and Interpretation: Perspectives on the Philosophy of Donald Davidson*. Oxford: Blackwell.

—— (1995). 'Tensed Thoughts', *Mind and Language* 10: 226–49.

—— (2001). 'Why is Sequence of Tense Obligatory?', in G. Preyer and E. Lepore (eds.), *On Logical Form*. New York: Oxford University Press.

Hinterhölzl, R. (2006). *Scrambling, Remnant Movement, and Restructuring in West Germanic*. New York: Oxford University Press.

Hinzen, W. (2006). *Mind Design and Minimal Syntax*. Oxford: Oxford University Press.

—— (2009a). 'An Argument Against Compositionality'. Ms., University of Durham.

—— (2009b). 'A Naturalization of Truth'. Ms., University of Durham.

Hockett, C. F. (1960). 'Logical Considerations in the Study of Animal Communication', in W. E. Lanyon and W. N. Tavolga (eds.), *Animal Sounds and Communication*. Washington, D.C.: American Institute of Biological Sciences, 392–430.

—— (1963). 'The Problem of Universals in Language', in J. Greenberg (ed.), *Universals of Language*. Cambridge, MA: MIT Press, 1–29.

Hodos, W., and Campbell, C. B. G. (1969). '*Scala Naturae*: Why There Is No Theory in Comparative Psychology', *Psychological Review* 76: 337–50.

Hoekstra, T., and Mulder, R. (1990). 'Unergatives as Copular Verbs: Locational and Existential Predication', *The Linguistic Review* 7: 1–79.

Holmberg, A. (2009). 'Another Look at the Role of Inflection in Scandinavian Syntax'. Ms. Newcastle University.

Holy, T. E., and Guo, Z. (2005). 'Ultrasonic Songs of Male Mice.' *PLoS Biology* 3: 2177–86.

Hornstein, N. (1999). 'Movement and Control', *Linguistic Inquiry* 30: 69–96.

—— (2001). *Move! A Minimalist Theory of Construal*. Oxford: Blackwell.

—— (2009). *A Theory of Syntax*. Cambridge: Cambridge University Press.

Horowitz, N. H. (1945). 'On the Evolution of Biochemical Synthesis'. *Proceedings of the National Acadamy of Sciences of the United States of America* 31: 153–7.

Horrocks, G. (1997). *Greek: A History of the Language and its Speakers*. London: Longman.

Huang, C.-T. J. (1981/82). 'Move *Wh* in a Language without *Wh*-Movement', *The Linguistic Review* 1: 369–416.

—— (1999). 'Passive'. Ms., University of California, Irvine.

—— and Liu, L. (2001). 'Logophoricity, Attitudes, and *Ziji* at the Interface', in P. Cole, G. Hermon, and C.-T. J. Huang (eds.), *Long-distance Reflexives*. New York: Academic Press, 141–95.

Hurford, J. R. (2007). *The Origins of Meaning*. Oxford: Oxford University Press.

Huybregts, R. (1985). 'The Weak Inadequacy of CFPSGs', in G. de Haan, M. Trommelen, and W. Zonneveld (eds.), *Van Periferie naar Kern*. Dordrecht: Foris, 81–99.

Hyams, N. (1986). *Language Acquisition and the Theory of Parameters*. Dordrecht: Reidel.

—— and Wexler, K. (1993). 'On the Grammatical Basis of Null Subjects in Child Language', *Linguistic Inquiry* 24, 3: 421–59.

International Chicken Genome Sequencing Consortium (2004). 'Sequence and Comparative Analysis of the Chicken Genome Provide Unique Perspectives on Vertebrate Evolution', *Nature* 432: 695–717.

Ito, M. (2000a). 'Mechanisms of Motor Learning in the Cerebellum', *Brain Research* 886(1–2): 237–45.

Ito, M. (2000b). 'Neural Control of Cognition and Language', in A. Marantz, Y. Miyashita, and W. A. O'Neill (eds.), *Image, Language, Brain*. Cambridge, MA: MIT Press, 149–62.

Jablonka, E., and Lamb, M. (2005). *Evolution in Four Dimensions*. Cambridge, MA: MIT Press.

Jaccard, P. (1901). 'Étude comparative de la distribution florale dans une portion des Alpes et des Jura', *Bulletin de la Société Vaudoise des Sciences Naturelles* 37: 547–79.

Jackendoff, R. (1987). *Consciousness and the Computational Mind*. Cambridge, MA: MIT Press.

—— (1994). *Patterns in the Mind: Language and Human Nature*. New York: Basic Books.

—— (2002). *Foundations of Language: Brain, Meaning, Grammar, Evolution*. Oxford: Oxford University Press.

—— (2007). *Language, Consciousness, Culture: Essays on Mental Structure*. Cambridge, MA: MIT Press.

Jacob, F. (1977). 'Darwinism Reconsidered', *Le Monde*, September 6–8.

—— (1982). *The Possible and the Actual*. New York: Pantheon.

—— (1988). *The Statue Within*. New York: Basic Books.

Jakobson, R. (1968). *Child Language, Aphasia and Phonological Universals* (1st publ. 1941). The Hague: Mouton.

Janik, V. M., and Slater, P. B. (1997). 'Vocal Learning in Mammals', *Advances in the Study of Behavior* 26: 59–99.

Jarvis, E. (2004). 'Learned Birdsong and the Neurobiology of Human Language', *Annals of the New York Academy of Science* 1016: 749–77.

Jayaseelan, K. A. (1988). 'Complex Predicates and Theta Theory', in W. Wilkins (ed.), *Thematic Relations (Syntax and Semantics* 21). New York: Academic Press, 91–111.

Jelinek, E., and Carnie, A. (2003). 'Argument Hierarchies and the Mapping Principle', in A. Carnie, H. Harley, and M. Willie (eds.), *Formal Approaches to Function*. Amsterdam/Philadelphia: John Benjamins, 265–96.

Jenkins, L. (2000). *Biolinguistics: Exploring the Biology of Language*. Cambridge: Cambridge University Press.

—— (ed.) (2004). *Variation and Universals in Biolinguistics*. Amsterdam: Elsevier.

Jerison, H. J. (1973). *Evolution of the Brain and Intelligence*. New York: Academic Press.

Jerne, N. K. (1985). 'The Generative Grammar of the Immune System', *Science* 229: 1057–9.

Jespersen, O. (1970). *A Modern English Grammar on Historical Principles*. Part V. *Syntax* (Fourth Volume) (1st publ. 1940). London/Copenhagen: George Allen & Unwin, and Ejnar Munksgaard.

Johns, A. (1999). 'On the Lexical Semantics of Affixal 'Want' in Inuktitut', *International Journal of American Linguistics* 65: 176–200.

Joos, M. (ed.) (1957). *Readings in Linguistics*. New York: American Council of Learned Societies.

Joseph, B., and Salmons, J. C. (eds.) (1998). *Nostratic, Sifting the Evidence*. Amsterdam/Philadelphia: John Benjamins.

Jung, H.-S., Francis-West, P. H., Widelitz, R. B., Jiang, T. X., Ting-Berreth, S., Tickle, C., Wolpert, L., and Chuong, C. M. (1998). 'Local Inhibitory Action of BMPs and Their Relationships with Activators in Feather Formation: Implications for Periodic Patterning', *Developmental Biology* 196(1): 11–23.

Jung, Y.-J., and Miyagawa, S. (2004). 'Decomposing Ditransitive Verbs', *Proceedings of SICGG*, 101–20.

Jürgens, U. (1995). 'Neuronal Control of Vocal Production in Non-Human and Human Primates', in E. Zimmerman and J. D. Newman (eds.), *Current Topics in Primate Vocal Communication*. New York: Plenum Press, 199–206.

Just, M. A., and Carpenter, P. A. (1992). 'A Capacity Theory of Comprehension: Individual Differences in Working Memory', *Psychological Review* 99(1): 122–49.

Kahn, C. (1966). 'The Greek Verb "To Be" and the Concept of Being', *Foundations of Language* 2: 245–65.

Kako, E. (1999). 'Elements of Syntax in the Systems of Three Language-Trained Animals', *Animal Learning & Behavior* 27: 1–14.

Karsenti, E. (2008). 'Self-Organization in Cell Biology: A Brief History', *Nature Reviews Molecular Cell Biology* 9(3): 255–62.

Kauffman, S. A. (1993). *The Origins of Order: Self-Organization and Selection in Evolution*. Oxford: Oxford University Press.

Kayne, R. S. (1975). *French Syntax: The Transformational Cycle*. Cambridge, MA: MIT Press.

—— (1981a). 'On Certain Differences between French and English', *Linguistic Inquiry* 12(3): 349–71.

—— (1981b). 'Unambiguous Paths', in R. May and J. Koster (eds.), *Levels of Syntactic Representation*. Dordrecht: Foris, 143–83. [Reprinted in Kayne (1984)].

—— (1982). 'Predicates and Arguments, Verbs and Nouns', *GLOW Newsletter* 8: 24.

—— (1984). *Connectedness and Binary Branching*. Dordrecht: Foris.

—— (1989). 'Null Subjects and Clitic Climbing', in O. Jaeggli. and K. Safir (eds.), *The Null Subject Parameter*. Dordrecht: Kluwer Academic Publishers.

—— (1993). 'Toward a Modular Theory of Auxiliary Selection', *Studia Linguistica* 47: 3–31. [reprinted in Kayne (2000)].

—— (1994). *The Antisymmetry of Syntax*. Cambridge, MA: MIT Press.

—— (2000). *Parameters and Universals*. New York: Oxford University Press.

—— (2005a). 'Some Notes on Comparative Syntax, with Special Reference to English and French', in G. Cinque and R. Kayne (eds.), *The Oxford Handbook of Comparative Syntax*. Oxford: Oxford University Press, 3–69.

—— (2005b). *Movement and Silence*. New York: Oxford University Press.

—— (2006a). 'Expletives, Datives and the Tension between Morphology and Syntax'. Ms., New York University.

Kayne, R. S. (2006b). 'On Parameters and on Principles of Pronunciation', in H. Broekhuis, N. Corver, R. Huybregts, U. Kleinhenz, and J. Koster (eds.), *Organizing Grammar: Linguistic Studies in Honor of Henk van Riemsdijk*. Berlin/New York: Mouton de Gruyter, 289–99.

—— (2008). 'A Note on Auxiliary Alternations and Silent Causation'. Ms., New York University.

—— (In press). 'Why Isn't *This* a Complementizer?', in P. Svenonius (ed.), *Functional Structure from Top to Toe: A Festschrift for Tarald Taraldsen*. New York: Oxford University Press.

—— and Pollock, J.-Y. (2001). 'New Thoughts on Stylistic Inversion', in A. Hulk and J.-Y. Pollock (eds.), *Inversion in Romance*. New York: Oxford University Press, 107–62. [reprinted in Kayne (2005b)].

—— —— (2008). 'Toward an Analysis of French Hyper-Complex Inversion'. Ms., New York University and Université Paris-Est Marne la Vallée.

Keenan, E. (1994). 'Creating Anaphors: An Historical Study of the English Reflexive Pronouns'. Ms., University of California, Los Angeles.

—— (2000). 'An Historical Explanation of Some Binding Theoretic Facts in English'. Ms., University of California, Los Angeles.

Keenan, E. (2002). 'Explaining the Creation of Reflexive Pronouns in English', in D. Minkova and R. Stockwell (eds.), *Studies in the History of the English Language*. Berlin/New York: Mouton de Gruyter, 325–54.

Keller, E. F. (2002). *Making Sense of Life: Explaining Biological Development with Models, Metaphors, and Machines*. Cambridge, MA: Harvard University Press.

Kellogg, W. N. (1968). 'Communication and Language in the Home-raised Chimpanzee', *Science* 162: 423–7.

Kenrick, P., and Davis, P. (2004). *Fossil Plants*. Washington, DC: Smithsonian Books.

Kihm, A. (2000). 'Wolof Genitive Constructions and the Construct State', in J. Lecarme, J. Lowenstamm, and U. Shlonsky (eds.), *Research in Afroasiatic Grammar*. Amsterdam/Philadelphia: John Benjamins, 151–81.

Kimura, M. (1983). *The Neutral Theory of Molecular Evolution*. Cambridge: Cambridge University Press.

King, H. D. (1936). 'A Waltzing Mutation in the White Rat', *Journal of Mammalogy* 17: 157–63.

King, J., and Just, M. A. (1991). 'Individual Differences in Syntactic Processing: The Role of Working Memory', *Journal of Memory and Language* 30: 580–602.

Kiparski, P. (1973). '"Elsewhere" in Phonology', in S. Anderson and P. Kiparsky (eds.), *A Festschrift for Morris Halle*. New York: Holt, Rinehart and Winston, 93–106.

—— (1996). 'The Shift to Head-initial VP in Germanic', in H. Thráinsson, S. D. Epstein, and S. Peters (eds.), *Studies in Comparative Generative Syntax*, vol. 2, Dordrecht: Kluwer Academic Publishers, 140–78.

Kirschner, M. W., and Gerhart, J. (2005). *The Plausibility of Life: Resolving Darwin's Dilemma*. New Haven: Yale University Press.

Kiya, T., Itoh, Y., and Kubo, T. (2008). 'Expression Analysis of the FoxP Homo-logue in the Brain of the Honeybee, Apis Mellifera', *Insect Molecular Biology* 17(1): 53–60.

Kleene, S. (1956). 'Representation of Events in Nerve Nets and Finite Automata', in C. Shannon and J. McCarthy (eds.), *Automata Studies*. Princeton: Princeton University Press, 3–41.

Klima, E. S., and Bellugi, U. (1979). *The Signs of Language*. Cambridge, MA: Harvard University Press.

Knörnschild, M., Nagy, M., Metz, M., Mayer, F., and von Helversen, O. (2010). 'Com-plex Vocal Imitation during Ontogeny in a Bat', *Biology Letters* 6: 56–9.

Koopman, H. (2000). *The Syntax of Specifiers and Heads*. London: Routledge.

—— (2003). 'The Locality of Agreement and the Structure of the DP in Maasai', in W. E. Griffin (ed.), *The Role of Agreement in Natural Language. TLS 5 Proceedings, Texas Linguistic Forum* 53: 206–27.

—— (2005). 'On the Parallelism of DPs and Clauses. Evidence from Kisongo Maasai', in A. Carnie, H. Harley, and S.A. Dooley (eds.), *Verb First, On the Syntax of Verb-initial Languages*. Amsterdam/Philadelphia: John Benjamins, 281–302.

—— and Sportiche, D. (1991). 'The Position of Subjects', *Lingua* 85: 211–58.

—— and Szabolcsi, A. (2000). *Verbal Complexes*. Cambridge, MA: MIT Press.

Kornfilt, J. (2004). *Turkish*. London: Routledge.

Kouprina, N., Pavlicek, A., Mochida, G. H., Solomon, G., Gersch, W., Yoon, Y. H., Collura, R., Ruvolo, M., Barrett, J. C., Woods, C. G., Walsh, C. A., Jurka, J., and Larionov, V. (2004). 'Accelerated Evolution of the ASPM Gene Controlling Brain Size Begins Prior to Human Brain Expansion', *PLoS Biology* 2: e126.

Koyré, A. (1961). 'Du monde de l'"à peu près" à l'univers de la précision', *Études d'Histoire de la Pensée Philosophique* 19: 311–29.

Krause, J., Lalueza-Fox, C., Orlando, L., Enard, W., Green, R., Burbano, H., Hublin, J-J., Hänni, C., Fortea, J., Rasilla, M., Bertranpetit, J., Rosas, A., and Pääbo, S. (2007). 'The Derived FOXP2 Variant of Modern Humans Was Shared with Neanderthals', *Current Biology* 17(1–5): 53–60.

—— Orlando, L., Serre, D., Viola, B., Prüfer, K., Richards, M. P., Hublin, J-J., Hänni, C., Derevianko, A. P., and Pääbo, S. (2007). 'Neanderthals in Central Asia and Siberia', *Nature* 449(7164): 902–4.

Krebs, J. R., and Dawkins, R. (1984). 'Animal Signals: Mind Reading and Manipulation', in J. R. Krebs and N. B. Davies (eds.), *Behavioural Ecology*. Sunderland: Sinauer, 380–402.

Kreitman, M. (2000). 'Methods to Detect Selection With Applications to the Human', *Annual Review of Genomics and Human Genetics* 1: 539–59.

Krifka, M. (1999). 'Manner in Dative Alternations', *Proceedings of West Coast Confer-ence on Formal Linguistics* 18, Somerville: Cascadilla Press, 260–71.

Kuczaj, S. (1976). '-ing', '-s', and '-ed': A Study of the Acquisition of Certain Verb Inflec-tions. Ph.D. dissertation, University of Minnesota.

Kuhl, P., Williams, K., Lacerda, F., Stevens, K., and Lindblom, B. (1992). 'Linguistic Experience Alters Phonetic Perception in Infants by 6 Months of Age', *Science* 255: 606–8.

Kurlansky, M. (2003). *Salt: A World History*. New York: Penguin.

Kuypers, H. G. J. M. (1958). 'Corticobulbar Connections to the Pons and Lower Brainstem in Man: An Anatomical Study', *Brain* 81: 364–88.

La Fauci, N., and Loporcaro, M. (1989). 'Passifs, avancements de l'objet indirect et formes verbales périphrastiques dans le dialecte d'Altamura (Pouilles)', *Rivista di linguistica* 1(1): 161–96.

Labov, W. (1994). *Principles of Language Change: Internal Factors*. Basil: Blackwell.

Lai, C. S. L., Fisher, S. E., Hurst, J. A., Vargha-Khadem, F., and Monaco, A. P. (2001). 'A Forkhead-domain Gene is Mutated in a Severe Speech and Language Disorder', *Nature* 413: 519–23.

—— Gerrelli, D., Monaco, A. P., Fisher, S. E., and Copp, A. J. (2003). 'FOXP2 Expression During Brain Development Coincides with Adult Sites of Pathology in a Severe Speech and Language Disorder', *Brain* 126: 2433–62.

Lakoff, G. (1970). 'Global rules', *Language* 46: 627–39.

—— (1972). 'The Arbitrary Basis of Transformational Grammar', *Language* 48: 76–87.

Larson, R. (1988). 'On the Double Object Construction', *Linguistic Inquiry* 19: 335–81.

—— and Ludlow, P. (1993). 'Interpreted Logical Forms', *Synthese* 95: 305–55.

Lascaratou, C. (1998). 'Basic Characteristics of Modern Greek Word Order', in A. Siewierska (ed.), *Constituent Order in the Languages of Europe*. Berlin/New York: Mouton de Gruyter, 151–72.

Lasnik, H. (1981). 'Restricting the Theory of Transformations: A Case Study', in N. Hornstein and D. Lightfoot (eds.), *Explanation in Linguistics*. London: Longman, 152–73.

—— and Saito, M. (1984). 'On the Nature of Proper Government', *Linguistic Inquiry* 15: 235–89. [Reprinted in Lasnik, H. (1990), *Essays on restrictiveness and learnability*. Dordrecht: Kluwer Academic Publishers, 198–255.]

—— —— (1992). *Move α*. Cambridge, MA: MIT Press.

Leakey, R. E. (1994). *The Origin of Humankind*. New York: Basic Books.

Lebeaux, D. (1984). 'Anaphoric Binding and the Definition of PRO', in C. Jones and P. Sells (eds.), *North East Linguistic Society* 14, Graduate Linguistic Student Association. Amherst: University of Massachusetts.

Lees, R. B. (1963). *The Grammar of English Nominalizations*. Bloomington: Indiana University.

Legate, J. (2002). 'The Hows of Wh-Scope Marking in Warlpiri', handout of paper presented at North East Linguistic Society 33, MIT.

—— (2003). 'Some Interface Properties of the Phase', *Linguistic Inquiry* 34: 506–16.

—— and Yang, C. (2007). 'Morphosyntactic Learning and the Development of Tense' *Language Acquisition* 14 (3): 315–44.

Legendre, G. (2007). 'Optimizing Auxiliary Selection in Romance', in R. Aranovich (ed.), *Split Auxiliary systems*. Amsterdam/Philadelphia: John Benjamins, 145–80.

Leiss, E. (2000). *Artikel und Aspekt: Die grammatischen Muster von Definitheit. (Studia Linguistica Germanica* 55). Berlin/New York: Mouton de Gruyter.

Lenneberg, E. H. (1967). *Biological Foundations of Language*. New York, John Wiley & Sons.

Leu, T. (2008). *The Internal Syntax of Determiners*. Ph.D. dissertation, New York University.

Levelt, W. J. M., Roelofs, A., and Meyer, A. S. (1999). 'A theory of lexical access in speech production'. *Behavioral and Brain Sciences* 22(1)–75.

Levin, B. (2008). 'Dative Verbs and Dative Alternation from a Crosslinguistic Perspective'. Ms., Department of Linguistics, Stanford University.

Levitt J. J., McCarley R. W., Dickey C. C., Voglmaier M. M., Niznikiewicz M. A., Seidman L. J., Hirayasu Y., Ciszewski A. A., Kikinis R., Jolesz F. A., and Shenton M. E. (2002). 'MRI Study of Caudate Nucleus Volume and Its Cognitive Correlates in Neuroleptic-naive Patients with Shizotypal Personality Disorder', *American Journal of Psychiatry* 159: 1190–7.

Levy, Y., and Schaeffer, J. C. (eds.) (2003). *Language Competence across Populations: Towards a Definition of Specific Language Impairment*. Mahwah: Erlbaum.

Lewontin, R. C. (1983). 'The Organism as the Subject and Object of Evolution', *Scientia* 118: 65–95.

——(1989). 'Inferring the Number of Evolutionary Events from DNA Coding Sequence Differences', *Molecular Biology and Evolution* 6(1): 15–32.

——(1998). 'The Evolution of Cognition: Questions We Will Never Answer', in D. Scarborough and S. Sternberg (eds.). *An Invitation to Cognitive Science - Vol. 4 Methods, Models and Conceptual Issues*. Cambridge, MA: MIT Press, 107–32.

——(2000). *The Triple Helix*. Cambridge, MA: Harvard University Press.

——(2002). 'Directions in Evolutionary Biology', *Annual Reviews Genetics* 36: 1–18.

Li, G., Wang, J., Rossiter, S. J., Jones, G., and Zhang, S. (2007). 'Accelerated FoxP2 Evolution in Echolocating Bats', *PLoS Biology* 9: e900 1–10.

Lieberman, P. (1991). *Uniquely Human: The Evolution of Speech, Thought, and Selfless Behaviour*. Cambridge, MA: Harvard University Press.

——(2000). *Human Language and Our Reptilian Brain: The Subcortical Bases of Speech, Syntax and Thought*. Cambridge, MA: Harvard University Press.

——and Crelin, E. S. (1971). 'On the Speech of Neanderthal Man', *Linguistic Inquiry* 2: 203–22.

——Klatt, D. H., and Wilson, W. H. (1969). 'Vocal Tract Limitations on the Vowel Repertoires of Rhesus Monkeys and Other Nonhuman Primates', *Science* 164: 1185–7.

Liegeois, F., Baldeweg, T., Connelly, A., Gadian D. G., Mishkin, M., and Vargha-Khadem, F. (2003). 'Language fMRI Abnormalities Associated with FOXP2 Gene Mutation', *Nature Neuroscience* 6(1): 1230–7.

Lightfoot, D. (1991a). 'Subjacency and Sex', *Language and Communication* 11(1): 67–9.

Lightfoot, D. (1991b). *How to Set Parameters: Arguments from Language Change.* Cambridge, MA: MIT Press.

—— (1998). 'The Development of Grammars', *Glot International* 3(1): 3–8.

—— (1999). *The Development of Language: Acquisition, Change and Evolution.* Oxford: Blackwell.

Lin, J.-W. (2003). 'Temporal Reference in Mandarin Chinese', *Journal of East Asian Linguistics* 12: 259–311.

—— (2006). 'Time in a Language without Tense: The Case of Chinese', *Journal of Semantics* 23: 1–53.

Logan, K., Mayberry, M., and Fletcher, J. (1996). 'The Short-term Memory of Profoundly Deaf People for Words, Signs, and Abstract Spatial Stimuli', *Applied Cognitive Psychology* 10: 105–19.

Lohr, M. (1998). *Methods for the Genetic Classification of Languages.* Ph.D. dissertation, University of Cambridge.

Longobardi, G. (2001a). 'Formal Syntax, Diachronic Minimalism and Etymology: The History of French *chez*', *Linguistic Inquiry* 32(2): 275–302.

—— (2001b). 'The Structure of DPs: Some Principles, Parameters and Problems', in M. Baltin and C. Collins (eds.), *The Handbook of Contemporary Syntactic Theory.* Oxford: Blackwell, 562–603.

—— (2003). 'Methods in Parametric Linguistics and Cognitive History', *Linguistic Variation Yearbook* 3: 101–38.

Longobardi, G. (2005a). 'A Minimalist Program for Parametric Linguistics?', in H. Broekhuis, N. Corver, R. Huybregts, U. Kleinhenz, and J. Koster (eds.), *Organizing Grammar*, Berlin/New York: Mouton de Gruyter, 407–14.

—— (2005b). 'Towards a Unified Grammar of Reference', *Zeitschrift für Sprachwissenschaft* 24: 5–44.

Lopez, A. J. (1998). 'Alternative Splicing of pre-mRNA: Developmental Consequences and Mechanism of Regulation', *Annual Reviews of Genetics* 32: 279–305.

Loporcaro, M. (1999). 'L'ausiliazione Perfettiva nelle Parlate di Zagarolo e Colonna (Roma) e lo Studio della Sintassi dei Dialetti Moderni', *Contributi di Filologia dell'Italia Mediana*, 13: 203–26.

—— (2007). 'On Triple Auxiliation in Romance', *Linguistics* 45: 173–222.

Lorenz, K. (1959). 'Psychologie und Stammesgeschichte', in G. Heberer, (ed.), *Evolution der Organismen.* Stuttgart: Fischer, 131–70.

Lorenzo, G., and Longa, V. M. (2003). *Homo Loquens. Biología y Evolución del Lenguaje.* Lugo: Tris Tram.

Lukhtanov, V.A., Kandul, N. P., Plotkin, J. B., Dantchenko, A.V., Haig, D. and Pierce, N. E. (2005). 'Reinforcement of Pre-zygotic Isolation and Karyotype Evolution in Agrodiaetus Butteries', *Nature* 436: 385–9.

Luria, S. (1974). 'A Debate on Bio-linguistics', paper presented at Centre Royaumont pour une Science de l'Homme. Dedham MA: Endicott House.

Lynch, M. (2007). *The Origins of Genome Architecture.* Sunderland: Sinauer.

Lyons, J. (1967). 'A Note on Possessive, Existential and Locative Sentences', *Foundations of Language* 3: 390–6.

McCawley, J. (1974). 'On Identifying the Remains of Deceased Clauses', in J. McCawley. *Adverbs, Vowels, and Other Objects of Wonder*. Chicago: University of Chicago Press. 74–85.

McDonald, J. H., and Kreitman, M. (1991). 'Adaptive Protein Evolution at the *Adh* Locus in *Drosophila*', *Nature* 351: 652–4.

MacDonald, M. C., Pearlmutter, N. J., and Seidenberg, M. S. (1994). 'The Lexical Nature of Syntatic Ambiguity Resolution', *Psychological Review* 101: 676–703.

McGee, A. W., Yang, Y. Fischer, Q. S., Daw, N. W., and Strittmatter, S. M. (2005). 'Experience-Driven Plasticity of Visual Cortex Limited by Myelin and Nogo Receptor', *Science* 309(5744): 2222–6.

McGonigle, B. O., and Chalmers, M. (1977). 'Are Monkeys Logical?', *Nature* 267: 694–7.

————— (2007). 'Ordering and Executive Functioning as a Window on the Evolution and Development of Cognitive Systems', *International Journal of Comparative Psychology* 19(2): 241–67.

————— (2008). 'Putting Decartes before the Horse (Again!)', *Behavioral and Brain Sciences* 31: 142–3.

————— and Dickinson, A. (2003). 'Concurrent Disjoint and Reciprocal Classification by *Cebus Apella* in Serial Ordering Tasks: Evidence for Hierarchical Organization', *Animal Cognition* 6: 185–97.

McMahon, A. (2005). 'Introduction', *Transactions of the Philological Society* 103(2): 113–19.

——— and McMahon, R. (2003). 'Finding Families: Quantitative Methods in Language Classifying', *Transactions of the Philological Society* 101(1): 7–55.

————— (2005). *Language Classification by Numbers*. Oxford University Press, Oxford.

Mackridge, P. (1985). *The Modern Greek Language: A Descriptive Analysis of Standard Modern Greek*. Cambridge: Cambridge University Press.

MacNeilage, P. (2008). *The Origin of Speech*. New York, Oxford University Press.

MacPhail, E. (1982). *Brain and Intelligence in Vertebrates*. Oxford: Clarendon Press.

——— (1987). 'The Comparative Psychology of Intelligence', *Behavioral and Brain Sciences* 10: 645–95.

——— (1998). *The Evolution of Consciousness*. Oxford: Oxford University Press.

MacSwan, J. (2000). 'The Architecture of the Bilingual Language Faculty: Evidence from Intrasentential Code switching', *Bilingualism: Language and Cognition* 3: 37–54.

MacWhinney, B. (1995). *The CHILDES Project: Tools for Analyzing Talk*. Mahwah: Lawrence Erlbaum.

Maiden, M., and Parry, M. (eds.) (1997). *The Dialects of Italy*. London: Routledge.

Maini, P. K., Baker, R. E, and Chuong, C.-C. (2006). 'Developmental Biology: The Turing Model Comes of Molecular Age', *Science* 314(5804): 1397–8.

Manzini, M. R. (1986). 'On Italian *si*', in Borer, H. (ed.), *The Syntax of Pronominal Clitics* (*Syntax and Semantics* 18). New York: Academic Press, 241–62.

—— (2000). 'Sentential Complementation: The Subjunctive', in C. Peter, M. Everaert, and J. Grimshaw (eds.), *Lexical Specification and Insertion*. Amsterdam/Philadelphia: John Benjamins, 241–67.

—— (2007). 'The Structure and Interpretation of (Romance) Complementizers'. Ms., University of Florence.

—— (2008). 'Doubling by Clitics and Doubling of Clitics', in S. Barbiers (ed.), *Syntactic Doubling in European Dialects* (*Syntax and Semantics*), Amsterdam: Emerald, 69–101.

—— (2009). 'Pro, pro and NP-trace (Raising) are Interpretations', in K. Grohmann (ed.), *Phase theory: Features, Arguments, Interpretations*. North Holland Linguistic Series: Linguistic Variation. Amsterdam/Oxford: Elsevier, 131–80.

—— and Roussou, A. (2000). 'A Minimalist Theory of A-movement and Control', *Lingua* 110: 409–47.

—— and Savoia, L. M. (2001). 'The Syntax of Object Clitics: *si* in Italian Dialects', in G. Cinque and G. Salvi (eds.), *Current Studies in Italian Syntax: Essays to Honour Lorenzo Renzi*. Amsterdam: North Holland, 234–64.

—— —— (2005). *I Dialetti Italiani e Romanci: Morfosintassi Generativa* (3 vols.). Alessandria: Edizioni dell'Orso.

—— —— (2007). *A Unification of Morphology and Syntax* (*Studies in Romance and Albanian Dialects*). London: Routledge.

—— —— (2008). 'Non-active Voice in Albanian: Implications for the Theory of Movement', in L. M. Savoia (ed.), *Studi Sulle Varietà Arbëreshe*. Rende: Università degli Studi della Calabria, 111–49.

—— —— (2009). 'Mesoclisis in the Imperative: Phonology, Morphology or Syntax?', in V. Moscati, E. Servidio (eds), *Proceedings XXVIII Incontro di Grammatica Generativa, Studies in Linguistics on line 3*, Università di Siena: 51–76.

—— —— (2010). 'Syncretism and Suppletivism in Clitic Systems: Underspecification, Silent Clitics or Neither?', in R. D'Alessandro, A. Ledgeway, and I. Roberts (eds.), *Syntactic Variation: The Dialects of Italy*. Cambridge: Cambridge University Press, 86–101.

—— Roussou, A., and Savoia, L. M. (in press). 'The Morphosyntax of Non-active Voice in Albanian and Greek', in S. Ozsoy (ed.), *Proceedings of the Mediterranean Syntax Meeting* 2. Istanbul, Turkey.

Marantz, A. (1984). *On the Nature of Grammatical Relations*. Cambridge, MA: MIT Press.

—— (1995). 'The Minimalist Program', in G. Webelhuth (ed.), *Government and Binding and the Minimalist Program*. Oxford: Blackwell, 349–82.

—— (2000). 'Words'. Ms., MIT.

—— (2008). 'Words and Phases', in S.-H. Choe (ed.), *Phases in the Theory of Grammar*. Seoul: Dong, 191–222.

Maratsos, M. (2000). 'More Overregularizations After All: New Data and Discussion on Marcus, Pinker, Ullman, Hollander, Rosen, and Xu', *Journal of Child Language* 27: 183–212.

Marcus, G. F. (2001). *The Algebraic Mind: Integrating Connectionism and Cognitive Science*. Cambridge, MA: MIT Press.

—— (2006). 'Cognitive Architecture and Descent with Modification', *Cognition* 101: 443–65.

—— (2008). *Kluge*. Boston: Houghton Miffin.

—— Brinkmann, U., Clahsen, H., Wiese, R., and Pinker, S. (1995). 'German Inflection: The Exception that Proves the Rule', *Cognitive Psychology* 29: 189–256.

—— and Fisher, S. E. (2003). '*FOXP2* in Focus: What can Genes Tell Us about Speech and Language?', *Trends in Cognitive Science* 7(6): 257–62.

—— Pinker, S., Ullman, M., Hollander, M., Rosen, J., and Xu, F. (1992). *Overregularization in Language Acquisition,* Monographs of the Society for Research in Child Development, No. 57.

Martin, R. C. (1987). 'Articulatory and Phonological Deficits in Short-term Memory and Their Relation to Syntactic Processing', *Brain and Language* 32: 137–58.

—— (2006). 'The Neuropsychology of Sentence Processing: Where Do We Stand?', *Cognitive Neuropsychology* 25: 1–22.

—— and He, T. (2004). 'Semantic Short-term Memory and Its Role in Sentence Processing: A Replication', *Brain and Language* 89: 76–82.

—— and Romani, C. (1994). 'Verbal Working Memory and Sentence Processing: Multiple Components View', *Neuropsychology* 8: 506–23.

Matthewson, L. (2006). 'Presuppositions and Cross-linguistic Variation'. Ms., University of British Columbia.

—— (2008). 'Pronouns, Presuppositions, and Semantic Variation', paper presented at Semantic and Linguistic Theory 18, University of Massachusetts, Amherst.

Matushansky, O. (2006). 'Head Movement in Linguistic Theory', *Linguistic Inquiry* 37: 69–109.

Maynard-Smith, J., Burian, J. R., Kauffman, S., Alberch, P., Campbell, J., Goodwin, B., Lande, R., Raup, D., and Wolpert, L. (1985). 'Developmental Constraints and Evolution: A Perspective From the Mountain Lake Conference on Development and Evolution', *The Quarterly Review of Biology* 60(3): 265–87.

Mayol, L., and Yang, C. (2008). 'Regularities in Spanish Irregular Morphology'. Ms., Department of Linguistics. University of Pennsylvania. Philadelphia.

Mayr, E. (1970). *Populations, Species and Evolution*. Cambridge, MA: Harvard University Press.

—— (2004). *What Makes Biology Unique?: Considerations on the Autonomy of a Scientific Discipline*. Cambridge: Cambridge University Press.

Meader, C. L. and J. H. Muysken. 1950. *Handbook of Biolinguistics*. Toledo: Herbert Weller.

Millen, K. J., Millonig, J. H., Wingate, R. J. T., Alder, J., and Hatten, M. E. (1999). 'Neurogenetics of the Cerebellar System', *Journal of Child Neurology* 14(9): 574–81.

Miller, G. A. (1956). 'The Magical Number Seven, Plus or Minus Two: Some Limits on Our Capacity for Processing Information', *Psychological Review* 63: 81–97.

—— (2008). 'Living in a World of Unfamiliar Voices', *Science NOW Daily News*, April 14.

—— and Chomsky, N. (1963). 'Finitary Models of Language Users', in R. D. Luce, R. Bush, and E. Galanter (eds.), *Handbook of Mathematical Psychology* (419–92). New York: John Wiley.

Mitchell, T. (1982). 'Generalization as Search', *Artificial Intelligence* 18: 203–26.

Mitchener, W. G. (2003). 'Bifurcation Analysis of the Fully Symmetric Language Dynamical Equation', *Journal of Mathematical Biology* 46(3): 265–85.

Mithen, S. J. (1996). *The Prehistory of the Mind*. London: Thames and Hudson.

Mittwoch, A. (1982). 'On the Difference Between Eating and Eating Something: Activities Versus Accomplishments', *Linguistic Inquiry* 13(1): 113–22.

Miyake, A., Carpenter, P., and Just, M. A. (1994). 'A Capacity Approach to Syntactic Comprehension Disorders: Making Normal Adults Perform Like Aphasic Patients', *Cognitive Neuropsychology* 11: 671–717.

—— Emerson M. J., and Friedman N. P. (1999). 'Good Interactions Are Hard to Find', *Behavioral and Brain Sciences* 22: 108–9.

Monod, J. (1970). *Le Hasard et la nécessité*. Paris: Seuil.

—— (1972). *Chance and Necessity: An Essay on the Natural Philosophy of Modern Biology*. New York: Vintage Books.

Montell, D. J. (2008). 'Morphogenetic Cell Movements: Diversity from Modular Mechanical Properties' *Science* 322: 1502–5.

Moro, A. (1997). *The Raising of Predicates*. Cambridge: Cambridge University Press.

—— (2000). *Dynamic Antisymmetry*. Cambridge, MA: MIT Press.

Morpurgo Davies, A. (1996). *La linguistica dell'ottocento*. Bologna: Il Mulino.

Motapanyane, V. (1995). *Theoretical Implications of Complementation in Romanian*. Padua: Unipress.

Mukherji, N. (2010). *The Primacy of Grammar*. Cambridge, MA: MIT Press.

Müller, F. M. (1861). 'The Theoretical Stage, and the Origin of Language', in *Lectures on the Science of Language*. London: Longman, Green, Longman, and Roberts.

—— (1873). 'Lectures on Mr. Darwin's Philosophy of Language', *Fraser's Magazine* 7(8): 147–233.

Müller, G. (2007). 'Evo-devo: Extending the Evolutionary Synthesis', *Nature Review Genetics* 8: 943–9.

Murray, C. D. (1926). 'The Physiological Principle of Minimum Work. Part I: The Vascular System and the Cost of Blood Volume', *Proceedings of the National Academy of Sciences* 12: 207–14.

Murray, W., and Forster, K. (2004). 'Serial Mechanisms in Lexical Access: The Rank Hypothesis', *Psychological Review* 111: 721–56.

Nagorcka, B. N. (1983–4). 'Evidence for a Reaction-diffusion System as a Mechanism Controlling Mammalian Hair Growth', *Biosystems* 16(3–4): 323–32.

Nash, D. (1986). *Topics in Warlpiri Syntax*. New York: Garland.

Nerbonne, J. (2007). 'Review of McMahon, A., and McMahon, R.: Language Classification by Numbers', *Linguistic Typology* 11: 425–36.

—— and Kretzschmar, W. (2003). 'Introducing Computational Methods in Dialectometry', in J. Nerbonne and W. Kretzschmar (eds.), *Computational Methods in Dialectometry*, special issue of *Computers and the Humanities* 37(3): 245–55.

Newmeyer, F. (2004). 'Against a Parameter-setting Approach to Language Variation', *Language Variation Yearbook* 4: 181–234.

—— (2005). *Possible and Probable Languages*. Oxford: Oxford University Press.

Nichols, J. (1992). *Linguistic Diversity in Space and Time*. Chicago: Chicago University Press.

—— (1996). 'The Comparative Method as Heuristic', in M. Durie and M. Ross (eds.), *The Comparative Method Reviewed: Regularity and Irregularity in Language Change*. Oxford: Oxford University Press, 39–71.

Nicoladis, E. (2007). 'Acquisition of Deverbal Compounds by French-speaking Preschoolers', *The Mental Lexicon* 2(1): 79–102.

Nicolis, M. (2006). 'The Null Subject Parameter and Correlating Properties: The case of Creole Languages'. Ms., University of Siena.

Niemi, J., Laine, M., and Tuominen, J. (1994). 'Cognitive Morphology in Finnish: Foundations of a New Model', *Language and Cognitive Processes* 9: 423–46.

Nilsson, D.-E., and Pelger, S. (1994). 'Eye Evolution', *Proceedings of the Royal Society of London* 256: 53–8.

Niyogi, P. (2004). 'Phase Transitions in Language Evolution', in L. Jenkins (ed.), *Variation and Universals in Biolinguistics*. Amsterdam: Elsevier, 57–74.

—— (2006). *The Computational Nature of Learning and Evolution*. Cambridge, MA: MIT Press.

—— and Berwick, R. C. (1996). 'A Language Learning Model for Finite Parameter Spaces', *Cognition* 61(1–2): 161–93.

—— —— (2009). 'The Proper Treatment of Language Acquisition and Change in a Population Setting', *PNAS*, 106(25): 10124–10129.

Nowak, M. A. (2006). *Evolutionary Dynamics: Exploring the Equations of Life*. Cambridge: Belknap Press of Harvard University Press.

—— Komarova, N., and Niyogi, P. (2002). 'Computational and Evolutionary Aspects of Language', *Nature* 417: 611–17.

O'Neil, W. (1976). 'Clause Adjunction in Old English', *General Linguistics* 17: 199–212.

Ogihara, T. (1996). *Tense, Attitudes, and Scope*. Dordrecht: Kluwer Academic Publishers.

Origgi, G., and Sperber, D. (2000). 'Evolution Communication and the Proper Function of Language', in P. Carruthers and A. Chamberlain (eds.), *Evolution and the Human Mind: Language, Modularity and Social Cognition*. Cambridge: Cambridge University Press, 140–69.

Orr, H. (2002). 'The Population Genetics of Adaptation: The Adaptation of DNA Sequences', *Evolution* 56: 1317–30.

—— (2005a). 'A Revolution in the Field of Evolution?', *The New Yorker* October 24.

Orr, H. (2005b). 'The Genetic Theory of Adaptation: A Brief History', *Nature Reviews Genetics* 6: 119–27.

Otero, C. (1990). 'The Emergence of Homo loquens and the Laws of Physics', *Behavioral and Brain Sciences* 13: 747–50.

Ouhalla, J. (1991). *Functional Categories and Parametric Variation.* London: Routledge.

Owen, R. (1846). 'Report on the Archetype and Homologies of the Vertebrate Skeleton', *Report of the British Association for the Advancement of Science* 1846: 169–340.

Packard, M. G., and Knowlton, B. J. (2002). 'Learning and Memory Functions of the Basal Ganglia', *Annual Review of Neuroscience* 25: 563–93.

Pagel, M. D. (1992). 'A Method for the Analysis of Comparative Data', *Journal of Theoretical Biology* 156: 434–42.

—— Atkinson, Q. D., and Meade, A. (2007). 'Frequency of Word-use Predicts Rates of Lexical Evolution Throughout Indo-European History', *Nature* 449(7163): 717–20.

Palmer, A. R. (1994). 'Fluctuating Asymmetry Analyses: A primer', in T. A. Markow (ed.), *Developmental Instability: Its Origin and Evolutionary Implications.* Dordrecht: Kluwer Academic Publishers, 333–64.

—— (1996). 'From Symmetry to Asymmetry: Phylogenetic Patterns of Asymmetry Variation in Animals and Their Evolutionary Significance', *Proceedings of the National Academy of Sciences* 93: 14279–14286.

—— (2004a). 'Antisymmetry', in B. Hallgrimson and B. K. Hall (eds.), *Variation: A Central Concept in Biology.* Amsterdam: Elsevier, 359–90.

—— (2004b). 'Symmetry Breaking and the Evolution of Development', *Science,* 306: 828–33.

—— (2009). 'Animal Asymmetry', *Current Biology* 19: R473.

Panchen, A. L. (1994). 'Richard Owen and the Concept of Homology', in B. K. Hall (ed.), *Homology: The Hierarchical Basis of Comparative Biology.* San Diego: Academic Press, 21–62.

Papagno, C., Cecchetto, C., Reati, F., and Bello, L. (2007). 'Processing of Syntactically Complex Sentences Relies on Verbal Short-term Memory. Evidence From a STM Patient', *Cognitive Neuropsychology* 24(3): 292–311.

Parkes, A. P. (2002). *Introduction to Languages, Machines and Logic: Computable Languages, Abstract Machines and Formal Logic.* New York: Springer.

Parmley, J. L., Urrutia, A. O., Potrzebowski, L., Kaessmann, H., and Hurst, L. D. (2007). 'Splicing and the Evolution of Proteins in Mammals', *PLoS Biology* 5(2): e14.

Parsons, T. (1990). *Events in the Semantics of English.* Cambridge, MA: MIT Press.

Pearl, L. (2007). *Necessary Bias in Language Learning.* Ph.D. dissertation, University of Maryland.

Pearson, J. C., Lemons, D., and McGinnis, W. (2005). 'Modulating Hox Gene Functions During Animal Body Patterning', *Nature Reviews Genetics* 6: 893–904.

Penke, M., and Krause, M. (2002). 'German Noun Plurals: A Challenge to the Dual-mechanism Model', *Brain and Language* 81(1–3): 303–11.

Perner, J. (1991). *Understanding the Representational Mind*. Cambridge, MA: MIT Press.

Perruchet, P., and Rey, A. (2005). 'Does the Mastery of Center-embedded Linguistic Structures Distinguish Humans from Nonhuman Primates?', *Psychonomic Bulletin and Review* 12: 307–13.

Pesetsky, D. (1991). 'Zero Syntax. Vol 2: Infinitives'. Ms., http://web.mit.edu/linguistics/people/faculty/pesetsky/infins.pdf.

—— (1995). *Zero Syntax: Experiencers and Cascades*. Cambridge, MA: MIT Press.

—— and Torrego, E. (2004). 'Tense, Case, and the Nature of Syntactic Categories', in J. Guéron and J. Lecarme (eds.), *The Syntax of Time*. Cambridge, MA: MIT Press, 495–538.

Petitto, L. A. (1987). 'On the Autonomy of Language and Gesture: Evidence from the Acquisition of Personal Pronouns in American Sign Language', *Cognition* 27(1): 1–52.

Petkov, C. I., Kayser, C., Steudel, T., Whittingstall, K., Augath, M., and Logothetis, N. K. (2008). 'A Voice Region in the Monkey Brain', *Nature Neuroscience* 11(3): 367–74.

Phillips, C. (1995). 'Syntax at Age 2: Cross-linguistic Differences', *MIT Working Papers In Linguistics* 26: 325–82.

—— (2003). 'Linear Order and Constituency', *Linguistic Inquiry* 34(2): 37–90.

Piatigorsky, J., and Kozmik, Z. (2004). 'Cubozoan Jellyfish: An Evo/devo Model for Eyes and Other Sensory Systems', *International Journal of Developmental Biology* 48: 719–29.

Piattelli-Palmarini, M. (1974). 'A Debate on Biolinguistics'. Centre Royaumont pour une science de l'homme report. Conference held at Endicott House, Dedham, Massachusetts, 20–21 May 1974.

—— (1986). 'The rise of selective theories: A case study and some lessons from immunology', in W. Demopoulos and A. Marros (eds.), *Language learning and concept acquisition*. Norwood, NJ: Ablex, 117–30.

—— (1989). 'Evolution, Selection and Cognition: From "learning" to Parameter Setting in Biology and in the Study of Language', *Cognition* 31: 1–44.

—— and Uriagereka, J. (2004). 'The Immune Syntax: The Evolution of the Language virus', in L. Jenkins (ed.), *Variation and Universals in Biolinguistics*. Amsterdam: Elsevier, 342–72.

—— —— (2005). 'The Evolution of the Narrow Language Faculty: The Skeptical View and a Reasonable Conjecture', *Lingue e Linguaggio* 4: 27–79.

—— —— (2008). 'Still a Bridge Too Far? Biolinguistic Questions for Grounding Language on Brains', *Physics of Life Reviews* 5: 207–24.

—— —— and Salaburu, P., (eds.) (2009). *Of Minds and Language: A Dialogue with Noam Chomsky in the Basque Country*. Oxford: Oxford University Press.

Pierce, A. (1989). *On the Emergence of Syntax: A Cross-linguistic Study*. Doctoral dissertation, Massachusetts Institute of Technology.

—— (1992). *Language Acquisition and Syntactic Theory*. Boston: Kluwer Academic Publishers.

Pietroski, P. M. (2005). *Events and Their Architecture*. Oxford: Oxford University Press.

—— (2007). 'Systematicity via Monadicity', *Croatian Journal of Philosophy* 7: 343–74.

—— (to appear). *Semantics without Truth Values*. Oxford: Oxford University Press.

Pigliucci, M. (2007). 'Do We Need an Extended Evolutionary Synthesis?', *International Journal of Organic Evolution* 61: 2743–9.

Pinker, S. (1984). *Language Learnability and Language Development*. Cambridge, MA: Harvard University Press.

—— (1989). *Language Learnability and Cognition*. Cambridge, MA: MIT Press.

—— (1994a). 'On Language (Interview)', *Journal of Cognitive Neuroscience* 6(1): 92–7.

—— (1994b). *The Language Instinct*. New York: William Morrow and Company, Inc.

—— (1997). *How the Mind Works*. New York: W. W. Norton & Co.

—— (1999). *Words and Rules: The Ingredients of Language*. New York: Basic Books.

—— and Bloom, P. (1990). 'Natural Language and Natural Selection', *The Behavioral and Brain Sciences* 13: 704–84.

—— and Jackendoff, R. (2005). 'The Faculty of Language: What's Special About It?', *Cognition* 95: 201–36.

—— and Ullman, M. (2002). 'The Past and Future of Past Tense', *Trends in Cognitive Sciences*, 11(1): 456–63.

Pintzuk, S., Tsoulas, G., and Warner, A. (eds.) (2000). *Diachronic Syntax: Models and Mechanisms*. Oxford: Oxford University Press.

Plank, F. (ed.). (2003). *Noun Phrase Structure in the Languages of Europe* (*Empirical Approaches to Language Typology* 20-7). Berlin/New York: Mouton de Gruyter.

Poelwijk, F., Kiviet, D. J., Weinreich, D. M., and Tans, S. J. (2007). 'Empirical Fitness Landscapes Reveal Accessible Evolutionary Paths', *Nature* 445(25): 383–6.

Poeppel, D., and Embick, D. (2006). 'The Relation Between Linguistics and Neuroscience', in A. Cutler (ed.), *Twenty-first Century Psycholinguistics: Four Cornerstones*. Mahwah: Lawrence Erlbaum, 173–89.

—— and Wexler, K. (1993). 'The Full Competence Hypothesis', *Language* 69: 1–33.

Poletto, C. (1995). 'Complementiser Deletion and Verb Movement in Italian', *Working Papers in Linguistics*, University of Venice.

—— (2000). *The Higher Functional Field: Evidence from Northern Italian Dialects*. Oxford: Oxford University Press.

Poletto, C. (2001). 'Complementizer Deletion and Verb Movement in Standard Italian', in G. Cinque and G. Salvi (eds.), *Current Studies in Italian Syntax*. Amsterdam: Elsevier, 265–86.

Poole, J. H., Tyack, P. L., Stoeger-Horwath, A. S., and Watwood, S. (2005). 'Elephants Are Capable of Vocal Learning', *Nature* 434: 455–6.

Portner, P. (1997). 'The Semantics of Mood, Complementation and Conversational Force', *Natural Language Semantics* 5: 167–212.

Postal, P. M. (1966). 'On So-Called "Pronouns" in English', in F. P. Dineen (ed.), *Report of the Seventeenth Annual Roundtable Meeting on Linguistics and Language Studies*. Washington, DC: Georgetown University Press, 177–206. [reprinted in D. A. Reibel and S. A. Schane (eds.) (1969), *Modern Studies in English*. Englewood Cliffs: Prentice-Hall.].

Potts, C., and Roeper, T. (2006). 'The Narrowing Acquisition Path: From Expressive Small Clauses to Declaratives', in L. Progovac, K. Paesani, E. Casielles, and E. Barton (eds.), *The Syntax of Nonsententials: Multi-Disciplinary Perspectives*. Amsterdam/Philadelphia: John Benjamins, 183–201.

Pough, F. H., Heiser, J. B., and McFarland, W. N. (1996). *Vertebrate Life*. Upper Saddle River: Prentice-Hall.

Prather, G. F., Peters, F., Nowicki, S., and Mooney, R. (2008). 'Precise Auditory–Vocal Mirroring in Neurons for Learned Vocal Communication', *Nature* 451(17): 305–12.

Pulvermüller, F. (1999). 'Words in the Brain's Language', *Behavioral and Brain Sciences* 22: 253–336.

Pylyshyn, Z. W. (2007). *Things and Places: How the Mind Connects with the World*. Cambridge, MA: MIT Press.

Quer, J. (1998). *Mood at the Interface*. The Hague: Holland Academic Graphics.

Quine, W. V. (1968). *Ontological Relativity and Other Essays*. New York: Columbia University Press.

Quiring, R., Walldorf, U., Kloter, U., and Gehring, W. J. (1994). 'Homology of the Eyeless Gene of Drosophila to the Small Eye Gene in Mice and Aniridia in Humans', *Science* 265: 785–9.

Radford, A. (1997). *Syntax: A Minimalist Introduction*. Cambridge: Cambridge University Press.

Ralls, K., Fiorelli, P., and Gish, S. (1985). 'Vocalizations and Vocal Mimicry in Captive Harbor Seals, *Phoca vitulina*', *Canadian Journal of Zoology* 63: 1050–6.

Ramón y Cajal, S. (1999). *Texture of the Nervous System of Man and the Vertebrates*. New York: Springer.

Raposo, E. (2002). 'Nominal Gaps with Prepositions Modifiers in Portuguese and Spanish: A Case for Quick Spell-Out', *Cuadernos de Linguistica del U. Ortega y Gasset* 9: 127–44.

Rappaport Hovav, M., and Levin, B. (2008). 'The English Dative Alternation: The Case for Verb Sensitivity', *Journal of Linguistics* (44): 129–67.

Real Puigdollers, C. (2007). 'The Status of Cognate Objects in Romance', paper presented at the 17th Colloquium on Generative Grammar, Girona, Spain.

Reinhart, T. (1978). *Anaphora and Semantic Interpretation*. Chicago: University of Chicago Press.

—— (2000). 'The Theta System: Syntactic Realization of Verbal Concepts', *OTS Working Paper in Linguistics* February.

—— (2006). *Interface Strategies: Optimal and Costly Computations*. Cambridge, MA: MIT Press.

—— and Siloni, T. (2005). 'The Lexicon-Syntax Parameter: Reflexivization and Other Arity Operations', *Linguistic Inquiry* 36: 389–436.

Renfrew, C. (1987). *Archaeology and Language: The Puzzle of Indo-European Origins*. Jonathan Cape, London.

Restifo, L. L. (2005). 'Mental Retardation Genes in Drosophila: New Approaches to Understanding and Treating Developmental Brain Disorders.' *Mental Retardation and Developmental Disabilities Research Reviews* 11: 286–94.

Rice, M. L., Wexler, K., and Clieve, P. L. (1995). 'Specific Language Impairment as a Period of Extended Optional Infinitive', *Journal of Speech and Hearing Research* 38: 850–63.

Richards, M. (2007). 'On Feature-inheritance: An Argument from the Phase Impenetrability Condition', *Linguistic Inquiry* 38: 563–72.

Rigon, G. (2009). *A Quantitative Approach to the Study of Syntactic Evolution*. Ph.D. dissertation, Università di Pisa.

Ringe, D. (1992). 'On Calculating the Factor of Chance in Language Comparison', *Transactions of the American Philosophical Society* 82(1): 1–110.

—— (1996). 'The Mathematics of "Amerind" ', *Diachronica* 13: 135–54.

—— Warnow, T., and Taylor, A. (2002). 'Indo-European and Computational Cladistics', *Transactions of the Philological Society* 100(1): 59–129.

Ritter, E., and Wiltschko, M. (2005). 'Anchoring Events to Utterances Without Tense', in J. Alderete, C.-H. Han, and A. Kochetov (eds.), *Proceedings of the 24th West Coast Conference on Formal Linguistics*. Somerville: Cascadilla Press, 343–51.

—— and Wiltschko, M. (2008). 'Varieties of INLF: Tense, Location and Person'. Ms., University of British Columbia.

Riva, D., and Giorgi, C. (2000). 'The Cerebellum Contributes to Higher Functions During Development: Evidence from a Series of Children Surgically Treated for Posterior Fossa Tumours', *Brain* 123: 1052–61.

Rivest, R. (1976). 'On Self-organizing Sequential Search Heuristics', *Communications of the Association for Computing Machinery* 2: 63–7.

Rizzi, L. (1982). *Issues in Italian Syntax*. Dordrecht: Foris.

—— (1986). 'Null Objects in Italian and the Theory of pro', *Linguistic Inquiry* 17: 501–57.

—— (1997). 'The Fine Structure of the Left Periphery', in Haegeman (ed.), *Elements of Grammar 1*. Dordrecht: Kluwer Academic Publishers, 281–27.

—— (2007). 'Grammatically-based Target-inconsistencies in Child Language', *Proceedings of the Inaugural GALANA conference, UConn Occasional Papers in Linguistics #4*, Cambridge, MA: MITWPL: 19–49.

Roberts, I. (1998). 'Review of A. Harris and L. Campbell, Historical Syntax in Cross-linguistic Perspective', *Romance Philology* 51: 363–70.

—— (2004). 'Parametric Comparison: Welsh, Semitic and the Anti-Babelic Principle', lecture notes, University of Cambridge.

—— (2005). *Principles and Parameters in a VSO Language: A Case Study in Welsh*. Oxford: Oxford University Press.

—— (2007a). 'The Mystery of the Overlooked Discipline: Modern Syntactic Theory and Cognitive Science', Ms, University of Cambridge.

—— (2007b). *Diachronic Syntax*. Oxford: Oxford University Press.

—— and Roussou, A. (1999). 'A Formal Approach to "Grammaticalization"', *Linguistics* 37(6): 1011–41.

—— —— (2002). *Syntactic Change*. Cambridge: Cambridge University Press.

—— —— (2003). *Syntactic Change: A Minimalist Approach to Grammaticalization*. Cambridge: Cambridge University Press.

Rochefort, C., He, X., Scotto-Lomassese, S., and Scharff, C. (2007). 'Recruitment of FoxP2-expressing Neurons to Area X Varies During Song Development', *Developmental Neurobiology* 67: 809–17.

Rochon, E., Waters, G., and Caplan, D. (2000). 'The Relationship between Measures of Working Memory and Sentence Comprehension in Patients with Alzheimer's Disease', *Journal of Speech, Language and Hearing Research* 43: 395–413.

Roeper, T. (1996). 'The Role of Merger Theory and Formal Features in Acquisition', in H. Clahsen (ed.), *Generative Perspectives on Language Acquisition*. Amsterdam/Philadelphia: John Benjamins, 415–49.

——(2000). 'Universal Bilingualism', *Bilingualism: Language and Cognition* 2: 169–86.

——and de Villiers, J. (1994). 'Lexical Links in the WH Chain', in B. Lust, G. Hermon, and J. Kornfilt (eds.), *Syntactic Theory and First Language Acquisition: Cross-linguistic Perspectives*. Vol. II: *Binding, Dependence and Learnability*. Hillsdale. NJ: Lawrence Erlbaum, 357–90.

Rohlfs, G. (1966). *Grammatica storica della lingua italiana e dei suoi dialetti*. Vol. 1: *Fonetica*. Turin: Einaudi.

Romero, L. E., Walsh, V., and Papagno, C. (2006). 'The Neural Correlates of Phonological Short-term Memory: A Repetitive Transcranial Stimulation (rTMS) Study', *Journal of Cognitive Neuroscience* 18: 1147–55.

————and Cecchetto, C. (2008). 'The Role of STM in Sentence Comprehension: A Repetitive Transcranial Stimulation (rTMS) Study', paper presented at Congresso Internazione della Società di Linguistica Italiana, Scuola Normale Superiore, Pisa.

Ronshaugen, M., McGinnis, N., and McGinnis, W. (2002). 'Hox Protein Mutation and Macroevolution of the Insect Body Plan', *Nature* 415: 914–17.

Rosenbaum, P. S. (1967). *The Grammar of English Predicate Complement Constructions*. Cambridge, MA: MIT Press.

Ross, J. R. (1967). *Constraints on Variables in Syntax*. Ph.D. dissertation, MIT.

——(1969). 'Guess Who?', in R. I. Binnick, A. Davison, G. M. Green, and J. L. Morgan (eds.), *Papers from the Fifth Regional Meeting of the Chicago Linguistic Society*. Chicago: University of Chicago, 252–86.

——(1970). 'On Declarative Sentences', in R. A. Jacobs and P. S. Rosenbaum (eds.), *Readings in English Transformational Grammar*. Waltham, MA: Ginn, 222–72.

——(1976). 'To Have Have and to Not Have Have', in M. Jazayery, E. Polom, and W. Winter (eds.), *Linguistic and Literary Studies in Honor of Archibald Hill*. Lisse: Peter de Ridder, 263–70.

Roussou, A. (1999). 'Modals and the Subjunctive', in A. Alexiadou, G. Horrocks, and M. Stávrou (eds.), *Studies in Greek Syntax*. Dordrecht: Kluwer Academic Publishers, 169–83.

——(2009). 'In the Mood for Control', in J. Quer (ed.), *The Distribution and Interpretation of Indicative and Subjunctive*. Special issue, *Lingua* 119: 1811–36.

Rouveret, A. (1994). *Syntaxe du Gallois: Principes généraux et typologie*. Paris: CNRS Editions.

Rummelhart, D., and McClelland, J. (1987). *Parallel Distributed Processing*. Cambridge, MA: MIT Press.

Saccon, G. (1992). VP-internal Arguments and Locative Subjects. *North East Linguistic Society* 22: 383–97.

Saffran, J. R., Aslin, R. N., and Newport, E. L. (1996). 'Statistical Learning by 8-Month Old Infants', *Science* 274: 1926–8.

Saito, M., and Fukui, N. (1998). 'Order and Phrase Structure and Movement', *Linguistic Inquiry* 29: 439–74.

Sakas, W., and Fodor, J. D. (2001). 'The Structural Triggers Learner', in S. Bertolo (ed.), *Language Acquisition and Learnability*. Cambridge: Cambridge University Press. 172–233.

Saltarelli, M. (2008). 'Marsican Genitives', paper presented at the CISDID Conference on Italian and Dialects Today. Museo della Genti d'Abruzzo, Pescara.

Salvini-Plawen, L., and Mayr, E. (1961). 'On the Evolution of Photoreceptors and Eyes', in M. K. Hecht, W. C. Steere, and B. Wallace (eds.), *Evolutionary Biology* 10, New York: Plenum Press, 207–63.

Samuels, B. (2009). *The Structure of Phonological Theory*. Ph.D. dissertation, Harvard University.

Sauerland, U., and Gärtner, H-M. (eds.) (2007). *Interfaces + Recursion = Language?* Berlin: Mouton.

Savoia, L. M., and Manzini, M. R. (2007). 'Variazione sintattica nel costrutto ausiliare Arbëresh. La variazione come problema teorico', *Minoranze linguistiche: Prospettive, strumenti, territori.* Roma: Carocci, 85–102.

——— (2010). 'Lexicalization of 3rd Person Object Clitics: Clitic Enclisis and Clitic Drop', in R. D'Alessandro, A. Ledgeway, and I. Roberts (eds.), *Syntactic Variation: The Dialects of Italy*. Cambridge: Cambridge University Press, 102–18.

Scharff, C., and Haesler, S. (2005). 'An Evolutionary Perspective on FoxP2: Strictly for the Birds?', *Current Opinion in Neurobiology* 15: 694–703.

Schlenker, P. (2003). 'A Plea for Monsters', *Linguistics and Philosophy* 26: 29–120.

——— (2005). 'Non-Redundancy: Towards a Semantic Reinterpretation of Binding Theory', *Natural Language Semantics* 13(1): 1–92.

——— (2005a). 'The Lazy Frenchman's Approach to the Subjunctive: Speculations on Reference to Worlds and Semantics Defaults in the Analysis of Mood', in T. Geerts, I. van Ginneken, and H. Jocobs (eds.) 'Romance Languages and Linguistic Theory, Selected Papers from Œ︎Going Romance 2003', John Benjamins, 269–309.

Scorretti, M. (1994). *Complemetizer Deletion*. Ph.D. dissertation, University of Amsterdam.

Searls, D. (2002). 'The Language of Genes.' *Nature* 420: 211–17.

Sebüktekin, H. I. (1971). *Turkish-English Contrastive Analysis: Turkish Morphology and Corresponding English Structures*. The Hague: Mouton.

Segal, G. (1989). 'A Preference for Sense and Reference', *Journal of Philosophy* 86: 73–89.

—— (1998). 'Representing Representations', in P. Carruthers and J. Boucher (eds.), *Language and Thought: Interdisciplinary Themes*. Cambridge: Cambridge University Press, 146–61.

Séguy, J. (1971). 'La relation entre la distance spatiale et la distance lexicale', *Revue de Linguistique Romane* 35: 335–57.

Sereno, J., and Jongman, A. (1997). Processing of English Inflectional Morphology. *Memory and Cognition* 25: 425–37.

Shapiro, K. A., Moo, L. R., and Caramazza, A. (2006). 'Cortical Signatures of Noun and Verb Production', *Proceedings of the National Academy of Sciences* 103(5): 1644–9.

Sherman, M. (2007). 'Universal Genome in the Origin of Metazoa: Thoughts about Evolution', *Cell Cycle* 6(15): 1873–7.

Shieber, S. M. (1985). 'Evidence against the Context-freeness of Natural Language', *Linguistics and Philosophy* 8.

Shu, W., Cho, J. Y., Jiang, Y., Zhang, M., Weisz, D., Elder, G. A., Schmeidler, J., De Gasperi, R., Sosa, M. A., Rabidou, D., et al. (2005). 'Altered Ultrasonic Vocalization in Mice with a Disruption in the Foxp2 Gene', *Proceedings of the National Academy of Sciences USA* 102: 9643–8.

Shubin, N., Tabin, C., and Carroll, S. (1997). 'Fossils, Genes and the Evolution of Animal Limbs', *Nature* 388: 639–48.

Sick, S., Reinker, S., Timmer, J., and Schlake, T. (2006). 'WNT and DKK Determine Hair Follicle Spacing Through a Reaction-Diffusion Mechanism', *Science* 314(5804): 1447–50.

Sigurðsson, H. Á. (2009). 'Remarks on Features', in K. Grohmann (ed.), *Explorations of Phase Theory: Features and Arguments*. Berlin/New York: Mouton de Gruyter, 21–52.

Simpson, T. I., and Price, D. J. (2002). 'Pax6: A Pleiotropic Player in Development', *Bioessays* 24: 1041–51.

Skinner, B. F. (1957). *Verbal Behavior*. New York: Appleton Century Cross Inc.

Smith, C. (2007). 'Time With and Without Tense', in J. Guéron and J. Lacarme (eds.), *Proceedings, International Round Table on Tense and Modality*. Cambridge, MA: MIT Press.

—— and Erbaugh, M. (2005). 'Temporal Interpretation in Mandarin Chinese', *Linguistics* 43(4): 713–56.

Smith, L. (1982). 'An Analysis of Affixal Verb Derivation and Complementation in Labrador Inuttut', *Linguistic Analysis* 10: 161–89.

Snyder, W. (2007). *Child Language: The View from Parameters*. Oxford: Oxford University Press.

—— and Stromswold, K. (1997). 'The Structure and Acquisition of English Dative Constructions', *Linguistic Inquiry* 28(2): 281–317.

Somerville, M. J., Mervis, C.B., Young, E. J., Seo, E. J., del Campo, M., Bamforth, S., Peregrine, E., Loo, W., Lilley, M., Pérez-Jurado, L. A., Morris, C. A., Scherer, S. W., and Osborne, L. R. (2005). 'Severe Expressive-language Delay Related to Duplication of the Williams-Beuren Locus', *New England Journal of Medicine* 353(16): 1694–701.

Sonnenstuhl, I., and Huth, A. (2002). 'Processing and Representation of German *-n* Plurals: A Dual-mechanism Approach', *Brain and Language* 81(1–3): 276–90.

Sorace, A. (2000). 'Gradients in Auxiliary Selection with Intransitive Verbs', *Language* 76(4): 859–90.

Spelke, E. (2003). 'What Makes Us Smart? Core Knowledge and Natural Language', in D. Gentner and S. Goldin-Meadow (eds.), *Language and Mind: Advances in the Study of Language and Thought*. Cambridge, MA: MIT Press, 277–311.

Sperber, D., and Wilson, D. (1986). *Relevance*. Oxford: Blackwell.

Spinozzi, G., Natale, F., Langer, J., and Brakke, K. E. (1999). 'Spontaneous Class Grouping Behavior by Bonobos (*Pan Paniscus*) and Common Chimpanzees (*Pan Troglodytes*)', *Animal Cognition* 2: 157–70.

Spiteri, E., Konopka, G., Coppola, G., Bomar, J., Oldham, M., Ou, J., Vernes, S. C., Fisher, S. E., Ren, B., and Geschwind, D. H. (2007). 'Identification of the Transcriptional Targets of *FOXP2*, a Gene Linked to Speech and Language, in Developing Human Brain', *The American Journal of Human Genetics* 81(6): 1144–57.

Spruit, M. (2008). *Quantitative Perspectives on Syntactic Variation in Dutch Dialects*. Utrecht: Landelijke Onderzoekschool Taalwetenschap.

Stabler, E. P. (1997). 'Derivational Minimalism', in C. Retoré (ed.), *Logical Aspects of Computational Linguistics*. New York: Springer-Verlag (Lecture Notes in Computer Science 1328), 68–95.

——(2004). 'Varieties of Crossing Dependencies: Structure Dependence and Mild Context Sensitivity', *Cognitive Science* 28: 699–720.

Stávrou, M., and Terzi, A. (eds.) (2005). *Advances in Greek Generative Syntax: In Honor of Dimitra Theophanopoulou-Kontou*. Amsterdam/Philadelphia: John Benjamins.

Stent, G. S., and Calendar, R. (1978). *Molecular Genetics: An Introductory Narrative*. San Francisco: W. H. Freeman.

Sterelny, K. (2007). *Dawkins vs. Gould: Survival of the Fittest*. Cambridge: Icon.

Stevens, K. N. (1972). 'The Quantal Nature of Speech: Evidence from Articulatory-Acoustic Data', in E. E. David Jr. and P. B. Denes (eds.), *Human Communication: A Unified View*. New York: McGraw-Hill, 51–66.

——(1989). 'On the Quantal Nature of Speech', *Journal of Phonetics* 17(1–2): 3–45.

Stewart, I. (1995). 'Daisy, Daisy, Give Me Your Answer, Do', *Scientific American* 272: 96–9.

Stowell, T. (1981). *Origins of Phrase Structure*. Ph.D. dissertation, MIT.

——(1996). 'The Phrase Structure of Tense', in J. Roorick and L. Zaring (eds.), *Phrase Structure and the Lexicon*. Dordrecht: Kluwer Academic Publishers, 277–91.

Straus, K. (2008). *Validations of a Probabilistic Model of Language Learning*. Ph.D. dissertation, Northeastern University.

Striedter, G. F. (2004). *Principles of Brain Evolution*. Sunderland, MA: Sinauer.

Stromswold, K., and Zimmerman, K. (1999). 'Acquisition of Nein and Nicht and the VP-Internal Subject Stage in German', *Language Acquisition* 8: 101–27.

Sugisaki, K. (2007). 'A Note on the Default Value of Parameters', *Biolinguistics* 1: 114–17.

Sun, H., Rodin, A., Zhou, Y., Dickinson, D. P., Harper, D. E., Hewett-Emmett, D., and Li, W.-H. (1997). 'Evolution of Paired Domains: Isolation and Sequencing of Jellyfish and Hydra Pax Genes Related to Pax-5 and Pax-6', *Proceedings of the National Academy of Sciences* 94: 5156–61.

Sussman, G., and Yip, K. (1997). 'Sparse Representations for Fast, One-Shot Learning', paper presented at the National Conference on Artificial Intelligence. Orlando.

Suthers, R. A. (2004). 'Vocal Mechanisms in Birds and Bats: A Comparative View', *Annals of the Brazilian Academy of Sciences* 76(2): 247–52.

Suzuki, R., Buck, J., and Tyack, P. (2006). 'Information Entropy of Humpback Whale Songs', *Journal of the Acoustical Society of America*, 119(3): 1849–66.

Svenonius, P., and Ramchand, G. (2007). 'Mapping a Parochial Lexicon onto a Universal Semantics'. Ms., University of Tromsoe.

Swartz, S. (1988). *Constraints on Zero Anaphora and Word Order in Warlpiri Narrative Text*. M.S. dissertation, Pacific Center for Graduate Studies, with William Carey College.

Swinney, D., and Cutler, A. (1979). 'The Access and Processing of Idiomatic Expressions', *Journal of Verbal Learning and Verbal Behavior* 18(5): 523–34.

Szabolcsi, A. (1983). 'The Possessor that Ran Away from Home', *The Linguistic Review* 3: 89–102.

——(1994). 'The Noun Phrase', in F. Kiefer and K. E. Kiss (eds.), *The Syntactic Structure of Hungarian (Syntax and Semantics* 27). San Diego: Academic Press, 179–274.

Számadó, S., and Szathmáry, E. (2006). 'Selective Scenarios for the Emergence of Natural Language', *Trends in Ecology and Evolution* 679: 555–61.

Taft, M., and Forster, K. (1976). 'Lexical Storage and Retrieval of Polymorphemic and Polysyllabic Words', *Journal of Verbal Learning and Verbal Behavior* 15(6): 607–20.

Tager-Flusberg, H. (1997). 'Language Acquisition and the Theory of Mind: Contributions From the Study of Autism', in L. B. Adamson and M. A. Romski (eds.), *Communication and Language Acquisition: Discoveries from Atypical Development*. Baltimore: Paul H. Brookes Publishing Company.

——(2000). 'Language and Understanding Minds: Connections in Autism', in S. Baron-Cohen, H. Tager-Flusberg, and D. Cohen (eds.), *Understanding Other Minds: Perspectives from Developmental Cognitive Neuroscience*. Oxford: Oxford University Press, 124–49.

Taraldsen, K. T. (1981). 'The Theoretical Interpretation of a Class of "Marked" Extractions', in A. Belletti, L. Brandi, and L. Rizzi (eds.), *Theory of Markedness in Generative Grammar. Proceedings of the 1979 GLOW Conference*. Pisa: Scuola Normale Superiore, 475–516.

Tattersall, I. (1998). *The Origin of the Human Capacity*, series James Arthur Lecture on the Evolution of the Human Brain 68, New York: American Museum of Natural History.

——(2002). *The Monkey in the Mirror*. New York: Harcourt.

——(2005). 'Patterns of Innovation in Human Evolution, Evolution und Menschenwerdung', *Nova Acta Leopoldina* 345(93).

Teramitsu, I. and White, S. A. (2006). 'FoxP2 Regulation During Undirected Singing in Adult Songbirds', *The Journal of Neuroscience* 26(28 July 12): 7390–4.

—— Kudo, L. C., London, S. E., Geschwind, D. H., and White, S. A. (2004). 'Parallel FoxP1 and FoxP2 Expression in Songbird and Human Brain Predicts Functional Interaction', *Journal of Neuroscence* 24: 3152–63.

Terrace, H. S. (2005). 'Metacognition and the Evolution of Language', in H. S. Terrace and J. Metcalfe (eds.), *The Missing Link in Cognition: Origins of Self-reflective Consciousness*. Oxford: Oxford University Press, 84–115.

Terzi, A. (1992). *Pro in Finite Clauses: A Study of the Inflectional Heads of the Balkan Languages*. Ph.D. dissertation, City University of New York.

—— and Wexler, K. (2002). 'A-chains and S-homophones in Children's Grammar', in M. Hirotami (ed.), *Proceedings of NELS 32*, GLSA. University of Massachusetts at Amherst, 519–37.

Theissen, G. (2002). 'Concepts: Secret Life of Genes', *Nature* 415(6873): 741.

Thomason, S., and Kaufman, T. (1988). *Language Contact, Creolization, and Genetic Linguistics*. Berkeley/Los Angeles: University of California Press.

Thompson, D'Arcy W. (1992). *On Growth and Form*. (2nd repr. of 2nd ed. 1942; 1st publ. 1917, Cambridge: Cambridge University Press). New York: Dover.

Thráinsson, H. (1991). 'Long-distance Reflexives and the Typology of NPs', in J. Koster and E. Reuland (eds.), *Long-Distance Anaphora*. Cambridge: Cambridge University Press, 49–75.

Tickle, C. (2006). 'Making Digit Patterns in the Vertebrate Limb', *Nature Reviews Molecular Cell Biology* 7: 45–53.

Tomarev, S. I., Callaerts, P., Kos, L., Zinovieva, R., Halder, G., Gehring, W., and Piatigorsky, J. (1997). 'Squid Pax-6 and Eye Development', *Proceedings of the National Academy of Sciences* 94: 2421–6.

Tomasello, M. (1999). *The Cultural Origins of Human Cognition*. Cambridge, MA: Harvard University Press.

—— (2003). *Constructing a Language: A Usage-based Approach to Language*. Cambridge, MA: Harvard University Press.

—— and Call, J. (1997). *Primate Cognition*. Oxford: Oxford University Press.

Tomita, M. (1986). *Generalized LR Parsing*. Dordrecht: Kluwer Academic Publishers.

Trevisan, M. A., Cooper, B., Goller, F., and Mindlin, G. B. (2007). 'Lateralization as a Symmetry Breaking Process in Birdsong', *Physical Review E (Statistical, Nonlinear, and Soft Matter Physics)* 75(3): 031908–5.

Trivedi, R. P. (2001). 'Scientists Identify a Language Gene', *National Geographic News* Washington DC, October 4.

Trubetzkoy, N. (1939). *Grundzüge der Phonologie*. Göttingen: Vandenhoeck & Ruprecht.

—— (1969). *Principles of Phonology*, [trans. C. Baltaxe.] Berkeley: University of California Press.

Tsimpli, I. M. (1995). 'Focusing in Modern Greek', in Kiss, E. (ed.), *Discourse Configurational Languages*. Oxford: Oxford University Press, 176–206.

Turing, A. (1952). 'The Chemical Basis of Morphogenesis', *Philosophical Transaction of the Royal Society of London Series B, Biological Sciences* 237(641) 37–72.

——and Wardlaw, C. W. (1992). *A Diffusion Reaction Theory of Morphogenesis, The Collected Works of Alan Turing: Morphogenesis*1st publ. 1953). Amsterdam: North-Holland.

Ullman, M. T. (2004). 'Contributions of Memory Circuits to Language: The Declarative/Procedural Model', *Cognition* 92(1–2): 231–70.

——and Pierpont, E. I. (2005). 'Specific Language Impairment is Not Specific to Language: The Procedural Deficit Hypothesis.' *Cortex* 41(3): 399–433.

Uriagereka, J. (1995). 'An F Position in Western Romance', in K. Kiss (ed.), *Discourse Configurational Languages*. New York: Oxford University Press, 153–75.

——(1998). *Rhyme and Reason: An Introduction to Minimalist Syntax*. Cambridge, MA: MIT Press.

——(1999). 'Multiple Spell-out', in S. D. Epstein and N. Hornstein (ed.), *Working Minimalism*. Cambridge, MA: MIT Press, 251–83.

——(2008). *Syntactic Anchors: On Semantic Structuring*. Cambridge: Cambridge University Press.

Valian, V. (1991). 'Syntactic Subjects in the Early Speech of American and Italian Children', *Cognition* 40: 21–82.

Vallar, G., and Baddeley, A. D. (1984). 'Phonological Short-term Store, Phonological Processing and Sentence Comprehension: A Neuropsychological Case Study', *Cognitive Neuropsychology* 1: 121–41.

——and Papagno, C. (2002). 'Neuropsychological Impairments of Short-term Memory', in A. D. Baddeley, M. D. Kopelman, and Wilson B. A. (eds.), *Handbook of Memory Disorders*. Chichester: John Wiley & Sons, 249–70.

Van der Lely, H. K. J., and Stollwerck, L. (1996). 'A Grammatical Specific Language Impairment in Children: An Autosomal Dominant Inheritance?', *Brain and Language* 52: 484–504.

van Heyningen, V., and Williamson, K. A. (2002). 'PAX6 in Sensory Development', *Human Molecular Genetics* 11: 1161–7.

van Riemsdijk, H. (2002). 'The Unbearable Lightness of Going: The Projection Parameter as a Pure Parameter Governing the Distribution of Elliptic Motion Verbs in Germanic', *Journal of Comparative Germanic Linguistics* 5: 143–96.

Vargha-Khadem, F., and Passingham, R. (1990). 'Speech and Language Deficits', *Nature* 346: 226.

——Gadian, D. G., Copp, A., and Mishkin, M. (2005). 'FOXP2 and the Neuroanatomy of Speech and Language', *Nature Reviews in Neuroscience* 6(2): 131–8.

——Watkins, K. E., Alcock, K., Fletcher, P., and Passingham, R. (1995). 'Praxic and Nonverbal Cognitive Deficits in a Large Family with a Genetically-transmitted Speech and Language Disorder', *Proceedings of the National Academy of Sciences* 92: 930–3.

Vennemann, T. (2002). 'Semitic > Celtic > English: The Transitivity of Language Contact', in M. Filppula, J. Klemola, and H. Pitkänen (eds.), *The Celtic Roots of English* (*Studies in Languages* 37). Joensuu: Joensuu University Press, 295–330.

Vergnaud, J.-R., and Zubizarreta, M. L. (1992). 'The Definite Determiner and the Inalienable Constructions in French and in English', *Linguistic Inquiry* 23: 595–652.

Vernes, S. C., Spiteri, E., Nicoda, J., Groszera, M., Taylor, J. M., Davies, K. E., Geschwind, D. H., and Fisher, S. E. (2007). 'High-Throughput Analysis of Promoter Occupancy Reveals Direct Neural Targets of *FOXP2*, a Gene Mutated in Speech and Language Disorders', *The American Journal of Human Genetics* 81: 1232–50.

Vicente, L. (2007). *The Syntax of Heads and Phrases*. Ph.D. dissertation, University of Leiden.

Viertel, J. (1966). 'Concepts of Language Underlying the 18th Century Controversy about the Origin of Language', *Monograph Series on Language and Linguistics* 19: 109–32.

Vijay-Shanker, K., and Weir, D. J. (1994). 'The Equivalence of Four Extensions of Context-free Grammars', *Mathematical Systems Theory* 27: 511–46.

von Humboldt, W. (1827). 'Über den Dualis', [in A. Leitzmann (ed.) (1907), *Gesammelte Schriften, im Auftrag der (Königlichen) Preußischen Akademia der Wissenschaften*, VI.1, 1907, Behr: Berlin.]

——(1836). 'Über die Verschiedenheit des Menschlichen Sprachbaues und ihren Einfluss auf die Geistige Entwicklung des Menschengeschlechts', in E. Buschmann, (ed.), *Gedruckt in der Druckerei der Königlichen Akademie der Wissenschaften*, Berlin. [in A. Leitzmann (ed.), (1907) *Gesammelte Schriften, im Auftrag der (Königlichen) Preußischen Akademia der Wissenschaften*, VII.1, Berlin: Behr.]

Wada, K., Howard, J. T., McConnell, P., Whitney, O., Lints, T., Rivas, M., Horita, H., Patterson, M. A., White, S. A., Scharff, C., Haesler, S., Zhao, S., Sakaguchi, H., Hagiwara, M., Shiraki, T., Hirozane-Kishikawa, T., Skene, P., Hayashizaki, Y., Caninci, T., and Jarvis, E. D. (2006). 'A Molecular Neuroethological Approach for Identifying and Characterizing a Cascade of Behaviorally Regulated Genes', *Proceedings of the National Academy of Sciences* 103: 15212–15217.

Wade, N. (2006). *Before the Dawn: Recovering the Lost History of our Ancestors*. New York: Penguin.

Wagner, A. (2005). *Robustness and Evolvability in Living Systems*. Princeton, NJ: Princeton University Press.

Wallace, A. R. (1871). 'Commentary on the Descent of Man and Selection in Relation to Sex, by Charles Darwin, 1871', *The Academy* 2(20): 177–83.

Walls, G. L. (1942). *The Vertebrate Eye and Its Adaptive Radiation*. New York: Hafner.

Wang, Q., Lillo-Martin, D., Best, C., and Levitt, A. (1992). 'Null Subject vs. Null Object: Some Evidence from the Acquisition of Chinese and English', *Language Acquisition* 2: 221–54.

Wang, W. S. Y. (1994). 'Glottochronology, Lexicostatistics, and Other Numerical Methods', *Encyclopedia of Language and Linguistics*. Oxford: Pergamon Press, 1445–50.

Warnow, T., Evans, S. N., Ringe, D., and Nakhleh, L. (2004). 'Stochastic Models of Language Evolution and an Application to the Indo-European Family of Languages', 'Technical report, Department of Statistics, The University of California, Berkeley, 2004'.

Warren, W., Hillier, L., et al. (2008). 'Genome Analysis of the Platypus Reveals Unique Signatures of Evolution', *Nature* 453: 175–84.

Waters, G., and Caplan, D. (2005). 'The Relationship between Age, Processing Speed, Working Memory Capacity, and Language Comprehension', *Memory* 13: 403–13.

—— —— and Hildebrandt, N. (1987). 'Working Memory and Written Sentence Comprehension', in M. Coltheart (ed.), *Attention and Performance XII: The Psychology of Reading*. Hillsdale, NJ: Laurence Erlbaum Associates, 531–55.

—— —— —— (1991). 'On the Structure of Verbal Short-term Memory and its Functional Role in Sentence Comprehension: Evidence from Neuropsychology', *Cognitive Neuropsychology* 8: 81–126.

—— —— and Yampolsky, S. (2003). 'On-line Syntactic Processing Under Concurrent Memory Load', *Psychonomic Bulletin and Review* 10: 88–95.

Watkins, C. (1976). 'Towards Proto-Indo-European Syntax: Problems and Pseudo-problems', in S. Steever, C. Walker, S. Mufwene, (eds.), *Diachronic Syntax*. Chicago: Chicago Linguistic Society, 305–26. [reprinted (1994) in L. Oliver (ed.), *Calvert Watkins. Selected Writings*. Innsbruck : Innsbrucker Beiträge zur Sprachwissenschaft, 242–63].

Watkins, K. E., Dronkers, N. F., and Vargha-Khadem, F. (2002). 'Behavioral Analysis of an Inherited Speech and Language Disorder: Comparison with Acquired Aphasia', *Brain* 125: 452–64.

—— Vargha-Khadem, F., Ashburner, J., Passingham, R. E., Connelly, A., Friston, K. J., Frackowiak, R. S. J., Mishkin, M., and Gadian, D. G. (2002). 'MRI analysis of an Inherited Speech and Language Disorder: Structural Brain Abnormalities', *Brain* 125: 465–78.

Webb, D. M., and Zhang, J. (2005). 'FoxP2 in Song-Learning Birds and Vocal-Learning Mammals', *Journal of Heredity* 96: 212–16.

Webelhuth, G. (1991). *Principles of Syntactic Saturation*. Oxford: Oxford University Press.

Weinreich, D. M., Delaney, N. F., DePristo, M. A., and Hartl, D. L. (2006). 'Darwinian Evolution Can Follow Only Very Few Mutational Paths to Fitter Proteins', *Science* 7(312): 111–14.

Weiss, L. A., Shen, Y., Korn, J. M., Arking, D. E., and other members of the Autism Consortium (2008). 'Association between Microdeletion and Microduplication at 16p11.2 and Autism', *New England Journal of Medicine* 358(7): 667–75.

Weissengruber, G. E., Forstenpointner, G., Peters, G., Kübber-Heiss, A., and Fitch, W. T. (2002). 'Hyoid Apparatus and Pharynx in the Lion (*Panthera leo*), Jaguar (*Panthera onca*), Tiger (*Panthera tigris*), Cheetah (*Acinonyx jubatus*), and Domestic Cat (*Felis silvestris* f. *catus*)', *Journal of Anatomy* 201: 195–209.

Wellman, H. M. (1990). *The Child's Theory of Mind*. Cambridge, MA: MIT Press.

Wen, Q., and Chklovskii, D. B. (2005). 'Segregation of the Brain into Gray and White Matter: A Design Minimizing Conduction Delays', *PLoS Computational Biology* 1(7): 617–30.

Werker, J., and Tees, R. (1983). 'Developmental Change across Childhood in the Perception of Non-native Speech Sounds', *Canadian Journal of Psychology* 37(2): 278–86.

Wexler, K. (1994). 'Optional Infinitives, Head Movement, and the Economy of Derivation in Child Language', in D. Lightfoot and N. Hornstein (eds.), *Verb Movement*. Cambridge: Cambridge University Press, 305–50.

——(1998). 'Very Early Parameter Setting and the Unique Checking Constraint: A New Explanation of the Optional Infinitive Stage', *Lingua* 106: 23–79.

——(2002). 'Lenneberg's Dream: Learning, Normal Language Development and Specific Language Impairment', in Y. Levy and J. Schaeffer (eds.), *Language Competence across Populations: Towards a Definition of Specific Language Impairment*. Mahwah: Lawrence Erlbaum, 11–60.

——(2004). 'Lenneberg's Dream: Learning, Normal Language Development and Specific Language Impairment', in L. Jenkins (ed.), *Variation and Universals in Biolinguistics*. Amsterdam: Elsevier, 239–84.

——and Culicover, P. (1980). *Formal Principles of Language Acquisition*. Cambridge, MA: MIT Press.

——and Manzini, R. (1987). 'Parameters and Learnability in Binding Theory', in T. Roeper and E. Williams (ed.), *Parameter Setting*. Dordrecht: Reidel, 41–76.

Whelan, S. (2001). 'Molecular Phylogenetics: State-of-the Art Methods for Looking into the Past', *Trends in Genetics* 17: 262–72.

Wiese, R. (1996). *The Phonology of German*. Cambridge: Cambridge University Press.

Wik, B. (1973). 'English Nominalization in *-ing*. Synchronic and Diachronic Aspects', *Studia Anglistica Upsaliensia* 12.

Wild, J. M. (1993). 'The Avian Nucleus Retroambigualis: A Nucleus for Breathing, Singing and Calling', *Brain Research* 606: 119–24.

Williams, E. (1981). 'On the Notions "Lexically Related" and "Head of a Word"', *Linguistic Inquiry* 12: 245–74.

——(2003). *Representation Theory*. Cambridge, MA: MIT Press.

Williams, G. C. (1996). *Adaptation and Natural Selection*. Princeton: Princeton University Press.

Wilson, M., and Emmorey, K. (1997). 'A Visuo-spatial "Phonological Loop" in Working Memory: Evidence from American Sign Language', *Memory and Cognition* 25: 313–20.

Wilson, M., and Emmorey, K. (1998). 'A "Word Length Effect" For Sign Language: Further Evidence on the Role of Language in Structuring Working Memory', *Memory and Cognition* 26: 584–90.

Wind, J. (1976). 'Phylogeny of the Human Vocal Tract', *Annals of the New York Academy of Science* 280: 612–30.

Woodbury, A. (1977). 'Greenlandic Eskimo, Ergativity and Relational Grammar', in P. Cole and J. Sadock (eds.), *Grammatical Relations (Syntax and Semantics* 8). New York: Academic Press, 307–36.

Woods, R. P., Freimer, N. B., De Young, J. A., Fears, S. C., Sicotte, N. L., Service, S. K., Valentino, D. J., Toga, A. W., and Mazziotta, J. C. (2006). 'Normal Variants of Microcephalin and ASPM Do Not Account for Brain Size Variability', *Human Molecular Genetics* 15: 2025–9.

Woolley, S., and Doupe, A. J. (2008). 'Social Context-Induced Song Variation Affects Female Behavior and Gene Expression', *PLoS Biology* 6(3): e62 1–13.

Wright, S. (1932). 'The Roles of Mutation, Inbreeding, Crossbreeding, and Selection in Evolution', *Proceedings of the Sixth International Congress on Genetics* 1, 355–66.

Wunderlich, D. (1999). 'German Noun Plural Reconsidered'. Ms., University of Düsseldorf. Germany.

Wurmbrand, S. (2003). 'Syntactic and Post-syntactic Movement', in S. Burelle and S. Somesfalean (eds.), *Proceedings of the 2003 Annual Conference of the Canadian Linguistic Association*, 284–95.

Xu, F., and Pinker, S. (1995). 'Weird Past Tense Forms', *Journal of Child Language* 22: 531–56.

Yamada, J. E. (1990). *Laura: A Case of the Modularity of Language*. Cambridge, MA: MIT Press.

Yang, C. (2002). *Knowledge and Learning in Natural Language*. New York: Oxford University Press.

—— (2004a). 'Toward a Theory of Language Growth', in L. Jenkins (ed.), *Variation and Universals in Biolinguistics*. Amsterdam, Elsevier: 37–56.

—— (2004b). 'Universal Grammar, Statistics, or Both', *Trends in Cognitive Sciences* 8(10): 451–6.

—— (2005). 'On Productivity', *Language Variation Yearbook* 5: 333–70.

—— (2006). *The Infinite Gift*. New York: Scribner's.

—— (2009). 'Who's Afraid of George Kingsley Zipf?'. Ms., University of Pennsylvania.

Zagona, K. (1999). 'Structural Case and Tense Construal', in J.-M. Authier, B. E. Bullock, and L. A. Reed (eds.), *Formal Perspectives on Romance Linguistics: Selected Papers From the 28th Linguistic Symposium on Romance Languages*, Amsterdam/Philadelphia: John Benjamins, 305–27.

Zhang, J. (2003). 'Evolution of the Human ASPM Gene, a Major Determinant of Brain Size', *Genetics* 165: 2063–70.

—— Webb, D. M., and Podlaha, O. (2002). 'Accelerated Protein Evolution and Origins of Human-specific Features: Foxp2 as an Example', *Genetics* 162: 1825–35.

Ziolkowski, J. M., and Putnam, M. C. J. (2008). *The Virgilian Tradition: The First Fifteen Hundred Years*. New Heaven: Yale University Press.

Zucchi, S. (1997). 'Incomplete Events, Intensionality and Imperfective Aspect', *Natural Language Semantics* 7: 179–215.

Zurif, E. R., and Caramazza, A. (1976). 'Psycholinguistic Structures in Aphasia: Studies in Syntax and Semantics', in N. Avakian-Whitaker and H. Whitaker (eds.), *Studies in Neurolinguistics*. New York: Academic Press.

Zwart, C. J.-W. (2006). 'Local Agreement', in C. Boeckx (ed.), *Agreement Systems*. Amsterdam/Philadelphia: John Benjamins, 317–39.

Index

Fujita, H. 44 n4, 119
function 11, 19, 23, 25, 28, 36, 49, 62, 64, 71,
 73–4, 83, 90, 100, 111–12, 111 n10, 114
 n13, 118–9, 119 n23, 122 n27, 123–4, 124
 n30, 128, 130, 132, 135–6, 144, 146, 152–3,
 159–61, 163–5, 169, 183, 228, 255 n15, 261
 n18, 265, 306, 310
functional magnetic resonance imaging
 (fMRI) 9, 104, 112, 131, 171, 459
future-in-the-past 395, 409 n28

Galaburda, A. M. 128
Gallistel, R. 39
Garrett, M. 68, 78–9
Gartner, H. -C. 30
Gathercole, S. E. 458
Gazzaniga, M. S. 176
Gee, J. 459
Gehring, W. J. 28, 73–4, 155, 158, 310–12
gender 9, 103, 131, 247, 281–2, 322, 335 n10,
 339
gene
 homologous 136, 156, 159, 163, 174
 knock-down 120 n24, 121 n26, 488
 orthologous 159, 164, 479
 regulatory 82, 154–5, 164
 transcription factor 33, 462, 472, 477–8,
 480
Generalized Double Access Reading (DAR)
 395 n7, 397
generative
 power 13, 354
 procedure 27, 29, 30
genetic endowment
 toolkit 24, 151, 160
genetics 2, 10–11, 23 n2, 43 n3, 47, 63, 69, 100,
 105, 110, 110 n9, 113, 115, 118, 125–34, 136,
 154, 156, 166, 171, 174, 177–8, 219, 223,
 266–8, 275, 298, 307, 465
Genie 176
genitive 281, 320–2
genome, universal 23, 220, 220 n18
genotype 68–9, 90
Gentner, T. Q. 173
Geraci, C. 455
German 45 n8, 84, 142, 185–6, 195, 195 n17,
 196, 198, 231, 253, 276, 280, 283, 289–91,
 339 n28n, 346 n39, 347, 373–4, 379, 399,
 427
gerund 345, 353 n52
Ghomeshi, J. 339 n27

Gianollo, C. 213, 282 n29
Gibson, E. 182, 445, 450
Gilbert, W. 176
Gillespie, J. 35, 67, 77
Giorgi, A. 14, 111, 238, 392–416
Glenn, C. 451
global derivational constraint 364
Gopnik, M. 9, 69, 101, 103, 109–10, 110 n8,
 161
Gould, S. 23–4, 45 n8, 47–9, 49 n11, 52, 58,
 63, 67, 219 n16, 220, 466
Gozzi, M. 455
grammatical relation 70–2, 91, 98
Gray, R. 275 n17, 307
Greek
 Classical Greek 280, 290, 320
 Cypriot Greek 323
 Modern Greek 280, 317, 320, 322
Greenberg, J. 268–72, 275, 277, 281, 289 n40,
 292, 298, 307
Grenier, J. 68, 156
Grico 280, 288 n37, 290–1, 322, 322 n10, 323
gridline 482–5, 487
Grodner, D. 445
Grossman, M. 459
Groszer, M. 33
Guardiano, C. 11–13, 213, 266–304, 306 n2,
 307, 426 n6
Guasti, M. T. 188 n12, 449
Guéron, J. 394 n6
Guimarães, M. 332, 332 n3, 333, 333 n5
Gulli, A. 332 n3

Haesler, S. 120, 120 n24, 122, 124, 137, 160,
 162–3, 464, 478, 488, 490
Hagoort, P. 143
hair follicle spacing 127, 131
Haldane, J. B. S. 25, 35, 67, 73
Hale, K. 192, 199, 211, 246, 335 n11, 336,
 336 n13, 336 n16, 338, 352
Hall, D. H. 127, 136, 156, 159
Halle, M. 1, 62, 65, 181, 191, 193–4, 211, 218,
 356, 461–4, 481–7, 487 n6, 488, 490–1
Hallet, G. 177
HapMap 127
Harasaki, Y. 499
Harris, Z. 21, 335 n10
Hauser, M. D. 9, 25, 42, 45–6, 50–3, 57–9, 62,
 116, 119 n20, 130, 135, 138, 141, 145, 164,
 173, 204, 222, 310 n5, 329, 354, 422, 424,
 426, 465, 467–8